8·30·76

CLAUSEWITZ AND THE STATE

Clausewitz at fifty.
Lithograph by Franz Michelis the younger after a painting by Wilhelm Wach.

Peter Paret

CLAUSEWITZ
AND THE STATE

New York

Oxford University Press

London   1976   Toronto

Selections from Carl von Clausewitz, *On War,* ed. and trans. by Michael
Howard and Peter Paret. With commentaries by Peter Paret, Michael Howard, and Bernard Brodie (Princeton University Press, 1976). Reprinted by
permission of Princeton University Press.

ACKNOWLEDGMENTS

1927611

A YEAR AT THE INSTITUTE FOR ADVANCED STUDY IN Princeton and a fellowship at the Center for Advanced Study in the Behavioral Sciences at Stanford enabled me to do much of the preparatory work and some of the writing on this book. I am greatly indebted to these institutions and to my associates there—in particular to Felix Gilbert, whose comments on various parts of the manuscript have been, as always, precise and entirely undogmatic. My wife, who first suggested that I expand my articles on Clausewitz into a longer study, William Bossart, John Shy, my colleague Carolyn Lougee, my former and present students Nancy Padgett, John Alger, Lawrence Baack, Daniel Moran, and Hugh West, as well as Dan Davin of the Clarendon Press, and Dorothy Curzon, Ann Lindsay, and Herbert F. Mann of Oxford University Press, have been helpful in various ways, and it is a pleasure to express my thanks to them here. The editors of the *Journal of the History of Ideas* and of the *Journal of Modern History* kindly permitted me to incorporate material that first appeared in somewhat different form in their publications. I am also obliged to Princeton University Press for permission to quote extensively from the new edition of Clausewitz's *On War* that Michael Howard and I have prepared.

CONTENTS

ILLUSTRATIONS

A Note on Translated Passages.

Translations of Clausewitz's writings are my own except for quotations from *On War,* which are based on a translation by Michael Howard and me that will be published by Princeton University Press. As this work goes to press the Princeton edition is not yet available, and I am therefore unable to give page-references to it. To help the reader locate passages in the many different editions of *On War,* book and chapter-references are complemented with page-references, in parentheses, to the most recent scholarly German edition, *Vom Kriege,* ed. Werner Hahlweg, Bonn, 1952, thus: *On War,* book I, ch. 1 (p. 1). Clausewitz frequently italicized words and passages; unless otherwise stated, italics in quotations from his works and letters are his.

EPIGRAPH

"Truth is relative, and time is nothing but the condition in which truth exists, de-
velops, functions, survives. Every organism known to us is confined within this con-
text: each man in his times. Our age is the age of self-consciousness, of self-reflection
pushed to imbalance and infinity. [Today] *the strongest potential for heroism, the*
most capable and effective personality, will dry up, shrivel, evaporate in smoke and
flame if he should happen to be doubly gifted, if he should be truly rich in human
qualities—that is, if his strength should be joined by a speculative, reflective spirit,
by sharp and intelligent comprehension, a mobile poetic imagination, by a powerful
but tender heart. In the fragmented modern world . . . only one option is left to the
enlightened individual: the heroism of scholarship."

Rahel Levin to Alexander von der Marwitz, 17 May 1811.

CLAUSEWITZ AND THE STATE

INTRODUCTION

CLAUSEWITZ REGARDED THE GROWTH OF THE MOD-
ern state as the most significant process in history. The manner in which
societies had generated and distributed political energy in the past, and
their political practices during his lifetime, served as organizing elements
for much of his theoretical work. As a symbol of profound emotional authority, the state also constituted a major element in his psychological con-
figuration. Throughout his life he alternated between action and the study
of the force that underlay all action, the force of politics, which he believed
could be understood only through its history. Before he was thirty, personal experience and reflection on past events had convinced him that political history was a story of perpetual creation and decline, of states carrying
out the task of making civilization possible, at times achieving great advances in rationalizing concepts and institutions, but also suffering reverses—a story that would never conclude with the ideal type of government. As a young soldier, survivor of the war that had ruined the
Frederician monarchy, he adduced the great religions of mankind and the
constitution of Sparta as instances of historical impermanence: "For however many centuries they may exist and function, even the most sublime
creations of society carry within themselves the element of their own destruction." [1] No doubt the centralized state, which only recently had
emancipated itself from a tangle of inhibitions to gain unfettered use of its
energies, would also decline. He did not speculate on forms that the state
might assume in the future; but in the last years of his life, in an analysis of
one crucial expression of state power—war—which ranged from antiquity
to post-Napoleonic Europe, he indicated his belief that while systems
might emerge that would again shun the concerns and contributions of the

1. Letter to his fiancée, Marie v. Brühl, 5 October 1807, in *Karl und Marie von Clausewitz: Ein Lebensbild in Briefen und Tagebuchblättern*, ed. K. Linnebach, Berlin, 1917, p. 142. This work is henceforth
cited as *Correspondence*.

mass of the people, and thus lessen the amount of political energy available
to the state, such diminution seemed unlikely. Whether gradually a separation between government and people will again take place is difficult to determine, "but the reader will agree with us when we say that once
barriers—which in a sense consist only in man's ignorance of what is possible—are torn down, they are not so easily set up again." [2] Whatever the
characteristics of political society, however, he held it was the duty of men
in public life to guard and improve the polity, and to help government understand the nature of its tasks. The importance and fragility of political
organization called for a high sense of responsibility in the citizen; its ever-
changing history justified his refusal to accept unreflectively the authority
of the present.

Not only was the European political system transformed in the course
of Clausewitz's life; his generation had reason to assume that further great
changes within societies and in their relations with each other were imminent. In France especially the claims of governmental authority had risen to
new heights, and everywhere ideological and institutional developments
were bringing about a more intrusive exploitation of society for the state's
purposes. Many of these innovations were linked to wars, from the War of
the First Coalition to the Waterloo campaign twenty-three years later.
Some states—France and Poland in the early 1790's, Prussia after 1806, are
examples—reached points in their history at which, in different respects,
fundamental issues of political existence came into question. Military institutions and war seemed at these times to regain the significance that they
had possessed in the early evolution of society, when political organization
first developed around the functions of defense and attack. In France and
Prussia the reshaping of political and military institutions had progressed
sufficiently for Clausewitz to characterize its outcome as a reversal of previous conditions. Military power, he wrote a few years after Napoleon's
downfall, had once been held by the nobility, later by the absolute monarchs; "but in recent times it had become the expression of total national
energy." [3] At least so far as events preceding the French Revolution are
concerned, the interpretation summarized in this statement is hardly original, being drawn mainly from the works of such authors as Montesquieu,
Schiller, and Clausewitz's acquaintance Johannes von Müller, the historian
of the Swiss Confederation. Nor was Clausewitz alone in recognizing that
the social and political world was changing radically and in feeling the need
to understand the forces involved in the process. But few men identified as

2. *On War*, book VIII, ch. 3B (pp. 870–871). A similar thought is expressed in military terms, *ibid.*,
book IV, ch. 11 (p. 368). Page numbers in my citations of *On War* refer to the 16th edition of the German original *Vom Kriege*, ed. W. Hahlweg, Bonn, 1952.
3. In the last of several efforts to interpret an event that occupied him throughout much of his mature
life, the collapse of Prussia in 1806, *Nachrichten über Preussen in seiner grossen Katastrophe; Kriegsgeschichtliche Einzelschriften*, vol. x, Berlin, 1888, p. 425.

clearly as he the dynamic and logic that caused a self-sufficient aristocracy to give way to the absolute monarchs, who in turn were being replaced by the nation-state; and his originality is even more apparent in his attempt to understand the transformation of contemporary Europe by a historical and theoretical analysis of its military component.

This analysis was as much the result of action and experience as it was of speculative effort. Measured by the norms of the age of the French Revolution and the Napoleonic Empire, Clausewitz's military career—his public life, as he occasionally termed it—was eventful but not exceptional. In common with thousands of officers in armies across Europe, he served from boyhood on, experienced defeat and captivity as well as victory, changed his allegiance and fought against his former sovereign, survived both physical and political dangers, was awarded the usual decorations, and rose to respectable rank. On the whole, his were the not uncharacteristic stations of a generation whose way was punctuated by war and the rise and fall of states. But at times his path departed from the ordinary. Between 1808 and 1815, in the Prussian reform era and the Wars of Liberation, and again during the last year of his life, when the French and Polish revolutions of 1830 tested the stability of Europe, he had a hand in decisions of considerable political as well as military significance. The part he played was at most of secondary magnitude, but it was one that influenced the course of events.

Far greater, however, was the impact his actions had on his own thought, whose importance outweighs anything he achieved in his public life. It is also more difficult to trace and interpret. His theories have been subjected to close and sophisticated analyses, notably by Hans Delbrück, Hans Rothfels, and more recently by Eberhard Kessel and Werner Hahlweg, but even their studies lack comprehensiveness and have not always succeeded in placing and interpreting Clausewitz's ideas among the diverse conceptions and attitudes that fought to dominate his age. The difficulties scholars face are symbolically prefigured by Clausewitz's reluctance to publish during his lifetime, a hesitation compounded of intellectual arrogance and unwillingness to push himself forward, which removed the man and his ideas from the normal testing interchange with colleagues and critics. The senior officers and bureaucrats among whom he lived were conscious of an unusual talent in their midst, but it required the posthumous publication of his historical and theoretical writings, his political essays, and his correspondence to reveal him for what he was: a forceful, exceptionally creative member of the generation of Germans whose fate was determined by Napoleon and Goethe, a soldier who had assembled an intellectual armory that in some respects was unique. Stated in the most summary form, it consisted in his ability to combine values and some of the philosophic method of German idealism with a pronounced sense of reality, in his individualizing view of the past, which approached that of historicism, and in his understanding of the way states functioned, particularly in their foreign relations and in war.

Clausewitz lived at a time when the educated German was emerging from a century and a half of paternalistic parochialism to rediscover the value of political power. More often than before, the individual's personal and professional development was proceeding in step with his feelings toward the state. The sublime indifference to politics that still marked some of the most creative among Clausewitz's contemporaries was growing rarer, as was the sense of complete independence with which Alexander von Humboldt, for example, refused to allow questions of ideology, nationality, and war to place limits on how and where he lived. More indicative of the way ahead was the attitude of Alexander's brother, Wilhelm. Clausewitz was too critical of moral ambiguities to be able to feel genuine affection for someone of Wilhelm von Humboldt's convoluted sensuality; but the two men respected each other's abilities, and their lives show remarkable affinities in their mixture of intellectual and cultural cosmopolitanism, idealization of the harmonious individual, involvement in public affairs, and fascination with the power of the state. There can be no doubt that significant areas of Clausewitz's work are beyond our comprehension, and that we cannot understand the achievements and problems of his career and his private life unless we recognize that for him, even to a greater extent than would be true for Humboldt, the state and its basis, the political vigor of society, occupied places very near the center of his thought.

Clausewitz held differing views of the state at different times in his life, but usually it was the power of the central agencies and the effectiveness of the state's institutions that mattered most to him. Ideologies, and social and economic issues, were of less compelling concern, which is not to suggest that they failed to interest him or that they did not occasionally influence his behavior. His own family, to improve its status, had taken steps of a kind that might justify the claim that he and his brothers began their careers with a deception. He himself was among the more egalitarian members of the reform party, and even after his political hopes and energies had been damped down by the Restoration he could be scathing in his criticism of the state's treatment of the poor. In an essay on ideologies in Germany written in the early 1820's, he concluded his account of the near starvation he had observed some years earlier in the Eifel Mountains with the comment that "anyone who has looked such misery in the face will forever be filled with a sense of obligation, which the government, too, should possess and act on in such calamities. It is for that reason that the author has never been able to recall without bitterness and an outraged heart the lack of scruple that led the Prussian government to drop the matter." [4] But his wish to rid society of restrictions and injustice not only

4. "Umtriebe," in C. v. Clausewitz, *Politische Schriften und Briefe,* ed. H. Rothfels, Munich, 1921, p. 191.

derived from compassion for the individual; it was also linked to his concern for the ethical rectitude and for the power of the Prussian state. A class-structure based on legal privilege appeared to him to deprive the political leadership of potential sources of ability and energy it could ill afford to lose. The strength of the monarchy would increase if its subjects could identify their interests more closely with those of the government. By rationalizing and humanizing its institutions, by learning to protect and educate its citizens more equitably and efficiently, the state would better carry out its mission of making civilized life possible, of justifying itself by providing scope for the full and harmonious development of the individual, and of responding to the urge for self-preservation and growth innate in every political organism.

If Clausewitz's realism was often put in the service of his political ideals, it also shaped what may be called the products of his creative or constructive idealism—his historical and theoretical writings. The interaction between realism and idealism in his life and work constitutes a major theme of this book, and it would be premature here to do more than indicate the importance of the relationship, and—as a suggestive rather than substantive illustration—point once more to the realms of society and economics, this time to the economic analogies with which he liked to elucidate his arguments. The idea of dividing one's troops on the march with the intent of bringing them together in action he calls "the small change, so to speak, of the strategic budget," while major battles are described as its gold and silver. A defeated army carrying out a time-consuming retreat is likened to a bankrupt incurring additional debts. At Borodino, Napoleon broke off the battle before the Russian army was destroyed, "not because he thought the issue was still in doubt, but because total victory would have cost him more than he was able to pay"; and at Waterloo he "spent every last penny, and then fled like a beggar from the battlefield and the Empire." [5] No one who believes in the impact of ideals on violence has taken a less romantic view of fighting, insisting on fitting even such imponderables as honor, morale, and genius into the "balance sheet of war"; and the terms that Clausewitz borrows from commercial life, or at other times from mechanics or the fine arts, fit easily into an interpretation that treats war as an act of social intercourse, as a political act.

For a soldier brought up on the brief and martial history of the Prus-

5. *On War*, book IV, ch. 7 (p. 346); ch. 12 (pp. 378, 382); ch. 9 (p. 357). See also the characteristic passages in book II, ch. 3 (p. 201); book III, ch. 1 (p. 251); book VI, ch. 7 (p. 551) and ch. 29 (p. 729); and book VIII, ch. 6A (p. 886). Elsewhere Clausewitz compares war with litigation, as in book VI, ch. 1 (p. 512) or ch. 30 (p. 733), where lawsuits are called the battles of civilian life. Comparisons of war with commercial activity appear in Clausewitz's earliest writings, long before *On War*, e.g., in 1804 (see p. 90 below). Some years later he wrote: "Battle is money and property, strategy is commerce; it is only through the former that the latter becomes significant, and he who wastes his master's estate (who doesn't know how to fight) should give up trade and commerce, otherwise he will soon be bankrupt." Letter to Gneisenau, 17 June 1811, in C. v. Clausewitz, *Schriften—Aufsätze—Studien—Briefe*, ed. W. Hahlweg, Göttingen, 1966, i, 647. This work is henceforth cited as *Schriften*.

sian monarchy, it was not difficult to conceive of the modern state as an organism created in large part by military institutions, whose continued existence depended on its ability to wage war. More unusual were the implications that flowed from this idea. Even Clausewitz's earliest writings expressed a sense of the bond between military and political power, which gradually came to inspire all his thoughts on war. Very few writers and soldiers since his day have held as steadily as he did to the view that because the purpose of war is political, the standard by which all military institutions and actions must ultimately be judged is that of political utility. But political and social concepts could only dimly illuminate the actual mechanics of war. To understand these, Clausewitz developed a technique of inquiry that sought to identify and separate the numerous components of military organization, decision-making, and action, and to reduce each to its essential core before fitting them together again into larger and dynamic structures. It was his manner of combining the political and social view of war—which might also be called the historical view—with a structural analysis of the way men fought that gave Clausewitz's theories their strength and, despite their many transitory aspects, helped make them stimulating to later generations. As the century progressed, his major and unfinished manuscript, *On War,* came to be regarded as the work that more successfully than any other in the literature showed that war was susceptible to historical and logical analysis, which could accommodate both general propositions of conflict and the constant changes introduced by new weapons and by new social and political phenomena. But these same qualities also rendered *On War* more difficult to understand than the customary, purely military analyses of battles and campaigns, or the sociological investigations by Herbert Spencer and his successors, who largely disregarded the strategic, operational, and tactical sides of war. Every theory that outlasts its creator tends to be reinterpreted unhistorically, according to the constantly changing concerns of later days; Clausewitz's writings have suffered the attendant distortions more than most. No doubt new facets may be revealed when men ignore the original intent and logic of a work, and the condition of its author and his times; but it would be difficult to imagine an age whose intellectual efforts lend themselves less to being torn out of their environment than the years in Germany between the 1780's and Goethe's death. The fruitfulness of this period derives in large part from the successful manner in which many of its most gifted figures combined qualities of intense inwardness with the effort to develop and express universal values. It would be presumptuous to attempt an explanation of this phenomenon here; but perhaps it is not too surprising that those in whom it revealed itself included a man who was both soldier and intellectual.

I have written this book neither to evaluate the adequacy of Clausewitz's theories nor to trace their impact on the conduct of war in the 19th and 20th centuries. Much remains uncertain in these matters, but they are not the only ones to be studied. Nor do economic and sociological issues— let alone ideological concerns—exhaust the possibilities of research in the history of the Prussian state and the Prussian people. Rudolf Stadelmann's essays on the personality and the intellectual world of Clausewitz's mentor, Scharnhorst, are recent reminders of the wealth of general relevance contained in the existence of the creative individual. Clausewitz, whose efforts to understand his own character and feelings can rarely be separated from his attempts to gain intellectual mastery over his environment, offers us in his life a window that opens on some of the most interesting aspects of the age of Neoclassicism in Germany. At the same time his life shows us an individual struggling to reach the psychological goals that the age idealized. That, too, is worth study. Finally, can we penetrate far into his writings without knowing something about the author and his world? The bare structure of his theories stands on its own; but how much is obscured or becomes meaningless when he is read as though he were a late-20th-century defense analyst who chooses to think and express himself in a peculiar manner. In turn, any interpretation of his political and military actions, to say nothing of his personal development, is pointless unless Clausewitz's writings are brought to bear on his life.

Despite admirable studies of facets of Clausewitz's thought, the literature is still so fragmented and contradictory in its findings that the need to return to the sources and to the historical environment cannot be doubted. That is what I have tried to do in this book. The first four chapters deal with Clausewitz's immediate background and surroundings more than with Clausewitz himself. Just as Prussia's foreign policy in the years of his adolescence and early maturity retained for him a cautionary exemplariness that never ceased to influence his political thinking, the institutions and doctrine of the post-Frederician army remained forces that he studied, and reacted against, throughout his life. It seems advisable, therefore, to treat these and other elements of his early environment at length, even if this requires shifts in focus. With the fifth chapter, which discusses his first political, historical, and military writings, the emphasis changes and for the rest of the book remains on Clausewitz and his work.

In many respects what I have written is little more than a preliminary outline, which may help others go farther. If I have explored some topics in detail—for instance, Clausewitz's early education, which has been largely ignored—I am far from claiming to have analyzed in depth each of the many aspects of his life, of his scholarship, and of his theories. But while the book does not aim at exhaustiveness it does try to be comprehensive, to touch on his social and intellectual antecedents, his surroundings, his experiences, and the ways in which they influenced his attempts to understand and explain politics and war. Not the interpretation of Clausewitz's theories but their psychological and historical genesis constitutes my central theme. That the discussion of his ideas, and of the events and institutions among which they developed, is joined to a biographical study must narrow its scope; on the other hand, this connection gives us access to the richness and to the ultimate precision of thought that are never found in intellectual movements, in attitudes held by groups or society, but exist only in the feelings, ideas, and actions of the individual.

PART I

1

CLAUSEWITZ'S PRUSSIA

AT CLAUSEWITZ'S BIRTH HIS FAMILY HELD A PRECARI-
ous place, at best, in the military elite with whose help Frederick II had
raised the Prussian state to new significance in Europe. Clausewitz's father,
Friedrich Gabriel, had entered the army in 1759 as officer-cadet, was
promoted to ensign, and soon after the end of the Seven Years' War to lieutenant.[1] By that time the crisis that had threatened the state was overcome,
officer complements no longer needed to be kept at war strength, and the
king again pressed for strict observance of the nobility's claim on positions
of military authority. The middle-class volunteers who had been welcomed
during the war were now subjected to review, which in most cases meant
reassignment to garrison-battalions—a type of home-guard unit—and an
end to further advancement, or outright dismissal. In 1766 the name of the
elder Clausewitz appeared on a list of officers of the 47th Infantry Regiment
"who are not of the nobility."[2] The following year he was retired from the
service and given a minor appointment as tax collector in Burg, a small
town seventy miles southwest of Berlin. Despite the army's reason for dis-
missing him, he did not relinquish the *von,* the mark of nobility he had
adopted as a young man, and his claim to noble status seems to have been
accepted at face value by the subaltern functionaries and former officers who
made up the society in which he moved for the rest of his life. At the
beginning of his new career he married Friederike Schmidt, about whose
family little is known except that her father may have been a subordinate
official in Burg, or alternately a village bailiff. The couple had four sons

1. The literature on Clausewitz is full of misinformation about his family. The two most important
sources on Clausewitz's antecedents are E. Kessel, "Carl von Clausewitz: Herkunft und Persönlichkeit,"
Wissen und Wehr, XVIII (1937), 700–706, 763–774; and, despite several errors, H. Banniza v. Bazan
and R. Müller, *Deutsche Geschichte in Ahnentafeln,* 2 vols., Berlin, 1940–42, ii, 143–145. Also useful,
though often inaccurate, is K. Schwartz, *Leben des Generals Carl von Clausewitz und der Frau Marie von
Clausewitz,* Berlin, 1878, i, 1–31.
2. Kessel, "Clausewitz," pp. 764–765.

and two daughters, the fifth child and youngest boy, born on 1 June 1780, being christened Carl Philipp Gottlieb. The few documents concerning him that have survived suggest that Friedrich Gabriel von Clausewitz was an enterprising individual; but he proved unable to rise in the administration. Nor did he succeed in his efforts at rejoining the army, or in obtaining commissions for his sons, as long as Frederick II lived. An appeal for one of his sons, submitted in 1786, was answered by the king: "If his son wants to serve in the artillery, he must report there and serve from the bottom up"—an insulting response that can be explained only by Frederick's belief that the Clausewitzes were bourgeois.[3]

This was not the conception Carl von Clausewitz had of his antecedents. In 1806, in a letter to his fiancée, he wrote that his father descended from a noble family in Silesia, which, he assumed, had lost its property during the Thirty Years' War. His grandfather was compelled to enter a profession, and, following the custom of the times, no longer used his title. Of his two elder sons, one studied theology, the other law; the youngest, Friedrich Gabriel, joined the army, was invalided in the Seven Years' War, and as a result received a post in the civil administration.[4] This account was inaccurate in two respects. Nothing linked the Silesian family von Clausnitz with Clausewitz's grandfather, professor of theology at Halle, who spelled his name Clauswitz. On the contrary, the theologian's father and grandfather are now known to have been Lutheran ministers in Silesia, each of whom had married a parson's daughter. His great-grandfather, the earliest documented member of the family, was mayor of the town of Troppau near the Silesian-Moravian border, who presumably for religious reasons emigrated north, to more secure Protestant territory, during the Thirty Years' War. It was in this move that the legend of impoverished nobility seems to have originated. Nor was Clausewitz correct in believing that his father had suffered a wound, which cut short his military career. Friedrich Gabriel von Clausewitz is not named in the casualty lists of his regiment; his claim of having been wounded was evidently meant to provide a socially acceptable explanation of his early dismissal. We can assume that even during Professor Clauswitz's lifetime the family vaguely believed, or hoped, that it was related to the Clausnitzes, who had been on the rolls of the Silesian nobility since the 1560's. In the course of the 18th century, as a title became increasingly useful for advancement in Prussia, this hope easily changed to certainty. The elder Clausewitz may have regarded his lie as nothing more than a necessary defense of his family's noble status, which, as was not unusual at the time, could not be adequately documented and for that reason was being called into question. His sense of being a nobleman was reinforced by an important change that oc-

3. *Ibid.*, p. 765.
4. Clausewitz to Marie v. Brühl, 13 December 1806, *Correspondence*, p. 73.

curred in the family's circumstances shortly before his dismissal. Professor Clauswitz had died in 1749. Fifteen years later his widow married again, this time a Prussian officer, Captain von Hundt.[5] By an earlier marriage Clausewitz's stepfather had seven sons, who also served in the army. There was nothing uncertain about their social standing—the Hundts had been squires in Mecklenburg for generations—and the new connection could be expected in time to solidify the position of the Clausewitz family. It was not yet sufficient to save the elder Clausewitz's career. But in the more lenient atmosphere that followed on the death of Frederick the Great some two decades later, Hundt's influence enabled three of Clausewitz's sons to enter the army as officer-cadets. During the revolutionary wars one of the three considered applying for official recognition of the family's nobility; but older comrades dissuaded him from a course of action that was unnecessary, seemed contrary to the enlightened spirit of the age, and might have an awkward outcome.[6] Thirty years later, however, the application was submitted, and in 1827 a cabinet order signed by Frederick William III finally attested the family's "legal claim to noble status." [7]

The royal order did not signify that the claim was believed; it was issued in recognition of something more important than genealogical truth: the continuing ascent of the Clausewitzes to positions of rank and dignity, and their proliferating ties by marriage and friendship to persons of the highest standing in the monarchy. Nor was the process that had carried the family upward in any sense exceptional. Since the days of the Great Elector the Protestant ministry had been one of the major channels by which able peasants and burghers were brought into the service of the Brandenburg-Prussian state. Beyond the middle ranks of the bureaucracy, promotion and its usual concomitant—social advancement—became very difficult; nevertheless in each generation a significant number of men did succeed in entering the nobility, which in Prussia more than in many German regions was prepared to assimilate newcomers. To move from parsonage to government bureau or regimental headquarters was facilitated, and indeed encouraged, by changes in religious attitudes that at the time were affecting most segments of Protestantism in Germany. Even for orthodox Lutherans, justification by faith was being transformed under the urging of the Enlightenment and the absolute monarchy into justification by virtue, work, and the fulfillment of duty. Inwardness and observing one's public obligations achieved a more intense synthesis in the Pietistic movement, some of whose leading spirits came to see the state as God's instrument for the education and betterment of man, and thus deserving of selfless service, regardless of

5. On Gustav Detlev, or Detlof, von Hundt and his family, see H. Kneschke, *Neues allgemeines Deutsches Adels-Lexicon*, Leipzig, 1929, iv, 525.
6. Clausewitz to Marie v. Brühl, 13 December 1806, *Correspondence*, p. 74.
7. Schwartz, *Leben des Generals Clausewitz*, i, 1.

one's economic interests and station in life. Many of the nobles and bourgeois who came under the influence of Pietism from the end of the 17th century onward linked social awareness and responsibility with a new urge to acquire professional expertise—a combination that played a part in shaping the emerging type of civil and military servant of the Prussian crown.[8] The old Protestant ethic, profoundly marked by the world of petty principalities in which it had developed, was changing to meet the new demands of the absolute monarchy. As the unification of Germany and two world wars were to show, beyond a certain point the expansion of territorial and political power, and the increasingly revolutionary efforts to maintain it, placed unbearable burdens on the Germans' ethical values. With the more modest claims of the Frederician monarchy, however, a temporary accommodation could be achieved, a merging of interests under which the good Christian might join God and state as objects of his allegiance without pangs of conscience. If the state was to grow, this infusion of new ideals and energies was essential. So far as society was concerned, the entry of middle-class soldiers and officials into the nobility meant that the dominant groups could retain their aristocratic posture while coming to terms with the new supremacy of the centralized state.

By the last decades of the 18th century, the Clausewitzes' adherence to the state had largely taken the place of their earlier theological commitment. To please his mother, the eldest of the four brothers prepared for the ministry, but he soon changed his field of study, and ended his career in the respectable obscurity of a councillor in the financial administration. Religion, at least in its institutional form, played an insignificant role in Carl von Clausewitz's adult life. Possibly his interest in education and his broad social sympathies owed something to his grandfather's association with the University of Halle.[9] Not only was Halle the intellectual center of Pietism in Germany; the orphanage and institute that August Hermann Francke founded in the town helped guide the gradually awakening concern of the state in the education of its less-privileged subjects as well as of the new bureaucratic elite. But the inwardness of Pietism and its longing for moral renovation could scarcely have been prominent in the family's daily existence. Decades later, in an analysis of attitudes in Prussian society that

8. The connections between Pietism and the Prussian army and administration have been repeatedly explored. I am especially indebted to the relevant studies by Carl Hinrichs, contained in his collected papers, *Preussen als historisches Problem,* ed. G. Oestreich, Berlin, 1964, and in his posthumous work, *Preussentum und Pietismus,* Göttingen, 1971.

9. On Benedikt Gottlob Clauswitz see the entries in C. G. Jöcher's *Allgemeines Gelehrten Lexicon,* i, Leipzig, 1750, which, incidentally, states that his father was a parson, and in the *Allgemeine Deutsche Biographie.* Clauswitz is also mentioned in the autobiography of the rationalist theologian J. S. Semler, who succeeded him at Halle, *Lebensbeschreibung von ihm selbst verfasst,* n.p., 1781. Other references to Clauswitz can be found in A. Ritschl's *Geschichte des Pietismus,* Bonn, 1884, ii, 561, 568, and in W. Schrader's *Geschichte der Friedrichs-Universität zu Halle,* Berlin, 1894, i, 276, 279, 291 (where he is characterized as a faithful representative of the Pietistic approach), and 338–339.

helped bring about the disaster of 1806, Clausewitz described his own early environment in these words: The author "grew up in the Prussian army. His father, an officer who had served in the Seven Years' War, was full of the prejudices of his class. In his parents' house the author saw almost no-one but officers, and not exactly the best-educated ones at that ... . In short, from the beginning *national* feeling and even *caste* sentiment were as pronounced and firmly rooted in him as could be expected ... ." [10] We should not ignore the unspoken message in this description. The attitudes to which Clausewitz was exposed in childhood may well have been enriched by elements of a new political ethic—the belief in the moral value of the state, and a sense of communion with this spiritual and temporal force—but his father's "prejudices" were certainly not those of the state's elite. The retired lieutenant, a man whose position depended on the accurate performance of his duties, had nothing in common either in manner of thought or style of existence with the head of a noble clan who wielded patriarchal authority over his peasants and dependents, and even under Frederician absolutism retained a sense of preeminence and independence. The Junker might wear the king's uniform, but on his land he was still absolute master, and the provincial diets of which he was a member constituted in fact, not merely by law, the first estate of the realm. The elder Clausewitz was simply a subaltern servant of the state. That is not to say that the growing habit of command and the consciousness of his value to the monarchy could not, in time, invest him too with a touch of aristocratic freedom. In his sons this process seems to have been aided by an absence of any sense of social inferiority. Although as a young officer Carl von Clausewitz was conscious of his father's lack of influence, and delighted whenever he or one of his brothers gained a mark of recognition and "made an unknown name better known," his letters indicate that he did not seriously question his noble antecedents, even while knowing that all proof was lacking.[11] Since his peers accepted him, and since in manners and ability he was not their inferior, he felt at ease with privilege; but it could never carry for him those quasi-feudal overtones and the assumption of permanency in the order of things that derived from hereditary ownership of land and from the Junker's sense of personal association with the Hohenzollern dynasty. Rather, privilege was the result of effort and a sense of allegiance that bound him and his family to the state.

Little is known about Clausewitz's first twelve years. When he was a grown man he confessed to his fiancée with a touch of self-criticism that even as a child he had been exceptionally ambitious.[12] Other passages in

---

10. Clausewitz, *Nachrichten*, pp. 428–429.
11. The quoted passage occurs in a letter to Marie v. Brühl, 15 June 1807, *Correspondence*, p. 124.
12. See, among others, his letters to Marie v. Brühl of 9 April and 3 July 1807, *ibid.*, pp. 110–111, 127.

his letters indicate that he grew up in an affectionate home, an impression further borne out by the unusual sadness he felt when he left his parents to enter the army. "The sad emotions that weighed down my heart on that occasion," he wrote long afterwards, "have never quite disappeared ... . I shall never entirely overcome them." [13] His father was so badly paid that even in Burg, a country town where life was not expensive, his family must have lived on the edge of poverty. [14] The town was the garrison of the 47th Infantry Regiment, the regiment in which the elder Clausewitz had served, and a modest center of cloth manufacture. It was a disciplined, hard-working community, like countless others on the north-German plain, affording its artisans, officials, and soldiers few means with which to broaden their narrow horizon. Fifty years after Clausewitz had left Burg, it could still be regarded as the typical provincial nest: with a glance at its wool industry, an enlightened visitor from Berlin wrote that the town resembled nothing as much as an enormous stable inhabited by good citizen-sheep. [15] The municipal school that Clausewitz attended as a boy was an inferior institution, which in the 1780's had reached the nadir of a long decline. Some seventy pupils, ranging in age from six to sixteen and grouped into three classes, were taught the fundamentals of grammar and arithmetic, together with a smattering of Latin. [16] The curriculum was modeled after Hecker's *Realschule* in Berlin, which sought to turn the sons of the nonacademic bourgeoisie into useful subjects of the crown by preparing them for commercial life or for the lower reaches of government administration. The school's most gifted pupils, the principal reported at the time of Clausewitz's attendance, aspired to the career of village schoolmaster. [17] A modest change for the better occurred in 1788. New teachers were appointed and the number of classes was doubled, with some academic subjects being of-

13. Clausewitz to his wife, 18 May 1821, *ibid.*, p. 410.
14. Until 1787 the elder Clausewitz received 180 taler annually, afterwards, 225 taler, together with certain rations and payments in kind. Kessel, "Clausewitz," p. 766, n. 31. How difficult it was to maintain a large family on such a sum is indicated in several memoirs of the period, for instance in the early chapters of *Karl Friedrich von Klöden's Jugenderinnerungen*, ed. K. Koetschau, Leipzig, 1911. Klöden, a pioneer of trade education in Prussia, was the son of a retired NCO who in the 1790's occupied a subaltern position in the West Prussian revenue service similar to that of the elder Clausewitz. It is possible that the Clausewitz family tried to improve its economic situation by maintaining a small stand of mulberry trees for the production of silk. At least this is stated by P. Burg in his fictionalized biography, *Feder und Schwert: Der Philosoph des Krieges, Carl von Clausewitz*, Berlin, 1939, pp. 7–9, but Burg gives no sources for his information, and I have been unable to trace it.
15. T. Fontane, "Burg," *Sämtliche Werke*, 27 vols., Munich, 1959–70, xx, 660. The following is based on my article "Education, Politics, and War in the Life of Clausewitz," *Journal of the History of Ideas*, XXIX, No. 3 (July–September 1968).
16. W. Sens, "Die Schulen der Stadt Burg, Bez. Magdeburg, zu Beginn des 19. Jahrhunderts," *Geschichtsblätter für Stadt und Land Magdeburg*, LXVI–LXVII (1931–32), 130.
17. Reply dated February 1788, to a royal questionnaire, cited in G. Thile, *Geschichte der Preussischen Lehrerseminare*, *Monumenta Germaniae Paedagogica*, lxii, Berlin, 1938, pp. 122–123.

fered in the upper three grades.[18] Either during these years or in adolescence Clausewitz also learned French, in which he became fluent during his internment in France in 1807.

It was not unusual for a boy to enter the army at the age of twelve or thirteen, but Frederick II's unwillingness to admit the young Clausewitzes as officer-cadets delayed the beginning of their military careers until after his death.[19] Finally, in 1787, the second and third oldest succeeded in gaining admission at the desired rank of *Gefreiterkorporal*—lance corporal, serving with the expectation of promotion to ensign. Friedrich Volmar, already sixteen years old, entered one of the new light-infantry battalions that were being raised to add some flexibility to the volley and shock tactics of the Prussian line; Wilhelm Benedikt, two years younger, was accepted by the more prestigious 34th Infantry Regiment.[20] Its *commandant en chef* was Prince Ferdinand, a brother of the late king; the actual commanding officer was Lieutenant-Colonel von Hundt, son of the man who had married Professor Clauswitz's widow, and thus a stepbrother of the elder Clausewitz. Hundt, who was already in his sixties, soon retired from active service to head a reserve battalion; but he retained his connections with the regiment, in which his young relative rose rapidly to the rank of ensign and in 1792 to that of lieutenant. It was a likely unit in which to place the youngest of the Clausewitz brothers. In the spring of 1792, shortly before Carl von Clausewitz's twelfth birthday, his father presented him to the new commanding officer, who accepted him into the regiment.[21] The French Constituent Assembly had recently declared war on Austria, and Prussia was already drawn into the conflict; but the 34th Infantry remained in garrison near Berlin and did not participate in the fighting that followed during the summer and fall. It was not until January 1793 that the regiment, the two Clausewitz brothers with it, marched to the Rhine, where the field army was being reinforced and reorganized after a campaign that had posed unexpected problems to Prussia's political and military leadership.

18. Sens, p. 130. An examination commission which visited the school in 1794 pronounced itself "reasonably satisfied" with the new conditions. See P. Schwartz, *Der erste Kulturkampf in Preussen um Kirche und Schule: 1788–1798, Monumenta Germaniae Paedagogica*, lviii, Berlin, 1925, pp. 318–319.
19. A survey of the fifth volume of K. v. Priesdorff's biographical dictionary, *Soldatisches Führertum* (10 vols., Hamburg, 1936–42), shows that of 130 Prussian generals of Clausewitz's generation who began their careers as officer cadets, 17 entered the army between the ages from sixteen to twenty, 15 were fifteen years old, 85 were between twelve and fourteen, and 13 between nine and eleven.
20. When Clausewitz joined the regiment it ranked fourth in order of precedence behind the Guards; C. Jany, *Geschichte der Preussischen Armee*, 2nd ed., Osnabrück, 1967, iii, 11, n. 21.
21. The date of Clausewitz's entry into the army is not known. A letter to Marie v. Brühl, of 2 June 1807, indicates that it must have taken place before June 1792; *Correspondence*, p. 117.

❧ 2 ❧

THE FRENCH REVOLUTION

THROUGHOUT HIS ADULT LIFE, CLAUSEWITZ'S OPIN-
ions on the French Revolution were firm and at the same time complex. It
is hardly surprising that he disliked the origin of forces that he spent a lifetime combating. Nor could someone whose greatest ambition was to understand the reality behind appearances feel anything but scorn for the theatricality and rhetoric of the revolutionary leaders and of the emperor who
succeeded them. But Clausewitz's sarcastic comments on the self-
proclaimed saviors of humanity in Paris went hand in hand with admiration
for the energies they generated. In his fascination with the magnitude of
the political and military achievements of the Convention we can also find
the reason that he would not—unlike many Germans of reformist, progressive bent—separate the Revolution into an early moderate and desirable
phase and its destructive aberrant successor. Indeed he doubted whether the
latter—brutal and catastrophic though it turned out to be—could be considered an aberration rather than the almost inevitable consequence of the
events of 1789, which in turn were the far from unreasonable results of
severe social and political maladjustments that had preceded them. Clausewitz's interpretation of the origins of the French Revolution in an essay
written a few years after Waterloo, at the height of Legitimist reaction, indicates how remote his opinions were from party spirit: "After nearly all
European states had developed into absolute monarchies during the 17th
and 18th centuries," he wrote, "the nobility retained its privileges only in
relation to the rest of society, not in relation to the prince. The noble dominated the peasant and enjoyed advantages over the bourgeois, but he no
longer held a share of sovereign power and had become a subject like the
others. This gave his relationship to bourgeois and peasant the appearance
of privilege pure and simple, of a kind of unwarranted favor." [1] After dis-

---

1. The opening sentences of the above-mentioned essay "Umtriebe," printed in H. Rothfels's selection
of Clausewitz's writings *Politische Schriften und Briefe,* p. 153. The following quotation is from p. 162.
In the essay Clausewitz responds to the Restoration's panic of revolutionary plots by developing the his-

cussing conditions under Louis XIV and his successors, Clausewitz continues: "Thus the totally changed condition of the nobility, the unhealthy place it was given in the new framework of the state on the one hand, and the cultural advance of the bourgeoisie on the other, created such tension that a resolution in one form or another became necessary—either gradually through voluntary changes, or suddenly by force. This tension we consider to be the most significant cause of the French Revolution. The other is the abuse of administrative power."

His sympathetic recognition of the interaction of social and political forces that led to the upheaval did not make Clausewitz any less determined in opposing the spread of French power over Europe. But here too he was not blinded by the battle. At least in retrospect he found little to recommend in the policies by which France's neighbors tried to stem the tide. The views he expressed as an adult on the early phases of the revolutionary wars may be summarized as follows: He echoed the belief commonly held in Berlin in 1792 that the war which had broken out between France and Prussia was not in the best interest of either state. Such ostensible causes of the conflict as French expropriation of German feudal privileges in Alsace or, on the other hand, the offensive behavior of *émigrés* assembled in Trier and Coblenz were amenable to negotiation, and indeed were in the process of being resolved. However deeply Frederick William sympathized with the captive royal family, his feelings scarcely deserved to be transformed into state policy, and were too vague ever to have proven decisive if they had not been joined by other considerations. Both French and Prussian *raison d'état* demanded peace, which did not prevent some political factions in France from deluding themselves that an open break between the powers was desirable. The blindness of Louis XVI, who had come to believe that only war, whatever its outcome, could restore his authority, was matched by the political cupidity of the Girondins, who failed to see how insubstantial their position was if it required war to maintain it. But as Brissot and his colleagues fell victim to their political combinations, they drove the Revolution forward. Unlike the state, the Revolution had need of war, without which its impetus, rhetoric, and terror would never have reached their peak. Having enemies abroad helped define the enemy at home and made him more vulnerable; the reciprocity of politics and war infused each with greater energies. And aside from its contribution to the revolutionary process, the war soon gained a certain popularity among those Frenchmen who did not directly suffer from it, if only by diverting their

torical logic of the French Revolution. When it was published, nearly sixty years after it had been written, Delbrück admiringly compared Clausewitz's interpretation of the limited historical facts known to him at the time to the result of Tocqueville's later detailed research; "General von Clausewitz," reprinted in *Historische und politische Aufsätze*, Berlin, 1887, p. 214. I discuss the essay in part II, ch. 10, iii, below.

attention from the nation's internal difficulties and by providing a new, and for many a more acceptable, outlet for the Revolution's missionary zeal.

It was characteristic of the dynamics of violence, the mature Clausewitz thought, that once fighting began, Prussia's interests became more immediately engaged. An Austrian defeat in Belgium would endanger the Prussian territories of Cleve and Mark; Prussia's authority in the Empire might diminish unless she took steps to protect the German principalities along the Rhine—though Clausewitz argued that there was nothing in Alsace that Prussia was called on either to defend or conquer.[2] In the final analysis, he believed, neither territorial ambitions nor chivalrous instincts led the king and his advisers to enter the war on Austria's side, but concern for the balance of power and for the traditional modes of intercourse between governments. These views coincided with those of a historian whose first works appeared in the last years of Clausewitz's life. The French Revolution, Ranke writes in a passage that echoes the calm tones of the chancelleries of the *ancien régime,* "had in its early phases moved in a direction that could perhaps still be reconciled with the political conditions of the old Europe. To contain the revolutionary forces in this system was the true objective of the campaign of 1792." [3] The result, on the contrary, was the rapid dismemberment of the system, and the extension of French power over most of the continent. Soon the nation occupied a position of unequaled grandeur; but its very universality made it untenable. Only at the cost to France of irreplaceable human and political assets could it be maintained for the next two decades.

From the outset the Prussian officer corps was divided in its feelings about the war. Many men, particularly in the junior ranks, were at one with the young Clausewitz in welcoming any campaign as an opportunity for distinction and advancement, and cared little whether the opponent was France, Austria, Denmark, or Russia.[4] Others, the senior commanders among them, were critical of the king's decision, and were joined in this attitude by most of the ministers, the bureaucracy, and educated society in general.[5] In these circles, sympathies with the efforts of the French to reform their government and social institutions were reinforced by an awareness of French strength, and by dislike of the new Austrian alliance, which was interpreted as an abandonment of the principles of Frederician policy for no clearly defined gain. Preparations for the campaign got under way in a spirit of professional confidence, but with a sense among the leadership that this was not Prussia's war—a feeling that necessarily affected

2. *On War,* book VIII, ch. 9 (p. 928).
3. L. v. Ranke, *Hardenberg und die Geschichte des preussischen Staates,* Leipzig, 1879, i, 122.
4. Expressions of this attitude abound in memoirs of the period; for example, *Erinnerungen aus dem Leben des General-Feldmarschalls Hermann von Boyen,* ed. F. Nippold, Leipzig, 3 vols., 1889–90, i, 26–27, and *Denkwürdigkeiten des Generals Friedrich von Eisenhart,* ed. E. Salzer, Berlin, 1910, p. 12.
5. O. Tschirch, *Geschichte der öffentlichen Meinung in Preussen,* Weimar, 1933, i, 10–63.

the course of events. The Duke of Brunswick, generalissimo of the forces mobilized against France, agreed with Frederick William that only by a rapid advance could the Allies save Louis XVI, but his doubts about the enterprise and about his fitness to lead it resulted in very different actions. In January 1792 he had rejected an offer of the supreme command over all French armies in favor of the Prussian appointment, but he told the emissary from Paris that he would take care not to act precipitately: "Why risk a battle? If the French are the victors it will ruin us; if they lose they will still have other resources. My plan is to move numerous armies into your border regions, station them there for an extended period, have them take up unassailable positions, and await your defeat from internal troubles and bankruptcy." [6] After the initial Prussian offensive had recoiled to the Rhine, this was in fact the strategy Brunswick adopted. The senior officer next to the duke, Field Marshal Möllendorff, opposed the war from the start as an unnecessary adventure with no prospect of success. A few weeks after Valmy, an English diplomat reported him as saying that it was beyond all human capacity to return the French to calm and good order: the best that could be done was to establish a defensive line just within the eastern borders of France.[7] When he came to replace Brunswick as commander-in-chief he considered the defense of the Rhineland his main obligation. Even the Prussian victories in the summer and fall of 1793 did nothing to alter the view of the antiwar party that the struggle with France was a "dreadful labyrinth" which would "exhaust the king's finances and destroy his army." [8] By 1794 Frederick William's attention had become fixed on Poland, and operations in the west came gradually to a halt.

Not only politically, but militarily as well, the war broke with Frederician tradition. During his lifetime Prussia had rarely attained independence of action to the extent Frederick thought desirable; that he had been able to pursue his own course as often as he did, despite the restraints imposed by far more powerful allies, was, indeed, one of the distinctions of his reign. Under his successor Prussia entered a war without clear political purpose, and with such limited freedom in strategic planning and the conduct of operations that she soon became the junior member of the alliance. The campaign of 1792 introduced Prussia to the role she was to play until the final defeat of Napoleon—that of an important but never preeminent partner. She cast it off only once, in 1806, in a desperate, belated show of independence that led to disaster; but in the absence of an exceptionally gifted monarch the role of subsidiary did, in fact, accord with her true strength.

6. Jany, *Preussische Armee*, iii, 240.
7. Morton Eden to Grenville, 13 October 1792, in E. Herrmann, *Diplomatische Correspondenzen aus der Revolutionszeit 1791–1797*, Gotha, 1867, pp. 300–301.
8. Minutes of the cabinet minister P. K. v. Alvensleben, 1 October 1793, *ibid.*, pp. 405, 409.

Brunswick's area of operations, first in the Champagne, later in the Rhineland, flanked in the north and south by Austrian armies, seemed to symbolize the new, dependent position of the monarchy. To a considerable extent Prussian actions were shaped by events in the Austrian Netherlands and in Alsace. Divergent policies and inadequate arrangements for the co-ordination of the three armies increased the precariousness at the center. The network of interlocking dependence that the Allies stretched from Switzerland to the Channel coast was a perilous substitute for a rapid and determined offensive; but such an advance would have called not only for different attitudes on the part of the governments and their commanding generals but also—as long as the French intended to fight seriously—for a reorganization of allied military institutions.

The campaign of 1792 was a demonstration rather than a true offensive. Pressed by Frederick William, Brunswick had allowed the *émigrés'* confidence of an easy victory to override his better judgment, but the first sign of serious opposition recalled him to his convictions. In the middle of September strong enemy forces assembled at the western edge of the Argonne Forest to block his road to Paris. The Prussian army sought to dislodge them by marching around their flank and threatening their lines of communication—a movement soundly planned and executed, which even Napoleon later found worthy of praise. But although Brunswick was prepared to maneuver his way to Paris, he was unwilling to risk a major battle. When the French showed that they would disregard prudence and make a stand, he had seen enough; as he had more than half-expected, the demonstration had failed. The Prussians withdrew; bad weather, epidemics, and the breakdown of the supply system turned their retreat into a disaster. Cautiously the French followed in their wake, crossed into Germany, and occupied Mainz and Frankfurt. Brunswick's first need now was to regain these cities, and with them control of the Rhine. The establishment of a broad base of operations in the area between Coblenz and Heidelberg, with its navigable streams and good roads, would enable him to launch a limited offensive to the south of his earlier thrust, which might exert pressure on the revolutionary government while helping to protect the Empire. In contrast to the advance on Paris, this mission lay well within the capacity of his command, which even after being reorganized would not constitute more than one-third of the entire Prussian army. That the character of the French forces was gradually changing and breaking out of the mold of the *ancien régime* did not yet appreciably increase the Prussians' difficulties.

The French and Prussian armies of 1789 can be compared to two branches of the same tree: both were military instruments of absolute monarchies, nurtured by states whose rise had been linked to, and had even depended on, the armies' own development. They had given the central authority of the state permanence at home and new weight abroad, while their financial, economic, and human requirements—increasing enormously over the preceding century—had provided a powerful stimulus to the growth of governmental expertise and the expansion and proliferation of its agencies and controls. At the same time the armies were aristocratic institutions, which by now played a vital part in the nobility's way of life. Their aristocratic character was further sustained by the nature of the rank and file. The troops were either foreign mercenaries or forcibly enrolled sons of the native poor; the gulf between them and their officers was rarely bridged. Since their training was a time-consuming process and it was difficult, even in the populous French monarchy, to obtain men in adequate numbers, long-term service was essential, as was the greatest possible avoidance of risk in the troops' operational employment. Hired and drafted soldiers were a mixture that called for stringent supervision; this, together with the limited effectiveness of weapons, suggested that men were best used in mass formations. In both services the most important branch, the infantry, maneuvered in shallow, closely packed lines, the individual being encapsulated in formations that thought and acted for him. Mass and shock were also the means with which the cavalry carried out its primary tasks of protecting friendly infantry, disrupting the enemy's attacks, and accelerating his retreats. Except in siege warfare, artillery and engineers still played a subsidiary part. In contrast to their tactical cohesion, the organization of the two armies continued to be fragmented, their administrative and operational units generally being no larger than the regiment or even the battalion. Numerous boards, agencies, temporary and permanent commissions, frequently overlapping in authority, administered the forces; but such unifying bodies as a general staff or a supreme supply directorate were still in their infancy. Neither army had yet succeeded in combining effective central control with the administrative initiative and responsibility that was needed on all levels.[9]

The affinity of the two armies was not compromised by differences in particulars. Though the population of France was four and a half times that of Prussia, the two forces were approximately equal in strength, so that rather than dominating society, the French army was merely one of numerous powerful institutions in the nation.[10] As was the case with other of-

9. For a more detailed discussion of 18th-century military thought and policy see my *Yorck and the Era of Prussian Reform*, Princeton, 1966, pp. 12–46.
10. In 1789, France with a population over 26 million had 181,230 effectives in the peacetime establishment; Prussia, with somewhat less than six million inhabitants, had 170,738. P. Boiteau, *État de la France en 1789*, Paris, 1861, pp. 225, 247; Jany, *Preussische Armee*, iii, 181. In view of the reorganization of the *maison du roi* at that time, the total of French effectives might have been a few thousand men less. Comparative figures claiming a French superiority of 80,000 to 100,000 men occasionally appear in the literature; see, for example, E. Léonard, *L'Armée et ses problèmes au XVIIIᵉ siècle*,

fices, military commissions could still be purchased in France, a practice
that Saint Germain's reforms were only now phasing out, generations after
it had been abolished in Prussia. The much greater number of French officers, particularly in the senior grades, is another indication of the influence exerted by social and financial considerations at the expense of efficiency. In 1789 the Prussian army contained 123 officers of general rank,
while in France there were 1159.[11] Between this corps of senior officers and
the many thousands of subalterns, barriers existed that could scarcely be
found in Prussia, where differences of rank within the nobility were less
marked, and the officer corps, in consequence, was more homogeneous. Influence and protection at court played a role in both countries, but in Prussia promotion by merit and seniority to even the highest positions was not
exceptional. Neither army did much for the education of the line officer,
but the training of engineers, gunners, and other specialists was superior in
France—a reflection of her greater technological sophistication and higher
standard of living. Both armies contained tens of thousands of foreign mercenaries. The French, however, had fewer of them, and they were usually
isolated in special regiments; in the Prussian service there were one or two
exotic squadrons of Asians and eastern-Europeans, while all other units in-
discriminately combined Prussians and non-Prussians. The French were led
to separate native and foreign troops because of their traditional political
connections with such groups as the Irish, the Rhinelanders, and the Swiss,
and also because of their own more advanced sense of nationhood. One
benefit derived from this division was greater tactical flexibility. Rightly or
wrongly, conventional military opinion held that disciplinary problems and
the danger of desertion increased in units made up of men with dissimilar
backgrounds. The existence of such formations inhibited the evolution of
open order tactics, and worked against the expansion of other activities in
which the soldier was less closely supervised and to some degree had to fend
for himself. In France the more homogeneous character of the troops encouraged tactical experimentation, which was further stimulated by dissatisfaction with the army's performance during the Seven Years' War. While
Frederick and his generals could see little need to make extensive changes
in the linear system, the French developed maneuver columns and attack
columns to supplement the line. At the same time they paid new attention
to light troops, both foot and horse, whose indifference to terrain obstacles,
and ability to patrol and forage, had always been an important aid to the
effective functioning of the linear patterns. By 1789 the French army pos-

Paris, 1958, p. 287. The mistake results from choosing strengths from different years for the comparison, and from including the militia in the French total while not adding equivalent second-line units to
the Prussian figures.
11. *État militaire de France*, Paris, 1789, p. 83; *Kurzgefasste Stamm- und Rangliste der Königlich Preussischen Armee für das Jahr 1789*, Berlin, 1789, pp. 173–175, 185–186, 192–193.

sessed twelve battalions of *chasseurs à pied* which could fight entirely in irregular formations, and every line battalion contained a few dozen men who
were taught to skirmish and fire at will. From this it was only a step to the
integration of close order and open order, the system that was to dominate
infantry tactics in the later campaigns of the revolutionary wars and of the
Napoleonic era. In the Prussian army the introduction of light infantry battalions and company sharpshooters was undertaken in too formalistic a
manner to achieve the same results. Here, as in all areas of organization and
doctrine, the two armies were searching for similar solutions to common
problems, but in almost every instance they moved at a different rate of development. Of the two forces in 1789, the Prussian army was the more
unified and internally consistent organization, and therefore less susceptible
to change; the French army was more diverse, less efficient for the moment,
but pliant and receptive to innovation.

In war, these forces and the tactical and strategic systems they adhered
to proved remarkably adaptable, as they repeatedly demonstrated under a variety of conditions; but they reached their highest effectiveness when facing
opponents of their own kind. They were designed to carry out the deliberate
working of the *raison d'état* in central and western Europe. A war of limited
objectives was the usual military corollary of the balance of power: the
conquest or defense of a province, or the occupation of a border region for
bargaining purposes. More ambitious aims that affected the very existence
of the opposing state were generally beyond the armies' capabilities—at
least if the opponent was a major power. Here lies one explanation for the
failure of the grand coalition to defeat Prussia during the Seven Years' War.
Despite the greater resources at their disposal, the military organizations of
Russia, Austria, and France were not constituted to overwhelm a determined opponent who refused to negotiate after the loss of a province or
even the partial destruction of his army. Similar limitations shaped Frederick's strategy. Since he fought on interior lines, much of the time on his
own territory, he could shift fronts rapidly and seek to defeat or repel his
enemies one by one: but to decide the war by a strategic offensive against
Vienna or Paris was beyond his means. Even had commanders gone against
the spirit of their times and seriously considered such far-reaching
schemes—and Frederick, the intruder in the concert of the great powers,
was sufficiently desperate to attempt them twice—they would have failed.
The armies of the absolute monarchies were too small, too difficult to
replace, and their supply systems were too cumbersome to sustain mobility
for any length of time.[12] The expense and the unreliability of the troops

12. Why the supply systems were so poor is a question whose solution would add to our understanding
not only of operational concepts but of general attitudes of the 18th and the early 19th century. That
the transport of supplies on campaign was the least efficient aspect of every European army was due
largely to the absence of permanent organizations charged with this task. In peacetime, supply trains

demanded that they be well cared for at every stage of the campaign. The burden this placed on the supply organizations could have been alleviated by requisitions and the levying of contributions; but this was kept to a minimum. Otherwise, so Gerhard Ritter sums up the inhibiting factors, "there would have been no end to looting, deserting, and pillage—abuses that had horrified every responsible government since the *Landsknecht* era. Aimless destruction also conflicted with the new concept of *raison d'état*. Wars were waged without national passion. So far as possible, occupied territory was treated considerately, if only because wars could be expected to continue for long periods ... ." [13] Besides, troops could not be trusted to live off the country and retain the peculiarly intense discipline necessary for the proper functioning of the linear formations. They were therefore largely dependent on the regular supply system; in turn the difficulties of storage, transportation, and distribution further limited combat strengths. The problem was so severe that late-18th-century theorists postulated an ideal size for field armies beyond which additional strength became a hindrance rather than an asset—a concept Clausewitz was to ridicule when it continued to be advocated under the very different conditions of the Napoleonic wars. [14] The poor roads and the inadequacy of wagon transport in mobile operations added to the importance of depots and magazines. Armies could not safely move more than a few days' march from their supplies; their advance, even if unopposed, had to come to a halt until depots and field bakeries were shifted forward to provide a base for the next step. Every mile added to the supply routes heightened the likelihood of breakdown, loss, or seizure by enemy patrols, and gave greater scope to the play of chance and surprise, which generals of the *ancien régime* feared more than did later generations, because their small, cumbersome forces were not good at dealing with the unforeseen. The spoilage of land and people, the willingness to trade lives for rapid, deep penetrations, and the destruction of the enemy had to await a new ruthlessness in political intercourse and a new strategic ideal, which no longer considered the utmost exclusion of chance a major achievement of command but actively sought chance in-

were entrusted to a few officers and civilian officials; for maneuvers and in time of war the necessary personnel had to be especially enrolled. The confusion this caused may be imagined from the fact that in 1792 the Prussian supply- and hospital-train alone required 3,348 drivers, none of whom had been instructed in his duties before mobilization. Conditions in other armies were similar; but although every commanding general from Frederick to Napoleon seems to have complained about the inadequacy of these *ad hoc* bodies or of the civilian contractors who often took their place, nothing was done to establish permanent train units and to standardize their equipment and drill. The reliability of Prussian supply increased markedly with the formation of train battalions in 1812, but they were again disbanded at the end of the war, and it was not until the early 1850's that permanent supply units became a regular part of the Prussian peacetime establishment. In the American Civil War the Union and Confederate armies still relied to a considerable extent on commercial haulers.

13. G. Ritter, *Frederick the Great*, ed. and trans. P. Paret, Berkeley and Los Angeles, 1968, pp. 135–136.
14. *On War*, book III, ch. 8 (p. 274).

stead. A fluid situation would create unsuspected opportunities for decisive results, which expendable mass armies could exploit.

By December 1792 the French invasion of the right bank of the Rhine had been brought to a halt. Frankfurt was soon liberated, and the French commander in chief, Custine, withdrew to the Palatinate; a strong garrison in Mainz, which in the course of the winter reached 23,000 men, supported by the *armée du Rhin* operating in the valleys of the Mosel and Saar rivers, might be able to hold the newly proclaimed Rhenish Republic. In the meantime the Prussians reorganized their forces in preparation for the siege. Clausewitz's regiment arrived on the Rhine toward the end of January; a few weeks later he saw his first combat when the regiment took part in the shelling of a village some miles from Mainz.[15] In the last days of March the main army crossed the Rhine north of the city; but instead of trying to destroy Custine's outnumbered forces, Brunswick was content to fight a number of limited engagements, which drove the French several days' marches farther west, beyond easy reach of the city. It required another six weeks for the necessary guns and siege equipment to be assembled; until then a costly war of ambushes and sorties was waged among the outlying villages which the garrison had converted into strongpoints. On 6 June, a few days after Clausewitz's thirteenth birthday and his promotion to ensign, one battalion of his regiment stormed the village of Zahlbach, after which the siege trenches could be opened. By the end of the month the earthworks had come to within 800 paces of the main walls, and the bombardment began. Goethe, who had accompanied the Weimar contingent to the siege, observed the bombardment from the headquarters' redoubt, pitying the stricken city and appreciating the beauty of the incendiary bombs as they lost themselves in the starry sky before dropping on their targets, while in a trench below, Clausewitz joined in the cheers of his soldiers at the sight of the first flames.[16] Violent fighting during the next weeks led to the capture of the remaining outworks, and on 23 July the garrison surrendered the city, obtaining for itself the freedom to return to France.

The Prussians now wished to advance on the Saar, in conjunction with

15. A list of the regiment's more important engagements in 1793 and 1794 is printed in G. Gieraths, *Die Kampfhandlungen der Brandenburgisch-Preussischen Armee*, Berlin, 1964, p. 113. There is no good modern history of the Rhine campaign. For the following I have relied on the standard works of Jomini and A. Chuquet; the two excellent studies by J. Colin, *La Tactique et la discipline dans les armées de la Révolution*, Paris, 1902, and *Campagne de 1793 en Alsace et dans le Palatinat*, Paris, 1902; *Pirmasens und Kaiserslautern; Kriegsgeschichtliche Einzelschriften*, xvi, published by the Historical Section of the German General Staff, Berlin, 1893; and Jany, *Preussischen Armee*, iii, 259–300.

16. Goethe describes the bombardment in his *Belagerung von Mainz*, *Werke*, 14 vols., Hamburg, 1956–60, x, 374–375. Clausewitz's self-critical recollection of his behavior is contained in his letter to Marie v. Brühl, 28 January 1807, *Correspondence*, p. 83.

an Anglo-Austrian offensive in the Austrian Netherlands; but Vienna, which had begun to lose interest in her exposed northern possessions, decided instead on an offensive in Alsace, and Brunswick marched south-west to cover the Austrian flank. For the rest of the year the Prussian army operated in the hilly rectangle outlined by the Rhine, Mosel, and Saar rivers, and the northern end of the Vosges Mountains, its 45,000 men much of the time dispersed over forty miles, fragmented into tendrils of outposts and detachments, probing the enemy, but without energy or will to exploit the opportunities they discovered. Twice Brunswick concentrated his forces to repel major French attacks, but since he had no wish to launch a major offensive his victories at Pirmasens and Kaiserslautern were not followed up, and had no lasting effect. Lack of agreement between the Prussians and Austrians compromised even the limited actions they undertook. Their failure to co-operate, Jomini writes, "saved France on her eastern frontiers as it did in the north, because at that time the *armée du Rhin* and the *armée de la Moselle* were so to speak disorganized [by] the systems of terror and distrust ... ." [17] The siege of Landau, possession of which would have given Brunswick an advanced operational base, dragged on until winter came and supply difficulties compelled the army to withdraw to its depots. Austrian defeats in Alsace caused the retreat to continue to the Rhine. By the end of the year the opposing armies occupied essentially the same positions they had held after the recapture of Mainz in July. Möllendorff, when he succeeded Brunswick in January 1794, sought to do no more than establish a line on the Saar River which would link up with allied forces in the Austrian Netherlands and cover the Rhineland. He retraced Brunswick's advance of the previous year; once again the French were defeated in several engagements; but the campaign continued to consist primarily of minor actions designed to interfere with the build-up of enemy forces and to prevent the launching of a serious offensive. At the same time, Möllendorff, without the king's knowledge, was negotiating with Paris to bring the fighting between Prussia and France to an end. [18] French victories in the Netherlands, Prussia's exhausted finances, and the contradictory interests of the allied powers were breaking up the First Coalition. The king himself lost heart. In late fall the French and Prussian governments began official talks, which in the spring of 1795 led to the Peace of Basel.

The campaign of 1792 and 1793 had shown few significant differences in the Prussian and French armies' manner of fighting. [19] Both sides con-

17. A. H. Jomini, *Histoire critique et militaire des guerres de la Révolution*, 15 vols., Paris, 1820–24, iv, 78.
18. Ranke, *Hardenberg*, i, 223. Ranke notes that it was in "striking and yet easily explicable contrast that the republic punished any departure from the government's instructions with the most extreme measures, while the monarchy tolerated a degree of independence among its officers which extended even to the major issues of foreign affairs."
19. A more detailed discussion of French and Prussian doctrine during the 1790's can be found in my *Yorck*, pp. 63–98.

tinued to think in terms of limited strategies. The French nearly as often as the Prussians deployed their infantry in linear formations, though the hilly terrain and the wide dispersion of the forces made the conventional extended line of battle a rarity. French use of skirmishers and attack columns increased slowly; their co-ordination of close order and open order showed some improvement; but their tactics were still too unformed to master the Prussian light troops and the smoothly firing Prussian line. The impetuousness of their attacks could suddenly change to panic. A subsequent German evaluation of the French army at the battle of Pirmasens is valid for the entire period: "The French attacks present the picture of a transitional era. A new doctrine is struggling to emerge, but it is not yet understood; it causes confusion and misunderstanding everywhere, and fails against a method of fighting that may be outdated, but is familiar and executed with confidence." [20] Contemporaries noted the reduced baggage train of the French and their efficient horse artillery—both indispensable if mobility was to increase—but these were still little more than indications of things to come. At the time, the most striking French weakness in combat was their "total lack of mobility and the total lack of combined operations"—that is, of co-ordinating infantry and cavalry.[21] The soldiers on the Rhine and in Alsace were perhaps better trained than French troops in other theaters of war, and units often fought well on their own; but their officers—many of whom had only recently taken the place of their aristocratic predecessors—lacked experience, and did not yet know how to act together for the common purpose. Their inexperience was equally damaging to the army's administration. The irregularities of pay and supply, and the high incidence of desertion to which this contributed, prevented the French commanders from exploiting the numerical superiority that they were coming to enjoy with increasing frequency.

Lack of discipline and the poor relations between officers and their government seemed in 1793 to constitute the most notable features distinguishing the French from the Prussian army. It was difficult to believe that the laxness, confusion, and terror which marked the opposing side in such contrast to one's own unchanging routine did not presage the collapse of army and state. Custine, who had failed to relieve Mainz, was guillotined, as were other officers. During the reverses of the autumn, the commander in chief and most of the generals of the *armée de la Moselle* were suspended from duty, while in the *armée du Rhin* few officers of field-grade or above escaped being denounced to the representatives on mission or to the Convention.[22] Political interference, which ranged from matters of personnel and administration to tactical decisions, was often enough capricious or mistaken; it hindered operations and hurt morale. But the impulses emanating

---

20. *Pirmasens und Kaiserslautern*, p. 312.
21. Colin, *Campagne de 1793*, p. 26.
22. *Ibid.*, pp. 424–425, 460.

from Paris also carried a message of determination, and infused officers and troops with so much energy that the patchwork armies continued to function. To a correspondent who complained of injustices suffered by noble officers, Bouchotte, the sansculotte minister of war, wrote in August 1793: "When those who possess [military] ability oppose the popular system, other men must be chosen to make it work; men who at first seem not to have great ability, but who end by acquiring it, and who, finally, have the greatest talent of all: the will to make the system work." [23]

Since the revolutionary *volonté de faire aller le système* was opposed by commanders who, as Clausewitz later wrote, were delighted to do nothing so long as they could put a decent face on it, the new and the traditional elements in the French army were given the time to achieve equilibrium. [24] By the end of 1794 the French nation's return to relative order had been matched by the growth of discipline and know-how among its troops; and with the maturation of new policies of manpower procurement and officer selection, and more dynamic tactical and strategic concepts, the army grew away from its Prussian twin. The new political aim—conquest and the destruction of old political entities—brought with it a new strategic and tactical mission: the destruction of the enemy's military power. The run of French successes throughout Europe demanded that other armies understand the workings of these innovations. In addition they posed two questions: how much did the new methods of war contribute to the victories; and to what extent were they necessarily dependent on political and social change. To men persuaded of the adequacy of their own arrangements, it was tempting to give greatest weight to the advantages France drew from her geography, the size of her population, and the lack of unity among her enemies; but already in the 1790's a few observers—notably Clausewitz's later teacher, the Hanoverian gunnery officer Gerhard Scharnhorst—called attention to the significance of her coherent, aggressive strategy, which served interests that could be expressed in national rather than dynastic terms, the rapidity with which troops now moved, the willingness to accept huge casualties, and the freedom and enthusiasm of the individual soldier. [25] That this and more was connected with political change was difficult to deny. By revolutionizing society, the state was able as never before to exploit the energies of society for war. And better military tools were now available to it. With the restraints of the monarchy falling away, the speculations and experiments of generations of soldiers could be brought to their full potential. It was the task of the reform-minded in other countries

23. *Ibid.*, p. 29.
24. Clausewitz, *Nachrichten*, p. 448.
25. See Scharnhorst's long essay, "Entwicklung der allgemeinen Ursachen des Glücks der Franzosen in dem Revolutionskriege," first published in 1797 and reprinted in *Militärische Schriften von Scharnhorst*, ed. C. v.d. Goltz, Dresden, 1891.

to learn how the energies of their own societies, without which any innovation might be nothing more than a new variant of the old formalism, could be aroused by other than revolutionary means. Purely technical and organizational adjustments in one's military institutions would hardly meet the new challenge. A decade after the defeat of Napoleon, Clausewitz wrote: "When that remarkable change in the art of war took place, when the best armies saw part of their doctrine become ineffective and military victories occurred on a scale that up to then had been inconceivable, it seemed that all mistakes had been military mistakes. It became evident that the art of war, long accustomed to a narrow range of possibilities, had been surprised by options that lay beyond this range, but that certainly did not go against the nature of war itself ... . Clearly the tremendous effects of the French Revolution abroad were caused not so much by new military methods and concepts as by radical changes in policies and administration, by the new character of government, altered conditions of the French people, and the like. That other governments did not understand these changes, that they wished to oppose new and overwhelming forces with customary means: all these were political errors. . . . In short, we can say that twenty years of revolutionary triumph were mainly due to the mistaken policies of France's enemies. . . . It is true that war itself has undergone significant changes in character and methods, changes that have brought it closer to its absolute form. But these changes did not come about because the French government freed itself, so to speak, from the harness of policy; they were caused by the new political conditions which the French Revolution created both in France and in Europe as a whole, conditions that set in motion new means and new forces, and have thus made possible a degree of energy in war that otherwise would have been inconceivable." [26]

These were reflections of the mature man. When the Peace of Basel was signed Clausewitz was not yet fifteen; what he thought about war at the time, and what being a soldier meant to him, can only be guessed at from a few statements made in later years. The campaign had not been easy for him. Of the three ensigns in his regiment, two died of illness, and his superiors suspected that Clausewitz, too, lacked the stamina to survive.[27] He was repeatedly under fire, taking his place in the regimental line of battle, or acting with a measure of independence when he accompanied a section on detached service. From one such episode—an ambush or skirmish so commonplace that it is not mentioned in the regimental records— he barely extricated himself.[28] Clausewitz's feelings as he came to know the infantry soldier's war can be reconstructed from a diary entry made in

26. *On War,* book VIII, ch. 6B (pp. 894–896).
27. According to a note once contained in the Clausewitz papers, quoted by H. Rothfels in his masterly study, *Carl von Clausewitz: Politik und Krieg,* Berlin, 1920, p. 5, n. 9.
28. Clausewitz to Marie v. Brühl, 2 June 1807, *Correspondence,* p. 117.

1807, which in its manner of fusing his environment with his fears and dreams reads like the prose version of one of Caspar David Friedrich's analytic-Romantic landscapes. A voyage through the French Jura had reminded Clausewitz of his first campaign: "With much pleasure I still recall ... an experience when the Prussian army in 1793 left the Vosges. We had spent half a year in these thickly wooded, raw, poor, and melancholy mountains, and with a kind of resignation our eyes had grown accustomed never to see more than a few steps of the path that we followed. Our psychological existence was similar: the physical surroundings perfectly reflected our mood. The soldier's extremely restricted horizon barely permits him to survey the next few hours. Often he hears the voice of battle, which is near and yet remains invisible, and he approaches his fate like a danger in the night.—At last, after an arduous march, we suddenly reached the peak of the last mountain ridge, and before and beneath us stretched the magnificent valley of the Rhine, from Landau to Worms. At that moment life seemed to me to change from ominous gravity to friendliness, from tears to smiles." [29]

Unmistakable in this reminiscence is the writer's desire to reconstruct and understand a feeling experienced long ago. The approach, if not its elegiac tone, is characteristic of the personal memories and reflections that Clausewitz often introduced into his letters and his historical and theoretical writings. No attempt is made to beautify his experiences or minimize their psychological difficulties and ambiguities. On the contrary, Clausewitz's objective view of himself is at times blurred by exaggerated self-criticism, or at least by a very ready acknowledgment of his personal traits, whether these might appear more or less admirable to the outside world. The evocation of a fourteen-year-old's very natural relief at having left danger behind suggests that even in adolescence Clausewitz was learning to face his anxieties openly; as an adult he was conscious of the violence and death that are part of war, to the point of stressing them again and again. But he also sought war. Only active service gave him the opportunity to rise in the world. "I grew up," he wrote to his fiancée, "on the stage of great events, where the fate of nations was decided. Not the temple in which family-life celebrates its serene happiness caught my gaze, but the triumphal arch through which the victor enters while a wreath of fresh laurel cools his brow. Perhaps," he added, "nature endowed me too richly with that vanity we call ambition." [30] His sense of the brutality of war and his longing for military distinction were joined by a third force: the need to understand the workings, purpose, and possible justifications of violence. No doubt this wish to know was not yet clearly evident during the Rhine

29. "Diary of a Journey from Soissons over Dijon to Geneva," in Schwartz, *Leben des Generals Clausewitz,* i, 90.
30. Clausewitz to Marie v. Brühl, 9 April 1807, *Correspondence,* pp. 110–111.

campaign; but it began to reveal itself as peace returned and the adolescent came to reflect on the meaning that war and the profession of arms held for himself and the state. What he had done and observed in 1793 and 1794 provided the impulse of personal experience to his early studies and his first theoretical speculations, written under the continuing impact of French aggression. Whatever the political condition of Europe and of Prussia, he would have looked to education as a means to improve and understand himself; but the onslaught of the Revolution and of Napoleon intensified the intellectual and emotional urgency of acquiring knowledge, until Clausewitz's individual development became inseparable from his effort to comprehend his political and military environment, its past, the changes that were occurring, and its constants. He had been present at the opening clash of two antagonistic systems—or, as he later was to believe, of two epochs in history—and as time went on the decisive significance of his experience in the revolutionary wars for his entire intellectual development became apparent. It dominated his youth, and its influence—usually creative but sometimes limiting—remained with him to the end of his life.

1927611

❧ 3 ❧

GARRISON LIFE AND
THE PERFECTIBILITY OF MAN

GERMAN WRITERS ON EDUCATION DURING THE LAST decades of the 18th century liked to refer to the "pedagogic century" in which they lived, or even, in a phrase Herder used in his *Humanitätsbriefe,* to their "political-pedagogic age." Optimistic designations such as these reflected not only the rapidly growing interest that society was showing in all aspects of education, the new concern of governments with educational policy and the administration of schools, and the enormous increase in the relevant literature, but, most important, a new way of considering the subject. It was at this time, a modern reformer of education writes, that pedagogic theory began to take on a more encompassing character, after it had dealt fragmentarily for some centuries with the universities, with family upbringing and elementary schooling, with the education of princes and of upper-class youths.[1] The psychological and intellectual potential of the individual, and a larger view of the society in which he was to function, now joined traditional considerations of class and calling to guide German pedagogic theorists in their efforts to rationalize educational practice.

Their innovations were propelled by, and responded to, changes in society and in the scope and apparatus of the state. The expansion of opportunity in government, trade, and the professions, with a concomitant need for greater specialization, called for appropriate training; as their activities proliferated, the middle classes, the primary beneficiaries of the process of modernization, sought intellectual and ethical support for their claim to a more independent and advantageous role in society. Neither could be provided by the old Latin schools, the academies of nobles, and the church-dominated universities. A bourgeoisie that was growing ambitious and self-

1. S. Bernfeld, *Sisyphus or the Limits of Education,* ed. P. Paret, Berkeley and Los Angeles, 1973, p. 9.

assertive demanded training for its sons that was secular and realistic, and that would breach some of the restrictive, aristocratic walls encapsulating German society. Pietism, with its rejection of external, formal standards of thought and conduct for the sake of achieving a rich inner development, was one major source of the new education, which came to mingle with Philantropism and, later, neohumanism to create the main body of German pedagogic theory in the second half of the century. Basedow's short-lived institute in Dessau, the Philantropin, indicates the general forms that these concepts at first tended to assume in real life. Although Basedow had been inspired by Rousseau's appeal to allow human nature to ripen gradually, and by his indictment of the corrupt bondage of class, the Philantropin's pupils were still drawn entirely from polite society, and were often subjected to academic forced feeding. Nevertheless, in comparison with prevailing standards Basedow's teaching methods were more relaxed; he limited learning by rote, and instead sought to nurture comprehension and independent judgment. His consciously utilitarian curriculum, emphasizing modern languages, mathematics, history, geography, and even sports, had the aim of creating successful, happy burghers and useful subjects of the state. Numerous schools followed Basedow's pattern—which, at once liberating and stilted, was probably better suited to imparting knowledge than to helping its pupils through puberty to adulthood—until at the end of the century German pedagogic thought found its richest, most human expression in Herder's declaration that the child was not an incomplete adult but possessed its own values and needs, and in Pestalozzi's schools, with their inclusion of children from poor as well as wealthy families, their attempt to translate parental love and careful observation into institutional terms, and their effort to achieve a genuine and constant bond between the processes of teaching and learning and the child's physiological and psychological development.

The new bourgeois schools benefited the state, its finances and its administrative machinery, even as they helped bring about a certain adjustment of the nobility's position; but the state also found it advisable to enter more actively into the business of educating the mass of its population. Memorizing the catechism and learning the alphabet no longer seemed sufficient schooling for the peasant. Some instruction in reading and writing, in adding and subtracting, learning the names of the state's rulers and the battles they had won, coupled with theological teaching heavily charged with the message of obedience and satisfaction in one's station in life, could turn the peasant into a more productive member of society, and reinforce and extend his patriarchal loyalties into a sense of obligation to the dynasty and the state. The threat to the status quo that might lurk in mass education was recognized, and contributed to the defeat of proposals for a common school system, already being advanced in Prussia and elsewhere, which children of many backgrounds would attend for some years to learn the basic knowledge needed in the modern world. But even in its severely controlled and restricted scope, elementary education encouraged intellectuals and pedagogues in their new ambition to create in society a sense of cultural community, an awareness of shared German values, which to some degree transcended class differences. As yet their thinking was still vague, its uncertainties and contradictions scarcely masked by the term *National-erziehung,* which was gaining currency; but the armed aggression of France in the 1790's and the first years of the new century simplified the issues and led to a purposeful effort to integrate, through education, human values and German values with service to the state.

Education, both of the mass and of elites, no matter how utilitarian, added the support of experience and tangible evidence to another, still more truly universal concept: that men, whatever their condition, were educable, and possessed the right and even duty to develop their abilities to the fullest. The purpose of education was thus raised beyond economic well-being, professional competence, or political strength to the harmonious development of intellect and personality. It was true that the most impressive writers who formulated the neohumanistic ideal of the serene, free spirit—notably Goethe—suggested that the ideal could be approached only by men who were economically and socially secure, that the highest degree of internal growth demanded independence from the state and from the press of daily business—even, as the young Wilhelm von Humboldt seemed to argue, that it could take place only in opposition to the state. And yet the ideal, profoundly unaristocratic, at least in the sense of elevating the merit of achievement over the merit of birth, had from the outset a strong impact on broader, less privileged circles in German life. Thousands of men in the service of great, impersonal institutions—parsons, teachers, bureaucrats, officers—sought to live by the Greek vision of the spirit that gained freedom and harmony by responsibly obeying its autonomous laws. Some members of the new cultural brotherhood separated their inner and their external lives. Others believed that by striving for a personal ideal they spiritualized and ennobled the work they performed for the state. As their narrow provincial condition expanded to a universe that spanned Periclean Athens and the discoveries and energies of the modern age, much seemed attainable for all levels of the community once polite society had embraced the serenity and intellectual sovereignty which German Classicism, the concept of *Bildung,* and pedagogic theory were holding up as the highest aims of man.

Clausewitz's first experience with the new trends in education probably occurred in early childhood. A family influenced by its Pietistic tradition, whose members lived on good terms with one another, was more likely to respect a child's particular qualities and respond to his needs for love than the higher nobility, among whom the earlier pattern of a cool distance between parents and children—much of whose upbringing was entrusted to tutors—still remained prevalent. Clausewitz again benefited from the new currents at the town school at Burg, which during his attendance underwent the broadening of the curriculum that was characteristic of the modest reforms of the Prussian state schools in the last decades of the century. His third experience occurred at the end of the Rhine campaign. In the spring of 1795 the main Prussian army withdrew from France to the area between the Ems River and Osnabrück, and for several months before returning to his permanent garrison near Berlin, Clausewitz was quartered in a Westphalian farmhouse. He was impressed by the patriarchal, self-sufficient existence of the farmers with whom he stayed. Years afterwards he wrote to his bride that the peace and simplicity of country life, following the turbulence of war, led him for the first time into prolonged introspection: "We were in the neighborhood of Osnabrück; books could be obtained from there; I began to read, and by chance some Illuminati pamphlets and other books on human perfectibility came into my hands. Suddenly the vanity of the little soldier was transformed into extreme philosophic ambition." [2] It is one of the very few statements by Clausewitz that we possess concerning his first twenty years, and the fact that he singled out this experience—a "unique, brief episode," he calls it, "apart from which my inner life . . . was perfectly ordinary, like that of most people"—indicates the magnitude of the impression that it made on him.

Clausewitz does not name the books that he read. In the 1780's a small lodge of Illuminati had been founded in Osnabrück.[3] The circulating library that supplied Clausewitz with books, and stocked Illuminati literature, evidently was connected with this group, and presumably belonged to the network of reading circles and lending libraries that some members tried to organize in the late 1780's to spread the views of the order.[4] During the second half of the century, secret societies such as the Freemasons and the Illuminati served to bring together men who were, or felt themselves to be, representatives of the new Enlightenment in Germany. To those who opposed the ideologies of the Reformation and Counter-Reformation, which still dominated much of everyday life in the German principalities, the secret societies offered some sense of community, functioning, it has been said, as a substitute church, which relieved men of their

2. Clausewitz to Marie v. Brühl, 3 July 1807, *Correspondence*, pp. 127–128. The memory of that episode remained with him when he wrote *On War*. In the chapter on guerrillas, book VI, ch. 26 (p. 699), he turns to the sparsely populated Westphalian countryside, dotted here and there with large farms, as the prime example of an area suited to irregular warfare. The following paragraphs are based on my previously cited article "Education, Politics, and War in the Life of Clausewitz."
3. R. le Forestier, *Les Illuminés de Bavière et la franc-maçonnerie allemande*, Paris, 1914, pp. 346, 396.
4. On this scheme see the anonymous article "Das Projekt der deutschen Union der XXII," *Latomia: Freimaurerische Vierteljahrsschrift*, XXI (1862), esp. pp. 34–35.

sense of loneliness and isolation as they struggled for new spiritual and intellectual certainty.[5] But they were more than havens; by their very nature, communities of the like-minded might work toward goals that lay beyond the capacity of society at large. The purpose of the Masons, Fichte wrote at the time, was to "remedy the flaws of education as it was generally practiced, to blend one-sided training that was suited to a particular class and profession with the general cultivation of humanity and to combine it with the universal education of the human being as human being." [6] When in the 1770's Adam Weishaupt, professor of canon law at the University of Ingolstadt, founded the Order of the Illuminati, or Perfectibilists, in close imitation of the Freemasons, he too was driven by the hope that a secret association of disciplined idealists might become a powerful force for intellectual and social good.[7] By being part of an elite which demanded that men use their intelligence freely, obeying only the majestic authority of nature as it was symbolized and represented by a hierarchy of superiors, the Illuminati would ennoble their own character, spread wisdom throughout Germany, and lead all mankind toward the goal of perfection. As perfection was approached, the true nature of man would break out of the snares in which it had been entangled by selfish and evil forces. Mankind, rid of prejudice and ignorance, would become happier, and when its existence was completely harmonized with the laws of nature, the old religious and political institutions that had enslaved it would crumble. Utopian prophecies of this kind facilitated attacks on the order as an "invisible conspiracy against the Christian religion and monarchical government." [8] Though a loose organization, lacking both political program and firm organization, the Illuminati were outlawed in Bavaria in 1785. After the beginning of the French Revolution, in which many claimed to detect its hand, the order was accused of scheming to betray Germany's independence to the Jacobins, and in the political and military tempests that ushered in the new century it ceased to exist.

Throughout his life Clausewitz scorned secret societies.[9] Even at the age of fifteen he could not have found much of specific value in the rhap-

5. The description is H. Schneider's, in "Lessing und die Freimaurer," reprinted in his *Lessing: zwölf biographische Studien*, Berne, 1951, p. 173.
6. J. G. Fichte, *Philosophie der Maurerei*, Leipzig, 1923, p. 17. Fichte had entered the Masons in 1793. His essays on masonry were written six years later, while he was a member of the Lodge Royal York in Berlin.
7. Essays, memoranda, and letters by Weishaupt and other members concerning the aims of the Order are printed in L. Engel, *Geschichte des Illuminaten-Ordens*, Berlin, 1906. Among Weishaupt's numerous writings, two books are especially interesting for their pedagogic analyses: *Geschichte der Vervolkommnung des menschlichen Geschlechtes*, Frankfurt and Leipzig, 1788, and *Über die Selbstkenntniss, ihre Hindernisse und Vortheile*, Regensburg, 1794. It may be noted that Pestalozzi, who was to figure in Clausewitz's intellectual development, entered the Order of Illuminati in 1783.
8. The title of an anonymous pamphlet against the Illuminati, first published in 1794, and later reprinted several times.
9. Letter of 21 May 1809 to Marie v. Brühl, *Correspondence*, p. 235.

sodic message of the Illuminati, and he probably ridiculed its occult acces-
sories, if one can judge from his subsequent comments on such matters.[10]
But his description of his first encounter with the literature of perfectibility
shows how much, as a youth, he was impressed by the idea that man could
learn to understand himself, could improve himself, and consequently
could improve society. In shallow and theatrically enticing form, with re-
petitive but easily understandable arguments, the Illuminati transmitted to
the young Clausewitz a general ideal of the educated German of his day:
that man could, and should, liberate himself from self-imposed mental
tutelage—from the inability, for lack of determination and courage, to use
his intelligence freely, without the guidance of others.[11]

Six years as a subaltern in the town of Neuruppin followed before
Clausewitz received a further great intellectual impulse from the outside
world. Hardly any biographical material has survived from this period, and
every biographer has passed over the years at Neuruppin in a sentence or
two. But there is no lack of information on the physical, social, and intellectual aspects of Clausewitz's existence in Neuruppin. As it is assembled, a
few specifically biographical facts emerge from the general picture, and
even some hints of ideas he was to express decades later in *On War*. Clausewitz himself dismissed the time from his fifteenth to his twenty-first year in
a few contemptuous and self-critical phrases: "Caged in a small garrison,
surrounded and influenced by nothing but prosaic conditions and prosaic
individuals, my existence was distinguished in no way from that of the better sort of my comrades—and even they were still very ordinary people—
except by a somewhat stronger tendency toward thought, toward literature,
and by military ambition, the one remaining trace of my earlier *élan*. But
ambition, too, was more of a handicap than beneficial to my inner development, as long as there seemed to be no way to satisfy it." [12] The note of
disappointment is caused by the failure of these years to fulfill the expectations that exposure to the ideas of the Enlightenment had aroused in the
boy. Presumably it also reflects later intellectual and social experiences of
the writer, who now looks back with disdain at this humdrum, provincial
period of his life. In reality, however, Neuruppin counted as one of the
more agreeable garrisons in the monarchy, as might be expected, seeing
that the regiment was among the most prestigious in the service, and possessed the distinction of having as its colonel-in-chief a brother of Frederick

---

10. See, for instance, his attack on "the newest sects" whose "mysticism, on which they pride themselves, is too shallow, too artificial ... . They want to subordinate human understanding to the dark
images of fantasy and to vague emotions, because they themselves lack sound intelligence and wish to
seem novel ... . I have no qualms about rebelling against that unseemly mysticism which always trans-
ports man to a dark shore, where it might be as well not to land, and where he remains like a feeble
child." "Historisch-politische Aufzeichnungen (1807–1808)," *Politische Schriften und Briefe*, p. 59.
11. I am paraphrasing the opening sentences of Kant's "Beantwortung der Frage: Was ist Aufklärung?"
12. Letter of 3 July 1807 to Marie v. Brühl, *Correspondence*, p. 128.

the Great. While the little town did not offer the stimulation of the capital, it was far from being one of the isolated nests that served as home for much of the army—overgrown villages whose dreariness and uninterrupted routine, particularly in the newly acquired Polish territories, were notorious and dreaded. Neuruppin was surrounded by estates of the Brandenburg nobility: Rheinsberg, where Crown Prince Frederick had spent his happiest years and now the residence of another of his brothers, Prince Henry, lay within easy riding distance; Berlin and Potsdam were less than forty miles to the southeast. Perhaps without being aware of it, Clausewitz was exposed to the breath of new ideas even here, while he underwent what was to be the final stage of his training in the mundane realities of Prussian military society and institutions. After his tour of duty in Neuruppin he was never again to come into close, regular contact with the common soldier and the line officer, as he was never again to live in a small provincial town. For the last time in his life he found himself at the base, rather than near the controlling center, of the kingdom's political and military power.

The condition of Neuruppin at the end of the 18th century, and its preceding history, reflect in small compass many of the periods in the growth of the Brandenburg-Prussian state.[13] In the first half of the 13th century, German colonists, who expelled or subjugated the Slav population, founded the town on the shore of one of the attenuated, riverlike lakes that are typical of the area. The settlement soon became the center of the new county of Ruppin, held in fief from the margraves of Brandenburg by nobles who had left their central-German properties for the greater opportunities of the East. The bonds of authority between margrave, vassal, and town were in general rather loose. Although the counts disposed over most of the judicial authority, the burghers governed themselves, formed the militia that defended the town, and dominated the economy of the region through their market, breweries, and spinneries. A Jewish community, first documented in 1315, strengthened the town's financial energy and credit until it was driven out in 1510 as part of the general expulsion of the Jews from Brandenburg. For three centuries thereafter, until the Prussian emancipation law of 1812, no Jew was permitted to enter Neuruppin. In 1524 the last Count of Ruppin died, and the fief reverted to the Elector of Brandenburg. The new demands on the town for money and services which this change brought were not too onerous at first; but throughout the century the community's vitality suffered from the religious conflicts of the Reformation, and from the general economic decline of the area, which led

13. On Neuruppin, see F. W. A. Bratring, *Statistisch-Topographische Beschreibung der gesamten Mark Brandenburg*, Berlin, 1804–09, reprinted Berlin, 1968; F. Heydemann, *Die neuere Geschichte der Stadt Neu-Ruppin*, Neuruppin, 1863; the excellent modern study by J. Schultze, *Geschichte der Stadt Neuruppin*, Neuruppin, 1932; and various historical and autobiographical accounts by Theodor Fontane, who was born there, collected in his *Wanderungen durch die Mark Brandenburg: Die Grafschaft Ruppin*, vol. ix of his *Sämtliche Werke*, Munich, 1960.

to quarrels and eventually open violence between the wealthy families that dominated the town council and the poorer inhabitants. In the surrounding countryside—as throughout northeastern Europe at this time—the peasants were losing much of their old independence to the large landowners, a change that also adversely affected the town's autonomy. With the increasing importance of firearms and of professional military expertise, the traditional defense arrangements became inadequate, and mercenaries replaced the armed burgher. The Thirty Years' War nearly destroyed Neuruppin. Between the outbreak of fighting and the 1640's the number of heads of households sank from 600 to 142. The crippled community needed help from the elector, and ceased to defend its liberties against his inroads. The council became dominated by electoral, and later royal, officials. Reluctantly the town accepted a permanent garrison; the town walls no longer guarded against external enemies, but now served to prevent smuggling and the desertion of soldiers, who were tempted by the proximity of the Mecklenburg border. In 1732, Neuruppin, by now fully incorporated into the system of Prussian absolutism, began its closer association with the royal family when it was chosen by the king as the residence of his son, Crown Prince Frederick, after Frederick had been pardoned for his attempted escape to England. For a few years the town basked in the modest rays of the crown-princely court. After Frederick's accession to the throne, one of the new units created in the course of the army's expansion—the 34th Infantry Regiment—was assigned to Neuruppin, with the king's youngest brother, Prince Ferdinand, as *commandant en chef*. In the community, whose civilian population rose to 4,400 by the end of the century, the military became a major social and economic force. The regiment numbered 2,180 men, of whom 837—mostly foreigners—were permanently on duty; the rest were on leave for ten and a half months of the year, working as farm laborers or artisans in the country, returning to the colors for intensive drill before the annual inspections and autumn maneuvers. The permanent complement was augmented by more than 400 soldiers' wives and 700 children, most of them living in severe poverty at the edge of town—one of the many such rootless groups throughout the kingdom, predecessors, in Meinecke's phrase, of the proletariat of late-19th-century Germany.[14]

In 1787 fire destroyed most of the town. Rebuilding was financed largely by the central government, which also appointed a special commission to draw up a comprehensive plan and supervise the work. The irregular network of streets and alleys that had spread in the course of centuries was replaced by a symmetrical grid of avenues, broad cross-streets, squares, and a drill field. The homes of the burghers, as well as government and

14. F. Meinecke, *Das Leben des Generalfeldmarschalls Hermann von Boyen*, 2 vols., Stuttgart, 1896–99, i, 94. The fine book by O. Büsch, *Militärsystem und Sozialleben im altem Preussen*, Berlin, 1962, unfortunately has little to say about this segment of military society.

municipal offices, were rebuilt of stone in a spare Neoclassic style, lightened here and there by a late-Rococo portal or cupola. In the center of town an imposing hall was erected for the Gymnasium, dedicated, according to the inscription on its façade, to "The Citizens of the Future." The walls of the main church, dating from the 13th century, had survived the fire, and restoration of the structure was considered; but since it lay diagonally across the new grid, the church was demolished, its stones being used in the construction of a drainage canal which finally dispelled the recurring epidemics and the constant stench from which the community had suffered throughout its existence.

Much of the rebuilding had been completed when the 34th Regiment, and with it Clausewitz, returned to Neuruppin in the summer of 1795. The troops that were not demobilized were quartered in barracks; officers moved into their own houses or, if they were subalterns, rented rooms in private residences. Their garrison duties were not arduous. In rotation the junior officers commanded the guard detachment that controlled traffic through the town gates and served as the community's main police and fire-fighting unit. Every weekday morning the men were drilled for four or five hours, in sections, companies, and battalions, occasionally the entire regiment being brought together. The officers' primary concerns were to achieve the utmost rapidity and precision in deploying their men from marching columns into various lines of battle—straight, oblique, parallel—to change direction without losing cohesion, and to break off the line again into marching columns. The motions of loading, firing, and reloading were practiced to produce rapid, smooth volleys, alternating by rank or section, although, for lack of money, powder and ball could be issued only once or twice a year. The few soldiers in each company who carried out the duties of sharpshooters were trained separately, and if an officer wished, he might drill his entire section or company in skirmish tactics, as Clausewitz did—though this was exceptional, and difficult to justify in the context of the army's linear doctrine.[15] In the afternoons some officers were occupied with instructing the cadets of the regiment, and with the administrative tasks and household chores of a large organization; the rest were free to pursue their own interests. The regimental commander persistently urged his officers to improve their knowledge, and a contemporary writes that subalterns in particular took advantage of the opportunities afforded by the library of the Gymnasium, consisting of nearly 2,000 volumes, and by the four reading clubs and circulating libraries of the town.[16] The proximity of Rheinsberg, where Prince Henry maintained a small

---

15. On the whole question of Prussian infantry doctrine and drill during this period, see my *Yorck*, pp. 53–61.
16. H., "Nachricht über den Fortgang der militärisch-wissenschaftlichen Bildungs-Anstalt, bey dem Regiment Prinz Ferdinand zu Neu-Ruppin," *Jahrbücher der preussischen Monarchie*, Berlin, 1800, p. 697.

orchestra, opera company, and theater, as well as one of the best libraries on military matters in the kingdom, attracted many—with harmful effects on their morals, according to a later chronicler.[17] Extended leaves, though they had to be approved by the king, were not uncommon. Clausewitz, for instance, was permitted an absence of six weeks in the summer of 1797, to accompany one of his step-uncles, Major-General von Hundt, brother of the former commander of the regiment, on a visit to Hundt's new estate in Prussian Poland—his introduction, incidentally, to Polish society, to which he took a permanent dislike.[18] The pace of this relaxed existence quickened when recruits arrived and the majority of the regiment's soldiers returned from their long leaves for the annual drill period preceding the reviews and maneuvers that climaxed the military year. Later, in his essay on the last decades of the old monarchy, Clausewitz observed that it was the formalistic, ceremonial character of these maneuvers that helped awaken his doubts about the state of Prussia's military institutions, and first stimulated the independence of his judgment. "In youth," he writes, "the author had experienced war, without—to be sure—understanding it, but he had retained a general impression. Even a modicum of reflection on these exercises during the autumn maneuvers in Potsdam and Berlin was bound to lead at once to the realization that none of this had taken place in the war that we had fought. What caused the author the greatest pain was that these sham battles, long practiced in advance, carefully discussed, arranged in every detail, were carried out by the most distinguished men in the service . . . with total absorption, and a degree of seriousness and energy that bordered on weakness." [19]

At a time when intellectual ferment in Prussia was additionally exacerbated by the quietism of the political leadership, Clausewitz was far from the only soldier to believe that if the army was to remain effective it must modernize. Even during Frederick's lifetime, suggestions for reform had been put forward; since his death, and since the outbreak of the revolution in France, they had multiplied. The most promising expression of this widespread concern was the creation, in 1795, of a special body reporting directly to the crown, the *Immediat-Militär-Organisationskommission,* which initially supervised the expansion of the army's administration into the newly acquired Polish territories, but soon brought every aspect of Prussia's

17. Heydemann, pp. 40–41.
18. The royal order is excerpted in the article on Hundt, Priesdorff, ii, No. 901.
19. Clausewitz, *Nachrichten,* p. 429. A statement in the same work suggests that the proposition in *On War* particularly distressing to 19th-century soldiers—that the defense rather than the attack is the stronger form of fighting—has a root in Clausewitz's early reaction to the doctrine fashionable in Prussia since the days of Frederick: "It had been taught, recommended, and preached a hundred thousand times that in war the offensive was always the best and afforded great advantages, that Prussian troops had a special aptitude for this way of fighting, while the attack in echelons constituted Prussian tactics raised to the level of the sublime, so to speak ... ." *Ibid.*, pp. 504–505.

military arrangements under review. During the ten years of its existence the commission was, in effect if not in law, the administrative head of the army, subject only to the king, and succeeded in carrying out numerous changes: the conscription districts were reapportioned, the number of foreigners in the ranks was reduced, some abuses of recruiting and conscription were abolished, discipline became more humane, a start was made on the modernization of the supply services, the entire administration of the army was simplified by reducing the number of units while increasing their strengths. In the area of equipment and tactics and commission also performed useful work, without ever instituting basic reforms, which alone would have made possible the quick mobilization, rapid strategic movements, and tactical flexibility that the new conditions in Europe seemed to demand of the army of a medium-sized and exposed state. To bring these about would, however, have called for a reduction in direct royal control over the military, and the transformation of Prussia's social conditions. Revolution being out of the question, the army continued to function much as it had since the end of the Seven Years' War, experimentation and improvement in matters of detail notwithstanding.

The 34th Infantry Regiment was known throughout the service for its role in one of these areas of innovation: the education not only of its young officers but also of its soldiers and of their dependents. In view of Clausewitz's enthusiasm for the *Bildung* and perfectibility of the individual, this aspect of his immediate environment must have interested him. Possibly he was even stimulated by it: the education of the officer and the common man was to occupy much of his thought during the years of reform after 1807. The regiment's reputation in this field was due almost entirely to the efforts of one individual, Friedrich Wilhelm Alexander von Tschammer und Osten, who had entered the regiment at the beginning of the Seven Years' War, and in the summer of 1793, after the recapture of Mainz, succeeded to its command.[20] Tschammer did not aim high in his educational work, but even the conventional, austerely practical manner in which he regarded the needs of his men was an improvement over the indifference shown by many of his fellow officers.

In Prussia, as everywhere in Europe, the economic condition and prospects of the common soldier and of his dependents were deplorable. Through most of the century what assistance veterans received was largely given by the municipalities, and by ecclesiastical, guild, and private charities. The state's energy, it was claimed, was fully taken up with maintaining its fighting force, and could spare little for the care of individuals who did not directly contribute to it. Private and local resources, on the other hand, were inadequate for the increasing numbers of people whom the

20. On Tschammer's service record, see Priesdorff, iii, No. 1015.

army withdrew from the economy, returning them only when they were no longer capable of heavy work and had become strangers to the community. Absolutism had weakened the sense of community responsibility for its poor, and the resultant need was not yet met by the central government, though the necessary provisions existed on paper. Under Frederick II, veterans with certificates of good conduct were to be cared for by admission to an invalid home, appointment to a position in the civil administration, or payment of a small pension. Able-bodied men qualified for land in one of the state's colonizing projects. The budgets assigned to these programs were so limited that at Frederick's death many thousands of eligible veterans of the campaign of 1778, and even some survivors of the Seven Years' War, still awaited help. His successor declared at the beginning of his reign that henceforth all men enrolling in the army could look forward to lifelong economic security. New old-age homes were built, invalid companies were organized for each regiment, the pension budget was raised by nearly a third; in addition, serving soldiers with children under the age of thirteen now received a small increment in pay, and a sum was set aside in each regiment for the children's schooling. Similar improvements were taking place in other countries—notably in Austria, under Joseph and Leopold—as governments began to acknowledge a broader responsibility for the physical and spiritual needs of people who in the service of the state had become excluded from the traditional institutions of society.[21]

Pedagogic ideals of the late Enlightenment helped stimulate the growth of the regimental schools, which began in the 1770's, but the immediate impetus came from men like Colonel Tschammer who wanted to alleviate the economic misery of the soldier families in their command.[22] For decades a few regiments and garrisons had maintained classes for the children of soldiers, which were usually conducted by service chaplains when they could spare time from their other duties. Frederick mildly encouraged these activities, but since he entrusted the local commanders with full authority and provided neither a budget nor overall supervision, very little was done. At the time of the brief War of the Bavarian Succession a few officers tried to organize more effective programs. Writers on education became interested and published proposals that called for trained and salaried teachers to instruct the children in reading, writing, and in simple economic tasks such as gardening and farming. The decisive step was taken

21. It may be noted that it was at the same time in Prussia that disabled or over-age officers who lacked an adequate private income were first granted a legal claim to pensions, which until then had been acts of royal grace and favor. For the widows of officers an insurance fund was established, made up of government contributions and monthly deductions from the officers' payroll.

22. For the general history of the education of the common soldier in 18th-century Prussia, see B. v. Poten, *Geschichte des Militär-Erziehungs- und Bildungswesens in den Landen deutscher Zunge,* iv, *Preussen; Monumenta Germaniae Pedagogica,* xvii, Berlin, 1896; and F. Wienecke, *Das preussische Garnisonschulwesen,* Berlin, 1907.

in 1780 when the commandant of Potsdam, Friedrich Wilhelm von Rohdich, and Johann Kletschke, the army's senior chaplain, visited the model
school that a Prussian landowner, Friedrich Eberhard von Rochow, had
opened on his estate to teach his peasants good agricultural practices and
pride in their German heritage.[23] Rohdich persuaded Frederick II to autho-
rize reformation of the existing garrison school at Potsdam according to
Rochow's principles, and a suitable building and funds for its upkeep and
other expenses were made available. Under the regulations drawn up by
Rohdich and Kletschke, all soldier children of the Potsdam garrison between the ages of five and thirteen were to attend the school. Their tuition
was paid by the parents or out of special regimental grants; textbooks and
writing materials were provided by the state. The school was divided into
four classes, and employed four male teachers and a schoolmistress, who
were expected to refrain from corporal punishment and to keep in mind the
social value of their work. They taught reading, writing, arithmetic,
proper pronunciation of German (local dialects being regarded as a handicap in making one's way in the world), Prussian geography and history,
religion, singing, and the writing of short essays. Girls with particularly
good records were given special instruction in sewing and knitting. The
end of the academic year was marked by a public examination, the singing
of hymns and patriotic airs, and a banquet.[24]

Under Frederick William II the program of soldier education expanded, the new schools following the general pattern set by Potsdam,
though more frugally and on a smaller scale. A central budget was established for the program, and with tuition entirely free, compulsory attendance could be enforced with some success since the child's education no
longer imposed an economic burden on his parents. Each school was supervised by a local commission, usually headed by a company commander,
whose members included two men who were not commissioned officers—the
unit's chaplain and its quartermaster. Contemporary descriptions of curricula and final examinations suggest that even in the more ambitious institutions, such as the Potsdam garrison school, instruction did not go beyond
what was deemed suitable for the training of future artisans and noncommissioned officers. Indicative of the program in smaller schools is the
purchase of textbooks for a one-class school in 1784: 50 spelling books, 50
reading books, 12 Old Testaments, 12 New Testaments, and 25 song-
books.[25] But the less authoritarian, more dialectical methods employed by

---

23. Rohdich's career illustrates the rise in status that military service made possible. His father was a
noncommissioned officer, and Rohdich himself served for some years in the ranks before being commissioned. He distinguished himself in the Seven Years' War, became a confidant of Frederick, the commanding officer of the 1st Regiment of Footguards, and ended his career in the 1790's as a minister of
state. Cf. Priesdorff, ii, No. 657.
24. The school is described by J. Stuve in the *Berliner Monatschrift*, 1783, no. 2. Stuve, the director of
the Gymnasium in Neuruppin, was a well-known writer on pedagogic questions.
25. Wienecke, p. 25.

many of the teachers seemed to point to higher possibilities, and some officials grew concerned that the schools were creating dissatisfied subjects. Their feeling that it was high time to revert from the sentimental humanism of the age to simpler standards found an echo in the prosaic, matter-of-fact paternalism of the crown prince. Soon after his accession, Frederick William III issued an order reducing the scope of the military schools. The decree stated that "true enlightenment, to the extent that it is desirable for the individual's own good and for the common good, is possessed by those who thoroughly understand the conditions and duties of the sphere of life in which they have been placed by fate, and who have the abilities to satisfy them. All elementary education should be restricted to this goal ... ." [26]

No doubt the king's warning that the regimental schools must not disturb the existing social system had its effect on the army. A civilian champion of the new education, however, writing anonymously from the security of Leipzig, beyond the Prussian frontier, used the occasion to launch an extensive counterattack on the restrictive pedagogic tendencies that were again becoming pronounced as the Enlightenment ossified, and the new regime in France presented Germany and Europe with hitherto unimagined challenges.

"Who can determine with certainty what fate has firmly decided?" asked the author, J. Z. Hahn. "Just because someone is born into a lower class can I say that fate has placed him into that low estate and thus limited his measure of enlightenment? ... Nature knows no social classes according to which she distributes her gifts and abilities among mankind. [Consequently] wisdom and higher education must not be made into a privilege of certain levels of society." [27] Though his sympathies lay with the individual rather than with the state, Hahn agreed that public education had to accommodate the interests of both. On the one hand, "every breast harbors feelings which, if they are nurtured, developed, made conscious, are vitalized and ennobled by advanced education, can ripen into the most glorious deeds ... . The powers and abilities of intelligent creatures should be developed as fully as possible ... ." However, even if the development of individual qualities should prove detrimental to the social status quo, it would greatly benefit the state: "Recent experience has shown that the best-trained and disciplined armies, equipped with every tactical art, armed with the full force of terrible weapons, enjoying every advantage of position, even fighting with courage, nevertheless often could not withstand some hurriedly mobilized host, made up of men who knew what they were fighting for, and what lay behind the present conflict between the

26. "Circular-Verordnung Sr. Königl. Majestät von Preussen an Allerhöchstdero sämmtliche Regimenter und Bataillons den Unterricht in den Garnisonschulen betreffend," *Jahrbücher der preussischen Monarchie*, Berlin, 1799, p. 161.
27. J. Z. H[ahn], "Bescheidene Prüfung der Circularverordnung Sr. Königl. Majestät von Preussen ... ," *Monatsschrift für Deutsche*, 1800, no. 7, 185–186. The quotations which follow are taken from the same essay, which appeared in installments, no. 6, 146; no. 7, 180; no. 5, 139–140.

powers, and who drew from this conflict the enthusiastic conclusion that they were fighting for the just cause."

Hahn's words repeated the emotional message of the free man irresistibly triumphing over the slave, which was common coin among the adherents of the French Revolution, and which such Prussian advocates of military regeneration as Heinrich Dietrich von Bülow were spreading in more technical language at this time.[28] It was a message received with tolerant amusement in the army, where experienced soldiers had little difficulty in pointing out the artificiality and exaggeration of arguments that in less than a decade were to become part of the standard terminology of the Prussian civil and military reformers.

Clausewitz's regiment was one of the earliest to follow the lead given by Rohdich in Potsdam. Around 1780, Tschammer, at that time still a captain, had organized a Garrison and Industrial School for the children of other ranks, which was soon praised in the *Berliner Monatschrift* for its effective combination of academic and practical instruction—the first of several discussions of Tschammer's educational activities in the contemporary literature. In later years many units in the army adopted the regulations he drew up for his school, which seemed particularly suited to the conditions of smaller garrisons. After the regiment returned from the Rhine, Tschammer, by now its commanding officer, enlarged the curriculum and added courses in lace-making and spinning for the soldiers' wives and daughters, who were paid for the finished product.[29] He divided the children attending the school into four classes, writes a contemporary, "each of which spent half the day doing lessons and the other half in the industrial workshop, which made it possible for two civilian teachers to manage four classes. As subjects of instruction he chose reading, writing, arithmetic, religion, natural history, and geography—the latter three subjects he taught himself." [30] Boys who showed military potential were organized into a special corps and clothed in a uniform in the colors of the regiment, paid for out of donations from officers and men, and gifts from the princes Henry and Ferdinand.[31] Tschammer's paternalism went so far as to oblige his officers to visit the quarters of married soldiers in their companies to see for themselves how the children were brought up at home. The school year ended with public examinations attended by the officer corps, the town

28. On Bülow see pp. 91–94 below.
29. "Nachricht von der Garnison-Schule und den Industrie- und Erwerbs-Anstalten für die Soldatenkinder und gemeinen Soldaten bei dem Infanterieregiment Sr. Königl. Hoheit des Prinzen Ferdinand von Preussen," in J. W. Kosmann and T. Heinsius, *Denkwürdigkeiten der Mark Brandenburg,* Berlin, 1797, iii, 502–509.
30. *Ibid.,* p. 495.
31. *Ibid.,* pp. 499–502.

council, and the faculty of the Gymnasium. Undoubtedly the school became an important institution in the life of the regiment and the town, even though it was far from accommodating all school-age children of the rank and file. Two hundred and forty was the maximum number admitted; the others—who must at least have equaled this figure—went to the town schools or received no education at all.

The edict of August 1799, which set precise limits on the curricula of the regimental schools, singled out Tschammer's policy as the proper model for the army to follow.[32] In what Meinecke has called the "interesting conflict between the principle of defending the old social barriers and the ideas of Rationalism," Tschammer's program served as a welcome support of the conservative position—indeed, as its humane and fatherly expression.[33] Its restricted purpose, directed largely to satisfying the basic economic needs of the military proletariat and the social and disciplinary interests of the absolutist state, could not have inspired a young man like Clausewitz who had recently been dazzled by the image of unending search for intellectual and moral perfection. That is not to say that Clausewitz gained nothing from experiencing at first hand the problems and rewards of teaching the underprivileged. Equally mixed was his experience with his own education.

For much of Frederick's reign the state had ignored not only the instruction of the rank and file but had shown little concern for the education of future officers and for their continued professional training. The cadet academies in Berlin and Potsdam, later supplemented by smaller institutions in Pomerania and West Prussia, taught the sons of the nobility the fundamentals of tactics, the traditions of the service, and a smattering of geography, mathematics, and French. Some 3,258 cadets passed through these schools in the course of Frederick's reign. After the Seven Years' War the king founded the *Académie militaire,* also called *Académie des nobles,* where a small number of highly recommended boys were prepared for service at court, in diplomacy, and in the army by a faculty made up largely of officers and French and Swiss savants. As Max Jähns observes, the curriculum, mainly of philosophic subjects and belles lettres, which Frederick devised in consultation with d'Alembert, was hardly suitable for boys between the ages of twelve and eighteen; military matters were scarcely touched on.[34] Except for some courses in such subjects as mathematics, fortification, and map-making, which so-called institutes in the military sciences offered during the winter months in the larger garrisons and for the king's own occasional seminars on the duties of the general staff, no

32. "Circular-Verordnung," *Jahrbücher,* 1799, p. 165.
33. Meinecke, *Boyen,* i, 97.
34. M. Jähns, *Geschichte der Kriegswissenschaften vornehmlich in Deutschland,* 3 vols., Munich and Leipzig, 1889–91, iii, 2455–2456.

provision existed for systematic study. After Frederick's death the cadet schools were reorganized, with the provincial academies now sending their graduates to the main school in Berlin. In the twelve years between 1786 and 1798, and some 1,022 boys entered the cadet corps, of whom 977 became officers.[35] The *Académie militaire* continued to train a favored few, and schools for engineers and gunners—each with one or two dozen officers attending—were founded near the capital. Like other functions of the state, military education was gradually standardized and centralized. But many Prussian officers—perhaps a majority—still did not undergo even this limited training; like the Clausewitz brothers, they continued to enter the army without first attending a cadet school. Whatever their subsequent education, young officers received it in courses that were occasionally offered in their own regiments or by higher military authority in the towns where they were stationed.

That a service already touched by a genuine sense of professionalism could ignore the education of its members may be explained by the fact that men were still far from agreement on the value of academic knowledge for the average infantry and cavalry officer. No one denied that gunners and engineers required technical professional training. But did their special needs apply to the infantry and cavalry? Indeed, the significance of mathematics, ballistics, or architecture to members of the technical corps, whose social status tended to be inferior to that of their comrades in the line, and whose opportunities to reach superior rank were more limited, formed an additional argument against serious professional training for aristocratic infantry and cavalry officers. And social considerations were reinforced by tactical and operational realities: as long as the officer's primary task was to maintain his men's cohesion, movement, and uniformity of action under fire, it could at least be argued that education, which would give him not only additional knowledge but a wider point of view and would develop his independent judgment, was unnecessary and quite possibly might damage his fighting qualities.

And yet, the debate over the possibilities and limitations of officer education, which became pronounced in the military literature by the 1770's, indicated that changes were on the way. Again Clausewitz's regiment was prominent in the new development. In October 1799 Colonel von Tschammer, having asked for and received the king's assurance that his work would not be discontinued when he left the regiment, opened a school for his lance corporals, who were soon joined by the regiment's ten ensigns. A contemporary report suggests that the lieutenants, among them Clausewitz, also took part in some of the studies.[36] The school was supervised by

35. *Ibid.*, p. 2469.
36. H., "Nachricht über den Fortgang der militärisch-wissenschaftlichen Bildungs-Anstalt bey dem Regiment Prinz Ferdinand zu Neu-Ruppin," *Jahrbücher der preussischen Monarchie*, Berlin, 1800, p. 697.

Major von Sydow, who had been among the first students of the *Académie militaire*, and who in a speech on the occasion of the first public examination of the pupils described the school as a continuation of Frederick the Great's concern for military excellence appropriate to the changed conditions of the age.[37] He was assisted by a commission of two officers, the regimental chaplain, the regimental quartermaster, and a civilian teacher, who also acted as regimental librarian.[38] The period of instruction, first ten, then fifteen hours a week, was divided into disciplines considered to be essential preparation for a soldier and those referred to as "auxiliary sciences." The former category included principles of arithmetic, geometry, trigonometry and its application to practical geometry, principles of mechanics, some knowledge of optics, and mathematical geography to the extent it was needed for reading maps, simple surveying, and enlarging and reducing existing maps. Auxiliary sciences comprised political geography, with an emphasis on Prussia and her immediate neighbors, as well as physical geography, recent Prussian and German history, European statistics, and the writing of German essays.[39] Some of these were taught in conjunction with the curriculum of the town's Gymnasium. Since the school quickly aroused great interest among the local gentry, Tschammer opened it to boys not connected to the regiment; their parents were asked to make a monthly contribution to the library fund and to the chaplain's salary.

We do not know precisely how Clausewitz was involved in the school: whether as auditor, supervisor, or even occasional instructor. That he did participate to some extent seems certain, since by his twenty-first year he had gained a modest degree of competence in such subjects as geometry, trigonometry, and surveying. The conduct reports, which his commanding officer annually submitted to the king, also refer in routine terms to his studies. In 1799 Tschammer wrote: "An excellent young man, useful and eager in the performance of his duties, who is intelligent and seeks to acquire knowledge of all sorts." [40] The following year the report stated: "His conduct is good; he is in every respect a very good officer, is intelligent and seeks to acquire knowledge." If Clausewitz later complained about the spiritual paucity of his years in Neuruppin, he was no doubt thinking of the neglect that the "auxiliary sciences" suffered in Tscham-

---

This is a continuation of an article begun in the preceding number of the journal, which in part responded to references to Tschammer's school in an article by C——r (apparently an academic) on military education, "Über die wissenschaftliche Bildung des Officiers," *ibid.*, pp. 44–57.

37. "Nachricht ... : Rede des Herrn Major v. Sydow," *ibid.*, pp. 687–693. The examination was held on the anniversary of Frederick's birth.

38. "Nachricht von der bei dem Infanterie-Regiment Prinz Ferdinand zu Neuruppin errichteten militärisch-wissenschaftlichen Bildungsanstalt für künftige Offiziere, und der damit verbundenen Regiments-Schulkommission," *ibid.*, 1799, pp. 267–269.

39. "Reglement für die Junkerschule des Infanterie-Regiments Prinz Ferdinand zu Neu-Ruppin," *ibid.*, 1799, pp. 259–263.

40. Clausewitz's conduct reports of these years are printed in Priesdorff, v, No. 1429.

mer's scheme of things and in Neuruppin society. Few regiments in the
army combined to the same degree military efficiency, concern for the soldier's well-being, and attention to learning—it was in these years that one
of the future heads of the reform party, then still a company commander in
a remote Silesian garrison, wrote an essay praising Tschammer's regiment
as a model for all Prussian soldiers.[41] But good intentions and energy
notwithstanding, Tschammer and his associates never fully understood
their own efforts: they proclaimed neohumanistic ideals but their school
was directed toward utilitarian gains, and they could hardly aspire far
beyond the sound second-rate—a level of insight and achievement that
Clausewitz rejected, first instinctively and later on the basis of superior understanding.

Yet it scarcely needs saying that Clausewitz did retain ideas and attitudes that he encountered in Neuruppin, or again met with there, after
having first discovered them in his father's house. There was, for one, the
insight into the political and constructive role of armies that the growth of
their state had given to Prussian officers. Major von Sydow expressed a
common point of view when he declared, "Our state is a military state ... .
What was our state before the reign of Frederick William, the Great Elector? Naked, poor, miserable, and so insignificant that its name was hardly
mentioned in the ranks of the European powers. Without strength, always
suffering, designed to be a follower ... ." It was the army, under the leadership of inspired rulers, that had turned the satellite into an equal. Now
Prussia "provided the strongest historical proof that the arts of peace dwell
by preference in the camp where the arts of war have pitched their
tents ... . In a military state the army is the strong foundation on which
the state's happiness and well-being are based." [42] Or again, Tschammer's
praise of education as the means of advancing the individual and society,
his plea that the soldier should not stand apart from the general progress of
civilization, and especially his belief that the primary function of education
was not the acquisition of knowledge but the development of judgment,
without which the soldier was only an animal. Courage and coolness,
Tschammer wrote, result from a healthy self-confidence, which in turn is
the product of education and experience. "Any sense of power that is not
founded on theoretical and practical knowledge and on genuine psychic
energies [*wirklich vorhandene Stärke der Seelenkräfte*], is rashness ... ." [43] In
the same vein Sydow distinguished between raw and educated courage.
"Raw courage is a wild horse that has shed its reins; it is a form of senseless
drunknness, a rage that throws itself thoughtlessly into danger because it

41. N. v. Gneisenau in a memorial of November 1806, G. H. Pertz and H. Delbrück, *Das Leben des
Feldmarschalls Grafen Neithardt von Gneisenau*, 5 vols., Berlin, 1864–80, i, 621.
42. "Nachricht ... : Rede des Herrn Major v. Sydow," *Jahrbücher*, 1800, pp. 688–689.
43. "Reglement ... ," *ibid.*, 1799, p. 264.

does not know how to judge either the danger itself or the means with which danger can be overcome." [44] This distinction between rashness and courage, which was not unknown to 18th-century military literature, Clausewitz adopted and refined, though his individualistic psychology could hardly retain the rationalist certainty that courage and knowledge were easily combined. In *On War* he was to define the two basic qualities that man needs to act effectively in war—even at the lowest level, increasingly so with greater responsibility—as the two opposites courage (by which he meant moral as well as physical bravery) and intelligence (the highest form of which he regarded to be intuitive understanding resulting from study, reflection and experience). It was man's harsh task to bring these two forces into harmony. Only genius—the true hero, in whom, Clausewitz wrote, courage is led by a dominant intelligence—could fully combine them. [45]

It was not easy for Clausewitz to move from Neuruppin to an environment more in accord with his ambition and ideals. In 1797 his older brother Wilhelm Benedikt, who had distinguished himself during the Rhine campaign, was promoted to first lieutenant, which necessitated his transfer from the 34th Infantry Regiment to a new unit that was being raised in Danzig. Clausewitz could not look forward to promotion for some years; on the other hand, transfer unaccompanied by promotion to a unit in the capital or in one of the other larger cities was difficult to arrange and, if brought about, might reduce his seniority and thus set back his career. In 1801 a different opportunity presented itself. The Hanoverian artillery officer and military writer Gerhard Scharnhorst had recently entered Prussian service. Among other duties he was entrusted with the reorganization of the small and moribund Berlin "Institute in the Military Sciences for Young Infantry and Cavalry Officers," which he soon turned into the army's central institution of higher education. With other interested subalterns throughout the monarchy, Clausewitz applied for admission and was among those accepted for the first three-year course. Toward the end of 1801 he left Neuruppin, to which he was to return only for short visits, though he remained attached to the 34th Infantry Regiment for some years to come. In 1802 Tschammer's successor in command of the regiment wrote in his annual report on Clausewitz, already based largely on outside opinions: "His conduct is good; he is a good officer who seeks to acquire knowledge. Is presently in Berlin to attend the military courses, where he is supposed to be very industrious and according to the judgment of Colonel von Scharnhorst one of the brightest minds."

44. "Nachricht ... : Rede des Herrn Major v. Sydow," *ibid.*, 1800, p. 690.
45. *On War*, book III, ch. 6 (p. 267).

4

SCHARNHORST'S MEDIATION BETWEEN OLD AND NEW

In the six years that had elapsed since the peace of Basel the political condition of Germany had suffered a fundamental change. The European balance of power was breaking down as France regained, and was passing, the former high point of her strength under Louis XIV. After years of bearing the main burden of the war on the continent, Austria was exhausted. Soon after Vienna submitted to the Peace of Lunéville in 1801, Great Britain and Russia also withdrew from the struggle. With her victory over Austria and the acquisition of the left bank of the Rhine, France gained a dominant voice in German affairs. Dozens of small sovereignties disappeared in the territorial exchanges that now began, and as French patronage allowed Bavaria, Württemberg, and Baden to expand to new significance, it became evident that after many centuries the existence of the German Empire was drawing to a close. The influence of the state that only two generations earlier had risen to become the Empire's second leading power now seemed again confined to northern Germany. Since 1795 Prussia had pursued a policy of neutrality that removed not only herself but all territories north of the Main from the conflict, emphasized their governments' common interests, and brought the smaller courts into closer dependence upon Berlin. This course, which could be interpreted by its adherents as a careful consolidation of Prussia's position in the north, lost its basis with the defeat of Austria and the commencing dissolution of the Empire. The system of north-German neutrality held out a promise of success only while France and her opponents were in some balance, and as long as a compromise peace remained a possibility.[1] Now

1. Ranke, *Hardenberg*, ii, 75–76.

Prussia's role, not alone in Europe but in Germany, was being called into question.

Ever since the accession of Frederick the Great, Prussia's position had owed much to her ability to play off the German princes against Austria. With the Habsburg threat replaced by that of a far more dangerous France, which had already destroyed numerous ecclesiastical and secular members of the Empire, and the new weight of the French client-states in the south, the old rules of the game greatly changed to her disadvantage. The hope of Hardenberg, who shared with Count Haugwitz the direction of the foreign ministry, that the monarchy might benefit from the redrawing of the German political map by at least gaining a defensible and commercially useful foothold south of the Main, was frustrated by Napoleon's support of Bavaria. In March 1801 a Prussian corps entered Hanover to preclude a possible French or Russian occupation, and to redress the diplomatic defeat suffered over the Franconian bridgehead. By October the troops had been recalled, since the government grew alarmed at the prospect of a concerted response on the part of Great Britain, Russia, and France. To be sure, the Imperial Diet, in what turned out to be its final session, confirmed Prussia's ownership of valuable but disjointed territories in Westphalia as indemnity for renouncing her possessions on the left bank of the Rhine. But when the French in turn occupied Hanover in the spring of 1803 they not only interposed themselves between these new acquisitions and the main body of the state, and pushed French forces to within eighty miles of Berlin, but demonstrated the feebleness of Prussia even in northern Germany. Negotiations for a withdrawal, or at least reduction, of the French garrison came to nothing, and in April 1804, his schemes for Franco-Prussian collaboration having collapsed, Count Haugwitz resigned.

The only feasible policy now seemed to be to defend one's own frontiers and to safeguard the state's immediate interests and obligations in the neighboring territories. But even such an obviously necessary step as protesting the kidnapping by French agents of the British Resident in Hamburg could be taken only after overcoming an increasingly influential group at court and in the administration, which warned against any step that might offend Napoleon. The cold light of political reality with which French aggression had pierced the conventions and mutual considerations of the old Europe was beginning to illuminate the discrepancies between Prussia's claim of being a major power and her limited strength. In population, wealth, and military potential she was far inferior to France, and she did not enjoy the geographic remoteness that enabled a power of the second magnitude such as Sweden to act with a measure of self-assurance and independence. An alliance with France that removed the differences outstanding between the two governments possessed great attractions; but the restless ambition of Napoleon spoke against it. Yielding to increasing Rus-

sian pressures and joining a new coalition against France could involve the
state in a war whose outcome, judging by the experience of the past decade, might easily be catastrophic. Frederick William III's own shortcomings as a diplomat, his abhorrence of violence, and the weakness of his
realm in the face of new dangers combined to dictate a cautious, suppli-
cant, essentially passive policy. Prussia had rarely played a leading role in
the concert of Europe; but now her actions, and even her existence, seemed
to depend on the will and energy of others.

"In the midst of all this—we sleep!" wrote one of Berlin's most gifted
political observers soon after the French triumphs of the summer of 1800.[2]
This note of impending catastrophe was not, however, representative of
public opinion. On the whole the political literature of the day, which a
mild censorship did not seriously inhibit, expressed satisfaction with Prussia's neutral posture, and showed no lack of confidence in her future. Here
and there a writer called for more active policies; the word that England on
the oceans and Prussia on the continent were the natural champions of European liberty was already heard; Arndt, shocked out of his early cosmopolitanism by the conquest of the Rhine, sang of the day

". . . when sacred German rage
scatters the vain French like chaff before the wind."

But these voices carried little weight in the chorus of approbation. Prussian
society at the turn of the century was not in a mood of crisis. Internal affairs were its primary concern, and here only a few men seriously disap-
proved of the government's performance. On the contrary, a sense of modest progress prevailed, at least superficially: an appreciation of economic
well-being and cultural growth, guarded and nurtured by the state, whose
greatest recent achievement was the security it provided in a time of un-
precedented troubles. In Berlin the skepticism of the influential Huguenot
colony, and the dissatisfaction the Jews felt over the narrow limits set to
their assimilation, qualified the optimism of the middle class only to a
degree. Nor were army, administration, and the nobility in general troubled by the evidence of Prussia's diminishing power. The government saw
matters differently. Frederick William, in whose mind the monarchy still
figured largely as a dynastic possession and obligation, and the high ministerial bureaucracy, which already regarded the state as an independent organism with its own requirements and even dynamic, anxiously watched the
deterioration of Prussia's position. Their concern, together with widespread
regret over the brutal political rearrangement of Germany, fed an uneasy
fin-de-siècle feeling that lay beneath much of the calm optimism. Prussia's
immobility at a time when other states were engaged in enormous efforts

---

2. Friedrich v. Gentz to Marquis Lucchesini, September 1800, cited in O. Tschirch, *Geschichte der
öffentlichen Meinung in Preussen*, Weimar, 1934, ii, 5, n. 1.

was too marked not to affect men's emotions and thoughts. In France the reestablishment of internal order and the modernization of administrative and economic institutions were achieved by the same energies that were transforming the character of her diplomacy and her wars. That some of her ventures failed appeared less significant than the daring expansiveness with which they were conceived and carried out. An attempt such as the Egyptian expedition was itself a victory over the old restrictive forms of international intercourse, an adventure that in spite of its costs seemed only to add to the vigor of the nation. In Prussia, in the meantime, everything was being renounced for the sake of tranquility.

And yet, despite her lapse into passivity, Prussia continued to attract men from all regions of Germany to her service. Nothing is more far-fetched than to interpret this tide of ambition and talent as responses to a feeling—possibly not even consciously recognized—that the future lay with Prussia. A similar pull was exerted by Austria and by the expanding south-German states, any of whose administrative and military institutions provided a range of opportunities that in the minor principalities was available, if at all, only to a few. Certainly Prussia's potential for further territorial growth and for assuming the political leadership of central Europe was not as important in attracting the three men who were to dominate the struggle for reform after 1807—Stein, Hardenberg, and Scharnhorst—as were the extensiveness and authority of her institutions, which offered them the greatest possible scope for their work. It can be assumed that external political possibilities weighed even less with the average officer and with the administrators who entered the service of the king of Prussia in large numbers. The high percentage of non-Prussians in the various branches of the army was striking. In 1805, one-third of all infantry officers holding the rank of lieutenant-colonel or higher were foreigners; of the 57 senior light-infantry officers, 28 were not natives of Prussia, and ten of these were not German at all; among the senior officers in the corps of engineers, native Prussians were even in the minority, seven of seventeen being Prussian by birth, the others, including the commandant of the corps, coming from France, Holland, and from Alsace and other German-speaking territories. In the cavalry, the percentage of foreign officers was somewhat lower, but with about one-fourth of the total in the higher grades, their presence was still significant.[3]

The circumstances surrounding Scharnhorst's transfer to the Prussian army, which took place in May 1801, were characteristic of the process that had recruited these men. A competent soldier in a foreign service attracts the attention of Berlin: after an evaluation of his record and his promise for

---

3. Figures are based on the *Rangliste der Königl. Preussischen Armee für das Jahr 1805*, Berlin, 1805, pp. i–xxxii. At the same time, foreigners in the ranks, though their number was being gradually reduced, still amounted to about 36% of all troops; Jany, iii, 436.

the future, he is offered an appointment; his frustrations in his present condition and the advantages held out by the Prussians lead him to accept their offer. The extensive negotiations with Scharnhorst, which lasted several years, nevertheless contained an unusual undertone that was due to the extraordinary character of the man involved and also to a certain difference in the motives of the negotiating parties. Frederick William III and his intermediaries believed they were acquiring a gifted gunnery officer who would benefit the Prussian artillery and in addition might improve the army's training program for officers, which, it was felt, stood in some need of change. Scharnhorst's expectations, on the other hand, were not necessarily as limited. Throughout his career his skepticism about the true worth of worldly success, and a pronounced sense of realism, had restrained his ambitions without ever diminishing them. He was confident that he could carry out the highest military tasks of the age. By joining a powerful, sophisticated military organization, which gave scope to talent and application, he placed himself in a more advantageous position to grasp the opportunity should it arise.[4]

He was born near the city of Hanover in 1755, the son of a retired noncommissioned officer in the Hanoverian cavalry who had married the daughter of a well-to-do free peasant. The elder Scharnhorst inherited from his father-in-law a small estate, which carried with it membership in the *Landschaft,* the association of the county's noble and free landowners, and raised him into the middle levels of local society. His son at eighteen was admitted to the military academy that Count Wilhelm zu Schaumburg-Lippe-Bückeburg had established in his small principality, just beyond the Hanoverian border. The instruction and stimulation Scharnhorst received there during the next five years led him directly into a career of military education, and thirty years later still exerted an influence on his reform programs and policies.

Schaumburg-Lippe belonged to those small states of German absolutism in which the genius or single-mindedness of the ruler had brought one aspect of civilization to full flower: chamber music, horse-breeding, archae-

---

4. Scharnhorst freely acknowledged his pronounced ambition to himself and his family, for instance, in his letters written during the early years of the revolutionary wars: *Scharnhorsts Briefe,* pp. 19, 85, 93, 162. Of particular importance for our knowledge of his life are the following works: C. v. Clausewitz, "Über das Leben und den Charakter von Scharnhorst," *Historisch-politische Zeitschrift,* I (1832); G. H. Klippel, *Das Leben des Generals von Scharnhorst,* 3 vols., Leipzig, 1869–71, the first serious full-length biography, with much valuable documentation; M. Lehmann's classic, monumentalizing interpretation, *Scharnhorst,* 2 vols., Leipzig, 1886–87; and the brilliant fragment by R. Stadelmann, *Scharnhorst: Schicksal und Geistige Welt,* Wiesbaden, 1952. Scharnhorst's private correspondence was edited by K. Linnebach under the title *Scharnhorsts Briefe,* Munich–Leipzig, 1914. A planned second volume of official correspondence never appeared. Excerpts from the voluminous Scharnhorst papers, now deposited in Freiburg, are contained in C. v.d. Goltz's already cited edition of Scharnhorst's military writings, and I have published three essays from his *Nachlass* in *Yorck,* in which additional references to works on and by Scharnhorst can be found.

ological excavation, or—as in this case—military organization and training. Count Wilhelm enjoyed an international reputation as a soldier.[5] He had successfully defended Portugal against Spain during the Seven Years' War, held the rank of field marshal in the British army, and had written an important work on the theory and practice of defensive operations, fortifications, and gunnery. Joined to this passionate involvement in war was a marked moral concern about violence. The count believed that cruelty and avarice were the motives for most wars; only defensive wars could be justified, and by improving the defensive capabilities of smaller states, he hoped the aggressive tendencies of the major powers might be neutralized and eventually eradicated. Early in his reign he had reorganized the military institutions of his state according to principles that seem to combine the advantages of autocratic rule with Rousseau's ideal of the free citizen defending his homestead. He introduced universal military service, reduced the regulars' time with the colors, organized a volunteer militia, and devised a system of quasi-Roman honors, medals, and other distinctions to reward faithful service. His school, in which he himself acted as the principal instructor, was one of the first in Germany to approach gunnery and military engineering as scientific subjects; at the same time he tried to raise the prestige of their practitioners, whom most German armies still tended to regard as uniformed technicians rather than genuine soldiers. Gneisenau, next to Clausewitz Scharnhorst's closest personal associate in the years of reform, once took the opportunity of a visit to Bückeburg to explore the bond between Count Wilhelm's teaching and Scharnhorst's work. To an early biographer of the count he wrote: "You have given Count Lippe very high praise, but still far from his true deserts: he was even greater than you suggest ... . Our whole program of mobilizing the people in 1813, *Landwehr* and *Landsturm,* all of modern warfare from broadest principle to the most minute detail was exhaustively treated by this man; everything was already understood, taught, and put into effect by him. Imagine the kind of man he must have been whose mind so early on developed the most important ideas about war, ideas whose subsequent realization were to cause the collapse of Napoleon's power." [6] Gneisenau was referring less to specific changes in organization and tactics than to the innovation that alone would render them fully effective: the establishment of the army on a broader popular basis, with the necessary compulsion of conscription being made more palatable by appealing to the individual's sense of a community

5. On Count Wilhelm see K. A. Varnhagen von Ense, *Biographische Denkmale,* Berlin, 1845, i; Klippel, i, 34–61; and Lehmann, *Scharnhorst,* i, 12–29. Some interesting information is also contained in the ill-organized and rather fantastic work of a modern descendant, F. C. Prinz zu Schaumburg-Lippe, *Zur Ehre des revolutionären Menschen: Wilhelm Regierender Graf zu Schaumburg-Lippe,* Stadthagen, 1960. Recently C. Harraschik-Ehl has explored the most important period of Count Wilhelm's active service in *Scharnhorsts Lehrer: Graf Wilhelm von Schaumburg-Lippe in Portugal,* Osnabrück, 1974.
6. Varnhagen von Ense, *Biographische Denkmale,* i, 78–79.

of interests with the state. It did no harm to the development of Scharnhorst's judgment that at the beginning of his career, years before the American and French revolutions, a sovereign German prince taught him to value the people in arms. To be sure, Count Wilhelm did not push his military schemes to their full political consequences; but that too may not have been without bearing on Scharnhorst's later view of human affairs as a process of gradual change, in which both the old and the new deserved respect, or on his use of history as a tool for change. It was to become a favorite device of his in Prussia both before and after Jena to make reforms palatable to conventional superiors and a reluctant monarch by presenting his proposals as practices that, far from revolutionary, had already been accepted during the reign of Frederick the Great.

In 1777 Count Wilhelm died and Scharnhorst returned to Hanover as ensign in a cavalry regiment, which needed a qualified teacher for its recently established regimental school.[7] Four years later he transferred to the new artillery academy in the capital; at the age of twenty-eight he was promoted to lieutenant, and nine years later, in 1792, to brevet captain, an honor that did not carry with it the economic advantages attached to the command and so-called proprietorship of a company. During these years of slow ascent in a service that was notorious for holding out few rewards to bourgeois officers, Scharnhorst established a reputation throughout the armies of central Europe as a knowledgeable and prolific writer on military subjects, inventor of technical improvements in gunnery, and editor of several military periodicals. For soldiers whose professional horizon was circumscribed by the drill field and the stable, it was not difficult to dismiss him as an academic, learned but of little value in battle, of a type common among the middle-class members of the technical branches of the service. Scharnhorst's theoretical interests, however, only strengthened his very considerable practical gifts, as he was to prove in the revolutionary wars, and as he demonstrated in different fashion in a book he published just before his first experience with actual war. This work, a manual written to help officers execute independent assignments on campaign, contained statistical, geographical, and technical information, instructions for drawing maps and writing reports, as well as tactical guidance on such matters as placing outposts, leading patrols, and setting ambushes, illustrated with hundreds of examples drawn from military history. The presence of a large body of historical material in a practical guide, meant to be carried in the

---

7. Scharnhorst was fortunate to find in his new regimental commander, E. O. v. Estorff, another officer who was interested in professional military education, and himself the anonymous author of a sensible, very well written work, *Fragmente militairischer Betrachtungen über die Einrichtung des Kriegswesens in mittlern Staaten,* Frankfurt–Leipzig, 1780. Scharnhorst's development seems prefigured in Estorff's description of the ideal soldier as one "who combines the academician and the officer inseparably in his person" (p. 108).

officer's saddlebag, indicates one of Scharnhorst's major pedagogic concerns—the difference that often existed between theory and practice—and his use of history to bridge the gap between the two. That in this instance he succeeded is suggested by the popularity the manual enjoyed among officers of the allied armies; it went through at least four editions during the next years.[8]

In the spring of 1793 Hanover entered the war against France, and Scharnhorst went on active service as a supernumerary battery commander. He hated the suffering and destruction that now became part of his daily existence. "I am not made to be a soldier," he wrote to his wife. "I can face danger without difficulty; but I am enraged and thrown into an insupportable mood by the sight of innocent people moaning in their blood at my feet, by the flames of burning villages, which men have put to the torch for their own pleasure, by the other horrors of this universal devastation." [9] Throughout the campaign, similar comments recurred in his correspondence; but his disgust with killing, which he retained to the end of his days, was not permitted to interfere with the determination to excel in his profession. After he had proved his competence under fire in several engagements, he did not hesitate to admit to himself and to his family that he "almost found pleasure in this shameful activity." [10] Nor could he doubt that war offered him the only hope for achieving higher rank.

He first gave clear evidence of his superior qualities of command in the battle of Hondschoote, in September 1793, when he took control of several weakened Hanoverian units fleeing the battlefield, and turned their rout into an orderly rear-guard action that helped preserve the entire corps. His great opportunity, both as organizer and combat soldier, came the following spring. The Hanoverian general Hammerstein had received orders to occupy the town of Menin in southern Belgium, which lay in the path of an expected French offensive. Menin's fortifications had been neglected; in a short period, and with inadequate materials, Scharnhorst improvised a system of ditches and barricades that enabled the garrison of 2,400 men to make a stand. In the second half of April, Pichegru crossed the Lys, and Menin was encircled by 20,000 men under Moreau. Several assaults were beaten back by the garrison; an offer of capitulation under honorable conditions was rejected; but the impossibility of holding out against such numbers was evident, and Hammerstein decided to save his troops by breaking through the siege. Scharnhorst acted as his chief of staff and took

8. G. Scharnhorst, *Militairisches Taschenbuch, zum Gebrauch im Felde,* Hanover, 1792. An English edition, *Military Field Pocket Book,* was published in London in 1811.
9. Letter of 22 May 1793, *Scharnhorsts Briefe,* p. 36. For related passages see *ibid.,* pp. 42, 46, 58–59, 113–114, etc.
10. Letter to his wife of 28 August 1793, *ibid.,* p. 66.

command of part of the corps in the attempt, which was successfully carried out against strong French opposition in the night of 30 April.[11] Though Menin was lost, as had been expected, the deliverance of the garrison was seen by the Allies as a moral victory and became a feat of arms famous in the military chronicle of those years. Scharnhorst was singled out by Hammerstein as the man primarily responsible; his reputation was established, he advanced to major and was transferred to the general staff.

During the rest of the war he served with distinction in increasingly responsible posts, without, however, receiving further promotion. The polite but tenacious resistance of senior generals and officials to his advancement, which persisted after the Peace of Basel, sprang not only from social but also from professional considerations. On his return to Hanover, Scharnhorst had begun to draw the sum of his recent experiences and to clarify his ideas about the revolution in warfare that was obviously taking place in Europe. An early product of his speculations was an essay of fifty pages, "The Basic Reasons for the French Success," which he and his friend Friedrich von der Decken published in their periodical the *Neue Militärische Journal* as an analytic introduction to a detailed history of the War of the First Coalition.[12] The obvious inadequacies of the Allies did not push Scharnhorst into an uncritical admiration of everything that was new and French; in Max Lehmann's words, he was "equally opposed to radical innovators and to the incurable admirers of the old system."[13] He took note of the advantages France had enjoyed over the Allies: a more favorable strategic position, superior numbers, unified political and military command, and greater incentive—"the struggle was indeed too unequal: one side had everything to lose, the other little."[14] But he also delineated with objectivity and precision the superior effectiveness of French organization and tactics; and beyond the military instrument he pointed to the greater strength possessed by a freer society, the element on which, in the end, all depended: "The reasons for the defeat of the Allied powers must be deeply enmeshed in their internal conditions and in those of the French nation," adding that he referred to psychological as well as physical factors.[15]

Some of the sting was drawn from these criticisms by the fact that they appeared in the relative obscurity of a scholarly journal. Simultaneously with their publication, however, Scharnhorst advanced the same arguments in memoranda to his superiors and in lectures and discussions as

11. Hammerstein's report on the action is printed in Klippel, ii, 104–114. Scharnhorst's later account, "Die Vertheidigung der Stadt Menin und die Selbstbefreiung der Garnison unter dem Generalmajor von Hammerstein," *Neues Militärisches Journal,* XI (1803), became a minor classic in the literature on the revolutionary wars.
12. See above, p. 32.
13. Lehmann, *Scharnhorst,* i, 226.
14. *Militärische Schriften von Scharnhorst,* p. 203.
15. *Ibid.,* p. 195, and note.

part of specific proposals for the modernization of Hanover's military institutions. He advocated better education for officers and noncommissioned officers, promotion to the rank of lieutenant by examination, the abolition of nepotism and favoritism, a more equitable and sensible application of military justice, expansion and reequipment of the artillery, transformation of infantry tactics from the linear system to a combination of attack columns, line, and skirmishers, institution of a permanent general staff, reorganization of the army into divisions of all arms to ensure flexibility and operational independence, realistic and intensified training, and finally the diminution of the mercenary character of the army by the introduction of conscription.

To bring about such changes would have required important political adjustments no less than a revolution in the service. Even if his superiors had been convinced of the justice of Scharnhorst's arguments, which they were not, the government of George III would have been reluctant to test the resistance of the Hanoverian aristocracy and the estates in the defense of their long-standing privileges. Scharnhorst was disregarded as a visionary or ambitious troublemaker, and vacancies in the higher ranks continued to be filled with men who were no match for him. Inquiries from other services consequently found him in a receptive mood. He turned down the first invitation from Prussia after Hanover agreed to go some way toward matching the offer by promoting him to lieutenant-colonel. But the reluctance with which it was done deepened his suspicion that he would be forever deprived of the highest prizes of the service. He reopened negotiations with his Prussian contacts, and resigned his Hanoverian commission after Frederick William III had met his terms: appointment as lieutenant-colonel in the artillery stationed in Berlin, a respectable pension for himself and his wife, and the promise of being raised into the nobility, a step which he requested for the sake of his two sons, but also, no doubt, to satisfy his own self-esteem and to facilitate his future advancement and effectiveness.[16]

Scharnhorst was a man of forty-six when he arrived in Berlin in the late spring of 1801, in robust health, accustomed to work half the night, with a mind that had reached the full powers of maturity while retaining its early receptivity and suppleness. To his new comrades he presented an unusual figure. He carried himself negligently, his trunk and massive head bent slightly forward. His speech, too, lacked elegance of form; it was low-keyed, deliberate, at times halting, with a Hanoverian intonation that sounded slurred to Prussian ears. Even on the parade ground he displayed none of the physical tautness and smartness of manner that was becoming fashionable among some Prussian soldiers. An artillery officer was soon

16. The course of the negotiations can be followed in some detail in *Scharnhorsts Briefe*, pp. 206–217.

heard to say that in service matters any NCO was superior to the new-comer.[17] The old battles over the academic in uniform, of the outsider and the reformer, had to be fought once again. He himself recognized the need for caution in the new environment. "I am following a policy of being agreeable to everyone," he wrote to his wife, who with their children remained in Hanover until he had found a house in Berlin. "I simply will not join any faction . . . but shall always remain a neutral. Admittedly that has its disagreeable side, but in the long run it gets you farthest." [18] Possibly this statement of good intentions was meant to reassure his wife; in fact, he had already made clear his general position by submitting very far-reaching reform proposals to the king and to the senior artillery commanders, which aimed at bringing Prussian organization, equipment, and operational and tactical doctrine into closer agreement with those of the French. The matter-of-fact tone of his memoranda did not obscure their revolutionary message: each denied the continued validity of a particular aspect of the Frederician system, and each was potentially damaging to special interests. All were rejected. Frederick William did not withdraw his favor from a man who impressed him with his detailed knowledge of weapons and organization, but Scharnhorst recognized that for the time being comprehensive reforms were beyond his reach in Prussia as they had been in Hanover. He was afforded real freedom only in the marginal and neglected field of higher military education. It characterizes his determination and resourcefulness that he did not limit his efforts to the Berlin Institute for Young Officers, in which it had always been expected that he would play a part, but set about almost immediately to create a second vehicle for spreading his message of the need for reform.

After a few meetings in the summer and fall of 1801, Scharnhorst with seven fellow officers and two professors of the Berlin Institute founded a society for the study of military affairs on 24 January 1802, the anniversary of Frederick the Great's birthday.[19] The purpose of the *Militärische Gesellschaft,* according to the first article of its by-laws, was "to instruct its members through the exchange of ideas in all areas of the art of war, in a manner that would encourage them to seek out truth," and, in language characteristic of Scharnhorst, "that would avoid the difficulties of private studies with their tendency to one-sidedness, and that would seem best suited to place theory and practice in proper relationship." The society, a club outside the institutional structure, was both more sophisticated in its activities and more prestigious than a service academy for junior officers

---

17. See the recollections of a contemporary who despite his conservatism was sympathetic to Scharnhorst, the later General J. H. Menu v. Minutoli, in his *Beiträge zu einer künftigen Biographie Friedrich Wilhelm III.,* Berlin, 1843, pp. 118–120.
18. Letter of 24 July 1801, *Scharnhorsts Briefe,* p. 231.
19. Paret, *Yorck,* pp. 84–86.

could hope to be. Its membership, never quite reaching two hundred, included officers of all ranks, two princes of the royal house—August and Louis Ferdinand—as well as civilian officials whose duties brought them in touch with the army, among whom Baron vom Stein was the most prominent. If no single direction, let alone program of reform, could be developed in the brief existence of the society—it broke up after three and a half years when the army mobilized in 1805—the lectures, discussions, and essay competitions conducted under Scharnhorst's guidance at least gave his ideas a sounding-board of considerable resonance, and allowed his personality to become widely known.

The work of the society might eventually heighten the army's receptivity for innovation, and in the meantime could influence the actions of a few of its well-placed members. An opportunity to affect not personalities but the structure of the service itself was afforded Scharnhorst through his connection with the Berlin Institute for Young Officers. If few men in the Prussian army saw the crisis of traditional military institutions of Europe in as broad a social and political context as he, a surprisingly large number agreed with him in believing that the quality of senior military leadership in Prussia presented a problem. Indeed, for many officers the disquiet they felt about the military capabilities of the monarchy reduced itself to this single issue. In times such as these was a new extraordinary figure needed to preserve the state, which only the genius of Frederick had raised to the heights of a European power? This question became even more critical after a soldier of supreme ability had placed himself at the head of the French nation, and was molding the Revolution's energy and enthusiasm into a force that was at once dynamic and reliable. Could a traditional army withstand this force unless it, too, was in the hands of an inspired leader? The widespread belief in the importance of the great man—in some cases a reflection of the cult of genius, which since the period of *Sturm und Drang* had not vanished from the world of literature and scholarship—no doubt helped motivate the anxious defense by many officers of every aspect of the Frederician system, from linear drill and machinelike responsiveness to the dominance of aristocratic rather than professional values in the officer's ethos. In an age of epigoni, for men to remain faithful to the great king's work, and thus benefit from his spirit, might still prove the best assurance of victory. After the collapse, Queen Louise pronounced a striking judgment on an entire generation: all had fallen asleep on Frederick's laurels. But often it had been fear rather than arrogant confidence that caused men to guard what they took to be the essence of Frederick's success. When Scharnhorst came to Berlin he quickly played on these anxieties to advance his particular solution to the problem of military leadership. "What will happen," he asked one of his young associates in the *Militärische Gesellschaft,* "when the men Frederick II trained during the Seven Years' War are no longer with us?

The crisis can be met only by educating our officers." [20] He was thinking not only of the officer corps in general but also of a program that prepared an elite for the duties of superior command. This elite was to be divided into two groups: the men who rose to the higher positions of command, and those who served in a reorganized and strengthened general staff.

In 18th-century armies the duties of the general staff—or general-quartermaster staff, in official Prussian terminology—tended to be less clearly defined than the functions of the fighting branches or of the exclusively technical services; on the whole, they consisted of subordinate, auxiliary activities. During Frederick's reign, officers on his staff were rarely more than adjutants employed to transmit orders and to assist in such technical tasks as the arranging of march routes and the placing of camps. As the field forces grew in strength and operated over progressively larger areas, officers were more frequently attached to the commanders of separate corps to counsel them according to the intentions of the commander-in-chief. This phase of the staff's development was completed with the appointment of advisers for the commander-in-chief himself, officers who without special training had, in the course of their careers, established a reputation for competence in operational planning and tactical dispositions. Their powers were left undefined, and depended on the widely differing attitudes of their superiors, but even the king and his entourage held that in the absence of a new military genius the needed improvement in leadership could be provided only by some form of staff. The precise character that this organization ought to assume remained, however, in question. Scharnhorst's answer was a further increase in the general staff's responsibilities, to be justified by advanced training of its members in the conduct of war. While not yet declaring his intentions fully, he wished to create an institution that would educate staff officers whose duties no longer were limited to technical matters or to strengthening the commander's control in battle, but who assisted in working out strategic plans and were empowered to advise the individual commanders as responsible and authoritative spokesmen of the overall strategic policy. During his last difficult years in Hanover, Scharnhorst had already declared that the function of a general staff was to provide the energy that set the motor of the army in motion. Now, as a substitute for Frederick, and to meet the challenge of Bonaparte, he proposed to remove the general staff from its former subsidiary position and educate it for a role of central significance.

The Institute in Berlin had to be entirely recast for this purpose. In 1801 its permanent faculty consisted of two men: Major Ludwig Müller of the Engineers, a veteran of the Seven Years' War, learned but decrepit,

---

20. To Lieutenant J. G. v. Rauch, 15 August 1802, quoted in R. Höhn, *Revolution-Heer-Kriegsbild*, Darmstadt, 1944, p. 493. Rauch became minister of war in the 1830's.

who lectured on military geography, the defense and attack of fortified places, and field encampments; and Johann Gottfried Kiesewetter, an influential popularizer of Kantian philosophy, whose classes in mathematics and logic were jointly sponsored by the Institute and the Royal College of Military Physicians and Surgeons.[21] The school was supervised by Lieutenant-General von Geusau, one of the most overworked administrators in the service. Besides holding numerous other responsibilities, he commanded the Engineers (though not an engineer himself), was inspector-general of fortifications, and the army's chief of staff, in which capacity he dealt with such matters as mobilization schedules, budgets for the field forces, and the topographical survey of the monarchy. Geusau was relieved when Scharnhorst expressed the willingness to take over the burden of the school, and supported his proposals for expanding its staff and curriculum. In the fall of 1801 Scharnhorst was appointed director under Geusau's nominal supervision, and given a small annual budget with which to transform the institution from an instrument of the Berlin garrison to a national academy. The number of students rose to about forty; to accommodate the increase and add to the prestige of the school, Frederick William was persuaded to provide a room in the royal palace as a lecture hall. The new course of instruction ran from October to April for three consecutive years. Müller and Kiesewetter continued on the faculty; a new instructor was brought in to teach applied mathematics, which enabled Kiesewetter to deal more effectively with pure mathematics and logic, subjects to which Scharnhorst ascribed basic pedagogic importance. Instruction in these fields, he stated, "should aim principally at forming the intelligence and at exercising the power of judgment. Since it is as important for a soldier to possess these qualities as it is to acquire knowledge more directly related to the practice [of war] ... , every officer will attend these lectures without interruption throughout the first two winters. It is extremely important to guide the student toward independent thought." [22] Kiesewetter strongly influenced Clausewitz's awakening interest in philosophic method; later chapters will discuss some aspects of his teaching that helped shape central elements of Clausewitz's theories on war. He was not a profound thinker, but his mind was exceptionally clear and he knew how to make his lectures so interesting that, as one of his listeners wrote, "one forgot that one had to spend the cold winter mornings in an unheated classroom." At his lectures Clausewitz met many young men who were to play a part in his later life: Prince

21. On Müller and his various writings see Jähns, iii, 1879–1880, 2459–2460, and 2740–2741; and Poten, iv, 113–115. A brief biographical essay on Kiesewetter by C. G. Flittner is included in the fourth edition of Kiesewetter's outline of Kantian philosophy, *Darstellung der wichtigsten Wahrheiten der kritischen Philosophie*, Berlin, 1824.
22. [Scharnhorst], *Verfassung und Lehreinrichtung der Akademie für junge Offiziere ...* , privately printed, Berlin, 1805, § 15. Scharnhorst's regulations are reprinted in Klippel, iii, 237–255; and excerpted in Poten, iv, 116–122.

August of Prussia; Duke Karl of Mecklenburg, the brother of Queen Louise; and on a different social level Varnhagen von Ense, who a decade later was to marry Rahel Levin, and whom Clausewitz still visited occasionally in the 1820's when both men had become political outsiders.[23] Scharnhorst himself lectured on strategy, tactics, and the duties of the general staff. Visiting speakers such as Colonel von Phull from the general staff presented their own, frequently differing, views. With the assistance of an artillery lieutenant, Scharnhorst also gave courses on the theory and practice of gunnery, which included demonstrations with live shot, something of a novelty in the training of Prussian officers who were not themselves preparing for this branch of the service, and another instance of Scharnhorst's attempt to break down artificial barriers in the study of war.

In 1804, the year Clausewitz completed the course, Scharnhorst reorganized the school once more. It was now divided into two sections: the Institute for the Berlin Inspection, where officers stationed in Berlin could, if they wished, learn the basics of logic, geography, and military history; and the Academy for Young Officers, for more advanced study, which was open to talented men from the entire army. In the Institute, material was taught by recitation and the question-and-answer method, while the Academy resembled a small university, where students attended formal lectures and tutorials. Müller died in this year. The subjects he had taught were divided between two young instructors from the artillery, and Professor Stützer, one of the founders of the *Militärische Gesellschaft,* who also lectured on the history of war. Another newcomer was the Hanoverian artillery lieutenant von Ziehen, who was commissioned as a Prussian captain, and with whom Scharnhorst shared his own courses. The organizational changes and the expansion of the faculty further strengthened the advanced part of the curriculum. Only a formal examination for admission was still lacking to complete the professionalization of the school. It still seemed difficult to reconcile such a hurdle with the aristocratic character of the fighting arms of the service, though it was accepted in branches requiring technical expertise; but Scharnhorst interviewed all applicants and had the power to reject those he judged unsuitable.

In the work of the school and in his own teaching it was Scharnhorst's main concern to help the young officer acquire the necessary technical and academic knowledge without enslaving him to a particular theory of war. To the surprise of some, the director of the army's institute for the advanced study of war discounted the authority of theoretical systems; whether classic works or the products of contemporary revolutionaries, all were fit objects of critical and historical analysis. "He taught that part of

23. Poten, iv, 114; K. A. Varnhagen von Ense, *Denkwürdigkeiten des eigenen Lebens,* Leipzig, 1843, i, 254; and the autobiography of another fellow-student, M. v. Brünneck, *Von Preussens Befreiungs- und Verfassungskampf,* ed. P. Herre, Berlin, 1914, pp. 144–145.

the art of war," Clausewitz later wrote, "which until then had scarcely been dealt with on the lecture platform and in books, war as it actually is—*der eigentliche Krieg.*" [24] In Clausewitz's eyes it was Scharnhorst's great merit "that he was not in the least impressed by the pretentious theories [of Bülow, Mathieu Dumas, and Jomini], which at that time were attracting everyone who was not unthinkingly holding fast to tradition. He recognized both the unchanging elements in the present age and the inadequacies of old methods, but he wanted the new to emerge from the old so that he might achieve as quickly and with as little fuss as possible a method that accorded with reality." [25]

No military theorist of the time was as conscious as Scharnhorst of the innate conflict between theory and reality. His elaboration of this fundamental issue, and his refusal to seek its solution in increasingly complex abstractions, constitute the most important lesson he taught Clausewitz. Scharnhorst himself never fully resolved this conflict in his own mind, at least not in a systematic, formal manner. His lectures at the Academy still presented the traditional argument that theory should eliminate accident and chance—that theory could dominate reality—a concept that still appears in Clausewitz's earliest writings, though in the company of very different thoughts. But in practice Scharnhorst had long given up this belief. Rather than emphasize that sound theory could eliminate accident, which obviously was sometimes the case, it might be pedagogically more productive, he thought, and far more realistic, to stress the ability of theory to help men deal with surprise, to help them exploit the unforeseen. From there it was only a short step, which Clausewitz was soon to take, to recognize the fortuitous not as a negative but as a positive force, an indispensable part of reality. But on what could a realistic theory base itself? Not on logic and mathematics: they were primarily important in training the intellect. In the classroom—that is, in the absence of experience—Scharnhorst believed that the study of war had to be based on history. That, too, was a legacy of the first importance to Clausewitz. In Scharnhorst's mind, history was the most complete intellectual representation of reality, and it was so natural for him to see contemporary events with the eyes of the historian that neither then nor later did he hesitate to incorporate historical references and interpretations in operational orders; his order of the day of 8 April 1813, after the battle of Möckern, is an example.

Scharnhorst's conviction that the study of history must lie at the center of any advanced study of war confirmed Clausewitz's tentative attitudes on military theory and on the role of education, and guided them further. Scharnhorst also deepened his awareness of the social forces that deter-

---

24. Clausewitz, "Über das Leben ... von Scharnhorst," *Historisch-politische Zeitschrift,* I (1832), 177.
25. *Ibid.,* p. 198.

Scharnhorst in 1813, painted by Friedrich Bury. Landesgalerie Hannover.

mined the military style and energies of states. Scharnhorst's early personal experience did not, as we have seen, turn him into a democrat, nor, having achieved professional success, did he fall into facile acceptance of privilege. What counted in his eyes was not the particular structure of society or the form taken by its institutions, but the spirit that animated them. In the regimental school for soldiers' children at Neuruppin, Clausewitz had witnessed something of the humanitarian, paternalistic concern for the poor that was such a pronounced feature of the late Enlightenment in Prussia. Scharnhorst taught him that this was adequate neither for the individual nor for the state. If the French Revolution had proved anything, it was that states wishing to preserve their independence must become more efficient in tapping the energies of their populations. Elites existed in every society, and were justified so long as they strengthened the community, remained open to talent, and rewarded merit. But nothing could justify the continuation of privilege that protected mediocrity while depriving the state of the abilities and enthusiasm of the common man. It was this attitude that a few years later was to determine the direction of the Prussian reform movement—less perhaps in civil matters than on the military side. In the genesis of Clausewitz's ideas the essentially unideological view of social and political arrangements that he had learned in part from Scharnhorst and that he expressed, as we shall see, as early as 1804 and 1805, clearly parallels his undogmatic approach to war. Statesman and soldier, a preliminary outline of this view might formulate, must shed tradition, convenience, any influence that interferes with their achieving the major objective. Similarly the theorist, wishing to understand the nature of the state and the nature of war, must never allow his thoughts to diverge far from the element central to each—power in politics, violence in war.

Scharnhorst was an unprepossessing lecturer, but to those of his students who, like Clausewitz, could overcome their initial impression of awkwardness he opened the way to a firm understanding of war: "He repeated his point, employing different expressions, so that one statement might make up for anything left vague in the other, he did not shrink from this seeming prolixity, and in the end never failed to establish his thought with the utmost clarity. ... The time lost in the use of words and turns of phrase is repaid a hundredfold by a substantial idea. His written work showed not a trace of diffuseness, for he kept correcting and revising his text until his exceptionally fine mind was entirely satisfied and not one word seemed out of place. ... Elegant society, not excepting some able and intelligent men, considered him a dry scholar and pedant; the military took him for an indecisive, impractical, unsoldierlike scribbler. Never was a judgment so mistaken—exactly the opposite qualities distinguished him. Far from being a pedant, he placed little value in the raw substance of knowledge, and paid attention only to the intellectual and spiritual values that can develop from it; nor was anyone ever more practical and active. This showed unmistakably in his judgment and selection of men for important assignments; native intelligence, common sense, even the crude child of nature counted for more with him than any amount of learning that had not yet proved its aptitude and usefulness. How lovable and inspired is this preference for natural abilities in a man who devoted his entire life to penetrate and encompass the body of knowledge of his profession." [26]

Clausewitz was a few months past his twenty-first birthday when he entered the Institute. He is described at the time as being of medium height, thin and erect—which he remained throughout his life—with full brown hair, to which, until 1806, he was obliged to tie a short tail when on duty. At first he seems to have known no one in Berlin. Officers stationed in the capital were still expected to have private means or to receive an allowance from home; but as his father could add nothing to his lieutenant's pay he was limited to a frugal, withdrawn existence. At times he was forced to earn money by taking the place of more affluent comrades when it came their turn to mount guard.[27] He was shaken to find the work at the Institute more difficult than he had expected; his studies in Neuruppin suddenly seemed inadequate to him, and he believed himself incapable of following the lectures. Now that he was finally offered the freedom and opportunities he had wanted, his self-assurance broke down. After his death his widow wrote that during these months he was near despair and might have left the school if Scharnhorst had not taken notice of him, and with characteristic kindness and empathy helped the troubled young man recover his confidence.[28] Soon teacher and student grew very close. In Scharnhorst, Clausewitz recognized qualities and achievements to which he himself aspired: a successful career in spite of humble beginnings, intellectual authority, manliness—a soldier who was not the passive agent of events, but one who tried to understand and guide them. Scharnhorst found in Clausewitz a promising and sympathetic mind, the unusual speculative bent of which sought as its objects the most complex political and military issues of the age. Personal elements further intensified the relationship. Clausewitz's father died in 1802. In February 1803 Scharnhorst's wife died, and soon afterwards his younger daughter; he was left with two half-grown sons and his daughter Julie, a fifteen-year-old girl of great charm and maturity, who soon took her mother's place as the human being in whom Scharnhorst felt free to confide without reserve not only his professional concerns but

26. *Ibid.*, pp. 194–195.
27. According to a note in the Clausewitz papers, which are now dispersed or destroyed; cited by Rothfels, *Carl von Clausewitz*, p. 12, n. 26.
28. In her "Erinnerung an den General Clausewitz und sein Verhältniss zu Scharnhorst," printed as a supplement to Clausewitz's essay in the *Historisch-politische Zeitschrift*, I, pp. 214–215.

also his emotions. In this period of profound loss Clausewitz's gratitude and admiration may have been especially valuable to the older man, who accepted his pupil as a new member of the family. Except for his children, he said, no person on earth was so close to him as Clausewitz, and by no one was he understood so well. He occupied himself with Clausewitz's future as though he were a son, while Clausewitz now saw in Scharnhorst his second father—"the father and friend of my spirit," he explicitly called him.[29]

Once he had regained his psychological balance, Clausewitz progressed rapidly. He believed that his life had passed a turning point. His duties now perfectly matched his interests, and he was able to pursue them in conditions that except for his continued poverty could hardly have been more favorable. Scharnhorst's guidance and friendship, to which he also owed admission to the *Militärische Gesellschaft,* were reinforced by the atmosphere of the Institute, which in its blend of a self-assured military style with middle-class scholarly attitudes repeated the most creative strains that had been present in Clausewitz's childhood. Similar antecedents linked him and his instructors. Major Müller's father had been a Reformed parson in Brandenburg; Kiesewetter, son of a sexton who also taught in a regimental school, had studied at Halle and taught at Francke's orphanage before coming to Berlin. The four artillery officers were men without family connections, who had struggled to reach the edge of military respectability. Everyone, from Scharnhorst on, had experienced the sparse existence of subaltern service for the state, which Clausewitz had known for the first two decades of his life. The values that had dominated his father's house and Colonel von Tschammer's regiment persisted in the lecture hall in the royal palace, but now their context was infinitely more important, and more promising to Clausewitz personally.

The first official intimation that Clausewitz could look forward to a career that might lift him above the average came in the spring of 1803, when after completing the second term at the Institute he was temporarily assigned as adjutant to Prince August of Prussia. The prince, twenty-four years old at the time, was the youngest son of Prince Ferdinand, head of the 34th Infantry Regiment, who had known something of Clausewitz since the revolutionary wars. During the summer the position was made permanent, "by request of Prince Ferdinand," as the king wrote in the cabinet order notifying Clausewitz of the appointment.[30] Since Prince August commanded a grenadier battalion stationed in Berlin, Clausewitz was able to continue his studies. The conditions of his existence changed radically. His new pay was 360 taler, considerably more than his father had ever received, and he was given quarters in a royal palace on the Wilhelms-

29. *Ibid.,* p. 215; and Clausewitz to Marie v. Brühl, 28 January 1807, *Correspondence,* p. 85.
30. The cabinet order of 8 August 1803 is printed in Priesdorff, v, No. 1429.

platz—the Palace of the Order of St. John, of which Prince Ferdinand was Grand Master.[31] It is not known how much Scharnhorst's views contributed to the appointment, but his judgment of his students, which he regularly submitted to the king, undoubtedly played a part. When he ranked the members of the class in the winter of 1803, he reserved the first category for Clausewitz and for another young infantry officer, Karl von Tiedemann, whose life from this time on was to be closely linked with Clausewitz's. Some weeks later Scharnhorst reaffirmed his opinion in a report to the king on the students' written work: "The performance of Lieutenant von Clausewitz is characterized by an unusually good analysis of the whole, and by a modest and agreeable style of presentation. Furthermore he possesses a thorough knowledge of mathematics and of military science." In the spring of 1804, Clausewitz left the Institute at the head of his class.[32]

The completion of the first three-year course coincided with the reorganization of the general-quartermaster staff. The reorganization was instigated not by Scharnhorst but by Colonel von Massenbach, a Württemberger who had entered the Prussian army during the last years of Frederick's reign, and in the succeeding two decades had established a reputation as a learned and emotional admirer of the Frederician system. The staff was expanded to 34 officers and divided into three sections, headed by general-quartermaster-lieutenants, each responsible for the topographic and strategic analysis of a prospective theater of war. The first section, under Phull, was assigned East Prussia; the second, under Massenbach, the area extending from Pomerania south over Silesia and Saxony to Bavaria; the third section, which dealt with the most likely zone of operations in a future war, the territory between the Elbe and the Rhine, was given to Scharnhorst, who was transferred from the artillery to the staff, and promoted to the rank of colonel. In an examination held to fill the twenty-two junior positions of the new organization, nine of the Institute's graduating officers gained admission, after four of their fellow students with particularly strong records, including Clausewitz and Tiedemann, had already received assignments as adjutants and as officers for special duties.[33]

Scharnhorst's appointment as general-quartermaster-lieutenant and the successes of his students were triumphs for himself and for his efforts to regenerate the army's leadership. Giving the staff its new form meant an im-

---

31. The city directory gives Clausewitz's address during these years. See, for instance, the 1805 edition of the *Adress-Kalender der Königlich Preussischen Haupt- und Residenz-Städte Berlin und Potsdam*, p. 25, where his name is spelled Clausswitz.

32. On Scharnhorst's ranking of his students, see Lehmann, *Scharnhorst*, i, 525–526; and Clausewitz's letter to Marie v. Brühl, 9 April 1807, *Correspondence*, p. 111.

33. *Rangliste der Königl. Preussischen Armee für das Jahr 1805,* Berlin, 1805, pp. lviii–lx. Of these thirteen officers, two were killed in the last years of the Napoleonic wars; eight of the remaining eleven rose to general rank.

portant advance toward unified control of strategic policy; but, as was almost always the case in Prussia before 1806, the innovation stopped short of what was needed. Geusau remained as chief of staff, a position which both he and the king continued to regard as administrative in nature. The three general-quartermaster-lieutenants, who disagreed among themselves on almost every issue of strategy and tactics, were left free to pursue their individual concerns, so long as they attempted nothing out of the ordinary. If anything guided their activities, it was not a clear idea of how the inevitable war with France was to be fought but a policy of misplaced caution. When Scharnhorst proposed, in the spring of 1806, to carry out a thorough reconnaissance of Westphalia and the Thuringian forest, where six months later Napoleon was to shatter the Prussian armies, Geusau demurred; he feared the expense, and that the presence of Prussian officers on foreign territories would cause comment and might give rise to misinterpretations.[34]

34. Priesdorff, ii, No. 820.

❧ 5 ❧

EARLY WRITINGS

CLAUSEWITZ'S EARLIEST WRITINGS DATE FROM HIS AT-
tendance at the Institute and from the following years when he served as
Prince August's adjutant, a period of immense psychological and intellectual importance, which ended with the war of 1806. The pieces that have
survived in print or in manuscript comprise two tactical school-exercises;
some random observations concerning politics; an essay on the strategic
principles to be followed in a war against France; essays on the Thirty
Years' War, on the Russo–Turkish war of 1736–39, a long study of Gustavus Adolphus in the years 1630 to 1632; some thirty notes and brief
essays grouped under the heading *Strategy;* and a review-article of one of
Heinrich von Bülow's many books on the theory of modern war.

The tactical discussions are brief answers to problems that Scharnhorst
regularly set his students. Clausewitz's solutions contain nothing remarkable, unless it be their practical note: men going on reconnaissance at night
are "not to carry packs, and if possible to be given dark trousers. They are
promised a monetary reward." [1] To turn from these useful subaltern exercises to Clausewitz's private political reflections is seemingly to enter another world. The twenty-three-year-old lieutenant who has just submitted a
carefully worked-out route for a seven-man patrol now speculates on the
fate of the European continent, and does so with imagination and verve.
His observations, put down in a notebook to express and clarify his ideas,
with no thought of publication, range from aphoristic paragraphs to short
essays. They are given emotional urgency by the writer's anxieties over
Prussia's future and over the character of the state he serves. [2] Are the

1. "Auflösung der 26ten Aufgabe," 3 December 1803, printed in C. v. Clausewitz, *Schriften*, i,
57–58. Another of Clausewitz's tactical solutions from 1803 is in the possession of the library of the
University of Münster.
2. A selection of these notes was first published by H. Rothfels in *Carl von Clausewitz*, pp. 197–204; a
few are also reprinted in his edition of Clausewitz's *Politische Schriften und Briefe*, pp. 1–5. Additional
passages were published by W. M. Schering in his edition of Clausewitz's selected writings, *Geist und*

France the new Romans? he asks in 1803. Their successses over the past decade do not by themselves prove this similarity, and the characters of the
two peoples are entirely different; but their politics are as alike as the passage of two millennia will permit. "No one can deny a nation the right to
fight for its interests," he continues, ". . . even France cannot be criticized
if she plants her foot on our back, and extends her realm of frightened vas-
sals to the polar sea." [3] It is the first statement of a political attitude—
derived perhaps from his reading of Machiavelli and Frederick at this
time—that was to fascinate him to the end of his days, even though he
came to recognize its limitations: every major power must necessarily wish
to increase her strength, though caution and moderation may restrain her
in practice. There is an evident parallel between this conception and the
argument he developed in later years that war in theory must seek the extremes of violence, but that its drive toward totality is modified by the limitations and considerations of the real world. It lies at the root of the cold
view of international relations that he soon developed, unclouded by partisanship, fears, or ideologies; but it is also the basis for some of his disappointments and misinterpretations. The potential of power seemed to him
almost to demand its use, and he found it difficult to accept the fact not
every statesman thought as exclusively in terms of power as he. The fragment concludes on the Kantian note that however frightening the power of
France, the magnitude of her challenge ought to lead not to surrender but
to an equally great response.

Other observations deal with coalitions, the balance of power, the
identity of interests of monarchs and their states, and Germany's political
condition—in which in a historical survey of less than a page in length he
traces the roots of Germany's political fragmentation, concluding, "Though
these reasons might seem adequate, the German national character must
contain a force that has contributed to this result." [4] With increasing clarity the later pieces mirror Clausewitz's concern over the continuing train of
French successes and his disgust at the passivity of Prussia's foreign policy.
"We must not fear—or rather, we must not hope for—the condition of
total subservience," he wrote in 1805, "but that shameful, languid period
in which our civil existence is not yet threatened while independence and
dignity of the state have already been lost." [5] In the same year he commented that perhaps the only principle of Roman policy that Bonaparte had
not adopted was to permit freedom of speech in the conquered nations.

Tat, Stuttgart, 1941, pp. 7–10, 12–15, 17–19. Professor Schering's commentaries in this volume as
well as in his work *Die Kriegsphilosophie von Clausewitz,* Hamburg, 1935, which pretends to find a "philosophy of action" in Clausewitz's writings, are distasteful examples of the brutalization and perversion of
German scholarship during the Third Reich.
3. *Politische Schriften und Briefe,* p. 2.
4. *Geist und Tat,* p. 13.
5. *Politische Schriften und Briefe,* p. 4. The following quotation is from the same page.

This could be an error on the part of the French, since men who are allowed to criticize do not think of themselves as being oppressed; "but if tyranny grows so heavy that no man dares to talk then misery swells and becomes the seed for great deeds ... ." Another passage questions the value of intrigue and stratagems, which marked Prussia's diplomatic style: "Political methods must always be vigorous, and worthy of the state, when an important issue is at stake."

From 1803 to the crises of 1805 and 1806, Clausewitz's political reflections express a consistent interpretation of the European condition, a view in which a sense of grave danger is balanced by trust in energetic measures. But when Clausewitz sought to apply his ideas to the central problem, he was unable to resolve the difficulties that lay in the path of developing an effective policy. His essay on war with France, written almost certainly just before the outbreak of the War of the Third Coalition, pursues a realistic argument to an abstract and vague conclusion.[6] Clausewitz began with the assumption—soon to prove false—that any major power could defend itself against France, but that it would require an alliance to wage a successful offensive war against her. Since the appearance of a great general could not be counted on, he set himself the task of eliminating the flaws that had proved fatal to the anti-French alliance in the early 1790's. A plan ought to be devised that would enable each member of the alliance to fight for his particular interests, without endangering the alliance. The theater of operations of each major power should therefore be located near its borders, so that a defeat could not be shrugged off as a purely military act but would directly endanger the state, while on the other hand a successful campaign could lead to desirable territorial acquisitions. Self-interest, provided reasonable leeway, would thus to some extent take the place of an overall plan of operations. Ideally, a high degree of coordination would be desirable, but no plan attractive to every member of the alliance could be a good one. "We must somewhat depart either from the principles of the art of war or from the self-interest of the powers. I prefer the former since that would damage only the perfection of theory, while were we to disregard the self-interest of the powers we would deprive the military operations of their soul, of the force that gives them life."[7] This last sentence is an interesting example of the readiness with which the young Clausewitz adopted Scharnhorst's skeptical view of the validity of military dogma. The subordination of military concerns to political interest also appears as a firmly established, self-evident concept. Clausewitz's distribution of the theaters of war is, however, schematic, based on geography rather than on true political interest, especially since his concept of the *raison d'état*—or, as he calls it, the *in-*

6. "Considérations sur la manière de faire la guerre à la France," *Schriften*, i, 58–63. The essay is written in fairly fluent French.
7. *Ibid.*, p. 63.

térêt naturel des états takes for granted each power's willingness to permit its allies to make important conquests. The essay ends abruptly with the hope that perhaps a plan for concerted action can, after all, be devised.

Both Clausewitz's political reflections and his "Considérations sur la manière de faire la guerre à la France" place great weight on history. But history is used not merely as a source of illustrations or examples; for the young officer the study of the past apparently played a more fundamental role than that of a clarifying addition to his argument. Even if the historical evidence took the form of flawed chronicles or of sentimental, abstract modern accounts, he believed it would provide him with insights into political and military conflict and change far transcending contemporary affairs in scope and variety of detail, a mass of facts and interpretations that alone can lead, in the course of analysis, to a universally valid comprehension of force in the intercourse of governments and the clash of armies.

During these years in Berlin, and probably earlier during his tour of duty in Neuruppin, Clausewitz read widely in European historical literature—not solely accounts of wars but also diplomatic, political, and cultural studies.[8] His early writings refer to such authors as Machiavelli, Montaigne, Montesquieu, Robertson, Johannes von Müller, Ancillon, and Gentz. The ideas and knowledge he drew from their works were easily incorporated into an emerging concept of history, which was given encouragement by the individualizing view of the past that Scharnhorst offered his students. Scharnhorst opposed schematic systems of strategy since he could not believe that any law of action could ever match the diversity of the real world. Instead, his lectures stressed the individuality of each campaign, which almost inevitably led him to a measure of recognition of the particularity of different historical epochs and of social and political systems. The strength of his interpretation of the revolutionary wars derived from his willingness to accept such differences rather than to posit a universally valid standard, which the opposing sides observed to greater or lesser extent. All this, to be sure, was the expression of a profoundly pragmatic mind, and pragmatism alone did not satisfy Clausewitz for long. Soon he was to insist that the fullest recognition of diversity should not render a general theory of conflict impossible. But his first efforts at scholarship could hardly have

8. In *Carl von Clausewitz,* pp. 29–30, n. 5, Rothfels mentions the following military writers as appearing in Clausewitz's early papers and reading lists: Montecuccoli, Feuquières, Santa-Cruz, Folard, Maurice de Saxe, Puysegur, Turpin, Guibert, Lloyd, Tempelhoff, Mauvillon, Venturini, Berenhorst, Prince de Ligne, de Silva, memoirs of the campaigns of Turenne, Condé, the Duke of Brunswick, and of Frederick the Great, and the military histories of Nast and Hoyer. To these should be added the writings of Bülow, Frederick (his *General Principles of War*), Scharnhorst, Gualdo Priorato's history of the Thirty Years' War, and works on the same subject by a number of other authors (see note 22 below), Mathieu Dumas, and Jomini—all of whom are mentioned in texts written before 1806. Passages in his *Strategie aus dem Jahr 1804* (see note 25 below) make it highly probable that by this time Clausewitz had also read Caesar and Polybius. The remainder of this paragraph and the following three pages are based on my previously cited article "Education, Politics, and War in the Life of Clausewitz."

occurred in a more auspicious environment than that created by Scharnhorst's undogmatic, open-minded approach to the old and the new. Even
Clausewitz's first manuscripts are entirely free of that criticism of other centuries which derives from a sense of alienation, a consciousness of superiority, on the part of the later observer. Instead, Clausewitz's pronounced bent
for logical analysis is given direction by a willingness to consider the ideas
and actions of previous generations as phenomena that were closely linked
with the general conditions of their age, and often, indeed, proved to be
their necessary outcome.

An early impulse toward this attitude, in which he found himself at
one with the historical school, came to him in 1795; indeed, the accident
of military operations that carried him to Westphalia may have opened his
eyes not only to the future but also to the past. The self-sufficient, patriarchal peasant-family, mentioned in the letter of 3 July 1807 to his fiancée,
showed him how great the human and social achievements of a way of life
could be that had not appreciably changed for centuries and that had little
in common with the cultural standards of the Enlightenment. Possibly
Justus Möser was among the authors with whom the circulating library
acquainted him; it would not have been surprising since Möser was Osnabrück's most eminent publicist, and had died there only the previous
year. Then or later, in any case, Clausewitz made some of Möser's ideas his
own. In an important essay of 1807 on French and German character, for
instance, a central section is a variant of Möser's argument that the German's individuality, his bonds with the particular culture that his native
region had developed since the days of Arminius and Ulfilas, rendered him
unsuitable to become the citizen of a "great, uniform monarchy." [9] In decades of administering the affairs of the burghers, the old established nobility, and the free peasants in the territory of Osnabrück, Möser had been
inspired to construct a theory of history very different from that of his contemporaries. The bishopric's tangle of traditions, privileges, and duties that
most scholars could only pity as an obstacle to the spread of reason, Möser
welcomed as evidence of an organic and therefore genuine vitality. Accepting it, seeking its earlier stages, and penetrating to its essence would enable man to understand his past. In Dilthey's words, Möser replaced "the
abstract concept of progress, which had been held by the entire 18th century, with the concept of development ... . The frequently unhistoric posture of the Enlightenment, according to which the culture of the 18th century constituted the standard for all earlier periods, was eliminated. For
Möser, every age contained its own measure." [10]

Clausewitz came to share his belief in the individuality of historical

9. "Die Deutschen und die Franzosen," *Politische Schriften und Briefe,* pp. 35–51, esp. pp. 46–47, 49.
Compare also the early observation on Germany's political fragmentation cited above, p. 79.
10. W. Dilthey, *Studien zur Geschichte des deutschen Geistes,* Leipzig and Berlin, 1927, pp. 256–257.

epochs and in the concept of historical evolution. But he rejected the particularist principles, and the conservative view of politics to which they gave rise, that had done so much to generate Möser's historicism. German cultural individuality—outcome of a process that had been at work for thousands of years—was a factor to be reckoned with, but it need not be accepted as a political guideline; on the contrary, the young Clausewitz regarded it as a tendency that Germans must be taught to modify for the sake of regaining their independence in a hostile world.

The energy with which Clausewitz studied the past, and the uses to which he put his knowledge, reveal the major role that history played in the process of self-education which had been his ideal since as an adolescent he happened on Illuminati tracts on returning from his first campaign. To identify this role more precisely we must touch on other forces in Clausewitz's thought to which his study of history was joined. We do not know when his general aim of intellectual development became refined to the intellectual mastery of specific problems; perhaps his desire, strong but vague, was not given direction until he arrived at the Berlin Institute and came under Scharnhorst's influence. From that time on he never ceased, in his words, to try to create for himself "a sound, encompassing and practical view of life and of its connections with the ordinary world. . . . I compared myself with my class and my profession, and measured my class against the great political events that govern this world, and in this way I have learned to recognize clearly what goals I should strive for." [11] The tone that distinguishes this observation from other programmatic statements of the Goethe period lies in its peculiar practicality. There was nothing unusual about thinking that the ideal of a mature and wise humanity could be achieved only by harmonizing action and reflection; where Clausewitz stood apart was in his definition of the "ordinary world," in which man must learn to function, as a political world with its inevitable military dimension. Once he had settled in the new life of the Institute he sought to educate and to understand himself by studying mathematics and philosophic method, and applying his new knowledge to the world of social and political intercourse and of military effort. His was not a mind that in the final analysis employed the world to illustrate its thought, let alone one that feared—as a few years later he accused Fichte of fearing—to compare the conclusions reached by reasoning with history and present experience. [12] For Clausewitz, then and later, the world was the object on which thought was tested, as well as the stage for the necessary complement of the speculative side of education: action.

11. Letter to Marie v. Brühl, 3 July 1807, *Correspondence*, pp. 128–129.
12. Letter to Marie v. Brühl, 15 April 1808, *ibid.*, pp. 154–155. Clausewitz's comment is part of an otherwise favorable reference to an unnamed work of Fichte's—either the *Patriotic Dialogues* of 1807 or, more likely, his *Addresses to the German Nation*. See below, p. 159.

The philosophic strain, which was so powerful in him, is of a singular, practical kind. In his writings, at least, it exists not for its own sake but as a means to an end. He freely used concepts learned from other writers, together with ideas that were the common property of his generation. Both in method and terminology he was influenced by the philosophers of the Enlightenment and of German idealism. But unlike the great creators of transcendental systems who were his contemporaries, his purpose and manner were realistic, to use the term in its naïve sense.[13] He was concerned with what is, and with what might develop, not with the metaphysical significance of day-to-day events. He never questioned the reality of the objects on which his attention centered. German philosophy gave him the means of subjecting war to logical inquiry, and no doubt also contributed to his desire to do so, but it did less to shape the result than might be assumed. Such thinkers as Kant, Herder, and Fichte inspired him not only directly through their works but also through the filter of German historical writing that was influenced by them—interpretations in which their metaphysics and ethics were forced to express themselves through men and events. Clausewitz's profound belief—stated even in his first manuscripts—in the causal importance of individual psychology, of genius, led in this direction; but it is notable how often his argument and style gained a special power when their general subject could be identified with an individual—with William Tell, Gustavus Adolphus, Wallenstein, William of Orange, Frederick, or Napoleon. Schiller, the dramatist and historian of charismatic leaders, is the author most often mentioned in his letters. An outcome of this tendency is Clausewitz's habit of regarding the state as an organism, an individual whose life extended through centuries—another quality he shares with the historical school.

How could he come to understand the political world sufficiently well to act effectively in it? By observing its appearances, searching out their functions and relationships, and by discovering the permanent qualities of its temporary phenomena. Even in his early twenties Clausewitz had come to believe that only historical inquiry joined to the observation of the current scene would make possible the kind of comprehensive analysis that alone interested him. Only history could illuminate the timeless forces in politics and war, and only in history could be found the key to the meaning of each particular detail, both past and present. The intensity of Clausewitz's search for universals, and of his need for a perspective that measured the present and future by relating them to what had gone before, is sug-

13. The frequently voiced supposition that Clausewitz's dialectic owes something to Hegel misses the point. The dialectical method in a variety of forms and with a variety of purposes was standard equipment of German idealistic and Romantic philosophy. More specifically, in contrast to Hegel, the dialectic of thesis and antithesis in Clausewitz's theoretical writings does not insist on resolution; its intent is to clarify differences: it is not part of a necessary progression that both gives expression to and moves toward a state of infinite harmony.

gested by the topic he chose for his first long scholarly work. It did not deal with a recent or contemporary occurrence—the war against the French Revolution, or one of Napoleon's campaigns would have been likely choices—but with a phase of the seemingly chaotic Thirty Years' War.

"Gustavus Adolphus's Campaigns of 1630–1632" was written during Clausewitz's first years in Berlin, but did not appear in print until 1837, when the ninth volume of his posthumous works was published.[14] According to the editor, the manuscript had never received a final revision; it is nevertheless a polished work, in which complex events are subjected to considered analysis and delineated in precise and sometimes striking language. Although Clausewitz does not hesitate to criticize opposing views or to employ his historical interpretations as the basis for commenting on ideas and policies of his own day, the tone of the study is very different from the sarcasm that marks many of his political reflections. His immediate aim is to interpret the strategic policy of the Swedish king. He notes, but does not elaborate upon, the social, economic, and technological conditions of the time, and the effect they exerted on the organization of the fighting forces and on their tactics; he says almost nothing about the battles and sieges that in other accounts are treated as the great poles around which the war swirled in confused and indeterminate devastation. The decisive encounter at Lützow, in which Gustavus Adolphus was killed, is dismissed in one sentence. The clash of arms is replaced in his pages by the clash of wills and of motives. In his opening chapter Clausewitz writes that scholarship usually ignores such "subjective forces" as the psychology of the commander, his ambitions, his awareness of his own abilities, "and yet it is precisely they that are most decisive." [15] Consequently his interpretation of Swedish strategy rests largely on an analysis of Gustavus Adolphus's personality.[16] Equally, it is psychological factors that guide the behavior of the Catholic party. Clausewitz takes account of the character of its political and military leaders, but also of general human responses to important events, which he believes are passed over or misunderstood by "scientific" soldiers and historians: "It is true, at the battle of Breitenfeld the emperor could have opposed the king of Sweden with over 60,000 men instead of 32,000, because a short time later he really did raise a force of this size, and nothing

---

14. "Gustav Adolphs Feldzüge von 1630–1632," *Hinterlassene Werke*, Berlin, 1832–37, ix, 1–106. Clausewitz's posthumous works are henceforth cited as *Werke*. For the date of composition of the manuscript on Gustavus Adolphus, see the preface of the editor, C. v. d. Groeben, p. vi, and his notes on pp. 20 and 104 of the text. The essays on the Russo-Turkish War, published in volume x of the posthumous works, were presumably written in connection with Clausewitz's studies at the Institute. They are primarily exercises in the organization and narration of complicated material, and contain relatively few interpretations.
15. "Gustav Adolphs Feldzüge," *Werke*, ix, 8.
16. *Ibid.*, p. 7. In his introduction, p. v, General v. d. Groeben, known throughout the service for his profound piety, regrets that Clausewitz's interpretation emphasized ambition rather than religious faith as the basis of the king's greatness.

about this army made it impossible to organize it a few months earlier. But did the emperor already possess the motive to raise and assemble such a force before the battle of Breitenfeld? Had conditions already driven him to that degree of energy and will that was required to produce such an effect? Is it not wiser to pay less attention to what the enemy *can* do, and pay more attention to what he *will* do? ... Sensible men will agree with us that this constitutes a more instructive topic for strategic thought than the degrees of the angles formed by operational lines." [17]

The character of Clausewitz's history of Gustavus Adolphus's campaigns in Germany is above all antidoctrinaire. Its author approached each event with the assumption that good reasons existed for it, and that it was at least conceivable that what had been done in the 1630's was preferable in attitude and execution to the standard of later generations. In discussing the operations of the imperial general Torquato Conti against strong Swedish forces, he comments that Conti's tenacity points "to the courageous spirit of the times, which certainly is worth more than the sham art [*Afterkunst*] of later wars." Far from agreeing with some modern authors, he continues, "that the Thirty Years' War went on interminably only because the generals did not know how to bring it to an end, we are convinced that recent wars were so brief only because people lacked the courage to fight to the finish." [18] An interpretation of the past based solely on whatever intellectual fashion reigns at the moment must mislead. A similar principle held true for the present: in military operations, abstract strategic and tactical systems were the enemies of natural, effective action. Neither the psychology of the individual nor chance could ever be controlled by science. [19] Clausewitz the historian and Clausewitz the serving soldier were guided by the same preference for reality over systematization, and possibly it was Clausewitz's sense of realism in military affairs that lay at the root of his historicist approach to the past. No doubt his decision to write about the Thirty Years' War was meant as a protest against such systematizing military savants as Bülow and Massenbach, who could regard this emotional, formless struggle only with a sense of horror and superiority. Clausewitz's

17. *Ibid.,* pp. 45–46. Compare the earlier programmatic statement (p. 8): "The careful reader of military history will have noticed that these reasons [which determine major decisions] are usually contained in moral and psychological elements, less often in the mathematical appraisal of physical factors. Those who want to restrict the art of war to the latter will regret it! Further, our attention is called to the influence that subjective reasons possess. These are usually overlooked in interpretations that are imposed on military events ..., nevertheless they are the most influential. Anyone who fails to recognize the spirit and character of his opponent will never guess his decisions. Proof again how despicable is a theory of war that erects its structure only of materials dragged up by the five senses, and also how difficult it is to treat this art theoretically."
18. *Ibid.,* p. 18. See also the comparison on pp. 101–102 between his age and that of the early 17th century, whose military attitudes rose "above the narrow arithmetic of physical forces."
19. "Gustav Adolphs Feldzüge," *Werke,* ix, 67.

caution in criticizing another century contrasts with his readiness to condemn the attitudes of his own generation. In a characteristic slap at the adherents of methodical warfare, he wrote in the opening chapter that Gustavus Adolphus "like all generals of the time, and like *sensible* generals still today, held to the principle that war must support itself." [20] He returned to this issue of requisitions, which constituted a major difference between Prussian and French policy, at the end of his study, and then proceeded in his concluding sentences to remind Frederick William III of the subjective forces that Germany could muster despite her political fragmentation and geographic defenselessness. If the monarch were to make use of the energies and courage of his subjects, if he were to bypass routine to draw on the talented leadership that could be found in the army, he would have no cause to fear any war. [21]

In the German military literature of the beginning 19th century, "Gustavus Adolphus" is exceptional for the decisive significance it ascribes to the moral and psychological qualities of the commander, and for the manner in which comments on current policy arise from an informed, balanced interpretation of the past, without distorting the evidence. A comparison with works of the mature Scharnhorst, such as his history of the siege of Gilbraltar or the account of the revolutionary wars, reveals a far higher degree of abstraction on the part of Clausewitz. Scharnhorst bases himself on a greater number of sources; he presents more illustrations, demonstrates a stronger interest in tactics and perhaps also a deeper concern for the individual soldier. His books show a strong affinity with the intellectual and aesthetic manner of the 1760's and 1770's; they recall buildings of the late Baroque in northern Germany, in which a wealth of detail—stylized and yet filled with a sense of nature and of everyday life—embellishes without ever obscuring the clarity of the design. In the writings of his student, everything is simplified and reduced to a few great themes, with the concept of the interaction of political motives and strategy providing the overall pattern. To continue the architectural simile: in Clausewitz's early writings the change from Baroque to German Classicism has been achieved.

The manner of "Gustavus Adolphus" forecast Clausewitz's subsequent historical method and style. For sources he relied on a balanced selection of printed documents, contemporary accounts, and later interpretations; but evidently he did not consider it essential to make use of all existing material. In "Gustavus Adolphus" he does not, for instance, cite the important contemporary history, based on Swedish sources, by B. P. v. Chemnitz. Possibly the rare work was not available to him. Nor does he refer to

20. *Ibid.*, p. 15.
21. *Ibid.*, pp. 105–106.

Schiller, whose interpretation of Gustavus, if not his teleological view, he would have found sympathetic.[22] A similar selectivity can be observed in the later works. Clausewitz's mature style was to differ from its precursor largely in its richer allusiveness and more powerful dialectic. But if method and style were to remain relatively constant, his ideas developed considerably; and yet much of their growth consisted in the enlargement of views already held—in their adaptation to fresh experiences and increased knowledge—rather than in the creation of new concepts. Some of the major themes of *On War* can already be found in Clausewitz's first historical study, and in his concurrent writings on the military issues of his day. Often they are set down in remarkably similar terms. We cannot refrain, he writes after rejecting criticism leveled at one of Gustavus Adolphus's decisions, from adding "a remark that touches on what seems to us one of the most essential principles of the art of war. Trusting wholly in those concepts that in the course of calm contemplation one has abstracted from the nature of the subject or from a mass of experience, one must never permit oneself to desert these concepts in times of action. Human intelligence is liable to self-deception and error, and never more so than in the press of events. At such times *character* must serve to steady conviction, and a new impression must not triumph over the completed thought-process for the simple reason that events seem more vivid in reality than in recollection, and because at the moment of action it is often impossible to run through once more the whole sequence of ideas that had led to the original conviction." [23]

The same argument is elaborated a decade later in an essay on "Principles of War," and achieves its final form in the chapter on genius in *On War:* "Only those general principles and attitudes that result from clear and deep understanding can provide a *comprehensive* guide to action. It is to these that opinions on specific problems should be anchored. The difficulty is to hold fast to these results of contemplation in the torrent of events and new opinions. Often there is a gap between principles and actual events that cannot always be bridged by a succession of logical deductions. Then a measure of self-confidence is needed, and a degree of skepticism is also salu-

---

22. Clausewitz's abbreviated references do not always indicate which edition of a particular work he used, but in "Gustavus Adolphus" he cites and discusses the following contemporary accounts and collections of documents: Khevenhiller's *Annales Ferdinandei;* the *Theatrum Europaeum;* Gualdo Priorato's history of the Thirty Years' War, either in Francheville's French translation, which appeared in Berlin in 1771, or in the German version of Francheville, published in Göttingen in 1794; and C. v. Murr's *Beyträge zur Geschichte des dreissigjährigen Krieges,* Nuremberg, 1790. Later interpretations mentioned are: W. Harte's well-known history of the Swedish king, presumably in the German version of 1760–61; J. Ar[c]kenholz, *Histoire de Gustave Adolphe,* ed. E. de Mauvillon, 1764; Mauvillon's subsequent *Essai historique sur l'art de la guerre pendant la guerre de trente ans,* Brunswick, 1780–89, which had been favorably reviewed by Scharnhorst; Grimoard's *Histoire des conquêtes de Gustave Adolphe* or his *Campagnes de Gustave Adolphe;* and J. G. Hoyer's *Geschichte der Kriegskunst,* Göttingen, 1797.
23. "Gustav Adolphs Feldzüge," *Werke,* ix, 49–50.

tary. Frequently nothing short of an imperative principle will suffice, which is not part of the immediate thought-process, but dominates it: that principle is in all doubtful cases *to stick to one's first opinion and to refuse to change unless forced to do so by a clear conviction.* A strong faith in the overriding truth of tested principles is needed; the *vividness* of transient impressions must not make us forget that such truth as they contain is of a lesser stamp. By giving precedence, in case of doubt, to our earlier convictions, by holding to them stubbornly, our actions acquire that quality of steadiness and consistency which is termed strength of character." [24]

More complex ideas—the meaning of strategy and tactics, the political interpretation of war—find their first expression in Clausewitz's review of Bülow's book and in his *Strategy*. Each contains important theoretical discussions, but neither matches the unity and balance that was achieved in the study of Gustavus Adolphus. The attack on Bülow is marred by the one-sidedness of all polemical writings; while the remarks and aperçus that Clausewitz set down in a notebook under the heading "Strategy" are a random collection on a wide variety of topics, some little more than variants of Scharnhorst's arguments, others the product of an increasingly independent mind. Like his political observations, the notes were intended at most for private circulation, and the manuscript remained unpublished until the 1930's. [25] In the space of thirty-two printed pages almost as many topics are treated, from the defense of rivers and the organization of a system of outposts to the military history of the ancient Swiss and the function of violence in national policy. Through this diversity run several common threads, the most prominent of which proclaims the value in war of battle and of energetic activity in general. Two forces are reflected in this theme: the author's reaction against the systematic character of 18th-century operations, valid in the conditions of that age but now clearly inapplicable. Joined to this is Clausewitz's response to the immediate political situation, which he regards as close to catastrophic, to be resolved, if at all, only by renouncing passivity and by daring to resort to the supreme effort. Theoretical and political considerations support one another; we may guess, though no evidence for it exists, that his early political instincts, his rage at finding himself and the Prussian state in a passive, victimized position, helped open his eyes to the time-bound quality of maneuver strategy, and thus to the unreality of universalist pretensions of any theoretical system, two opinions which were to become fundamental elements of his thought.

24. *On War*, book I, ch. 3 (p. 143). In the same chapter (p. 150) the discussion of the difficulties the historian faces in reconstructing the past is nearly identical with comments on this problem in "Gustavus Adolphus," pp. 95–96.

25. C. v. Clausewitz, *Strategie aus dem Jahr 1804, mit Zusätzen von 1808 und 1809*, ed. E. Kessel, Hamburg, 1937. Professor Kessel's valuable introductory essay is especially suggestive in its exploration of the bonds between the military theory of the later 18th century and the writings of the young Clausewitz.

Several passages in *Strategy* indicate that Clausewitz had not yet liberated himself completely from rationalist doctrine—the assertion, for instance, that progress in the art of war was possible only if the realm of chance could be reduced. On the other hand, he found no difficulty in exposing the feebleness of maneuver strategy and of its latter-day variants. "Three characteristic things that should no longer occur in strategy" is the heading of a section that critically outlines the major features of current Prussian doctrine: exaggerating the importance of enemy fortresses; the related tendency to use sizable detachments to protect one's own strongpoints, thus weakening the field army; and what he castigated as "Fabian temporizing." [26] Criticism constitutes the most persuasive aspect of the notes; positive elements of Clausewitz's thought are stated with equal force, but they are not yet fully developed, and there are some inconsistencies. Once again he stressed the psychology of the general, of the aggressive leader on whom his hopes for Prussia center: "Above all he must be fearless, calm, firm, cold-blooded, ambitious—in short, he must possess a powerful, striving soul—cunning and constant activity are two additional qualities I should like to see in him." [27] In opposition to the claim of Frederick's epigoni that great generalship was a science, he writes that the supreme commander needs "a very little knowledge and much practice in judgment, few abstract truths and many ideas that have become so intimately joined to his spirit that often he can no longer separate and distinguish them from his own nature—in short, as the philosophers would say: little intellectual content, but much intellectual form." How, he continues, "can the mind acquire this form? In constant occupation with history! So the general must after all be an academic researcher? Heaven help us, no! He should have studied history, he should have strengthened his mind in wrestling with the past; but whether or not he retains particular historical facts is entirely insignificant." In this variation on the theme of military genius he discounts the value of formal education in somewhat stronger terms than he was to use in later years; but the basic point will remain unchanged: only men of independent and powerful character can liberate themselves from dogma, can suit their actions to their special circumstances, and can willingly resort to battle, which, potentially or in reality, is at the basis of all wars. This last thought was illustrated with an early version of the simile that so impressed Friedrich Engels when he read *On War:* "Battle is for strategy what cold cash is for commercial transactions." [28] The ultimate purpose of war is political. One fights either "to

---

26. *Ibid.,* pp. 45–47.
27. *Ibid.,* p. 41. The following two quotations are from the same page.
28. *Ibid.,* pp. 62–63. Compare the passage in *On War,* book I, ch. 2 (p. 124): "The decision by arms is for all major and minor operations in war what cash payment is in commerce. Regardless how complex the relationship between the two parties, regardless how rarely settlements actually occur, they can

destroy one's opponent, to terminate his political existence, or to impose conditions on him during the peace negotiations"—a distinction that Clausewitz subsequently developed into the concept of the dual nature of war. "In either case the intention must be to immobilize the opposing forces ... . Thus destruction of the enemy's fighting power is the more immediate purpose of war ... which can be achieved *by occupying his territory, by depriving him of military supplies, or by destroying his army.*" [29]

New meanings for the terms "strategy" and "tactics" are proposed in another paragraph: "Tactics constitute the theory of the use of armed forces in battle; strategy forms the theory of using battles for the purposes of the war." [30] This definition, which Clausewitz was to repeat in identical words in this review of Bülow's book, and later in *On War,* was formulated in opposition to the distinction between the two terms that Bülow had recently developed. Heinrich von Bülow, retired Prussian lieutenant, world-traveler, and author of more than a dozen works on military and political subjects, was seeking to create order in the ways men thought about modern war by introducing universally valid propositions into military theory, and by developing a generally accepted vocabulary, in which his definitions of "strategy" and "tactics" proved particularly influential. [31] "Strategical" he defined as all "military movements out of the enemy's cannon range or range of vision. Tactical are all movements within this range." [32] Bülow felt the need for change in the Prussian army more strongly than most; but his unsystematic reasoning, and his emotional, insulted rejection of the military hierarchy in which he himself had failed to make his way, limited the value of his writings. He took pleasure in elevating Carnot and Napoleon for his German readers as the supreme modern heroes, who conquered because they expressed the ultimate individual freedom in war. He grasped the value of such tactical developments as skirmishing in large numbers, rapidity of movement, and aimed fire; at the same time he discounted the

---

never be entirely absent." The comparison of war and trade is repeated in book II, ch. 3 (p. 201). Engels' comment occurs in a letter of 7 January 1858 to Marx; K. Marx and F. Engels, *Briefwechsel,* Moscow and Leningrad, 1936, ii, 336. Clausewitz may have borrowed the idea from Scharnhorst, who occasionally employed commercial references to bring out the reality of political intercourse—for example, in his memoir to Hardenberg of 2 December 1804: "A state resembles a commercial firm; if its credit is lost it is near collapse." Lehmann, *Scharnhorst,* i, 341.

29. *Strategie,* p. 51.
30. *Ibid.,* p. 62.
31. On Bülow see the biography by his friend J. v. Voss, *Heinrich von Bülow,* Kölln [i. e., Berlin], 1806; the two introductory essays in *Militärische und vermischte Schriften von Heinrich von Bülow,* Leipzig, 1853, by the two editors, E. Bülow and W. Rüstow; Jähns, iii, 2133–2145; R. R. Palmer's chapter "Frederick the Great, Guibert, Bülow: From Dynastic to National War," in *Makers of Modern Strategy,* ed. E. M. Earle, Princeton, 1961; and my discussion in *Yorck,* pp. 80–82. E. A. Nohn has analyzed the relationship of Bülow's and Clausewitz's ideas in *Der unzeitgemässe Clausewitz;* Beiheft 5 of the *Wehrwissenschaftliche Rundschau,* 1956. Nohn's wide-ranging essay contains interesting observations, but does not take sufficient account of the confusions and contradictions in Bülow's writings.
32. [H. D. v. Bülow], *Lehrsätze des neuern Krieges,* Berlin, 1805, p. 1.

effectiveness of battle in the new age, and instead postulated a strategic system of points of domination and angles of approach, whose geometric patterns combined in a fantastic manner with his paeans on the natural, unfettered fighting man. Clausewitz acknowledged Bülow's merit in clarifying concepts, which "until now ... had been employed with great vagueness," and agreed with many of his criticisms of 18th-century strategy, but he found Bülow's logic self-deceiving.[33] The virulence with which he developed this point is due in part to his recognition that Bülow, despite his façade of radicalism, was in reality of the same mold as the military savants he claimed to demolish.

Clausewitz's first task in his essay was to demonstrate the weaknesses of Bülow's method. "No separation of concepts," he wrote, referring to the definitions of strategy and tactics, "however logically correct, can be useful so long as its purpose is not stated."[34] What does range of vision have to do with the matter? he continued. Bülow had made the valid point that distance from the enemy affected behavior: once within range, units would concentrate, formations would be aligned, and men would place themselves in readiness to fight. But, Clausewitz responded, freqently in battle units are not concentrated nor are men aligned, while one is always more or less prepared to defend oneself. "The internal arragements of a formation, that is, the distribution of weapons, etc., are and remain tactical dispositions, whether they are carried out one year before the battle and a thousand miles from the enemy, or in point-blank range."[35] Not only were Bülow's definitions inapplicable to the actual occurrences in war, but since they were in part based on contemporoary technology—the range of cannon—they lacked validity for the past and the future. The definition "brushed close to truth, but is nevertheless entirely mechanical, and in the highest degree unscientific."[36] After this preliminary, Clausewitz proceeded to his main purpose, the destruction of the central feature of Bülow's theories.

Bülow claimed that the success of a military operation depended largely on the angle formed by two lines running from the extremes of the base of operations to its objective. If the base of operations was suitably placed, and sufficiently extended for the lines to converge on the target at an angle of 90° or more, victory was as certain as could reasonably be expected. In reply, Clausewitz wrote that Bülow's historical illustrations proved only that campaigns could be won from an inadequate base of operations, and lost with a base that answered all of Bülow's requirements; that the system made impossible demands on a state's network of depots and

33. [C. v. Clausewitz], "Bemerkungen über die reine und angewandte Strategie des Herrn von Bülow," *Neue Bellona*, IX, No. 3 (1805), 252–287. The approving passage is from p. 255. A similar comment occurs on the preceding page.
34. *Ibid.*, p. 256.
35. *Ibid.*, pp. 258–259.
36. *Ibid.*, p. 258.

fortresses, which could not always be advantageously situated; and most important, that for the sake of establishing a perfect system of supply lines, and by seeing everything from the point of view of geography, Bülow ignored the actions of the enemy, the results of success or failure in battle, the physical and moral effects of fighting. Strategy, however, "is nothing without battle, for battle is the raw material with which it works, the means it employs." [37] In his urge to understand war, to rationalize the use of violence, turn it into a science and make it predictable, Bülow overlooked much that actually took place in war. But, Clausewitz concluded, strategy must concern "not only the forces that are susceptible to mathematical analysis; no, the realm of the military art extends wherever in psychology [*der moralischen Natur*] human intelligence discovers a resource that can serve the soldier." [38]

It was not unusual to attack Bülow in print. Though much of his impact was on the general public, he did not lack for champions among the military; but ever since his first book he had been the target of severe and often violent criticism. He himself thrived on notoriety, and would rather have been denounced than ignored. In the same year that Clausewitz's essay appeared, Bülow published yet another book on war, the last 125 pages of which contained condemnations of his ideas under the title "Anti-Bülow," which he introduced with a few good humored, tolerant sentences. [39] In this voluminous literature Clausewitz's article could not cause much comment; in tendency, if not specific content, it was the kind of discussion to be expected from any intelligent officer who wished to take part in the public debate on the major issues of his profession. Nor was the intemperate tone to which he occasionally succumbed exceptional in the polemics of the day, though it did suggest an unusual degree of personal engagement on the part of the reviewer. Bülow's theatrical combativeness obviously offended Clausewitz; his motives for writing the review, he stated rather ponderously, were "to deprive error of the influence over public opinion which it had usurped, to cleanse vanity of its greasepaint, and to oppose with calm reflection the arrogance of an overheated babbler." [40] His feelings did not, however, prevent him from studying Bülow and learning from him. The most interesting though not the most important impulse may have been transmitted by Bülow's awkward attempt to define the relationship between war and politics, which Clausewitz subsequently reduced to a clas-

37. *Ibid.*, p. 271. See also pp. 272–274. Some of this probably repeated arguments Clausewitz had heard at the Institute, where Bülow's dogmatism made him a frequent target. See, for example, the reference to one of Clausewitz's instructors in J. v. Voss's biography of Bülow, p. 40: "Major von Müller sharply opposed Bülow's main principle of operational bases and angles in his lectures." A refutation by Scharnhorst is cited in Lehmann, *Scharnhorst*, i, 318.

38. [Clausewitz], "Bemerkungen," *Neue Bellona*, IX, 276.

39. [H. D. v. Bülow], *Neue Taktik der Neuern*, 2 vols., Leipzig, 1805.

40. [Clausewitz], "Bemerkungen," *Neue Bellona*, IX, 254–255.

sic formulation. Political strategy, Bülow wrote, "relates to military strategy as military strategy to tactics, and political strategy is the highest of all. Military strategy determines the operations of a campaign, or at most of a war, but political strategy concerns itself with the glory of empires for centuries and millennia." [41]

That an author whose work was filled with absurdities also uttered statements that were intelligent and suggestive could not help but be disagreeable to Clausewitz both in a general and in a personal sense. Bülow made a poor ally in the campaign for innovation; he preempted ideas that he was incompetent to develop, and undermined one's self-esteem. Finally, in this case, as repeatedly throughout his life, Clausewitz was less tolerant of half-truths, which he fought with a bitter sense of betrayal, than of outright error or honest traditionalism. In Bülow he attacked the adherent of maneuver strategy who masqueraded as a revolutionary: the theorist who applied logic to the problem of war, but did so inadequately; the writer who praised genius, but intrepreted this quality as a boundless, violent force, shattering every law, sufficient unto itself. Clausewitz's view of genius was a very different one. "We *never* rise above the rules," he wrote in his essay. "Where we seem to *transgress* a particular rule we are either in the *wrong,* or the case in point *no longer falls under this rule.* The rules of strategy are based on the means at one's disposal; these comprise not only *cannon, soldiers, fortresses,* but also the *psychological* advantages that we may possess, and one of these is the genius of the commander. Whoever possesses genius should make use of it; *that is entirely according to the rules!*" [42] In agreement with his other early writings, Clausewitz's comments on Bülow argue that the irrational in war should neither be denied, nor hedged in by restrictive doctrine; nor, on the other hand, should theory abdicate before it.

The essay on Bülow, the history of Gustavus Adolphus, and Clausewitz's other early manuscripts are scarcely inferior to the best military literature of his day. If they lacked the sophistication of his later writings and occasionally exhibited a note of callousness and self-righteousness, which he was soon to excise, they nevertheless constituted a remarkable achievement for a novice. He passed through the briefest of apprenticeships as writer and theorist. His intellectual powers continued to expand throughout his life, but by the time he was twenty-five he had progressed far toward maturity. A contributing factor in this early development was the great volume of his work. From the beginning he experienced little difficulty in expressing himself on paper. Although he revised his manuscripts

---

41. "Der Feldzug von 1805," reprinted in part in *Militärische und vermischte Schriften von ... Bülow,* p. 99. Bülow introduced this discussion with the statement that "political strategy—not diplomatic strategy, for diplomats are rarely politicians—is as yet an unknown science, which I shall establish by communicating principles of political strategy to the world." *Ibid.,* p. 98.
42. [Clausewitz], "Bemerkungen," *Neue Bellona,* IX, 276. This idea recurs in identical form throughout Clausewitz's writings.

carefully, even the first drafts are taut, and show in style and content the determination to link abstract and concrete as closely as possible that distinguished him among German soldiers and statesmen of the period. Even as a student at the Institute he viewed the political condition of Europe and the immediate as well as the timeless issues of war somewhat differently than did the great majority of his contemporaries. The difference is attributable in large part to the concept of the state that he formed in these years—a cluster of political opinions, insights, and expectations, which brought a special dynamic to his sense of history, his speculative bent, and his realism, and which helped shape his ideal of individual growth. Even his first writings rarely treat war simply as a craft or technique; their tendency is to explore war as the application of state power, as the violent expression of the state's energies. At some time in the 1790's, during the campaigns against the French, or more probably in Neuruppin while reflecting on his experiences, Clausewitz grew aware of the political purpose or effect of each particular military act; and soon he could not think of one in isolation from the other. It was his consciousness of the interactions of politics and war, and a still vague sense of the potential that resided in governments and societies, to be exploited once the barriers of absolutism had been eroded, that led him to interpret international affairs in exclusive, uncompromising terms of power.

The young Clausewitz did not, to be sure, think of the state simply as a machine producing energy for the men at its controls. The state, and the national community which it should represent, stood for him in a relationship of mutual obligation, a connection that was so close in his mind that he frequently used the term "nation" in referring not only to a people but also to its government and administrative structure. That his concept of the state not only affected his interpretation of political intercourse but was also linked to very personal feelings further increased its complexity. The psychological nature of his view of the state is clearly evident in the demands repeatedly made in his early notebooks and manuscripts for the state to maintain dignity, strength, and frankness in its foreign relations. These passages expressed his reaction to the timidity of Prussia's policies; but it is notable that his response showed none of the matter-of-fact manner in which he habitually discussed violence; on the contrary, his arguments were couched in strikingly emotional terms, which otherwise are to be met with only in his attack on Bülow. The impression given is that of an angry man, who judges the state, its leaders, and the community, according to absolute criteria that have little to do with day-to-day political events, and who is offended and anxious because his standards are not met. "The honor of the state must be regarded as sacred," he wrote in 1805.[43] A discussion

---

43. *Politische Schriften und Briefe*, p. 4.

of the monarchical form of government from the same period declares that "a nation which purchases physical advantages at the expense of its honor must be in such a decline that without great upheavals it cannot continue for long among other nations." [44] A later passage in the same discussion runs: "The monarch who succumbs with shame defiles the nation and renders it miserable; the monarch who is gloriously vanquished exalts the nation, and his exalted name is balm on the nation's wounds."

The state, in short, must pursue energetic policies not only because they afford the best chance of success but also to satisfy the expectations of those of the state's subjects who, like Clausewitz, place ideal, ethical demands on its actions. In return—and this, too, is repeatedly expressed and implied in Clausewitz's early writings—the state is owed a measure of loyalty far exceeding the Frederician monarchy's demands for the obedient and competent execution of orders. The formal obligations of absolutism are replaced by joint service to a cultural and national ideal, a combination in which the state dominates, but in which the individual as well is invested with ethical authority that enables him to judge his own and the state's actions according to general principles. That this emancipation might be of value for the individual is obvious; but what would be its usefulness to the state? Conservatives of an old-Prussian cast denied that such changes could be anything but destructive; to a new generation of patriots, who sought to combine service to the particularist state with service to the great, inchoate German nation, the decline in Prussian leadership since the death of Frederick the Great coincided with—and perhaps even reinforced—the growth of political potential in German society, and the new need to defend oneself against France and keep pace with French internal development. The genius of Frederick had created a European power with a race of slaves; inferior leaders in a more dangerous age could preserve the state only by exploiting and giving rein to the genius of their subjects. On a larger stage the force that drove progressive soldiers to conceive a new kind of general staff also pressed for the development of new political arrangements.

To prepare of their new, active role in public life men must educate themselves in new ways. Clausewitz's political ideals and his personal goal of *Bildung* thus led to the same conclusion. His conviction that action was an essential part of education took him far beyond the Frederician concept of the *Staatsbürger,* and of the type of education that the state had lately decided would be beneficial to the subject. Zedlitz, Frederick II's minister of education, had written earlier that "the entire life of man is an education. Theology and politics contain the rules of this great process." [45] But to the young Clausewitz religion was a matter of small moment, and poli-

44. *Geist und Tat,* p. 18. The quotation which follows is from p. 19 of the same collection of Clausewitz's writings.
45. Dilthey, p. 168.

tics no longer simply signified rendering the subject useful to the state. For himself political education had become, as it should become for all men, a reciprocal process that was not solely governed by the principle of utility for the dynasty and its policies.

Out of this array of feelings, ideas, and ambitions emerged the originality that is already evident in Clausewitz's first writings. His cultural and political idealism and his belief in the autonomy of the gifted individual were values common enough among his contemporaries, and indeed drew much of their strength from the wide currency they had achieved in a multitude of forms throughout German society. A few exceptional men—Wilhelm von Humboldt and Friedrich August von der Marwitz, for instance—combined this idealism with an interest in the mechanics of state power and a sense of the dynamics of politics.[46] Clausewitz was the only one of his generation to add war to these forces, and to subject their interaction to systematic and historical inquiry. But the same qualities that freed his intellect carried a potential threat to his peace of mind. The intensity with which he was attached to his ideal of the state might render him captive to the ideal. Success or failure in his life would then depend not only on his personal development and on the external circumstances of his career but also on the moral character of the state. It did not augur well for his future that he had come to regard the political community and his relationship to it as factors of the most profound personal meaning, the more so since from the day when as a twelve-year-old he entered the service of the state, experience had shown him that Prussia in her foreign relations, her military policies, and her internal character was likely to fall short of his desires.

46. But characteristically the young Humboldt thought about war in an unrealistic, even antihumanistic manner, which Clausewitz would have scorned. Note, for example, his statement in a letter to Gentz, written in 1791 or 1792: "War appears to me among the phenomena most beneficial for the education of the human race. ... It is the admittedly dreadful extreme that tests and strengthens every active courage against danger, labor, and misfortune ... ." A. Leitzmann, "Politische Jugendbriefe Wilhelm von Humboldts an Gentz," *Historische Zeitschrift*, CLII (1935), 72.

❧ 6 ❧

THE COLLAPSE OF
THE FREDERICIAN STATE

CLAUSEWITZ'S INTELLECTUAL CONSISTENCY, THE early emergence of ideas that occupied him throughout his life, was paralleled by the development of personal relationships as a young man that were to dominate his maturity. He found a second father in Scharnhorst at the age of twenty-one. Two years later, as a result of his introduction to the Prussian court, he made the acquaintance of Marie von Brühl, his future wife. On his return from France in 1807 he met Gneisenau, who next to Scharnhorst was to be the most important man in his life. Not surprisingly, the affinity of thought and feeling that he recognized in Marie von Brühl and Gneisenau initially made the two significant to him, and his association with them reinforced his ideas and helped nurture them. It was more of an accident that the position he assumed in Berlin society during the years from 1803 to 1806, as adjutant of a prince belonging to a collateral line of the royal house, placed him in a sphere that increasingly developed its own particular outlook on the social and political issues of the day: a special environment that influenced his views, and was to influence the impression that others formed of him.

Clausewitz first met Marie von Brühl in December 1803 in Bellevue, one of Prince Ferdinand's two residences in Berlin, at a dinner which Clausewitz attended as adjutant of Prince August, Ferdinand's son.[1] Several days later they saw each other again when Clausewitz accompanied Prince August on a visit to the queen mother, among whose ladies-in-waiting was

1. Marie v. Brühl described the early stages of her acquaintance with Clausewitz in undated notes, which were evidently written between March 1811 and the beginning of 1812; *Correspondence*, pp. 39–52. Allusions to this period are also contained in their letters. Interesting references to her social life before the war can be found in the excerpts from Sophie v. Bray's diary, "Aus der Berliner Hofgesellschaft der Jahre 1805 und 1806," *Deutsche Rundschau*, XXIX (1903), No. 5.

Countess Brühl. The festivities surrounding the marriage of the king's brother, Prince Wilhelm, on 12 January, brought them together repeatedly at banquets, the opera, and at balls; Clausewitz told her of his early career, talked about Goethe's *Werther,* and indicated, as they were dancing a quadrille, that she had made an impression on him. Their acquaintance was assuming importance for both when the younger Countess Brühl, recently married to Friedrich August von der Marwitz, died in childbed, and her sister withdrew from society for some months. For the rest of the year she and Clausewitz saw each other only in passing; after the death of the queen mother in February 1805, which terminated Marie von Brühl's position as lady-in-waiting, the occasions for meetings became even less frequent, though she and her mother continued to be invited to court functions.

The reception of Tsar Alexander in October brought them together again; each sensed the significance of the encounter, but reserve and lack of privacy kept them from declaring themselves, until the mobilization of the army in December and Clausewitz's imminent departure acted as a catalyst. The daily roll-call of Prince August's battalion was taken in a street off the royal palace. With the hope of meeting Clausewitz, Marie von Brühl writes, she accompanied her small niece and her nurse to one of the row of luxury shops that faced the palace square: "I had scarcely been there for a few moments when I experienced the indescribably joyous surprise of seeing him enter. . . . Other customers came and went, and made it possible for us to stand unnoticed in a corner of the shop." [2] In a few words, which would have sounded insignificant to strangers, they communicated their feelings: "We understood each other, and the union of our souls was silently formed." After parting, Clausewitz mounted his horse and crossed the square, so preoccupied that he rode into the palace yard under a low side-portal designed for pedestrians rather than through the main gate.

This almost wordless declaration of love was the beginning of a lasting relationship, which the principals as well as their friends always felt to be an exceptionally happy one. Yet the marriage did not take place for another five years. The war and Clausewitz's internment in France contributed to the delay; a second and possibly more serious impediment was their difference in background and condition, which repeatedly put their joint future in question. On her father's side Marie von Brühl descended from a Thuringian family that had been settled on the same lands since the 15th century.[3] Her grandfather had been prime minister of Saxony, and established the anti-Prussian policy that Saxony followed during the 1740's

2. *Correspondence,* p. 47. The quotation which follows is from the same page.
3. Information on the two generations of the Brühl family that are of interest to this study is contained in *Karl Graf von Brühl und seine Eltern,* ed. H. v. Krosigk, Berlin, 1910; P. Seidel, "Karl Adolph Graf von Brühl," *Hohenzollern-Jahrbuch,* I (1897), 199–202; and R. Lehmann, *Geschichte der Niederlausitz,* Berlin, 1963. References to the Brühls' connection with the Rosicrucian order can be found in Seidel's article and in several studies concerning the order—for instance, J. Schultze, "Bischoffwerder," *Mittel-*

and '50's. Frederick II pursued Count Brühl and his family vindictively;
the sack of the Brühl estates at the beginning of the Seven Years' War
caused unfavorable comment even among the king's adherents. The count
died a few months after the end of the war; his four sons devoted the next
two decades to salvaging the family's fortunes, in which they were aided by
their many connections among the high aristocracy of central and eastern
Europe. The oldest son served as quartermaster-general of the Polish crown
and governor of Warsaw; his three brothers entered Prussian service after
Frederick's death, their paths to Berlin being smoothed for them by the
new king's Saxon confidant, Bischoffwerder.

   At the end of 1786, Marie von Brühl's father, Charles (he had been
christened with the French form of a first name frequently used in the family) was appointed governor to the crown prince, with the rank of lieutenant-general. The following year a second brother assumed the Prussian
embassy in Munich, and later served as brigadier of light troops in East
Prussia. The youngest brother, Hans Moritz, who possessed some knowledge of engineering, and shared with the king an interest in magnetism
and spiritualism, was put in charge of the state highways in the Mark and
Pomerania. He and his wife enjoyed a wide acquaintance among German
writers and artists; even Goethe had recently addressed three occasional
poems to the couple. Their son, Karl, became in turn chamberlain to
Prince Henry, the queen mother, and Queen Louise, and subsequently rose
to be intendant-general of the royal theaters in Berlin, in which capacity he
continued and strengthened the family's connection with Goethe. Only a
few years after the death of Frederick, the Brühls were firmly implanted in
the service of the Prussian crown. It was an astounding reversal, perhaps
the most striking example of the new ruler's tendency to show favor to men
whom his predecessor had slighted or who had opposed him. That at least
two of the brothers—Charles and Hans Moritz—had leanings toward mysticism, and like the king were members of the Rosicrucians, presumably
helped recommend them to Frederick William II; nevertheless the Brühls
were talented men, with verve, self-assurance, and a breadth of outlook rare
amont the Prussian nobility.[4]

   The most prominent position was undoubtedly held by Charles. Some
Prussians, such as Clausewitz's friend in later years, the young Hermann von
Boyen, regarded his appointment as an affront, because of his Catholic faith

---

deutsche Lebensbilder, III (1928), 134–155, and A. Marx, *Die Gold- und Rosenkreuzer,* Zeulenroda and
Leipzig, 1929, pp. 47–48.
4. The style of the Brühls is exemplified by an anecdote of one of the brothers who dined with the royal
family in Charlottenburg. On leaving the palace he changed his silk stockings for woollen ones, which
he had carried in a pocket of his court-dress, took out his pipe and a treatise on mysticism, and began
walking the two miles back to Berlin. Cries of "bon soir, comte Brühl!" made him look up from his
book. He saw that he was crossing the path of the king and his family, returned their greetings, and
continued on his way. *Karl Graf von Brühl und seine Eltern,* pp. 161–162.

and his father's opposition to Frederick the Great, an attitude that derived further support from the posthumous appearance of Frederick's *Histoire de mon temps,* in which the minister was vilified.[5] But the newcomer soon showed himself to be honorable and discreet, with moral standards that differed advantageously from the laxness into which the court was now falling. It also became evident that the crown prince, who was sixteen at the time, was already too set in his dour, self-centered ways to be significantly influenced by anyone. He seems to have felt little affection for Brühl, but came to respect him; when he succeeded to the throne in 1797, his former governor was among the first to be decorated with the Order of the Red Eagle. In the following year he was promoted to the rank of full general, which made him one of the senior officers of the army.[6]

Brühl was not very fortunate in his economic affairs and remained largely dependent on his army pay and on occasional favors from the king, but until his death in 1802 he and his family assumed an important place in Berlin society—a position which, despite her reduced circumstances, his widow attempted to retain. Brühl had met his wife in St. Petersburg, where her father, William Gomm, a contractor for the Russian government, served as British consul and secretary to the embassy.[7] Since her father had recently suffered reverses in business, Miss Gomm could bring only an insignificant dowry to her marriage; but she was attractive, carefully educated, and vivacious—a nervous ailment, which in her old age developed into a severe hysteria, was not then apparent.

Three of the Brühls' seven children survived infancy: a son, who entered the Prussian army and ended his career as lieutenant-general, and two daughters, Marie, born in 1779, and Fanny, born four years later. In his memoirs, Friedrich August von der Marwitz, who married the younger daughter in 1803 and never recovered from the blow of her death one year later, analyzed his mother-in-law's social concerns with the calmness of a man who knew his own condition to be beyond all need of justification or explanation: "Because of the position and seniority of her husband, she had

5. In the first German edition Brühl is described as a minister who "knew nothing but the cunning and plots that make up the politics of minor princes. He was the man who possessed the most clothes, watches, lace, boots, shoes, and slippers in this century. Caesar would have counted him among those carefully combed and perfumed heads that he never feared. It required a prince of the quality of August II to enable a man such as Brühl to play the role of prime minister." *Hinterlassene Werke Friedrichs II., 5* vols., Frankfurt and Leipzig, 1788, i, 61. Elsewhere Frederick accused Brühl of being unfaithful, a coward, and a traitor. Some of his most cutting insults remained unknown until Preuss published them in the second volume of his authorized edition, *Œuvres de Frédéric le Grand,* 26 vols., Berlin, 1846–56, for instance, ii, 26.

6. Priesdorff, ii, No. 751; *Stammliste aller Regimenter und Corps der Königlich Preussischen Armee,* Berlin, 1798, p. 261.

7. On Sophia Gomm and her marriage to Charles von Brühl see F. C. Carr-Gomm, *Letters and Journals of Field Marshal Sir William Maynard Gomm, G.C.B.,* London, 1881; *Karl Graf von Brühl und seine Eltern;* notes by Marie v. Brühl in Schwartz, *Leben des Generals Clausewitz,* i, 175–181; and F.A.L. v.d. Marwitz, *Lebensbeschreibung,* ed. F. Meusel, Berlin, 1908, pp. 179–189.

almost the highest rank in Berlin. She was considered a model of strict, noble, and distinguished breeding and manners, and soon set the fashion in this regard in Berlin. If she criticized someone, the damage remained; anyone she accepted, or—even better—praised, was regarded as someone special; and indeed her judgment could be trusted so long as her egotism did not interfere. Nothing repelled her more than the appearance of even the slightest trace of meanness, low manners, or bad habits. Consequently she was greatly feared. She was proud of her position, proud of her husband's family, and even proud of the nobility as such. At times it was whispered behind her back that this was highly absurd, since she herself was not noble, indeed—as the daughter of a merchant—could never have appeared at court if she hadn't suddenly emerged from Saxony and been installed in the palace, but no one dared to say it openly." [8]

Countess Brühl readily welcomed Marwitz as her son-in-law; besides his exceptional personal qualities, he was comfortably situated and the head of one of the oldest and most distinguished families in Brandenburg. Clausewitz, on the other hand, had little to recommend him in her eyes. At the outbreak of war in 1806 she agreed that he and her daughter might correspond; but for years afterwards she opposed their marriage. Clausewitz met her antagonism patiently, but was in no doubt about her motives: "My name, my social position, my economic condition are the true considerations, whether she admits it or not," he wrote on one occasion when the countess with the help of her friend Stein, then the king's senior minister, was trying to arrange a match between her daughter and a Count Dohna. [9] "Even though your mother goes a little too far," he continued, "when she interprets your love for me as something out of a novel, as though I were a vagrant fortune hunter, I can understand quite well that it pains her to renounce such a desirable connection for you, and I won't criticize her in the least for it. Logically, I must excuse her displeasure far more readily in such a situation than when she opposes our union on pure principle, without having a better arrangement in mind for you."

Clausewitz could take this tone because of his confidence in his fiancée's character, and in their feelings for each other. By the time of their third meeting, he wrote years later, he knew that she would be the ideal wife for him, and his instinct was sound. She was not the great beauty her sister had been; contemporaries describe her as slender, graceful, an energetic dancer and good horsewoman. She had received the education usual for young girls of good families, was musical, sketched and worked in wa-

8. Marwitz, pp. 175–176. The description of Sophia Gomm as the daughter of a merchant is somewhat misleading. Her paternal grandfather had been lord of the manor of Nethercote House, Lewknow, Oxon.; her maternal grandfather was a Baltic baron.
9. Letter to Marie v. Brühl, 5 August 1808, *Correspondence,* p. 160. The quotation which follows is from the next page.

tercolors, and had been taught by her mother to speak fluent English as well as French and German. What distinguished her from most of her peers was the depth of her interest in art, music, and especially in modern literature, in which her marked intelligence found a congenial vocabulary. Her reactions to life, public as well as private, received their specific form from the ideas and language of German Classicism; quotations and literary allusions fill her letters, which themselves are superior examples of the informal prose style of the period, at once logical and unmannered. She did not hesitate to use adjectives and superlatives that might have given a male writer pause, but they only point up the precision of her narrative and analysis. Her correspondence, like her entire adult life, reveals a woman who as fully as any man in her environment recognized the cultural ideals of the age, and who was serious in her efforts to achieve them. In these central concerns of their lives she did not passively obey Clausewitz's guidance, but met him as an independent personality, on equal terms; indeed, it seems to have been she who taught him to love the works of Goethe's maturity, and helped him to complete the process of education, followed by so many of his contemporaries, which led from the ethical dramas of Schiller to Goethe's universality.

The psychological and intellectual affinities that made their relationship possible were accompanied but not disturbed by great differences in temperament. Marie von Brühl had the gift, as she wrote, to take people as they are, while Clausewitz increasingly encountered others with skepticism, which only too often turned to disdain and suppressed rage.[10] Her ease with others derived a particular quality from her long residence at court, where she had lived since her seventh birthday. Questions of protocol and precedence were taken seriously by her—Clausewitz even good-humoredly alludes to her passionate interest in external distinctions and rewards—and like many courtiers she was able to combine recognition of the human frailties of the men and women who reigned with a profound sense that they, indeed, were the founts of honor.[11]

But in her relations with Clausewitz, and in her feelings about public issues, these considerations lost all significance. In later years she seems never to have sought to dissuade him from actions that would place him in opposition to the king; at the turn of the century the political opinions she was then beginning to develop took a direction that went counter to the Prussian government's policy of neutrality. In her recollections, Caroline von Rochow, the youngest sister of Friedrich August von der Marwitz, described Marie von Brühl's politics during the period of her first acquaintance with Clausewitz: "We saw much of Countess Brühl, my brother's mother-in-law, English by birth, holding strict principles, and a narrow

10. Letter to Clausewitz, 22 October 1808, *ibid.*, p. 176.
11. The phrase "Dein ordenssüchtiges Herz" occurs in a letter to his wife, 8 May 1813, *ibid.*, p. 334.

point of view. Because of the deaths of her husband and daughter she led a withdrawn existence, but was stimulated by all the hatred of Napoleon that characterized English people at that time. She and her daughter, Marie Brühl, later Frau von Clausewitz, known for her excellent artistic and aesthetic education, lived entirely in the fervour of politics and the passionate hatred of the French." [12] The elder Countess Brühl's English origins and her influence were propelling her daughter into attitudes that were increasingly critical of the king's policy.

Marie von Brühl's intellectual interests expanded this process beyond the specific wish for the defeat of French imperialism into vague, universal hopes for Germany. It helps define her position in the partly overlapping, often antagonistic circles clustered around the throne that an older friend, Caroline von Berg, who had influenced her own education, was attempting to exert the same impact on Queen Louise, and to break down the cultural isolation in which the royal couple found itself. Niece of a minister of state under Frederick II, and wife of a courtier, Countess Berg was also the friend and patron of Herder and Fichte, personally acquainted with Goethe, Jean Paul, and other writers, whose work she furthered through financial assistance and her social connections, and was as well a confidante of Stein, who counted her among the three human beings with whom he found himself "in a complete accord of feelings and concepts." [13] She was an intelligent, intense, sentimental woman, saturated, Gerhard Ritter writes, "with the cultural atmosphere of Weimar ... who considered it to be her life's task to bring Queen Louise, and through her the Prussian court, in touch with the great literary movement of the age." [14]

The queen became strongly attached to her dedication and her motherly qualities, and from the turn of the century on, Countess Berg with a few like-minded members of the court, Colonel Massenbach and Marie von Kleist, cousin of the dramatist, guided the queen's reading, and acquainted her with the artistic and intellectual currents of the time. Louise, still in her twenties, burdened with court routine and constant pregnancies, was not always able to master the material that was ceaselessly brought to her tea table; but she had an instinct for the freedom and beauty of modern German literature, and persevered even in the face of her husband's disapproval. The king, on the other hand, could never have enough of ballet and French comedies, and despised the serious writers of his time as "eccentric, fashionable litterateurs"; he feared that education would estrange his wife from him, and he hated Countess Berg for her, as he put it, "unauthorized meddling." [15]

12. C. v. Rochow and M. de la Motte-Fouqué, *Vom Leben am preussischen Hofe,* ed. L. v.d. Marwitz, Berlin, 1908, p. 27.
13. G. Ritter, *Stein: Eine politische Biographie,* Stuttgart, 1958, p. 31. P. Bailleu discusses Countess Berg's life in his work *Königin Luise,* Berlin and Leipzig, 1908, especially pp. 117–120.
14. Ritter, *Stein,* p. 52.
15. Bailleu, p. 120.

Inevitably, the new reading exposed the queen to social and political ideas that sat ill with the dynastic concepts of the king. The free, sovereign individual of Herder's essays and historical speculations, of Schiller's and Goethe's dramas, could co-exist with the monarchical system—but hardly with its absolutist, exclusively dynastic form; just as a reawakening pride in the qualities of the German life and spirit were insulted by the rigid *raison d'état* that traded peoples and territories in accord with the narrowest of political calculations. That the poet whose vitality and inexhaustible riches were only now becoming apparent to the general educated public—Goethe—was himself apolitical did nothing to lessen the political implications of his works: like a part of the German earth, his existence was statement enough; it inspired, and it laid demands on the actions of princes and cabinets.

Sentiments of this kind, which the king ridiculed, and continued to scorn a decade later when they were no longer expressed by ladies-in-waiting but by his most distinguished soldiers, found a favorable reception among other members of the royal family, who in varying degree criticized the king's policies, methods, or personality: Prince Wilhelm and his wife, and the children of the king's great-uncle, Prince Ferdinand. Prince Wilhelm, an uncomplicated, modest young man, who was frequently puzzled by the harshness of his older brother, and Wilhelm's bride, Princess Marianne of Hesse-Homburg, were Stein's favorites among the Hohenzollern. Stein admired the princess's intelligence, her genuine interest in literature and scholarship, and her hatred of "everything that is shallow and mean, even though it be surrounded by the gloriole of the throne." [16] Soon after her marriage, the princess formed a lasting friendship with Marie von Brühl. The two women had much in common, not least similarly forceful characters loyally placed at the service of retiring, solitary husbands. Decades later, after Clausewitz died and his widow stood in need of companionship and economic security, Princess Marianne appointed her as her senior lady-in-waiting. She and her husband possessed little influence, and except in a few crises limited their opposition to muted statements among intimates.

Much more overt, occasionally explosive, were the tensions between the king and Prince Ferdinand's family.[17] Prince Ferdinand had shown personal courage in the early campaigns of the Seven Years' War, but illness

---

16. Ritter, *Stein*, p. 53. Princess Marianne is the subject of a naïve dissertation by L. Wuppermann, *Prinzessin Marianne von Preussen ... in den Jahren 1804–1808*, Bonn, 1942, which contains some interesting documents from the Hessian State archives, including references to the extensive correspondence between the princess and Marie v. Brühl.

17. The most important source of information on Prince Ferdinand and his children is the memoirs of his daughter Louise Radziwill, *Quarante-cinq années de ma vie*, ed. Princess Castellance-Radziwill, Paris, 1911. Also useful are the collection of documents by H. Wahl, *Prinz Louis Ferdinand von Preussen*, Weimar, 1917; and E. Poseck, *Louis Ferdinand, Prinz von Preussen*, Berlin, 1943, a slovenly biography, which nevertheless contains interesting archival material on the 1780's and 1790's.

and disagreements with Frederick led to his withdrawal from public affairs, and he persisted in his grumbling from afar during the subsequent reigns. All observers of the Berlin scene from Mirabeau to Boyen agreed that he was a man of limited abilities—a soldier interested in the minutiae of drill and uniforms, attached to wealth to the point of parsimony, but inviolable in his dignity of royal prince, which he did not hesitate to assert against his grandnephew on the throne. From his marriage with a daughter of his own elder sister he had seven children, of whom two sons and a daughter reached maturity. The union of his daughter, Louise, with Prince Anton Radziwill had been opposed by some of the king's advisers on the grounds that the partitions of Poland had compromised the sovereign status of the Radziwill family which thus was no longer a suitable connection for a Hohenzollern. The king approved the marriage, but under conditions that reduced the official position of Prince Radziwill and of his future children in Prussia—restrictions that Prince Ferdinand interpreted as an affront to his family, but which the groom accepted with equanimity. Radziwill was a man of wide intellectual and artistic interests: a gifted mathematician, portraitist, cellist, and composer; his incidental music to *Faust* and the vocal pieces he wrote for the Berlin *Singakademie* were esteemed in their day, and continued to be performed throughout the century. He and his wife were as close to Marie von Brühl as was Princess Marianne; after 1815, when the Clausewitzes lived in Berlin, Prince and Princess Radziwill were among their small circle of intimates, though Clausewitz and the prince did not always agree on Prussian policies in eastern Europe. Being a Pole, Radziwill showed a natural interest in the conditions in Prussia's Polish territories, a concern which in 1798 Count Haugwitz, the foreign minister, chose to interpret as treasonable political activity. Frederick William III had ordered a search of Radziwill's papers, which revealed nothing damaging; the king was obliged to apologize, but the episode did not improve relations between the two families.

At the same time Frederick William experienced difficulties with Ferdinand's older son, Louis Ferdinand. As a twenty-year-old general in the revolutionary wars the prince had demonstrated energy and an aptitude for charismatic acts, such as his rescue under fire, of a wounded Austrian musketeer before Mainz. Despite his eagerness to serve the state, Louis Ferdinand was, however, kept from the serious affairs of the army and government. After the war he wasted years in provincial garrisons, keeping mistresses, constantly in financial difficulties, quarreling with Frederick William II and his successor over money and marriage plans to the point of being placed under house arrest. The rumors of his dissolute life were nevertheless exaggerated; he tried to broaden his knowledge of political and economic theories and of military affairs, requested men such as Stein and Scharnhorst to guide his education, and was a gifted and hard-working composer and pianist. Beethoven praised his piano-playing as "not at all royal or princely," and of his compositions Schumann could later write that the prince "was the Romantic of the Classical age," and link him with Schubert as exerting particular influence on the new directions in music.[18]

From the turn of the century, Louis Ferdinand regularly spent longer periods in Berlin, still without suitable occupation but quickly becoming a leading figure in those circles that were interested in the arts and in public affairs. He was a member of the *Militärische Gesellschaft,* frequented Countess Berg's house, where he regularly met Stein and other ministers, and such writers and scholars as Gentz, Johannes von Müller, and Alexander von Humboldt. Some of these men he and Anton Radziwill saw again in the circle gathered around Varnhagen von Ense's future wife, Rahel Levin, to whom he was soon linked by their mutual recognition of each other as outsiders and independent spirits. Rahel, the daughter of a Jewish merchant, could not appear at court, but apart from social condition and wealth she was Frau von Berg's superior. The countess was an enthusiastic agent of the new literature, particularly of its rigorously ethical voices—Goethe's heathen qualities rather discomfited her—but she was uncritical and not creative. As she herself said, she could feel and love but not write, an admission borne out by the mannered and lachrymose, immensely popular essay she devoted to Queen Louise after the queen's death. Rahel, on the contrary, responded to the new writers with a strong intellect as well as with her feelings. Her passion for Goethe, and for literature in general, was the counterpart of her need to understand herself and the men and women of her circle. Conversation and correspondence were the tools with which to carry out this process. If her reactions were sometimes clouded by self-consciousness and by a sense of unhappiness that could assume hysterical forms, they were more often than not marked by realism, honesty, and a precision of analysis that owed much to her courageous spontaneity. The perfectibility of the individual, for which the Enlightenment had laid the rational foundations, which Classicism had raised as an ideal, and which Romanticism experienced as the revelation of transcendental powers, was accepted by Rahel as the natural and self-evident task of humanity. In her attic apartment in the Jäger Strasse, among her friends and visitors, she pursued this task, and demonstrated to Berlin society that it was neither utopian nor the exclusive privilege of the inspired, but susceptible of general realization.[19] To Louis Ferdinand she was, if not a spiritual guide, at least a trusted, uncensorious friend.

After Clausewitz was appointed adjutant to Prince August, he often met Louis Ferdinand at their father's residences in Berlin, and at the Rad-

---

18. Wahl, p. 175.
19. The last two sentences paraphrase I. Drewitz's analysis in her admirable study, *Berliner Salons,* Berlin, 1965, p. 52.

ziwell palace. He was fascinated by Louis Ferdinand, and observed him closely. In his account of Prussia before 1806 his analysis of the prince is by far the longest of the many character sketches with which he tries to recreate the Frederician monarchy and interpret its demise: "He was the Prussian Alcibiades. A somewhat disorderly way of life had prevented him from maturing fully. As though he were the first-born son of Mars he possessed huge gifts of courage, daring, determination; but like the head of an old family, who, proud of his wealth, neglects other matters, he too had not done enough to educate and develop his mind seriously. The French called him *un crane*. If by this they meant to say that he was empty- and hot-headed, they misjudged him badly. His courage was not a brutal indifference toward life but true longing for greatness—genuine heroism. He loved life, and enjoyed it only too much, but at the same time *danger* was a *necessity* for him. It had accompanied him since childhood; if he could not find danger in war, he searched for it on the hunt, in raging streams, on wild horses, etc. He was extremely clever, with refined manners, full of wit, widely read, talented in many fields, among them music. On the piano he ranked as a virtuoso.

"...Young, handsome, a general and prince, nephew of Frederick the Great, distinguished by audacity and courage and a high-spirited enjoyment of life, he was soon idolized by the soldiers and the younger officers—but the old, cautious generals in their long waistcoats shook their heads doubtfully over such a young gentleman, and judged that until his exuberant gifts were properly subordinated to the rules and garrison-routine of military service they were of no use.

" ... So he continued his gay life, made heavy debts, wasted his energies on nothing but pleasure, did not always keep the best company; nevertheless he never succumbed to these forces, but kept his head above water, and in spirit remained in nobler regions, always attracted to the great affairs of the state and the fatherland, always longing for glory and honor. ... The result was only that he made himself a nuisance to the government. The king, in any case, did not especially care for him. His wild way of life was repugnant to the king's seriousness; he suspected the prince of an equally boundless ambition, which naturally will always cause a monarch some concern; and his brilliant qualities appeared insufficiently solid to the skeptical mind of the king." [20]

His younger brother, August, shared neither his genius nor his recklessness. He was the most conventional of Ferdinand's children, content with the largely French cultural values that had become traditional for Hohenzollern princes since Frederick's reign, holding strong views on the

---

20. Clausewitz, *Nachrichten*, pp. 437–440. Cf. the similar analysis of the prince by Marwitz, pp. 288–290, which ends with the words: "Mentally and physically endowed like no other, he was destroyed by the conditions of the age."

maintenance of Prussia's position in Germany, intelligent and industrious. He had early come under Scharnhorst's influence, and then and in later years supported modernization of the army, even when this placed him in opposition to the king. But he usually knew how to pursue his goals without seriously affronting Frederick William.[21] While acknowledging his many qualities, Clausewitz could never entirely overcome the feeling that he himself was the superior. In his eyes the prince was too much the unreflective, practical optimist, and perhaps also too obviously cut out for success. August, in turn, respected his adjutant's probity and competence, but seems to have found him too speculative to be truly congenial.

It was his appointment as adjutant to Prince August that made Clausewitz a familiar figure in those groups around the throne in which Marie von Brühl moved by right of birth. Yet their social standing remained very different. Clausewitz's background was obscure; his family did not own land, he himself was poor. He did not lack useful connections—his uncle by marriage, General von Hundt, who was awaiting retirement in the honorable but scarcely distinguished sinecure of town commandant of Thorn on the Vistula, after more than fifty years of active service, could do something to further his interests, as could Scharnhorst. At the early age of twenty-five, in November 1805, he was promoted to brevet captain—Gneisenau was thirty when he reached this rank, and Scharnhorst thirty-seven—an advance that took him a short step up the hierarchy and gave him a few taler more a month, but it scarcely rendered his uncertain place in society more secure. The great republic of the Prussian officer corps, a communality still symbolized by the absence of grade distinctions below the rank of general, numbered many men at the higher levels who would never have aspired to marriage with the daughter of an imperial count and intimate of the royal family. But if there was a marked difference in their positions in Berlin society, Clausewitz and his fiancée represented similar intellectual and political directions. Circumstance and personal inclination had led them to those members of the royal family who did not mechanically follow the king's political decisions. Their hatred of Napoleon and their larger German loyalties found echoes in the attitudes of the princes and princesses whom they served. For Clausewitz, this bond foretold the role he was to play in the years after Prussia's defeat; as has already been suggested, it may also have contributed to the estimate that Frederick William and conservative courtiers and soldiers were to form of him. The king came to know Clausewitz not as a member of his own entourage, nor as an officer who was proving himself in a sequence of conventional appointments, but as a military intel-

21. An example of his diplomatic independence from a much later period, when he had become commander-in-chief of the artillery, is his protection of the Jewish artillery officer Meno Burg, whom he helped rise to the rank of major in the face of Frederick William's pronounced dislike of Jews who refused to be converted.

lectual connected with whatever opposition sentiment might be said to exist in the state.

The events of 1805 and 1806 could only strengthen this unfavorable association in the king's mind. To Clausewitz, on the contrary, these same years always remained a terrifying example of political disaster resulting from weak leadership and inadequate governmental and military institutions. As the likelihood of a new war with Russia and Austria increased, France sought to bring Prussia on her side, but although tempted by the prospect of acquiring Hanover, which Napoleon offered as inducement, the king and Hardenberg refused to abandon their policy of neutrality. In September war broke out. Soon it was learned in Berlin that Russian forces were preparing to enter Prussia and compel her to join the coalition. A conflict with Russia seemed imminent when early in October a French corps under Bernadotte, hurrying to disrupt the build-up of Austrian forces in Bavaria, crossed Prussian territory and caused Berlin to shift policy again. Frederick William opened his borders to the Russian army, and ordered Prussian forces into Hanover, where the few French units, left behind as a token garrison, took care to avoid clashes with them. At this stage of the crisis, with Tsar Alexander expected in Berlin, and the Austrians suffering their first defeats, the king recalled Haugwitz to take joint charge with Hardenberg of the foreign ministry. On 3 November he reluctantly signed a treaty with Alexander and the Austrian ambassador, Metternich, which committed his state to still another line of action—that of armed mediation.

Haugwitz was sent to Napoleon's headquarters to demand French withdrawal from the war and a substantial reduction of her presence in Germany; should the emperor refuse, Prussia would join his opponents. Napoleon did not receive Haugwitz until the battle of Austerlitz had destroyed the coalition; under the changed circumstances, Haugwitz felt compelled to sign an agreement which both weakened Prussia and tied her firmly to France. When Frederick William could not bring himself to ratify the treaty in the period specified, though he demobilized to demonstrate his peaceful intent, Napoleon presented an ultimatum demanding that Prussia accede to the French conquests of the past years and close the ports in the North Sea and the Baltic to English shipping. Now defenseless against the threat of immediate invasion, the king agreed. Hardenberg resigned—a hero to those groups that had advocated war with France—while the windows of Haugwitz's residence were smashed by hostile mobs, and young guards officers insulted him at court.

In reality, the political views of the two men were not dissimilar; both had been overly attracted by the prize of Hanover and neither trusted

Napoleon, but neither had proved able to develop a firm policy and persuade the king to implement it with the necessary energy and consistency. It was Haugwitz who, in July 1806, in the face of continued French pressure, including the refusal to withdraw their forces from Germany, advocated renewed mobilization of the army, which on the receipt of alarming dispatches from Paris was ordered on 9 August, to the astonishment of Europe, three days after Francis II had announced the demise of the German Empire.

Clausewitz later judged the mobilization to have been an act of despair.[22] But characteristically, Frederick William did not apply it to the entire army, only to the units stationed in the west and center of the monarchy. Napoleon was being warned, without being threatened. "Prussia cannot wage a defensive war," Scharnhorst wrote. "Her geographic position and lack of natural and artificial defensive means do not permit it." In the face of these and other arguments that mobilization was suicidal unless it led to an immediate offensive, the king and his political advisers persisted in regarding partial mobilization as a defensive measure until the realities of the situation overcame their intentions, and pushed the course of events toward offensive operations.[23] The concentration of Prussian forces gave rise to French countermeasures, which in turn called for Prussian responses, until open hostilities could have been averted only at the price of a major diplomatic defeat, which Napoleon had no cause to accept. It is true that the isolation in which Prussia found herself was strategic rather than diplomatic—both Russia and England being eager to come to her support—but the strengths and positions of the opposing armies now counted for more than slowly maturing political combinations. No doubt England, Austria, and particularly Russia—with her eagerness to fight in November 1805 rather than concert moves with Prussia—had done much to bring about Prussia's isolation, nor is it clear whether after Austerlitz any policy could have fully succeeded for Prussia. But the magnitude of the failure was due to blindness and floundering in Berlin. The king neither clearly understood what his state could and could not achieve militarily and politically, nor were he and his advisers capable of committing themselves vigorously to any given line of action. By 1806, in any case, it was no longer the choice of policy that was decisive, but, as Clausewitz recognized, the way decisions were arrived at, and the mechanics of their implementation. Neither process was adequate for a state that in the past decade had lost nearly

---

22. *Nachrichten*, p. 463.
23. See, for instance, Louis Ferdinand's letter of 9 January 1806 to his sister, but intended for the queen, Wahl, pp. 286–292. The quotation from Scharnhorst is from a letter of 16 April 1806 to General v. Rüchel, *Scharnhorsts Briefe*, p. 273. Scharnhorst repeated his arguments against a defensive war in a memorandum of 19 April 1806 addressed to Hardenberg, Lehmann, *Scharnhorst*, i, 370–373. Scharnhorst's advice that Prussia must defend herself by taking the offensive is also mentioned in the Duke of Brunswick's memorandum to the king of 22 August 1806, *ibid.*, pp. 400–402.

all of its outlying bastions and buffer zones, and was now directly threatened by a vastly superior power.

The governmental system obtaining in Berlin accorded both with the vacillating character of the king, and with his unwillingness to seem to depart from the personal regime of his great predecessor. Frederick William was not averse to listening to uninformed and incompetent courtiers, among whom at this time, and for some years to come, his first personal adjutant, Köckritz, exerted a particularly unfortunate influence. It was even more damaging that, except for a period between 1801 and 1804, he continued the Frederician tradition of having two ministers share responsibility for the conduct of foreign affairs, an arrangement that enabled him to turn now to Haugwitz, now to Hardenberg, and made it impossible for Prussian diplomacy to pursue a positive, firm line. But the most serious defect of the system was Frederick William's practice of governing from his cabinet rather than with and through his ministers. The royal cabinet consisted of four officials: two general adjutants, responsible for military affairs, and two cabinet councillors, who handled internal and external matters respectively. Together with Köckritz they controlled access to the king in the mass of routine business. Although certain senior generals and officials possessed the right of regularly reporting to the king in person, they ordinarily communicated with him through the general adjutants and the cabinet councillors, who screened and passed on their reports, requests, suggestions, and queries. It was in the spring of 1806, for instance, that one of the general adjutants, Colonel Kleist, failed to transmit a memorandum of Scharnhorst—possibly his radical scheme for a militia or national guard—on the grounds that in different form most of the proposals it contained had already been suggested to the king.[24] In turn, Frederick William's responses and orders frequently were guided by the advice of the members of his cabinet, and were almost always couched in their words.

Though often criticized, the authority of the general adjutants, which in a sense went against hierarchical principles of rank and seniority, rested on Frederician precedent; and to some degree their influence was mitigated by the close relationship between crown and army, which still made it easier for the individual officer than for the government official to break through institutional barriers and appeal directly to the king. The position of the cabinet councillors, on the other hand, was an innovation that had gradually developed from that of the subaltern secretaries whom Frederick II had employed for his correspondence. Officially the bourgeois councillors, Beyme and Lombard, were no more than heads of the royal secretariat; in fact, they had become advisers as well as the men who controlled a central link in the transmission of information and orders. In these func-

24. F. H. v. Kleist's letter of 5 July 1806 to Scharnhorst, Lehmann, *Scharnhorst*, i, 389, n. 1. See also Stadelmann, p. 74, and p. 180, n. 74.

tions they were charged with a vast amount of work, which they performed conscientiously. Beyme, in particular, was a gifted and reliable administrator, as had been his predecessor, Mencken, Bismarck's maternal grandfather. They regarded themselves, Clausewitz writes, "as popular tribunes of a sort, placed beside the throne to keep tight rein on the aristocratic sentiment of the noble ministers, and to enable the government to act in the spirit of the [democratizing, enlightened] age." [25] Since Beyme and Lombard saw Frederick William daily, and possessed his complete confidence, their power was considerable; often enough they formulated policy in place of the departmental ministers, and thus tended to reduce the ministers to administrators and executants of their policies, while bearing no formal responsibility themselves. But this very lack of responsibility, and the relatively modest rank they held, made possible the fiction that the king still ruled alone.

Under such a system a consistent foreign policy could have been maintained only if it were generated by the monarch, or if no serious differences of opinion existed in court circles and among the senior generals and high bureaucracy. Since neither was the case, a nervous and increasingly embittered, self-defeating neutrality was perhaps the best that could be expected; but by 1805 the balance of contending views that underlay Prussia's immobility began to shift under the weight of new internal pressures as well as of events abroad.

Prussia's participation in the war against the French Revolution had encountered some opposition in the army and administration. At times an advantageously placed individual could privately affect policy, as Möllendorff had done in Alsace in 1794. Open criticism, however, remained strangely abstract; only rarely had men conceived of the possibility that their views, refined in continuing debate, could affect the great lines of government policy. But since that time more people had begun to show an interest in foreign affairs, and the events of 1805 seemed to afford new scope to this fresh element in Prussian life. In his account of Prussia at that time, Clausewitz identifies three separate attitudes toward Franco-Prussian relations: one party admired French institutions and French glory, and "deemed it a blessing for Europe to be placed under French tutelage." A second group feared the dislocation and danger of war. A third group interpreted French progress as leading toward universal rule and the destruction of Prussia, and therefore counseled war. [26] Bernadotte's march through Ansbach intensified this feeling, and Clausewitz concludes that by 1806 the

25. *Nachrichten*, p. 424. Compare Ritter's evaluation in Stein, p. 142: Like the *conseillers de Parlement* of pre-revolutionary France, the cabinet councillors were "conscious of defending the general interests of the state against absolutist arbitrariness and the special interests of the nobility. Their opposition to tax exemptions for the nobility and their fight for freeing the peasants had from the outset made them hateful to aristocratic ministers."

26. *Nachrichten*, pp. 466–467.

war party had become strong. Its leaders were Stein, Louis Ferdinand, and a few senior officers, notably Blücher. Scharnhorst and Hardenberg supported these men with ideas and advice, but retained their independence of action.

In Berlin, the residences of Louis Ferdinand, Anton Radziwill, and Countess Berg served as the group's principal meeting places. It is no doubt exaggerated to write of Frau von Berg's circle that "Austerlitz transformed this literary salon into a political club." [27] The number of men who actually attempted to change the king's policy was small; they remained unorganized, and tried to keep their actions confidential; but there is no denying the connection of cultural and political concerns, and the evolution of the former into the latter. The target of the group was Count Haugwitz and the cabinet system, which was recognized as inefficient, and interpreted—not always accurately—as the center of pro-French sentiment. The group's program thus combined by implication, and often explicitly, several goals: reform of the government's machinery, dismissal of the advisers whom the king found most congenial, and change of the king's foreign policy. Underneath these aims lay a disparaging comparison of Frederick William with Frederick the Great and Napoleon, and the conviction that the pretense of absolute rule by an incompetent was ruining the state. Stein and some others went further, and believed that whatever the ability of the king, absolutism in Prussia must make way for a freer society and an extension of political authority.

Scharnhorst's plan of April 1806 for expanding the army and bringing crown and people into closer union through the establishment of a militia was followed some days later by a condemnation of the cabinet system, which Hardenberg submitted to the king on the occasion of his quitting the post of foreign minister. [28] On 27 April, in conjunction with Hardenberg's memorial, Stein drafted his first great reform program, which combined violent and insulting attacks on Haugwitz, Köckritz, Beyme, and Lombard, with a careful critique of the role of the cabinet councillors, whom he wanted replaced by a council of ministers possessing executive authority. Stein sent an expurgated version to the queen, who replied that she agreed in principle; but evidently she found the proposals and language too radical for the king's eyes. Eventually she suggested that the text be revised, and that other personalities in the king's confidence sign it jointly with Stein. Throughout May, Frederick William received alarmist and bellicose notes from Blücher, and, at the end of the month, two reports by

27. K. Schib, *Johannes v. Müller*, Schaffhausen, 1967, p. 239.

28. Scharnhorst's memorandum on the militia is printed in C. v.d. Goltz, *Von Rossbach bis Jena*, Berlin, 1906, pp. 543–549. Other reform proposals to the king during these months can be found in such documentary publications as *Die Reorganisation des Preussischen Staates, unter Stein und Hardenberg*, part I, *Allgemeine Verwaltungs- und Behördenreform*, ed. G. Winter, Leipzig, 1931; and *Freiherr vom Stein: Briefe und amtliche Schriften*, ii, part I, ed. P. Thielen, Stuttgart, 1959.

Stein, which ironically and with crude allusions to the king's advisers unfavorably compared Prussia's power and independence to that of Portugal. In the course of June, July, and August the king was subjected to dozens of verbal and written appeals by the army's commander-in-chief, the Duke of Brunswick, and by Louis Ferdinand and other senior officers, calling on him to dismiss Haugwitz and Lombard, and to turn against France. Participating with a whole sheaf of notes was Colonel von Massenbach, who thus joined the army's other general-quartermaster-lieutenants, Scharnhorst and Phull, in suggesting not only military reforms but far-reaching changes in the monarchy's political institutions.[29] Mobilization did nothing to bring these unauthorized and often badly informed and unrealistic communications to a halt; on the contrary, the king's refusal to respond, other than by angrily asserting his authority, led to more extreme steps. On 2 September, Frederick William was handed a memorial, composed by Stein's close associate, the historian Johannes von Müller, which was based on Stein's April memorandum, though the proposal of a ministerial council and Stein's personal attacks were deleted.[30] It had been intended that Countess Berg would consult the queen for an auspicious moment in which to present the note, but a mix-up resulted in its being delivered by an adjutant of one of the signatories instead, and without advance preparation the king read a document whose import was unique in the history of the Prussian state.

After castigating the policies that had brought the monarchy to her present "dreadful crisis," the memorial claimed that the "entire army, the entire public, and even well-disposed foreign courts regard the royal cabinet as presently constituted with extreme distrust." Whether, as was suspected, the cabinet was bribed, was unimportant; for whatever reason, the cabinet was in collusion with Napoleon, "and either will purchase peace through the most despicable subservience, or in war will take the feeblest of measures, or, if Your Majesty prescribes vigorous steps, and honorable generals wish to carry them out with energy, the cabinet will cripple if not betray them." Only the removal of Court Haugwitz and the two cabinet councillors held out promise for a favorable outcome. The memorial concluded that the signatories did not speak only for themselves but voiced public sentiment. These arguments were not unusual; what was new was the fact that more than one man signed the document—that men had come together to criticize the king's policies, and acted in unison to persuade him to change—and the identity of the signatories. The memorial, which was accompanied by a supporting letter by the Duke of Brunswick, bore

29. For instance, in his two memorials of 2 and 8 July 1806, which proposed a reorganization of the ministries and personnel changes in various offices, *Allgemeine Verwaltungs- und Behördenreform*, pp. 15–17, 20–24.
30. The memorial is printed in *Stein: Briefe und amtliche Schriften*, ii, part I, 259–263.

the names of five royal princes: the king's brothers, Wilhelm and Heinrich; his brother-in-law, the Prince of Orange, the future king of the Netherlands; and Louis Ferdinand, who also signed in the name of his brother, August. Other signatories were Stein; General Rüchel, commander of one of the field armies; and General Phull, the senior general-quartermaster-lieutenant. Clausewitz and other contemporaries wrongly believed that Scharnhorst had also signed.[31]

Frederick William's reaction was unequivocal. In the first flush of anger he called the memorial an act of mutiny. The signatories were informed of his extreme displeasure, similar group actions were prohibited once and for all, and those princes who held military commands were ordered to join their units.[32] Prince Wilhelm wrote Stein that a disagreeable interview with his brother had shown him that nothing could change matters. When Louis Ferdinand presented himself at the palace for a farewell audience, he was received neither by the king nor by the queen, who now blamed him for his role in the revolutionary *démarche*—to use Hardenberg's description—that had so enraged her husband.[33] A brief letter of justification, which he sent her through his sister Louise Radziwill and Countess Berg, closed with the statement that he was prepared to spill his blood for king and fatherland, without hoping that Prussia could still be saved.[34] At the same time he wrote Massenbach that to bring about change, men must unite more firmly than before. On the evening of the 6th he took leave from his parents at their residence, Bellevue, where he also found Prince and Princess Radziwill, Clausewitz, and an intimate of Prince Ferdinand, General Schmettau.[35] Louis Ferdinand spent much of the evening persuading Schmettau to join in a new appeal to the king that was being prepared. Nothing better indicates the decline of Frederick William's authority than the fact that such a step was contemplated in disregard of his explicit prohibition. The new memorial, written by Stein, repeated the content of the earlier note in more forceful terms: the government must regain public confidence, "without which salvation is not possible"; Haugwitz and the cabinet councillors must be dismissed, and a responsible council of ministers instituted. If the king did not agree, the signatories would

31. *Nachrichten*, p. 441. See also Boyen, *Erinnerungen*, i, 146; and Marwitz, p. 286. Actually Scharnhorst was in Hanover during these days. Clausewitz had at least one close source of information, Marie v. Brühl, who according to a letter of Princess Marianne to her husband of 7 or 9 September 1806 "knew everything." His former teacher at the Institute, Kiesewetter, who occasionally dined with Louis Ferdinand and Wilhelm, had also been told of the memorial. Letter of Princess Marianne to Prince Wilhelm of 12 September 1806, Wuppermann, p. 51.

32. The king's responses to the appeal are printed in *Allgemeine Verwaltungs- und Behördenreform*, pp. 42–44.

33. Prince Wilhelm's note is printed in *Stein: Briefe und amtliche Schriften*, ii, part I, 265; Hardenberg's words, *ibid.*, p. 266.

34. Radziwill, p. 203.

35. *Ibid.*, p. 204.

resign from his service.[36] On the advice of Hardenberg and Blücher, however, this outspoken threat was never sent. It was impossible, Blücher wrote, to push matters to the extreme of leaving one's post when war was upon Prussia.[37]

The war party was being overtaken by the dynamic of the partial mobilization that Frederick William had ordered in August. As Napoleon concentrated very strong forces in southern Germany, the rest of the Prussian army was mobilized, and by the middle of September it could hardly be doubted that this time war would not be avoided. Much of the opposition's efforts of the past months had been needless; its fear that Prussia would again back down derived from inadequate knowledge of diplomatic developments, and an exaggerated suspicion of Haugwitz and the cabinet councillors, who themselves had gradually come to favor an alliance with Russia directed against France, without, to be sure, making adequate political preparations for the imminent conflict.[38] The rest of the opposition's program, however, remained an open issue. The failure to remove the king's advisers, and to reform his method of governing, caused most of the senior commanders to begin the campaign without confidence. Some shared with Prince Louis Ferdinand a sense of approaching disaster.

This was not the general attitude among their subordinates. Correspondence and memoirs of the time indicate that among the junior officers in particular, many were filled with confidence, rejoicing that the Prussian eagle was at last unfolding its wings, even disdainful of the French, who would now learn what it meant to face the Prussian line.[39] Clausewitz, with better information at his disposal, and with his aim of seeing events in their political and strategic context, thought otherwise. A letter he had written in May indicates that even before the crisis broke in the summer he had considered war more than probable. It was addressed to the publishers and editors of one of Germany's most prestigious scholarly periodicals, the *Allgemeine Jenaische Literatur-Zeitung,* and incidentally casts further light on the confidence Scharnhorst placed in his student:

"Colonel v. Scharnhorst has kindly forwarded to the undersigned a

---

36. The draft is printed in *Stein: Briefe und amtliche Schriften,* ii, part I, 266–269.
37. *Ibid.,* pp. 269–270.
38. Cf. Clausewitz's admission in his letter of 26 September 1806 to Marie v. Brühl, *Correspondence,* pp. 63–64: "I recognize that I was *somewhat* mistaken in my view of our cabinet; the situation is generally somewhat better than I had believed."
39. Representative are the memoirs of three officers who were subalterns in 1806: C. F. v. Blumen, *Von Jena bis Neisse,* ed. C. M. v. Unruh, Leipzig, 1904, pp. 9–10; K. v. Wedel, *Lebenserinnerungen,* ed. C. Troeger, Berlin, 1911, i, 33; and F. L. v. Wachholtz, *Aus dem Tagebuch des Generals Fr. L. von Wachholtz,* ed. C. F. v. Vechelde, Brunswick, 1843, p. 110. A more differentiated evaluation is given by Marwitz, pp. 300–301. He singles out as "bellicose and therefore useful" those officers serving in regiments stationed in the core provinces, in the Berlin garrison, or under sound generals, while officers in the newly acquired territories, or who were exposed to French propaganda, or those who were "contaminated by associating with the educated middle classes, had become useless and unwarlike."

contract, which the publishers of the Jenaische A. L. Z. were good enough to draw up on his suggestion.

"I am grateful for this sign of their confidence, and feel too much honored by the proposed connection not to agree to it. Therefore I return a signed copy of the contract to the publishers, and add only a comment, which incidentally does not conflict with its terms: in case of war, which would remove the undersigned from his garrison, he would scarcely be able to write for the Journal, not so much for lack of time, but because he would be constantly on the move and would have no books available. This eventuality now seems imminent since the local units have received orders to put themselves in readiness for moving at twenty-four hours' notice; in any case, the present state of Europe seems hardly to promise a calm future.

"In conclusion I permit myself the avowal that truth and knowledge are too sacred to me not to pursue them always with the purest zeal." [40]

When the campaign did begin, he could not repress his anxieties. To Marie von Brühl he wrote in a note on 30 August that no one had the right to lose courage, but that the situation was "infinitely wretched." [41] A week later he left Berlin with Prince August's grenadiers; on their march through the city he was able to see his fiancée once more. "All our political hopes are fading," he wrote on 11 September, while his unit rested near Magdeburg, not far from the place of his birth. [42] But as the main army slowly moved south, toward the Thuringian mountains beyond which French reconnaissance detachments were already operating, his spirits rose. "A weak gleam of warlike expectation again enters my soul," he wrote on the 18th. [43] He was moved by the sight of men marching calmly to battle, by the vision of manifold individuality combined with impersonal cohesiveness and unity of purpose that he was afforded by every passing battalion and regiment. But most significant to him was the new concurrence of the state's intent with his own ideals, as well as with his desire for distinction, the fulfillment of which would not only satisfy old ambitions but would also facilitate his marriage: "My fatherland needs war, and—to put it plainly—war alone can bring me to my goal. In whatever way I have sought to link my existence with the rest of the world, my path always leads to a vast battlefield. Unless I enter this field there can be no permanent happiness for me." He ended his letter abruptly on hearing that his battalion was ordered to break camp and continue its advance. "As little as my intelligence can expect from the prospect," he concluded, "as powerfully does it engage my imagination."

40. Letter of 23 May 1806, in the collection of the late Basil Liddell Hart. The letter has been published by W. Hahlweg in "Clausewitz bei Liddell Hart," *Archiv für Kulturgeschichte*, XLI (1959), No. 1.
41. *Correspondence*, pp. 52–53.
42. *Ibid.*, p. 56.
43. *Ibid.*, p. 57. The quotations which follow are from pp. 58–60.

The degree of insight these letters indicate is considerable; and Clausewitz was already sufficiently realistic to make the best of his very circumscribed personal situation. But that did not diminish the severity of his internal conflict. His ambitions, his need to trust the state, his confidence in his second father, but also his sense of the difficulties that Scharnhorst faced and his recognition of Napoleon's genius—these contradictions could be reconciled only in hope. War, he had written, was that part of the world in which he needed to make his mark, and under the pressure of this exigency the possibility of the state's defeat faded, to be replaced by the prospect of personal distinction.[44] That did not put an end to his eager observation of the reality around him, or to the reflective process by which impressions were condensed into formal analytic conceptions. Just as the years leading up to the war left a deep imprint on his political views—in particular the belief that efficient, clearly articulated political institutions mattered more than monarchical absolutism or any other ideology—so the campaign itself was subsequently reflected in numerous facets of his thinking on war. It is during these weeks that the concept of friction is first alluded to in his letters.[45] But for the moment the personal element remained paramount. When the fighting ended in disaster for Prussia, and knocked away the psychological prop that the state had provided, Clausewitz was at a loss. His recovery, after a period of extreme stress, took two forms: a further intensification of his concept of the state as a heroic autonomous being in the political world, paralleled by an energetic, often reckless effort to bring Prussia closer to that ideal.

44. An echo of this mood returns two decades later in the analysis of the effects of a major victory in *On War,* book IV, ch. 10 (pp. 360–361). Clausewitz outlines the likely events during the opening stage of the retreat, which match precisely the experience of the defeated Prussian army in October 1806, and then turns to the psychological reactions of the individual soldier: "One may have been aware of [the likelihood of defeat] all along, but for the lack of more solid alternatives this awareness was countered by one's trust in chance, good luck, Providence, and in one's own audacity and courage. All this has now turned out to have been insufficient, and one is harshly and inexorably confronted by the terrible truth."

45. See below, p. 124.

PART II

CAPTIVITY AND THE
IDEAL OF GERMAN LIBERTY

IN THE FIRST OF THREE ARTICLES ON THE CAMPAIGN of 1806, published soon after the campaign had been lost, Clausewitz wrote that, critical though the situation of the Prussian army had become by the second week of October, it might still have been restored by rapid, energetic measures.[1] His trust in the overriding power of initiative and of determined action echoes through his many subsequent discussions of the campaign, notwithstanding his strictures on the army's antiquated and inefficient organization, administration, equipment, and tactics. He recognized the differences between the French and the Prussian way of waging war as clearly as did his teacher Scharnhorst; but unlike many later historians he did not regard 1806 as a laboratory test in which the superior system was the more successful, an experiment that conclusively demonstrated the decay of the old regime. Even as he raged sarcastically against a military leadership that was unwilling to learn the lessons of the age, he never forgot that for Prussia war against the far stronger Napoleonic Empire was at best a considerable gamble. And yet French superiority might have been balanced by inspired leadership; the triumph of the French, he maintained, was due less to modernity or numerical weight than to Napoleon's genius, abetted by the "intellectual poverty" and moral cowardice of his opponents.[2] Scharnhorst, the one man on the Prussian side whose ability approached that of the emperor, had still not risen above the rank of colonel,

1. [Clausewitz], "Historische Briefe über die grossen Kriegsereignisse im October 1806," *Minerva*, I (January and February 1807) and II (April 1807). Cited passage: I, 17. His most comprehensive analysis of the campaign is the above-mentioned study *Nachrichten über Preussen in seiner grossen Katastrophe*, written in the 1820's. Comments on the strategic features of the campaign can also be found in *On War*, e.g., book VI, ch. 14 (pp. 603–604) and ch. 28 (pp. 718–720).
2. *On War*, book II, ch. 4 (p. 209). Among numerous similar judgments, the entry in his journal of 25 August 1807 is particularly interesting. Schwartz, *Leben des Generals Clausewitz*, i, 99–110.

chief of staff of an army whose decisions in fact emerged from councils jointly chaired by the king and the Duke of Brunswick, and attended by any number of corps commanders, staff officers, adjutants, and advisers. It is hard to imagine, Clausewitz wrote at the time, under what conditions Scharnhorst labored; but some idea of the difficulties could be gained "if one realizes that *three* commanders-in-chief and *two* chiefs of staff serve with the army, though only *one* commander and *one* chief of staff ought to be there. ... How much must the effectiveness of a gifted man be reduced when he is constantly confronted by obstacles of convenience and tradition, when he is paralyzed by constant friction with the opinions of others." [3] Whether Scharnhorst could ever have imposed his personal authority on this assemblage is doubtful; but he did not even attempt it. In the week before the twin battles of Jena and Auerstedt he seemed to succumb to depression as he saw that his work over the past five years had scarcely dented the old preconceptions, and perhaps he came to believe that his superiors could learn only from unmistakable experience. Consequently he did little more than to make certain that the army's staff machinery continued to function. As the climax approached at Auerstedt, he used the pretext of attending to affairs on the left wing to quit the staff altogether, assumed command of a few regiments, and fought a successful local action while the battle was being lost for want of central leadership. When his battered troops were at last forced to retreat, he gave his horse to a brother of the king, whose own horse had been killed, picked up a musket, and left the field on foot with the last of the infantry—an episode full of personal glory, symbolic, it might be thought, of the army's future regeneration by this newcomer to Prussia, but also a renunciation of responsibility on Scharnhorst's part that makes it easier to understand the moral exhaustion of many lesser men. [4]

By the second week of October, the French had traversed Franconia, crossed to the east bank of the Saale River, and were advancing north toward Leipzig, leaving the widely separated Prussian forces to one side in Thuringia, west of the Saale. Each army was in doubt about the other's exact location and intentions. On the 10th, Prince Louis Ferdinand, who commanded the Prussian advance guard, was attacked by the extreme left column of the French. Misleading orders caused the prince to believe that

3. Clausewitz to Marie v. Brühl, 29 September 1806, *Correspondence,* p. 65. Two decades later, in his *Nachrichten,* p. 492, Clausewitz again used the term "friction" to characterize the conditions at Prussian headquarters in those days. Rothfels, *Carl von Clausewitz,* p. 90, points out that the passage in the letter of 29 September 1806 is Clausewitz's earliest known use of the term to describe the effect of reality on ideas and intentions in war—a theme he was to develop in the following years and discuss comprehensively in *On War,* where friction is called "the only concept that more or less corresponds to the factors that distinguish real war from war on paper." *On War,* book I, ch. 7 (p. 160). See also the discussion below, pp. 201, 230, 362–363, 367–368, 372–375, etc.

4. Stadelmann's remarkable interpretation of Scharnhorst's attitude in *Scharnhorst: Schicksal und Geistige Welt,* pp. 9–35, is borne out by the letters Scharnhorst wrote just before and after the battle.

he must stop the French at all costs; his outnumbered, badly placed corps was destroyed and he himself killed, succumbing, Clausewitz later wrote, "to the iron force of circumstances." [5] Two days later French patrols had reached the outskirts of Leipzig, the lines of communication to Magdeburg and Berlin were threatened, and the Prussians decided to withdraw to the northeast, just as Napoleon wheeled his forces to the west. On the 14th he succeeded in concentrating greatly superior numbers against the Prussian divisions under Hohenlohe, which were still strung out between Weimar and Jena, and defeated them completely. On the same day, fifteen miles to the north near Auerstedt, the main Prussian army was turned back in its attempt to regain its lines of communication. Although outnumbering their opponents by nearly two to one, the Prussians failed to exploit their superiority; confusion grew after the Duke of Brunswick was shot through the eyes, and it was decided to break off the battle. Instead of retreating toward the Magdeburg highway, which was still open, Frederick William directed the army southwest to rejoin Hohenlohe. The king was still unaware of the disaster at Jena, but even under the best of circumstances this move would have been fatal since it took the army toward the French and away from its reserves and depots in the north. When word of Napoleon's victory arrived during the evening, new and contradictory orders were issued, and by morning the exhausted and disorganized troops had for the moment lost any capacity to fight.

Early in the battle of Auerstedt, tactical control of the leading divisions was already slipping out of the hands of their generals. As Scharnhorst helped restore the situation on the left flank, so Prince August on the right assumed command of three grenadier battalions in addition to his own. The broken terrain and French snipers disrupted and immobilized their serried ranks—a characteristic encounter between old and new tactics that was being repeated across the whole of the battlefield. Since Prince August's battalion was among the few in the army that had been trained to copy some of the French methods, Clausewitz was able to form a third of the men into lines of skirmishers that preceded the attacks and covered the withdrawals of the compact formations. [6] As casualties mounted he took charge of the entire battalion, the largest command he was ever to hold in combat. The battalion survived the first days of the retreat, though on a night march the prince lost his way and was separated from the men, whom Clausewitz managed to lead to an assembly point where efforts were

---

5. *Nachrichten*, p. 499.
6. The activities of Prince August and Clausewitz during the October campaign are mentioned in *Aus dem kriegsgeschichtlichen Nachlasse Seiner Königlichen Hoheit des Prinzen August von Preussen; Kriegsgeschichtliche Einzelschriften*, ii, Berlin, 1883; L. v. Puttkammer, *Erinnerungsblätter aus dem Leben Seiner Königlichen Hoheit des Prinzen August von Preussen*, Gotha, 1869; in Clausewitz's *Nachrichten*, pp. 543–548; and in August's letter of 16 February 1809 to Frederick William, recommending Clausewitz's promotion, printed in Schwartz, *Leben des Generals Clausewitz*, i, 126–127.

made to fuse the surviving fragments of the army into new units. In the meantime the French pursuit continued unabated; the breakdown of command and of the supply system left each unit to fend for itself, and every day thousands of men deserted or were captured. The network of Prussian fortresses and depots with their sizable garrisons that stretched across the north-German plain might have afforded the troops an opportunity to reorganize; instead the strongpoints were swept away in an orgy of capitulations that long impressed contemporaries as a particularly shameful and inexplicable episode among the many that marked the French wars. A corps of some 22,000 men, which Blücher pieced together with Scharnhorst's help, fought its way to Lübeck, where it was defeated and the remnant disarmed. A second improvised army under Hohenlohe sought to reach Prussian reserves on the Oder River. Prince August and Clausewitz with 240 grenadiers formed part of its rear guard. On the 28th, near Prenzlau, halfway between Berlin and the Baltic coast, they were cut off from the main body by several pursuing regiments, and surrendered after they had repelled seven cavalry charges. That same evening the prince and his adjutant were taken to Berlin, where Napoleon now made his headquarters. While August had a brief audience with the emperor, Clausewitz waited in an anteroom, "in completely ruined clothes among the brilliant, as it were, disdainful uniforms of the imperial adjutants." [7] For a time the prince and Clausewitz were permitted to remain on parole near Berlin. Toward the end of the year this arrangement was changed to internment in Nancy.[8]

The ten months that Clausewitz passed in France and Switzerland before returning to Prussia had a lasting effect on his career and life. During this period the remaining Prussian forces, squeezed into Silesia and East Prussia, resisted the French with surprising tenacity. For the first time in this war reputations were made rather than lost, the most significant rise being that of Scharnhorst. Captured with Blücher's corps, he had the good fortune of being exchanged at once, and immediately returned to active service. His part in the battle of Eylau, in February 1807, at which Napoleon suffered his first check, confirmed his new fame of being as good a fighting soldier as he was a savant and administrator. He was promoted, decorated, and was clearly marked as a coming man by the confidence that the king now showed in him. Many of the officers on whom he later relied in reforming the army also proved themselves in the fighting that continued

7. Clausewitz, *Nachrichten*, p. 547.
8. On 27 December 1806 the prince interrupted his voyage to France in Weimar to pay his respects to Goethe. Clausewitz missed the opportunity since he did not leave Berlin until the 30th. A decade later Marie v. Brühl, by then his wife, was to meet Goethe at Stein's residence in Nassau, where she stopped on her way to join Clausewitz in Paris.

until spring, when Prussia at last sued for peace. Clausewitz was too young to hope for important assignments; only distinguished service in the field would bring him rapid advancement at a time of great opportunities, but being forced to accompany Prince August to France robbed him of the chance. Although it was not to be apparent for some time to come, he could never make up the lead that others gained while he was immobilized in captivity, the more so since some years later he was again to be absent during a critical period in the army's affairs. He himself felt bitterly frustrated. All he wanted on earth, he wrote to his fiancée in the spring of 1807, was to embrace her and to rejoin the army. He continued the letter by deploring not only his exile but also the ponderous system of advancement, based largely on seniority, that was still being followed in the Prussian army: "Now in the plenitude and strength of my spirit, when no great name frightens me, because I know that superior daring, novelty, rapidity hold out a justified expectation of victory (and the advantage possessed by a young general consists in his ability to surprise the opponent with the full originality and newness of his talent), now I can't move forward; but someday when my arm trembles with the feebleness of age, I, like so many others, may be entrusted with the safety of the state, with the leadership of the army." The paean to the young genius, who like Napoleon can turn the advantages of youth into supreme achievement, changes at the end of the letter to a more realistic note: all Clausewitz wants is the chance to distinguish himself, to become known as a promising young officer to his seniors.[9]

His frustration and the hurt to his patriotism were deepened by his shame at being obliged to live among his conquerors. The intimate bond between the state and himself that he had recently discovered in his thoughts and feelings now revealed its destructive side. Prussia's defeats threatened his self-esteem. "Children of a lost fatherland, we wander aimlessly like orphans," he wrote to his fiancée soon after leaving Berlin, and continued with an explicit denial of the nonpolitical ideal of humanism: "I always think it egotistical for man to be so proud of his human qualities that he becomes indifferent to the quality of citizenship."[10]

To keep from grieving over the political situation, he threw himself into an intensive study of mathematics. Soon he recovered a degree of confidence. He did not believe that Napoleon's position was entirely secure: in

9. Clausewitz to Marie v. Brühl, 2 April 1807, *Correspondence*, pp. 105–106. The long letter opens with an equally interesting passage of self-analysis. Clausewitz had reacted with deep satisfaction to his fiancée's statement that Scharnhorst's ability was now widely recognized; then he began to doubt whether this really was so or whether she only wrote it to cheer him up. He thought it typical that his pleasures were always qualified by contrary emotions, but did not know whether this common reaction was caused by his grief over Prussia's misfortune, by an innate "dreary instinct," or by realism and common sense. *Ibid.*, p. 103.

10. Clausewitz to Marie v. Brühl, 9 January 1807, *ibid.*, p. 79.

the very extensiveness of the French conquests lay potential military and political weaknesses that might be exploited if only Austria would re-enter the war. A campaign plan developing this possibility dates from the early spring of 1807.[11] A more personal statement of discouragement overcome concluded the last of his articles on the October battles, which he wrote in February: "I freely admit, I myself and all of us desired the war, and we did not consider a successful outcome to be impossible. We cherished the most sublime hopes, for never would an army's blood have earned a more noble fame than that of having saved the honor and liberty of the German nation, and the happiness of its citizens. On the other hand, we were far from a vain self-confidence that could ignore the reefs on which our hopes might founder, and the recognition of that possibility deeply saddened some of us. Now our magnificent hopes, our whole beautiful relationship to Germany, have been destroyed. We have been deprived of our civic happiness, our careers are ended, our strength lies idle, and the unjust judgment of the whole of Europe rests heavily upon us. Thus redoubled courage is needed to bear—together with the nation—the misfortune and shame of the times! And yet I want to call out to all Germans: *Honor yourselves*—that is: *Don't despair at your fate!*" [12]

As the shock caused by defeat gave way to reflection and analysis, it had a further, very different impact as well. Before the war Clausewitz had committed himself to the political ideal of a strong, self-reliant, and honorable state, which was justified in placing heavy demands on its citizens since it served cultural and national ends and thus enabled both the individual and society to achieve their innate potentials. That he also felt a very personal need to be part of such a force—a son who owes all to his fatherland—clearly emerges from his notebooks and letters of the time. This ideal Clausewitz now reformulated in sharper outline and deeper colors, and for some years after 1806 his ideas of what the state, particularly his state, ought to be touch on extremes of power and authority.

As never before, fantasies vigorous with political energy suffused his thoughts about the nation and society, and even his image of himself, so that he could end a declaration of love for Marie von Brühl with the words: "*I sense within myself a specific striving after a noble purpose;* and in me—as in a well-administered state—all energies *shall obey and serve* this striving." [13] No doubt this peculiar analogy, by which for an instant he incorporated the state into his own person, simply suggests his political preoccupations; but

---

11. "Skizze zu einem Operationsplane für Oesterreich, wenn es jetzt Theil an dem Kriege gegen Frankreich nehmen wollte," Schwartz, *Leben des Generals Clausewitz*, i, 67–72.

12. "Historische Briefe," *Minerva*, II (April 1807), 25–26. Clausewitz quoted the final sentence in his letter to Marie v. Brühl of 28 February 1807, *Correspondence*, p. 92.

13. Clausewitz to Marie v. Brühl, 29 March 1807, *ibid.*, p. 102.

while comparing himself to a state he extended the personification of the state itself far beyond the point reached in his earlier writings.[14] The state now appeared as a supreme individual—the mass of its citizens becoming effective through the leadership of the few—"existing free and feared" in a community of states.[15] Like all men and all institutions, the state was doomed to eventual decay, brought about by the very elements that originally gave it vigor; until then it must bend all efforts to gain strength and use it effectively with its peers and rivals. "It must never be the object of generous pity" if it is to achieve great things, "unless we are speaking of a small, pacific pastoral tribe."[16] External strength derived from an increase in internal authority, since the state could not be powerful unless the citizen was prepared to renounce his autonomous goals of individual perfection. Here Clausewitz broached a theme to which he was to return often in the following years: the hypercritical, self-willed nature of the Germans, which inhibited their striving and fighting together for a common end. "The poverty of the German spirit is revealing itself more and more," he wrote some months after the amistice; "the feebleness of character and principle emerging everywhere is enough to make one weep. I write this with infinite sadness, for no one on earth feels a greater need for national honor and dignity than I do; but it is impossible to be mistaken, the facts cannot be denied. . . . That the attitudes of our people are not marked by greater nobility is not the fault of nature, but the fault of men. Had those who led the nation shown themselves to be better men, then the nation would have been animated by a different spirit." But, he continued, ways existed to change men's beliefs, "and if I am to express my innermost thoughts I would say that I favor the most extreme [measures]. With whips I would stir the lazy animal and teach it to burst the chains with which out of cowardice and fear it permitted itself to be bound. I would spread an attitude throughout Germany, which like an antidote would eliminate with destructive force the plague that is threatening to decay the spirit of the nation."[17]

The health of the state suffered no limits to be placed on efforts in its behalf if—to revert to Clausewitz's emotional needs—the state was to

14. Elizabeth Stevenson's evaluation of Henry Adams also holds true of Clausewitz in these years: "The national self was a second skin . . . ; what wounded the nation wounded him."
15. Letter to Marie v. Brühl, 5 October 1807, *Correspondence,* pp. 140–141. Compare Rothfels, *Carl von Clausewitz,* p. 103. Without wishing to minimize the many differences in interpretation, I am greatly indebted to the subtle analysis of the political ideas of the young Clausewitz contained in this work. Some disagreements between Rothfels's views and my own are indicated below, and in the last chapter of this book.
16. Letters to Marie v. Brühl, 28 February and 5 October 1807, *Correspondence,* pp. 91, 141–144.
17. Clausewitz to Marie v. Brühl, 1 September 1807, *ibid.,* p. 135. Six years later, in more hopeful circumstances, Clausewitz returned to this simile and wrote of the pestilential air that had been dispelled by Prussian and Russian arms. See below, p. 241, n. 50.

become once more an all-powerful, feared person, with whose authority he could identify and from whom he could gain the self-confidence he required to attain his goals. Emotional need and intellectual recognition went hand in hand. Clausewitz's despair at Napoleon's triumph over Prussia had helped him arrive at the thesis that the essence of the state is power, and that no convention or consideration of any kind could be permitted to stand in the way of power when independence or survival were in question. But as Napoleon's star began to set, Clausewitz returned to more moderate views, without ever losing sight of the political absolute that he had discovered in the year of Prussia's deepest crisis. At the end of the Wars of Liberation he was able to advocate policies in Germany and toward the defeated French that ranged him on the side of the diplomats against the uncompromising, vindictive demands raised by some of the soldiers. He never wrote a theory of politics as he was to develop a theory of war. But if he had, the concept of the absolute state would have paralleled his thesis of absolute war—a war of total violence, the necessary extreme in theory, the ideal that permits us to understand the manifold forms of reality—but an abolute that is reduced, moderated, and limited in practice.

The easy conditions of their internment—the prince and Clausewitz were supervised guests of the government rather than its prisoners—gave Clausewitz the opportunity of becoming acquainted with French provincial society, first at Nancy, then for six months at Soissons. The people he met left him with a general impression of slyness and superficiality, though there was much in their way of life that he found agreeable. Of greater interest were the workings of the national and departmental administrations, whose first aim, he said, was to discern and carry out promptly the will of the feared ruler, but which nevertheless had not turned Frenchmen into dedicated and efficient servants of the state.[18] Most significantly, the emperor's military despotism had not succeeded in militarizing the French people. "It is true," Clausewitz noted in his journal, "that in France all administrative processes are characterized by extreme military tendencies; but there is no trace of these in the character of the nation. Two or three gendarmes leading thirty or forty conscripts, tied two by two, on a single rope to the prefectures, proves both points at the same time. The first, because this economical method saves gendarmes; the second, because the shameful procedure suggests [the need for] extreme compulsion."[19] From such observations Clausewitz drew the comforting conclusion that Germans had no need to fear the French, who were far from being the invincible warrior race of revolutionary and Napoleonic propaganda. But he also came to appreci-

18. Entry in his journal of 25 August 1807, Schwartz, *Leben des Generals Clausewitz,* i, 107–108.
19. *Ibid.,* p. 108. See also my article "Nationalism and the Sense of Military Obligation," *Military Affairs,* XXXIV, No. 1 (February 1970), 4.

ate how effective a rationally designed and guided bureaucratic machine could be, even when it dealt with inferior, recalcitrant human material. How much more might be achieved if efficient methods of government were combined with idealistic rulers and politically educated subjects!

A visit of three weeks to Paris did not, contrary to expectations, prove the high point of his stay in France. Prince August's insistence on seeing everything of interest irritated and exhausted Clausewitz; his letters to his fiancée are largely devoted to such standard topics as the Louvre and the theater, the latter stimulating speculations on the differences between the French and German languages and psychologies. More important was a visit to Abbé Sicard's institute for the deaf and dumb, where Clausewitz was once again struck by the potential power of education. The training of the patients suggested, he thought, how a teacher-philosopher could transform a primitive man into a moral human being.[20] At the end of July, a few weeks after Prussia had signed the Peace of Tilsit, the prince finally received permission to leave France; but the voyage had to be interrupted in Switzerland until the necessary passports arrived, and they spent two months in Coppet, near Geneva, as guests of Mme. de Staël, who was also entertaining Mme. Récamier, with whom Prince August had fallen in love in Paris. In his letters to his fiancée Clausewitz never so much as hints at this relationship, which the prince took seriously enough to suggest marriage, except for once referring to Mme. Récamier as "a very ordinary cocotte."[21] But Coppet offered other attractions. Despite his impatience to return to Berlin and Marie von Brühl, Clausewitz enjoyed being among people to whom art and philosophy were not the small change of social intercourse but matters of fundamental importance. With his hostess he compared the qualities of French and German literature; her friend, August Wilhelm Schlegel, introduced him to the poetry of the German Middle Ages; and he made the acquaintance of Pestalozzi, whose school at Yverdun was in the vicinity. A visit to the institute resulted in the most thoughtful analysis of the problems of education Clausewitz had yet written.[22] His appreciation of Pestalozzi's theories, and his uneasy recognition of the degree to which they were coarsened in application, presage a concern over the relationship between changes in men's attitudes and changes in their institutions, which occupied him throughout the years of reform.

20. Clausewitz to Marie v. Brühl, 5 April 1807, *Correspondence*, pp. 106–108. In his memoirs one of Clausewitz's acquaintances, the publicist Wilhelm Dorow, gives a detailed account of the kind of public examination that Clausewitz attended at this institute; *Erlebtes*, Leipzig, 1845, iv, 35–41.
21. Clausewitz to Marie v. Brühl, 16 August 1807, *Correspondence*, p. 132.
22. "Pestalozzi," Schwartz, *Leben des Generals Clausewitz*, i, 110–113. The essay is discussed below, pp. 184–186. Clausewitz's interest in educational methods and institutions is further attested to by his visit to another school, directed by Fellenberg, a former associate of Pestalozzi.

When Clausewitz returned to occupied Berlin in November 1807, his experiences in France had strengthened an intellectual approach that was to become central to his work—the comparative method. Even in adolescence he had looked to conditions outside Prussia to help him understand and evaluate his native military environment. The progress of the French Revolution made such references more than ordinarily pressing, and in the first years of the new century his reflections on politics and war were often based on comparisons between contemporary elements or between past and present. But exile in France lent a degree of richness and concreteness to his analyses that he otherwise might have found difficult to attain. The first important product of his new skill was an essay on the national character of the French and the Germans, which he wrote in the winter months of 1807 while he and Prince August waited for orders to report to Königsberg, where the Prussian government and its central military agencies were temporarily established. The essay deserves to be discussed at this point rather than in the following chapter since it is primarily a psychological statement, the expression of an attitude that underlay the policies, both toward France and within Prussia, which Clausewitz was soon to advocate. It presents in polished, highly structured form ideas that had first been expressed in his letters and notebooks; and it applies his current elevated concept of the state to the relationship of the two antagonistic nations, which "face each other like human beings." [23]

Clausewitz begins by asking the question that at the moment was the most vital to him: was French domination of Germany accidental and temporary or did it result from strengths and weaknesses in the character of the two nations, which would suggest that their present relationship might continue for generations? His answer is, first, to repeat the view he had stated a year ago in his articles on the campaign of 1806, that some causes of the defeat were fortuitous—Napoleon's genius, for one. But, he continues, returning to an idea he first jotted down in 1803, more permanent factors such as national character must also have played a significant part. What are the main elements in the psychology and intelligence of the French and German peoples? The French he considers to have lively but shallow emotions; their intelligence, too, is quick but superficial. Men who do not seek to probe beneath the surface will not find it difficult to agree

---

23. "Die Deutschen und die Franzosen," *Politische Schriften und Briefe*, pp. 35–51. The quotation is from p. 36. Precursors of the essay, apart from passages in letters to Marie v. Brühl between January and October 1807, are "Journal einer Reise von Soissons über Dijon nach Genf," Schwartz, *Leben des Generals Clausewitz*, i, 88–110, particularly the section written after Clausewitz had met Mme. de Staël and Schlegel, and entries in his notebook, which were published by Rothfels as an appendix to his *Carl von Clausewitz*, pp. 221–229. Clausewitz may have intended to publish the essay, but it was first printed in Schwartz's biography. Among discussions of the essay, the following should be noted: Rothfels, *Carl von Clausewitz*, pp. 108–119; P. Roques, *Le Général de Clausewitz*, Paris, 1912, pp. 31–33; and A. Raif, *Die Urteile der Deutschen über die französische Nationalität im Zeitalter der Revolution und der deutschen Erhebung*, Berlin and Leipzig, 1911, pp. 120–123.

among themselves; indeed, "originality of mind is so rare in France that the expression *un original* has become a mark of ridicule." [24] Their superficiality, however, makes Frenchmen not only easier to govern but also more practical. Their uniformity is conducive to *esprit de corps*; their concern for externals lies behind their politeness and courage; they are cruel, and "since little labor suffices to maintain life in their fertile land" they are content with little and at the same time fill their many free hours pursuing shallow pleasures. [25] If French emotions can be compared to a flickering flame, German feelings are like embers, calmer and richer. The German intellect is marked by a similar calm profundity; it pursues ideas below their surface appearance, and seeks to comprehend them totally. "Of the intellectual riches with which nature has endowed man, this trait of abstract analysis is certainly the highest, and it will always be the most magnificent ornament of the German character. But while it elevates the human being it often damages his usefulness in practical—particularly in political—life." [26] Echoing Justus Möser, Clausewitz argues that the great variety in German attitudes—a historical profusion that he compresses into the abstract term "originality"—would be difficult to reconcile with a uniform national spirit. Still it would be wrong to assume that, in its absence, national character and nationality must also be lacking. The German spirit would not suit citizens of a great uniform empire such as the French. It would be least opposed to the republican type of government, which suits the German's individual and critical tendencies, and would educate him by involving him in public affairs, thus counteracting his innate cosmopolitanism. "But his true element, in which he can follow all his natural leanings ... , is the recently lost confederation." [27] Unfortunately, large continental states cannot survive as republics or federations and, because of her geographic location, Germany least of all: "Therefore we can only wish her the greatest uniformity of political activity and political institutions. Political variety [*Parteiungen*], which in other countries may be beneficial, must in Germany—the target of constant foreign interference—always lead to great divisions that would cause the collapse of the Reich." [28] Clausewitz con-

24. *Politische Schriften und Briefe*, p. 38. The French Revolution, which might have suggested an extreme diversity of views and a profound search for political ideals among the French people, was dismissed by Clausewitz with the argument that the ease with which republicans turned into enthusiastic supporters of the emperor demonstrated the shallowness and theatricality of their political convictions.
25. *Ibid.*, p. 42.
26. *Ibid.*, pp. 43–44.
27. *Ibid.*, p. 46. It again illustrates the essay's partisan qualities, unusual among Clausewitz's writings, that he believes in the possibility of political education for the German, but regards the Frenchman as an unchanging, absolute type.
28. In light of this passage it is difficult to agree with Leonard Krieger's argument in *The German Idea of Freedom*, Boston, 1957, pp. 198–199, that Clausewitz's "celebration of German individualism" in this essay illustrates "the narrow political assumptions of the military reform party before 1808." Clausewitz clearly argues that while the political arrangement best suited to the German psyche is some

cludes that their shallowness, frugality, and vanity enable Frenchmen to combine more easily into a uniform society; they are easier to discipline for the purposes of government, and in general make a better political instrument than do the Germans with their many individual differences, their originality, their urge to reason and argue, their love of work, their endless striving after higher, personal goals. In a pendant made up of historical allusions, Clausewitz ends his essay with a comparison that was frequently made at the time: the superiority of the practical French over the morally and intellectually richer Germans is akin to the relationship between Roman and Greek.[29]

Although expressing the belief that the German character "in more than one respect ... would be highly suited to wind a unifying bond around the separate members of the German nation," Clausewitz does not suggest how the national character of the two peoples might be exploited or altered to make possible the recovery of German independence.[30] The essay, in Hans Rothfels's apt phrase, is no more than "a kind of inventory of the forces availabe to the two sides. ... What Machiavelli attempted in the *Ritratti* with early, primitive categories—to reduce the power of the two nations into their constituent elements and to estimate their extent—the Prussian officer undertook with far more refined instruments and a full spectrum of colors. For him, too, everything is determined by the political and military impact." [31] Rothfels goes on to suggest certain affinities between Clausewitz's essay and the works of contemporaries. Wilhelm von Humboldt judged the French character in very similar terms; Clausewitz shared with Fichte a belief in the political significance of language, and his regard for German as the supremely natural and creative tongue; while his dismissal of French superficiality and uniformity is paralleled in the writings of the Schlegel brothers, from which, perhaps, it is borrowed in part. What distinguishes Clausewitz's essay in Rothfels's eyes is its rigorously systematic structure and its political concern. Rothfels does not, however, take the further step of pointing out that the political message of the manuscript radically distorts the fundamental tenets of German idealism, whose concepts it incorporates. When Fichte emphasizes the differences between languages, from which he derives the existence of a specifically German cultural mission, he seeks to establish the German's fitness for these tasks, not the inferiority of non-German cultures. Nor does Rothfels in-

---

form of federalism, practical needs demand another solution. Clausewitz's opposition to German particularism, especially in these years, was so strong that he could condemn Frederick the Great's policies in extreme terms, e.g.: "Frederick II's constant screaming against the universal rule of Austria is nothing but egotism." Preliminary draft of the essay, quoted by Rothfels, *Carl von Clausewitz*, p. 119.
29. *Politische Schriften und Briefe*, pp. 49–51.
30. *Ibid.*, p. 46.
31. Rothfels, *Carl von Clausewitz*, p. 112.

quire into the validity of Clausewitz's description of the two peoples.[32] That the question should not be dismissed is evident if one considers the possible consequences of an attitude that in part consists in underestimating the French and exaggerating the qualities of the Germans. How did this affect Clausewitz's political judgments? And, to rephrase the question in more general terms, what might be the historical results of a nationalism that depended so heavily on the vilification of the foreigner?

And yet, like his elevated concept of the state, Clausewitz's idealization of German qualities was an outgrowth of the defeats of Jena and Auerstedt that did not figure permanently in his thought. In the years before the war he had refused to accept his country's political weakness as inevitable: innately, Germans were as capable as the French of securing for themselves a powerful place in Europe. Now he went further, claiming that morally and culturally they were incomparably superior to the victors, whom he simultaneously disparaged with an extravagant smugness that stands comparison with the more disagreeable effusions of German Romantic writing of the day. Clamorous though it was at times, however, his aggressive patriotism even then formed only a subordinate aspect of his thought. Clearly it was yet another way of compensating for the army's fate, as well as that of Prussia, and of restoring his self-esteem, which had suffered through its close association with the beaten state. Soon he also used patriotic exhortations to persuade others to act. But even in the years when the future of Prussia as an independent power seemed in doubt, his desire to understand the phenomena of politics and war remained far stronger than his urge to give way to pathos. It is suggestive that at the very time that he was stimulated by such Romantic writers as Friedrich and August Wilhelm Schlegel, especially by their interpretation of French culture as a force destructive of individuality, he was repelled by their surging, allusive boundlessness—by "the forced enthusiasm that is so frequent in today's writing." [33] Besides, he was too critical of his German and Prus-

---

32. Rothfels, *ibid.*, pp. 114, 117, raises the point but does not pursue it, being more interested in the political energy expressed in the essay than in the form that the energy takes. Here as elsewhere in his excellent study, Rothfels's own strong patriotic sentiments are apparent.

33. "Now and then [August Wilhelm] Schlegel reads some of his works to me, which gives me great pleasure. ... In spite of this, nothing can bring me nearer to his point of view, nor have I come to appreciate the poetry of his brother, though some good things are among it." Clausewitz to Marie v. Brühl, 5 October 1807, *Correspondence*, p. 147. The quotation in the text is from another letter to his fiancée of 4 September 1809, *ibid.*, p. 261. See also an entry in his notebook, dating from 1808 or 1809, which attacks the Romantic writers' elevation of "dark pictures of fantasy, vague feelings" over reason; Rothfels, *Carl von Clausewitz*, p. 228. The profound division in attitudes that separated Clausewitz from the Romantics is further illustrated by their opposing views of a psychological phenomenon that was of great importance to both. Such writers as Friedrich Schlegel proclaimed an absolute difference between ordinary man and genius, whose highest achievement consisted in God-like pleasure (*Genuss*). Clausewitz, on the contrary, regarded genius as the highest expression of the universal creative qualities of man. See below, pp. 160–161. After Clausewitz returned to Prussia in November 1807 he exchanged

sian environment to be able to insist on its absolute superiority for long. By
the end of the Napoleonic wars, his objectivity and his analytic energies
had fully matured, and had vanquished the strain of national arrogance
with which the younger man had responded to Prussia's humiliation and
his own.[34]

at least one letter with August Wilhelm Schlegel, but soon contact between the two men ceased completely. See his letter to A. W. Schlegel of 23 January 1808, and the letter of 4 February 1808 to the
same recipient by Louise Voss, Marie v. Brühl's friend, in *Krisenjahre der Frühromantik,* ed. J. Körner, 2
vols., Bern, 1969, i, 496–497, 502.
34. His objective attitude toward the defeated French in 1815 is discussed on pp. 252–254 below. His
views had moderated even earlier. See, for example, a comment written in the course of the 1814 campaign, which also provides an interesting insight into the early emotional roots of his approach to history: "I am a strange person in relation to the past. I love it even when it wasn't worth much. When I
first came to know France I really did not care much for the country, nor had any reason to do so; nevertheless I have always had agreeable recollections of France. On the whole, the strangeness of manners
has many attractions if one can observe them as traveller (not as an exile), and these together with many
small favorable characteristics have remained in my grateful memory, while the unpleasant impressions
have disappeared." Letter to his wife, 17 March 1814, *Correspondence,* p. 364. Later historical writings
are, as might be expected, free of chauvinism. Cf. the characteristic description of French military competence and bravery in his history of the campaign of 1814, *Werke,* vii, 386 and similar comments in
On War—for example, book I, ch. 3 (p. 130), book IV, ch. 7 (p. 341), and book VI, ch. 16 (p. 621).

∞ 8 ∞

THE YEARS OF REFORM

I. THE MILITARY REFORMERS

In the last days of March 1808, Prince August and Clausewitz left Berlin for Königsberg, where they arrived on 1 April. For Clausewitz and Marie von Brühl it was the beginning of another long separation, which—except for some meetings in Berlin in the summer of 1808—was to last for nearly twenty months. During this time they continued to keep their engagement hidden from her mother, who had not changed view that Clausewitz was an undesirable suitor. Countess Brühl, Clausewitz wrote with some bitterness, claimed to dislike his "exalted" moods, but in reality objected to his poverty and his obscure family.[1] Marie von Brühl's friends sought to arrange a more advantageous match for her—attempts that she rejected, but which caused Clausewitz anguish, though he never doubted her love. In letters that constantly passed between them they continued the affectionate, trusting exploration of their own and each other's character and temperament that makes their correspondence such an unusual monument to the inner life of German Classicism.[2] Clausewitz suffered from their separation; but at least he had returned to active service at the center of affairs, and he was near Scharnhorst—the other of the two human beings who, he said, meant most in his life.

By this time the plans for the administrative and military reorganization of the state had been completed. The king had in principle accepted essential parts of the great reform proposals drawn up by Stein and his collaborators, and by the Military Reorganization Commission under Scharnhorst's chairmanship, and the first steps were being taken to carry them out. Their common intent was to break up the old absolutist system, which had inhibited the rational execution of public business, and to achieve a

---

1. Clausewitz to Marie v. Brühl in his above-cited letter of 5 August 1808, *Correspondence*, p. 160.
2. Though many letters have been lost, the surviving correspondence between April 1808 and the end of 1809 takes up nearly 120 printed pages.

fuller exploitation by the state of social and psychological energies that the Frederician class-structure had repressed. Whatever form the new or changed institutions were to assume, they must give the state more direct access to the subject, who, in turn, must be persuaded that a closer connection existed between the well-being of the state and his own condition and opportunities. This general purpose was pursued by men holding very different views, ranging from Stein's patriarchal sympathies for the political organisms of the old estates and municipalities to the Whiggism of such men as Theodor von Schön. The personalities involved, the tenacity with which influential groups opposed even the most modest proposals for change, and Stein's forced departure from office in November 1808 insured that for the time being what was actually done did not go far beyond the common denominator of increasing bureaucratic and social efficiency. By abolishing the legal privileges of the nobility, creating new opportunities for the middle classes, and strengthening the authority of the civil service, the reforms laid the foundations for further liberalization, which, some men hoped, might be crowned in the future by economic policies less disadvantageous to the small landholders and former serfs, by the formation of a council of state, and by a constitution.[3]

In Prussia perhaps more than in most states, civil and military change were irrevocably connected. The issue of widest impact linking the two was conscription. If the army, in Clausewitz's words, was to be reorganized "according to a new spirit," universal obligation for military service had to be introduced "so that the burden ... was carried on all shoulders," a proud civic duty, which turned the cause of the state into the cause of every man.[4] But even among the military reformers some—most notably Scharnhorst—only gradually relinquished more or less restrictive militia schemes to accept the desirability of general conscription without exemption for privileged groups, and elsewhere resistance to the concept of universal military obligation was intense. Few things discomfited Frederick William more than the thought that by broadening the subject's obligations and simultaneously enlarging his dynastic loyalties to include the more abstract values of fatherland and nation, absolute royal control over the army might be compromised. The nobility feared conscription as an egalitarian force, especially if it was coupled with a limitation of their favored access to officer rank. Nor did the middle classes evince much eagerness to serve the state in uniform. The principle of conscription was officially adopted in August 1808; but only the urgent need for men during the campaigns of 1813 and 1814 at last compelled the king to put it into practice.[5] Never-

3. On the opening phase of the reforms see my *Yorck*, pp. 117–140.
4. *Bekenntnisdenkschrift* of 1812, *Schriften*, i, 698.
5. Paret, "Nationalism and the Sense of Military Obligation," *Military Affairs*, p. 4.

theless, the social restrictions that formerly had made the army a dynastic instrument and military authority a preserve of the nobility were beginning to be breached at several points: the nobility lost most of its legal rights to preference in the appointment of officers and the principle of promotion by strict seniority was at least weakened by placing new emphasis on military education and performance, so that, Scharnhorst wrote, superior positions would no longer be filled by "worn-out ancients and junior positions by children." [6] The significant economic privileges of company commanders and senior officers, who until 1807 had themselves purchased and distributed at a personal profit much of the equipment of their men, were abolished, as was the employment of foreign mercenaries. To make military service less onerous for men in the ranks, the length of service was reduced, the code of military justice was made more humane, corporal punishment was largely done away with, and discipline eased by a degree or two. Step by step, the administration of the army was being brought into closer conformity to the civilian ministries and agencies. But more than these changes were needed to improve its fighting quality. Better equipment had to be designed and manufactured. The many segments of the service had to be brought together into larger combinations to make cooperation between infantry, cavalry, and artillery less haphazard than in the past. Realistic training had to be introduced, and new operational and tactical doctrines worked out, which—to a greater degree at the top, to a lesser extent in the ranks—placed new emphasis on the initiative of the trained, committed, thinking soldier.

As head of the commission that had been appointed to propose measures for the reorganization and modernization of the army, Scharnhorst had now become the political as well as the intellectual leader of the military reformers. In essence his program differed little from the proposals he had put forward in Hanover a decade earlier, but it was still thought to be revolutionary. His powers were narrowly circumscribed; he remained dependent on the trust or toleration of the king and the senior generals. Nor was it clear until the terms of the Treaty of Paris had been agreed on whether Prussia was to retain an army of any significance, and before the outlines of the new military establishment were known Scharnhorst felt unable to offer Clausewitz a regular appointment. For the time being he employed him as an unofficial assistant and propagandist, and set in motion the "little intrigue" that Clausewitz predicted would be required to detach him from Prince August's service without causing hurt feelings. [7] The agree-

---

6. In a letter of 12 November 1810 to a close friend of his youth, the Saxon general Heinrich v. Zeschau; *Scharnhorsts Briefe*, p. 407.
7. Clausewitz to Marie v. Brühl, 15 September 1807, and 4 September 1808; *Correspondence*, pp. 137, 170–171.

ment Clausewitz had concluded with the *Jenaische Allgemeine Literatur-Zeitung* a few months before the war finally led to results. In Scharnhorst's name Clausewitz wrote an analysis of some of the most significant military reforms that had already been instituted: the new articles of war, the revision of the army's penal code, and the new regulations on appointing ensigns and junior officers, which for the first time accorded elementary education and competitive examinations a genuine role in their selection.[8]

In the summer of 1808, Scharnhorst at last succeeded in bringing about a change in the army's structure that was crucial to the subsequent course of reform. The office of general adjutant—the military equivalent of the cabinet councillors—was abolished, and replaced by two departments with executive responsibility and authority—an early stage in the evolution of a ministry of war.[9] Scharnhorst was made head of the first department, the *Allgemeine Kriegsdepartement*, with responsibility for all but economic matters. At the end of the year the two bodies, under the combined name of War Department, became one of the five ministries into which the government was being reorganized; and although Frederick William, jealous of his role of supreme commander, refused for the time being to appoint a minister of war, a major step had been taken toward the creation of ministerial supervision of the army. Scharnhorst now possessed the agency he needed to carry out his schemes for modernizing the service. In February 1809, Clausewitz was appointed to Scharnhorst's office in the new ministry with simultaneous promotion to the rank of captain. From this time until he resigned his commission at the start of the War of 1812, he served as Scharnhorst's closest personal assistant.[10] His duties during the first months are not fully known, but he assisted Scharnhorst in the drafting of memoranda and letters, kept minutes at committee meetings, and twice a week drew up a report on the progress of the wars that continued to rack Europe. An early task was to defend in a memorandum for internal circulation the *Allgemeine Kriegsdepartement* against the "king's distrust of the persons employed there."[11] He also worked, possibly in a key role, on the secret rearmament measures by which Scharnhorst evaded the military clauses of the Treaty of Paris. In spite of all this he could write his fiancée,

8. The article, "Die preussischen Kriegsartikel," signed "S——st." (Scharnhorst), appeared in the *Jenaische Allgemeine Literatur-Zeitung*, no. 238, 11 October 1808. It was reprinted with a few changes in the *Hallesche Allgemeine Literatur-Zeitung*, 2 November 1808.
9. In the same year Scharnhorst abolished the official central administrative agency of the army, the Supreme War Council, which had never been able to fulfill its intended role since to do so would have meant a reduction in the monarch's prerogative. A similar body, established in 1795 to succeed where the Supreme War Council was failing, had already been disbanded before Jena. See my *Yorck*, pp. 98–101, 138–139. Until 1808 the true administrative head of the army was the king, advised by the general adjutants, who were responsible to him alone.
10. H. v. Boyen, *Beiträge zur Kenntnis des Generals von Scharnhorst*, Berlin, 1833, p. 44.
11. Undated memorandum (May–July 1809) in Clausewitz, *Schriften*, i, 677–678.

no doubt with some exaggeration, that he spent a great part of every day reading books on history and government.[12]

The reorganization of the army was the work of hundreds of men, but in developing the great lines of his policies Scharnhorst relied on the help of only a very few. All had been his pupils at the Institute in Berlin, or had come to his notice by distinguishing themselves in the midst of the general debacle. The most important among them was Gneisenau, in 1806 a forty-six-year-old captain, whose defense of Colberg against seemingly impossible odds had by 1808 brought him a seat on the Reorganization Commission and command of the Corps of Engineers. Other members of the commission were Boyen and Grolman, who had proved themselves at Auerstedt, and Count Goetzen, whose partisan operations had successfully defended Silesia against Jerome. Gneisenau, Boyen, and Grolman also served as section heads in the new ministry. Boyen, a member of the *Militärische Gesellschaft,* had been one of Scharnhorst's earliest adherents while the younger Grolman had been a student at the Institute. Another former student was Braun, an artillery officer, who became Scharnhorst's principal assistant in the design and manufacture of weapons. Finally, Scharnhorst transferred three of his former students to his personal staff: Count Dohna, Clausewitz, and Tiedemann, who with Clausewitz had shared the distinction of graduating at the head of the class of 1803.

The social antecedents of this inner circle reflected the blend of old and new, native and foreign, in the changing army. Dohna was the scion of one of the first families in East Prussia. Goetzen, Boyen, and Tiedemann belonged to established Prussian families with strong military traditions. The Grolmans were West German patricians who from the 17th century on occupied increasingly senior positions in the Prussian legal administration, Grolman's father being ennobled in 1786. Gneisenau's background closely resembled that of Clausewitz, except that he was the first of his family to enter Prussian service. He descended from a long line of Saxon jurists and municipal officials; his father, a subaltern in the service of the Prince-Bishop of Würzburg, claimed nobility on the basis of a pretended connection to a family of imperial counts with a similar name. Scharnhorst's ancestors were Hanoverian peasants; and Braun—who was never ennobled, though he ended his career as a lieutenant-general—was the son of a Prussian advocate who had married the daughter of a noncommissioned officer.[13]

12. Boyen, *Scharnhorst,* p. 44; Clausewitz to Marie v. Brühl, 2 January, 23 February, and 10 May 1809, *Correspondence,* pp. 198–201, 214–215, 230–231. Clausewitz's literary interests remained intense and catholic during this period. His letters refer to memorizing a poem by Schiller and reading his *History of the Revolt of the Netherlands;* for recreation he read *Tristram Shandy.* Immediately after the first part of *Faust* appeared he borrowed Gneisenau's copy, promising to return it the following day. Clausewitz to Gneisenau, 6 January 1809, *Schriften,* i, 616.

13. On the genealogy of Goetzen, Dohna, Boyen, Grolman, and Gneisenau, see Banniza v. Bazan and

Gneisenau during the reform era, drawn by Prince Anton Radziwill. Formerly in possession of the Gneisenau family.

Scharnhorst's supremacy among this group was unquestioned, though opinions on particular issues often diverged. He alone had both a detailed understanding of the requirements of every branch of the service and a vision of what the new army as a whole ought to be, and his determination and sense of the possible made him the best hope for bringing such a force into being. His political wisdom—most strikingly apparent in his sure handling of the king—extended to the choice of his principal assistants, each of whom possessed great technical expertise and the necessary human qualities to make him an effective representative of the reform program. But unlike his counterparts in the civil administration—Stein, Altenstein, and Hardenberg—Scharnhorst needed to reinforce the identity of purpose that existed between him and his colleagues and subordinates by strong emotional bonds. That need was answered in particular by Clausewitz, Tiedemann, and Dohna. His feelings toward these three, each his junior by more than twenty years, can be described as being akin to fatherly love. The care with which he watched over their lives may be guessed at from his letters to them, in which respect for their independence and the frankest expressions of affection are associated with unselfconscious authority. He was delighted when his daughter Julie accepted Dohna's proposal of marriage. The special intellectual affinity that he had always felt for Clausewitz had been intensified through the experience of the war. "Your views are mine, or become mine through your letters," the fifty-two-year-old general wrote to the twenty-seven-year-old captain. "Your opinions give me the courage not to deny my own." [14] Of all his associates, he said, Clausewitz was the most loyal and dedicated. In turn, Clausewitz was particularly dependent on him, and not only intellectually. Dohna and Tiedemann belonged to large families that gave them emotional as well as social support of a kind that Clausewitz could not hope for from his three older brothers, all struggling to make their way.[15] Except for Marie von Brühl, Clausewitz stood alone, and he was fortunate that Scharnhorst gave him the encouragement and affection as well as the patronage that he needed. His social world, too, centered on Scharnhorst and the inner circle of reformers. A faint royal luster was added by his intercourse with the Radziwills—in whose house he came to know Stein—and with Prince Wilhelm and Princess Marianne, whose lack of influence in state affairs was now even

---

Müller, ii, 104–105, 122–123, 136–138, 139–141, 191–196. Information on Braun's ancestry is contained in Priesdorff, iv, No. 1263.

14. Letter of 27 November 1807, *Scharnhorsts Briefe*, pp. 333–334.

15. In 1809 Clausewitz's oldest brother served as *Rendant*—an official of middle rank in the revenue service—in the family's hometown, Burg. Clausewitz appears to have had little contact with him in adult life. In a letter to Marie v. Brühl of 23 February 1809, *Correspondence*, p. 214, he even refers to the second of the four brothers, Friedrich, as the oldest. In February 1809, at the age of thirty-eight, Friedrich had just been promoted to major. The third oldest, Wilhelm Benedikt, served as company commander in an infantry regiment.

more apparent than it had been in the months leading up to the war of 1806. Most important among his personal relationships, next to his bond with Scharnhorst, was his new friendship with Gneisenau, whom, like the Radziwills, he came to admire as a secret Prussian Napoleon, and the German personification of his ideal of military genius.

Events beyond Prussia's borders soon disrupted the group. Goetzen and Tiedemann were sent to Silesia to assure the defense of the province, which was endangered by the prospective war between France and Austria. When war did break out in April 1809, Grolman resigned from the army to take service with the Austrians, and Clausewitz, fearing that Prussia would be compelled to support the French, decided to follow his example. He approached an Austrian emissary with the request for an appointment to Archduke Charles's staff, and arranged for letters of recommendation; at the same time he busied himself with studies on the possibility of popular uprisings throughout Germany in support of the Austrian armies. When Charles's defeat at Wagram and the subsequent armistice ruined his Austrian prospects, he asked Gneisenau, who had left on a mission to England, to find him a position in the British service. But this plan, too, came to nothing, though at the end of October, when he accompanied the court and government on their return to Berlin, he still had not given up all hope of fighting the French in Spain.[16]

Soon after their arrival in Berlin, Scharnhorst made Clausewitz his *chef de cabinet* at the ministry, a post that he occupied for the next two and a half years. The areas of responsibility in Scharnhorst's office were not clearly defined. Much of the work Scharnhorst handled himself, often without the knowledge of even his closest subordinates; other fields were parceled out, with some overlapping between individuals. But as head of the office, Clausewitz had a hand in much of Scharnhorst's official correspondence; he summarized incoming reports and presented them to Scharnhorst, and drafted or edited the answers and outgoing orders. Many of the papers that passed through the office have been lost, nor do we possess a complete register of the correspondence; of the material that remains, the greater part deals with the development and manufacture of weapons. Other matters range from strengthening the defensive works of the city of Breslau to the drawing up of tactical regulations and the introduction of conscription. Usually Scharnhorst would indicate the purport of a response or order with a few key words, which Clausewitz then expanded into a full text. The wording might be corrected by Scharnhorst; more often Clausewitz's draft

---

16. Clausewitz's efforts to enter the Austrian or British service are described in his letter to Gneisenau of 12 April 1809, *Schriften,* i, 617; and in his letters to Marie v. Brühl of 23 April, 6 May, 19 June, 26 June, 20 July, 31 July, 21 August, and 9 October 1809; *Correspondence,* pp. 224–226, 228–229, 246–249, 249–250, 253, 254–255, 259, 265. The last letter mentions that he is about to begin the study of English, a language in which he appears to have reached some fluency.

would be dispatched unchanged, sometimes even without Scharnhorst's signature, simply in his name. The freedom with which Clausewitz disposed of important questions affecting senior officers and agencies is striking; but rather than being a reflection of his own authority, his independence was due to his thorough understanding of Scharnhorst's intentions, and to Scharnhorst's confidence that he would carry them out accurately.[17] This work placed him at the center of the army's administration; his other duties during these years involved him deeply in the reformers' efforts to create common views on war according to which the new army would be employed against a future enemy. In the summer of 1810 he was appointed to the general staff and to the faculty of the new war college the *Kriegsschule für die Offiziere,* usually called *Allgemeine Kriegsschule,* which was established with the purpose of introducing promising junior officers to the new operational doctrines that were being developed. "Half against my will," Clausewitz wrote, "I have become a professor." [18] The curriculum was supervised by a directorate of studies under the chairmanship of Tiedemann, who together with Clausewitz gave the school's two courses on strategy and tactics.[19] The general staff continued to be what it had been before 1806, a small body of uncertain authority.[20] Scharnhorst, now its head, hoped however that its members, who were to serve both at headquarters and with the individual corps, would strengthen the links between these and the center, guide the commanding generals according to the intentions of the high command, raise the quality of the army's operational leadership, and help bring about a wider comprehension and acceptance of the new forms of war.

It was in line with these appointments, and again indicates the significance of Scharnhorst's inner circle, that in February 1811 Clausewitz was placed on the commission which under Scharnhorst's chairmanship worked

17. That Clausewitz worked in Scharnhorst's office has always been known, and his authorship of letters or memoranda in Scharnhorst's name has been noted in individual cases; see, for instance, my *Yorck,* p. 148, n. 79, p. 164, n. 17, and p. 180, n. 81; but it is Werner Hahlweg's merit to have recognized the surprising extent of Clausewitz's participation. Professor Hahlweg has printed or excerpted the surviving Scharnhorst correspondence in Clausewitz's hand, together with a valuable introduction and notes, in his edition of Clausewitz's *Schriften,* i, 90–208.
18. Clausewitz to Gneisenau, 24 June 1810, *ibid.,* p. 682.
19. To broaden the social basis of the officer corps and to raise its professional standards, the Reorganization Commission instituted two examinations—one for promotion to ensign, the other for promotion to lieutenant. Military schools in Königsberg, Breslau, and Berlin were founded to prepare ensigns for the second examination; the *Kriegsschule für die Offiziere* functioned as the institution for advanced education. These reforms only partially realized the intentions of the liberal majority of the commission: the nobility continued to dominate the officer corps, but now had to accommodate itself to a system of educational selection.
20. When Clausewitz joined the staff it consisted of less than twenty officers. At the outbreak of the War of 1812, by which time the army had grown to about 65,000 effectives, the staff still numbered little more than thirty men, including officials of the map and drafting sections. *Rang- und Quartierliste der Preussischen Armee von 1812,* reprinted Osnabrück, 1968, pp. 39–40.

out new operational and tactical regulations for the infantry and cavalry.[21]
Some months earlier he had also been appointed tutor in the "military art"
to the crown prince.

The knowledge of military administration and the insights into the
interdependence of military and civil policies that Clausewitz acquired as
head of Scharnhorst's office and in his other tasks strongly affected his later
writings. But his appointments also led to a sizable literary output at the
time. His lectures at the *Kriegsschule* and the syllabus for the crown prince
alone run to nearly 400 printed pages. Together with his essays and notes
on theory and on political topics, the military writings constitute an important intellectual achievement of the reform movement, and form a
bridge between Clausewitz's early ideas and the works of his maturity.

21. Paret, *Yorck,* p. 179.

II. STUDIES IN POLICY AND THEORY

The call for specific actions and faith in activity as such are at the center of Clausewitz's writings in the reform era. Together they dominate his discussions of political issues and of his memoranda on military organization and policy; they provide the interpretive principle for his studies of the uprising of the Vendée against the Revolution and of Spanish resistance to Napoleon with which he illustrated his argument that Prussia, too, should renew the struggle.[1] On an early occasion, while he was still waiting for an assignment that would engage him in the practical work of reform, his urge for action pushed him onto the path of pure speculation, unaffected by any consideration of political and military probability. In an essay on Prussia's prospects in the event of a new war, written sometime before he arrived in Königsberg in the spring of 1808, he proposed that since the French would be able to occupy Prussia at will, the state should be abandoned altogether while the struggle was carried on by the army, operating wherever in central Europe it could support itself: "A state that can no longer be defended should be sacrificed in order to save the army. Consequently ... I would select a well-organized army of fifty to sixty thousand men, whose maintenance throughout the war is my primary concern, a force that represents the kingdom I have lost. If it still exists in some strength at the end of the war, it will constitute a secure bill of exchange for the restitution of this kingdom." [2] Logic and indifference to the way men actually behave could

1. E.g., a position paper that his new friend Gneisenau submitted to the king in 1808, favoring the resumption of war with France but also recognizing the possibility of negotiations, elicited Clausewitz's comment that to present the king with alternatives necessarily led to half measures. Instead, Gneisenau should appear as the uncompromising prophet of action. "Denkschrift zu Gneisenaus Erhebungsplan von 1808," *Politische Schriften und Briefe,* p. 67. A plan for the defense of Silesia in 1811 expresses confidence that the far stronger French could be resisted if the troops were aggressively led and were supported by the armed population. "Die Operationen in Schlesien," *Schriften,* i, 663–666. This sentiment is given even stronger expression in Clausewitz's letters to Gneisenau during this period: *ibid.,* pp. 650–663, 667–669. In November of the same year, Clausewitz drafted a proposal to establish a German legion, financed and equipped by England, to provide a nucleus for a general uprising against the French. Pertz-Delbrück, ii, 685–688. The historical studies of successful operations by an aroused populace against strong regular forces also date from this time. The brief outline of the Spanish war was written in French, "Précis de la guérre en Espagne et en Portugal," *Schriften,* i, 604–611; the more extensive account of the first phase of the war in the Vendée, "Übersicht des Krieges in der Vendée 1793," was included in the tenth volume of his collected works.
2. "Über die künftigen Kriegs-Operationen Preussens gegen Frankreich," *Schriften,* i, 66–90; the quoted passage is from p. 81.

hardly be pressed further. No doubt these words should be interpreted as yet another expression of despair at the impotence of the state, which Clausewitz experienced with particular intensity during this period. But it is indicative of a growing tendency in his writing—that of paying closer attention to the *manner* in which principles are established and propositions arrived at—that his uncompromising proposal, far from being an isolated aperçu, resulted from a careful review of the political, economic, and military potential of the major powers.

The note of action is also sounded in Clausewitz's lectures and writings on the theory and practice of war. Whether his subject is the individual rifleman or the supreme commander, he teaches that success depends on activity, exertion, the willingness to take risks—on the use rather than the possession of force. But again the call for action is accompanied by an intense search for "scientifically valid" methods of analyzing and interpreting the reality of war. The pervasive interest in methodology—which also sets Clausewitz apart from his fellow-reformers—emerges as a second major theme of his thought at this time, with consequences for his work that go far beyond his reactions to the political and military challenges of the moment.

Since adolescence Clausewitz had sought more than purely pragmatic goals in his studies. His first writings show that even in his early years career considerations and his growing anxiety for the state were repeatedly illuminated by more detached speculations about the problem of war. These scholarly impulses were not unrelated to concerns of great importance to the young man in other areas: exploring the elements that determine health and sickness in society and state, the pursuit of human perfectibility. The French triumph in 1806 enormously increased the pressures on Clausewitz's pragmatism, while offering him the most graphic of lessons in the dynamic of violence and the interaction of politics and war. No one after Jena and Auerstedt could have suffered more from Prussia's defeat than he, nor trusted more fanatically in the restorative function of continued fighting. But even as he witnessed from exile the last unavailing resistance of Prussian forces in the eastern corner of the monarchy, he did not relinquish his conviction that wars must not only be won, they must also be understood. The effectiveness of the reforms that now began depended in the last analysis on the accuracy of the reformers' perception of modern war. But the purposes and rewards of understanding far transcended the practical. It is these broader considerations that help explain why Clausewitz by 1808 was no longer satisfied with the enlightening insight and the useful idea. Indeed, at this time he explicitly criticized other writers on war—Bülow and Jomini, for example—for building their doctrines around thoughts and recognitions haphazardly arrived at. They were one-sided, he wrote, since they generalized from ideas that possessed only limited validity.[3] Instead, the cognitive value of ideas rested on their being part of a theoretical system whose components and totality could stand the test of experience, historical interpretation, and logical analysis.

Clausewitz's debt to the philosophy and science of his time is obvious. In the study of war, as in biology or geology, theoretical constructions unsupported by demonstrable evidence or the industrious but unsystematic collecting and cataloguing of data were no longer satisfactory. Clausewitz's thought clearly reflects a concept of science as the ordering of observable facts by means of certain logical assumptions—Kant's principles of understanding—as well as the conviction that complete knowledge was unattainable. From Kant and his successors he acquired his tools of speculative reasoning, and learned to have confidence in their power. But the affinity went deeper. Clausewitz did not regard war simply as a craft, with techniques and conditions peculiar to it, but as a prism in which all of life was refracted. If the breadth of his vision did not equal the universality of German idealism, it was nevertheless related to it. War defined that segment of the world which the accident of his birth and training had made into the object of his inquiry. It was the part that stood for the whole; and it was his awareness of the whole and of the interconnections of all phenomena that was later to enable him to think of war as an act of social intercourse, "concerned with living forces and moral forces," with all the political and psychological implications that flow from such a conception.

In the great movement of Romantic idealism that dominated German intellectual life at the turn of the century, Clausewitz's position is easily recognized. He rejected the popular Enlightenment, with its doctrinaire faith in rationality and progress, and found no difficulty in acknowledging limitations to human understanding, an acceptance that made reason all the stronger in those areas left to it. He benefited enormously from the liberating emphasis that the early Romantics placed on the psychological qualities of the individual; but he did not follow such writers as Novalis or the Schlegel brothers in their surrender to emotion. The religious wave of Romanticism did not touch him; nor did its mysticism, nostalgia, and its sham-medieval, patriarchal view of the state. In feeling and manner he was far closer to the men who had passed through the anti-rationalist revolt of the *Sturm und Drang* to seek internal and external harmony, and who gave expression to their belief in the unity of all phenomena—"the marvellously structured organic whole of all living nature," as Clausewitz once wrote— not in rhapsodic musings after the infinite, but in disciplined mastery of thought and form. The ideal of antiquity that inspired Goethe and Schiller

3. Clausewitz, *Strategie*, p. 72.

had, however, no hold on Clausewitz; its place was taken by a fascination with political and military reality.

The lines that distinguish him from his contemporaries are most nearly obliterated in his manner of reasoning. His argumentation was characterized by the dialectical forms that were the common property of his generation. Men thought in terms of thesis and antithesis, contradiction, polarity, the separation and connection of active and passive, positive and negative. For Clausewitz to write in the opening chapter of *On War* that a principle of polarity was at work whenever two parties to a conflict tried to defeat each other, or in a later chapter to explain salient features of the attack by discussing its antithesis, the defense, was to play variations on a then familiar theme. The separation of a force into opposites, and their reunification, was basic to Goethe's view of nature; for Schelling the absolutes of nature and spirit were composed of polarities; and Hegel wrote of the necessary relationship between two opposites, which were actually one since the existence of one also necessitated the existence of the other. Concepts such as these, which clarified individual phenomena and their reciprocal processes, also expressed men's belief in the unity of life—the principle of polarity, it was said, alone could overcome the infinite distance between the positive and negative.

Even had Clausewitz wished to do so, he could not for long have separated method and view of the world in the writings of his philosophic mentors. But this was not his intention, nor was it necessary as long as their methods of exploration and testing could be applied to his particular area of study. It is in these years that he works hardest to achieve the transfer of analytic techniques from the realms of ethics, aesthetics, and pure reason to politics and war. His preoccupation with mathematics points in this direction; and essays, letters, and critical commentaries on other writers leave no doubt of the significance that methodological questions possess for him. After 1815 some essays as well as passages in longer manuscripts attest to his continued fascination with the refinements of dialectical processes and with the relationship between theory and reality; but their conclusions do not appreciably alter the analytic system he was developing during the reform era.

In its components this system was derivative. Clausewitz's originality lay in the manner in which he combined separate analytic strands and applied their integrated force to the issues of conflict. Perhaps for this reason we cannot point to any single ancestor of his theoretical method among German philosophers. Clausewitz in any case was not a trained philosopher. We have no evidence that he read such works as the Kantian critiques or one of the versions of Fichte's *Science of Knowledge.* If he did, we have no assurance that he—any more than Goethe, Schiller, or Humboldt—could confidently follow the crystalline snail's path of their abstractions. Rather, he was a typical educated representative of his generation, who attended lectures on logic and ethics designed for the general public, read relevant nonprofessional books and articles, and drew scraps of ideas at second and third hand from his cultural environment. But beyond the affinities that could be expected in those years to link a German of his social class with the central metaphysical and artistic statements of Neoclassicism, we can infer, and in certain cases identify, sources of his methodology and even of his concepts in the philosophy of German idealism and in the aesthetic theories of the late Enlightenment.

In one respect, however—purists might regard it as the only one that matters—Clausewitz differed completely from the transcendental philosophers: as has already been noted in the discussion of his writings before 1806, he accepted the reality of concrete phenomena. It was the naïve reality of politics and war that circumscribed his sphere of action, and that he sought to understand through systematic analysis. During the reform era he even poured invective on some scholars whose metaphysical speculations seemed to him alibis for political passivity. A note of 1808, entitled "In reference to well-meaning German philosophers," begins: "Contempt and derision are merited by presumptuous philosophy, which seeks to raise us high above the activities of the day, so that we can escape their pressures and cease all inner resistance to them." The note continues that detached speculation and passive faith in the future are unjustified: "Generations ... do not exist in order to observe the world; by constantly striving for rational goals they *are* the world. ... The times belong to you; what they will become, they will become through you!" [4] With the defeat of Napoleon this mood abated; but Clausewitz would never reinterpret everyday appearances as abstractions, just as he would not follow Bülow and other rationalist theorists of war in formulating doctrines that ignored or condemned parts of reality. Nor had he much difficulty in identifying reality: it consisted of those physical, moral, and psychological phenomena that were contained in the record of history and that everyday experience presented to us. To make these comprehensible was the task of theory. A prefatory note to a collection of essays he wrote soon after the Wars of Liberation states his mature position:

"In the formal sense the present work contains no ... system; instead of a complete theory it offers only material for one.

"Its scientific character consists in an attempt to investigate the essence of the phenomena of war and to indicate the links between these phenomena and the nature of their component parts. No logical conclusion has been avoided; but whenever the thread became too thin I have preferred to break it off and go back to the relevant phenomena of experience. Just as

---

4. Clausewitz, *Politische Schriften und Briefe,* pp. 65–66.

some plants bear fruit only if they don't shoot up too high, so in the practical arts the leaves and flowers of theory must be pruned and the plant kept close to its proper soil—experience." [5]

Even a decade earlier Clausewitz was in no doubt about the consequences for methodology as well as for the selection of topics to be studied that resulted from the rigorous concern for naïve reality, proper to a "practical art" such as war. Much remained to be done before he was ready to formulate a comprehensive theory; but his notes and brief essays already identified major elements of an integrated system that existed in his mind long before it was openly stated or fully developed.

His additions of 1808 and 1809 to the notebook on *Strategy,* which he had kept since 1804, introduce several of these ideas. [6] An essay on "Abstract Principles of Strategy" declares that "strategic theory can posit few abstract principles, or even none; not, as is commonly thought, because the matter is too difficult, but because one would drown in trivialities. So many petty circumstances occur in war and affect events that anyone who wants to treat them fully and properly in his abstractions would appear as the biggest pedant." On the other hand, to ignore such details would be unrealistic.

Clausewitz illustrated the problem, and expanded it in an unexpected direction, by referring to Jomini's "very recent ... attempt to formulate theory in general statements." Clausewitz did not name the specific work he had in mind; presumably he meant Jomini's *Traité de grande tactique,* four volumes of which had appeared by 1807, and probably also the pamphlet *Résumé des principes généraux de l'art de la guerre,* which Jomini wrote and published in 1807, while stationed in the Silesian town of Glogau, and which he later used as the final chapter of the *Traité des grandes opérations militaires.* [7] This work, which in its repeated revisions was to have an impact on generations of soldiers, turned into general principles of war several practices that Jomini claimed he had identified in the operations of Frederick and Napoleon, and elevated Napoleon above commanders of earlier periods. Clausewitz objected that Jomini's principles would lose the absolute validity claimed for them if it could be shown that earlier generations

5. The note was written between 1816 and 1818 to introduce a collection of studies on strategy, from which *On War* developed. Under the title "Preface of the Author" the note is usually printed in editions of *On War,* although it refers to another and very different kind of work.

6. Clausewitz, *Strategie,* pp. 71–82. The quotation which follows is from p. 71.

7. The printing history of Jomini's *Traité* is confusing because the title of the work changed with the third volume, the fifth volume was published before the third and fourth, and the concluding chapter appeared separately, in several versions and under different titles, before being incorporated into the final volume of the 2nd edition. It is more than likely that by 1808 Clausewitz was familiar with this summary of maxims, since not only was it printed as a pamphlet in Glogau but it also appeared in the spring 1808 issue of a new journal, *Pallas,* which the former Prussian lieutenant Rühle von Lilienstern was editing in Weimar. On the history of Jomini's works, see the recent study by J. Alger, *Antoine-Henri Jomini: A Bibliographical Survey,* West Point, 1975.

had good reason to ignore them. Not that Jomini "stated anything that is wholly wrong, but often he has presented the incidental as the essential." At the same time, Jomini's evaluation of Frederick and Eugene left out of account particulars that determined or influenced their operations. Several years earlier, in his defense of Gustavus Adolphus and Wallenstein against rationalist critics, Clausewitz had referred to political, social, and technological differences between earlier centuries and the Napoleonic age, but declared that the military historian or analyst must also pay attention to the commander's personality and feelings. Now he reverted to the psychological factor and again made it the central point of his criticism. If Frederick remained on the defensive in the second half of the Seven Years' War, it was not only because of Prussia's limited strength but also because the king was reacting to his experiences in earlier campaigns: "The commander's psychology greatly influences his actions. ... A man acts boldly not from reflection but because he happens to be bold. ... A commander who has been affected by numerous unlucky experiences is no longer as daring as one who has always been fortunate." Jomini's schematic evaluation of Napoleon and Frederick was flawed because it passed over their respective situations, and ignored the manner in which two very different individuals responded to conflicting experiences.[8]

Since Clausewitz's views were anything but relativist, he did not appeal to the particularity of men and events in order to dismiss the possibility of comparison. Rather, he held that the analyst must liberate himself from the fashions and constraints of his own age to discover those elements that are comparable, that are present in every war. A note of 1809 compares the psychological features of Caesar and Napoleon, and finds the greatest similarity of the two men to lie in their "common good fortune, and the panic and sense of discouragement they induce in their opponents." The note also points to a specific tactical element to which much of Caesar's success is attributed—field fortifications. Some of the techniques the Romans employed could still be useful in the 19th century, Clausewitz believed; but he added: "By that I don't mean to suggest that we should entrench ourselves as often and in the same manner as the Romans did. That would scarcely suit the wealth of marches and movement, the great complexities, of modern war."[9] In short, the presence or absence of such factors as field entrenchments or Jomini's principle of concentrating a major part of one's available forces at the "decisive point" cannot serve as the basis of theory; they are transitory phenomena, deriving their value from the particular conditions of the age. Theory must assign them their proper place;

8. Clausewitz, *Strategie*, pp. 72–73. In later writings, Jomini did take some account of these factors. Their appearance in his analyses is an interesting indication of the development of his thought, but they always remain of marginal significance.
9. "Caesar," *ibid.*, pp. 77–78.

but they are not the constants or absolutes—such as the psychology of the commander—which a general theory of war must above all seek to identify and understand.

Another essay elaborates on the definitions of strategy and tactics Clausewitz had first formulated in 1804 and in his review-essay of Bülow. Tactics, he repeated, refers to the engagement, while strategy is the doctrine of combining individual engagements to achieve the purpose of the war. Consequently, strategy is concerned with (1) the analysis of tactical successes and their effect on subsequent events; (2) the manner in which separate engagements can be combined for the general purpose; (3) the organization of the forces; (4) their maintenance and supply; and (5) the major man-made obstacles to movement: fortified cities and fortresses. The first two of these categories are the most important since they deal directly with the consequences of battle, which is "the essential raw material of strategy." Matters to be analyzed in the first category include "the effects of minor engagements and of major battles . . . of combat in the plains and in the mountains, the effects of an offensive or of a defensive victory, the effects of action by cavalry or by infantry; [strategy] will be concerned with the consequences that may result from these." The second category relates to the strategist's efforts to discover the most favorable points on which to give battle, and to seek ways of concentrating sufficient forces there: "Strategy will define and select the intermediary purpose—for instance, destruction of the enemy's army, conquest of his provinces, etc.—which connects the tactical success with the overall purpose of the war." [10]

But, Clausewitz continued, "the supreme importance that these matters have in actual war is very poorly served by theory. It is indeed in these two categories that the formulation of a genuine theory may be impossible. Theory can develop its teachings only on the basis of objective elements, and in the objective realm it can apply positive laws only to material phenomena." [11] However, "subjective elements—the courage of the commander, his self-confidence, and the effect of moral qualities—are precisely those that constantly appear among the factors that lead to decisions in war."

The essay does not directly pursue the psychological theme but reverts to the limitation of theory, which Clausewitz summarized in a sequence of precise statements: "*Example* and *formula* are essentially different. An example is a living occurrence; a formula is an abstraction. Where, as in mathematics, nothing is lost by abstraction it fully achieves its purpose.

---

10. "Strategie und Taktik," *ibid.*, pp. 78–80.
11. *Ibid.*, p. 80. That this sentence represents a simplified summary of Kantian teaching is obvious. But it may also be noted that the sentence paraphrases statements in a popular introduction to Kant by J. G. C. Kiesewetter, which appeared at the time that Clausewitz attended Kiesewetter's lectures in Berlin: *Immanuel Kants Critik der Urtheilskraft für Uneingeweihte*, Berlin, 1804, pp. 1–2.

But when abstractions must constantly discard the living phenomena in order to reflect the lifeless form (which, to be sure, is most susceptible to abstraction) the result is a dry skeleton of dull truths and commonplaces, squeezed into doctrine. It really is astonishing that people waste their time on such conceptualizations when we consider that it is exactly the factors that are most important in war and strategy—specifics, pronounced singularities, and local circumstances—that best succeed in evading abstractions and scientific systems." [12]

Not only the validity of the past but also the infinite potential of the future caused Clausewitz to reject theories of war that took Napoleonic practice as their analytic standard. An essay "On the State of Military Theory"—the author clearly profiled in the somber irony of its language—opens with the declaration that contrary to the belief of some writers the art of war had not yet attained perfection: "Any scientific discipline—unless like logic it is complete unto itself—must always be capable of growth, of constant accretion. In any event it is not all that easy to set limits to the human intellect." A glance at the way men fight today would suffice to show that the claim of perfection is "one of those boasts with which every generation occasionally seeks to ornament the events of its own time." Perhaps the writers in question find perfection not in the actual wars but in the books written on them. The books, however, are even worse. [13]

This leads into the essay's second section, headed "The great deeds in the history of warfare cannot be imputed to books." The vast majority of such acts are "the products of talent and of particular principles derived from the study of history." Most works of military theory are poorly organized, illogical, and unrealistic. These flaws are due less to the authors' lack of talent than to their lack of scientific training. Military careers do not reward study; officers who reach high command rarely analyze their art: "They read some history, and in the end do what they can according to their natural abilities." Furthermore, in war more than in most practical arts, it is difficult for the theorist to acquire the necessary practical knowledge. The workshop of war is battle, "but adequate knowledge cannot be gained in a *single* battle, and even in [lengthy] wars the opportunity to observe battles thoroughly is not all that common." In this respect the soldier may be compared to the actor, who has rarely received a literary education, is given little opportunity to learn the theory of drama, and instead tends to be mechanically drilled. [14]

It increases the importance of theory that, at least in some aspects of

12. Clausewitz, *Strategie,* p. 82.
13. "Über den Zustand der Theorie der Kriegskunst." The essay, some 2,400 words in length, was clearly intended for publication, but remained unknown until 1941, when W. Schering included it in his collection of Clausewitz's writings, *Geist und Tat.* The quotations in this paragraph are from pp. 52–53.
14. *Ibid.,* pp. 53–56.

war, practical training is hard to come by. But unlike practical training, which depends largely on demonstration, theoretical instruction must accomplish everything by definition and explication, and most military writers cannot even identify the fundamentals of their subject. "The writers themselves have sensed this weakness of their theoretical instruction, and quickly decided to make it more practical—that is, they have taught by relying on examples. Consequently their works consist mainly of historical examples, critically discussed." [15]

The essay ends with the statement that history is an essential part of theory, and that in the absence of a useful theory, teaching by historical example is the only practical approach: "But none of this prevents us from confessing our belief that the intelligent development of theory would greatly benefit the training of young students, and even more the progress of the art itself." [16]

The programmatic note of these words is apparent. Clausewitz obviously meant to develop theory beyond the level to which it had been brought by writers whose theoretical pretensions he was demolishing by the assiduous application of elementary logic. Despite his clear sense of the difference between knowledge and practice, he did not doubt that pedagogic and operational benefits would flow from scientifically defensible theories. But basically his faith in the practical value of theory was an expression of his general intellectual attitude, which also determined what he thought the character of such a theory ought to be. His letters, notes, and manuscripts show a mind at work that seeks to reach the irreducible elements of phenomena, and to discover the logical and dynamic links that bring them together into comprehensive structures. Whatever the psychological impulses behind this way of thinking, it found intellectual models and tools in the effort of German idealism to achieve syntheses of apparently separate elements.

Very different qualities—narrow scope, disjointed treatment—marked contemporary military theory, in Clausewitz's judgment. But it is noticeable that in his debate with other writers he was not content to call their methods and conclusions into question. Repeatedly he stressed not only the need for theoretical analysis but also its very great difficulties, to the point of speculating whether some aspects of war might not lie entirely beyond its reach. This attitude, too, was familiar to idealist philosophy, which held that rational understanding must be pursued to the utmost, while recognizing that a limit may exist, that some areas of inquiry will not yield to understanding, that reality may also be irrational. The young Clausewitz's rejection of Bülow's geometric interpretation of war may well have been based on the knowledge of the practical soldier, who had seen the

15. *Ibid.*, pp. 59–60.
16. Clausewitz, *Geist und Tat*, p. 60.

most refined strategic combinations overturned by the unpredictable effects of courage and violence; but certainly his pragmatism was supported and strengthened by Kant's destruction of the illusion of rationalism.

Even Clausewitz's earliest writings indicate their author's complete, indeed matter-of-fact, adherence to Kant's criticism of the rationalist view of the world, whose doctrine of cause and effect was justified in the sciences but could not fully apply to feelings and morality. The social world could not be regarded as consisting of deterministic sequences that left no space for freedom of action. This was as true of war as of other areas of social intercourse—even more so, Clausewitz came to believe. "No other human activity," he was to write in *On War*, "is so continuously or universally bound up with chance." [17] The area of immunity to "absolute—so-called mathematical—factors" comprised three zones: activity, which constantly generated new conditions, unforeseen opportunities and dangers; accident, which at least in part could be intellectually mastered if men recognized that execution never fully matched intention; and the psychology of armies and their leaders. All are mentioned in Clausewitz's early writings as factors that have the most far-reaching impact on the course of events, and that must figure prominently in any interpretation of war. All take their place in his discussions and proposals between 1807 and 1812; but for the time being he paid less attention to the theoretical analysis of the disparity between planning and execution, for which he later developed the doctrine of friction. Instead he concentrated on the role of psychology.

Clausewitz's treatment of this question exemplifies his part in the development of military theory in general. He was far from entering unknown territory. Every soldier knew the reality of courage, morale, fear, just as it was taken for granted that some generals were more able than others, and the military literature was filled with reflections on this common knowledge. Maurice de Saxe, in his *Rêveries,* had called the "imbécillité du coeur" the most significant among all aspects of war. Frederick advised his generals to exploit such forces as ambition, hatred, and fanaticism. More recently, Henry Lloyd had written on the effect of fear and other emotions, and on the psychology of the commander. Since the start of the revolutionary wars, the debates between innovators and traditionalists revolved around the attitude of the French troops, the share that enthusiasm and patriotism had in their victories, the conditions in army and society that encouraged or inhibited the unfolding of individual talent. [18] That men could not be expected to fight well unless their reason and emotions were engaged formed a basic tenet of the Prussian reformers. Napoleon's contemporaries were well aware of his belief that "à la guerre, les trois quarts sont des affaires morales," and of the crude methods by which he

17. Book I, ch. 1 (p. 105).
18. I have analyzed some facets of this discussion in *Yorck*, see especially pp. 74–98.

sought to maintain the spirit of his troops—honors, advancement, patriotic appeals, optimistic bulletins. But the treatment that the literature devoted to the role of psychology in war was haphazard, rarely more than an addendum to extended discussions of supply or of elementary tactics and, at least since the 1790's, far more interested in the morale of the soldier than in the talents of the commander. When faced with the genius of a Frederick the Great, military theory had in effect abdicated, acknowledging the king's determination and inventiveness, before proceeding to seek the reasons for his victories by minutely analyzing the arrangement of his marches and the deployment of his lines of battle.

The study of psychological forces, Clausewitz insisted, must move beyond the marginal acknowledgment of their existence to full integration into the theoretical structure. "A genuine need of our time," he wrote in 1807 or 1808, "[is] to return from the tendency to *rationalize* [*vernünfteln*] to the neglected riches of the emotions and of the imagination." [19] Investigating cause and effect of the troops' morale must be complemented by inquiries into the personality and gifts of the commander, and also by the study of political psychology, of the emotions of the people. Military doctrine that ignored the free working of the human mind and heart, that condemned Frederick for fighting a limited war, or Napoleon for transgressing against the principle of economy, belonged to the realm of literature rather than to that of science.

For Clausewitz's purposes, the descriptive, typological psychology of the early 19th century was not very useful. In time he developed a considerable capacity to delineate such attitudes as vanity, indecision, rashness; but his observations and insights were poured into traditional, static categories, similar to those that could be found, for instance, in Kant's pragmatically oriented *Anthropologie,* from which he could liberate himself only by means of the kind of unsystematic speculation he considered unworthy of theory. The result could nevertheless be suggestive in its awareness of the sweep and interaction of motives and behavior. "Why does human nature appear so detestable when the rabble collects in a mob?" he asked in a

---

19. "Historisch-politische Aufzeichnungen," *Politische Schriften und Briefe,* p. 59. At nearly the same time, a British officer expressed very similar thoughts. In the "Prefatory Essay" to his translation of General Latrille's *Reflections on Modern War,* London, 1809, Major H. Le Mesurier criticized the "pedantry observable in most of the German military writers, who strive to conceal their want of ideas by an affectation of science and the introduction of technical phrases. Some of these gentlemen would have us believe that war may be learnt like chess... ." General Latrille, on the contrary, founded his maxims "on an observation of the human heart, which is in its nature immutable" (pp. viii, xi). The text does not bear out this promise, however, being a haphazard collection of brief essays on a variety of topics, from "The Importance and Effects of Military Education," which the author regards as significant, to "The Celibacy of Troops," of which he approves: "If the celibacy of the troops be an evil, it is, notwithstanding, unavoidable. A married soldier cannot be a good soldier" (p. 184). The work, widely read at the time, provides an excellent illustration of the inadequacy of the pragmatic response to late rationalist military theory.

note written soon after his return from France. "Because fear and vanity are absent. When these two frequently ambiguous, frequently miserable emotions are withdrawn from man's psychological storehouse, they leave behind a detestable result—just as gun-metal becomes not harder but softer when soft tin is withdrawn from it." [20] Freud would have agreed with this conclusion, though he might have substituted "sense of reality and self-esteem" for Clausewitz's "fear and vanity."

Whatever scientific character psychology possessed was derived from philosophy, to which psychology owed not only its logic and structure but also its vocabulary, with such metaphysical postulates as force and effect. But Kant had depicted man's ethical existence in universal, impersonal terms. The categorical imperative, it has been said, achieved the triumph of ethical action "at the cost of suppressing every claim of individuality." [21] Like many of his contemporaries, Clausewitz responded strongly to the reassertion of individual values with which the neo-Kantians sought to complement the master's austere architectonic. He was especially drawn to Fichte, who continued to proclaim the absolute quality of duty, but insisted on the significance of the individual, of personal character and unique tendencies, of feelings, and of the irrational in man's effort to fulfill his ethical obligations and achieve intellectual and moral independence.

Clausewitz's ideas about his own growth into a mature personality, harmoniously combining reflection, knowledge, and action, and his views about the reciprocal obligations of individual and state, were very close to the pedagogic and political thoughts that Fichte was developing in his *Patriotic Dialogues* and his *Addresses to the German Nation* during these years. Clausewitz could feel only empathy with Fichte's teaching of the primacy of practical reason, and his call to Germans to lead active rather than contemplative lives in a time of political and cultural crisis. In April 1808 he wrote Marie von Brühl that he had read a work by Fichte, which in some respects he found very good; he did not mention the title, but it was almost certainly the *Addresses to the German Nation,* which had recently been published. However, Clausewitz continued, "the whole is pure abstraction—despite what Stein has said—and thus not very practical. Furthermore he [Fichte] evidently shied *very much* away from making comparisons with history and with present experience." [22] It helps characterize Clause-

20. "Historisch-politische Aufzeichnungen," *Politische Schriften und Briefe*, p. 54.
21. W. Windelband, "Die neuere Philosophie," in *Allgemeine Geschichte der Philosophie*, ed. P. Hinneberg, Leipzig and Berlin, 1913, p. 528.
22. C. v. Clausewitz to Marie v. Brühl, 15 April 1808, *Correspondence*, pp. 154–155. Rothfels, *Carl von Clausewitz*, p. 132, n. 23, argues that Clausewitz could not have referred to the *Addresses* since they had not been published in April 1808. However, as early as 2 January 1808 Fichte writes of his plan of publishing each lecture as a separate pamphlet. Although the Prussian authorities in occupied Berlin refused the official imprimatur to the first lecture, printed copies of the next six lectures were available by 1 February. Fichte to Beyme, 2 January and 1 February 1808, in J. G. Fichte, *Briefwechsel,* ed. H. Schulz, 2 vols., Leipzig, 1925, ii, 500–501.

witz's intellectual environment, and the difficulties he faced in applying philosophic concepts to war, that the man he criticized as unrealistic was more interested in directly affecting society and politics than any German philosopher of the time. But in the words of E. Bergmann, the activism of Fichte's personality and teachings "was joined to an almost total lack of practical sense." [23] Clausewitz's letter continued: "What he said about the purpose of mankind and about religion is very much to my taste; and all in all a course in philosophy with him would give me great pleasure if this were the time for it. He has a manner of arguing that I like very much. When I read this work I sensed my entire tendency toward speculative reasoning being awakened and stimulated again." Eight months later, after reading Fichte's new defense of Machiavelli, Clausewitz was to address the philosopher directly.

In Fichte's writings Clausewitz found a consistent and convincing philosophic elaboration of his own image of the sovereign individual, who recognized his duties to society and state, and strove to fulfill them without regard to personal consequences and also according to his own understanding and ability, independent of authority. But for the analytic tools that he needed to advance his inquiries into the psychology of the individual in his particular area of activity, war, Clausewitz turned back to Kant—or, more accurately, to the aesthetic theories of the German Enlightenment and to their concept of genius. The *Begriff des Genies* was doubly valuable because it not only stood for the gifts and effectiveness of the exceptional man but could also illumine the various abilities and feelings that affected the military behavior of more ordinary individuals. Clausewitz explicitly affirmed the wider application of the term in the chapter "On Military Genius" in *On War*: "But we cannot restrict our discussion to *genius* proper, as a superlative degree of talent, for this concept lacks measurable limits. What we must do is to survey all those gifts of mind and temperament that in combination bear on military activity. These, taken together, constitute *the essence of military genius.* We have said *in combination* since it is precisely the essence of military genius that it does not consist in a single appropriate gift—courage, for example—while other qualities of mind or temperament are wanting or are not suited to war; genius consists in *a harmonious combination of elements*, in which one or the other ability may predominate, but none may be in conflict with the rest." [24] Originality and creativity raised to their highest power were thus used by Clausewitz to identify and interpret universal qualities, just as they represented and helped explain the freedom of will and action that was potentially present in every human being.

In his conception of genius proper, Clausewitz retained the general

23. E. Bergmann, *J. G. Fichte der Erzieher*, Leipzig, 1928, p. 14.
24. Book I, ch. 3 (pp. 129–130).

view of the German Enlightenment. His teacher Kiesewetter chose familiar terminology when he defined genius as the union of imagination and reason, brought to life by the spirit. Clausewitz adopted this definition, adding moral and physical courage to imagination and reason to characterize military genius.[25] What implications did this hold for the theoretical treatment of those areas of activity in which genius was present? Possibly in Kant's *Critique of Judgment,* but certainly in Kiesewetter's lectures on the *Critique,* Clausewitz had learned that "genius is the talent (natural ability) that establishes rules for the arts. Since this talent, as an innate creative ability of the artist, is itself part of nature, we might also express ourselves in this manner: Genius is the innate psychological power (*ingenium*) through which nature establishes rules for the arts."[26]

Clausewitz had employed this idea to destroy the validity of geometric rules of war in his essay on Bülow, which he wrote at the time he attended Kiesewetter's lectures, or shortly afterwards. There could be no conflict between the actions of genius and the maxims of sound theory, he had argued, since genius was their source, or gave them expression. Now, in 1808 or 1809, in the course of yet another polemic against the rationalist school, he repeated the thought: "Genius, dear sirs, never acts against the rules."[27] In *On War* he was to elaborate on this idea, and once again the condemnation of rationalist theory provided the starting point: "Anything that could not be reached by the meager wisdom of such one-sided points of view was held to be beyond scientific control: it lay in the realm of genius, *which rises above all rules.* Pity the soldier who is supposed to crawl among these scraps of rules, not good enough for genius, which genius can ignore, or laugh at. No; what genius does is the best rule, and theory can do no better than show how and why this should be the case. Pity the theory that conflicts with reason!"[28] Theory and its resultant doctrines are thus subordinate to the great creative talent and to the universals he expresses. Quite apart from their positive tasks, theorists must accommodate themselves to this reality by taking care not to inhibit the action of genius in their doctrines, and by affording scope to freedom of action in general.

Genetically associated with the concept of genius were other features of the aesthetic theories of the German Enlightenment, which Clausewitz applied to the study of war. These borrowings did not carry the implication for him that war belonged among the arts. Even his earliest writings outlined a position he was never to abandon: that war, while not a science, should not on that account be considered an art. It was even less true to

25. Kiesewetter, pp. 402–403; Clausewitz, "On Military Genius," *On War* (esp. pp. 130–134).
26. I. Kant, *Kritik der Urteilskraft; Werke,* ed. E. Cassirer, 11 vols., Berlin, 1912–22, vol. v (1914), §46, p. 382; Kiesewetter, p. 396.
27. The manuscript, entitled "Taktische Rhapsodien," was never published and now appears to be lost. Rothfels cites passages in his work *Carl von Clausewitz,* pp. 156, 162.
28. Book II, ch. 2 (pp. 181–182).

think of war as an activity whose major elements were largely immune to analysis, as seemed to be suggested by a few writers such as Berenhorst, who saw modern war as an anarchic, primal force or as an expression of self-willed genius, able to ignore the realities that dominated the actions of lesser mortals. In its combination of scientific and material elements, which were given form and distinction by the creative imagination, war might be regarded, Clausewitz thought, as a practical art, akin perhaps to architecture. But war differed from all activities concerned with inert matter by resting on a mutuality of action and reaction, to which the response of the artist's public to his work was in no sense an equivalent. "War is a clash between major interests," he wrote in *On War,* "which is resolved by bloodshed," and then repeated a thought he set down in his notebook in 1804: "Rather than comparing it to art, we could more accurately compare it to commerce, which is also a conflict of human interests and activities; and it is *still* closer to politics, which in turn may be considered as a kind of commerce on a larger scale." [29]

But although war was not an art, aesthetic theory had something to say about the possibilities of any theory of action. Clausewitz might have turned to the writings of contemporary Romantics, Friedrich Schlegel, for instance, who was proclaiming a cult of autocratic genius; but his need for universals and the firmly systematic, and perhaps also his exposure to Kant in Kiesewetter's lectures, again led him to the Enlightenment. The thought of such writers as Lessing, Moses Mendelssohn, Sulzer, and through them Shaftesbury, is reflected in his writings, particularly their emphasis on the power of feeling and sentiment in aesthetics, but stripped of all moral and teleological implications. The aesthetic systems of the late Enlightenment not only helped him to clarify his ideas about theory, and further demonstrated how emotional factors might be analyzed; from them he also borrowed the standard concepts "means" and "purpose" with which to interpret the forms taken by military conflict and with which to evaluate the actions of the protagonists.

An undated essay "On Art and Theory of Art," in part clearly stimulated by Kiesewetter's lectures but perhaps not written until the reform era, contains such conceptual speculations as: "*Means* very frequently constitute the difference between the arts. Music, poetry, and nearly all the *fine arts* have the same purpose, but they achieve it by different paths. The distinguishing elements are sound in one art-form, colors in another, mental images in the third. Finally it is also the *purpose* that frequently distinguishes one art-form from another"—a point the essay illustrates by referring to the identity of means but difference of purpose in the design and construction of canals and dams on the one hand and fortifications on the other. [30]

29. Book II, ch. 3 (p. 201).
30. "Über Kunst und Kunsttheorie," *Geist und Tat,* p. 158.

A subsequent paragraph takes art as the starting point for an exploration into the precise role of theory: "Thus art is a developed [*ausgebildete*] capacity. If it is to express itself it must have a *purpose*, like every application of existing forces, and to approach this purpose it is necessary to have means. ... To combine purpose and means is to create. Art is the capacity to create; the theory of art teaches this combination to the extent that concepts can do so. Thus we may say: theory is the representation of art by way of concepts. We can easily see that this constitutes the whole of art, with two exceptions: *talent*, which is fundamental to everything; and *practice*. The latter cannot be achieved through theory; consequently it is practice and exercise [*Übung*] that distinguishes practical from theoretical instruction." [31]

That even realistic theory could never match reality remained a fact of crucial significance to Clausewitz, and he never ceased to emphasize the scientific and pedagogic consequences that flowed from the difference. Few other writers, however, seemed concerned with its implications. Their indifference undoubtedly contributed to the confusion in which military theory found itself at the time, and also to misinterpretations of Clausewitz's work later on. Clausewitz's position can be better understood if we follow him in separating the scientific and the pedagogic function of theory. In the former area it was the duty of the theorist to structure reality

31. *Ibid.*, p. 159. Three other fragments on the theory of art existed in the Clausewitz papers: "Über Kunsttheorie überhaupt und die Schwierigkeiten einer theoretischen Bearbeitung der Kriegskunst, vorzüglich der Strategie"; "Über den Begriff des körperlich Schönen"; and "Architektonische Rhapsodien." The latter two were published by Schering in *Geist und Tat*, pp. 166–178, the last also by Rothfels in a version that differs in many details from Schering's text: "Ein kunsttheoretisches Fragment des Generals von Clausewitz," *Deutsche Rundschau*, CLXXIII (December 1917). Rothfels places the writing of "Architektonische Rhapsodien" in the first half of the 1820's, and speculates that the other fragments were written around the same time (p. 375, n. 1). This seems to me unlikely in regard to the essay "On Art and the Theory of Art," in which Clausewitz labors to distinguish clearly between purpose and means, distinctions that he had completely mastered by the time he began to work on *On War* in the early 1820's.

The two published essays generally express the aesthetic values of Neoclassicism, with the significant exception that Clausewitz has no high regard for didactic works of art, apparently because he feels that the overt message places an inappropriate burden on the work's "inner necessity." It is often said, he writes, that the purpose of art lies in expressing an idea; but that is wrong: "Those paintings that express the greatest number of ideas, allegorical works, are the least effective of all." *Geist und Tat*, p. 169. Beauty he regards as the expression of that which is necessary [*das Notwendige*], not that which is willed. In the essay on architecture he shows himself particularly interested in the constant interaction between the aesthetically pleasing and the rationally appropriate, as well as in the allusive effect that certain forms and combinations of forms have on the beholder—an effect that is beyond the reach of rules. In a section headed "Character of Private Residences" he discusses architecture as a carrier of a sense of history; it serves to remind generations of each other, and "to crystallize the echo of their existence into definite form." This function has long been recognized by the architects of public buildings and palaces, and by their patrons: why should it not apply to private residences as well? The historic character of architecture, which expresses permanence, and reality, works against this extension. In the 14th century the Gothic style was appropriate; but it is not valid in the 18th, least of all in private residences. *Deutsche Rundschau*, pp. 378–379. Clausewitz obviously takes the past and the present too seriously to be able to accept romantic recreations of the Middle Ages or the Renaissance. Instead he calls for simplicity, and for designs and decorations that suit the specific purpose of the building.

intellectually without permitting himself and others to believe that the logic, and indeed validity, of his system possessed prescriptive power. Theory could provide only the universal analytic context for men's actions, feelings, and for the fortuitous. To be sure, the study of general theory had itself an important educational function—as had the act of creating theory—in that it helped to develop judgment. But this held true for no more than a few particularly gifted individuals. The general system could directly benefit the great majority of soldiers only in the form of certain deductions drawn from it—distillations of theory that provided points of reference and standards of evaluation in specific areas of action. In Clausewitz's view, these operational aids could only be an outgrowth of the analytic synthesis. For almost everyone else, defining and responding to practical issues was the aim and highest peak of theoretical endeavor. This was the task to which Jomini, for one, addressed himself. It was the confident empiricism of his arguments, sensibly organized according to subject matter, that made his writings so appealing to many soldiers trying to find their way in the new conditions brought about by mass armies and the increased incidence of major battles.

A note Clausewitz wrote during the reform era indicates how essential he felt it was to draw an absolute distinction between cognition and practical concerns. The arts, he declared, "seek an infinite goal; the activities of practical life seek a finite goal; anyone entering the realm of science must have no goal at all. For any goal would be nothing more than a preconceived opinion, something that is entirely alien to science. The innate [*reine*] element of science is *analysis;* the innate element of the arts is the *force of synthesis.*" [32]

He did not rule out maxims, but, as he wrote in his essay "On Art and Theory of Art," they could exist only as extensions of theoretical analysis, obeying the same logic that had created the structure from which they derived. Nor should they descend to the level of prescriptive rules: "A law is first of all a rule for action, i.e., the determination of the use of the available means for the intended purpose.

"From this follows that purpose and means determine the instance to which the rule is to apply. The instance changes as soon as a different purpose or different means are introduced. ...

"It further follows that the properties of purposes and means create the rule, i.e., are the sole *source* of all rules.

"Rules for *individual cases* have no place in theory, since theory cannot exhaust all possible cases (in logic: perceptions). ...

"As we have just seen, rules are not intended for individual cases, and action in the individual case can be determined only by purpose and means.

32. "Historisch-politische Aufzeichnungen," *Politische Schriften und Briefe,* p. 53.

If we wish to combine several cases under a common point of view, it can be done only be resorting to *purposes* and *means*." [33]

The common properties of individual cases spring from the relationship between energy and intention. Their recognition alone makes possible the conceptualization of dynamic universals. Principles of action and maxims are always subordinate to the understanding of the entire field of activity. To the extent that principles of war can be developed, Clausewitz concluded, they too derive from an analysis of means and purpose—not from "decisive points," geometrically expressed bases of operations, "key positions," or any other momentarily accepted way of thinking and writing about war. Genius and free will prevent this analysis from declining into a mechanistic exercise, just as free will and the fortuitous prevent the consequent actions from unfolding in a completely predetermined manner.

To restate Clausewitz's position in the simplest terms: laws which identify the relationships between parts of a whole are necessary and valid in the analytic, cognitive process. They lose much of their validity in the realm of action, since specific actions do not follow laws, or rules derived from them. This distinction is central to Clausewitz's theoretical work. The analysis of means and purpose, however, does permit generalizations of some practical value.

If we return to Clausewitz's earliest writings, we find two elements of exceptionally creative power active in the development of his theories from the outset. The manuscripts and notebook entries of the twenty-three- and twenty-four-year-old already indicate an approach to history that seeks to individualize past epochs, and to personify their societies and states, and— related to this approach in numerous ways—the concept of genius. The ubiquity of these two themes and the authority Clausewitz granted them suggest that they not only performed intellectual functions but also represented emotional concerns. It must be admitted that the immediacy with which his concepts of genius and of individuality and change in the past reflect psychological forces can only be inferred from the character of his writings, his responses to events in letters, and his behavior. Nor can we say much about the nature of the feelings involved. But speculation on the links between his feelings and his ideas is not gratuitous. To forget that Clausewitz's ambition for philosophic understanding coexisted with the intense desire to effect change in the real world would mean overlooking an essential strand in the history of his thought, whose origins can be fully accounted for neither by his studies nor even by the fusion of his individual tendencies with the world view of Neoclassicism.

Very likely it was his recognition in the 1790's that Frederick the Great, the armies of revolutionary France, and Napoleon all acted against

---

33. "Über Kunst und Kunsttheorie," *Geist und Tat,* pp. 161–162.

the doctrinal preconceptions of their times—that military writing was in conflict with their spirit—which stimulated the young officer's earliest theoretical efforts. He was not alone in this recognition, but his response to it was unique. Many soldiers felt the inadequacy of existing theory without turning to history and psychology for the answers. Scharnhorst's realistic, undogmatic instruction confirmed Clausewitz's criticisms of Prussian conditions and guided them into productive channels. But the views on the power of genius that Clausewitz expressed even before 1806 owed little to his teacher; on the contrary, they implied a certain divergence from the direction of Scharnhorst's interests. The empirical soldier who in Hanover, and later in Berlin, worked to raise the effectiveness of military institutions showed less concern with genius, the creation of which lay beyond his competence, than did his pupil. Talented individuals would emerge from collective change, as had happened in the course of the French Revolution. Indeed, the flowering of Clausewitz's gifts could itself be regarded as a product of Scharnhorst's policies. Serious as they were, the practical problems posed by Napoleon's genius could be solved, Scharnhorst insisted, by the reform of Prussia's army, government, and society.

Clausewitz certainly shared this view. But his letters from France and Switzerland, his essays, and other writings indicate that his commitment to reform was intensified by a uniquely personal sense of having been betrayed by the political and ideological shortcomings of Prussia's leadership. His sense of Frederick William's limitations, which were a cause for despair when contrasted with Napoleon's abilities, led him into ever greater independence, until by 1812 he was openly placing his own judgment of the state's interests above that of the king. If Frederick William could not be inspired or threatened to rise above his normal stature, the genius of the heroic collective—the Prussian state and people—must take his place. Clausewitz was driven in this direction by his personal identification with the state. That he came to recognize it as a dead end, and after 1812 ceased to invest extreme expectations in the state, constitutes a crucial advance in his emotional and intellectual maturation. But the evidence leaves no doubt that at the time his identification with the state possessed profound psychological meaning to him, even if it was not to be permanent, and even though we do not know the particular forces in his psychological makeup that lay behind it.

The willingness to invest state and society with the capacity for the exceptional and heroic stands in natural relationship with the insistence that man is not a predictable abstraction. Clausewitz's belief in the potential of the individual went hand in hand with his faith in the potential of the political and military community. Both derived from his sense of the particularity of individuals and societies, which observed their own laws rather than rationalist abstractions. And further, if individuals and collective unities could be understood only in their own terms, they could be understood only in terms of their history—a conclusion Clausewitz reached very early on.

We have already seen how his individualizing view of history, his respect for the uniqueness of the great man and of the conditions of his age, became a main force in his critique of rationalist military theory and in his own theoretical work. Only ideas and feelings could be universal and unchanging, but their human, social, and intellectual expression was in flux. That held true even for mankind's great ethical systems—a thought he found substantiated in Fichte's writings, and more specifically in the work of a personal acquaintance of these years, the theologian Friedrich Schleiermacher.[34] To his fiancée he wrote from Coppet: "Religious feeling in its elemental purity will eternally exist in men's hearts, but no positive religion can last forever. Virtue will eternally exert its beneficial influence on society; but the universality of this global spirit cannot be expressed in the restrictive form of a code of laws, and form itself will shatter sooner or later when the stream of time has washed away or reshaped the surrounding contours."[35]

In the final analysis, it was his sense of the interaction of past and present, permanence and change, that gave his theories their suppleness and dynamic. But to be sure, the concept of human potential was not related solely to Clausewitz's historical understanding; it was also a result of the demand for action, heroism, and sacrifice that he placed on man and the state: you are capable of anything, because you must be.

Feelings and ideas thus formed an unending chain. All nourished a common denominator in Clausewitz's concerns at this time—the element of activity. As he interpreted Prussia's political impotence and her social and institutional decay, only radical change, sacrifice, and war could save the

---

34. Although conclusive evidence appears to be lacking, it is safe to assume that the two men knew each other. Schleiermacher had confirmed Marie v. Brühl, and after his return from Halle to Berlin in 1807 their acquaintance was resumed. During the French occupation, Schleiermacher was active in patriotic societies. He knew most of the leading members of the reform movement; Scharnhorst called him a friend. In 1811 his name appears with Clausewitz's on a list of approximately 70 subscribers to the privately printed "Treatise on the Philistine," sponsored by the literary-patriotic club of which Clausewitz was a member (see below, p. 212).

Schleiermacher's lectures on religion, which were published in Berlin shortly before Clausewitz arrived there as a student, rejected dogmatic, positive religion as a creation of the calculating intelligence, attempting to express faith in words. Every religion, Schleiermacher taught, was a separate expression of religious feeling, which is universal in man—ideas that accord completely with Clausewitz's statements on the historical and ethical character of religion.

It may be added that certain features of Clausewitz's mature theoretical work show similarities with Schleiermacher's writings—for example, the nonprescriptive function of theory, the absolute concept of the subject studied, which is modified in reality, and the concern with the acting individual. See E. Weniger, "Philosophie und Bildung im Denken von Clausewitz," in *Schicksalswege deutscher Vergangenheit*, ed. W. Hubatsch, Düsseldorf, 1950, p. 143.

35. C. v. Clausewitz to Marie v. Brühl, 5 October 1807, *Correspondence*, pp. 142–143.

state—indeed, make it worth saving. His continuing attempts at gaining intellectual mastery of the processes and meaning of conflict led him to sketch out parts of a theoretical system that centered on the conceptualization of the freedom of action. And as he declared in constantly new formulations in his letters to Marie von Brühl, his personal ambitions could be fulfilled only through his own intense activity in a society that valued and shared in them. It is not going too far to suggest that after the disasters of 1806, activity had taken on the quality of a spiritual force in his thoughts. Religion itself, he wrote in the letter from Coppet that I have just cited, "should lead not to reflection but to activity in daily life. It is in this that I base my justification for not turning my eyes away from the earth, from the affairs of the day, but instead pay tribute to them with the feelings of my heart and with the products of my weak intellect." [36] With Goethe, he could have said of himself and of the kind of state and society he wanted to help create in Prussia: "The daily observance of difficult duties is all the revelation that we need." [37]

36. *Ibid.*, p. 142.
37. "Vermächtnis altpersischen Glaubens," *Westöstlicher Divan, Werke,* ii (1952), 105.

III. FICHTE, MACHIAVELLI, PESTALOZZI

In June 1807 an essay by Fichte, "On Machiavelli as Author," appeared in the periodical *Vesta*, which had recently began publication in Königsberg. Clausewitz did not see the issue until some months after he himself had arrived in East Prussia. When he did read the essay in the first days of 1809, the subject and Fichte's treatment of it so stimulated him that he wrote a long, anonymous letter to the author, whom he apostrophized in the final paragraph as the "great philosopher, the priest of this holy flame [of truth], to whom a beautiful privilege had granted access to the innermost—to the spirit of every art and science." [1]

As a student in Berlin, Clausewitz had read Machiavelli's *Discorsi* and *Arte della Guerra*, most likely in one of the several French translations that were readily available. Either during those years or soon after the war he had also read *The Prince* and Frederick the Great's early essay against Machiavelli, which, he commented in 1807, "quite bears the imprint of a young academic who is delighted for the first time to be able to write in the professorial mode." [2]

His brief essays and notes on strategy, written in 1804, contain several references to the *Discorsi*, all touching on issues of morale and psychology. The fourth article in *Strategy*, "On the critical moment for offering battle and for waging war," opens with the following paragraph: "Machiavelli, whose judgment in military matters is very sound, declares that for fresh troops to defeat an army that has just won a victory is more difficult than to defeat it earlier. He supports this with several examples, and quite correctly declares that the moral advantage gained fully makes up for the physical losses." In developing this thought, Clausewitz qualified Machiavelli's statement by pointing to differences in victories and to the relationship of a particular battle to the campaign of which it is only one part: a sequence of successes may expose the victor to disaster. It is in this connection that he made a prediction he was often to repeat: Napoleon

---

1. [Clausewitz], "An den Herrn Verfasser des Aufsatzes über den Machiavelli im ersten Band der Vesta," 11 January 1809, in J. G. Fichte, *Briefwechsel*, ii, 520–526. Cf. Clausewitz to Marie v. Brühl, 12 January 1809, *Correspondence*, pp. 208–209. At the time of writing his study of the young Clausewitz, Rothfels did not know of the letter to Fichte, the text of which goes far to invalidate his assertion (*Carl von Clausewitz*, p. 132) that Clausewitz was critical of "the soaring flight of the idealistic spirit" expressed in Fichte's works.
2. "Historisch-politische Aufzeichnungen," *Politische Schriften und Briefe*, pp. 63–64.

would meet disaster if he invaded Russia. The article ends with a renewed affirmation of Machiavelli's point.[3]

The following section, "On fundamental measures," elaborates Machiavelli's statement that military measures must suit their times and circumstances. Far from being a self-evident triviality, Clausewitz wrote, Machiavelli's argument refers to fundamental decisions, in which this maxim is usually forgotten: "Governments tend to appoint commanders-in-chief without paying attention to time and circumstance; and the commanders-in-chief are no better when they decide on their strategic system. This system is a pure expression of his [sic!] manner of thinking and feeling, hardly ever a course chosen freely and deliberately." As an illustration, he offered Machiavelli's example of Fabius Cunctator, who temporized against the Carthaginians not because this happened to be the appropriate strategy but because he was a procrastinator by nature.[4] The sixth article, "On the spirit of the art of war among the Swiss," discusses the idea that under certain conditions societies lacking military sophistication may produce better fighters than societies whose military institutions are highly formalized. Clausewitz had come across it in the *History of the Swiss Confederation* of his acquaintance Johannes von Müller, who, he wrote, was paraphrasing Machiavelli.[5]

It is not difficult to recognize what impressed the young Clausewitz on his first reading of Machiavelli. Every passage he chose for discussion serves to confirm his growing sense, stimulated by the experience of his generation, that in war, psychological forces cannot be repressed by convention and system. The reference to the superiority of the untutored Swiss over the late-feudal chivalry could hardly be improved on as a gloss on the recent French triumphs over the military institutions and practices of the *ancien régime*. Machiavelli's subject matter—the growth and decline of the Roman Empire and the conflicts of Renaissance Italy—was in itself of great value to Clausewitz, because it helped expand the comparative framework of his ideas. But the *Discorsi* provided more than significant historical interpretations. Of the authors whom we know Clausewitz had read before 1806, only Scharnhorst approached Machiavelli in the acute realism of his analyses of contemporary phenomena and their antecedents. But Machiavelli's range was far broader and—what was more important—he took as his starting point the fundamental force of politics, which he then pursued in its various military, social, and psychological expressions, while Scharnhorst approached political and social factors by way of war, and discussed

3. *Strategie*, pp. 41–42. Cf. below, p. 224. The passage by Machiavelli occurs in *Discorsi*, book II, ch. 22.
4. *Strategie*, pp. 42–43. Clausewitz's references are to *Discorsi*, book III, ch. 9.
5. *Strategie*, pp. 43–44.

them only insofar as they affected war.[6] From the beginning, as might be expected, Clausewitz studied Machiavelli for his political as well as for his military interpretations: a note of 1805 on Napoleonic policy in occupied and satellite territories alludes to accounts in the *Discorsi* on techniques the Romans employed to maintain order in their imperial possessions.[7] By the time Clausewitz returned from internment in France his interest in Machiavelli had come to center on the political.

In the manuscripts and notebooks that date from these years, Clausewitz treats Machiavelli as a theorist and historian many of whose thoughts possess contemporary and even permanent relevance. Their timelessness, to be sure, depended, according to Clausewitz's view of history, on the reader's recognition of the individuality of Machiavelli and of his age and culture. In a passing reference he might appeal to the Renaissance writer as though they belonged to the same generation. "Machiavelli would turn away in disgust from such a policy," he stated in an essay that attacked Russia's abandonment of Prussia in 1807 and the transparent dishonesties the Tsar's government put forward in justification.[8] But when he addressed himself to Machiavelli's theories, he took care to analyze them historically.

An untitled note, two paragraphs long, is devoted to the problem of their interpretation.[9] "No book on earth," it begins, "is more necessary to the politician than Machiavelli's. Those who affect disgust for his principles are a kind of humanistic *petit-maîtres* [*sic!*]. What he says about the princes' policies toward their subjects is certainly largely outdated because political forms have considerably changed since his day. Nevertheless, he gives some remarkable rules, which will remain valid forever. ... But this author is especially instructive in regard to foreign affairs, and all the scorn cast on him (to be sure, often out of confusion, ignorance, affectation) belongs to his teaching on the treatment of the citizenry, insofar as it is justified at all." The modern reader, Clausewitz continues, can understand Machiavelli only if he pays attention to the social and political conditions of Renaissance Italy, and to the characteristics of his style—precisely what Frederick failed to do in his polemic against *The Prince*.[10] "If we have regard for all these conditions, we will not be able to accuse him of more than that, with

---

6. It is characteristic of Clausewitz's wish to understand things as they are and were that he valued the historical writings of Montesquieu, which he had also read by 1805, while showing little interest in the political message and the speculations on first principles and a fundamental *droit naturel* of *De l'Esprit des lois*. On Montesquieu's stylistic influence on Clausewitz see below, pp. 361, 382.

7. "Historisch-politische Aufzeichnungen," *Politische Schriften und Briefe*, p. 4.

8. "Bei Gelegenheit der russischen Manifeste nach dem Tilsiter Frieden," *ibid.*, p. 62.

9. *Ibid.*, pp. 63–64. The exact date of writing is not known, but it was sometime in 1807, more than a year before Clausewitz read Fichte's essay on Machiavelli, which makes some of the same points.

10. See note 2 above.

a certain lack of decency, he called things by their proper name." The note concludes by contrasting Machiavelli's realism with the sentimentality and hypocrisy of his critics, the final sentence abruptly turning into an attack on the policy of neutrality of the continental powers toward France: "The 21st chapter of Machiavelli's *Prince* is the basic code for all diplomacy—and woe to those who fail to keep to it!" [11]

Obviously Clausewitz felt a strong intellectual affinity with a writer who insisted that, above all, the state was an institution created and maintained by the realistic use of force. Both men feared that their contemporaries overestimated the political effectiveness of historical and spiritual traditions and of ethical commitments, which, while placing important obligations on governments, could not be trusted in themselves to provide the power to implement these obligations. Machiavelli's assertion that conscience and other ethical concerns were extraneous to fundamental political realities was to find an echo in Clausewitz's statement in the opening chapter of *On War* that ethics were not part of war itself. Equally, Clausewitz could only be in profound agreement with a view of the political world as something permanently in flux, lacking finality. In the various notes and essays in which he developed historical analyses to cast light on the present, Machiavelli's name does not appear, but his ideas are frequently in evidence. Possibly the most interesting example of these borrowings occurs in a brief, untitled essay that compares the forceful character of the Middle Ages with modern times and traces the political evolution of Europe toward centralized, monarchical government in order to ask why Germany and Italy did not share in the general development: "Every social combination, unless ultimately subjected to the laws of reason, has a tendency toward monarchy." [12] In the case of Germany, the answer lay, he thought, in the warlike and freedom-loving character of her population in the early modern period, whose divisive potential was reinforced by the religious quarrels of the Reformation and the emergence of the European balance of power. The reasons for Italian disunity he sought in the country's degree of urban culture, resulting in the emergence of numerous small states, and in the divisive policies of the Papacy, reinforced by the special interests of the great powers. Both in the way Clausewitz poses his question and in the answers he puts forward he closely follows the interpretation of

---

11. As Rothfels points out in his edition of the *Politische Schriften und Briefe,* p. 64 note, the 21st chapter, "How a Prince Should Act to Acquire Great Reputation," emphatically warns against a policy of neutrality.
12. "Historisch-politische Aufzeichnungen," *ibid.,* p. 54. Subsequent passages show that by "laws of reason" Clausewitz means the rational decisions of a statesman such as Napoleon, which interfere with innate political tendencies. The argument is refined still further in the essay's final sentence (p. 58), which declares that confederations and leagues of states necessarily move toward union into large monarchies, though "this is contrary to the tendency of men and even of individual states, and handicaps the development of humanity."

Italian disunity Machiavelli offers in book I, chapter 12 of the *Discorsi*. Again the essay concludes with a sudden descent to the present: Although Napoleon had destroyed the balance of power, France might not be the permanent beneficiary. The "gigantic oscillations" of the political changes that were now occurring might create a new balance in which the small Italian and German states would coalesce in more natural form, at which time "Germany will become a single monarchy, or at most will separate into two large realms. This will unquestionably come to pass if France should fail to subjugate Germany—a presupposition whose probability, or lack of it, I shall not judge here." [13]

When Clausewitz came to read Fichte's essay on Machiavelli, at a time that he regarded as a significant stage in his intellectual development, he encountered ideas that were familiar and appealing to him. [14] He did not agree with every one of the essay's interpretations. Nor were his views on the nature of the state as expansive as Fichte's, whose universalistic idealism here led to the claim that "every nation wants to disseminate as widely as it possibly can the good points that are peculiar to it. And as far as it can it wants to incorporate [*einverleiben*] the entire human race, in accordance with an urge implanted in men by God, an urge on which rest the community of nations, the friction between them, and their development toward perfection." [15] Clausewitz discounted the missionary element as a motive of aggression other than as a hypocritical or self-deceiving factor. But he believed with Fichte that Machiavelli's politics deserved sympathetic study, and the letter he sent the author immediately after reading the essay shows how profound was the sense of affinity with which he welcomed his intermingling of idealism, recognition of historical individuality, and political realism.

Fichte begins in terms reminiscent of Clausewitz's note on interpreting Machiavelli: the essay's sole purpose is to defend an "honest, sensible, and meritorious man" against the prejudices of the vulgar and ignorant. [16] But that this is only the opening shot in a campaign with very different

13. *Ibid.*, p. 58.
14. The reference to "einen eigenen bedeutenden Abschnitt meines ... intellektuellen Lebens" is contained in a letter to Marie v. Brühl of 7 January 1809; *Correspondence*, p. 202. A letter of 12 January asks his fiancée to read "Fichte's essay on Machiavelli, and reflect on what has happened to us." *Ibid.*, p. 209. On the previous day he had written Fichte the letter that will be discussed below. The following quotations from the essay "On Machiavelli as Author" are based on the edition of Fichte's political writings by O. Braun, *Volk und Staat*, Munich, 1921, pp. 198–222.
15. Fichte, *Volk und Staat*, p. 216. Meinecke described this passage as being "one of the most profound and significant statements of this period. It brings both the reality of the old political struggles for power and the new national impulses into harmony with the cosmopolitan and universalistic ideals of German thought up to this time." *Cosmopolitanism and the National State*, Princeton, 1970, p. 79. I agree with O. Braun, *Volk und Staat*, p. xvii, that Meinecke overestimates the factor of realism in this statement, but the tendency of Fichte's thought to accept the autonomous and aggressive state is unmistakable, although it was temporary.
16. Fichte, *Volk und Staat*, pp. 198–199.

ends is indicated by recurring references to the contemporaneity of Machiavelli's ideas. The first of the essay's main sections deals with the "Intellectual and Moral Character of the Writer Machiavelli." Machiavelli's work rests wholly on reality. He is concerned with how things are, not with the way they ought to be. Consequently he can be understood only in his time: "Under no circumstances can he be judged according to concepts that he does not possess, according to a language that he does not know." Readers sensitive "to the way in which an author's ethical nature is reflected in his work without his willing it, will take leave of him not without love and respect, but also not without regret that this magnificent spirit was not granted a more pleasing environment for his observations." [17]

Subsequent paragraphs seek to make it easier for Fichte's readers to accept Machiavelli as a political guide by explaining some specific characteristics that might appear objectionable to them. He was not a doctrinaire republican. If he was an avowed pagan, so were "the Popes, and cardinals, and all able men of that period." [18] A section that contrasts Machiavelli's freedom from censorship with the restrictions under which even philosophers in Protestant states labor at the beginning of the 19th century introduces a discussion of Machiavelli's major works. Mention of the *Arte della Guerra* leads to a lengthy digression. Although he knows nothing about war, Fichte writes, he thinks it might be conducive to important consequences for the present if someone "with deep knowledge of military matters, who is both objective and influential" were to study this work. Specifically, might not today's faith in gunpowder and artillery be misplaced? "If we consider that changes in the relations between states have always resulted from changes in the conduct of war and in weapons, and if we realize that in today's manner of fighting—particularly that employed by the nation which so far has remained victorious—everything depends on artillery, it becomes apparent that if an army were to appear suddenly, as though stamped out of the ground, which had no artillery at all, this army would at first gain the upper hand, quickly and without encountering opposition, and would enable its ruler to give Europe that form which he thought proper." [19] It was this daring application of speculative reasoning to military affairs—which must have struck the practical men Fichte was hoping to influence as a typical professorial absurdity—that became the immediate occasion for Clausewitz's letter.

The last third of Fichte's essay, for which the preceding discussion laid the groundwork, asks the question "To what extent do Machiavelli's Politics still apply to our Day?" The opening passage firmly links the Renaissance writer and the German philosopher: "The basis of Machiavellian poli-

17. *Ibid.*, pp. 199–203.
18. *Ibid.*, pp. 205–206.
19. *Ibid.*, p. 211.

tics, and we add without hesitation the basis of our politics as well, and of every theory of state that has insight into its own workings, is contained in the following words of Machiavelli: 'Anyone who establishes a republic (or any state) and gives it laws, must presuppose that all men are vicious, and that without exception they will express their inner viciousness as soon as they find it safe to do so.' It is quite unnecessary to debate whether or not people really are constituted as this sentence makes them out to be; what matters is that the state as an institution possessing coercive powers necessarily assumes that they are, and this assumption alone forms the basis for the state's existence." [20] If in the 19th century domestic affairs are no longer characterized by the war of all against all, this continues to hold true for the relations between states. Fichte thus makes the same point that occurs in Clausewitz's notebook: order and the rule of law now characterize relations between rulers and subjects, but Machiavelli's depiction of inter-state relations retains validity.[21] From the fact of international anarchy both Fichte and Clausewitz draw the same conclusion—that states must pursue wary, energetic policies, and not shirk risks—even expressing themselves in identical turns of phrase: "A courageous defense can make good every loss, and if you fall, at least you fall with honor." [22]

The essay ends with a series of statements from which Machiavelli almost disappears: Societies must prepare and train for war; rulers must distinguish between private morality and the higher ethical requirement to maintain the state; enlightened, humane minds must rid themselves of faith in the golden mean and recognize the reality of force.

This was rather different from the detached world view of well-meaning German philosophers, and in another sense also from Kant's writings on political theory—his *Perpetual Peace,* for instance, which suggested that once an international league of republican states dominated the world, war would disappear. Fichte's analysis of state power through the medium of Machiavelli's works extended the support of idealistic philosophy at the very time that Clausewitz was calling on Prussia to take heroic risks, and was wrestling with the difficulties of applying philosophic methodology to the analysis of war. Given the intellectual and political conditions of his life

---

20. Fichte, *Volk und Staat,* p. 214.

21. *Ibid.,* pp. 215–216. In applying Machiavelli's arguments primarily to foreign affairs, Fichte and Clausewitz reflect a general tendency of the time. See the interesting article by T. Schieder, "Niccolò Machiavelli. Epilog zu einem Jubiläumsjahr," *Historische Zeitschrift,* CCX, No. 2 (April 1970), esp. 273–275.

22. Fichte, *Volk und Staat,* p. 219. The following short paragraph may be the source for Clausewitz's grim joke in *On War,* book VI, ch. 5 (p. 532), that aggressors love peace since they prefer to make bloodless conquests. It is the people who defend themselves that start wars. Aggressors, Fichte writes, "love peace indeed—that is, their own—and they really do not wish to encounter resistance while they wage war against everyone, and continue and complete it." Cf. the theoretical argument in *On War,* book VI, ch. 7 (p. 543) that it is the attacked party, by using force to defend itself, that "first commits an act that really fits the concept of war."

at the beginning of 1809, it was not surprising that reading the essay tore him out of his customary reserve, and led him to address its author.

Clausewitz's letter to Fichte began: "To the gentleman who wrote the essay on Machiavelli in the first volume of *Vesta.* I have read this essay, and while I am not the man of profound insights into the art of war, and even less of influence, whom you call on to study Machiavelli's book on the art of war, I believe I am without prejudice, the more so since I have seen the traditional opinions and forms among which I grew up come apart like rotten timber, and collapse in the swift stream of events." [23] He is writing him because today more than ever all citizens should acquire a sound general view of what war is all about, and men on the path to this understanding should communicate with one another. In response to Fichte's observations on artillery, Clausewitz agrees that this arm, like all others, "certainly has been badly employed here and there, mainly by the Prussian army in 1806, less so by the French, who do not have much artillery judged by present standards." But since Machiavelli's time the effect of artillery has considerably increased; one can no longer do without it, and experience will eventually indicate the most appropriate proportion of guns to troops. So much for Fichte's argument. In 1813, when the essay was reprinted, Fichte did not delete the two pages that suggested a modern army might dispense with cannon altogether, but he did correct his statement that in the French service "everything depends on artillery."

Clausewitz continued that he had often found sound and original opinions on military matters in the *Discorsi,* and instances the comment on Fabius Cunctator, which he had discussed in his *Strategy* in 1804. "But so far as Machiavelli's book on the art of war itself is concerned, I recall missing the free, independent judgment that so strongly distinguishes his political writings. The art of war of the ancients attracted him too much, not only its spirit, but also in all of its forms. The Middle Ages could easily develop an exaggerated regard for the Greek and Roman art of war. At that time war had fallen into profound decline and become a kind of craft, as is best shown by the hired armies and generals of the period." Improvement, today as always, should never be sought by returning to an earlier pattern, but by restoring the true spirit of war, which will create its own appropriate forms and techniques. [24]

What is this spirit, and how can it be developed? Clausewitz answers with a thumbnail sketch of his concept of the Prussian reform program: "This true spirit of war seems to me to consist in mobilizing the energies of every soldier to the greatest possible extent, and in infusing him with bellicose feelings, so that the fire of war spreads to every component of the army instead of leaving numerous dead coals in the mass. To the extent

23. Fichte, *Briefwechsel*, ii, 520–521. The quotation which follows is from p. 521.
24. *Ibid.*, pp. 522–523. The quotation which follows is from p. 523.

that this depends on the art of war, it is achieved by the manner in which the individual is treated, but even more by the manner in which he is employed. The modern art of war, far from using men like simple machines, should vitalize individual energies so far as the nature of its weapons permit—which, to be sure, establishes a limit, for an essential condition of large forces is to have the kind of organization that permits them to be led by a rational will without a superfluity of friction.

"But we should not go further and, as was the tendency particularly in the 18th century, turn the whole into an artificial machine, in which psychology is subordinated to mechanical forces. ... That by stimulating individual energies infinitely more is gained than by artificial forms is shown in the history of nearly all civil wars, particularly the Swiss war for independence and the wars of the French Revolution." Fortunately modern weapons favor this approach: "especially in the most beautiful of wars, in the war that a people wages on its homeground for liberty and independence," large numbers of individual fighters equipped with modern firearms can be employed to great advantage.[25] "The two wellsprings, which we must clear again so that the warlike spirit will return to us and make us feared among our neighbors ... [are] civil conditions, which are a matter of political arrangements and of education; [and] the appropriate use of military potential, for which the art of war is responsible." Military reform, Clausewitz concludes, will create an army that is vital rather than mechanical, in which the individual counts: *"Then preconceived views on weapons and on the basic forms* [of war] *will disappear by themselves;* for as we know, the natural enemy of mannerism in every art is the *spirit."* [26]

Fichte and Clausewitz thus met in their common view of Machiavelli as a witness to political truths that they thought were inadequately understood in Germany. They believed that Machiavelli's writings could help a blind or corrupted generation recognize the primacy of force, including military force, in political life. Napoleon's demonstration of the superiority that power enjoyed over inadequately armed ideals they opposed with Machiavelli's timeless statement that this was the nature of politics—a lesson that had the not unimportant consequence of reducing the emperor to everyday proportions. Napoleon was unique only to the extent that he eagerly resorted to means that were available to all, and that honest men should not hesitate to employ in defense of their interests. Neither Fichte nor Clausewitz, following an Enlightenment tradition that went back at least to Rousseau and Herder, found it difficult to link Machiavelli's teachings to the defense of liberty.[27] But they reached this broad area of agreement by

25. *Ibid.,* pp. 523–524.
26. *Ibid.,* pp. 524–525.
27. Cf. A. Elkan, "Die Entdeckung Machiavellis in Deutschland zu Beginn des 19. Jahrhunderts," *Historische Zeitschrift,* CXIX, No. 3 (1919), 428–430.

different paths. Fichte's turning to Machiavelli was not the inconsistent rejection of earlier ideas, as it has sometimes been termed, but it did represent an extreme development of one strain of his thought, and it was not lasting. From an essentially negative view of the state in the early 1790's, Fichte had moved to an appreciation of the state's role in uniting individuals into an organic whole, and in enabling them singly and as a nation to create the highest possible cultural values. This expanded concept of politics went together with a new sense of the state's individuality and with growing emphasis on the constraints that the state must exert in order to carry out its tasks. In the essay on Machiavelli, Fichte reached the peak of his recognition of power politics. Under the crushing experience of the Prussian catastrophe, Meinecke writes, he rose "to a radicalism that sought the most effective weapons and found them in Machiavelli." [28] But the prominence he gave to the absolute struggle of state against state soon waned, and earlier ethical considerations returned to dominance, until in his last lectures on the theory of the state in 1813 he again taught that while the state must pursue forceful policies, its ultimate task was to secure the absolute moral and intellectual independence of every citizen. As society gradually progressed toward freedom, the state would become unnecessary.

Despite its unique confluence of ethical and political motives, Fichte's interpretation of the state accorded with general views held by many whose thought was rooted in the political theories of the late Enlightenment in Germany, or continued to be influenced by them. Kant had taught that the state was the ultimate goal of history, insofar as the state recognized the progressive realization of liberty as its highest mission. The young Wilhelm von Humboldt regarded the state as a mechanism that enabled the individual to develop and perfect himself; even in later years he gave the cultural nation precedence over its political institutions, which were merely one of its visible expressions—now, to be sure, granted vastly expanded powers—safeguarding and fostering the intellectual and moral development of its individual members.

Clausewitz, too, shared in this common outlook; but he combined it with very different elements. If his ideas on the state were suffused with ethical motives, they lacked the universalistic grandeur that had found in the state's cultural mission the driving force of political action at home and abroad. Rather they flowed in narrower channels, which circumscribed the state's obligations as making it possible for the individual to progress toward intellectual and psychological harmony, and maintaining the community as a secure, respected body in a dangerous world. He did not consider the state as an agent in the service of an ultimate purposeful scheme

28. *Cosmopolitanism and the National State*, p. 78.

for humanity, dominated by universal historical and ethical principles; he neither imputed spiritual qualities to the state nor believed that the state would eventually dissolve. He was thus far closer to Machiavelli's incipient *ragione di stato* than was Fichte, since what really concerned him were the means by which states survived.

It does not contradict his emphasis on the power bases of political existence that at this time of his life he still attached important symbolic qualities to the Prussian monarchy. The demands Clausewitz placed on his own state were psychological in nature, rather than expressions of an ethical system, and they reached their peak in those years when his personal fate and that of the state were intertwined in defeat and weakness. Nevertheless, in the dissimilar history of Fichte's and Clausewitz's political thought a parallel can be drawn between the radicalism Fichte achieved in his essay on Machiavelli and the younger man's intensely combative, personal radicalism of the same period, both stimulated by the common experience of Prussia's collapse. For neither man did this remain the final word. In his *Staatslehre* of 1813 and in the fragments and reflections he jotted down in the last months of his life, Fichte progressed to a vision of an ultimate cosmopolitanism, in which man graduated from the political school of the state to acquire citizenship in the realm of freedom. Clausewitz, by contrast, moved more deeply into the realistic exploration of contemporary phenomena of political power, which after 1815 achieved a cosmopolitanism of its own—that of professional detachment, now unclouded by his former psychological needs.

As we know, Clausewitz's interest in Fichte antedates the essay on Machiavelli. Fichte's writings on the individual and the nation, his effort—in Eugene Anderson's phrase—to transport idealism from the realm of theory to the world of social reality, had attracted Clausewitz's attention soon after his return to Prussia, and further stimulated him to exploit the philosophic method in his own writings.[29] Yet another bond is suggested by their common concern with education, though it was pure coincidence—rendered more likely by the intellectual fashions of the society in which they lived—that both men decided at the same time to write about Pestalozzi's educational innovations.

For both Fichte and Clausewitz, education was closely related to politics. In 1801 Schiller, responding to Napoleon's triumph at Lunéville, could still claim that political impotence would not prevent the Germans from leading the eternal effort of educating humanity. Fichte, on the contrary, and with him Clausewitz, held that only the state, with its protec-

---

29. E. Anderson, "Die Wirkung der Reden Fichtes," *Forschungen zur brandenburgischen und preussischen Geschichte,* XLVIII (1936), 398.

tive, regulative, and supportive power, made education possible—a thesis that Fichte extended into the very justification of the state itself. The consequence of this point of view was to ascribe two tasks to education: individual improvement, and service to the guarantors of cultural development—society and the state. As Germans began to bring their ideas of the state into closer accord with their ideas about society and culture, a further step was taken. The concept, long familiar to the Prussian bureaucracy, that education was the responsibility of the state, was now complemented by the conviction that it was through the schools and universities that society would develop into that new form of the state, the nation.

This task could never be achieved by the old educational system, which was designed to prepare different segments of society for their particular role in life. The leaders of educational reform in Prussia—Fichte, Humboldt, Schleiermacher, Nicolovius, Süvern, Schulze—were united in their belief that education should aim at the full development of man's positive dispositions and capacities, whatever his class. Education, Fichte thought, meant giving man the opportunity to make himself the master and ruler of his energies; and Schleiermacher wrote: "It is the task of education to individualize [man]. Not until the end of her efforts does she establish this individuality, and that achievement is her greatest triumph." [30] But the reformers did not wish to isolate educated man. Isolation would deprive the state of his talents, while his individuality could develop only through exposure to a multitude of conditions, in interaction with others. Education, Schleiermacher said, must enable man to achieve the greatest degree of autonomy consistent with life in society and state, and give him "the motive and ability to improve all incomplete aspects of public life." [31]

It was hardly possible to establish the individuality of German culture, the existence of national character, and to define the responsibilities this imposed on the state, without wishing for significant improvement in the education of the lower classes. That, indeed, was implied in the humanistic critique of 18th-century pedagogic practices, though some men found it possible to evade the logic. In Fichte's eyes the greatest flaw of education under the *ancien régime* was that in general it had been limited to elites. A degree of universal schooling, the exact measure and substance of which could be debated, was essential to bring about a culturally and politically united society, in which even the least privileged member shared certain values with the most advanced, and in which men were no longer the powerless or indifferent subjects of governmental bureaucracy. The point was stated clearly in a passage of Stein's proclamation of 21 October 1808 on the achievements and future of the reform program, which had been

---

30. F. Schleiermacher, "Zur Pädagogik. 1813," *Erziehungslehre*, ed. C. Platz, Berlin, 1849, p. 593.
31. F. Schleiermacher, "Die Vorlesungen aus dem Jahre 1826," *ibid.*, p. 43.

drafted by Süvern: "Educating our youth into a vigorous race, in which the sublime purposes of the state are maintained and developed further, is already an object of serious attention and action on the part of the relevant agencies of government, and will continue to be so in the future. At last Prussia's youth will benefit from national education [*Nationalbildung*], which has long been in preparation, and which now rests on a new and secure basis." [32]

The methods by which this new race was to be created could be adapted, many pedagogues thought, from Pestalozzi's educational practices, which for some time had been the subject of discussion in Germany. Fichte had read Pestalozzi's treatise on elementary education *Lienhard und Gertrud* when he was in his twenties; later he had visited his boarding school outside Zürich and had written a commentary on Pestalozzi's system. In the second of his *Patriotic Dialogues,* written soon after the battle of Jena, he declared that Pestalozzi's ideas, far from being restricted to the poor and oppressed, should be applied to everyone's primary education. In his *Addresses to the German Nation* this proposition was repeated and developed. [33]

Fichte's advocacy was not uncritical. He expatiated at length on what he held to be Pestalozzi's inconsistencies, theoretical and methodological errors, and on the limitations that local Swiss conditions and lack of funds imposed on his work. He went far beyond Pestalozzi in valuing the boarding school as the most desirable arena for reformed education. Pestalozzi believed that the mother was the child's best teacher, and the loving family its best school; children who for whatever reason were compelled to attend a boarding school should be instructed under conditions that re-created to the fullest possible extent the affection and security afforded by family life. The *Addresses* declared, on the contrary, that at least during the first generation of educational reform, all children should be taken from their families and taught in coeducational school communities, isolated from the influences of an as yet unregenerate society. But Fichte was in complete accord with Pestalozzi on the tasks of education, as well as on the principles of concrete observation, demonstration, and active interchange between student and instructor that underlay the new method. Instruction should begin by helping the child understand its immediate environment, not by drilling it in abstractions. Once the child had gained some understanding

32. "Proklamation an sämtliche Bewohner des preussischen Staates," *Stein: Briefe und amtliche Schriften,* ii, part 2, ed. P. Thielen, Stuttgart, 1960, p. 905.
33. J. G. Fichte, 9th, 10th, and 11th lectures, *Reden an die deutsche Nation,* Munich, 1922, pp. 182–243. It exemplifies the affinities between some of Fichte's ideas and the ideas of the reformers that in the period of the second *Patriotic Dialogue* and the *Addresses* Gneisenau suggested the introduction of Pestalozzi's method to the regimental schools for children of the rank and file. See his undated memorandum of 1807 or possibly earlier in *Die Reorganisation des Preussischen Staates unter Stein und Hardenberg.* Part II, *Das Preussische Heer vom Tilsiter Frieden bis zur Befreiung; 1807–1814.* Ed. R. Vaupel. *Publikationen aus den Preussischen Staatsarchiven,* vol. xciv, Leipzig, 1938, pp. 186–187.

of a particular object, it would be stimulated to develop its own abstractions and associations. The child's inherent capacities should be released and guided at whatever rate was appropriate to it, with physical and moral abilities progressing in unison, instead of holding the child to a fixed program designed to meet arbitrary external standards. The teacher should develop the child's natural desire for understanding and clarity, and its equally innate love for its fellow human beings and for rational society. Moral education, not professional training, was what mattered. In their mixture of rejection, agreement, and adaptation, Fichte's proposals constituted a bold attempt to turn Pestalozzi's educational work among the Swiss poor to the use of creating a new national society.

Although Pestalozzi's system—or rather the "natural," undogmatic approach associated with his name—had become fashionable in Prussia, it also aroused opposition. If the program at Yverdun was famous, its effectiveness remained uncertain; the language instruction of the very young seemed to consist of the very memorizing that Pestalozzi condemned; for a group motivated by love, the teaching staff proved remarkably prone to rivalries and disputes. Much criticism was directed against Pestalozzi's unwillingness to make distinctions between children of different social backgrounds. Even such a sympathetic educator as Karl von Raumer, who, inspired by Fichte, became a teacher at Yverdun, left the school when Pestalozzi refused to separate the children of indigent families in a poorhouse.[34] It was the democratic tendency of educational reform, and its confidence in the ability of educators to effect basic changes in man and society, that Heinrich von Kleist, the incomparable dramatist of patriotism, duty, and sacrifice, attacked in an epigram a few months after Fichte delivered the *Addresses:*

P[estalozzi] and F[ichte]
Assume you were right, and could educate youth to become men like yourselves: what, dear friends, would that amount to?[35]

Kleist renewed the attack in an article published in five installments in his newspaper, the *Berliner Abendblätter,* at about the time Clausewitz returned to Berlin and the two men came to know each other. "The child isn't wax, which the hands of man can mold into any desired shape," Kleist's article concluded. "It is alive, it is free, it possesses an independent and singular capacity for development, and carries the model for all internal shaping within itself." Whether children are educated under one system or another is incidental; some will prosper, others will spoil, and "everything on earth will stay the way it is."[36]

34. *Karl von Raumers Leben von ihm selbst erzählt,* Stuttgart, 1866, pp. 106, 125, n. 1. R. Steig, *Heinrich von Kleists Berliner Kämpfe,* Berlin and Stuttgart, 1901, pp. 326–328.
35. H. v. Kleist, "Epigramme," *Phöbus,* I, No. 6 (June 1808), 46.
36. C. J. Levanus [i.e., H. v. Kleist], "Allerneuester Erziehungsplan," *Berliner Abendblätter,* Nos.

Clausewitz did not think it important or even desirable to maintain caste differences in the classroom at the very time that their significance was being reduced in the bureaucracy and the army. Nor did he share the conservatives' distaste for educators as social and political reformers. He himself would scarcely have accepted an assignment at the new *Kriegs-schule* if he had not regarded teaching as an opportunity to influence men's thinking and their future actions. He had long ago freed himself from the limitations of his own early education, which both at Burg and in the regimental school at Neuruppin had been defined by the social standing of the pupils and by their social and professional prospects. Latin schools, academies of nobles, and cadet institutions did not unify society but prolonged its fragmentation, which, he thought, might be psychologically damaging to the individual and sapped the political energies of the nation. The military changes that Clausewitz was helping to bring about were related in many ways to the changes that were being considered or were already taking place in the educational activities of the state: all aimed at a greater degree of independence and self-reliance of the individual, and at the same time sought to create a firmer psychological link between the individual soldier and citizen and those in authority over him.[37] To be sure, spiritual and practical contradictions existed between increasing the autonomy of the individual and strengthening the bond between citizen and state; but they could be mitigated by emphasizing the role of the state in advancing the development of man.

Nor was Clausewitz alone among military reformers in believing that the new schools ought to disseminate and strengthen the concept of the cultural, and thus of the political, nation. That the particularist Prussian monarchy should more adequately reflect the values and interests of the greater cultural nation was an article of faith of Scharnhorst, Boyen, Gneisenau, and of most if not all of their closer associates. In the minds of these men, changing the character of the state and increasing its power were mutually dependent parts of the same process. But Clausewitz was unique in the group in the way in which pronounced pedagogic concerns informed the entire range of his activities. As all reformers did, he tried to educate his environment in the values of the new concepts and institutions. But he also was a teacher in the narrower sense of the term, educating his students at the War College and the princes to whom he lectured privately in

25–27, 35–36 (29–31 October, 9–10 November 1810). On the article and on Kleist's political views at the time, see Steig, pp. 330–336; H. Meyer-Benfey, "Kleists politische Anschauungen," *Schriften der Kleist-Gesellschaft*, vols. xiii–xiv, Berlin, 1932, especially pp. 28–34; and H. Sembdner, *Die Berliner Abendblätter Heinrich von Kleists,* vol. xix of the *Schriften der Kleist-Gesellschaft*, Berlin, 1939, p. 66.
37. It is possible to recognize these affinities without accepting the uncritical, idealizing interpretations of the connection between pedagogy and politics in the reform era that were prominent in German historiography before 1945. A realistic, balanced analysis of the matter is developed by K. E. Jeismann in " 'Nationalerziehung'," *Geschichte in Wissenschaft und Unterricht*, vol. xiv, no. 4 (1968), and the same author's collection of texts *Staat und Erziehung in der preussischen Reform 1807–1819*, Göttingen, 1969.

the realities of modern war. At the same time he pursued his own education, both in his historical and theoretical writings, and by continuing his earlier self-conscious efforts to achieve greater intellectual and emotional independence.

We possess two manuscripts in which Clausewitz addresses himself to the theory of education and to its application in specific circumstances: a long memorandum to the minister of war on the curriculum of the War College in Berlin, submitted in 1819, after he had been appointed director of the college; and an essay on Pestalozzi, written soon after he and Prince August had visited Yverdun in August 1807.[38] Unfortunately the second part of this essay is lost; it ends after some one thousand words, in the middle of a sentence. But the fragment makes plain Clausewitz's approval of Pestalozzi's ideas, an approval complemented by a letter dating from the same period which comments with admiration on Pestalozzi's personal simplicity, frankness, and moral courage.[39]

Since he lacks pedagogic expertise, Clausewitz began his essay, he cannot offer definitive judgments on Pestalozzi's work, only hypotheses. Pestalozzi proceeds on the principle that the pupil's moral qualities should be fostered before the acquisition of knowledge becomes the main purpose of education. Both his method of teaching and the organization of his school are designed primarily with the former in mind. For that reason alone, the frequently voiced criticism that Pestalozzi's method consists essentially of mechanical, mindless drill is erroneous, though Pestalozzi does not ignore academic exercises. The pupil's ability to think is promoted largely through the study of mathematics. Some observations on the pedagogic uses of this discipline, which develops inventiveness, and the capacity for logical and abstract reasoning, brought Clausewitz to his main point: "The method has been accused of neglecting or even of stifling the imagination. That is unfair to the method, but the criticism does apply to the school. I don't, in fact, know of any system of education that is particularly effective in stimulating the imagination. I suspect that imagination, especially the more advanced kind—aesthetic imagination—develops best on its own, provided the environment is not hostile. But, to be sure, it must be given scope; and the school sins against this requirement by tying down the children to too full a schedule." [40] Children who attend eleven classes a day will not have time for the free play of their imagination, and it is for just that reason that Pestalozzi keeps them busy: "The vague roaming of the spirit appears to him the seedbed of many moral evils. No doubt he is

38. "Pestalozzi," Schwartz, *Leben des Generals Clausewitz,* i, 110–113. The memorandum of 21 March 1819 is discussed on pp. 272–279 below.
39. Clausewitz to Marie v. Brühl, 16 August 1807, *Correspondence,* p. 133.
40. "Pestalozzi," Schwartz, *Leben des Generals Clausewitz,* i, 111. The quotation which follows is from p. 112.

right; who can deny that in young years the intercourse of heart and phantasy constitutes a grave threat to man's psychological makeup [*den ganzen inneren Menschen*], nor that the beautiful fruit of imagination are not to be picked without risk. The only antidote is the careful guidance of emotions—and that can hardly be expected of a large educational institution."

Clausewitz conceded that a child sent to Yverdun from his "eighth to the tenth year" would not lose the potential of imagination; the child would acquire mental discipline and training without, Clausewitz thought, suffering permanent damage. "But nothing prevents us from transferring the essence of this method to education in the home" by having tutors or teachers trained in Pestalozzi's method instruct the child without separating child from parent.

A more detailed analysis of Pestalozzi's teaching method was begun in the final, incomplete paragraph of the fragment: Pestalozzi seeks to have his students advance by the shortest possible steps, avoiding large leaps, so as to minimize the child's efforts of attention and conceptualization, and because otherwise mediocre students would never completely master their subject. Clausewitz was in full accord with this "very significant principle." Far from believing that it makes things too easy for the student, he thought it absurd to argue that children must become accustomed to difficulties: "To acquire an intellectual advantage at great cost, if it can be attained more cheaply, is unnatural, and human intelligence would always rebel against such an insane policy." [41]

The essay, which breaks off at this point, thus responds to Pestalozzi's work in a manner very different from that of Fichte's *Addresses.* Clausewitz had the individual in mind, not society. The child, he believed, would benefit less from a boarding-school education than from education in the home, which alone could combine Pestalozzi's superior teaching techniques with the parents' "careful guidance" of the child's developing fantasy-life. Once again Clausewitz's appreciation of reality enabled him to recognize the assumptions on which theoretical speculations were based, and to sense their implications for real human beings. It was not difficult for him to penetrate and reject the arguments of such an uncompromising pedagogic reformer as Fichte, who for the sake of ideology did not hesitate to accept the destruction of the family. We may guess that here, as elsewhere, Clausewitz's ability to abstract without losing sight of mundane reality was nourished by fortunate experiences in his own childhood; at least, it seems unlikely that a man who had not himself received in childhood affectionate support from his parents would stress the value of the family in education and human development. To elevate the family above the school obviously was not meant as a criticism of Pestalozzi, who offered a refuge to children

41. *Ibid.*, p. 113.

who otherwise might have been neglected or abandoned; but Clausewitz did condemn the exaggerated institutionalization and the discrepancy between ideas and policy that he had observed at Yverdun. His comments reflect a concern common to all reformers—how to put ideas into practice without losing too much of their substance—but here they were made on pedagogic not ideological grounds, and it may be noted that soon after Clausewitz's visit Pestalozzi raised many of the same objections himself.[42]

Clausewitz applauded Pestalozzi's policy of developing the child's innate potential without paying overly great attention to external standards, and welcomed the efforts of the staff at Yverdun to teach by example, demonstration, and the free interaction between adult and child. These procedures, so different from passive learning by rote, may have impressed him, as they impressed Fichte, as a specific means by which the general process of human perfectibility could be advanced. Indeed, the essay, though stimulated by his visit to Yverdun, is not so much a critique of conditions there as a discussion of some basic problems of education.

The careful accretion of knowledge, "by short steps," which Clausewitz praised in Pestalozzi's method, is an early characteristic of his own theoretical writings, and we will soon encounter it in his teaching as well. His distaste for a multiplicity of courses, which, he fears, results in shallow knowledge and prevents the student from exploring his own thoughts, recurs in his criticism of the curriculum of the War College twelve years later. Underlying the discussion of Yverdun is Clausewitz's concern that closely organized training, the rigid implementation of doctrine, stifles the free, creative expression of feelings and ideas—a concern that by this time, as we know, occupied a central place in his thinking about the possibilities and limitations of a theory of war.

Until his thirty-first year Clausewitz had studied military theory and practice, and begun to write on it, but had never taught it—if we exclude the possibility that during the 1790's he had helped instruct the ensigns in his regiment in elementary mathematics and surveying. This changed when he and his friend and former fellow-student at Scharnhorst's Institute, Karl von Tiedemann, were appointed to the faculty of the new War College. Tiedemann offered the course on general tactics, Clausewitz the course on the so-called "little war," on general-staff duties, gunnery, field entrenchments, and the construction of bridges. He met his class four times a week from October 1810 to June 1811, for a total of 156 hours; field trips, written assignments, and weapon demonstrations supplemented the lectures. In October 1811 he began to repeat the course for the new first-year students,

42. In his extremely self-critical New Year's message of 1 January 1808, printed in *Heinrich Pestalozzis Lebendiges Werk*, ed. A. Haller, Basel, 1946, iv, 315–322.

but ended it prematurely in the spring of 1812, when he quit the Prussian service.[43]

Clausewitz's manuscripts on the general staff, entrenchments, and bridge construction seem not to have survived, with the exception of a lecture on foraging parties, the organization of which was at the time regarded as an elementary staff duty.[44] His lectures on the little war and on gunnery have recently been published.[45] The brief manuscript on gunnery, comprising possibly three lectures, offers an introductory survey for infantry and cavalry officers, derived from Scharnhorst's *Handbuch der Artillerie* and a few other standard works. The lectures with their detailed diagrams and tables suggest that Clausewitz had acquired a more than superficial acquaintance with the subject, but his treatment does not go beyond the elementary level. His lectures on the little war, by contrast, offer an advanced interpretation based on comprehensive knowledge.

The courses of Tiedemann and Clausewitz, which the two men were careful to coordinate, introduced the officers attending the War College to the significant innovations in the employment of troops that were occurring in the army: a more flexible command-system, the combined use of different branches of the service, and—most important—a new integrated form of infantry fighting, which brought together skirmishers, march and attack columns, and massed fire. At the same time, the lectures themselves constituted a further step in the development of doctrine; their discussion of concepts and methods provided additional material to the commissions and advisory bodies that Scharnhorst had formed to draft the army's definitive regulations. The reformers were in no doubt about the importance of acquainting the abler junior officers with the most advanced thinking in the army. Scharnhorst wrote that what Tiedemann and Clausewitz were offering their students was neither more nor less than an analysis of war as it actually is; and Clausewitz could joke about the numerous suggestions that he and his friend were putting forward by referring to the "Tiedemann-Clausewitzian factory of tactics." [46] But, no doubt, he would have preferred an assignment with greater executive authority. In June 1810 he wrote Gneisenau: "Half against my will I have become a professor; together with Tiedemann I am to teach tactics in the new Military Academy for Officers. In addition I am tutoring the crown prince—as you see,

43. On the *Allgemeine Kriegsschule* and Clausewitz's duties there, see G. Friedländer, *Die Königliche Allgemeine Kriegs-Schule und das höhere Militair-Bildungswesen 1765–1813*, Berlin, 1854, pp. 228–313; and L. v. Scharfenort, *Die Königlich Preussische Kriegsakademie, 1810–1910*, Berlin, 1910, pp. 6–24.
44. "*Fouragirungen,*" Clausewitz, *Schriften*, i, 450–456.
45. Excerpts of Clausewitz's and Tiedemann's lectures were printed and discussed by me in *Yorck*, pp. 170–179. Shortly afterwards the whole of Clausewitz's lectures, *Meine Vorlesungen über den kleinen Krieg, gehalten auf der Kriegs-Schule 1810–1811.—Artillerie. Geschütze*, were published in Clausewitz, *Schriften*, i, 226–599. The editor, W. Hahlweg, added extensive notes to the text, as well as an informative introduction, *ibid.*, pp. 208–225.
46. Clausewitz to Gneisenau, 17 June 1811, *ibid.*, p. 644.

my activities are nearly as peaceful as planting cabbage." The following September, after his hopes for a command in Silesia had been disappointed, he wrote Gneisenau: "The time for the opening of the Berlin Military Academy draws near, and I suppose it is inevitable that once again I will invoke the ghosts of my abstract wisdom, and project them like smoky clouds, faintly gleaming, in feeble, uncertain outlines before the eyes of the class." [47]

Eighteenth-century military theory had codified the principal subject of Clausewitz's lectures, the *kleine Krieg*—war of detachments, or little war—as those actions that guarded an army on the move and in camp, disturbed the enemy, and gathered information. In his definition, Clausewitz characteristically avoided a list of specific tasks and based himself instead on the element of power; what mattered was the proportion of force committed: "By *little war* we understand the employment of small units in the field. Actions involving 20, 50, 100, or 300 or 400 men belong to the little war, unless they form part of a larger action." [48] The later 19th century retained this point of view, a representative definition holding that "the little war is that manner of fighting which attempts to achieve the secondary aims present in all wars by means that are small in relation to the over-all military effort." [49]

These secondary aims were to be realized by patrols, raids, outposts, ambushes, and the capture of prisoners. In the armies of the *ancien régime,* whose effectiveness depended on the exact movements and rapid volleys of infantry fighting in close order, such missions had in the main been entrusted to specialists—hussars and *Jäger*—who had been augmented in the second half of the 18th century by light-infantry battalions. The decisive step in the modernization of infantry fighting throughout Europe during the wars of the French Revolution consisted of the line-infantry's more frequent use of the methods of these specialists, which led to the amalgamation of linear tactics with the attack column and with skirmishing, sniping, and other actions characteristic of the little war.

It is this development which explains the prominent place the little war occupied in the curriculum of the War College. Most of Clausewitz's listeners would never take part in patrols or ambushes. But a course of lectures on the little war provided an effective way of inducing line and staff officers to think with greater indepencence than had been their custom. "The individual hussar and *Jäger*," Clausewitz said in an early lecture, "possesses an enterprising spirit, a degree of confidence in himself and in his luck, which someone who has always served in the line can hardly

47. Clausewitz to Gneisenau, 24 June 1810, and 24 September 1811, *ibid.*, pp. 628, 668.
48. *Ibid.*, p. 231.
49. W. Rüstow, *Die Lehre vom kleinen Kriege*, Zurich, 1864, p. 3. For the place the little war occupied in the military operations of the *ancien régime* and the Napoleonic period, see my *Yorck*, pp. 21–46.

imagine. ... This is an absolutely essential quality of light troops ... [in whom] the most extreme daring must alternate according to circumstances with intelligent caution. ... This free play of intelligence, which operates in the little war, this clever union of boldness with caution (I should like to say this fortunate combination of daring and fear), is the quality that renders the little war so extraordinarily interesting." [50] Lectures on this subject would also of necessity address themselves to issues relating to the cooperation between infantry, cavalry, and artillery, which in the Napoleonic age had become far more significant at all levels of command. In short, the little war was a useful introduction to modern war as such.

In his opening lecture, Clausewitz promised his listeners that he would try to remove any preconceived opinions and prejudices on their part. What mattered above all, he thought, was to demolish the belief that war consisted of discrete actions carried out by different groups of specialists. Just as his definition of the little war would not draw a numerically precise line between small and large units, so the little war and major operations were not inherently different, but tended to blend into one another.[51] As soon as he had distinguished the psychology of individual fighters from that of the line-infantry, he went on to argue that in modern war much of the difference ought to disappear. The same principles applied to the little war and to major operations; their differences were not absolute, but a matter of emphasis. In future, skirmisher and grenadier must use each other's tactics, and this meant that each had to assume qualities of the other. The light-infantryman must renounce some of his hit-and-run methods; the line-infantryman must add a good measure of caution and deception to his exact drill. As we know, this concept of amalgamated tactics and operations was held by most of the Prussian military reformers; its analysis in Clausewitz's course drew added strength from the lecturer's view that all forms of fighting were interconnected, that theory should reflect their interconnection, that war was an activity in which each aspect influences and is influenced by others, and that this interrelationship extended to the social and political matrix of war. The purposes of Clausewitz's lectures—to bring out the value of independent action and the interdependence of all actions—thus fit well into the general ideas on war and society that he was developing in the reform period.

50. "Über den Charakter des kleinen Krieges," *Schriften*, i, 237–239. It was, to say the least, unusual for a Prussian officer to depict fear as a natural, even beneficial, military quality. Since it helps to characterize Clausewitz's environment, I cannot refrain from mentioning the only parallel that comes to mind: the episode, shocking to contemporaries, in Kleist's *Prinz von Homburg* in which the hero, a German prince and Prussian general, is eager to renounce glory, rank, and honor if his life is spared. This scene was the main reason why the play, which Kleist wrote between 1809 and 1811, was not performed in Berlin until 1828, and then only after the verses expressing the hero's panic had been heavily cut and rewritten.

51. "Einleitung in den kleinen Krieg," *Schriften*, i, 231, 233.

After several introductory lectures, outlining the program of the course, defining means and purpose of the little war, and establishing its relationship to other kinds of fighting, Clausewitz proceeded to its tactics: operations of infantry and cavalry, separately and in combination; use of artillery; exploitation of terrain; methods of planning actions; and special problems affecting attack and defense. By repeatedly contrasting features common to all types of combat with those peculiar to small groups, the lectures continued to emphasize the unity of war. Only after this systematic survey were the traditional topics of the little war taken up: advance and rear guards; outposts; reconnaissance and combat patrols; the gathering and transmission of intelligence; observation and defense of river crossings, roads, mountain passes, forests, villages; use of field entrenchments; surprise attacks; ambushes; retreats and pursuits; breaking out of encirclements; destruction of bridges, depots, and roads.[52] To enrich the illustrations and references already thickly scattered through the lectures, Clausewitz collected longer examples and whole scenarios in separate folders, dealing with operations in the Seven Years' War, the revolutionary campaigns, and the war of 1806. Some of this material consisted of notes he had taken in Scharnhorst's classes, or was based on independent studies before 1806; other analyses were the results of new research. Together they form an impressive collection of thorough explorations in the detail, the minutiae, of the way soldiers actually behave in combat.[53]

At the end, rather than summarizing the main points of the course, Clausewitz looked ahead, encouraging his listeners to think for themselves and alerting them once more to methodological aspects of the study of war. His words reflected the approach he took to teaching and his suspicion of abstraction as a hindrance to understanding with such clarity that the first part of the final lecture, except for a few marginal passages, is here quoted in full: "Herewith I conclude the little war, gentlemen," he began, "hoping that you deem the principles, observations, and rules that I offered you worthy of further reflection. For only personal reflection, coming to terms with one's own ideas rather than memorizing rules, leads to knowledge of

---

52. *Ibid.*, pp. 239–443. An error in transcribing my notes on Clausewitz's lectures, at that time still unpublished, led me to state in *Yorck*, pp. 178–179, that Clausewitz had devoted an entire lecture to guerrilla warfare. In reality, references to this type of war occur in several lectures but are not treated comprehensively. Professor Hahlweg nevertheless believes that Clausewitz's discussion of the operations of partisans and small detachments constitutes an important phase in the development of the theory of revolutionary war. Repeated reading of the lectures confirms me in my view of their essentially apolitical, "regular" approach to the little war, on which I already commented in *Yorck*—e.g., by the term "partisans" (*Partheygänger*) Clausewitz means not guerrillas but regular soldiers (*Schriften*, i, 435). The difference on this score between the lectures and the later *Bekenntnisdenkschrift* (see p. 218 below) is striking but quite natural. In the lectures Clausewitz instructed regulars in modern operations and tactics; in the *Bekenntnisdenkschrift* he tried to convince his readers, and himself, of the military potential inherent in civilians to justify his call for a national uprising against the French.
53. *Schriften*, i, 456–588.

the subject and to the capacity of acting accordingly. I very much hope that from time to time in the course of your studies you will return to these statements and subject them to the test of your increasingly mature judgment. ...

"I wasn't able to promise you much at the beginning of these lectures, and I must conclude with the admission that these hours would have been far more useful to you if I could have clarified the web of individual circumstances and shown you the spirit of the whole—its guiding principle— by means of a circumstantial account of events in which I myself had taken part. Instead, I simply stated the principle, and demonstrated it with a few meager examples. Principles are truly understood by us and become useful only if we associate individual events with them, or at least if we have a general conception of the way things occur in war. That, too, is the reason why I hope that you will return to these matters after you have spent some time familiarizing yourselves with the history of war.

"I considered it my duty to tell you nothing that went against my beliefs. In military affairs we are too easily seduced into repeating what others have said—as is shown by the great number of books of this kind appearing even today. About these we can say that many authors have written many things that they themselves did not understand, the primary reason being that most of them were simply compilers.

"I believe I need not accuse myself of this. Whatever I did not understand, did not clearly perceive, I left out; just as I left out the many longwinded, vague *Raisonnements*—saying everything and nothing—with which most authors accompany their principles.

"It is my greatest ambition that you will find my rules to be natural— that is, to come as close to the matter as possible, and not in contradiction with the course of events in war. As little combat experience as I have, it is enough to give me an accurate view of the way most episodes in war unfold, as well as of the numerous chance incidents, which touch everything, and of the numerous difficulties that inhibit accurate execution of the precise plans that theory tends to formulate. We might term these the friction of the whole machinery, which, as is the case with any other friction, can be recognized only through experience, and which so many authors ignore completely.

"In short, the little personal experience that I do possess will, I hope, guard me against the dangers of pedantry." [54]

The second part of the lecture concerns the literature on the little war, most of which, Clausewitz repeated, was not worth bothering with. A descriptive list of the better books, articles, and journals singled out Scharnhorst's writings for their wealth of historical examples and classical

---

54. "Schlussbemerkung über den kleinen Krieg," *ibid.*, pp. 443–445. The discussion of the literature referred to in the paragraphs below and Clausewitz's concluding remarks follow on pp. 445–449.

conciseness, and the works of the Hessian *Jäger* officer Johann von Ewald, which Clausewitz liked for the many examples drawn from the author's own experiences.[55] Not on the same level, according to Clausewitz, but nevertheless of some merit, was the *Abhandlung über den kleinen Krieg* by his contemporary Georg Wilhelm von Valentini, who had recently left Prussian service to fight with the Austrians, and then accepted a Russian commission before returning to Prussia in the spring of 1812 to succeed Clausewitz as military instructor to the crown prince.[56]

Clausewitz ended his discussion of the literature by advising his listeners once more not to read too much theory: "The time you wish to devote to reading might be better spent on military history. Only later, when you again feel the need to clarify and develop your ideas systematically, would you be well advised to consult the authors I have recommended. You can then ask yourself: if I disregard all preconceptions and do not bind myself to conventional rules, which of the author's statements remain true?" The lecture ended with the words: "Finally, I hope you will also occasionally recall this course, and think further about it."

What is conventional and what is original in Clausewitz's approach can best be recognized by comparing his treatment with Valentini's, whose book on the little war, first published in 1799 and reprinted twice in the following decade, is in the opinion of at least one scholar "the most distinguished and mature work on the subject that the 18th century produced."[57] Both Valentini and Clausewitz discussed more or less the same

55. In his writings on the little war Scharnhorst had relied on Ewald for examples from the American War for Independence; see my *Yorck,* p. 42 and n. 109.

56. For basic information on Valentini's career see Priesdorff, iv, No. 1268. The professional lives of Valentini and Clausewitz followed remarkably similar paths; but at almost every point Valentini had better luck, and his intelligent, moderate conservatism smoothed his way to greater external success. He was five years older than Clausewitz, served with distinction as a *Jäger* lieutenant in 1793 and 1794, and at the age of twenty-four published his first book, which was favorably received. In 1806 he managed to evade captivity, and continued on active service through the critically important first years of reform. His resignation in 1809 was motivated by professional rather than political considerations, and thus did not offend the king, especially since Valentini returned to Prussia at the very moment when such activists as Gneisenau, Boyen, Tiedemann, and Clausewitz either retired or joined the Russian army. During 1813 and 1814 Valentini served as chief of staff with various commands, but unlike Clausewitz never in areas of marginal importance. In the campaign of 1815 both Valentini and Clausewitz were chiefs of staff of segments of Blücher's army, but on 18 June Clausewitz's corps covered the army's lines of communication while Valentini was with the Prussian column whose arrival put the outcome of Waterloo beyond doubt. Valentini returned home a highly decorated major-general, and for the following thirteen years served as commandant of the Silesian fortress of Glogau, during which time he published several works on the theory of war. After being promoted to lieutenant-general, he was appointed in 1828 to one of the few posts in the service which by that time might still have appealed to Clausewitz: inspector-general of military education and training. Valentini remained skeptical about many of the army's reforms; he considered Scharnhorst an overrated, impractical theorist, nearly fought a duel with Gneisenau, and found Clausewitz "highly repugnant." Clausewitz, in turn, liked to refer to him as "the schoolmaster." The letters that Valentini exchanged with the military theorist Georg Heinrich von Berenhorst between 1802 and 1814 contain some of the most telling contemporary evaluations of Clausewitz (see below, pp. 205–206, 214).

57. Jähns, iii, 2724.

topics, cited many of the same writers, and even referred to the same episodes to illustrate their arguments. But Valentini organized his material in the arbitrary and inconsistent manner that characterizes so much of the military writing of the time. His book begins with a chapter on the movement of troops, since, as the opening paragraph has it: "Every military operation commences with a march by which the troops are brought to the point where they are to act, be it in the offensive or defensively. Consequently we must begin with a consideration of the march; first with the organization of the march itself, then proceeding to measures of security and precaution taken for its protection." [58] If a chapter on marches is a logical starting point, one might think that it ought to be followed by chapters on such topics as supply and camps; instead, the second chapter surveys general tactics, its discussion alternating between broad principles and details, interspersed with historical and technical illustrations, and anecdotes. The focus narrows again in the remaining chapters, which deal with patrols, reconnaissance, outposts, camps, surprise attacks, and ambushes. Throughout, the reader is in the company of an urbane, pragmatic commentator, who moves easily from topic to topic, drawing on his experiences and studies, but who rarely rises to interpretation and never attempts to synthesize.[59] Nothing approaching Clausewitz's systematic analysis, which seeks to open the student's eyes not only to the specifics of fighting in small groups but also to means and purpose of all types of fighting, and their mutual relationships, can be found in Valentini's work.

What the lectures tell us about Clausewitz's pedagogic ideas and the development of his military theories is best considered in conjunction with the parallel evidence contained in the tutorials he gave the crown prince. This course of three weekly one-hour sessions began in October 1810, about the same time as the lectures at the War College, continued through spring, resumed in October, and ended in March 1812.[60] In October 1810 the crown prince had just turned fifteen; his brother William and

58. Having failed to locate a copy of the first edition, I am citing from the sixth, which appeared under a slightly amended title, *Der kleine Krieg,* Berlin, 1833. The quotation is from page 10. The table of contents of the first edition given by Jähns, iii, 2724, and Valentini's introduction to the sixth edition indicate that few significant changes occurred in the work between 1799 and 1833, except for the discussion of general tactics, which was expanded and moved to the end of the text.
59. It might be noted that the expanded chapter on tactics in the 1833 edition contains passages in which Valentini's characteristic approach incorporates a more modern—Clausewitzian—spirit, e.g., this discussion of cavalry attacks: "The old learned definition 'shock is the product of velocity and mass' is wrong because not everything valid for inanimate objects and mechanical forces can be applied to living beings, who act according to the laws of the will. The consequences drawn from this proposition, according to which force and resistance were measured and compared on the basis of the weight of soldiers and horses, and the speed of the attack, must be regarded as the kind of academic aberration that tends to develop during long periods of peace. Fortunately in war we recover from the feebleness of speculation.

"Not the laws of mechanics but moral reasons explain why the side that assaults the opponent with greater violence is usually victorious ... " (pp. 340–341).
60. Clausewitz to Gneisenau, 20 October 1810; 2 September 1811; *Schriften,* i, 634, 658.

Prince Frederick of the Netherlands, who joined the tutorials in 1811, were two years younger, so that Clausewitz faced the challenge of presenting his thoughts in the simplest terms possible. In a course outline he submitted to the prince's governor, his aims were formulated modestly as the imparting of some provisional knowledge of war to the young man to enable him to understand recent military history without overly taxing his capacities: "My greatest concern will be, on the one hand, always to remain comprehensible to the prince, since otherwise even the most attentive student soon grows bored, inattentive, and disgusted with the subject; secondly, not to give him false ideas on any matter, which would create difficulties for more detailed instruction or independent study [later on]. For the sake of the former I shall always try to link the particular topic and natural common sense as closely as possible, and in so doing expect to depart frequently from scientific spirit and academic forms." The course would open with a survey of weapons and the various branches of the service, and then proceed to their employment, moving from a general description of war to small-unit tactics and the order of battle of larger units. Here a halt would be called to consider the general context again, and indicate more closely the interrelationship of the various components of a campaign. The treatment of the remaining tactical subjects would follow. Finally, the discussion of strategic issues would again start with a general analysis of a campaign, which would provide a new point of view from which to consider the previously presented material.[61]

If Clausewitz prepared notes for his sessions they have not survived; but in April 1812, shortly before leaving Prussia, he sent the crown prince an essay that covered the topics he had dealt with in the second part of the course: "The most important Principles for the Conduct of War, to supplement my Lessons to His Royal Highness, the Crown Prince."[62] The essay offers a synthesis of Clausewitz's ideas on tactics, strategy, and the relationship between study and reality, reduced to simple declarative sentences and brief numbered paragraphs, which, as he wrote in an introductory note, were designed to stimulate thought rather than offer a complete body of instruction. The short opening part, "Propositions Dealing with War in General," states that theory is concerned with the manner in which physical preponderance can be gained at decisive points, and with the way in which psychological factors can be evaluated and exploited. Since it is not

61. "Entwurf der dem Herrn General von Gaudi vorgelegt wurde," printed as an appendix to *On War* (pp. 941–943). The text is probably based on a subsequent copy of Clausewitz's outline, since in 1810 the prince's governor, Friedrich Wilhelm von Gaudi, had not yet reached the rank of general. The essay Clausewitz wrote in connection with his tutorials (see note 62 below) was copied several times, the copies being circulated among interested officers.

62. "Die wichtigsten Grundsätze des Kriegführens zur Ergänzung meines Unterrichts bei Sr. Königlichen Hoheit dem Kronprinzen," printed as an appendix to *On War* (pp. 945–984). A translation by Hans W. Gatzke, *Principles of War*, was published in Harrisburg in 1942, and has been frequently reprinted.

always possible to act on the probability of success, one must be prepared to act against it if no better option should be available. Activity and daring are of the essence: "Some people believe that theory always counsels the most cautious path; that is false. If theory were to advise anything, it would be in the nature of war that it would always advise the most decisive—that is, the most daring—option. But theory leaves it to the commander to decide according to his own courage, enterprise, and degree of self-confidence." [63]

The second part, "Tactics or the Theory of Combat," begins: "War consists of a combination of many separate engagements. This combination may or may not be wise, and success depends greatly on the degree of its soundness; but for the moment the individual engagement must be our most important concern. For only a combination of successful engagements can lead to good results. Thus the art of defeating your enemy in an engagement remains the most important thing in war." On the defensive, it is a basic principle never to remain passive: the defense is always the preliminary for an attack. On the offensive, concentration of force, concentric attacks on the critical target, and surprise hold out the greatest promise of success. Sections on the use of troops and the exploitation of terrain summarize the doctrine of the Prussian reformers: testing the opponent's position, gradual application of force, withholding strong reserves for the decisive blow. [64]

The third part, "Strategy," defines its subject as the art of "combining the separate engagements that make up a war to achieve the purpose of the campaign and of the war." Wars are waged to achieve three main purposes: defeat the enemy's armies, acquire his resources, and gain the acquiescence of the population. Consequently one must operate against the enemy's major armies, and against his capital and significant fortresses and depots; public opinion will be won over if one gains major victories and occupies the capital. "The first and most important principle to observe in order to accomplish these purposes is to make every possible effort to mobilize *all* resources available to us. Any moderation would leave us short of our aim. Even if success were already fairly probable, we should be unwise not to make the greatest effort in order to assure success *without doubt*. Such an effort can never have negative results. Even if the country were to suffer severely from this policy no real disadvantage would follow, for the heavier the burden the sooner it would be lifted.

"The moral effect of these actions is of infinite value. Everyone becomes confident of success; it is the best means for quickly raising the nation's morale." [65]

---

63. "Die wichtigsten Grundsätze," *On War* (pp. 945–947).
64. *Ibid.*, pp. 947–967.
65. *Ibid.*, pp. 967–968. The sentence beginning "The first and most important principle ... " is a translation of: "Der erste und wichtigste Grundsatz ... ist der: *alle* Kräfte, die uns gegeben sind, mit

Having mobilized all one's strength, one should, secondly, concentrate one's forces against the major targets, even at the risk of weaknesses elsewhere; thirdly, operate rapidly and create surprises; and, fourthly, exploit fully any success gained. After enumerating these desiderata, Clausewitz returned to the point that appeared fundamental to him: true caution consists in completely mobilizing one's physical and psychological strength; on that basis even a small power like Prussia, which can no longer engage in wars of conquest, can very well wage defensive wars. This statement ushered in a series of comments on Prussia's history and on her present condition, which Clausewitz presented in favorable terms. He agreed that on the tactical plane a concentric action such as simultaneously attacking front and flank of an enemy's position, was effective, but it was less advantageous strategically, since forces operating considerable distances apart may be defeated separately. "Strategically, the side surrounded by the enemy {i.e., Prussia} is better off than the side which surrounds its opponent, especially with equal or even weaker forces." Clausewitz added that Jomini was correct to advocate operating on interior lines, "and if Herr von Bülow demonstrated the opposite so convincingly it is only because he exaggerated the immediate impact that the disruption of supply {caused by concentric operations} has on the strategic situation, while completely and thoughtlessly denying the inevitable effects of battle." [66]

The section on the strategic defensive opens with a definition of exemplary clarity and subtleness: "In the political sense a defensive war is a war waged for one's independence; in the strategic sense, a defensive war is a campaign in which I limit myself to opposing the enemy in a theater of operations I have prepared for that purpose. Whether I fight offensive or defensive battles in that theater of operations makes no difference." [67] The political aim of self-preservation may coexist with the tactical or even strategic offensive. Both this and the following section on the strategic offensive are replete with contemporary allusions.

In its last pages the essay turns to the "Application in Time of War of the Principles just discussed." The lucid argument, progressing swiftly to a

---

der höchsten Anstrengung aufzubieten." Clausewitz's words might be interpreted as referring not to mobilization but to combat. In this sense Gatzke (p. 46) translated them: "The first and most important rule ... is to use our entire forces with the utmost energy." But the subsequent allusion to the recommended policy placing heavy burdens on a country makes it apparent that Clausewitz is talking of conscription, requisitions, and other mobilization measures.

Possibly this ambiguity contributed to misinterpretations of this passage and the following paragraphs as Clausewitz's four "principles of war," akin to the various lists of principles or rules formulated by Jomini and his successors. It would have amused Clausewitz with his scorn for dogma that his words to a seventeen-year-old boy became the precedent for the conventional checklists of rules and laws by which military academies and staff schools in the 20th century try to make war comprehensible and manageable to their pupils.

66. "Die wichtigsten Grundsätze," *On War* (p. 970).
67. *Ibid.,* p. 973.

climax that is at once logical and emotional, makes the concluding section a masterpiece among Clausewitz's writings of the reform era. The first two paragraphs state the paradox that had come to underlie all of his thinking about war: "The fundamental concepts of the art of war are actually extremely simple, closely allied to common sense; and although in tactics— rather more so than in strategy—they rest on some special expertise, this expertise is so circumscribed in variety and profundity that it can scarcely be compared to other scientific disciplines." [68]

A variety of examples reinforce the statement that war calls for little theoretical knowledge; Then Clausewitz abruptly changes course: "Waging war in reality is very difficult, no doubt about it; but the difficulty is not that erudition and great genius are needed to understand the basic principles of warfare. Any well-organized and objective intellect, which is not entirely unfamiliar with the subject, can manage it. Even the application of these principles on the map and in memoranda presents no problem, and there is no great art to devising a good plan of operations. The entire difficulty is this: *To remain faithful in action to the principles we have laid down for ourselves.*

"To call attention to this difficulty," Clausewitz continued, "is the purpose of these closing remarks, and to give Your Royal Highness a clear idea of it I regard as the most important object of this essay.

"The conduct of war resembles the workings of an intricate machine with tremendous friction, so that combinations which are easily planned on paper can be executed only with great effort.

"Consequently the commander's free will and intelligence find themselves hampered at every turn, and remarkable strength of mind and spirit are needed to overcome this resistance. Even then many good ideas are destroyed by friction, and we must carry out more simply and modestly what in more complicated form would have given greater results." [69]

Since the Jena campaign, when Clausewitz had first applied the term "friction" to the difficulties with which Scharnhorst labored, he had turned the word into a comprehensive theoretical concept, most recently in his concluding lecture on the little war. The originality and usefulness of this concept were greatly increased by his argument that however friction showed itself, it had a psychologically inhibiting effect and consequently could be overcome only by psychic energy. He listed eight major sources of friction. The first is insufficient knowledge of the enemy, which creates doubts and anxiety, as does the second, rumor—Clausewitz's term for information gained by remote observation and spies. He went so far as to claim that *all* external influences on the commander tend to heighten his confusion. To regain certainty the general must critically analyze every-

68. *Ibid.,* p. 977.
69. *Ibid.,* p. 978.

thing he is told; if this does not suffice he must rely on probability and not hesitate to make mistakes. The third source of friction is uncertainty about his own strength and position; the fourth, that his troops, too, are uncertain, and tend to exaggerate the difficulties of their situation. "To resist these pressures requires confidence in your own insights and convictions. At the time this usually gives the impression of stubbornness, but in reality it is that strength of mind and character we call firmness."

The fifth source of friction lies in the difference between expectation and reality. Unforeseen obstacles, errors, troops not marching as rapidly or fighting as effectively as intended, mean that we never achieve exactly what we had hoped for. The sixth source of friction is that one's own army is never as strong and effective in reality as it appears on paper—but that also holds true of the enemy. Seventh, supply, however organized, always presents great difficulties; indeed, it constitutes the main reason why the whole machinery of war is so unwieldy, and why its product always falls far short of the initial design. Finally, it cannot be sufficiently emphasized that "in action our physical images and perceptions are more vivid than the impressions we gained beforehand by mature reflection. But they are only the outward appearances of things, which, as we know, rarely match their essence precisely. We therefore run the risk of sacrificing mature reflection for first impressions.

"That these first impressions tend to incline toward fear and exaggerated caution is due to man's natural timidity, which recognizes only one side to everything.

"We must fortify ourselves against this danger, have blind faith in the results of our own earlier reflections, in order to strengthen ourselves against the debilitating impressions of the moment.

"All these difficulties of execution make it essential to have confidence and firm convictions. That is why the study of military history is so important, for it enables us to see things as they are and as they function. The principles that we can derive from theoretical instruction are only useful to facilitate the study of military history, and to call attention to its most important aspects." [70]

Once again we encounter a view of history different from that held by most military writers of the time. Military history, according to this formulation, is not a pool of material for the theorist; on the contrary, Clausewitz reversed the functions of history and theory: one purpose of the latter is to help us understand the past. Where theory contradicts history it must be corrected or even rejected: to test theory was the second function of history. Its third and most important function was to serve as a substitute for experience: "Only the study of military history is capable of giving those

70. *On War* (pp. 978–982).

who have no experience of their own a clear perception of what I have here called the friction of the whole machine." The kind of history he meant, Clausewitz added, was not propaganda or broad surveys, the products of historians "who make history rather than write it," but the detailed, factual account of a few engagements, which is more useful than any number of generalized treatments of whole wars. Scharnhorst's account of the defense of Menin and the breakout of its garrison was a fine example, "which will provide Your Royal Highness with a standard for the way military history should be written." [71]

Clausewitz directed the attention of the crown prince to Scharnhorst's work not only because it was objective and thorough; the content of the piece and the fact that its author was the guiding spirit of military change in Prussia were equally significant: "No battle in history has convinced me as much as this one that we must never despair of success in war. It proves that the effect of sound principles—which in any case does not manifest itself as regularly as we might expect—may suddenly reappear, even in the most critical situations when we have given up any hope of their influence." Theoretical speculation could scarcely combine more closely with allusions to contemporary Prussian reality.

By logical progression, imperceptibly, the discussion had moved from its starting point—war as an object of study—to the purpose of war, its tactical and strategic characteristics, and to the permanent friction between plans and reality, until the analysis turned into a paean on the qualities of self-confidence and heroism, rising in the essay's final sentences to a personal appeal: "A powerful emotion must stimulate the talents of the commander, whether it be ambition as in Caesar, hatred of the enemy as in Hannibal, or the proud acceptance of a glorious end as in Frederick the Great.

"Open your heart to such an emotion. Be audacious and cunning in your plans, firm and perservering in their execution, ready to meet a glorious end, and fate will crown you with a gloriole—fitting ornament for a prince—whose light will carry your image into the hearts of your last descendants, who for millennia will continue to perpetuate your glorious name." [72]

Clausewitz's politics are as apparent in the words he addressed to the crown prince as they had been in his writings of 1807 and 1808. They

71. *Ibid.*, p. 983. The quotation which follows is from the same page.
72. *Ibid.*, pp. 983–984. The quoted passage was added in Clausewitz's hand to the clean copy that Scharnhorst's orderly wrote for him. The last ten words of the quotation are not included in printed versions, possibly because of the grammatical ambiguity of the original. In a letter to his wife of 12 April 1812, *Correspondence*, p. 274, Clausewitz reported the completion of the essay, and included the final exhortation in full.

emerge in his advocacy of complete rather than partial mobilization, a first principle whose universal validity he was to deny when circumstances changed, in the value he assigns to interior lines, or in his evocation of Frederick the Great and in his appeal to a seventeen-year-old boy, who at any time might ascend the throne, to dare and conquer or perish. The political message expressed or implied in these statements remained what it had been since the beginning of the reform period. Whatever the momentary diplomatic constellation, it faded into insignificance before Clausewitz's conviction that Prussia must try to liberate herself even if the odds seemed against her, and that there could be no peace in Europe as long as Napoleon ruled France. More movement, though no change of view, is evident in his pedagogical and theoretical concerns. Ideas that he had expressed in the fragment on Pestalozzi, the letter to Fichte, or the notes on strategy were developed and achieved new clarity by being applied and tested in his lectures on the little war and in the essay in which he summarized his tutorials.

His experiences as a teacher confirmed Clausewitz in his belief that the function of education lay not in the transmission of a fixed body of knowledge, but in sensitizing the student to aspects of reality and in strengthening his capacities of understanding and dealing with these aspects. When he criticized learning by rote he did not, of course, mean that memorizing and mechanical drill could be dispensed with; his notebooks and manuscripts show to what an extent repetition and systematic review formed part of his own education. What he objected to was the view that education consisted primarily in the more passive kind of intellectual effort. Its ultimate aim always remained the development of the student's intellectual and emotional powers, which would enable him to progress from knowledge to judgment and action, and thus to further knowledge. In his lectures, and increasingly in those of his writings that addressed an audience, he sought to stimulate and liberate the mind and the imagination; but it goes without saying that intellectual freedom was at every point disciplined by intense concern with reality, which encompassed technical expertise in the relevant fields of study.

It was in harmony with these ideas that Clausewitz shunned rapid surveys and sweeping arguments. Instead he was at pains to erect an analytic framework in his lectures and writings that would help the listener or reader develop the subject according to its inherent laws, "out of inner necessity," exploring one point thoroughly before taking a short step to the next. To make learning difficult in the hope of stretching the student's mind he considered a mistake; what mattered was to give the student confidence in his teacher and in himself.

How much success Clausewitz enjoyed with this approach is not entirely clear. Evidently he shed his habitual reserve on the lecture platform, was animated, witty, and conversed rather than orated. His manner and personality impressed some young officers at the War College, who became and remained his friends through the vicissitudes of the Wars of Liberation and the Restoration. With the king and among senior officers he acquired the name of a gifted teacher, a reputation that had a bearing on his career after 1815.

His instruction of the crown prince was probably less effective. Though impressionable, and receptive to his tutor's message of the supremacy of the gifted and determined commander, the future Frederick William IV was not a serious soldier. Clausewitz had occasion to lament over "crown-princely deaf ears." [73] After the lessons concluded, the prince's governor, Colonel von Gaudi, nevertheless reported that Clausewitz had "accomplished an incredible amount," and except for some unpleasant remarks the following year when Clausewitz appeared at the king's headquarters in Russian uniform, the prince seemed to retain friendly feelings for his tutor. A farewell letter that Clausewitz addressed to him in 1812 suggests the close attention he had paid to his pupil's emotional as well as intellectual development in the course of the tutorials, and affords us further insights into his concept of education.

The rich qualities with which the prince was endowed, Clausewitz wrote, as well as his station in life, were meaningless unless they were joined by the determination to become an exceptional human being. Many men with remarkable attributes achieved less than an ordinary but disciplined worker. "Only the will, which governs strong natures like an absolute ruler, can prevent unusual gifts and abilities from being lost among the multitude of daily phenomena, like a single ray of light losing itself in immeasurable space. As light converges on a focus so willpower brings together man's separate abilities. ..." Neither the study of history nor that of any other discipline possessed meaning unless the student was determined to perfect himself. That determination would render any lesson attractive: "You will gain an inner freedom that liberates you from your teachers. ... Had I enjoyed the good fortune of continuing to instruct you I should not have tried to burden you with *my* art of war—but by developing *my* views would have hoped to awaken *yours:* you would rise above me and learn to judge me. ..." [74]

Clausewitz's fear that the boy he had come to know over two years might never acquire sustained determination and consequentiality was to be borne out by Frederick William IV's life and reign. But apart from the specific pedagogic message contained in the letter to his pupil, and the con-

---

73. Clausewitz to Gneisenau, 2 September 1811, *Schriften*, i, 658.
74. Clausewitz to the crown prince, 29 March 1812, published by Hans Rothfels with a brief but notable introduction in "Ein Brief von Clausewitz an den Kronprinzen Friedrich Wilhelm aus dem Jahre 1812," *Historische Zeitschrift*, CXXI (1920), 282–286.

cept of education in general that it expressed, it offers yet another gloss on Clausewitz's belief that determination was an essential component of military genius, and thus of war itself. The thoughts he had drawn from his early analyses of Gustavus Adolphus and of strategic theory, and developed in his tutorials and the lectures on the little war, were here restated in personal terms. In *On War,* the chapters "Military Genius" and especially "Friction in War" gave final expression to this idea: only "iron determination" could overcome friction. "The proud spirit's firm will dominates the art of war like an obelisk dominates the town square on which all roads converge." [75]

In their essentials, the chapter on friction in *On War* and the treatment of friction that runs through the entire work are derived from the concluding part of the essay for the crown prince, "Application in Time of War of the Principles just discussed," in which Clausewitz first developed this concept systematically. Thus by the beginning of 1812 one of the most important elements in Clausewitz's image of war—chance—had been rendered subject to theoretical analysis. Insofar as friction interfered with one's own actions, to be sure, it stood only for the negative aspects of chance; the positive aspects of chance were represented by means of its equally pervasive power on the enemy's side. To appreciate the significance of Clausewitz's conceptual development, we should recall that the military writers of the Enlightenment, while often acknowledging the power of the fortuitous—Frederick's "Sa Majesté le hazard"—developed their theories with the purpose of reducing as much as possible the scope of chance. Their spiritual successors Bülow and Jomini strove for the same goal by means of systems that extended the enormously detailed rules of 18th-century march, camp, and tactical arrangements to strategy. Success could be assured, they claimed, by choosing the correct operational base, or by operating on interior lines against the enemy's main force. Valentini's friend Georg Heinrich von Berenhorst, who during the Seven Years' War had served as adjutant both to Frederick and to his brother Prince Henry, denied the validity of any such system. In his long work *Betrachtungen über die Kriegskunst,* which appeared in three volumes in 1798 and 1799, and in subsequent collections of essays and aphorisms, Berenhorst condemned all dogma. [76] Far from being scientific, war was anarchic, dominated by accident and the personalities of its leading actors. Efforts to control, let alone abolish, this primeval wildness were absurd. In his sarcastic, sophisticated debunking of systems, Berenhorst was an intellectual ally of Scharnhorst and Clausewitz; they dif-

75. *On War,* book I, ch. 7 (p. 160).
76. On Berenhorst see in particular his correspondence and diaries published in two volumes by E. v. Bülow, *Aus dem Nachlasse von Georg Heinrich von Berenhorst,* Dessau, 1845–47; and E. Kessel, "Georg Heinrich von Berenhorst," *Sachsen und Anhalt,* vol. ix (1933), pp. 161–198. Much inferior to Kessel's admirable study is the pretentious work by E. Hagemann, *Die deutsche Lehre vom Kriege; I: Von Berenhorst zu Clausewitz,* Berlin, 1940.

fered from him in their conviction that war was not anarchic, and thus impossible to cope with other than by empirical means, but was a natural social phenomenon, susceptible to analysis. If the theorists of the rationalist age had tried to hedge in the fortuitous, and Berenhorst had tried to elevate rationalism to anarchism, Scharnhorst held that the natural behavior of societies and individuals in war could be understood and thus to some extent guided, and Clausewitz gave this belief theoretical form. In their view, to exclude or deny chance was to go against nature; indeed, chance was to be welcomed because it was part of reality. Despite its terrible, constant power, chance was more than a danger: it was a positive force to be exploited. Napoleon expressed this idea perfectly in his operational dictum, "On s'engage, puis on voit," as did Sir John Moore in Spain in 1808 when he explained the reason for a maneuver by saying, "I shall be in fortune's way." The commander put himself in the path of chance; the power at his disposal and his determination to use it enabled him to turn chance into a new reality.[77]

The force that could most effectively create and exploit this reality was genius. Thus the concept of friction came to form the counterpart in external life to the result of Clausewitz's earlier analyses of the psychology of the individual, which had led him to elevate military genius—the soldier who possessed exceptional intellectual and emotional qualities in harmonious combination—to a key position in the conceptualization of war.

As we know, Clausewitz regarded the study of history, which transcended the narrow limits of personal observation, as the only trustworthy means of acquiring an understanding of chance, friction, and genius. Consequently the variety and reflected reality of history, which alone could place the present in perspective, lay at the center of his theoretical work. The emphasis on history—with the intellectual products of historical study, the dual concepts of friction and genius—became the force that more effectively than any other restricted the authority of principles or rules of war, even in those years when for political as well as pedagogic reasons Clausewitz might have been most willing to concede their validity. Characteristically, in his essay for the crown prince he treated principles less critically than he was ever to do again; but even here he sounded a clear warning: "The principles that we can derive from theoretical instruction are useful only to facilitate the study of military history ..."—i.e., to help us understand reality. "The effect of sound principles ... does not manifest itself as regularly as we might expect." [78]

---

77. That chance and the irrational formed not only an inevitable but also a healthy part of life was an idea that was still sufficiently in doubt at the time to require frequent reiteration. Cf. W. v. Humboldt's statement: "Policy must never resort to measures that are meant to be absolutely certain." Quoted by E. Kessel in *Zeiten der Wandlung,* Darmstadt, 1953, pp. 250–251.

78. See pp. 198 and 199 above.

The limitations of rules of whatever kind, which he had first explored in such works as his essay "On Art and Theory of Art," and which had been a major motif in subsequent writings, he was to define systematically in the chapter "Method" in *On War,* which distinguishes between laws, principles, rules, regulations, and method.[79] Here Clausewitz concludes that the concept of law is useless for military theory, "since no prescriptive formulation universal enough to deserve the name of law can be applied to the constant change and diversity of the phenomena of war." [80] "Objective" principles, which could help educate and guide judgment, might represent the spirit of law, but never assume its prescriptive form. "Subjective" principles were identical with maxims, applicable, if at all, only to a particular individual.

The essence of this approach, which acknowledges the infinite variety of war, as of life, without surrendering to it, is perhaps best appreciated by comparing it with Jomini's confident codification in the concluding chapter of his *Traité des grandes opérations militaires.* This chapter, "The Art of War Brought Back to Its True Principles," a refinement of several earlier versions, begins with the statement: "The fundamental principle, whose application renders all combinations effective, and without which all are defective, consists in combining the greatest amount of one's forces against the decisive point." The study of Napoleon's and Frederick's wars demonstrates how this can be achieved. Ten maxims result from this historical review: (1) Take the initiative. (2) Move against the most important weak point in the enemy's position. (3) Do not direct your offensive forces against more than one point. (4) Concentrate your forces in preparation for the attack so that all can act together. (5) Infantry must form in such a manner as to combine the greatest possible mobility with the greatest possible depth. (6) Induce the enemy to extend and fragment his front. (7) Acquire intelligence and information. (8) When attacking engage all of your forces, except reserves, simultaneously. (9) A defeated army must be vigorously pursued. (10) Take care to keep the morale of your men high.

The chapter ends with the statement that "the science of war consists in three general combinations," which respectively concern operational planning, strategy, and tactics: (1) Choose the most advantageous lines of operations. (2) Move your forces as rapidly as possible against the decisive strategic point. (3) Simultaneously employ the major part of your forces against the most important point in your enemy's position.[81]

What is striking in this codification, based on a view of history that discerns no difference between the frequently cautious operations of the

---

79. *On War,* book II, ch. 4 (pp. 203–204).
80. *Ibid.,* pp. 204–205.
81. Ch. xxxv, "Conclusion de l'ouvrage: l'art de la guerre ramené a ses véritables principes," *Traité des grandes opérations militaires,* Paris, 1811, iv, 275–286.

18th century and the sweeping campaigns of the Napoleonic era, is the muddle of tactical and strategic categories, the silence on motives and political objectives, the meandering argument, the platitudinous character of much that is recommended, and the confused relationship between the "fundamental principle" at the beginning of the chapter and the three "general combinations" comprising the science of war at the end. Indeed, the third "general combination" appears to be identical with the "fundamental principle," indicating once again the essentially tactical basis of Jomini's thought. Jomini, like Bülow and the theorists of the *ancien régime* before them, pursued an arbitrary number of facts and observations through a disorganized argument to a dogmatic end. Clausewitz developed his ideas as logically as he knew how to produce not a system but insights into the nature and interaction of military phenomena, which enabled the student to progress further through the infinite variety of dangers and opportunities.

Presumably it was this quality that led Berenhorst, who, incidentally, had studied Jomini's books, to declare that Clausewitz was the first to have fully explained Napoleon's generalship.[82] In a letter to Valentini, who had sent him a copy of Clausewitz's essay for the crown prince, he first criticized the organization of the argument and the use of the term "applied tactics," in part, perhaps, because he was aware of Valentini's dislike of Clausewitz, and then continued: "The most significant parts of his wisdom he [Clausewitz] abstracted from the wisdom, the actions, and the maxims of Napoleon. Indeed, his relationship to Carnot's and Napoleon's method or system of war, today's art of war, is like the relationship of Reinhold, Kiesewetter, and Berg to the philosophy of Hume and Kant. ... He certainly has the merit of explaining the new art of war very well and intelligibly, and he should be recognized as the first to have done so." Berenhorst added that Clausewitz's politics were revealed in the passage "in which he seeks to make the crown prince believe in the possibility of a weak and small state successfully waging a defensive war. ... But I must admit that I don't regret having been able to read this disquisition on war. Apart from the system, maxims, and examples of the great Napoleon, Herr von Klausewitz [*sic!*] has his own ideas, which do him honor and reveal him as an author who certainly has the right to express himself on his

---

82. On Berenhorst's knowledge of Jomini, see his letter to Valentini of 29 March 1809, *Aus dem Nachlasse*, ii, 295–296, mentioning copious notes he had taken on three of the four volumes of the *Traité* that had appeared by that time. The letter continues with a brief outline of Jomini's system, concluding that his maxims, though far from original, were sound, but owed their effectiveness solely to the fact that only one commander was observing them, while his opponents still adhered to inappropriate concepts. Once everyone fought in the same manner, Jomini's maxims would no longer assure success: "Wouldn't [Jomini's theory] then yield to the impact of numbers, of the troops' courage or cowardice, of the lucky star of their leader—to those three powerful phenomena whose influence it had vainly sought to displace?"

chosen subject, although the last lines of his testament are nothing but convoluted pathos. But tell me, who is he actually? That is, what is his family, in which regiment did he serve, how did he educate himself, what were his recent activities, and what is his present assignment with the Russians?" [83]

The young Clausewitz had attacked the validity of systems and dogma from the time he began to write on war. During the reform era he completed the destruction of their authority to his satisfaction, while perfecting earlier ideas and developing new concepts which could nevertheless render war comprehensible and manageable. The emotional and intellectual forces that had expressed themselves before 1806 in effective criticism of tradition or of the "scientific" soldier, and as isolated insights into the manner in which conflict actually occurred, now became enveloped in conceptual structures that after 1815 would coalesce into a general theory of war in which such absolutes as friction and genius coexisted with permanent change.

The development of his ideas was characterized by continuity and elaboration rather than by a turning away from earlier views. I have previously commented on the recurrence in *On War* of thoughts first expressed in 1804 and 1805, or during the reform period, and many similar repetitions exist that may be said to stitch together the writings of Clausewitz's youth and maturity. The comparison of war to commerce, first made in 1804 in the notebook on *Strategy,* is stated somewhat differently in the lectures on the little war—"We believe that in war battle more or less represents what cold cash does to major commercial transactions"—before it is given a final and expanded formulation in chapter 3, book II of *On War.* [84] The same lecture, "Introduction to the Little War," defines strategy and tactics in terms that Clausewitz had originally proposed in *Strategy* and the review-essay of Bülow, and continued to apply throughout the historical studies of the 1820's and *On War.* In the lecture he adds that strategy is defined according to its means and not according to its purpose, "because the means (that is, combat) is universally employed by strategy, is unique, and cannot be disregarded without destroying the entire concept of war, while the possible purposes [of strategy] are too diverse to be enumerated"—ideas that originated in his speculations on the theory of art, and

---

83. Berenhorst to Valentini, 1 November 1812, *ibid.,* ii, 353–354. Some months earlier Valentini had written that Clausewitz believed there was no great art to devising a good plan of operations. On 18 June 1812, (*ibid.,* ii, 336) Berenhorst replied: "So far as plans of operations are concerned, I tend to agree with him. They resemble the pedagogues' plans of education: the former are rendered absurd in one way or another by unforeseen circumstances; the latter, by the potential and peculiarities of the individuals to be educated. 'Then should we proceed without any plan, just into the blue?' I wish I could reply 'yes,' but fear of the gentlemen who think in formulae holds me back."

84. *Schriften,* i, 236. Related comments are noted above, pp. 7, 90.

recur in chapters 1 and 2 of book II in *On War*.[85] The point of view informing these lectures, that every military phenomenon reflects universal aspects of war, is of course fundamental to Clausewitz's fully developed theory, as is the essentially political and social nature of war, which he demonstrated in a variety of ways in the lectures and in his essay for the crown prince.

The strengthening and elaboration of these ideas resulted largely from advances in his ability to use theory for his special purposes. It was during the years of reform that Clausewitz acquired mastery of his methodological tools, and that he came to understand clearly the relationship between reality and abstraction, the limitations of theory, and the difference between its pedagogic and scientific functions.[86] The latter—cognition without utilitarian professional motives—was growing in importance to him even while he continued to involve himself deeply in the pedagogic activities that made up a large share of his official duties. In a sense the entire reform movement was a pedagogic program, and was regarded as such by its leaders as well as by Clausewitz. "We must train the nation to manage its own affairs," Stein wrote toward the end of 1807, "and to grow out of this condition of childhood in which an ever-restless and officious government wishes to keep the people." During the same weeks and in terms that echoed Clausewitz's views on the education of the child in the Pestalozzi fragment, Scharnhorst wrote Clausewitz that the reformers' purpose must be to "kindle a sense of independence in the nation; we must enable the nation to understand itself and to take up its own affairs; only then will the nation acquire self-respect and compel the respect of others. To work toward that goal is all we can do. To destroy the old forms, remove the ties of prejudice, guide and nurture our revival without inhibiting its free growth—our work cannot go further than that." [87]

Specifically, the reform program was an enterprise in political education, which sought to turn the absolute monarchy and corporative society, with their mutual limitations and barriers, into a less restrictive, more efficient power-generating organism. By affording greater scope to the individual, the state gained strength; growth of state and individual were thus interdependent. Urging the bureaucratic and military elites to welcome talent and to make their institutions more independent and responsible, writing memoranda and articles to justify innovation, were means by which Clausewitz participated in the education of society, and enabled the state to pursue policies that he believed were alone worthy of it. If in the ministe-

---

85. *Ibid.*, pp. 235, 237.
86. See above, pp. 147–168.
87. Stein to Hardenberg, 8 December 1807; Scharnhorst to Clausewitz, 27 November 1807. Quoted by me in *Yorck*, pp. 118–119.

rial and political realms education progressed slowly, the army offered somewhat greater scope. All of Scharnhorst's activities may be interpreted as an endless demonstration to the king and the officer corps that the changes he and his assistants proposed were necessary and effective. At the same time, the scheme of universal military service, joined to decent treatment of the man in the ranks and appeals to his patriotism, were ways of educating—that is, changing—the people. The army, Clausewitz wrote, should be regarded "as a school for military training and for the development of national spirit." [88] He considered his duties in Scharnhorst's office, his service on the general staff, his contributions to the development of operational and tactical doctrine, in much the same light as his lectures and tutorials—as ways by which soldiers could be helped to perfect themselves, and thus in turn help perfect the state. Indeed, his view of the condition of the Prussian state appeared similar to his feelings about himself, to the extent that both state and individual depended on education to achieve a harmonious intellectual and moral maturity.

In Clausewitz's personal education, however, the development of theory played a greater role than did teaching or the performance of his other duties. The cognitive effort was itself educational, regardless of where it led. The sounder understanding of war, and of the political and moral world, which resulted was the means by which he could satisfy the need to achieve intellectual independence that he had felt in Neuruppin, earlier as an adolescent on the Westphalian farm, and no doubt earlier still.

88. In *Der Feldzug von 1813 bis zum Waffenstillstand,* Glatz, 1813, p. 7. The short book was written in the summer of 1813.

IV. THE LOGIC OF PATRIOTISM

By the time he reached his thirtieth birthday, on 1 June 1810, Clausewitz had become a man of some significance in the army and the state. As long as disaster did not overtake Prussia, his prospects seemed reasonably assured. The only reservation concerned his health. Since 1807 he suffered from arthritis, occasionally accompanied by colic-like convulsions; hemorrhoids; and what his doctors diagnosed as "neuralgic fever," a broad term that on one occasion—in January 1809—was applied to what may have been malaria and at other times to severe headaches. The treatment usually prescribed consisted of opium drops, ether, rest, and a diet; several times he took the waters at a Silesian spa. When his duties were pressing, however, he managed to ignore his ailments, and his constitution, while "not excessively strong," still seemed sound enough.[1] His rise in stature induced Countess Brühl to renounce her opposition to his marrying her daughter, though she remained less than enthusiastic.[2] The engagement was made public in June, and Clausewitz applied to the king for the necessary permission to marry, which he received in August, together with promotion to major. On 17 December he and Marie von Brühl were married. Their life together continued the close, trusting relationship that had early grown up between them; and despite periods of great stress in Clausewitz's career, it was to remain exceptionally happy, the only serious disappointment being their failure to have children. Both frankly hoped for them, and Clausewitz found it difficult to believe that children would be denied a woman who would make such a good mother. "One boon I want to beg for us," he wrote in a New Year's poem at the beginning of 1812, "a sweet child, playing on the mother's breast."[3]

By his marriage to a lady whose father had been governor of the crown prince and present monarch, who herself had been a lady-in-waiting, and

---

1. Clausewitz to Marie v. Brühl, 17 March 1807, *Correspondence*, p. 98. The fluctuations of Clausewitz's health during these years can be followed in his letters to his fiancée, *ibid.*, pp. 209–218, 263–266; and in his letters to Gneisenau, Clausewitz, *Schriften*, i, 627, 637–638, 650. See also the letter of Princess Louise Radziwill to Stein of 27 June 1811, in Stein, *Briefe und Amtliche Schriften*, iii, ed. W. Hubatsch, Stuttgart, 1961, p. 527; and Caemmerer, pp. 18, 30.
2. Stein to Princess Louise Radziwill, 2 October 1810, *Briefe und Amtliche Schriften*, iii, 411.
3. *Correspondence*, p. 270. Other expressions of their hope for children are contained in Marie v. Clausewitz's reminiscences of her engagement and marriage, written on 1 January 1813, and in his letter to her of 25 April 1813; *ibid.*, pp. 312, 314, 330.

who was a close friend of Princess Marianne, Clausewitz was thought by some to have strengthened his already useful connections with the royal family, an impression further increased by his association with the crown prince. But he had never cared for life at court, and since returning from France had shed whatever qualities of courtier he had once possessed. He now made little effort to control what he himself recognized as his tendency to appear preoccupied and saturnine.[4] Unlike his friend Gneisenau, who could spend all day in committees or on the parade ground and in the evening captivate a dinner party with his vitality and charm, Clausewitz found it impossible to mask his seriousness in company. His wife's young relative Caroline von der Marwitz, whose memoirs have been cited earlier and who was living with the Brühls at the time of the wedding, described his personality as "unfortunate in every respect. There was something cold and negative in his demeanor, which often went so far as to imply disdain of others. He said little, usually because he seemed to feel that people and ordinary topics were not worthy of his attention. At the same time he was animated by poetic passion and sentiments that were expressed in the most idealized love ... for his wife, in verse, and in occasional outbursts of speech. He was filled with a burning ambition, and strove for the self-denial of antiquity rather than for modern ways of stimulation and enjoyment. He had few, but close and firm friends, who expected and hoped more from him than he was able to achieve—whether because of fate, circumstances, or his off-putting personality."[5] If this was an extreme judgment, recollected over the distance of four decades by an ultraconservative grande dame, the general impression it conveyed was borne out by too many contemporaries to be doubted. Stein's characterization of Clausewitz as "un brave homme, mais froid et méthodique" reflected the common view.[6] Younger officers who served under him after the Wars of Liberation commented on his awkwardness and stubborn or embarrassed silence, even in familiar military surroundings. "He lacked the gift of rousing troops to enthusiasm," one subordinate wrote. "When one saw him with soldiers one could actually sense a certain uneasiness in him, which disappeared again as he left them. ... When he was inspector of the Silesian artillery ... he would walk up to officers at assemblies to talk to them; but it often hap-

4. Clausewitz to Marie v. Brühl, 5 October 1807, *ibid.*, p. 144.
5. Caroline v. d. Marwitz later married the Prussian minister of the interior G. A. v. Rochow. The quotation is from the above-cited volume *Vom Leben am preussischen Hofe*, in which her memoirs were published together with those of M. de la Motte-Fouqué. She was the sister-in-law of Marie v. Brühl, her brother F. A. v. d. Marwitz having married Marie's younger sister Franziska in 1803. Franziska died in childbirth and for some years her little daughter was brought up by Marie v. Brühl. Although Marwitz and Clausewitz were on opposite sides on most issues in the political and military reform programs, the relationship between Clausewitz's wife and Marwitz remained very close. See also my *Yorck*, pp. 129, 146–147, 227, 232–234.
6. Stein to his wife, 3 February 1813, *Briefe und Amtliche Schriften*, iv, ed. W. Hubatsch, Stuttgart, 1963, p. 30.

pened that he would stand before this or that one, look at him without saying a word, and then walk on. The officers said that he went to them in order to be thoroughly silent." [7] His lack of facility in military small talk was strengthened by his admiration for Scharnhorst, whom he later described as having been deficient in such "superficial minutiae" as "an authoritarian tone in everyday speech," and with whom he also shared the feeling that parades and other military ceremonial were slightly ridiculous.[8] Only in small groups was his arrogance or indifference replaced by what one subordinate called his "urbanity," and among friends he could be gay, affectionate, and even exuberant. There were times when he would succumb to such violent attacks of laughter that he had to leave the company.[9]

The marriage did little to change the frugality of his bachelor existence. His mother-in-law depended on a royal pension, and his wife was almost without private means; he had nothing but his pay, out of which he helped support his mother until her death in 1811.[10] Caroline von der Marwitz recalls how pleased the young couple was with the sparse furnishings of their new flat, some of which had been wedding presents: "A sofa, six chairs covered in calico, and a few other pieces made up the entire household. Marie ... was delighted when she could entertain a few relatives or good friends with a leg of mutton." [11] When Clausewitz left Berlin for Russia in 1812 he found it difficult to finance the journey; he hoped that his tutorials would bring him a present from the crown prince, and borrowed a small sum from Gneisenau as a reserve.[12] His social life also con-

---

7. *Aus dem Leben des Generals der Infanterie z. D. Dr. Heinrich von Brandt,* ed. H. v. Brandt, Berlin, 1869, ii, 107–108. Similar observations can be found in the recollections of Major Steinmann v. Friederici, who served as Clausewitz's adjutant for some years, *Was sich die Offiziere im Bureau erzählten,* Berlin, 1853, p. 36.

8. Clausewitz, "Über das Leben von Scharnhorst," *Historisch-politische Zeitschrift,* I, 207.

9. Brandt, ii, 104, 136–137. In the second reference Brandt repeats an anecdote that caused Clausewitz and Gneisenau paroxysms of laughter when he told it to them in 1831. It was one of the many versions of the Polish legend of a nobleman named Twardowski, who sold his soul to the devil, after which he invented the art of printing. Years later the devil returned to collect his due; Baron Twardowski raised objections, but the devil replied, while dragging him to hell: "Oh Pani Twardowski, verbum nobile debet esse stabile." Underlying the anecdote and the excessive laughter it occasioned is obviously a sarcastic view of aristocratic concepts of honor. The fact that both Clausewitz and Gneisenau could not feel wholly confident of their own right to a title might have added a painful element to the joke: not only could the word of a noble not be trusted; the nobleman himself might be a fraud.

10. As captain, Clausewitz's annual pay was about 820 taler after deductions, which rose to 1,150 taler on his promotion to major. In addition he received a housing allowance, oats and hay for his horses, and was provided with an orderly; on the other hand, he had to purchase his uniforms and horses, both very expensive items. Since he served on the general staff his pay was between 25 and 30 percent below that of equivalent ranks in the line, to make up for the greater opportunities for advancement enjoyed by officers such as himself, whose duties brought them in close contact with the army's senior generals. *Das Preussische Heer im Jahre 1812,* ed. by the Historical Section of the Great General Staff, Berlin, 1912, pp. 330–332, 542–543. It helps to determine Clausewitz's economic status to compare his pay with professorial salaries at the new University of Berlin. The so-called normal salary for an *Ordinarius* was 1,500 taler; some men received less, others more. Fichte, for example, received 2,000 taler a year.

11. Rochow, pp. 40–41; Marie v. Clausewitz's reminiscences, *Correspondence,* p. 313.

12. Clausewitz to Gneisenau, undated (early 1812), *Schriften,* i, 670–671.

tinued the pattern he had established in Königsberg, though it was expanded somewhat by his wife's acquaintances among Berlin's literary and intellectual circles. It was probably she who introduced him to Wilhelm von Humboldt, the poet Achim von Arnim, and others who frequented the house of her good friend Louise von Voss, the daughter of her old patroness, Countess Berg.[13] They in turn invited him to join the *Christlich-Deutsche Tischgesellschaft,* a group whose members and guests met every second Tuesday to discuss literature and politics. Among them were Fichte and Schleiermacher; Heinrich von Kleist and his partner in the newspaper venture of the *Berliner Abendblätter,* Adam Müller; Stein's confidant Eichhorn, with whom Clausewitz remained on good terms when he returned to live in Berlin in 1818; the poets Brentano and Fouqué; the jurist Savigny; the artist Friedrich Bury, Goethe's associate in Italy and Weimar, who later was to paint a notable portrait of Scharnhorst; and Clausewitz's army friends Tiedemann, Dohna, Röder, and Gerlach.[14] "Philistines," women, and Jews were excluded. The anti-Jewish clause in its statutes was not central to the group's concerns; rather it reflected an increasingly common association between the cultural and political patriotism of the German Romantics and anti-Semitism, which after the Congress of Vienna was to find its most assertive expression in the liberal student movement of the *Burschenschaften.* Nevertheless, it raises the question of Clausewitz's anti-Semitism, which on the slim evidence available is perhaps best answered by saying that he was antagonistic to Jews when he thought of them as Jews, but could be on good terms with Jews who had become assimilated. On the occasion of Napoleon's first abdication he characterized the emperor as being "as tough as a Jew, and equally shameless." [15] Infinitely more disturbing to generations whose experience or historical consciousness has been marked by the Third Reich is a passage in a letter written two years earlier, when Clausewitz was traveling through Poland on his way to Russia. "The whole existence of the Poles," he wrote to his wife, "is as though bound and held together by torn ropes and rags. Dirty German Jews, swarming like vermin in the dirt and misery, are the patricians of this land. A thousand times I thought if only fire would destroy this whole anthill [*Anbau*] so that this unending filth were changed by the clean flame into clean ashes." [16] The

13. Marie v. Brühl to Clausewitz, 17 March 1809, *Correspondence,* pp. 219–220; Rothfels, *Carl von Clausewitz,* p. 131.

14. Clausewitz also subscribed to the volume of essays and poems *Der Philister,* which the *Tischgesellschaft* published privately in May 1811. Fichte's presence at a meeting of the association on 24 January 1812, honoring the hundredth anniversary of the birth of Frederick the Great, is mentioned in Fouqué's memoirs. On the history of the association see Steig, pp. 21–40, 607–639.

15. Clausewitz to his wife, 11 April 1814, *Correspondence,* p. 371.

16. Clausewitz to his wife, 15 May 1812, *ibid.,* p. 287. Clausewitz continues by remarking on the incomprehensible German the Jews speak, and on their high birth rate. While comments of this nature, though not of such violence, are frequent in the correspondence of the time, it is instructive to compare the passage in Clausewitz's letter with Boyen's objective description, in the second volume of his *Erinnerungen,* of the Galician Jews and Poles he encountered in 1812.

prophetic nature of this statement is less significant as evidence of his attitude than its brutality, which is rare in Clausewitz's writings, and suggests strong feelings of dislike, not only of Jews but of Poles as well. Jews who had become assimilated in German society were another matter. After 1815 he was close to at least two couples, the O'Etzels and the Ermans, in which the men had married Jewish wives. O'Etzel was to be a co-editor of Clausewitz's posthumous works, which were published by a firm that had been founded by O'Etzel's Jewish brother-in-law, Julius Eduard Hitzig. This distinction between baptized and unbaptized Jews may also explain why there is no indication that Clausewitz knew Rahel Levin, the friend of Prince Louis Ferdinand, even though he might have felt a stronger affinity to the literary tastes of her circle than to the sentimental medievalism of such writers as Arnim. As was true before the war, several of his friends and close acquaintances frequented Rahel's salon in the Jäger Strasse, among them Prince Radziwill, and Alexander, the gifted younger brother of Friedrich August von der Marwitz, to whom she was linked by particularly close bonds of sympathy and understanding. But perhaps it was consideration for his wife that lay behind his absence—until Rahel was baptized and married Varnhagen von Ense in 1814 she was doubly objectionable to higher society—or he simply preferred to pass his few free hours in the company of men who were passionately patriotic at a time when the state was about to confront new dangers.

Less than a year after Napoleon's triumph over Austria the fragile equilibrium of his system was again in jeopardy. The emperor could neither resolve the conflict in Spain nor reduce it to acceptable proportions, and gradually, in spite of everything that told against it, a new war between France and Russia was accepted in the ministries of Europe as likely, if not yet as inevitable. Since any invasion of Russia depended on Prussia for its communications and supply lines, the political reliability of the monarchy once more became a matter of immediate concern to Napoleon. The energy with which Prussia was reorganizing her army and strengthening her fortresses he found unnecessary, and he was irritated by reports of continuing antagonism to his policies among her political and military leadership. In June 1810, after the French ambassador in Berlin had repeatedly warned the Prussians that Scharnhorst was among the individuals whose attitudes displeased the emperor, Scharnhorst felt compelled to resign as head of the *Allgemeine Kriegsdepartement,* though secretly he carried on most of his functions as *de facto* minister of war and he remained head of the general staff. As part of the intensifying preparations for war, France opened negotiations designed to move Prussia from her official policy of neutrality. Despite impassioned resistance from the reform party and Frederick William's Russian sympathies, the outcome could not be in doubt. By the treaty of 24 February 1812 Prussia was incorporated into Napoleon's front as firmly as any state of the Confederation of the Rhine; depots and staging areas in her territory were placed under French control, as were the major highways running from west to east, and she committed herself to contributing an auxiliary corps of 20,000 men to the new *Grande Armée*.

In the debate over Prussia's policy in the coming war, carried on in secrecy at court and in the ministries, the minority that favored a Russian alliance experienced difficulties in translating its hatred of Napoleon into realistic political terms. The closest collaborators of Scharnhorst—Gneisenau, Boyen, Tiedemann, and Clausewitz—proposed a guerrilla campaign on the Spanish model, waged by regular forces and the armed population, and backed by Russian armies and a British expeditionary corps. The argument that this was a counsel of despair which, if followed, would ruin society while destroying the state they countered by declaring that the state was already doomed, Napoleon having decided on its final dissolution. Their belief is now known to have been unfounded. But, as Clausewitz wrote, so long as the destruction of the state was a possibility, it did not matter whether it was more or less likely. Here he reverted to the thought he had expressed before the war, and subsequently with greater emphasis during his internment in France: no nation should depend for its existence on the good will of another power. If Prussia's future was for Napoleon to decide, she was lost in any event. A war against the tyrant, even if it almost certainly led to defeat, would at least save honor and create the moral strength that alone might inspire the rebirth of the state at some future date. "Whatever our condition, it is essential that we decide to fight to gain our independence ... . It does not matter at all whether we have more or less means with which to save ourselves; the decision should arise from the need for salvation, not from the ease of gaining it"—words in the spirit of Kant's moral imperative, but an imperative that Clausewitz transferred to the ambiguous realm of public affairs without inquiring whether it was necessary or desirable for thousands of others to pay the price of turning his personal convictions into reality.[17] That such views could convince neither the king, the government, nor the army is obvious; and when it became apparent that Frederick William would range himself on the side of France the position of the most determined members of the reform group became untenable.

These developments dealt a severe shock to Clausewitz's psyche. A decade earlier, when he was twenty-one and twenty-two, the uncertainties

---

17. *Bekenntnisdenkschrift*, in *Schriften*, i, 707. During this period Valentini wrote Berenhorst that Clausewitz and his wife were known to have a favorite expression: "To commit one's life to an idea"—a Fichtean statement that Valentini evidently considered absurd or irresponsible. Berenhorst replied by inquiring whether it was the husband's or the wife's favorite expression, and continued by mildly casting doubt on the ideals of the old Prussian school, which Valentini had praised. He concluded that the Frederician Prussians and their ideals "form a category to which, it seems to me, Clausewitz, his other merits notwithstanding, does not belong." Valentini to Berenhorst, 30 November 1812, Berenhorst to Valentini, 9–11 December 1812, Berenhorst, ii, 358.

and the lack of self-confidence that plagued him had been resolved by a double alliance. He had bound himself closely to the most impressive man he had yet encountered, Scharnhorst. Scharnhorst took the place of his father, who had just died, and by intense intellectual labor Clausewitz succeeded in winning him as his teacher and protector. The second supportive power had been the state, to whose strength and honor he committed a good share of his personal self-esteem. Prussia's defeat in 1806 again threw him into dejection. His emotional response certainly went far beyond that of even the more political and idealistic officers. It is unimaginable, for example, that his brother-in-law, Friedrich August von der Marwitz, who had served with distinction in the Jena campaign, experienced personal shame or felt inferior because he was the subject of a state that happened to have been defeated in war. Clausewitz's reunion in 1808 with Scharnhorst, who was now working to regenerate the state's military power, and his collaboration in this task, carried Clausewitz to new heights of confidence and energy. For four years his actions were guided by the principle he himself expressed: "Since the Peace of Tilsit anyone wishing to restore the Prussian state should think about nothing except preparations for a renewal of the struggle, about that and about nothing else." [18] Prussia's surrender to Napoleon in 1812, the removal of Scharnhorst from administrative control of the army, the defeat of the reformers' political hopes: all these Clausewitz could experience only as personal hurts that were unbearable to him.

In the last few weeks before the alliance was concluded, Clausewitz drafted an apologia for those officers who, like himself, were unbending in their opposition to France. The manuscript, parts of which he dictated to his wife, was based on discussions with Gneisenau, Boyen, and others, who added marginal comments and corrections; but even though it was essentially the manifesto of a group holding common views, sections of it were openly personal in tone, and the title he gave to the whole, *Bekenntnisdenkschrift*—memorial of confession, or of belief—accurately reflected the combination of emotional testimony and staff officer's appraisal that made up its contents. [19] A preliminary note declared that the memorial was addressed to "sympathetic friends ... but, further, to other fellow-citizens as a formal protest against any kind of participation in [the policies that] will be decided on, and in what might ensue and will one day be deeply regretted and expiated. Perhaps these lines will also stimulate a feeling of duty and honor in some breasts." [20] In short, the explanation of a political

18. *Ibid.*, p. 694.
19. The memorial, which was completed on or just before 16 February, has been published repeatedly. The most accurate version, indicating variants and corrections, is contained in W. Hahlweg's edition of Clausewitz's *Schriften*, i, 678–751.
20. *Ibid.*, p. 685.

view that had suffered defeat was linked with efforts to change people's minds even at this late date, and these conflicting purposes also affected plans for the memorial's distribution. It was written to be circulated among a few dozen men at most; but there were thoughts of printing another version, necessarily much revised and toned down. In the end, only a few copies passed from hand to hand; but word of the document spread, and it exacerbated the feelings of some of the men who obeyed the new policy against those who, like Clausewitz, decided to quit Prussia and fight Napoleon, even if this meant taking up arms against their own king. Frederick William, who seems to have seen a copy of the operational parts of the manuscript, might easily have regarded the memorial as a repetition of the appeal for reform and action in September 1806, which he had rejected as an impermissible challenge to his authority.

The *Bekenntnisdenkschrift* consists of three separate parts. The first and much the shortest, only twelve manuscript pages in length, is an emotional declaration of independence from the attitudes dominating Prussian society. It opens by castigating the blindness of public opinion in the current international crisis, which is exploited by reactionaries, who appeal to a falsely conceived ideal of Frederick the Great to justify submission to France: "The upper classes are corrupt; court and government officials are the most corrupt." [21] With "irreconcilable hatred" they pursue those who are prepared to fight Napoleon. "Anyone who does not agree that only the most unconditional, shameful submission is one's duty" can count on being "hated, persecuted, publicly accused, denounced before the king, and—betrayed to the French ambassador," this being a reference to Scharnhorst's fate. Only the government can cure Prussia's diseased public opinion; but "in the main it is the lack of confidence in the government that causes general discouragement. Equally, the government has little confidence in its subjects, and even in itself." [22] From this mood of feebleness and impotence Clausewitz dissociates himself and his comrades in a litany of exceptional violence: "I renounce the facile hope of being saved by chance ... the childish hope of taming the tyrant's anger by voluntarily disarming ... the false resignation of a repressed intellect ... the foolish mistrust in our God-given abilities ... the ignominious sacrifice of every honor due to the state and people, of every personal and human dignity." Instead, "I believe and confess that a people can value nothing more highly than the dignity and liberty of its existence. That it must defend these to the last drop of its blood. ... That the shameful blot of cowardly submission can never be erased. ... That the honor of the king and government are at one with the

---

21. *Ibid.*, p. 687. Cf. Gneisenau's description in 1815 of "so-called good society" in Berlin as consisting "mostly of those who supported France." Gneisenau to J. Gruner, 10 April 1815, Pertz-Delbrück, iv, 492.
22. *Bekenntnisdenkschrift*, in *Schriften*, i, 687–688.

honor of the people, and the sole safeguard of its well-being. That a people courageously struggling for its liberty is invincible. That even the destruction of liberty after a bloody and honorable struggle assures the people's rebirth. It is the seed of life, which one day will bring forth a new, securely rooted tree." [23]

We know that Clausewitz would have welcomed war against France under almost any circumstances; but with these sentences he expressed not only his own emotional need to belong to a heroic, autonomous state but also the considered political views of the leaders of the reform group. The belief that an honorable defeat creates the moral strength to build a better society had long been a tenet of the reformers; Scharnhorst had even used it as an argument for war in 1805 and 1806.[24] A few years later to advocate war against Napoleon expressed not only the conviction that the question resolved itself into a moral issue but also the historical experience that it was the lost war of 1806 that alone had opened the door to basic change in Prussia.

The second section, thirty-eight pages long, is less emotional in tone, though it contains barely veiled criticisms of the king. It surveys events since 1806, argues that Napoleon is seeking the destruction of the state, and weighs the advantages and disadvantages of the French alliance, concluding that at best the link with France would increase Prussia's dependence on Napoleon. The king's advisers are blamed for counseling policies which for the moment seem the easier alternative but which can only result in tearing apart monarch and nation. "The king who perishes shamefully insults the nation and is the cause of its misfortunes; the king who succumbs gloriously elevates the nation and is balm on its wounds." [25] Clausewitz greatly exaggerated if he claimed that a conflict between ruler and

23. *Ibid.*, pp. 688–689. I have earlier (p. 133, n. 28) expressed disagreement with Leonard Krieger's interpretation in *The German Idea of Freedom* of Clausewitz's political views during the first years of the reform era. His interpretation of this passage of the *Bekenntnisdenkschrift* strikes me as equally mistaken. He writes, p. 199, that Clausewitz "declared that the whole people must participate militarily in the state for their freedom, but he then insisted that 'the honor of the king and the government is one with the honor of the people and the only palladium of its good,' since the king represents not only 'the moral person of the state but the nationality of the whole people.' " Krieger explains his first quotation, taken from the *Bekenntnisdenkschrift*, with a second quotation from a note Clausewitz wrote nearly three years earlier, in itself a doubtful procedure, to support his general argument that Clausewitz regarded the king's authority as supreme. The message of this segment of the *Bekenntnisdenkschrift* is obviously quite different. It appeals to the king's sense of duty and honor: such dishonorable policies as Prussia's military support of Napoleon also dishonor the monarch personally—a theme repeated in stronger terms in the second memorial. Clausewitz certainly did not believe in popular sovereignty, which indeed would have made him exceptional in early-19th-century Europe, but his position calls for more differentiated analysis than it receives in Professor Krieger's generally admirable study.
24. For instance, in his letter to Prince Hohenlohe of 4 February 1806, *Scharnhorsts Briefe*, p. 270. This belief still echoes through *On War*. See, for example, book VI, ch. 26 (pp. 703–704): "No matter how small and weak a state may be in comparison with its enemy, it must not forgo these last efforts, or one would conclude that its soul is dead."
25. *Bekenntnisdenkschrift*, in *Schriften*, i, 703.

nation was a genuine possibility. In the spring of 1812 only a few men elevated the uncompromising defense of Prussia's independence into the moral absolute that he regarded it to be; but for him policies that compromised the independence of the state actually did call the authority of the monarch into question. He reiterated the point by stressing that "the king is the representative of the nation." His authority is not absolute; it derives from the coincidence of his policies with the public good, even if the public good is not recognized by the majority of the upper and educated classes, as Clausewitz believed was the case in 1812.

The third and longest section is a positive evaluation of Prussia's ability to wage the war that the preceding sections declared to be a moral and political imperative. It begins by listing the state's normal military assets: the adequate number of trained officers and men available, their equipment and supplies, the fortresses on which they could base their operations, and Prussia's geographic advantages—a coastline open to allied vessels, and the relative remoteness of her richest provinces from the main Franco-Russian theater of operations. Then Clausewitz turns to the state's extraordinary asset that would have to be employed in this war: the armed population. Drawing on the fighting in the Vendée and Spain he develops a plan for guerrilla warfare, the size and organization of the irregular force to be raised, the tactical instructions to be issued, and the missions it should be assigned. These concrete proposals are followed by a theoretical discussion of strategy, tactics, and the concept of territorial defense against a superior enemy. The discussion contains much of the argument later to be developed in the relevant chapters of *On War,* but here it is pointed toward an immediate pragmatic end: in 1812 a defensive war fought by the Prussian army and by armed, hurriedly trained civilians could be successful against the French.

The *Bekenntnisdenkschrift* does not lack inconsistencies. On the one hand, it proclaims the identity of king and nation; on the other, the monarch is threatened with the consequence of pursuing unheroic policies: "What will happen when [the king], overwhelmed by violence and disgrace, abandoned by his people, deserted by public opinion, stands alone, a poor prisoner?" [26] Nor does Clausewitz resolve the contradiction of calling public opinion corrupt and submissive while seriously proposing that the people take up arms. Except for remarking that German "patriotic enthusiasms" is not innately inferior to that of the French, which recalls his essay on national character, Clausewitz minimizes the task of rousing the people to wage this most socially destructive type of war. The answer may lie in his judgment of the differences in political outlook of various social groups. The upper classes will have to be taught to support a war against France;

26. *Ibid.,* p. 703.

but he takes it for granted that the vast majority of the population is patriotic and obedient, and that the peasants will follow a royal command to wage guerrilla warfare under their elected or appointed leaders, who, as in the Vendée, would be drawn from the gentry and the church. But his inconsistencies and his asymmetrical treatment of the various topics vanish before the revolutionary message that unifies the three sections into a combative whole. The argument proceeds logically and in a manner that we have come to recognize as characteristic of its author. From a forcefully defined emotional source it flows out to historical interpretations, and on to a combination of theoretical analysis and practical suggestions by which the original desire for action may be satisfied. In the *Denkschrift* Clausewitz's concept of the state and his view of his own relationship with the state, as these had developed since his early observations on politics and war, reach a point of culmination: the idea of the state had become far more important than its reality at a particular moment, and those who recognize the ethical essence of the state now have the right to judge its formal political leaders—even the king.

That men holding such beliefs would refuse to observe the new policy of collaboration with France followed almost inevitably. To Tiedemann, who in these weeks left the army to accept a Russian commission, Scharnhorst wrote: "I cannot condemn your decision, because everyone must first see that he remains true to himself." [27] Stein, writing from St. Petersburg to Princess Radziwill, acknowledged that "at this moment it is very difficult to reconcile the duties of the citizen with those of the moral man." [28] But Clausewitz went a step farther by denying that a conflict existed. The moral duties that he and his friends recognized were identical with their political duties and their obligations as Prussian subjects. They believed that by fighting the incarnation of the "principle of destruction," even if this meant facing their former comrades, they were saving the state's honor and morally as well as politically assuring its survival.

On 31 March, after the Franco-Prussian alliance had been ratified by Frederick William, and after a corps of the French army had entered Berlin, Clausewitz quit the city. Suffering from severe neuralgic pains, "cursing every rock over which I drove," he traveled to Silesia, where he passed the next month with Scharnhorst and Dohna.[29] His decision to leave Prussia was as firm as ever, but he had not yet sent in his resignation, and he spent the time writing the essay that summed up the lessons he had given the crown prince. When he sent the manuscript to his former pupil, he added the note, already cited above, exhorting the prince to be daring, cunning, persevering, and always ready for a glorious death. He considered

---

27. Letter of 28 April 1812, *Scharnhorsts Briefe*, p. 428.
28. Letter of 13 March 1812, Stein, *Briefe und Amtliche Schriften*, iii, 619.
29. Clausewitz to his wife, 2 April 1812, *Correspondence*, p. 270.

it his duty, he wrote to his wife, "to have at some stage breathed a spark into his soul—whether or not it is taken amiss or people find me ridiculous. What do I care since I must leave this land in any case, and should leave it more gladly if such a statement were to be taken as a crime." [30] On 18 April he submitted his resignation, couched in terms that concealed rather than clarified his reasons and future plans: "Private affairs compel me to take this step, which is one of incredible difficulty for me, but perhaps will determine my life's happiness. ... The gratitude, the sense of closest allegiance and of most loyal devotion to His Royal Majesty's person that at the present moment inspire me more than ever, will never be extinguished." [31] The king granted the request with a single, cold sentence. Scharnhorst, who had also tried to resign, was given indefinite leave instead. Gneisenau and Boyen were sent on confidential missions to foreign courts, while Tiedemann and Dohna, like Clausewitz, entered Russian service. Of the approximately thirty officers who left the army at the time in what could be regarded as a kind of protest, Frederick William singled out Clausewitz both then and later for especially harsh treatment. It was as though he were exacting revenge from one of the most vulnerable members of the reform party for the affronts that his dynastic self-esteem had suffered through the many changes of the past years. That he could associate Clausewitz with the suppressed antagonism of Prince Ferdinand's family before 1806, and with the broader German sympathies of Princess Marianne, the Radziwills, and of Countess Berg, who for a time had made Queen Louise doubt his judgment, may have contributed to the king's antipathy, which now openly revealed itself. Finally, Clausewitz made himself into a likely target not only through these associations and by his emotional, uncompromising attitude, which neither rank nor family connections could excuse, but also by his disregard of certain legal obligations. In his letter of resignation he failed to state his intention to enter Russian service, and to request permission to do so. Some months later charges were, in fact, drawn up against him, and he was ordered to defend himself at a court hearing in Berlin on pain of suffering confiscation of his property in case of nonappearance. [32] But long before the judicial wheels began to turn he had

---

30. Clausewitz to his wife, 12 April 1812, *ibid.*, pp. 274–275.
31. Quoted by M. Lehmann in *Knesebeck und Schön*, Leipzig, 1875, p. 54, n. 1.
32. *Ibid.*, p. 54. On 20 August 1812 the *Kammergericht*, Berlin's highest court, issued the following citation, which was published in the Berlin and Königsberg newspapers: "Since the retired General Staff Major and teacher at the local War College, Herr Carl Philipp Gottlieb v. Clausewitz, born near Magdeburg, departed from these territories contrary to regulations, and also entered Imperial Russian service without permission of His Majesty the King, this court not only calls on him to return at once to Prussian territory but also cites him to appear before the court ... to account personally for his departure. Should the individual named above report neither in person nor in writing within the period specified, and in the latter case request an extension for returning, he can expect that no extension will be granted. On the contrary, according to law he will be deprived of all property within these territories, as well as of any inheritance he may receive in the future ... ." A second demand by the court for

left Silesia and the Prussian state. On 20 May he reached the Tsar's head-quarters in Vilna, where letters of recommendation from Gneisenau and Count Lieven, the Russian ambassador to Prussia, assured him a ready wel-come.

Clausewitz's appearance was published as late as 2 March 1813. The citation was quashed by order of the government on 19 March. P. Czygan, *Zur Geschichte der Tagesliteratur während der Freiheitskriege*, 2 vols., Leipzig, 1909–11, ii, 60.

ᏇᏇ 9 ᏗᏗ

NAPOLEON'S DESTRUCTION

IN A LIFE OF FIFTY-ONE YEARS AND A MILITARY CA-
reer that lasted nearly four decades, Clausewitz went to war three times. As
an adolescent in 1794 and 1795 he was swept, passive and uncomprehending, into a stream of exertion, violence, and suffering, from which he
emerged determined to understand the process of which he had been a part,
to which his life was committed, and which by shaping the interaction of
great states guided the course of world history. His second experience of
war was the brief interlude of the campaign of 1806. His third exposure
lasted the longest and was the most significant, not only for its content but
because now he possessed both intellectual maturity and the technical and
political information essential for an understanding of the manifold character of modern war. Between 1812 and 1815 he took part in, or was able to
observe at close hand, the unfolding of great strategic combinations, as well
as major battles, detached operations, arming of the people, and political-
military negotiations; and he witnessed, underlying these expressions of
state power, the human reality of "corpses and dying men among smoking
ruins, and thousands of ghostlike men [who] pass by screaming and begging and crying in vain for bread." [1] The range and depth of his experiences in Russia and in central Europe, as the French were slowly pushed
back into their own country, taught him a great deal, as he himself repeatedly noted. His education was given impetus by the pronounced emotional
satisfaction of seeing that the force that had disrupted his life and his society since adolescence was at last on the decline. Napoleon and revolutionary France were being destroyed by their own weapons and ideas, which
were turned against them in the service of national liberty, a cause whose
justice could not be questioned.

Before these intellectual and emotional triumphs, disappointments in

---

1. Letter to his wife, 29 November 1812, *Correspondence,* p. 305.

other respects waned in importance, though that is not to say that they were not strongly felt. Clausewitz was outspoken in his scorn at the selfish and narrow policies with which German princes, among them the king of Prussia, compromised the cause of German freedom; he was increasingly bitter over the bad luck and injustice that handicapped his own career. The letters he and his wife wrote to their friend Gneisenau, who in these years reached the pinnacle of glory, make clear the extent of Clausewitz's discouragement. By the time of Waterloo he had become resigned to the fact that his ambitions for exceptional distinction in war had finally come to nothing. But the sometimes angry and depressed recognition that he would never achieve what had been perhaps the most cherished goal of his youth did not lead to inactivity. He overcame the disappointment by the intense intellectual labor of studying and interpreting the final campaigns between the Napoleonic Empire and the rest of Europe. Until 1812 the wish for success in politics and war had gone hand in hand with the wish to master politics and war intellectually; now ambition—frustrated by circumstance and royal disfavor—was very largely sublimated in mental effort.

Shortly after he arrived in Vilna, where he encountered several friends—among them Gneisenau, who soon left on a mission to England, and Tiedemann—Clausewitz realized that though he was now on the right side of the conflict it would be difficult to gain an appointment in which he would be more than a uniformed bystander. Unresolved rivalries among the senior Russian commanders, and their disagreement over the strategy to be adopted against Napoleon, made headquarters an awkward place for a stranger, particularly if he spoke only a few words of Russian. Clausewitz was commissioned a lieutenant-colonel on the general staff and initially assigned to help General Phull, in former years Scharnhorst's colleague as general-quartermaster-lieutenant, who had entered the Russian service in 1807 and now acted as a personal adviser to the Tsar. Clausewitz, who had been his student at the Berlin Institute, thought him honest but ineffectual, "an abstract genius." In his history of the War of 1812 he wrote that he had "never known anyone who so easily lost his head, who while thinking only of great matters was so easily overwhelmed by the smallest aspect of the real world." [2]

Phull had drafted a plan that called for the main Russian force to

---

2. "Der Feldzug von 1812 in Russland," *Werke,* vii, 8, 10. Together with his letters to his wife from Russia, only a minority of which have survived, Clausewitz's history of the War of 1812 is the most valuable source on his Russian experiences. The sections dealing with his own activities were written soon after the event, perhaps as early as 1814, and the operational accounts some years later. Passages from letters to his wife, Stein, and others are repeated almost verbatim in the text. Additional information is contained in the memoirs and correspondence of such acquaintances as Stein, Arndt, Dorow, and Wolzogen, and in the official diary of the Prussian auxiliary corps with the *Grande Armée,* A. v. Seydlitz, *Tagebuch des Königlich Preussischen Armeekorps unter Befehl des General-Lieutenants von York,* 2 vols., Berlin and Posen, 1823.

withdraw into a fortified camp at Drissa near the Duna River, between the roads to Moscow and St. Petersburg, where it would either halt the French advance or threaten its flank and rear. Work had begun on the fortifications, but much doubt persisted about the soundness of the scheme, and Clausewitz's first task was to inspect the camp and its lines of communication. He found the position even less suitable than he had expected, and on his return tactfully indicated as much to the Tsar, thus adding another small voice to the chorus opposing the camp and favoring instead a further retreat.[3] With Scharnhorst, Boyen, and other Prussian officers, Clausewitz shared the belief that only a strategic withdrawal, possibly beyond Moscow, would save the Russians, and his major concern during the opening weeks of the war was that no artificial schemes should interfere with what he took to be the natural course of fighting, which compelled the Russians, even against their wishes, to give way before Napoleon.[4] As he had suspected years before, the emperor might eventually be driven to overestimate the significance of victorious battles and the conquest of political and administrative centers. "If Bonaparte should someday reach Poland," he had written in 1804, "he would be easier to defeat than in Italy, and in Russia I would consider his destruction as certain." [5]

Now the expected had arrived. "At heart," he was to write in *On War*, "all Europe was opposed to Bonaparte; he had stretched his resources to the very limit; in Spain he was fighting a war of attrition; and the vast expanse of Russia meant that an invader's strength could be worn down to the bone in the course of five hundred miles' retreat. Tremendous things were possible; not only was a massive counterstroke a certainty if the French offensive failed (and how could it succeed if the Tsar would not make peace nor his subjects rise against him?), but the counterstroke could bring the French to utter ruin. The highest wisdom could never have devised a better strategy than the one the Russians followed unintentionally." [6]

Phull was one of the sources from which continued interference in what Tolstoy was later to call the inevitable march of events might be expected; and since in any case he had lost much of his influence over the Tsar, Clausewitz persuaded him to leave the army. Clausewitz himself sought an appointment away from headquarters, and through the good offices of Count Lieven and yet another German serving with the Russians, Colonel von Wolzogen, he was made chief of staff of the Russian rear

3. Nothing justifies K. Linnebach's statement in the introduction to his edition of Clausewitz's letters, *Correspondence*, p. 18, that Clausewitz's report "contributed significantly to the renunciation of the unfortunate scheme of making a determined stand in the Camp of Drissa." Clausewitz, on the contrary, attributes little or no importance to his mission but stresses the widespread Russian dissatisfaction with Phull's plan.
4. Meinecke, *Boyen*, i, 235; Clausewitz, *Werke*, vii, 15, 28.
5. Clausewitz, *Strategie*, p. 42.
6. *On War*, book VIII, ch. 8 (p. 905).

guard. His lack of Russian condemned him to virtual inactivity, and he was soon superseded by an officer of higher rank.[7] When the retreating armies united at Smolensk, where severe fighting took place on 16 and 17 August, Clausewitz was present as an officer on the staff of the First West Army. On 29 August, Kutuzov took command over the combined armies, and a week later fought a major battle near the village of Borodino, which Clausewitz attended in yet another capacity, as nominal chief of staff of a cavalry corps of some 2,500 men. The corps was sent on a pointless mission, so that Clausewitz, devoid of power and responsibility, "thanked God that under such circumstances he had been reduced to a complete zero." [8] But perhaps the very fact that he was excluded from the routine of staff work and of tactical decisions helped him to see more clearly than most the natural, inevitable character of the campaign, which he was to emphasize so strongly in his history of 1812 and in *On War*. Borodino itself impressed him as a remarkable episode of mutual attrition and exhaustion, which Kutuzov neither wanted nor needed to fight, since by invading Russia "Bonaparte had become involved in such a serious business that for the Russians things began to go well by themselves, and a successful outcome would necessarily result without much additional effort." [9] For the remainder of the retreat, Clausewitz served with the rear guard, his horse being shot from under him during one "violent ... action, which lasted far into the night," and even though the French appeared invincible, he was confirmed in his belief that only a premature peace could now save them.[10] When, after the fall of Moscow, Kutuzov marched southwest to Tula and then to Kaluga, he thought it certain that Napoleon would soon relinquish the city.

On the march from Moscow to Kaluga, Clausewitz received the news that Karl von Tiedemann had been killed in action, shot by a hussar of the Prussian auxiliary corps that was attached to the *Grande Armée*. Tiedemann had served as chief of staff to the Russian forces covering Riga and the approaches to St. Petersburg, and during the third week of September Clausewitz learned that he was to take his dead friend's place. His journey, circling Moscow over Tula, Yaroslavl, and Novgorod, was made more perilous by the suspicions of Russian militia detachments, which in one town held him as a French spy and sent him back to Kutuzov's headquarters.[11]

Clausewitz finally reached St. Petersburg in the middle of October, where he encountered Boyen, Dohna, Stein, and the poet Arndt among the many Germans gathered at imperial headquarters. From them he learned of

7. L. v. Wolzogen, *Memoiren*, Leipzig, 1851, p. 96; Clausewitz, *Werke*, vii, 42–44, 104–105.
8. *Ibid.*, p. 157.
9. *Ibid.*, pp. 135, 158.
10. Letters to his wife, 30 September and 4 November 1812, *Correspondence*, pp. 296–297, 300–301.
11. Clausewitz, *Werke*, vii, 189.

the proceedings that had been opened against him in Berlin. His feelings at being singled out for punishment among the members of the reform party are unmistakable in his letters to his wife, even though he expressed himself with some restraint since anything sent by diplomatic mail was liable to be read by government agents. In his anger, and no doubt encouraged by such men as Stein and Arndt, he seemed for a time to reject the Prussian monarchy in favor of a united German fatherland, which he believed would remember him with gratitude, and "even at our graves will praise the good intentions to which we sacrificed our fortunes and lives. If we should fall victim to these hard times I think we will find it easier to bear honorable misfortune, while so many others submit to dishonor." [12] Meinecke, describing the mood of the German patriots in Russia during these weeks, comments that "as Clausewitz had written in the spring, a drop of poison really had entered the bloodstream of the Prussian state when it submitted to France. Stein and Clausewitz felt this in the strongest possible manner in those autumn days of 1812. ... Clausewitz [as well as Stein] was at that time in danger of relinquishing his fatherland." [13] Meinecke concludes by quoting a passage from a letter Clausewitz sent his wife on hearing that a Prussian tribunal was about to convict him: "Let them do it in God's name! Anyone who has witnessed the scenes of misery and need here, which the German governments helped bring about, will not feel his pride broken by their condemnations." [14] His German rather than Prussian mood contributed to the decision of again seeking a change in assignment. Instead of proceeding to Riga, Clausewitz applied for admission to the Russo-German Legion, which was being organized in St. Petersburg, and was designated as its chief of staff. [15]

The genesis of the Russo-German Legion began with various attempts inspired by Austria during the War of 1809 to employ regular troops and free corps on expeditions deep into French-held territory, where they would disrupt the enemy's lines of communication, prepare the ground for major allied operations, especially for a British landing on the German coast, and stimulate popular uprisings. We have noted the interest that Gneisenau and Clausewitz, among others, showed at the time in the possibility of irregular operations on the Spanish model, an interest that had not waned in intervening years, and that Clausewitz had again fully explored in the third *Bekenntnisdenkschrift.* In 1809 the most prominent examples had been the expedition of the Duke of Brunswick-Oels from Bohemia across Germany

12. Letter to his wife, 27 October 1812, *Correspondence,* pp. 298–299.
13. Meinecke, *Boyen,* i, 248–249.
14. Clausewitz to his wife, 29 November 1812, *Correspondence,* p. 305.
15. On the Legion see in particular B. v. Quistorp, *Die Kaiserlich Russisch-Deutsche Legion,* Berlin, 1860; and G. Venzky, *Die Russisch-Deutsche Legion in den Jahren 1811–1815,* Wiesbaden, 1966, which contains valuable documents on the intentions of its political and financial sponsors, on the recruiting of its members, and on other aspects of its history before it went on active service in 1813.

and the smaller actions by Dörnberg, who tried to overthrow Jerome in Westphalia, and by the Prussian Major Schill, who without orders left Berlin with his hussar regiment and a company of *Jäger* to engage French troops in former Prussian territories with the hope of starting an insurrection and forcing Frederick William to enter the war on Austria's side. These and other attempts failed because French military superiority was too great and because the civilian population refused to take up arms in what appeared to be a hopeless enterprise.[16]

By 1812, the Prussian officers who believed in the military and political potential of insurrection, Gneisenau at their head, had come to appreciate that to Prussia and Germany the Spanish guerrilla could be an inspiration but not a model. They now held that if only because the north-German plain was not as favorable to irregular operations as the peninsula, Prussia should not choose the slow road of guerrillas gradually weakening the security of the occupying forces, but rather resort to a well-integrated campaign of regular troops and armed civilians, under firm central control, seeking to defeat the French armies in battle. In this process the Legion was to act as an early regular force that provided a focus for insurrection, mobilized the population and engaged in minor operations preparatory to the arrival of the main armies. The founder and provisional head of the Legion was the Duke of Oldenburg, uncle of the Tsar, who was compelled to relinquish his position when it became apparent that his views and methods did not accord with those of Stein, who had become interested in the Legion as a suitable instrument for his own political purposes. For a time Gneisenau was considered for the post of commanding general; eventually the appointment went to Count Wallmoden-Gimborn, a cousin of Stein. In the military sphere, the Legion may be said to have paralleled the anti-particularist orientation of the Committee for German Affairs that Stein had founded in Russia; and indeed his committee became the political agency responsible for the Legion, acting as its representative in negotiations with Russian authorities, and administering the substantial sums with which the force was subsidized by Russia and Britain. The all-German spirit of the Legion was bluntly affirmed by Stein and his collaborators. Arndt, who served as the Legion's paid publicist, expressed both his personal hopes and Stein's intentions when he wrote that "the German Legion is designed to further a union of German hearts and energies, and to

16. In the last two decades some East German historians have attempted to refurbish, with different ideological decoration, the old nationalist thesis of significant popular participation in the wars against France in 1809 and 1813, but their arguments, based on inadequate and contradictory evidence, seem to me entirely unconvincing, while their political motives are only too apparent. I share the conclusion of such historians as Meinecke and Ritter, as well as of such recent studies as R. Wohlfeil's *Vom Stehenden Heer des Absolutismus zur Allgemeinen Wehrpflicht*, Frankfurt, 1964, and the same author's *Spanien und die Deutsche Erhebung, 1808–1814*, Wiesbaden, 1965, that broad patriotic sentiment in the population at large had very little direct impact on recruitment or on the course of military operations.

abolish the evil separation and division of Germans. Its name indicates that it encompasses all Germans ... . It is a focus where [Germans] can gather and learn that only one Germany exists and should exist." [17]

That such views did not merely express the poetic enthusiasm of a civilian propagandist but were taken seriously by many is shown, for example, by Scharnhorst's son-in-law, Friedrich von Dohna, who had been commissioned a lieutenant-colonel in the Legion. The Legion, he wrote in a report to Stein, "is a glorious center round which little by little a sizeable mass can and undoubtedly will collect. ... [In it] the prejudices of a fragmented German nationalism are extinguished, and everyone will be guided by a common German love and faithfulness. It will suit everyone in Germany to whom ordinary military pedantry and aristocracy seems unbearable." [18] But despite the idealism and energy of its leading members and the financial support it received, the Legion grew slowly. The German prisoners of war who were to provide its rank and file were decimated by hunger and epidemics, some Russian authorities obstructed the efforts of the Legion's recruiting officers, and by the end of the year the Legion still numbered less than 1,700 men. [19] Until it was operational, which could not be expected before the spring of 1813, the Legion's chief of staff had little to do. Consequently Clausewitz asked for a temporary assignment to one of the Russian field armies, and on 11 November received orders to report to Wittgenstein, whose army was interposing itself between the left wing of the *Grande Armée*—Macdonald's X Corps before Riga—and the main French force retreating from Moscow.

When followed on the map, the movements of the French and Russian forces in the autumn of 1812 seemed to trace patterns of strategic opportunities and dangers; but for the small armies of some tens of thousands of men, marching and fighting over the vast Russian plain, at times separated by hundreds of miles from their comrades north and south, the theoretical complexities resolved into a few realities of supply, physical effort, and tactical confrontation. By November the Russian objective had been reduced to the destruction of the French columns that were withdrawing from Moscow, a task that did not call for strategic combinations. If, nevertheless, destruction could not be achieved because the Russians were fatigued and cautious and because of Napoleon's continued daring, the alternative was to chase out of the country whatever French remnants could extricate themselves from the fighting and could survive hunger and the weather. When Clausewitz joined Wittgenstein's army on the 16th or 17th of November, the Russians had just repelled the last attempt of the French reserve under

17. E. M. Arndt, *Zwei Worte über die Entstehung und Bestimmung der teutschen Legion*, n. p., 1813, pp. 23–24.
18. F. v. Dohna to Stein, January 1813, quoted in Venzky, pp. 69–70.
19. *Ibid.*, p. 74.

Oudinot and Victor to clear the path for the main force. Had Wittgenstein exploited his success by immediately advancing southwest toward the Berezina he would have rendered Napoleon's escape unlikely. His orders, and fear of facing the emperor himself, delayed him so that Napoleon slipped through once more, though at heavy cost. While Kutuzov slowly followed the main army, Wittgenstein again turned north to cut off the French in Lithuania. The French viceroy at Vilna had waited very late to order Macdonald to withdraw; the incompetence of a messenger extended the delay, so that Macdonald did not receive definite word until 18 December. He began his retreat to Tilsit at once; by this time advance units of Wittgenstein's army, one of which was accompanied by Clausewitz, had approached the East Prussian border, and were about to move between Macdonald and his goal. Nevertheless it could be expected that the French, who were marching rapidly despite the terrible weather, would escape or fight their way through the thin barriers that the Russians might throw in their path. What complicated this simple operational equation of distance, time, and numerical strengths, and made it significant out of all proportion to the numbers involved, was the fact that nearly two-thirds of Macdonald's force consisted of 14,000 Prussians, the greater part of the auxiliary corps that Prussia contributed to the *Grande Armée* under the terms of the French alliance. These troops were under the immediate command of Lieutenant-General von Yorck, a man who was strongly opposed to the French, and who in the years before 1812 had supported most of Scharnhorst's program without himself belonging to the radical reform party.[20] In his hatred of Napoleon, his grasp of military realities, and the popularity he enjoyed among his soldiers he resembled Blücher, though he was more cerebral, less the happy warrior. As senior officers deeply rooted in the Frederician tradition, who nevertheless welcomed the revolution in war, the two men played an important part in shaping the character of the Prussian army after 1806.

Since September, Yorck had been in intermittent contact with the Russians, who provided him with information on the progress of the war and assured him of the continued friendship that the Tsar entertained toward Prussia. The desirability of Yorck's quitting the French cause had been muted, but Yorck quite correctly had gained the impression that even severe French reverses in Russia would not induce Frederick William and Hardenberg to abandon the alliance. Now a change of sides was again proposed by General Diebitsch, an officer of Prussian descent, who commanded Wittgenstein's advance guard. The tactical situation of the retreat favored Diebitsch's attempt. The Prussian troops had been the last to

20. On Yorck's relations to the reformers, on his contributions to tactical and technical modernization, and on his support of conscription and arming the population, see my *Yorck*, especially the concluding discussion on pp. 220–245.

withdraw and were several marches behind Macdonald. On Christmas Day, Diebitsch moved between the two columns. Yorck could easily have pushed Diebitsch's small force aside; but at least on paper the Prussians now appeared cut off, which seemed to justify talks between the two sides. Negotiations began in earnest, with a view to neutralizing the Prussian corps for the time being. Clausewitz served as Russian representative, supported by his friend Dohna, whom the commander of the Russian army covering Riga had sent to Yorck with similar intentions. On the 29th, Yorck's first adjutant returned from Berlin to Prussian headquarters in the village of Tauroggen to report that the attitude of the king had not changed. On the same day, Clausewitz brought Yorck dispatches from Wittgenstein, which he himself characterized as *ultima ratio,* indicating that within forty-eight hours additional Russian units would arrive in the area and pose a genuine threat to the Prussians. To Yorck's question of whether Wittgenstein's troops would really reach the indicated positions on the 31st, Clausewitz replied with words that can stand as a precise exegesis of the concept of friction that he was later to propound in *On War*: "I guarantee the honesty of the letter ... ; whether these intentions really will be fulfilled I can, of course, not guarantee, since Your Excellency knows that in war with the best will in the world one must often fall short of the line one has set oneself." After a few seconds of reflection, Yorck took Clausewitz's hand and said, "You have me." The scene, in which the clash of conflicting loyalties had reached extremes, reminded Clausewitz of Schiller's *Wallenstein.*[21]

Yorck's decision to quite the French left Macdonald too weak to take a stand on the Niemen. He was compelled to continue his retreat across East Prussia, gathering the scattered French garrisons as he went. The Russians slowly followed. Soon they were joined by Yorck, who, ignoring orders from Berlin for his removal from command and arrest, renounced neutralization for overt support of the Russians. The war spilled into central Europe, and it grew likely that in any future campaign Napoleon would be limited to the western parts of Germany for his operational base. The Prussian government, however, continued to adhere to the French alliance.

21. Clausewitz, "Der Feldzug von 1812 in Russland," *Werke,* vii, 207–228; Paret, *Yorck,* pp. 191–196. A comparison of manuscripts and letters by Clausewitz with the document signed by Yorck and Diebitsch indicates that it was Clausewitz who wrote the text of the Convention of Tauroggen. Notwithstanding the claims of strict monarchists and lovers of the conspiratorial that Yorck acted in accordance with secret instructions from Berlin, the evidence conclusively demonstrates that the decision was his own. The documents and the secondary literature are exhaustively analyzed by W. Elze in *Der Streit um Tauroggen,* Breslau, 1926. Since 1945, East German historians have posited the patriotic "wishes and demands" of the Russian and German masses as an essential factor in Yorck's decision, without, however, presenting any new evidence. But, as one scholar frankly admits: "The problem is less a question of interpreting the sources than a question of one's concept of history: Do 'men' make history, or the masses? That is what matters. Not until the role of the masses is revealed everywhere can Yorck's deed be seen in the proper light." R. Röder, "Zur Geschichte der Konvention von Tauroggen," *Das Jahr 1813,* ed. F. Straube, Berlin (East), 1963, pp. 90–91.

"What kinds of opinions are held in Berlin?" Yorck wrote on 13 January. "Have men sunk so low that they will not dare break the chains of slavery that we have meekly borne for five years? Now or never is the time to regain liberty and honor. ... With bleeding heart I tear the bonds of obedience and wage war on my own." [22] He began to mobilize the resources of the province to provide himself with an adequate operational base, force the king into a break with France, and fill the political vacuum which the Russians might otherwise be tempted to exploit. Stein, who had arrived in Königsberg as Russian plenipotentiary, added his vast energy to drive the province further from its "rigid monarchical loyalty" into war with France. At a special session, the East Prussian Estates agreed to reinforce Yorck's corps with conscripts and volunteers, and to form a *Landwehr*, or militia, of 20,000 men backed by a *Landsturm*, or home guard, both organized according to a scheme that Clausewitz drafted, closely following the proposals he had developed in his *Bekenntnisdenkschrift* almost twelve months earlier. On 11 February the Königsberg newspaper published an order that all officers on half-pay in the province were to report to Clausewitz for assignment to the new force. [23]

German historians are agreed on the exceptional nature of the decision to establish the *Landwehr*. "What was undertaken here," Gerhard Ritter writes in a characteristic evaluation, "the raising of a popular army by a province, financed by the province, without prior permission of the king, was something unheard of in the absolutist state. It was undoubtedly a revolutionary act, all assurances of obedience and pious faith in the subsequent agreement of the king notwithstanding." [24] East Prussia in fact, if not officially, entered the war against Napoleon, and a shift in the monarchy's position became almost unavoidable. Toward the end of January the king and his ministers left Berlin, which was controlled by the French, for Silesia, and on 16 March Prussia declared war on France. In his memoirs Boyen wrote that "without Tauroggen and the rising of the East Prussian Estates, Scharnhorst very likely would not have succeeded in overcoming the French party [at court] and the king's indecision." Clausewitz's evaluation is more modest and shows greater awareness of the processes of history: "It would be unreasonable to believe that had it not been for the decision General Yorck reached at Tauroggen ... Bonaparte would still occupy the French throne and the French would still rule Europe. Such great results are the effects of an infinite number of causes, or rather forces, most of which would have retained their strength even without General Yorck. But

---

22. Yorck to General v. Bülow, quoted in Paret, *Yorck*, p. 193.
23. *Ibid.*, p. 194; R. Caemmerer, *Clausewitz*, Berlin, 1905, pp. 40–44; Czygan, i, 59. Count Alexander Dohna and his brother Friedrich, Clausewitz's friend, revised Clausewitz's draft and put it in final legal form.
24. Ritter, *Stein*, p. 423.

it cannot be denied that the decision of this general had enormous consequences, and in all likelihood very considerably speeded up the final outcome." [25]

In Clausewitz's life, 1812 marks the high point of his open allegiance to a political ideal, rather than to the reality of the politically inadequate Prussian state. From the beginning of the year he had not ceased to associate himself with actions that disregarded or opposed the king's will: he worked against the French alliance, quit the Prussian service, played a part in persuading Yorck to disobey orders, and helped to mobilize the East Prussian population for war against the French at a time when these were still officially allies of Prussia. His behavior was consistent and followed logically on far earlier attitudes, but more than ever it left him exposed to the accusation of being a disobedient and unpatriotic subject.

Clausewitz returned to Berlin with Wittgenstein's corps in the second week of March, and stayed with his wife and mother-in-law for a fortnight before joining Scharnhorst in Silesia, where the court and supreme headquarters were temporarily established. [26] His request for readmission to the Prussian army was turned down by the king, who quashed the legal proceedings outstanding against him, but wrote that readmission could be justified only by extraordinarily distinguished service in the coming campaign. [27] The crown prince and other members of the court followed the king's lead and treated him with "marked coldness," as Clausewitz indignantly wrote to his wife. [28] The young princes regarded his presence in Russian uniform as an affront to their father, and behind his back called him "Lausewitz"—a term standing in remarkable juxtaposition to Stein's simultaneous characterization of Napoleon's admirers in the royal entourage as "insects at court." [29] Among the royal family only his former superior, Prince August, and his friend Prince Wilhelm were sympathetic; but they were powerless to change the mind of the king, who remained adamantly opposed to Clausewitz's readmission, even in the face of appeals by Gneisenau, Scharnhorst, and Hardenberg.

Under these circumstances, the best that his friends could do for Clausewitz was to have him appointed Russian liaison officer on Blücher's staff, where in reality he again served as Scharnhorst's assistant. Once more,

25. Clausewitz, "Der Feldzug von 1812 in Russland," *Werke,* vii, 238–239.

26. When the French threatened Berlin in May, Marie v. Clausewitz and her mother left the city "convinced that as mother-in-law and wife of a well-known enemy of the French they would be exposed to special dangers." They spent the summer in Prague, as guests of Stein; Rochow, pp. 53–54.

27. Clausewitz's attempts to return to Prussian service are related in letters to his wife of 26 March, 1 April, 4 April, 9 April, 18 April, 22 April, and 11 and 31 June 1813, *Correspondence,* pp. 320, 322, 325–328, 340–343.

28. Letters of 4 and 9 April 1813, *ibid.,* pp. 325, 327.

29. Prince William [later Emperor William I] to the crown prince, 30 March 1813, in *Hohenzollernbriefe aus den Freiheitskriegen 1813–1815,* ed. H. Granier, Leipzig, 1913, p. 8; Stein to Princess Louise Radziwill, 12 April 1813, in *Briefe und Amtliche Schriften,* iv, 91.

and at a critical time, Clausewitz found himself near the center of the state's military energies, as Scharnhorst gradually overcame opposition and inertia to carry Prussia into the grand alliance against Napoleon. These months—from the French collapse in Russia to the opening battle of the spring campaign—constituted the climax of Scharnhorst's life. In 1811 and 1812 he had resisted the French alliance, not because he demanded that Prussia meet his psychological expectations, as Clausewitz did, but on the realistic grounds that German liberty could not be entrusted to the care of Britain, Russia, or even Austria. It was self-evident to him that France would never relinquish northern Germany unless Prussia turned against her. When Prussia became the emperor's ally instead, Scharnhorst retired from most of his positions and left Berlin. He might still take steps to improve the manufacture of weapons or to insure that those fortresses remaining in Prussian control were strengthened, but he was removed from any real authority. In his Silesian exile he felt, he said, like a transplanted tree. From afar he observed the progress of the war, followed the fates of his friends and pupils on both sides, and after an interruption of many years resumed work on his treatise on the theory and practice of gunnery, completing the third volume and beginning the fourth. His wife had died soon after he had entered the Prussian service; now he fell in love once more. His profound need for affection, which had always accompanied the deliberation and reserve of his public manner, once again burst into the open to fill a void, which, he wrote, even the closest friendship could not quite do. The woman was almost forty years younger than he, daughter not of an officer or official but of lower-middle-class parents, her background similar to the frugal, hard-working environment in which he himself had been brought up. "I am not ashamed to confess," he wrote to a friend, "that love can still shake me to my innermost being." [30] The episode seemed to crystallize the convictions of an entire life: he doubted whether he or anyone could achieve happiness for any length of time, but that was no reason not to strive for it with all one's power; this also held true for political and military success.

As the extent of Napoleon's disaster became apparent, Scharnhorst began to press for acceleration of the state's military preparations. Even those of his friends who had remained in Prussia found his urgency excessive; but to him it was obvious that if only the war did not come to a halt on the Russian frontier, if Prussia turned against the remnants of the *Grande Armée* and attacked its lines of communication, the French had no choice but to withdraw to the Rhine. Frederick William, however, could never be induced to make rapid decisions. In the negotiations with the Tsar that now began, Scharnhorst was the driving element on the Prussian side, overcoming the king's hesitations and disdainfully cutting through the ob-

---

30. Scharnhorst to A. E. v. Thile, 2 July 1812, *Scharnhorsts Briefe*, p. 435.

structionist diplomacy of the Prussian representative, Colonel von dem Knesebeck, whom he disliked as a hypocritical antagonist of reform. It is difficult to see how but for Scharnhorst's single-minded advocacy a Russo-Prussian army capable of major operations could have met the resurgent Napoleon on the Elbe in the spring of 1813. For the sake of assuring the Tsar's cooperation, Scharnhorst did not hesitate to accept a Russian as supreme commander and a plan of campaign that he judged to be defective. Even though he believed himself to be the best choice for commander of the Prussian field forces, he recognized the political desirability of appointing Blücher to this post: "a good man ... [who] understands nothing about leading the army." [31] But he took care to make Gneisenau Blücher's assistant. He himself again served as minister of war and as chief of the general staff, with final responsibility for expanding, equipping, and training the army. When the campaign opened in April, he joined Blücher in the field.

Frederick William regarded the expansion of the army to strengths far beyond the limit Napoleon had imposed in 1808 as an essentially normal organizational and administrative task, which merely needed to be carried out more rapidly than desirable because half of his state was occupied and some sort of conflict with France appeared imminent. Scharnhorst and other members of the reform party saw the task very differently. Fighting should start as quickly as possible, they believed, even at the cost of losing the early battles, so that new political and strategic conditions could be brought about which firmly committed the allied powers to the war, and operational opportunities could be created which their superior manpower might exploit. "Only toward the end of May will the army be able to achieve something," Scharnhorst wrote in the first days of April; in the meantime, "we try and we take risks." [32]

These political and military principles were reinforced by a motive of specific self-interest: of all members of the alliance Prussia was the most threatened, and the one that would benefit most from immediate and extreme efforts. It was obvious that she could influence her allies, who had less to lose from unhurried policies, only if she herself resorted to exceptional measures. These could not but help affect the state's political and social conditions. If the size of the army were to be doubled, or more, within a few months by incorporating tens of thousands of untrained short-term soldiers, its traditional character as a force of long-serving regulars would necessarily be diluted. The appeal to volunteers, the institution of conscription and of some form of militia—all became inevitable. The fighting would involve more groups of the population than had ever before been the

---

31. Scharnhorst to his daughter, 2 May 1813, *ibid.*, p. 473.
32. Scharnhorst to his daughter, 2 April 1813, *ibid.*, p. 465. See also his letter to her of 28 April 1813, *ibid.*, p. 469. I have discussed the willingness of the reformers to exploit the unforeseen as a characteristic of modern war in *Yorck*, pp. 215–218.

case in Prussia. Something akin to the conditions in France in 1793 and 1794 might be approached, and Gneisenau's and Clausewitz's call for insurgency and popular war might at last become reality.[33] The war would have to be made a concern of the people as a whole, not only to meet the demands of manpower and the pressure of time but also to make its conduct less dependent on the weak will of the monarch. Popular enthusiasm, which benefited the army by bringing in recruits and raising morale, might also lend impetus to the policy of the state and thus continue the line that began when Yorck's convention with the Russians and the subsequent mobilization of East Prussia had forced the king's hand.

Other than calling up half-trained reservists, the measures for enlarging the army meant further changes in the army's place in society. In the 18th century the army's character as the force that above all others represented the monarch largely depended on the social structure that had developed under absolutism. After Tilsit most of the legal props of this hierarchy had been knocked away; but privilege and special opportunities and exemptions remained, and the army as an institution continued in its former isolation. Now the reformers once more called into question the concept that the soldier was the king's man to the exclusion of other concerns and interests. All former exemptions from the obligation for military service were abolished, and universal military conscription became law. Conscripts were assigned both to the line and to the *Landwehr,* which with one or two alterations was adapted from the East Prussian model and instituted in all provinces. Members of the propertied and educated classes could, if they wished, equip themselves at their own expense and serve in special detachments of *Jäger*—a measure by which Scharnhorst sought "to chain the interest of all families to the war," something that could hardly have been achieved unless the bourgeois was given the means to serve in the ranks under privileged conditions and without losing status.[34] As a result the army, which in December 1812 was less than 60,000 men strong, three months later had a force of approximately 130,000 officers and men available for service in the field and in the fortresses, a number that increased to more than 270,000 by the beginning of the fall campaign. These figures were achieved with a population of somewhat under five million; in 1806, when the population was double that number, Prussia had mobilized a field army of no more than 164,000 men.[35] The most radical measure of the reformers, however, was the establishment on paper of the *Landsturm,* an ir-

---

33. In the historical survey with which he introduces his study of the campaign of 1815, Clausewitz compares Prussia's mobilization policies of 1813 with those of revolutionary France; *Der Feldzug von 1815 in Frankreich, Werke,* viii 4–5.
34. Scharnhorst to his daughter, 19 March 1813, *Scharnhorsts Briefe,* p. 462.
35. Jany, iv, 82, 93–94; R. Friederich, *Die Befreiungskriege 1813–1815,* 4 vols., Berlin, 1911–13, i, 103; *Das Preussische Heer im Jahre 1813,* ed. by the Historical Section of the Great General Staff, Berlin, 1914, p. 551. Cf. Clausewitz's comments in *On War,* book VIII, ch. 3B (p. 869).

regular force of all men between the ages of fifteen and sixty who had not been called up for service in the line or the *Landwehr*. Opposition to this *levée en masse* was widespread, on social and political even more than on military grounds. At times the debate verged on extremes of violence. A privy councillor on Hardenberg's staff challenged Gneisenau to a duel, a challenge that Gneisenau rejected with the king's approval. Clausewitz, whom both parties appealed to as the sole witness of their quarrel, took the occasion to write a memorandum that derisively countered the civilian official's arguments against the *Landsturm* and in the name of efficiency and social justice rejected all claims to exempt bureaucrats and the middle class in general from military service. Not only should all judges and lawyers fight in the *Landsturm,* he wrote; "To exclude tax administrators and assessors [on the grounds that they were needed to organize supply for the regular forces] is even less admissible. There can be no doubt that shoemakers, tailors, and peasants do more to meet the army's needs than do tax councillors. Consequently, if the needs of the army should suffer from the *Landsturm,* as is falsely claimed, it would be preferable to exempt one shoemaker than ten assessors. To exclude merchants from service would be a disgusting injustice to others ... ." etc.[36] The reformers gained a formal victory on the issue; but since the war in central Germany afforded few opportunities for guerrilla operations, the *Landsturm* was in effect revoked in the summer of 1813.

Even the more conventional measures by which the reformers tried to bring civilian society into the war were strongly resisted. The middle classes and the inhabitants of formerly exempt cities and towns objected to the loss of their privileges, which had limited their military contribution to the payment of taxes; conservative nobles disliked conscription since it weakened their authority over the peasantry, and turned the army from a dynastic instrument into a force possessing some national characteristics—an objection that was also raised against the *Landwehr,* which with its provision for short service and the election of junior officers by their men gave conservatives offense on other grounds as well. The great mass of the population, finally, obeyed authority. Indeed, workers, peasants, and subaltern officials made up 90 percent of the 30,000 volunteers who joined the army between the beginning of 1813 and August 1814; but, as could be expected, the majority remained passive.[37]

These reactions suggest that the reformers overestimated the strength

---

36. "Die Erklärung des Oberst-Lieutenants von Clausewitz," June 1813, Pertz-Delbrück, iii, 688–689.
37. R. Ibbeken, *Preussen 1807–1813,* Cologne and Berlin, 1970, pp. 393–450, contains a valuable statistical analysis of the Prussian volunteers, based on records that were destroyed during the Second World War. Although many of Ibbeken's interpretations have been questioned—I myself disagree with his repetition of the historical cliché that categorizes Yorc as "reactionary"—his data have demolished once and for all the legend, dear to German liberalism, that academics and university students played a leading part in the volunteer movement.

of patriotism in Prussia, or, more likely, that they claimed more for it than it could perform. They acted as spokesmen of attitudes that did not yet possess wide currency but were only emerging in Prussian society, often in response to their own propaganda and policies. The months that so often have been labeled a period of national rising against the French found Scharnhorst and his associates, as in earlier years, fighting for their own conception of state and society amidst an antagonistic nobility, an unsympathetic bourgeoisie, and a passive, largely uncomprehending population in the towns and the country. They could never have achieved as much as they did if they had not found supporters and sympathizers in all classes, and if the king had not reluctantly cooperated with them for a time; but the degree of antagonism and misunderstanding they encountered on all sides insured that they would fail in their ultimate social and political goals.

Only extreme exertion enabled Scharnhorst, aided by a few adjutants and secretaries, to direct the army's expansion and mobilization, and to intervene with some effect in the political and strategic debates. Before he joined Blücher in the field, his working day would begin at five in the morning. Usually, one of his adjutants writes, he "worked in his room, wrapped in a white cloak, generally kneeling at his desk, a position that afforded him a pleasant change from sitting. After ten o'clock he would join the king and the chancellor, rarely returning until lunch, which he usually ate by himself. Around four o'clock he again expected me in his office, where work lasted mostly until eight or nine in the evening. But if Scharnhorst still had to see the chancellor it might be midnight before he returned. I had to wait for him, since there were always orders to be issued or something to be dictated. Frequently his eyes would fall shut from fatigue; for ten minutes he would sink into what appeared to be a deep sleep, then he quickly roused himself and continued to dictate exactly where he had broken off." [38] He was still, as he had been in the years of reform, the only man in the army who combined mastery of technical and administrative details with a firm conception of the ideal and of the possible in Prussian policy and strategy. In his view of the whole and the courage with which he fought for it he equaled Stein, whose influence with the Tsar he successfully utilized for his own ends; but he far outshone him in his realism, his understanding of others, and his diplomatic powers. He was perhaps the strongest, and certainly the most gifted and effective personality among the reformers, and it is not surprising that with this example before him Clausewitz could believe that idealism might indeed dominate politics.

Toward the end of March, Blücher left Silesia, crossed the Elbe at Dresden, and occupied Leipzig. Other Prussian and Russian corps operated along the river from Saxony to the North Sea, covering Berlin, and observ-

38. *Denkwürdigkeiten aus dem Leben des Generals der Infanterie von Hüser,* ed. M. G., Berlin, 1877, p. 102.

ing the chain of French and Saxon bases on the river. The main Russian army was still reorganizing on the Polish border and did not reach the Elbe until the 26th. Napoleon in the meantime was assembling a much stronger force in Franconia, and by the end of April felt ready for a short and decisive campaign. He advanced northeast toward Leipzig, hoping to defeat the allied armies before they had combined, and to drive the Russians back to Poland. Instead, on 2 May the French columns, numbering nearly 130,000 men, were attacked on the march near Grossgörschen by 80,000 Russians and Prussians under Wittgenstein. When darkness fell after eight hours of fighting, and the battle came to an end, the Allies had inflicted disproportionately high losses on their enemies and remained in possession of the terrain captured at the beginning of their attack. Scharnhorst spoke of victory—justifiably, from his perspective, since the French momentum had been broken; but their great numerical inferiority obliged the Allies to withdraw to Dresden and beyond. To demonstrate to the Austrian government, which had not yet joined the alliance against France, that Prussia was far from defeated, Hardenberg thought it desirable for the army to fight another battle. In the night of the 14th to the 15th Gneisenau and Clausewitz, in the presence of a representative of the chancellor, reviewed the possibilities, and concluded that political and psychological considerations justified taking the risk, even though the Prussians were outnumbered.[39] As he had before, and was often to do in the future, Knesebeck counseled against accepting Gneisenau's advice. Envy of Gneisenau and an 18th-century dislike of battle made him an unchanging obstacle to aggressive action in Prussian headquarters. On this occasion, however, he failed, and on the 20th and 21st the Prussians and Russians fought a second major battle at Bautzen, which once again ended in their retreat but left the French seriously weakened. Five days later the slow French pursuit stumbled into an ambush, and Napoleon decided to gain time for the badly needed reorganization of his forces by agreeing to an armistice which the neutral Austrian government had recently proposed to the two sides. Gneisenau, Grolman, and Clausewitz attempted to persuade Frederick William and the Russians that now was the moment to turn on the French. "The situation of the enemy is desperate," Clausewitz wrote on 31 May, "and only the miserable pessimism of our leaders can see matters differently. ... The Emperor Napoleon has never played such a desperate game." Four days later, before he learned that the armistice had been signed, he repeated, "If we are afraid of Napoleon now, we deserve to be whipped."[40]

The spring campaign had ended inconclusively on the battlefield, but organizationally and even strategically the Prussians had gained a solid ad-

---

39. Pertz-Delbrück, ii, 615; A. v. Janson, *König Friedrich Wilhelm III. in der Schlacht,* Berlin, 1907, p. 159.
40. Clausewitz to his wife, 31 May and 4 June 1813, *Correspondence,* pp. 338–339, 340.

vantage. Clausewitz's contribution to this outcome was never officially recognized. But on at least one critical occasion his optimism and willingness to take risks had strengthened Gneisenau in his continuing struggle to hammer out a positive strategic policy. The two men worked as well together in the field as they had in committee meetings; but their collaboration came to an end during the summer, and Clausewitz was not again to influence major strategic decisions during the war.[41]

At the battle of Grossgörschen, Clausewitz wrote to his wife at the time, the senior Prussian generals and their staff, having no share in the overall conduct of the action, could do little else than encourage the troops by fighting in the first rank. He himself was unharmed, although at one point he found himself in the middle of a French battalion, warding off "a small Frenchman with a bayonet."[42] But Blücher suffered a contusion, Grolman was slashed by a bayonet, while Scharnhorst had one horse killed under him and a second wounded, bullets pierced his hat and coat, and in the early evening his leg was struck below the knee. At first the wound seemed harmless. Scharnhorst left the army for Vienna to speed negotiations for bringing Austria into the alliance; but his leg became infected, and he died in Prague on 28 June.

Two obituaries, which Clausewitz and Gneisenau wrote jointly, were refused approval by the relevant government office since they seemed to suggest that Scharnhorst's achievements were not sufficiently appreciated. Gneisenau was forced to protest to Hardenberg before the texts could be printed unchanged.[43] For the time being Clausewitz continued to serve on Blücher's staff. A plan for guerrilla operations in Silesia he drafted during this period provides a good example of the operational concepts of the reformed general staff in its combination of setting specific objectives and allowing the commander considerable latitude in his manner of achieving them.[44] Gneisenau asked that Clausewitz be appointed his senior assistant, but the king again refused to accept him into the Prussian army. Clausewitz was compelled to leave headquarters and report to the Russo-German Legion, which had joined the new allied Army of the North under Bernadotte. The king had already rejected a recommendation that he be decorated for bravery at Grossgörschen.[45]

41. During the armistice friends of Gneisenau—Heinrich and Amalie v. Beguelin—visited him in Silesia. One evening the couple joined Gneisenau, Clausewitz, Grolman, and others for tea. Afterwards Frau v. Beguelin noted in her diary: "Clausewitz exerts a decided influence on [Gneisenau] and seems to me to be the head of the faction, ambitious and intelligent." Elsewhere she quotes Gneisenau as telling her: "Clausewitz is a man whose advice always pleased me, whose talent I rate above my own," etc. *Denkwürdigkeiten von Heinrich und Amalie von Beguelin*, ed. A. Ernst, Berlin, 1892, pp. 275, 285.
42. Clausewitz to his wife, 3 and 8 May 1813, *Correspondence*, pp. 331–334. For the following see also Scharnhorst's letters and reports of 2, 3, and 5 May 1813, *Scharnhorsts Briefe*, pp. 471–477.
43. "Nachruf," and "Nekrolog," printed in Pertz-Delbrück, iii, 32–37.
44. "Über den Parteigängerkrieg des Majors v. Boltenstern," *ibid.*, pp. 689–692.
45. Clausewitz to his wife, 18 and 28 May 1813, *Correspondence*, pp. 335–336.

At the beginning of the armistice, before Clausewitz left for the Baltic, Gneisenau asked him to write an account of the spring campaign that would justify the conduct of the war to the public and raise enthusiasm for the fighting ahead. With his usual facility, Clausewitz needed only a few days to produce a manuscript of some 16,000 words, which was at once published and widely distributed.[46] The brochure achieved its propagandistic aims by sounding rich chords of patriotism and political morality—emotional appeals that the author embedded in a firm and analytic narrative. If the text lacks the concern with personalities, the sarcasm, and the sweep of social and political interpretation that distinguish Clausewitz's later study of Prussia before and during the war of 1806, it is due in part to the immediate purpose of the brochure, in part to the circumstance that depicting the decline of a system calls for a broader canvas than narrating a campaign. But even when he reports events that he had witnessed or in which he participated, Clausewitz retains his essentially historical point of view, and it is hardly surprising that he joins his account of the fighting in April and May 1813 to a survey of the reforms of the previous years. First, however, comes a brief introduction, which opens with a paean to man's inherent love of freedom, then pictures Yorck's small corps, "forgotten and abandoned by the hurriedly fleeing French, marching silently and calmly, with firm courage, through the snow and forests of Curland toward home," and ends by sketching the change in Prussia's policies: "The monarch and his ministers understood the voice of the people and shared its feelings. They recognized the duty to support the people now with all the power and authority of government ... and to begin once more the struggle for a free, honorable existence among the nations of Europe." [47] This is followed by an outline of the changes in the army's organization and training since 1808, and by the Prussian order of battle in the spring of 1813. Only then does the narrative proper begin.

Unexceptional though this approach seems to us, similar works written at the time suggest that Clausewitz's attempt to describe the political and strategic background and to combine significant detail with general analysis was far from typical in military history; indeed, it is not all that common today. A useful comparison is provided by a short study of the campaign that the Prussian staff officer Friedrich Karl Ferdinand von Müffling wrote during the armistice.[48] Müffling had served under Scharn-

---

46. Anonymous, *Der Feldzug von 1813 bis zum Waffenstillstand*, Glatz, 1813. A second and third edition appeared the following year in Leipzig, and a slightly modernized version was included in vol. vii of Clausewitz's collected works. The following references are to the first edition. An English biography, *The Life and Campaigns of Field-Marshal Prince Blücher*, London, 1815, "translated in part from the German of General Count Gneisenau ... with considerable additions by J. E. Marston, Esq. of the Hamburgh-Bürger-Guard," includes a free rendering of Clausewitz's history of 1813, which thus became his first work to appear in a foreign language.

47. Clausewitz, *Feldzug 1813*, pp. 1–3.

48. C. v. W., *Die preussisch-russische Campagne im Jahr 1813*, n.p., 1813.

horst from 1804 to 1806, and was then employed in the administration of Saxe–Weimar until 1813, when he returned to the Prussian army, in which he was to occupy increasingly influential positions during the following decades, rising to become chief of the general staff and a field marshall. In his text he tries to develop the great lines of the campaign, tests specific events against general principles, and is by no means free of criticism of his own side; but the historical discussion exhausts itself in a few references to the retreat from Moscow, and his discussion of strategy continually slides into tactics. Consequently the mass of detail in his pages provides the reader with remarkably little understanding. Nor does Müffling demonstrate a clear sense of what is and what is not significant information. He fails, for instance, to give the strengths of the opposing sides at Grossgörschen—in *On War* Clausewitz was to castigate indifference to figures as characteristic of old-fashioned history—while at other times facts are presented without indicating their meaning.[49] An example is his treatment of a preliminary phase of the battle of Bautzen on 20 May. On the preceding day two allied corps some miles apart attacked two French corps marching toward the main French army. Müffling depicts the attacks as two unconnected events. Clausewitz expands his description by adding that the "repeated attacks of General v. Yorck on the far stronger corps of Marshall Ney prevented the latter from coming to the aid of General Lauriston; and this effort, which continued until evening, contributed not a little to the success of General Barclay against General Lauriston." The evidence of the French commanders bears out this interpretation; but whether or not Clausewitz was correct is less important than his constant search for possible meanings of specific actions and for their relationship to the general purpose.[50]

In the autumn campaign, which ended with Napoleon's defeat at Leipzig and his expulsion from Germany, Clausewitz served in the least significant theater of operations. The missions of the Army of the North were to hold in check the sizable French forces in northern Germany that had recaptured Hamburg, protect Berlin, and extend its operations south to add to the pressures on Napoleon in the area around Leipzig. Bernadotte

49. "To show for how long the strength of armies was not considered to be of major significance, we need only point out that most of the histories of the 18th century—even the most extensive ones—either do not mention the size of armies, or do so only in a very casual way; certainly they never emphasize it." *On War*, book III, ch. 8 (p. 274).

50. Clausewitz, *Feldzug 1813*, p. 45; Müffling, pp. 35–36. The effect on the French is recorded in the *Journal des opérations des IIIe et Ve Corps en 1813*, ed. G. Fabry, Paris, 1902, pp. 22–23. Compare also a later work of Müffling, again published under his pseudonym C. v. W., *Betrachtungen über die grossen Operationen und Schlachten der Feldzüge von 1813 und 1814*, Berlin and Posen, 1825, pp. 32–33. Clausewitz devotes the last pages of his study to a comparison of allied and French strengths and strategic possibilities, admits that the Allies could have done more in the spring but points out that in war, no less than in other areas of life, one can never do more than approximate the ideal. In the final paragraphs he once more appeals to the patriotism of his readers, to whom the war should matter as much as it does to princes and generals: "The pestilential air of hopelessness which for so long has blown across Germany should be past now that the thunderstorm [of the Russian campaign] has swept clean the political atmosphere."

Clausewitz in his middle thirties.
The portrait, by an unknown painter, shows Clausewitz in Russian uniform with the Swedish decoration
he received in the fall of 1813. It must have been painted between that time and his readmission to the
Prussian army early in 1815. Formerly in possession of the Clausewitz family.

was also charged with covering the Allies' extreme northern flank and maintaining communications with Sweden. This household chore—necessary but unpromising of great decisions—was entrusted to Count Wallmoden, who was placed in command of an international force of some 22,600 men, of which the Russo-German Legion formed the elite. On his arrival in Mecklenburg, Clausewitz was appointed chief of staff of the entire force. Throughout the fall Wallmoden's corps waged an uneventful campaign of marches and countermarches, raids, and minor engagements, the original revolutionary intention of the Legion having long been put aside. The corps' most successful day was a sudden attack across the Elbe on a French column—the battle on the Göhrde on 16 September, in which Wallmoden and Clausewitz, with a force of 12,000, surprised the enemy, who numbered somewhat above 3,000 men. In the ensuing fighting, the French lost 1,500 men, an eagle, and six guns; but considering the great disparity of forces, this was a disappointing outcome, which the German general-staff history attributes to the "inexperience of the senior officers in coordinating the actions of separate units." [51] Clausewitz was promoted to colonel for his share in the victory.[52] During a lull in the campaign his wife was able to visit him for a few days.[53] Wallmoden's force slowly moved west. On 10 December it encountered a Danish corps near Sehestädt in Schleswig, again gaining a victory but failing to achieve the complete encirclement that had been planned. "It is a disgusting feeling to have been so close to a brilliant success and to have missed it," Clausewitz wrote to his wife, who had returned to Berlin. "The crown prince [Bernadotte] overwhelmed us with praise, but what kind of substitute is that!" [54]

In the early months of 1814, while Napoleon was being driven back to Paris, Wallmoden's corps blockaded Hamburg and then marched to the lower Rhine and Brussels on what was scarcely more than an armed demonstration. By that time Clausewitz had become resigned to the fact that he could neither participate in the last battles against Napoleon nor achieve a great measure of personal distinction; but he worried about his future in a corps that did not belong to the regular establishment of any army. Might not the Legion become the army of the new German Reich, he inquired of Gneisenau.[55] For a time he considered entering Dutch service. His wife

51. R. Friederich, *Geschichte des Herbstfeldzuges 1813*, Berlin, 1904, ii, 235; B. Schwertfeger, *Das Treffen an der Göhrde, Militär-Wochenblatt*, 1897, Beiheft 5–6.

52. Immediately after the battle he wrote his wife that "to become colonel is a great object of my ambition," but he feared that he would be put off with a decoration; letter of 21 September 1813, *Correspondence*, p. 356. The statement in Hahlweg, *Clausewitz*, p. 37, that Clausewitz had already been promoted to colonel during the Russian campaign is in error, as is the implication in the same paragraph that Tolstoy's passing reference to Clausewitz in *War and Peace* is a favorable one.

53. W. v. Haxthausen, Wallmoden's adjutant, to Gneisenau, 10 November 1813, printed in A. Pick, *Aus der Zeit der Not*, Berlin, 1900, p. 280.

54. Clausewitz to his wife, 13 December 1813, *Correspondence*, p. 360.

55. The suggestion is mentioned by Gneisenau in a letter to Rühle von Lilienstern, 29 December 1813, printed in *Aus den Papieren der Familie von Schleinitz*, Berlin, 1905, pp. 88–89.

found it more difficult than he to reconcile herself to his disappointments. After Napoleon's abdication she wrote to Gneisenau that in her pleasure at her friend's triumphs she sought solace for the fate of her husband, "who during this glorious period remained sadly deprived of joy." Gneisenau replied from Paris: " 'The race is not to the swift,' says the Bible. Our poor Clausewitz was equipped with the will and ability to take an active part in this war, and during the concluding phase was always kept from the main theater of operations. He must find comfort in the thought that the rest of us were still tortured by uncertainty while he already saw the humbled enemy flee [an allusion to Clausewitz's participation in the Russian campaign], that he shared in the greater and more dangerous task, while we were given the easier burden in the second half of the war." [56] At least Gneisenau was able to reassure the couple that the Legion would most probably be incorporated into the Prussian army; but Clausewitz was unwilling to "sneak back," as he put it, into Prussian uniform with an entire corps, and drafted a note to the king requesting a separate decision for himself in view of the king's attitude of the previous year. Probably this polite but assertive note was never sent. On 11 April 1814, the day before Clausewitz wrote his wife that he intended to query the king, his commission as colonel in the Prussian infantry was issued by the ministry of war.[57]

The winding up of the Legion's affairs was time-consuming and caused difficulties in which Clausewitz, who for part of the spring was the senior officer present, was necessarily involved.[58] In May, shortly before the Legion marched from Belgium to Aachen, some of the junior officers threatened to leave unless they received promotions that had been promised earlier. This so-called conspiracy of Masseyk was settled amicably, though as it became known, one of its officers later wrote, the Legion acquired the reputation of a volatile, unreliable body. By a convention concluded on 2 June between Stein, Hardenberg, and two representatives of the British government, which was paying the Legion's upkeep, its 5,697 men were placed under Prussian command, full administrative and financial responsibility not passing to Prussia until the second half of August. In the interval, the record of every man was checked before his discharge or transfer was approved. Two former Prussian officers, who had joined the Legion in September 1812, were court-martialed for desertion; some thousands of officers and men were discharged or departed on their own. The two thou-

---

56. Marie v. Clausewitz to Gneisenau, 20 April 1814; Gneisenau to Marie v. Clausewitz, 5 May 1814; Pertz-Delbrück, iv, 248–251. Clausewitz refers to his Dutch prospects several times—for instance, in his letter to Gneisenau of 22 April 1814, *ibid.*, p. 238.
57. Clausewitz to his wife, 12 April 1814, *Correspondence*, pp. 372–373; Schwartz, *Leben des Generals Clausewitz*, ii, 64. Hahlweg, *Clausewitz*, p. 40, incorrectly delays Clausewitz's readmission to the Prussian army to March 1815.
58. Clausewitz to his wife, 17 April 1814, *Correspondence*, p. 374. Venzky, pp. 107–113 and appendices, contains useful material on this period of the Legion's history.

sand who remained, now collectively known as the "German Legion," were divided into two brigades, intended as cadres for units to be raised later, of which the second was placed under Clausewitz's command. An order of the day of 22 July warned officers and men of the Prussian army on the Rhine against unseemly comment about their new comrades: evidently the reputation of the Legion had sunk very low. Immediately afterwards the brigades, together with other units, were sent to Hesse to compel the elector to honor his political and military agreements with the Allies and to maintain public order. [59]

The two brigades did not return to the Rhine until September, where they were reinforced by Prussian conscripts. Few of Clausewitz's letters from this period have survived. That he continued to serve with his brigade is shown by an order of the day, dated 7 October and signed by him, concerning the disposition of pay that his units were drawing for men who had deserted or were in hospital. [60] Shortly afterwards he was placed in charge of both brigades. In a letter to Gneisenau toward the end of the year he refers to himself as "provisional commander of a legion that is itself provisional," adding in a postscript that he had no expectation of receiving a more suitable assignment: "I see fairly clearly that the king's anger with me has not diminished." [61] He was disgusted with his "insipid position," he wrote the following February, which "removes me from important affairs while not involving me more closely with the sciences. ... If I were free to dispose over my time and energy, if I were not too old and [if my education were] not too neglected, I would throw myself wholly into the arms of scholarship." [62] In March he was still wearing Russian uniform, since the brigades had not yet been fully integrated into the Prussian army. On hearing the news of Napoleon's return from Elba he again wrote Gneisenau, begging for a regular assignment that would enable him to change to Prussian dress: "to take part in the campaign as a Prussian officer wearing Russian uniform would appear as though the king could not overcome his aversion to seeing me in his army." [63] Finally, on 30 March, he was transferred to the general staff, and two weeks later appointed chief of staff of one of the four corps that initially comprised the Prussian field army. Later, Gneisenau and

59. Venzky writes, p. 112, that the Legion was "used to execute political opponents in Hesse." I have been unable to verify this statement, which may with some exaggeration refer to fights in Marburg between students supporting the cause of German nationalism and troops stationed in the area. If Venzky's statement is correct, the failure of the national hopes of the Legion and of its sponsoring agency, Stein's Committee for German Affairs, could hardly have been demonstrated more conclusively.
60. "Tagesbefehl der Brigade: Königswinter den 7ten Oktober 1814," Berlin, Staatsbibliothek Preussischer Kulturbesitz: 2f 1820.
61. Clausewitz to Gneisenau, 21 December 1814, Pertz-Delbrück, iv, 303–305. In the same letter he describes Gneisenau as one of the "few channels of friendship and affection" still linking him to Prussia.
62. Clausewitz to Gneisenau, 27 February 1815, *ibid.*, pp. 324–325.
63. Clausewitz to Gneisenau, 17 March 1815, *ibid.*, pp. 476–477.

Boyen hoped, it might be possible to advance him to Blücher's staff.[64] A strange coda followed on this presumably coveted appointment: on 1 May, Clausewitz asked the king to transfer him to the line, a request that was refused.[65] Clausewitz's motive is not known; we can only speculate that he believed he had greater opportunity to distinguish himself at the head of a regiment or brigade than as adviser to a corps commander.

Clausewitz's final year of service with the Legion was interspersed with periods of treatment for various physical debilities, of which arthritis continued to be the most troublesome. His old complaints had been exacerbated by the severities of the Russian campaign. As early as August 1812 he wrote that he had not changed clothes for five weeks, was often compelled to drink dirty water, at times suffered arthritis, and almost constantly had toothache.[66] In November and December exposure to extreme cold left his face permanently discolored, so that in later years some men suspected him of being a secret drinker.[67] Throughout 1813 and 1814 he continued to have arthritic attacks. "Yesterday I was very ill," goes one characteristic passage in a letter to his wife. "Arthritis tortured me so horribly that I fell into the most violent convulsions. A competent surgeon administered opium and ether, which stopped the convulsions and eased the pain." [68] Three weeks later he wrote that he was obliged to use opium every evening. He worried about becoming dependent on the drug, but it was his only means of relief in the field, and he seems to have taken it fairly regularly for several years. Immediately after Napoleon's first abdication he asked his wife to meet him for a long sojourn at a spa.[69] Since he could not leave his post, he had to be satisfied with taking the waters at Aachen, the Legion's temporary headquarters in June and July. He returned to Aachen the following February for another six weeks' cure, which was cut short by Napoleon's return. When Paris had fallen the second time he again planned to visit a spa, "the sooner the better, since arthritis has returned with abominable violence." [70] His ailments, however, did not prevent him from drawing on reserves of physical energy in times of crisis—after the battle of Ligny on 16 June he spent all night in the saddle guiding the retreat of his

64. Boyen to Gneisenau, 15 April 1815, and Gneisenau to Clausewitz 16 April 1815, *ibid.*, pp. 496, 500. Schwartz, *Leben des Generals Clausewitz,* ii, 121.

65. Priesdorff, v, No. 1429. Unfortunately, Priesdorff prints only the briefest extracts of these documents, which were unknown before he discovered them and are now presumably destroyed.

66. Clausewitz to his wife, 24 August 1812, *Correspondence*, pp. 294–295. Cf. his comment in his history of 1812: "The author still retains a vivid recollection of the severe lack of water during this campaign. Never has he suffered from thirst to the same extent; water had to be drawn from the most disgusting sources to still the burning pain, and washing was often out of the question for a week at a time." *Werke*, vii, 171.

67. Steinmann v. Friederici, p. 35.

68. Clausewitz to his wife, 1 September 1813, *Correspondence*, p. 349.

69. Clausewitz to his wife, 21 September 1813 and 19 April 1814, *ibid.*, pp. 356, 374.

70. Clausewitz to Gneisenau, 9 February 1815, Pertz-Delbrück, iv, 317; Clausewitz to his wife, 29 June and 7 July 1815, *Correspondence*, pp. 384, 394–395.

corps, and the following day supervised the reorganization and provisioning of the troops on the march—and after the war the annual conduct reports described him as being in generally good health.[71]

The corps to which Clausewitz was assigned in April 1815 was led by Johann Adolph von Thielmann, who after a stormy career as fighting soldier and diplomat in the Saxon army had recently entered Prussian service.[72] The son of a middle-class official in the Saxon financial administration, he had studied at one of the best schools in Germany, the Academy of Princes in Meissen, and was exceptionally well versed in the literature and music of his time, interests that he combined with the qualities of a military adventurer on a grand scale. He reminded contemporaries of a Napoleonic marshal or a condottiere, seemingly out of place in the orderly bureaucratic environment of the Prussian army, to which, in reality, he adjusted with conspicuous success. Clausewitz found him very attractive— not least for his friendship with Schiller—and the two men got on well together. The corps was in the final stage of mobilization when Clausewitz, whose wife accompanied him until the campaign opened, arrived at Thielmann's headquarters in Luxembourg on 7 May.[73] Toward the end of the month its strength had been brought to 23,000 men and 48 guns, and it was marching through the Ardennes to join Blücher's other three corps in southern Belgium.[74] By the second week in June the Prussians were in loose contact with Wellington's left wing; but since a common plan of operations had not yet been adopted both armies remained dispersed over a wide area between the French border, Liège in the east, and Brussels and Ghent in the west.

In the night of the 14th to the 15th, Napoleon crossed into Belgium and drove back the 1st Prussian corps, which was observing the border. He hoped to defeat Blücher and Wellington separately, first attacking the Prussians, then turning west against the Anglo-Dutch army. On the 15th the Prussians had only begun to concentrate their forces. Both in his history of 1815 and in *On War*, Clausewitz criticizes their dispersal, but the Prussians might have united in time to meet the French assault if Gnei-

71. Priesdorff, v, No. 1429.
72. Thielmann is the subject of an excellent biography by H. v. Petersdorff, *General Johann Adolph Freiherr von Thielmann,* Leipzig, 1894.
73. See the memoirs of a friend and former student of Clausewitz, C. v. Roeder, *Für Euch, meine Kinder!*, Berlin, 1861, pp. 305–306.
74. Even when there was no fighting, strength figures fluctuated considerably during this period, and are difficult to work with; some returns include officers, musicians, and administrative personnel in their totals while others do not. Delbrück prints the official Prussian returns at the beginning and end of the Waterloo campaign in Pertz-Delbrück, iv, 680. On 15 June the army in Belgium consisted of 121, 959 combatants, 25,255 in the 3rd corps. Three weeks later the strength of the army had fallen to 86,226 combatants, and that of the 3rd corps to 18,810. At any one time the paper totals were, of course, larger than the number of men actually present for duty. For our purpose the precise figures are unimportant; what matters is to indicate the approximate magnitude of Clausewitz's responsibility as chief of staff of his corps, and the strength of the corps relative to that of the army as a whole.

senau's somewhat belated orders had been punctually carried out. Instead, one corps failed to appear at all, while only forced marches enabled the 2nd and 3rd corps to reach Sombreffe and Ligny on the morning of the 16th, where they joined the 1st corps, which had delayed the French advance as well as it could. The 86,000 men hurriedly deployed into a chain of defensive positions, which Napoleon attacked soon after two o'clock in the afternoon with 75,000 men, while Ney with 45,000 was pushing back Wellington's advance units at Quatre Bras a few miles to the west. The 3rd corps formed the left, eastern flank of the Prussian positions, covering the army's line of retreat, and remained out of much of the severe fighting that followed, Toward eight o'clock in the evening it attempted to help the hard-pressed center with a cavalry charge, which failed, and in the course of which Clausewitz barely escaped from counterattacking French cuirassiers.

Whether more could have been done is not clear. Thielmann's biographer acknowledges the difficult terrain and the restraint that its mission to guard the line of retreat imposed on the corps, but adds that while Thielmann's and Clausewitz's "conduct of the engagement cannot be faulted, it betrayed a certain anxiety and caution"—a judgment with which the German general-staff history concurs.[75] Clausewitz, on the other hand, criticizes Blücher, and by implication Gneisenau, for not ordering the entire 3rd corps to counterattack in the middle of the afternoon, even though this would have committed all reserves.[76] At about the time that Thielmann's cavalry tried to restore the situation, the Prussian center was driven in; in a counterattack Blücher was thrown off his horse and incapacitated, and the action had to be broken off. For some hours the 3rd corps was isolated from the rest of the army, but Thielmann and Clausewitz managed to extricate their units and keep open the roads to the rear, on which the army withdrew in reasonable order. The direction of the retreat now became of paramount importance. Toward the east lay Namur, Liège, and a chain of Prussian depots stretching to the Rhine; but Gneisenau directed the army northwest instead, toward Brussels and Wellington, which meant giving up his lines of communication but prevented the French from acting with a free hand. It was one of the significant decisions of the age: by ruining Napoleon's plan of beating the Allies separately it made his defeat inevitable.

French errors intensified the effect of Gneisenau's decision. Napoleon convinced himself that the Prussians were withdrawing to the east—perhaps because only this standard, un-Napoleonic move would have given him any hope for success. On the morning of the 17th he ordered Grouchy to pursue Blücher, while he combined with Ney to fight a decisive battle against the weaker Wellington. If Grouchy had operated between the main

75. Petersdorff, p. 294; O. v. Lettow-Vorbeck, *Napoleons Untergang 1815,* Berlin, 1904, i, 340.
76. Clausewitz, *Der Feldzug von 1815, Werke,* viii, 90–91.

French army and the retreating Prussians, he could have protected Napoleon's flank or rear against their unexpected return. Instead he was sent in a wide sweep toward the east, with the result that by the 18th the Prussian army found itself between him and Napoleon, who now had no means of controlling Grouchy's movements, and could not obtain his help when it was needed.

In the course of the 17th, the Prussian army converged around the village of Wavre on the river Dyle, some twelve miles north of the battlefield of Ligny, the 3rd corps arriving in heavy rain toward evening. At Wavre, Clausewitz learned from Grolman, Gneisenau's senior assistant, that while the rest of the army would join Wellington, who was preparing to meet Napoleon some eight to ten miles to the southwest, the 3rd corps was to act as reserve, or to hold Wavre if the village were attacked. By early afternoon of the following day, while the sound of cannon in the west indicated that a major battle had begun, Thielmann and his chief of staff became convinced that the entire French army had concentrated against Wellington, and that they should move closer to the fighting. The troops were already in march columns on the Brussels highway when Grouchy, who had unsuccessfully sought the Prussians in the east, at last found his way to Wavre. The corps resumed defensive positions along the river, where its approximately 16,000 men were attacked by Grouchy's 32,000. Throughout the afternoon and evening the Prussians held, opposing the massed French assaults with the flexible small-unit tactics that the reformers had introduced. The engagement, Jomini later wrote, did great honor to both sides; in fact, the much weaker Prussians succeeded in keeping nearly one-third of Napoleon's total force occupied to no useful purpose.[77] The only serious flaw in their performance, one that indicates some laxness at the center, was that the commander of the reserve misunderstood his orders and marched off unnoticed to join Blücher. Twice in the course of the afternoon Thielmann called for help. Blücher's response was to hold on as well as possible: the decision lay at Waterloo, not at Wavre. When fighting ceased, toward ten o'clock, the French had managed to cross the Dyle and were enveloping the corps' right flank. In the morning Thielmann learned that Napoleon had been defeated and that the 2nd corps was approaching to take Grouchy in the rear. Grouchy, however, continued to press his attack, and gradually developed irresistible force. Clausewitz was compelled to order the commander of the *Landwehr* regiment holding the most exposed section of the Prussian line to defend his position to the last man, and to counterattack the advancing enemy.[78] But when no help arrived by eleven o'clock, the situation became untenable; the corps disengaged itself from Wavre, and took up new positions two hours' march

77. A. H. Jomini, *Précis politique et militaire de la campagne de 1815,* Paris, 1839, p. 226.
78. Priesdorff, vi, No. 1763.

to the north. The knowledge that the rest of the army was pursuing Napoleon while he himself was forced to retreat made these hours among the worst in Clausewitz's life.[79] The Prussians spent the afternoon reorganizing—the last two days of fighting had cost the corps a further 2,500 casualties—and Clausewitz drew up dispositions for an advance the following morning. But at daybreak it was discovered that Grouchy had slipped away, and only the cavalry under Clausewitz's brother-in-law Marwitz was able to catch up with the French rear guard and capture some guns and prisoners. By not observing Grouchy's movements during their retreat, and perhaps by retreating too far. Thielmann and Clausewitz shared responsibility with the overly cautious and systematic leadership of the 2nd corps for letting the French escape.[80]

Clausewitz seems to have felt no need to apologize for his actions. As always in war, everyone had made mistakes, and in the end victory had gone to the side that was stronger and erred less.[81] But he regretted the bad luck that once again had kept him on the margin rather than at the center of great events; he commented on the "apparent injustice" of the official report, which minimized the contribution of the 3rd corps so that Blücher's triumph would appear the greater; and he was less than pleased with the Iron Cross second class—the lowest of Prussian decorations—with which his services were recognized.[82] The letters he wrote to his wife and to Gneisenau after Napoleon's defeat are noticeably restrained; even the choice of topics seems to indicate reserve, as though the writer were eschewing matters that for the moment are too painful or too important to discuss. To his wife he described in considerable detail the countryside between Belgium and Paris through which the corps was marching; personal reflections are rare, though occasionally his sense of triumph over the "unequalled debacle" breaks through. In the first days of July, quartered in a

79. See below, p. 431.

80. Petersdorff, pp. 300–302; Lettow-Vorbeck, i, 457–459. A more precise evaluation of the retreat from Wavre depends on the discovery of further evidence. Until that unlikely occurrence, one can only agree with the judgment of Clausewitz's French biographer, Paul Roques, that "the degree to which Clausewitz was guilty of this loss of contact, which may have saved Grouchy, is impossible to determine with certainty." *Le Général de Clausewitz*, p. 66. Among references in the extensive literature on Waterloo, the following may be noted: H. v. Treitschke, *Deutsche Geschichte im 19ten Jahrhundert*, Leipzig, 1923, i, 764; K. Linnebach, "Clausewitz' Persönlichkeit," *Wissen und Wehr*, XI (1930), 299, 315; J. Waller, *Wellington at Waterloo*, London, 1967, p. 204. W. Hyde Kelly, *The Battle of Wavre and Grouchy's Retreat*, London, 1905, like most English works on the campaign, ignores the relevant German literature, and does not mention Clausewitz's part in the events of 17 to 20 June.

81. Soon after the war an anonymous article, possibly written by Valentini, blamed the 2nd corps for letting Grouchy escape. Some officers of the corps regarded the tone of the piece as insulting and Clausewitz, together with other senior staff officers, was officially asked by the chief of staff, his friend Grolman, to disavow authorship. His discussion of the incident in a letter to Gneisenau of 27 December 1816, Pertz-Delbrück, v, 180, is completely detached, and betrays no hint of personal involvement or self-justification.

82. Clausewitz to his wife, 21 July 1815, *Correspondence*, pp. 404–405; Clausewitz to Gneisenau, 24 July 1815, Pertz-Delbrück, iv, 590.

suburb of Paris with the "gleaming pinnacles of the humbled capital of the world" before him, he wrote a factual summary of the preceding two weeks and brought his diary up to date.[83] On the 9th the corps entered Paris for one day, and then marched to Fontainebleau, where he was quartered in five rooms in the imperial palace, lonely in the "surroundings of princely beds and sofas." After a week and a half the corps moved to the neighborhood of Orleans, and then to Le Mans to assure public order in the northwest. Like Gneisenau and Boyen, Clausewitz continued for some time to fear the possibility of a popular uprising—a last sign of the exaggerated importance that the reform party attributed to guerrilla warfare. The country remained calm, however, the only development that disturbed Clausewitz being the return of peacetime spit and polish. "An object of real sadness to me," he wrote to Gneisenau on 11 September, "is the petty drill-spirit that now engulfs us. ... That the army is being worked into the ground by it may be all right, though inevitably useful matters are being slighted; but it is a real misfortune that the *Landwehr* is being repaid for its good will with this torture, which destroys its spirit and involves so much that is personally disagreeable. A respectable farmer, who leaves house and home ... to face the dangers threatening the state, is here drilled like a cadet, must goosestep, present arms blindly, study the signals and ruffles of the drummers, etc." [84] In August or September his wife joined him in Le Mans. They visited Paris together and before the end of the year returned to Germany, where he took up a new assignment.

If his letters during these months are unusually reticent about his personal feelings, they are uncommunicative on another score as well. In later years Clausewitz carefully studied the campaign of 1815, which he viewed as the outcome of historical processes generated in the last instance by the French Revolution and shaped by the genius and weaknesses of Napoleon. His history of 1815 and the many references to the campaign in *On War* developed a multifaceted interpretation of Napoleon's personality and leadership—though we might note that he never wrote a comprehensive study of Napoleon comparable to his biography of Scharnhorst or to his sketches of such lesser men as Prince Louis Ferdinand. To the historian Clausewitz, the figure of Napoleon blends into the wars that shook Europe for twenty-five years. But reflection on the events of the campaign, and their interpretation, lay in the future. In the months after Waterloo, Clausewitz's letters contain hardly a single observation on the historical and theoretical bases of the fighting. Very different in them is his treatment of politics. Such issues as the attitudes of the French population or the allied policy toward Louis

83. Clausewitz to his wife, 3 July and 7 July 1815, *Correspondence*, pp. 384–398.
84. Clausewitz to Gneisenau, 11 September 1815, Pertz-Delbrück, iv, 629. Clausewitz's comments presage Boyen's objections to the treatment of the *Landwehr*, which played a part in his resignation in 1819.

XVIII, he discusses with an attention to psychological and diplomatic elements and to historical antecedents almost wholly lacking in his references to military matters. Of particular concern to him was the future relationship between France and Prussia. He was at one with the entire army in calling for territorial gains along the Rhine, Mosel, and Meuse that would give Prussia a strong western frontier. In common with many politically aware officers, he was troubled by indications that her allies were preventing Prussia from gaining the fruits of victory, and that Prussia was being isolated in the concert of Europe. For this he tended to hold Austria primarily responsible, while Gneisenau cast greater blame on Alexander and Wellington; but both agreed that Prussia was being outmaneuvered. "The unity of the major allied powers is at present of the highest importance to the well-being of Germany and Prussia, and is worth every sacrifice," he wrote to Gneisenau on 29 July, and continued with an interesting economic analogy: "Our victories have given us great moral power. They have increased our credit, but not our resources, while enormously expanding our business; now flexibility and cleverness are absolutely essential." [85]

Where Clausewitz differed from many of his comrades, and certainly from Gneisenau, was on the two linked issues of Prussia's policy toward the new French government and on her treatment of the French population. Gneisenau hated the French—that "depraved, but capable and courageous people," as he described them in terms reminiscent of Clausewitz's essay on national character.[86] He felt himself as conqueror with the right to take revenge for the humiliations and sacrifices that Napoleon had imposed on Prussia over the years, and saw no reason why Prussia in turn should not now demand vast payments in money and goods, and encourage those tendencies in the country's affairs that might weaken French power. He resented Wellington's support of the Bourbon restoration as being at the very least unnecessary and premature. Clausewitz, on the contrary, regarded Prussia's neutrality among the parties as ineffectual, and saw no benefit in prolonging unsettled conditions. "It would be very stupid," he wrote his wife from Fontainebleau, "if we did not conclude a preliminary peace through the agency of Louis XVIII, and thus deprive the [French] nation of its weapons and spirit." [87] Nor did he approve of arrogant treatment of the population, whose pride and energy he respected. On 24 July he assured Gneisenau that even defeat and occupation "have not sufficed to reduce the people to humility and deception." [88] Three weeks later he wrote that initially the Prussians had been welcomed in Le Mans "with open arms, but

85. Clausewitz to Gneisenau, 29 July 1815, *ibid.*, p. 597.
86. Gneisenau to Hardenberg, 22 June 1815, Pertz-Delbrück, iv, 532. Similar statements recur in Gneisenau's letters during the months after Waterloo.
87. Clausewitz to his wife, 12 July 1815, *Correspondence*, p. 401.
88. Clausewitz to Gneisenau, 24 July 1815, Pertz-Delbrück, iv, 591.

the requisition of cloth and shoes, the confiscation of public moneys, the nature of foreign occupation, which has been unknown in these parts since the Hundred Years' War, the disarming of the National Guard and of the countryside to the extent already carried out—these measures have already alienated opinion, and I believe that inconsiderate treatment could easily provoke people into insurrection." [89]

In his letters to his wife he was more openly critical. He condemned Blücher and "his headquarters"—that is, Gneisenau—for snubbing Louis XVIII while simultaneously demanding contributions and making preparations for blowing up the Pont de Iéna across the Seine, the bridge being a particularly hated symbol of Napoleonic vainglory: "You can easily judge in how false and hostile a position this puts us toward the French and toward Louis XVIII, the more so since the English secretly favored the king's entry [into Paris], since they remain in camp, don't levy contributions, and don't loot. The worst seems to me that we fall between two stools—we spoil our relations with the French government and the French people simultaneously—and we don't really know what we want. Our king arrived in Paris the evening before last, and as he revoked the order to blow up the Pont de Iéna (after three small mines had been set off without the least effect) the drama turned to farce and French displeasure with us is not much increased. Be that as it may, I find our behavior lacking in that nobility that best suits the victor, and in the conflux of these peculiar actions and reactions it even acquires a degree of gaucheness and absurdity." [90]

After a lengthy analysis of the prospects for obtaining a lasting peace, Clausewitz concludes that history will record that the English played "the best part in this catastrophe, for they seem not to have come here, as we did, filled with a passion for revenge and retaliation, but rather like a punishing master, proud, cold, and completely pure—in short, they show greater nobility than we. ... But that lies in the entire role we have assumed; I could have imagined a more beautiful one."

As so often before, Clausewitz was dismayed by the reality of Prussian politics—both by its flawed policies and by the shortcomings of its individual agents—and in this instance he turned to another society as representative of his moral and political ideals. But more indicative of the manner in which he was coming to approach politics is another sentence toward the end of the same letter: "My greatest desire is that this epilogue will soon come to an end; for standing with one foot on another's neck is contrary to my feelings, and my intelligence abhors the endless conflicts of special interests and parties." To a man who was devoting himself to discovering the rational in war, and who had just passed through three years of intensive

89. Clausewitz to Gneisenau, 18 August 1815, *ibid.*, p. 608.
90. Clausewitz to his wife, 12 July 1815, *Correspondence*, pp. 399–400. The quotations which follow are from p. 401.

physical and intellectual experience with war, reason could not come to a halt when fighting stopped. The same detachment and objectivity—that coldness and rationality he attributed to his idealized Englishmen—were necessary in evaluating politics, the more so since he knew war to be nothing more than a force for political change, a part of the political whole.

10

THE RESTORATION

1. COBLENZ

In the spring of 1815, soon after he had taken up his appointment as chief of staff of the 3rd corps, Clausewitz wrote to his wife: "Anyone who now sees the Prussian army cannot recover from his amazement at the changes that have taken place in it since 1794. When I recall those days ... I am overjoyed that the plans and aspirations of my youth have now become reality. How much competence, how much good will and youthfulness can today be found in the army that used to be so dreary, stunted, and worn out! I don't know how far we would have come in these things without Scharnhorst; but it is impossible to see all this without constantly thinking of him." [1] The weeks of effort and fighting that followed confirmed his feeling of achievement. He might have been more fortunate personally, but the party among which he counted himself since his garrison days in Neuruppin had triumphed. The men who had worked to modernize the army and its manner of fighting had ultimately shown themselves superior to their great antagonist, the more so since their triumphs, unlike his, would not prove hollow. Prussia's victory could hardly be reversed in the next years, nor could the changes that had occurred within the country. The organizational forms that had been borrowed from the Revolution and the emperor were being animated, the reformers believed, by a healthier spirit than had been the case in France. That despite their successes against the French the plans and methods of innovation continued to be called into question by Prussian conservatives was only to be expected; the animosities that had marked the years since 1807 needed time to dissipate. More disturbing to the military reformers was the inability of their civilian peers to achieve further changes in the political arrangements of the Prussian state, and the diplomats' failure to create a stronger Germany in Europe. Ger-

---

1. Letter to Marie v. Clausewitz, 20 May 1815, *Correspondence*, p. 377.

many was subsiding into a condition little better than her former Legitimist fragmentation. The new Confederation seemed to the reformers a poor return for the German patriotism rather than Prussian sense of duty that had lent such impetus to their actions. Clausewitz, whose contempt for the German princes was now joined by the conviction that for the time being they would survive, accepted the outcome more calmly than did Gneisenau, Grolman, and other friends. At the same time he reconciled himself to ending his life in the service of the Prussian monarchy, a state whose political and spiritual parameters were unmistakably narrowing.

In view of Clausewitz's earlier insistence on the purity and heroism of the state, his new acceptance of Prussian realities can hardly be more striking. Not only is the change significant; with one notable exception, and that in the realm of theory rather than ideology, it was the last time that he changed his mind on a matter of fundamental importance. We may be justified in thinking that this development, which occurred between the spring of 1812 when he left the Prussian service and the Waterloo campaign three years later, places the seal on his maturity. No doubt the challenges and frictions that he encountered in the last three years of the Napoleonic wars strengthened his already pronounced realism. It is also apparent that the breakup of French imperialism, which he regarded as the actively evil element in European affairs, made it easier for him to tolerate the undesirable characteristics of the status quo. Two events that had a close bearing on his personal life might have been even more influential. The death of Scharnhorst in 1813 and the defeat and captivity of Napoleon removed the beloved and hated authorities, who together, in an intensely antagonistic relationship, had dominated Clausewitz's existence since late adolescence. With the departure of these two figures—one whom he called "father of my spirit," the other, whose destruction had been the object of his thought and actions, "the personification of war"—Clausewitz gained a new measure of independence. From now on an added breath of freedom is noticeable in his writings. The pressure of conflict was lifted; he ceased to wage war in his pamphlets and memoranda, nor was he any longer under the obligation of paying regard to Scharnhorst's opinions and politics. Even his letters to Gneisenau in 1814 and 1815, all friendship and respect notwithstanding, sound a new note of authority and detachment. It can hardly be surprising that with this gain in independence the Prussian state too, the idealized authority of his youth which had so often disappointed Clausewitz, lost some of its psychological hold over him. His criticism of Prussian policies was to be extensive in the coming years, but its tone gradually became very different, less emotional, increasingly objective, at times almost cold.

Since the beginning of 1815, Clausewitz's position in the army had been regularized, although not until August 1816 was it finally decided that the years he spent in Russian uniform should be credited to his Prussian seniority. He was no longer an outsider. If he was disappointed that he had not particularly distinguished himself in the last campaign, his rank of full colonel at the age of thirty-five scarcely made him appear a failure in the eyes of the world. Nor were his prospects poor. The king remained cool to him; but Clausewitz's closest associates had reached influential positions in the service, and could be relied on to keep his interests in mind: Boyen was minister of war; Grolman, now one of the most decorated younger officers, was charged with the reorganization of the general staff; and above all there was the connection with Gneisenau. The army's senior generals—Blücher, Yorck, and the other leaders of the Wars of Liberation—were near the end of their careers, and Gneisenau at the age of fifty-five could be considered the first soldier of the realm. After the army returned from France he was given a new assignment, and for his chief of staff chose Clausewitz, who regarded this as the best of all possible duties. With his wife Clausewitz arrived in Coblenz, seat of Gneisenau's new headquarters, in the late fall of 1815.

Under the terms of the second Peace of Paris, Prussia had regained most of her scattered possessions in western Germany, now consolidated and expanded into a territorial block that extended on both banks of the Rhine from Cleves to Coblenz, and continued along the Mosel to Saarbrücken. These acquisitions, which were to shift Prussia's interest to the west with fateful consequences, not only strengthened the state but served the restored balance of power by guarding the Netherlands and assuring a bridgehead for a British expeditionary corps on the continent. The Rhineland's political loyalty to Berlin remained in some doubt, and since it was still separated from the main body of the monarchy by a string of middle-sized and minor states, the task of its administrative, economic, and social integration was exacerbated. When the Prussian army was reorganized into seven territorial commands in the fall of 1815, Gneisenau was appointed commanding general on the Rhine, with additional authority over Thielmann, who commanded in Westphalia and over the Prussian contingent of the allied occupation army in France. This arrangement was meant to solidify political authority in the west and to insure a unified and sizable force should a new conflict with France errupt—a possibility few men were prepared to rule out completely.

The diversity of Gneisenau's political and military concerns was reflected in Clausewitz's activities. Besides carrying out such normal staff work as supervising training schedules and preparing contingency plans, Clausewitz kept an eye on the introduction of conscription in the new territories and on the relationship between the troops and the civil authorities and population. Gneisenau also involved him in larger political issues. In January 1816 he traveled to Frankfurt, where Wilhelm von Humboldt,

Prussia's representative at the German Territorial Commission, was engaged in settling the new Dutch-Prussian frontier. On 23 January, Humboldt wrote Gneisenau that he could not thank him enough for sending Clausewitz to advise him in his negotiations: he now understood the Prussian position perfectly.[2] Their meeting, which confirmed the good opinion that Humboldt had formed of Clausewitz before 1812 in Berlin, undoubtedly contributed to his political support of Clausewitz in the following years. Humboldt added in his letter that Clausewitz would verbally convey to Gneisenau Humboldt's reaction to the recent replacement of the civil governor of the Rhineland, Johann August Sack. The change of officials and Humboldt's suspicion that his letters might be opened were two signals among many of the gathering strength of reaction in Prussia.

The ideological tensions that touched Clausewitz's life in Coblenz from the beginning did not at first interfere with his personal relationships. Although he resented the transfer of Sack, a long-time associate of Stein and an energetic middle-class member of the reform party, he got on well with his successor, Karl Heinrich von Ingersleben, a man of very different stamp. Ingersleben, son of a Frederician general, was a conscientious but profoundly conventional senior civil servant, who bore with dignity the disgrace brought on his family by an older brother, who had been sentenced to death for surrendering a fortress to the French in 1806. Clausewitz seems to have valued his unassuming simplicity and great kindness. Ingersleben, representative of an older Prussia, and Gneisenau, who only a few years ago had fought his way out of obscurity to help save the state, were the two poles around which Clausewitz's personal circle formed.

Apart from Gneisenau his closest friends among the officers stationed in Coblenz were Count von der Groeben, who had been his student at the War College and served with him in the Russo-German Legion. Two decades later, after both Clausewitz and his wife had died, Groeben edited the last two volumes of Clausewitz's collected works. Another member of Gneisenau's staff who was to help prepare Clausewitz's manuscripts for publication was Captain O'Etzel, who had studied mineralogy and chemistry and gained the degree of D. Phil. at Wittenberg before entering the army. His wife was a daughter of the well-known Jewish publisher and jurist Hitzig. In later years O'Etzel was to be one of the founders of the Geographic Society of Berlin and a pioneer of telegraphy in Germany. From similar well-established middle-class backgrounds came Major Stosch, who had studied law at Halle and served as a *Landwehr* officer before Gneisenau chose him as his adjutant, and Major Hellwig, son of a mathematician, who had distinguished himself in 1806, and again in the Wars of Liberation as a leader of

2. *Wilhelm von Humboldts Politische Briefe*, ed. W. Richter, Berlin, 1936, ii, 102–103. See also the preceding letter of 22 January 1816 to Hardenberg.

partisan operations. A man of particular significance to the Clausewitzes was Scharnhorst's elder son, Wilhelm, who in 1818 married Gneisenau's daughter Agnes, after a difficult courtship in which Marie von Clausewitz acted as his motherly friend and adviser. Throughout these years Clausewitz vainly tried to persuade the state that land should be deeded or a pension paid to Scharnhorst's children in recognition of their father's great services.[3] Most junior of Clausewitz's friends was Lieutenant Leopold von Gerlach, the future leader of the Prussian conservatives and intimate of

3. An example of Clausewitz's concern which also provides a good illustration of the almost exaggeratedly formal manner in which he addressed his old friends, including Gneisenau, who now had far outdistanced him in rank, is the following letter, which he wrote to Boyen, the minister of war, on 29 November 1816:

"If this letter calls for an apology, Your Excellency will find it in [our] relationship of an earlier day. The subject itself, I believe, will not require an apology in your eyes.

"General Scharnhorst's achievements are acknowledged by the king, and his memorial is to be erected next to the statue of Count Bülow von Dennewitz. His closer friends—among whom I count the Chancellor, Prince Blücher, and General Count Gneisenau—used to speculate on the possibility of endowing the family with an estate. I don't know whether this thought ever reached the king. If those with a closer knowledge of the events in our state between 1806 and 1813 were formed into a jury, they would scarcely judge Scharnhorst to have had less merit than the most distinguished among the gentlemen who were made counts in 1814 [i.e., Gneisenau, Yorck, Bülow, Kleist, and Tauenzien]. The judges would find that his claims equal theirs in all respects, and in the eyes of the people he certainly would not appear less deserving. But undoubtedly at the time the matter was not seen in this light, otherwise it would not have been ignored, and I quite understand that what would be no more than justice according to my feelings cannot now be hoped for.

"I admit that opinions may differ, and that one individual does not have the right to impose his views as law; but today the matter seems to have been completely forgotten, there is the greatest danger that nothing at all will be done, and that could not be justified on any account.

"All those who were closely associated with him, owe it to his memory and to his family never to let this question vanish from their hearts. When I consider that Your Excellency, Prince Blücher, the Chancellor, Count Gneisenau, Lord Chancellor Beyme, General Grolman—all were close friends of General Scharnhorst, that all are profoundly conscious of his services, it seems incredible that he could be passed over completely. It should not be difficult to do enough to make his family economically independent; it would hardly require a third or a fourth of what other men received.

"The purpose of this letter is not to call Your Excellency's attention to the son, which certainly would not be necessary, but to beg you to have the kindness to inform me of your view of the matter and tell me whether you do not agree that if at present it really is dormant, a common appeal by General Scharnhorst's friends, especially through the good offices of Lord Chancellor Beyme, might not achieve something.

"It goes without saying that the children will never initiate this request; indeed, their noble pride goes so far that even toward me they have never as much as hinted at the matter. But the less they complain at the fate of being forgotten, which now seems to lie upon them, the more sensible will their friends be to the insult, and suffer with them.

"Your Excellency will undoubtedly share my feelings on this matter to such an extent that you will not regard my strong concern as unnatural. I believe therefore that any further apology is unnecessary, and with the assurance of my exceptional respect and devotion beg to remain in your continued favor. Clausewitz."

At the head of the letter, Boyen noted: "This request has been rejected twice by the king." Deutsches Zentralarchiv, Historische Abt. II, Merseburg, Rep. 92, Boyen d. Ä., XIII, a. Cf. also Clausewitz's letter to Gneisenau of 4 March 1817, Pertz-Delbrück, v, 192–193: "I had a strong compulsion to raise the matter again since I was as close to [Scharnhorst] as a son, without being an heir to his family glory and fortune."

Frederick William IV. Clausewitz, who had come to know him in Berlin before the war when both were members of the *Christlich-Deutsche Tischgesellschaft,* and had met him again in Blücher's headquarters in 1813, treated the younger man with an open affection that he rarely showed.[4] Groeben alone of these officers, all of whom rose to senior positions, came from an old noble family; O'Etzel, Stosch, and Hellwig were ennobled in the course of their careers or, like Clausewitz, had their claims of nobility confirmed.

Among civilians other than Ingersleben with whom Clausewitz was intimate were Karl von Meusebach, president of the Appellate Court, owner of one of the great private libraries in Germany, who wrote on Renaissance and Baroque literature, and the young legal official Max von Schenkendorf, who had been one of the editors of *Vesta,* which printed Fichte's essay on Machiavelli. Schenkendorf wrote poems and patriotic songs, a few of which still survive in anthologies. Cultivated and able as these men were, two others, whom Clausewitz saw only irregularly, were of far greater stature: Stein, whom he occasionally visited in nearby Nassau, and the scholar and publicist Joseph Görres, who lived in Coblenz until 1819 when a warrant for his arrest, issued because of his book *Germany and the Revolution,* compelled him to escape to Strasbourg.

The small contingent of Prussian officials, all newcomers to Coblenz, passed much of their leisure time together. The men met in the afternoons for coffee; accompanied by their wives they explored the valley of the Rhine on weekends, or came together for a frugal dinner. In his poem "Die Tafel am Rhein" Schenkendorf compares Gneisenau and his paladins to the medieval knights of whom he had dreamed as a boy. This was feebly fanciful, like most of Schenkendorf's verse; but the low-key conviviality, strongly shaped by music, literature, and the legend-filled countryside, does appear to have been touched by a genuinely creative note of German romanticism. All members of the group agree, Delbrück writes in his biography of Gneisenau, that this period of their lives was colored with "the glow of that poetic idealism that only seldom becomes reality, and then never for long." [5] Gneisenau spoke of his "headquarters of the vineyards." Another, less friendly description was at the same time making the rounds among conservatives in Berlin and Potsdam: Wallenstein's camp on the Rhine.

Ever since 1807, when Gneisenau, suddenly famous for his defense of Colberg, was named to the Military Reorganization Commission, he had been charged with being a Jacobin. His drive to modernize the army, his scorn of the mixture of brutality and family influence that characterized so

---

4. See, for instance, Clausewitz's letter to Gerlach of 9 March 1816, in which the recipient is addressed as "little one," "little friend with curly hair and a face that is alternately gloomy and cheerful," etc. Printed in the collection of letters and diaries of the Gerlach family, *Aus den Jahren Preussischer Not und Erneuerung,* ed. H. J. Schoeps, Berlin, 1963, pp. 556–558.
5. Pertz-Delbrück, *Gneisenau,* v, 7.

much of the old system, his espousal of a people in arms, all made enemies—the more so since in his dealings with others he had little of Scharnhorst's diplomatic reserve. His ability to hate, no less than his charm and
vitality, seemed inexhaustible. In 1813 and 1814 his single-minded pursuit of decision by battle, regardless of effort or casualties, created further
opposition, which in the minds of some was linked with envy at his rapid
rise to the highest distinctions in the service. His vocal condemnation of
the peace terms and his dissatisfaction with the continued division and
weakness of Germany caused such foreign observers as the Tsar, Metternich, and Wellington to express concern that the Prussian army had become politicized. With the increase of restorative tendencies in Prussia during the second half of 1815, rumors began to circulate that Gneisenau, a
non-Prussian himself, who surrounded himself with middle-class officers
and others who had renounced their commissions rather than support the
Franco-Prussian alliance, was becoming the head of a possibly subversive
movement in army and state.

These suspicions, accurately reflecting Gneisenau's preeminence
among the military reformers, were misplaced on two counts: Gneisenau
entertained no political ambitions; and, though he wanted the work of innovation to continue, his political attitudes were anything but revolutionary. As is true of Clausewitz and of most members of the reformers'
inner circle, his politics are not susceptible to easy categorization—least of
all if they are defined according to more modern conceptions. Indeed, as
Delbrück writes in analyzing this period of Gneisenau's life, even the majority of contemporaries did not fully understand his political views.

Doctrine, whether political or military, easily bored him. He believed
in the art of the possible, though he was far from permitting custom or
convenience to define its limits. That had been true of his participation in
the reforms, and again during the Wars of Liberation, when he repeatedly
transgressed against accepted practice, and realistically exploited the potential of the army to the utmost. His independence and pragmatism did not
diminish after 1815. He saw nothing sacred in the absolute authority of the
crown, nor in the traditional social and economic privileges of the nobility;
but neither was he impressed by liberal, let alone democratic, speculations.
In common with nearly every member of the reform group, he was repelled
by the noisy presumptuousness with which some students and gymnasts
were now proclaiming the unity of the German fatherland. A united Germany was his ideal too, but he no longer regarded it as attainable in ·the
foreseeable future. "That is the way it is with this class of men," he wrote
to Clausewitz in reference to Jahn's *Turner;* "constantly exaggerating, they
disdain the possible in order to chase after fantasies." [6] But it was absurd to

6. Letter of 8 November 1818, *ibid.,* p. 354.

see them as a serious political threat; on the contrary, they provided reactionaries with an easy opportunity to discredit moderate opinion. Such repressive measures as censorship seemed to him more likely to damage than to protect the interests of the state. When the Prussian government in January 1816 followed the lead of Bavaria, Baden, and Württemberg, and stopped publication of Görres's newspaper, the *Rheinische Merkur,* which in its brief existence had gained a European-wide reputation, Gneisenau wrote that even though he did not agree with half the editor's views, the prohibition was a serious error.[7] As early as 1808 he had sent a memorandum to the king that advocated the introduction of a constitution, and he continued to give emphatic support to the constitutional movement after the war. A good constitution, he wrote in 1818, is the only bond that can fuse the provinces of the Prussian monarchy into a solid whole: "Representation in two chambers, public trials, freedom of the press with guarantees against personal libel and assaults on morality, accountability of officials, abolition of the secret police, an end to the practice of opening letters and of arresting individuals without a hearing—these should be the pillars of the new constitution." [8] What Gneisenau had in mind was an upper chamber consisting of hereditary as well as of appointed members, and a lower house elected by limited suffrage, possibly on a corporative basis, possessing the right of free discussion, consultation, and legislative initiative, but not yet significantly sharing power with the executive. This body was to make possible the responsible participation in public affairs of a greater number of experienced and educated men; if it prospered it would inevitably acquire a measure of true authority. For the moment he thought it important to make a start; but by the grace of the monarch, not in response to popular demands and political agitation.

Clausewitz shared these feelings. When toward the end of 1817 Görres drafted a petition to Frederick William reminding him of the promised constitution, which was signed by many Rhinelanders, including judges and other officials, Clausewitz decided after some reflection that he could not approve the step since the signatories were self-appointed spokesmen: "It is my conviction that the people must never directly approach the throne. Its voice should reach the throne through the medium of the press or through representatives. A direct contact of people and throne is dangerously democratic [*ist demokratischer, gefährlicher Natur*], and in this sense the mob that gathered before the Tuileries on 10 August [1792] does not differ from the signatories of a popular petition. Their legitimization is identical." He had not yet seen a copy of the privately circulated address, but wrote Gneisenau: "We may assume that it is couched in intelligent and

7. Letter to Schleiermacher, 20 January 1816, *ibid.,* p. 73.
8. Gneisenau to Clausewitz, 20 August 1818. Cf. his letter of 20 May 1819 to his friend J. v. Gruner, *ibid.,* pp. 333–334, 372.

honorable terms, and that it seeks nothing but good." [9] Content, however, could not justify in his eyes the potentially revolutionary step of private citizens advising and even criticizing the king. Evidently he continued to think of politics after 1815 in terms of the reform era: change came from above. He must have differentiated between Görres's *Adresse* and his own *Bekenntnisdenkschrift* with the thought that in 1812 the state was in crisis, and that his memorial emanated from, and circulated among, a few members of the military elite, who during the reform era had come to assert a special moral and political authority in the state.

He believed that all Prussians should enjoy equality of rights as well as equality of duties—a condition that he thought the Third Estate had now "more or less" achieved. But he was opposed to a leveling of groups and classes.[10] His letters and his political essays do not go into specifics, but it is apparent that like Gneisenau he favored some form of limited franchise, dependent on residence, property, and professional qualifications, leading to a bicameral parliament, which at least for the moment should possess little initiative but had the right to discuss and advise. This was not very different from the French constitutional charter of 1814 or, indeed, from the position generally adopted by early German liberals. As Lothar Gall has recently stated: " 'Bourgeois society' was for them quite naturally *ständisch,* that is, structured according to talent and achievement, but also almost inevitably according to background and tradition." [11] Economic and educational differences were reflected as a matter of course in their political programs: "It was possible to be liberal without embracing the principle of popular sovereignty." [12] And if only because Prussian society still lacked a sizable and economically independent middle class, a parliamentary constitution on the English pattern, with elected representatives wielding direct political power, was a practical impossibility.[13]

An important element in the political position that Clausewitz shared with Gneisenau was the belief that a strong central authority was essential to a state in Prussia's exposed situation. But Gneisenau had genuinely aristocratic instincts, attitudes similar in some respects to those of the great

9. Clausewitz to Gneisenau, 12 November 1817, Pertz-Delbrück, v, 266.
10. Clausewitz to Gneisenau, 28 October 1817, *ibid.,* p. 265. The letter goes on to complain about the leveling effect of economic development, which itself leads to new kinds of inequality, and refers to the "truth" of K. L. v. Haller's contention that society can exist only on the basis of inequality. It is a peculiar way for Clausewitz to support his belief in class distinctions since nothing could have been more remote from his conception of the state than Haller's view of the state as a large family of sovereign property-owners. The letter appears to have been used by Gneisenau to allay Hardenberg's doubts concerning Clausewitz's political reliability (see pp. 266, 271 below) and it is not inconceivable that it was written with that purpose in mind.
11. L. Gall, "Liberalismus und 'bürgerliche Gesellschaft'. Zu Charakter und Entwicklung der liberalen Bewegung in Deutschland," *Historische Zeitschrift,* CCXX (1975), No. 2, 341.
12. F. Schnabel, *Deutsche Geschichte im neunzehnten Jahrhundert,* Freiburg, 1933, ii, 99.
13. Cf. R. Koselleck, *Preussen zwischen Reform und Revolution,* Stuttgart, 1967, p. 186, n. 82.

Whig peers of George III's reign, while Clausewitz put greater faith in the political potential of broader segments of society, and was more inclined to develop his political views systematically and historically. Despite these differences, both men saw themselves as treading a broad middle path between extremes. Gneisenau's exclamation in 1826: "What has not happened in Europe in the past decade! Insolence of democracy and insanity or idiocy of absolutism—on what false paths have they led us!" could as easily have come from his younger friend.[14]

The absence of politically organized and effective public opinion in Prussia meant that conflicts over policy—and, increasingly, between ideological positions—were waged by individuals and small, informal coalitions among those whose positions gave them a greater or lesser degree of influence in the administration, the army, and such other institutions as the schools and the church. The fragmentation of the reform years continued to characterize public affairs after 1815. Rather than being integrated into party programs, views on domestic issues—the constitution, press laws, university and church administration, agricultural policy, the relationship between regular army and *Landwehr*—expressed themselves in countless separate battles, success in any one of which tended to have limited carry-over. Personal relationships largely took the place of political organizations, and such matters as the bestowing of a decoration or the choice for a middle-level appointment assumed a significance out of all proportion, on the strength of which men estimated the political direction the country was taking. For even in the absence of clearly drawn party lines, there could be no doubt that Prussia was involved in a great struggle over the character of her government and society, which in turn had a bearing on her role in Germany and Europe. To the adherents of monarchical absolutism and to their social peers but frequent opponents, the politically active provincial nobles, who sought to diminish rather than increase the power of the central government, the changes introduced after 1806 had been essentially a counterstrategy to Napoleon. Once he had fallen, justification for change disappeared. To the reformers and their occasional allies on right and left—

14. Letter to the Hanoverian statesman Count Münster, 14 November 1826, *Lebensbilder aus dem Befreiungskriege*, ed. J. F. v. Hormayr, Jena, 1841, i, 146–147. Similar statements recur in his correspondence during these years. See, for instance, his letter of 22 October 1819 to Princess Louise Radziwill, discussing the response in Prussia to the repressive Karlsbad Decrees: "For the time being one can distinguish only three major parties. First, the more violent liberals, to whom must be added the genuine Jacobins and revolutionaries. . . . Their number is certainly not large. Then the violent persecutors, joined by the fearful. They accuse, arouse mistrust, collect statements and poison them by their interpretations. A third party, the most sizable, consists of loyal supporters of the monarchy who tend to favor the constitutional development of the state and fear that at Karlsbad more was decided than was necessary. ... I could mention ... a fourth party, but it is feeble indeed, consisting as it does only of General v. Clausewitz and myself. We believe that all three parties are more or less mistaken on many points; that the impudence of the first deserved to be punished; that the lust for persecution of the second as disgusting; and that the worries of the third are exaggerated ...." Pertz–Delbrück, v, 379–380.

the enlightened conservatives and, on the other side, men like Schön and Sack, who wanted to develop liberal institutions on a western-European model—the early reforms had proved themselves and, logically, should be continued and expanded. The reactionary faction at court, the chancellor's immediate circle, which worked for further innovation but without the regenerative fervor of the true reformers, the moderately liberal senior bureaucracy, and other such groupings were beginning to define the fronts more sharply, but what Clausewitz wrote early in 1816 of himself and Scharnhorst's other disciples held true for many throughout society: "So far as our army is concerned ... it can scarcely compare in spirit and attitude with the army of 1809 and '10. In those days six or eight people of spirit held together, ceaselessly repeated the same arguments, and in ways that they themselves were not aware of gained influence over the rest. Now everyone is completely isolated ... ." [15]

A passage in a letter by Groeben to Gerlach, who had been transferred to Berlin, illustrates the prevailing uncertainty, in which even friends might misinterpret each other's position: "Clausewitz, though I value him for his integrity, ossifies more and more. All of a sudden he becomes political and sly, takes the side of the court, opposes Görres because twenty years ago he had written some nonsense, and asks Councillor Sack to dine (who is universally hated by the people, and rightly so) to make certain that no one in Berlin might think him to be on the side of the people." [16] Groeben was mistaken in supposing that Clausewitz's criticism of Görres signified a sharp political shift. From the start Clausewitz had opposed Görres's corporative-national ideal, as he failed to share Stein's not dissimilar views, and in subsequent years both men's political attitudes grew further apart, without causing a personal rift or bringing them into complete political opposition. In 1817 Clausewitz wrote Gneisenau that while Görres was "more of a democrat than is fitting in a great monarchy ... he pursues his ideals and convictions with intentions that are entirely pure; he is not unfair in his judgments, although unrestrained, blunt, and loud; he is an upright and high-minded man." An influential position in government would tie him to the state and teach him the political realities. [17] As late as 1822, Görres returned the compliment. To a friend who was visiting Berlin to sound out the ministries on Rhenish issues, he wrote: "Do visit Clausewitz; a greeting from me can serve you as pretext. He is an intelligent, sensible, and good man." [18] Nor was Groeben correct in his comments on Sack, whose liberalism and consequent unpopularity at court are beyond question. [19] Groe-

15. Clausewitz to Gerlach, 9 March 1816; *Aus den Jahren Preussischer Not,* p. 557.
16. 29 April 1816, *ibid.,* p. 560.
17. 11 December 1817; Pertz-Delbrück, v, 272–273.
18. Görres to H. J. Dietz, 7 November 1822; J. v. Görres, *Gesammelte Briefe,* Munich, 1874, iii, 51.
19. See, for example, the account of Sack's fight for freedom of the press in the Rhineland, in E. Klein, *Von der Reform zur Restauration,* Berlin, 1965, pp. 211–214.

ben's suppositions can be explained only as an expression of the ominous, confused political atmosphere that was enveloping the country, a contributory factor possibly being his knowledge that the Gerlachs disliked Sack, who a few years earlier had been preferred to the senior Gerlach for an important appointment.

Gneisenau was irritated by the vague, persistent attacks on his loyalty. His protests that neither he nor Clausewitz had so much as belonged to the *Tugendbund,* a secret patriotic organization that had been officially tolerated for a time during the reform era, let alone to more recent and more radical associations, did not stop the talk.[20] Like many others, he was weary after years of intense activity—Hardenberg, who valued him greatly, diagnosed a spell of hypochondria—and in a mixture of fatigue and disgust he offered his resignation. At first he was given extended leave, and Clausewitz almost frantically urged him to withdraw his resignation; then, to his own surprise, he was replaced. Lack of coordination between the various authorities in their correspondence with him may have been responsible as much as the intrigue that he himself suspected. He left Coblenz in July 1816.

Clausewitz's regret at the departure of his friend was heightened by the identity of his successor, Albrecht Georg von Hake. General von Hake, whose career had in the main taken him through a succession of administrative posts, had been disliked by Scharnhorst for his opportunistic pliability and opposition to innovation. "If it can be done unnoticed," Scharnhorst once warned Hardenberg, "[he and his crony Knesebeck will] undermine the new organization of the army, shake it to its foundations, and reverse it."[21] That such a man now assumed Gneisenau's place, Clausewitz could interpret only as a further setback to the spirit of reform. He did his best to accommodate himself to the change, but would not deny that his views differed greatly from those held by Hake, who, besides, was such a stickler for detail that Clausewitz sighed he felt "like a trained poodle" in his efforts to execute accurately every minor order that he received. Years later he recalled him as "an excellent inspector of barracks." Marie von Clausewitz was less polite. To Gneisenau she wrote that with Hake's arrival, "a dry pedant is placed next to an imbecile writing machine"—the latter presumably referring to Ingersleben.[22] For his part, Hake, who was far from stupid, had little difficulty in evaluating his chief of staff. A few months

---

20. In his *Histoire de France sous Napoléon*, x, Paris, 1833, the former French *intendant* in Berlin L. P. de Bignon writes that in 1811 Gneisenau and Clausewitz were denounced to the French authorities as members of the *Tugendbund*. The rumor, though false, persisted throughout their lives and beyond.
21. Letter of 11 March 1812, *Scharnhorsts Briefe,* pp. 426–427.
22. Marie v. Clausewitz to Gneisenau, 30 August 1816, Pertz-Delbrück, v, 145; Clausewitz to Gneisenau, 11 December 1817 and 21 June 1825, *ibid.,* pp. 271–272, 516. The couple's correspondence with Gneisenau is a significant source of information on the remainder of Clausewitz's life, its importance being heightened by the fact that with one exception letters between husband and wife from the years 1816 to 1830 have not survived.

after he assumed his command, he wrote the following conduct report on Clausewitz for the year 1816: "Is not very communicative. I consider him a decent person. He shows much feeling for truth and justice, is generous, stimulated by honor, perhaps vain, and consequently likes to insist on his point of view. But, to be sure, his knowledge of military affairs is far from insignificant, and he was a useful teacher of young officers. He is primarily interested in ideas, nevertheless he carries out his duties with precision, and writes in a beautiful and clear style. Even though his own behavior is at times rather brusque, he expects to be treated with tact. If this is done, he presents no problems. So far I have always had reason to be satisfied with him, and regard him as a competent senior general-staff officer. I have not yet had occasion to come to know him outside the office on field duty. His health is good." [23]

The last statement was not wholly accurate, since Clausewitz continued to suffer from his old illnesses. A "cheerful and courageous spirit in a gouty body" was Arndt's description of him at the time, but he did not permit the occasionally severe pains to interfere with his heavy official schedule.[24] His social life, on the other hand, he now found uneventful and insipid. "Six jokes and scarcely two original thoughts come our way every six months," he wrote Gneisenau. "Herr v. Stein is our only solace." [25] It was at this time that he began to write the early drafts of what later became *On War;* his brief biography of Scharnhorst is another important work of these years.

The Scharnhorst biography and the essays on strategic theory will be discussed in chapter 11 below. Here something should be said about the more technical studies that Clausewitz wrote in his official capacity while stationed in Coblenz, papers addressing specific issues, from which his theoretical and historical writings continued to draw ideas and illustrations. An example is a long study on the Rhineland as a theater of operations, which analyzed Prussia's defensive options in a war with France.[26] Clausewitz regarded Cologne as the logical target of a French offensive; if the city fell, the barrier of the Rhine would be breached and the entire province might have to be surrendered. Consequently Cologne should be made secure and other significant towns on the Rhine fortified to create the framework for a mobile defense, within which the local commanders could operate according to circumstances. He castigated the habit of "thinking in systems," which had not been eliminated in the Prussian army; it was

23. Priesdorff, v, No. 1429.

24. Letter to Schleiermacher, 17 January 1818, in E. M. Arndt, *Ein Lebensbild in Briefen,* eds. H. Meissner and R. Geerds, Berlin, 1898, p. 171. In the spring of 1817 Clausewitz requested two months leave to take the waters in Nassau "because constant arthritic pains make this necessary for me." Letter to Gneisenau, 28 April 1817, Pertz-Delbrück, v, 217.

25. Letter of 28 April 1817, *ibid.,* p. 217.

26. "Preussens Kriegstheater am Rhein," Hahlweg, *Clausewitz,* pp. 42–43.

"more important to work on building up the means of resistance than to draw up plans." [27]

Almost as important as the location of defensive positions was the question of their design. Prussian military architects were rejecting Vauban's system of a national barrier of strong forts and fortified towns, each designed for close-in defense. The writings of Montalembert and Carnot, and such experiences in recent wars as Gneisenau's aggressive defense of Colberg in which he relied as much on sorties and counterattacks as on the fortifications themselves, led the army to develop a few major strongpoints, whose works did not follow a standard pattern but the local terrain and which were designed to support a mobile defense. The affinity between this concept of fortification and Clausewitz's view of war as a whole is obvious: both emphasize the uniqueness of the particular situation and believe that the forces engaged should seek the greatest possible scope for individual initiative. Characteristic of Clausewitz's opinion is his "Memoire über die Befestigung von Trier" of 1818, a subject on which he also corresponded with Gneisenau. [28] He did not believe that a town on the border of Luxembourg, some seventy-five miles west of the Rhine, was suited to be a major defensive position. Fortified camps and major citadels, he wrote to Gneisenau, who differed with him on this point, interfere with the freedom of operations if they are placed on the frontier; they should be located in the interior to support a defense of last resort. Trier should be used as a communications center; to make it secure against a surprise raid it sufficed to build a few blockhouses and to deepen the ditch in front of the existing town walls.

Of greater political interest than these operational studies was Clausewitz's evaluation of a proposal to exchange parts of Prussian territory for land of minor German states so as to create a corridor of Prussian sovereignty between the western and the central provinces of the state. [29] This scheme by Friedrich von Motz, soon to be Prussian finance minister, sought not only to link the two parts of the state but also to provide a belt that would hold together and separate northern Germany from the south-German states and Austria. Though conscious of certain disadvantages that resulted from Prussia's fragmented territories, Clausewitz opposed the plan. His memorandum, dated 20 January 1818, began by noting that Motz's political reasons for the exchange in reality "all have a military basis, and in the final analysis rely on arguments for greater military effectiveness." Motz's expectations of nonmilitary advantages appeared to be unrealistic.

27. *Ibid.*, p. 43.
28. "Memoire über die Befestigung von Trier," *ibid.*, p. 43; Clausewitz to Gneisenau, 29 July 1818, Pertz-Delbrück, v, 330–332. Cf. *On War*, book VI, chs. 10–11 (pp. 568–586).
29. "Über das vom Präsidenten von Motz angegebene Projekt,..." published by E. Kessel in "Clausewitz über den Gedanken eines Ländertauschs ...," *Forschungen zur Brandenburgischen und Preussischen Geschichte*, LI (1939), pp. 371–377.

Surely no territorial wall was needed to keep such small central-German states as Saxe-Weimar and Hesse in the Prussian orbit.[30] But the military arguments, too, Clausewitz held to be invalid. The fact that Prussia's territories were fragmented and extended hundreds of miles from east to west did not decisively inhibit the state's defense "against its main enemies, France and Russia." Combining the two separated areas would not increase their defensive strength: "What a totally separated state can achieve the two branches of the House of Austria have demonstrated in Belgium for three centuries. I doubt that it would have benefited the German Habsburgs if a narrow strip of land had been cut from the Belgian provinces and stretched to the Danube. This narrow strip would have weakened the solid mass [of Belgium] without in any real sense lessening her isolation." Nor would a strip of territory act as a barrier in time of war: "As soon as war is declared, the concept of a political frontier ceases to exist for all practical purposes, especially in the case of such a narrow strip, and we should be glad if we could withdraw the living fighting forces from it in time." [31]

After analyzing the geographic and economic details of the proposed territorial exchange, Clausewitz concluded that the only true advantage of the scheme lay in relieving both Prussia and the minor German states of the inconvenience of having Prussian units march from one part of the monarchy to another through non-Prussian territory, as was constantly happening. But the unfavorable impression that a territorial exchange would make on Germans everywhere was too high a price to pay to eliminate this irritation. In any case, better administration in the Prussian army could reduce "this endless marching back and forth." [32]

The quantity of Clausewitz's writing and the diversity of his topics, ranging from staff memoranda to political essays, and historical and theoretical analyses, indicate that after something of a hiatus filled by campaign and occupation duties he had entered into a new phase of creativity. It was to last without much interruption for the rest of his life. In his remaining sixteen years, whatever his obligations, he engaged in constant research and wrote many thousands of pages, and his productivity flowed steadily—affected, no doubt, but until 1830 rarely impeded by events of the external world. It would be wrong to assume that this intellectual harvest was bought at the price of his resigning himself to a stunted career. Certainly he was no longer as intensely ambitious for outward success as he had been in his twenties. He might now assure Gneisenau that he did not care whether he was a colonel or general, adding the characteristic proviso, "so

---

30. *Ibid.,* pp. 373–374.
31. *Ibid.,* pp. 374–375.
32. *Ibid.,* pp. 376–377. A year and a half earlier Clausewitz had condemned another project of territorial exchange with a similar emphasis on the importance of German public opinion: "We are wrong to expect benefits from [German] governments, we should expect them from the spirit of the people." Letter to Gneisenau of 9 August 1816, Pertz-Delbrück, v, 136.

long as I am being treated fairly"; but this did not mean that he had lost all desire for advancement.[33] He continued to pursue a variety of possible appointments, and for several years seriously hoped to exchange military service for a diplomatic post; but neither these attempts nor the failures in which they almost always ended brought his theoretical and historical studies to a halt.

In his efforts to be appointed to duties that were more agreeable and significant than working under Hake he was strongly encouraged by Gneisenau, who used his influence, which was still considerable, to advance Clausewitz's interests. In March 1816, when Gneisenau was already talking of resigning, he suggested the liberal-minded Prince Wilhelm as his successor, to be assisted by Clausewitz, whom he described to Hardenberg as an officer of rare political and military understanding. Some months later he asked Boyen to relieve Clausewitz of routine duties to give him time to write an official manual on strategy and major operations. Early the following year he recommended Clausewitz as companion to the crown prince, who was to take a month-long tour of the Rhineland. Unlike the preceding suggestions, this was accepted, and the trip enabled Clausewitz to regain the good will of his former pupil, which, he hoped, might stand him in good stead at some later time. After Gneisenau was appointed to the new council of state, created by Hardenberg to debate and initiate legislation and to coordinate the work of the various ministries, he repeatedly urged Clausewitz's co-option to this body, characterized by Clausewitz as a "birth-aid in the constitutional crisis in which we find ourselves." [34] He brought Clausewitz into closer contact with Hardenberg, and suggested him as permanent representative on the military council of the German Diet at Frankfurt, should the position fall vacant. A mission to Frankfurt that Clausewitz undertook in the spring of 1818 presumably had to do with the work of the military council. Immediately afterwards Clausewitz traveled to England, probably in connection with a scheme in which he was beginning to invest many of his hopes for the future: succeeding Wilhelm von Humboldt as ambassador to the Court of St. James. In his diary Humboldt mentions Clausewitz's presence at dinner on 22 June. But by that time another of Gneisenau's plans for his friend had come to fruition.[35]

On 21 September 1817, the administrative head of the War College in Berlin, General von Boguslawski, had died. Gneisenau proposed that Clausewitz be appointed to the post, which, though of no real importance, provided a base in the capital, carried with it promotion to major-general,

33. Clausewitz to Gneisenau, 29 October 1816, *ibid.*, p. 157.
34. Clausewitz to Gneisenau, 12 October 1816, *ibid.*, p. 152.
35. Gneisenau's efforts to help Clausewitz during these years are documented in his correspondence with Clausewitz and others, printed in the fifth volume of Pertz-Delbrück's Gneisenau biography. For Clausewitz's presence in London see Wilhelm v. Humboldt, *Gesammelte Schriften,* ed. A. Leitzmann, Berlin, 1918, xv, 498, 513, 515.

and might be made more significant by giving the incumbent a voice in the army's advanced training and strategic planning.[36] From the point of view of the army hierarchy, bringing one of the service's better-known learned officers to the War College had much to recommend it. Clausewitz, on the other hand, was not eager to make the move; he no longer much cared for Berlin—Gneisenau's presence seemed to him the city's only positive attraction—and he asked Boyen to consider him instead for an inspectorship of the *Landwehr*, where he might be useful in strengthening the institution of the army that was most threatened by conservative attacks. The directorship at the War College, however, was the only opening available, and the appointment process took its course. It included an investigation into the candidate's moral qualities and political reliability. In disgust Gneisenau wrote to Clausewitz that the king wished to know "whether young officers could be safely entrusted to you because of your political attitudes, and whether you too possibly belonged to the republican innovators, who are now threatening the thrones." The inquiry took some time; it was not until 9 May 1818 that the king signed the appointment.[37]

Before Clausewitz reported to his new post he was given the temporary assignment of commandant of Aachen for the duration of the congress that was to open there on 30 September. He and his wife left Coblenz early that month; on the 19th he was promoted to major-general, the highest rank he was to reach. At the congress he was responsible for "guard arrangements, issuing the password, and a few other trifles." He saw few people, and was not invited to the major festivities, but thought he was at least as well informed of the progress of the meetings as were the representatives of the minor states, whose lack of influence he compared to that of associate professors in universities.[38] He and his wife left Aachen toward the end of November. After brief sojourns in Coblenz, Erfurth, and Leipzig, they reached Berlin a few days before Christmas 1818.

36. Gneisenau to Clausewitz, 29 September 1817, Pertz-Delbrück, v, 243–244. See also Gneisenau's letters to Hardenberg of 25 November, and to Clausewitz of 23 December 1817, *ibid.*, pp. 268–269, 276–282.

37. Clausewitz to Gneisenau, 3 February 1818, and Gneisenau to Clausewitz, 23 February, 29 March, and 7 May 1818; *ibid.*, pp. 289, 292–293, 299–300, 312–313. Priesdorff, v, No. 1429.

38. Clausewitz to Gneisenau, 1 October and 25 October 1818; Pertz-Delbrück, v, 342, 351. A passage in a letter by Hardenberg to Prince Wittgenstein, one of the most influential representatives of ultraconservatism at court, suggests the existence of some opposition to Clausewitz's appointment to Aachen—an appointment that, unimportant though it was, could be interpreted as a sign of royal confidence. On 4 September 1818 Hardenberg writes, presumably in reply to a comment by Wittgenstein: "To be sure, I should have preferred to see Colonel Pfuhl as commandant here; but Clausewitz is also a clever man, though not I think as suitable to this position as the former." *Briefwechsel des Fürsten Karl August von Hardenberg mit dem Fürsten Wilhelm Ludwig von Sayn-Wittgenstein, 1806–1822,* ed. H. Branig, Berlin, 1972, p. 237.

II. KNOWLEDGE AND PERSONALITY

On 21 March 1819, three months after he had arrived in Berlin, Clausewitz completed a memorandum on the educational shortcomings of the *Allgemeine Kriegsschule,* and sent it to Boyen. The subject lay outside his official responsibilities. As director he was in administrative charge of the college, and had disciplinary authority over its students; educational policy was determined by a directorate of studies under the chairmanship of Colonel August Rühle von Lilienstern, with the minister of war retaining a watching brief. Rühle, the man in effective control, was in some respects the very opposite of Clausewitz: his intellectual interests were as broad, if not broader; but unlike Clausewitz he was not reluctant to make public the results of his research. His personality was as outgoing as his scholarship. He possessed great charm and enjoyed a very wide circle of friends and acquaintances; in the four years he spent as chamberlain at the court of Saxe-Weimar, in close proximity to Goethe, his intense involvement in art and learning had been overlaid with a rich patina of social sophistication. At the age of thirty-nine—he was born in the same year as Clausewitz—he had already published a large number of articles and more than half a dozen books, among them a work that applied philosophy and mathematics to the interpretation of political life, and a justly admired three-volume account of his experiences in the War of 1809, in which acute observations of military events alternated with essays on such topics as Gothic architecture, landscape painting, and the state of the arts in contemporary Vienna. His more technical studies on warfare and on military theory were superior to the average products in the field, without being marked by genuine originality in method or argument. His mind and character seemed to predestine him to the professional success that, in fact, he was rapidly achieving: he ended his career as inspector-general of military schools and colleges with the rank of lieutenant-general, holder of the Order of the Red Eagle, first class, with oak-leaf cluster and diamonds. That his presence at the War College might pose problems to the new director had been foreseen, the more so since the two men held opposing views on the proper role of the institution. When his appointment was first being considered, Clausewitz wrote Gneisenau that so far as the teaching program of the college was concerned, "Rühle ... obviously has older and perhaps also stronger claims than I." [1] If Clause-

---

1. Letter of 11 December 1817, Pertz-Delbrück, v, 271. On Rühle von Lilienstern see Priesdorff, iv, No. 1360; and E. Weniger, *Goethe und die Generale der Freiheitskriege,* Stuttgart, 1956.

witz nevertheless decided to express his views to Boyen, it was not only because education in all forms was a matter of intense interest to him but presumably also to test the assurance he had received that the duties of his new position would be enlarged beyond the purely administrative.

Clausewitz's main criticism of the War College was that it functioned more as a small university than as an institution of professional training. The issue to which his memorandum addressed itself, an issue that he had first encountered as a lieutenant in Neuruppin, underlies the entire history of military education: how to reconcile academic and cultural values with professional and technical preparation. To understand Clausewitz's position in 1819, we must recall the origins of the *Kriegsschule*—the Institute for Young Officers, which Scharnhorst revitalized in 1801. The task of the school, Scharnhorst declared at the time, was not solely to transmit facts, and certainly not to drill students in a particular theory of war, but above all to train intelligence and develop judgment. His approach, emphasizing practicality and intellectual independence, and expressing his recognition of the singularity of every war, was in opposition to that of the learned, system-building officer, who until then had dominated higher military education in Prussia. But since many of the academy's students possessed little more than an elementary-school background and were incapable of following the highly professional instruction of Scharnhorst and his associates, it was necessary, as well as socially desirable, to include courses in languages, philosophy, literature—which again brought the curriculum into closer agreement with late-Enlightenment views. When in 1810 Scharnhorst once more turned his attention to the task of officer education, the basic problems and his attitude toward them had not changed. To help raise the general educational level of the officer corps three preparatory schools were established; the War College for Officers, now incorporating the old artillery and engineering schools, was to give a select group advanced instruction covering the whole spectrum of war. To preserve the academic character of the school students were granted some flexibility in their programs, and electives were offered, but except for foreign languages, chemistry, physics, and mathematics the curriculum consisted of military subjects. Mathematics and military history continued to form its core since—quite apart from their practical benefits—Scharnhorst believed their study to be almost essential for the development of reasoning and judgment. After the second Peace of Paris the system was once again reorganized under Boyen's leadership and expanded to serve the needs of the greatly enlarged army. A new central coordinating authority was placed at its head, the Committee of Military Studies, chaired by an officer on the active list holding a senior appointment in the ministry of war, and reporting to the minister—the position that Rühle was eventually to occupy. The number of preparatory schools was increased to eighteen—a desirable growth in principle, whose effect, however, was largely nugatory since the schools were inadequately financed. A new combined artillery and engineering academy was founded, which left the *Allgemeine Kriegsschule* as the army's school for advanced study for officers in the infantry and cavalry, and for those preparing for service in the ministry of war, the general staff, and the topographical bureau. Boyen and Rühle, who was appointed to the college in 1815, departed from Scharnhorst's emphasis on practical knowledge (on this score alone Scharnhorst would have opposed the separation of the artillery and engineering courses from the curriculum) while seeking to continue in his tradition of developing officers with broad interests and an awareness of the links not only between all elements of warfare but also between war and society in general. Consequently the course offerings proliferated, especially in the academic fields. By the time Clausewitz arrived in Berlin, the institution was very different from the War College for Officers where he had lectured eight years earlier on the little war and on general-staff duties. The school year still ran from October to July, but the course now extended over three years, a typical program of studies averaging between twenty-five and thirty lectures a week. Slightly more than a hundred students were taught by a faculty of approximately twenty soldiers and civilians. Such a ratio should have encouraged tutorials and seminars; instead, instruction consisted almost wholly of formal lectures. In the academic year 1818–19 the lower two classes were offered forty hours a week in nonmilitary fields and only sixteen hours on military subjects. When the future chief of the general staff Helmuth von Moltke gained admission to the college in 1823 about 60 percent of all lectures dealt with general academic subjects.[2]

For a gifted student this intellectual variety might be stimulating, especially since some of the instructors had creative and original minds; but the average officer, Clausewitz believed, would only be confused by the range and the somewhat haphazard composition of the curriculum, while the policy of formal lectures, without much opportunity for discussion or practical work, might easily lead him to be satisfied with a superficial fulfillment of the requirements.

If, on the contrary, the student is compelled to "elaborate and develop his lecture notes," Clausewitz wrote to Boyen, "and if he is assigned rele-

---

2. In the academic years 1818–19 and 1819–20 the weekly program was as follows:

For first-year students: tactics, three hours; gunnery, three hours; military history and geography, five hours; mathematical subjects, ten hours; the "encyclopedic" course, four hours; history, two hours. For second-year students: gunnery, one hour; engineering, four hours; history of German literature, four hours; history, four hours; physics, four hours; mathematical subjects, twelve hours. For third-year students: military statistics, four hours; military history, two hours; applied tactics, four hours; general staff duties, two hours; siege warfare, four hours; advanced surveying, two hours; chemistry, four hours; history of foreign literature, two hours; care of the horse, two hours. L. v. Scharfenort, p. 387. See also the excellent discussion in E. Kessel, *Moltke,* Stuttgart, 1957, pp. 32–47.

vant problems to solve, then any particular course takes on such intensive force that officers can and must be given greater freedom in choosing their subjects. I am convinced," he continued, "that a young man who pursues three or four courses in this manner spends his time profitably. However, I also believe that students ought to find it attractive to attend some courses to which they cannot devote the same degree of interest, either to review topics already familiar to them, or simply to acquire some background in the discipline, for relaxation, a change of pace, etc. I would therefore consider it appropriate to draw a distinction between motives for taking a course. Those lectures that an officer has chosen for his real field of study he must attend without fail, he must regularly review and work up his notes, and turn in his practical assignments. The other courses he can visit, and the class register carries him as an auditor. In these courses it is left to his energy whether or not he does the written work and solves the problems, and there is less insistence on his regular attendance." [3]

For several reasons, Clausewitz continued, instruction at the college should have the character of a French polytechnic school rather than that of a German university. "First of all, the young men who attend a university have been intensively prepared for it for several years, and although the knowledge of nonphilological subjects that they acquire in the Gymnasia will not be extensive, at least their intellect is better fertilized and prepared, they have some practice in thinking and are inseminated with ideas. The officers who come to the *Kriegsschule,* on the other hand, have lain intellectually fallow for some years, with here and there something productive having shot up in the midst of many weeds.

"Because most university students study to acquire a profession, and at their own expense, they are diligent and exert themselves. The officer attends the *Kriegsschule* at the government's expense and is already assured of his livelihood. Hence it becomes necessary to occupy him with practical tasks, to know his educational background thoroughly, and to attune the lectures to it. The lectures themselves must be internally consistent and leave no gaps in the material, since it cannot be expected that the officer would always seek to fill them. In short, instruction must here take on more the form of rigorous schooling [*Schuldisziplin*] than would be the case in universities.

"Thirdly—and this is the main argument against instruction carried out in the manner of university lectures—after completing their studies jurists, bureaucrats, physicians move on to a practical internship of several years, during which the general education they have gained is given more positive form and turned into tangible expertise. The practical instruction not found at a university is now acquired. But that does not occur when the

3. Extensive passages of Clausewitz's memorandum are printed in Scharfenort, pp. 30–32, 35–37, and 40–41. See also Caemmerer, pp. 68–70.

officer returns to his drill field: he must acquire the practical aspects [of the subjects studied] at the time of instruction itself." Clausewitz concluded with a comparison that had helped to clarify his ideas on the relationship between theoretical knowledge and practical ability since he first employed it in his studies of aesthetics during the reform era: "Architects and artists do not learn their skills at a university."

That Clausewitz's criticism was more than an abstract discussion of opposing types of teaching is shown by the detailed nature of his accompanying evaluation of courses and instructors at the college. He agreed with Boyen that mathematics took up too large a part of the curriculum—one-fifth of the program for the first two years. Courses were offered in arithmetic, algebra, plane and solid geometry, plane and spherical trigonometry, conics, applied mathematics, optics, astronomy, finite analysis, differential and integral calculus, and elementary and advanced surveying. Mathematics is the soul of military studies, Clausewitz wrote, "but we must ask ourselves whether the students who now attend the advanced courses really learn the subject so well that they can apply it in the future. I doubt it. Furthermore, does it satisfy a genuine need of the army to instruct so many officers in higher mathematics if only those few need it who will occupy themselves with advanced surveying or with scientific research? Indeed, we may even raise the question whether the study of higher mathematics, if it genuinely attracts the student, doesn't render him useless for practical military life."

On the other hand, Clausewitz believed that all students at the War College ought to receive some systematic instruction in the fundamentals of academic work. He therefore approved of a four-hour weekly course that introduced the first-year student to the various disciplines represented in the curriculum and outlined their interrelationships—the so-called encyclopedic course, which in 1816 had been offered by his old philosophy teacher, Kiesewetter. To Clausewitz's regret the course was deleted after one year, since Kiesewetter fell seriously ill and was forced to retire. Something like it, he thought, or a course in the fundamentals of logic was essential: "How can one expect academic competence in young people who do not know the logical structure of their own language, who have never heard of a premise or a proposition, who have never learned how a sound syllogism is constructed?"

The significance of history, geography, statistics, and of military history and geography to the professional study of war was obvious. Unfortunately, Clausewitz noted, the last two subjects were taught by a civilian who had never personally experienced war or even belonged to a military organization, and whose lectures neither were realistic nor introduced useful theoretical observations. The instructor was Christian August Stützer, who had been Clausewitz's teacher at the Institute for Young Officers and subsequently his colleague at the War College for Officers. Stützer had won Scharnhorst's gratitude by supporting and encouraging him when Scharnhorst had first come to Prussia. He had been one of the founders of the *Militärische Gesellschaft* in 1802; probably on Scharnhorst's recommendation he later became tutor in history and military geography to the crown prince. His good connections, energy, and his administrative gifts made him something of a power in the local academic world, though his publications did not go beyond a few derivative articles.[4] Clausewitz not only disliked Stützer's view that military operations should be aimed at "watersheds" and "key geographic positions"—he was to dismiss this "elegant" doctrine in a biting chapter in *On War*—but objected even more to his mechanical style of teaching, a criticism borne out by one of Stützer's students, who wrote that year after year Stützer repeated his lectures verbatim, jokes and all, while many of his listeners followed the lesson with the aid of transcripts that circulated in the college.[5] "The true study of military history," Clausewitz's memorandum observed, "is in any case so extensive that it cannot be dealt with in one course. An introduction to it could be provided by a very detailed description of a single campaign, which can be given by the [present] instructor in tactics, who has sufficient time and competence." [6]

The courses in German and French literature, which had replaced earlier instruction in the grammar and vocabulary of the two languages, appeared to Clausewitz as little more than "hors d'oeuvres." Unless one intended to do academic research in the field, he wrote, literary works should not be the subject of study; it was sufficient—and essential—to read them. The instructors themselves felt this, and had shifted their emphasis from literary analysis to the history of ideas, an approach which, Clausewitz thought, usefully supplemented the general history course.

Finally, Clausewitz had mixed feelings about the work done in the more technical military fields—tactics, gunnery, siege operations, military architecture, duties of the general staff, horsemanship. He approved of the courses on tactics and staff work taught by the young infantry officer and military writer Captain von Decker. On the other hand, he thought that the instruction in fortification by Lieutenant-Colonel Meinert, who had been professor of mathematics and military science at the University of Halle before being commissioned in 1797, was antiquated and mechanical. In general, he felt, the courses should be more practical, and their sequence

---

4. A. v. Janson, "Ein vergessener Zivilstratege," *Militär-Wochenblatt* (1907), Beiheft 12, pp. 493–512; and Scharfenort, pp. 55–57.
5. *On War*, book VI, ch. 23 (pp. 664–668); Scharfenort, p. 56. As early as 5 October 1814, in a memorandum on military education that obviously reflected impressions formed when he and Stützer were colleagues in Berlin, Clausewitz discounted Stützer as a teacher because "he has become accustomed to touch on everything in passing, and never fully works through anything." Janson, p. 511.
6. Scharfenort, pp. 35–36.

rearranged to offer the student a more coherent development of relevant professional knowledge.

Clausewitz, in short, proposed a significant change of direction in the educational policy of the *Kriegsschule*. To the existing system of obligatory, formal lectures his memorandum opposed fewer courses, with the students given some freedom of choice in the mathematical and nonmilitary subjects. Furthermore, instruction was to be conducted as far as possible according to the so-called applicatory method, which turned the student from a passive listener into a participant, who—to give an example—learned geography not solely by memorizing lists of rivers and mountain ranges but by making clay models and maps of the terrain, by writing papers on its natural features and their influence on the inhabitants, and by actual travel and observation. As so often in Clausewitz's thinking, Scharnhorst had pointed the way here too, and he had not restricted the applicatory method to the curriculum. In 1809 he had introduced it to the large-scale exercises of the army by organizing maneuvers in which both parties acted independently instead of carrying out a prearranged scheme. Rather than having students acquire abstract knowledge by rote, Clausewitz now argued, the college should develop each individual student's potential by guiding and stimulating him to informed activity and independence. It is not going too far to say that the applicatory method transposed to officer education Pestalozzi's concept of the child learning by observing and doing, in a sympathetic, helpful environment. Many years earlier Clausewitz had learned from Pestalozzi that all methodology of education should aim at helping the pupil acquire a realistic view of the objects around him, and then to develop clear ideas about them, direct observation being the starting point of all sound education. At the same time, Clausewitz's condemnation of the excessive number of courses at the *Kriegsschule*, which inhibited genuine mastery of any one subject, repeated the criticism in his essay on Pestalozzi that the program at Yverdun, which kept students occupied from morning to night, prevented the unfolding and free play of their intelligence and imagination.

At least some of the weaknesses of the work done at the *Kriegsschule* that Clausewitz's memorandum pointed out had already been recognized by the minister of war. Boyen agreed with Clausewitz that courses and course sequences should be better integrated, that they should take a more practical approach, and that the program as a whole did not do enough to train officers to cope with the complexities of planning and leadership. But he placed greater faith in the individual's ability to overcome his educational weaknesses unaided than did Clausewitz, and he may also have been more impressed by the opportunity of raising the general educational level of a significant number of officers. In his discussion of Boyen's educational policies after 1815, Meinecke comments that Clausewitz recognized "the dilemma of the [War College] more precisely and soberly than did the idealistic Boyen, but perhaps it was fortunate after all that in the succeeding years his advice did not fully prevail." Meinecke continues that the criticism of the institution by professional soldiers was understandable; "but seen from a higher point of view the *Allgemeine Kriegsschule* ... was and remained that realm where the easily loosened bond between the officer corps' attitude and professional training and the general intellectual achievement of the nation could be tightened again and again—incompletely, but for all that, not ineffectually." [7]

Boyen might well have done something about those suggestions on which he and Clausewitz were in agreement, if the timing of the memorandum had been more fortunate. He himself, however, had originated many of the changes in educational policy and organization adopted in 1816; it was perhaps too soon for the most important institution in the system to alter course radically. A more dramatic consideration also intervened. On 23 March 1819, two days after Clausewitz signed his memorandum, Karl Ludwig Sand, member of an extremist student group, murdered the conservative playwright and occasional Russian agent August von Kotzebue. The deed, Görres wrote in *Germany and the Revolution,* "struck the German people like lightning." Not only did the assassination confuse moderates and liberals; it lent remarkable momentum to the repressive drive of the ultraconservatives, and soon Boyen was fighting for his political existence—a struggle that ended with his resignation nine months later.

Not surprisingly then, Clausewitz's memorandum did not result in immediate change. In 1826, when the program of the college was thoroughly reviewed, the applicatory method was at least formally adopted; but it was not until half a century later, in the activist, purposeful 1860's, that the institution became a professional school in Clausewitz's special sense of the term.

His reaction to the failure of his memorandum was to do nothing further to bring about changes in the policy of the *Kriegsschule.* Scharnhorst in his place would have collaborated and compromised with Rühle, and gradually implemented his ideas; Gneisenau would have stormed at the opposition with verve and irony. Few men, having made the effort to investigate the curriculum and develop a program for its improvement, would have simply dropped the matter—but Clausewitz resigned completely, both at the time and later. In the mass of memoranda and minutes that led to the changes introduced in 1826, the historian of the General War College did not find a single document from Clausewitz's hand. He observes that Clausewitz's passivity was a misfortune for the institution, but that Clausewitz was too kind to push his own point of view—a suggestion which, even if it

7. Meinecke, *Boyen,* ii, 111.

were accurate, describes but does not explain this striking renunciation.[8] It is reported by too many contemporaries to be doubtful that despite his reputation for conceit, Clausewitz's overt behavior was far from assertive, let alone aggressive, and that at least toward his subordinates he was considerate and sympathetic. That did not prevent him in 1812 from threatening the king in memoranda whose confidentiality was far from assured; nor did he appear reluctant throughout his life to think, speak, and act for himself. His kindness and gentleness were selective. But clearly he was not the man to operate effectively in a bureaucracy—not, at least, when he was on his own, rather than carrying out orders by Scharnhorst or Gneisenau. He was never a politician; his stand on particular issues was generally unambiguous, and there is no evidence that he worried greatly when his views did not suit the fashion of the moment; but after 1815 he tended to shrug his shoulders when their validity was questioned, rather than fight for them. Except in the years of reform, the soundness of his ideas meant more to him than did their acceptance. Nor, now that the wars were ended, did his ambitions retain their old force. That is not to say that he no longer wished to bring his position in life into closer agreement with his interests and abilities; but he found it difficult to recognize that his wishes— however realistic or justified—necessarily brought him into rivalry with other men. His competitiveness seems in any case always to have been the kind that found gratification less in outdoing and defeating others, or even in gaining official recognition, than in the quality of his own achievement. His statement to Gneisenau that rank was immaterial to him so long as he was fairly treated was not a unique confession to his closest friend. When he became a candidate for an ambassadorial appointment in 1819 he went so far as to request that his interest in the post not be made public. He must have known that this could scarcely be managed; but his dislike of being seen to struggle against others for prizes and distinctions was so pronounced that it overpowered even his sense of realism. After word of his candidacy became known, and he was left uncertain about its success month after month, he bore his equivocal position calmly, making no move to join the game of personnel politics and turn it to his favor. In this episode, as throughout his career, he was a good loser. His distaste for striving after professional success, which always involves a measure of acceptance of prevailing standards, was reinforced by his disgust at the new political climate. A few days after he learned of Boyen's resignation, he told his friend Groeben how discouraged he was at the backwardness and confusion of views that now dominated public affairs, adding bitterly that "the political principles of anyone whom the students and professors do not fill with fear and horror are totally suspect, a suspicion that frequently expresses it-

8. Scharfenort, p. 53.

self in an indecent manner." Hardly anything remained, he concluded, "but to withdraw indignantly into one's own innermost being and to shut onself off against the world." [9]

This statement—"cry of outrage" may not be too strong a term for it—accurately reflects Clausewitz's public demeanor in the Restoration. Does it tell us anything about his "innermost being"? If the lines just quoted are taken in connection with two comments in letters that he wrote to Gneisenau in the following year, they may suggest a sense of discouragement going beyond disgust with political developments to weariness with life itself. On 21 August 1820 a letter to Gneisenau begins: "The only pleasure and solace I find at this moment is the total leisure that I shall enjoy until the middle of October when the War College reopens. I intend to be very busy during this period, and thus gain some new courage for living and keep gloomy thoughts at bay." [10] Three weeks later, after Gneisenau had inquired what assignment he hoped for in the event of a new war, Clausewitz wrote: "I admit that it would most accord with my wishes if I could make a name for myself at the head of a column, sword in hand. An honorable death that would spare me a tired and paralyzed existence, which, in the words of Jean Paul, must be borne for years like a damaged arm in a sling, would then be a highly desirable fate." Should he not be killed, he continued, he would nevertheless find comfort in the knowledge that he had grown old in honorable and dangerous service. "I cannot count on [being given] a truly important assignment; it would be pure chance if this were to happen, and nothing gives me a claim to it. It is too late to drink from the fountain of science and develop all of its riches within me. In short, what greater satisfaction can I hope for in old age than the solace of having the reputation of a courageous soldier?" [11]

These lines express resignation, even depression. But they are accompanied by very different statements. In August he plans to be very busy, evidently with research and writing—it is, in fact, the time when he begins the manuscript of *On War*—and the letter continues with a discussion of his future prospects in the service, to which Clausewitz clearly is not indifferent, and with an extended joke comparing various staff officers, including himself, to different types of wagons, coaches, and carriages. In

9. Letter of 26 December 1819, published by E. Kessel in "Zu Boyens Entlassung," *Historische Zeitschrift*, CLXXV (1953), 53–54. Compare also an undated letter on politics, written four or five months earlier to Gneisenau, which concludes: "Today ... people respond to common sense in the way they treat someone who wears unusually old-fashioned clothes. I have only rarely the courage to show mine, but hundreds of times [I have] the feeling of someone who walks through London in odd clothes—it's not a question of being pelted by accusations, against which one might defend oneself, but of being pelted pure and simple, which at a minimum leaves stains." Pertz-Delbrück, v, 378. My translation falls far short of the imaginative strength of the original, which, as is often the case in Clausewitz's language, contains a play on words: *Vorwürfen* (accusations) and *Würfen* (pelted).
10. *Ibid.*, p. 438.
11. Clausewitz to Gneisenau, 16 September 1820, *ibid.*, p. 442.

the second letter, the phrases concerning bravery and an honorable death usher in statements of very different purport: Even more than a combat command, the writer hopes for the assignment of chief of staff of the field army, while in the event war does not break out he expects "sooner or later" to be given a diplomatic appointment. His other letters of 1820 and of the following years convey the same impression of an energetic individual, engaged in satisfying intellectual work, interested in the social and political world in which he lives, and—despite the unfavorable political atmosphere—full of confidence and plans for the future. Evidently whatever discouragement he sometimes felt was temporary rather than permanent and did not run deep.

That is not to say that the victory of conservatism in Prussia failed to have an impact on Clausewitz's feelings as well as on his behavior. As we have seen, the Restoration turned the unrepentant reformer into something of an outsider; it offended his moral and intellectual standards, and increased his tendency toward reserve. It also came to influence his attitude toward publishing his writings. In earlier years he had not been reluctant to appear in print. His review-essay on Bülow, his account of the campaign of 1806, the article or two he wrote on reform measures, his book on the spring campaign of 1813, all appeared anonymously; but many serving officers who published maintained a formal anonymity, and Clausewitz's identity as author of these pieces was generally known. After 1815 he would have published his biography of Scharnhorst if Gneisenau had not dissuaded him; and he continued to show his new manuscripts on military theory to those who expressed an interest in them. But as he began to devote more of his energy to scholarship, and perhaps as his ambitions concentrated on this aspect of his life, his reserve increased here too, and he came to restrict the expression of his intellectual efforts to a few intimates.

Clausewitz's manuscripts leave no doubt that far from being a writer's private mediations, they are addressed to prospective readers. The intention to publish existed; but without eagerness, without the urge to hurry into print. In 1817, in a letter accompanying an essay, he wrote Gneisenau that for the time being he was reluctant to publish his theoretical writings since he believed that people showed little sympathy for the extended analytic process needed to penetrate to the essence of a subject: "The crude objections of the initial superficial reactions too easily wound me, and it is difficult to fend them off since people have the habit of not letting anyone finish his thoughts who is not a preacher or professor." [12] Eventually he preferred publication to be delayed until after his death, though his notes to this effect, which were found with the manuscript of *On War,* and a supporting statement by his widow may not accurately reflect his attitude

12. Clausewitz to Gneisenau, 4 March 1817, Pertz-Delbrück, v, 192.

throughout the last fifteen years of his life.[13] Certainly his growing awareness in the mid-1820's that the manuscript of *On War* needed to be thoroughly revised played a part. In 1830 and 1831 he was to write political essays for immediate publication. What cannot be doubted, however, is Clausewitz's confidence in the intellectual superiority of his work, and his certainty that the theorists and historians of war who were his contemporaries had nothing significant to say to him. In consequence, and because he had no ambition to present himself as a military oracle in the fashion of a Bülow or Jomini, he wrote neither for the educated public nor for a small group of experts—not even in the sense that most scholars, concerned above all with illuminating their topics, also address their works to a few peers.

It would not be difficult to speculate on the psychological elements and their dynamic that underlie and create such attitudes. But we know far too little about Clausewitz's childhood to do so with any sense of assurance. Because the evidence for many episodes in his life and work is obviously incomplete, this study has tended throughout to underinterpret the data, rather than force conclusions from them. The available material is almost always suggestive but so very fragmentary that its seems preferable to point to the implications and let the reader draw his own conclusions. If firm patterns of thought and behavior nevertheless emerge clearly in Clausewitz's life, this is not surprising in a man who took ideas seriously enough to explore them as thoroughly as he could and who also attempted—instinctively and often consciously as well—to integrate his ideas completely with his feelings and actions.

Without seeking to do more than indicate some obvious parallels between the situation of the child and of the mature man, and recognizing the importance of the information that is lost to us, it may be helpful at this point to recall the little that we do know of Clausewitz's early years. He was the youngest and presumably the most gifted of four boys. As an adult he believed that he had been an exceptionally ambitious child. But he must have learned early on that whatever his abilities, and regardless of the intensity of his wishes, he could not successfully compete with his father and his older, stronger, and more knowledgeable brothers. To what extent he persisted in active competition, how far he withdrew into his fantasies, we do not know. His tendency in adult life to aim high, but to scorn open rivalries and yet never completely resign, suggests that the boy energetically, but without complete success, tried to find an equitable resolution

13. See the somewhat ambiguous statements by Clausewitz in two communications combined under the title "Notes" and printed before the author's preface in *On War*, and Marie v. Clausewitz's assertion in her preface to the work: "To complete [*On War*] was his dearest wish, but it was not his intention to communicate it to the world during his lifetime. When I would try to dissuade him from this decision, he often responded, half jokingly, but perhaps also with a presentiment of his early death: '*You* shall publish it'."

between his wishes and the loving and hostile, stimulating and frustrating reality. When Clausewitz was six or seven years old, a major change occurred in his life. His oldest brother, eleven years his senior, left home, and at about the same time his other two brothers entered the army: at the age of seven Clausewitz was the only boy in the family.[14] For five years he remained in this situation, which evidently was a happy one, for when he too entered the army just before his twelfth birthday, he experienced the separation from his family as a severe shock. Twenty-nine years later he wrote: "I still have the clearest impression of the sad emotions that weighed down my heart on that occasion." He continued with the remarkable statement that these emotions "actually have never quite disappeared. ... I shall never entirely overcome them." [15] We can be certain that anger accompanied his sadness over the separation, though we do not know whether the seemingly omnipotent father, who was compelling his son to leave home, was the primary object of his anger or whether it also flowed strongly toward the mother for allowing the separation to take place. That Clausewitz openly recognized the permanent psychic effect of the episode is not its least significant aspect.

Experiences such as these may completely convince a child that competing in the outside world is futile, leading only to an impotent and frightening anger, which must be coped with somehow, and by contrast how rewarding the pursuit of one's fantasies and ideas may be. Scope is afforded to open ambition only when the normal conditions of life are overturned—when the ever-present older brothers suddenly leave home, or when there is a war, in which one's seniors may be killed and exceptional

14. For references to the early careers of Clausewitz's brothers, see their entries in the Index. Little is known of the relationship between the four brothers in later years. Clausewitz's letters mention an occasional visit. A letter of condolence Gneisenau wrote on the death of the oldest brother (letter of 24 March 1830, Pertz-Delbrück, v, 582) indicates that Clausewitz felt some responsibility for his nephews. His second and third brothers were highly decorated officers who had good careers. Friedrich Volmar was promoted to the rank of major-general at the same time as Clausewitz, who was nine years his junior, and retired with the courtesy title of lieutenant-general in 1830. He died at the age of 83 in 1854. Wilhelm Benedikt, an unusually able and popular officer, became major-general in 1828, and ended his career as head of the section for veteran affairs in the war ministry. He, too, retired with the title of lieutenant-general, and died in 1849 at the age of seventy-six. Clausewitz was sufficiently intimate with him to show him his manuscripts, as is indicated by a copy in Wilhelm Benedikt's hand of the study on a future war with France of 1807/8, which used to be in the Clausewitz *Nachlass*. One of Wilhelm Benedikt's sons, a young officer, seems to have seen Clausewitz fairly often in the late 1820's. Schwartz, *Leben des Generals Clausewitz*, i, 20–27; Priesdorff, iv, No. 1326, and v, No. 1419.

    Countess Bernstorff, wife of the Prussian minister of foreign affairs, who knew Clausewitz well in the 1820's, presumably referred to his second and third brothers when she wrote in her memoirs that Clausewitz "felt humiliated by the oppressive conditions from which his parents had suffered. He could not bring himself to introduce his brothers—who were frequently in Berlin—to our house, even though they too were very decent and distinguished men, if in their ways perhaps less refined than our friend." *Gräfin Elise von Bernstorff*, ed. E. v. d. Bussche-Kessell, Berlin, 1896, ii, 102. The sparse evidence seems to suggest that, whatever Clausewitz's feelings and motives, in later life he was on good but not close terms with his brothers.

15. In the previously cited letter to his wife of 18 May 1821, *Correspondence*, p. 410.

opportunities present themselves. But these periods, too, contain frustrations and are circumscribed. When the boy is compelled to leave father and mother, when the mature idealist and rebel must return to peacetime service, the presence of authorities and constraints will again have to be accepted as immutable. Clausewitz's renunciation of the ambition, after 1815, to "make a name for himself and for his family" bears the mark of earlier psychic solutions, even while it can be justified by the hostile reality of the Restoration. An element of resignation is undoubtedly at work as he throws himself into the private sphere of scholarship. But as in childhood, this shell against the outside world is filled with intense, creative energy, now informed and disciplined by the experiences and efforts of the mature man. That Clausewitz was unable to achieve the transition to scholarship without a measure of exaggeration and rigidity in his behavior reduced his effectiveness with others and may at times have made him dissatisfied with himself, but does not compromise the essential soundness of the solution.

The nature of Clausewitz's scholarly work reinforces the view that early difficulties which the boy experienced while living in a circle of stronger, more effective males encouraged the adult to evade open competition and instead seek the supremacy he needed in the confines of his intellect. The systematic analysis of war, for which he had been preparing himself since late adolescence, and which in the Restoration became his primary concern, can scarcely have been unrelated to events in his childhood. Ambition, aggression, hostility, violence, and fear are, after all, always part of competition—whether carried out among individuals or between politically organized societies. Throughout his life Clausewitz resolved only imperfectly the problems these feelings posed, putting himself forward and repeatedly withdrawing from the contest. The insistence on being given his due, the uncomplicated love of conflict and of victory, that helped make his friend Gneisenau a nondaemonic, German version of Napoleon were not Clausewitz's way. But in his writings he frankly faced all aspects of violence. One of Clausewitz's most original and creative achievements was to recognize without aversion or reservation how fundamental a role emotion played not only in combat but also in the planning and conduct of military operations at every level; this psychological factor he systematically incorporated into his theories of war. If he did not express his own aggressive impulses with the naïve freedom of one of the swashbucklers whose personality he dissected with such care in *On War*, he did not deny their significance but regarded them as a part of reality that required analysis.[16] And his own feelings of violence, too, appear to have been sublimated to a considerable extent in his writings on war.

16. *On War,* book I, ch. 3.

III. POLITICAL WRITINGS

Clausewitz's response to the revival of conservatism and to the failure of the constitutional movement in Prussia emerges with some clarity from the letters he exchanged with his friends, and from their comments on his views; but his reactions were not restricted to private conversations and correspondence. For a time after the Karlsbad Decrees he sought to influence through memoranda the attitudes and decisions of senior officials. Subsequently he analyzed the political character and stability of postwar Germany in a long study that he may have meant to publish, but failed to complete for reasons that are not known. Apart from this ambitious essay in history and contemporary affairs, his manuscripts addressed questions on military policy, which, however, were closely bound up with political and social considerations, and which he discussed with that interaction uppermost in his mind. At stake, he believed, were the institutions and spirit of the reformed army, and thus much of the civil reforms as well. His memoranda, translating private opinions into positions for which he could be held accountable, add details to the stand he took on specific issues—though it is hardly surprising to find him defending the *Landwehr* or the reform program's reduction of special privilege in society. More important is the further evidence they offer on his basic social outlook, and on his attempt to establish a realistic—rather than an ideologically defined—political starting point for his analyses of military policy and institutions.

In 1789 the Prussian and French armies had been institutions of basically similar cast, the latter less efficient but more flexible, with a receptivity to innovation whose importance became apparent in the course of the Revolution. The wars of the First Republic and the campaigns that created the Empire and led to its collapse had changed both armies beyond recognition, the Prussians learning from the French but developing organizations and attitudes unique to themselves. After 1815 the two peacetime forces again came to resemble each other more closely, but their differences remained significant. The Prussian army was now not only the superior operational instrument; in the ability of its organizational forms to adjust to the coming industrial mass society, it possessed the greater potential for the future.

In France the physical and psychological disasters between the Russian invasion and Waterloo, the purges and strength-reductions under the Restoration, and the republican and Bonapartist conspiracies in the early 1820's left the army a divided service, uncertain of itself and of its place in the nation. Under the circumstances, a return to pre-Revolutionary concepts of an *armée de métier* was perhaps the only politically feasible solution. Saint-Cyr tried to make the army less of a professional and more of a national institution by reintroducing conscription and organizing a territorial reserve to back up the regulars, but these efforts failed because of the inequities of the draft—including the provision for paid replacements, which freed all but the poor from the obligation to serve—and because of the mutinies of reservists during the Spanish expedition. In 1824 the reserve was abolished, and French military policy committed itself for decades to come to a fairly sizable standing army of professionals who served for a minimum of six, later of seven years.

Increasing professionalization and bureaucratization were not without benefits: as a whole, the French artillery and engineers may have been the best in the world and technical education—at least for the elite of the officer corps—was of a high order; but the overwhelming desire for a return to calm and regularity prevented the needed reforms of the army's operational and tactical system, and of its methods of strategic planning and command. Napoleon's indifference to tactical details persisted under the new regime. Despite warnings of veterans and extensive debates in the literature, little was done to improve the clumsy mass and shock tactics of the later Empire, the loose integration of skirmishers and column, the notoriously poor outpost and security service. The interaction of components within the division and corps remained mechanical, especially in mobile operations, while in the direction of larger forces army headquarters aimed at an unrealistic degree of precision and control, which only resulted in confusion and consequent improvisation. This was due to the emperor's most damaging legacy, the effects of which the army still felt in 1870: his insistence on personal command, supported only by technicians, clerks, and messengers; that is, his failure to develop a central general staff and an articulated operational staff system that made it possible for the individual commander to act independently and opportunely, while hewing to the main lines of the strategic intention. As this last point suggests, it was only an apparent paradox that the men led by the greatest commander of the age had succumbed to routine, while the army that had suffered most at their hands was now the most unified and flexible force in Europe.

Aside from the tactical and operational doctrines developed during the reform era, and the new system of selecting, training, and promoting officers, the principal factors in the new superiority of the Prussian army were the general staff, conscription, and the *Landwehr*. None of these had reached maturity by the 1820's, but in each the essentials for growth were present. The general-staff network already extended through the army;

gradually the influence of the central staff and of its representatives in the
field would expand, so that by 1866 strategic and even operational control
had shifted to a significant extent from the supreme commander and the
field commanders to the chief of staff and his assistants. Conscription, although diluted by the institution of the one-year volunteer, which afforded
preferential treatment to the sons of the middle class and of the wealthier
peasants, was a universal obligation, borne by all levels of society, with few
permanent exemptions and no possibility of paid substitutes. Obligation to
serve in the standing army began with a young man's twenty-first birthday;
the period of service was for three years, followed by two years in the reserves and six years in the *Landwehr*. In the depression after 1816 about
one-third of the standing army's rank and file reenlisted; even so, a far
higher proportion of men passed through military service and returned to
an active civilian existence than was the case in France. Further assuring a
national character to the armed forces, rather than one that was exclusively
professional, was the *Landwehr*, a regionally organized body made up of
reservists who had passed their twenty-sixth year and of all those men who
had never been drafted, the annual quota usually encompassing only three-
fourths of eligibles. Since the state was in severe financial straits, the standing army was kept relatively small. In 1820 Prussian peacetime effectives
numbered approximately 128,000 officers and men, compared to 240,000
in France; by means of the *Landwehr*, however, Prussia could mobilize
300,000 men rapidly enough to answer any foreseeable defensive need. By
itself the standing army was too weak to take the offensive against a major
power and the *Landwehr* would require months of additional training to
make it fit for mobile operations; a preventive war of the kind that Frederick had launched in 1756 was out of the question for this mixed force.

If the strategic options of the Prussian army were limited, its ability
to change and grow with society was considerable, as was its power to influence society, with which it blended far more closely than did the *armée de
métier* with the variegated currents of French life. Standing army, reserve,
and *Landwehr*—based on universal conscription—provided the institutional
framework for one of the ideals of the French Revolution and of the Prussian reform era; with them the precondition for the nation in arms had been
created. But it was only to be expected that great practical and ideological
difficulties remained to be solved. The limited manpower needs of the
standing army, together with the rapid growth of the population, meant
that every year tens of thousands of young men were not called up. On
what basis was the selection among them to be made? Because the army
was small and because many veterans reenlisted, fewer trained men were
available to the *Landwehr*, and a greater proportion came directly from civilian life; these men could not be turned into proficient soldiers during the
Landwehr's brief training periods.

A solution might have been reached by integrating line and *Landwehr* more closely, the latter becoming a pool of trained men for the regular formations. But that went against the pedagogic and ideological mission intended for the *Landwehr* by its principal organizer and protector, Boyen. He did not want the regular army to dominate what he regarded as an essentially civilian force, which in the words of the *Landwehr* regulation of November 1815 was "always ready to defend the fatherland, but which assembled only when required by an enemy attack or by its own training needs." The *Landwehr* was to develop freely, each unit on the basis of its own local environment; common action with the line on maneuvers and in war would lead to a blending of professional and social values, and to a growing sense of national loyalty.[1] To achieve these goals, Boyen and other reformers were willing to accept a reduction in military efficiency and far greater civilian participation in military matters than had existed in Brandenburg-Prussia since the days of the Great Elector. As far as possible, the organization of the *Landwehr* was adapted to local administrative districts. Responsibility for the mobilization, maneuvers, and training sessions of the force was shared between the army and local civilian authorities. Boards of civilians, elected by the towns and the rural districts, selected the men for induction, and adjudicated exemptions. Officers below the rank of battalion commander were chosen by the men themselves. *Landwehr* inspectors with the rank of general or colonel supervised the force in each province: Clausewitz had applied for such a position. Although the crown and the regular army retained ultimate authority, and the system was surrounded with political and social safeguards, the *Landwehr* reflected the attitudes of new and increasingly significant civilian elements in Prussia, and was egalitarian to a degree.[2]

As such, the *Landwehr* and the principle of universal military service that it expressed were the objects of suspicion and attack. In the first years of peace many Prussians echoed Chateaubriand's denunciation of conscription as being "at the same time naturally suited to despotism and to democracy; to the former because it enlists men by force, violates political and individual rights, and necessarily is arbitrary in its implementation; to the other because it is concerned only with the individual, and establishes a metaphysical equality that does not exist in wealth, education, and manners."[3] In 1820 Clausewitz chanced to meet a "young jurist and noble-

---

1. After 1815 changes in the design of emblems, uniforms, and flags reduced the signs of a unit's regional origins and attachment while emphasizing its link to the supra-provincial state. That these changes were not always undertaken from consciously ideological motives does not diminish their significance as indications of the slow growth of political nationalism in Prussia.
2. E.g., NCO's in the regular army who were also landowners qualified for a commission in the *Landwehr*.
3. Speech of 2 March 1818, cited in J. Monteilhet, *Les Institutions militaires de la France*, Paris, 1932, pp. 4–5.

man" who hewed to the same line, waxing indignant at the servitude that conscription now imposed on the Prussian people. When Clausewitz pointed to the inequities that had existed before the reforms, he was answered that the old obligations were justified since they rested on positive law. In his letter to Gneisenau in which he related the episode, Clausewitz added: "This sanctity of positive law is now the motto of our ultras." [4] But similar arguments against conscription, particularly peacetime conscription, were put forward by middle-class and urban commercial interests. In December 1816 the Berlin town council petitioned for a return to the capital's former exemption from any military obligation whatever; the Breslau town council saw no need for sons of bourgeois families to be subjected to military training; and in the following year the rector and faculty of the University of Breslau opposed the induction of students into the peacetime army on the grounds, among others, that "the rich diversity of life is transformed into a dreary, indistinct, uniform mass when master and servant, educated and uneducated, moral and immoral are made equal."

Even supporters of conscription objected to the manner of its implementation. Clausewitz's protests, which began in the year the new system was introduced, differed little from those voiced by other members of the reform group, except perhaps in the message implied in his repeated complaints: the state and its military institutions should not reinforce the economic and educational inequalities already existing in the population. In October 1816 he was troubled that the method of selecting recruits— whether by lot, interview, or in some other way—had not been established; granting practical autonomy to small local commissions could only lead to the unequal administration of the law. [5] When the first group of recruits was called up the following month, he objected to the plan of choosing the best men for the guards before the remaining quota was filled by lot, which meant that all tall men faced the certainty of service while their shorter peers might escape: even if the scheme were rejected, "such proposals suffice to indicate the existing spirit of illiberality and arbitrariness." [6] In December he returned to the absence of standardized procedures: since vast numbers of exemptions were granted in one district and none in another, the population felt, and was, unfairly treated. This theme he took up again the following spring: permitting local boards to operate without guidance or supervision had predictably resulted in "graft, unimaginable arbitrariness, and injustice." [7] In April he went on an inspection tour of the Eifel Mountains, during which he witnessed severe, widespread poverty, which inefficient government measures did little to relieve, an experience

4. Clausewitz to Gneisenau, 23 October 1820, Pertz-Delbrück, v, 444.
5. Clausewitz to Gneisenau, 12 October 1816, *ibid.*, p. 153.
6. Clausewitz to Gneisenau, 14 November 1816, *ibid.*, p. 162.
7. Clausewitz to Gneisenau, 27 December 1816 and 18 March 1817, *ibid.*, pp. 178, 198–199.

that continued to haunt him for years afterwards. Conscription procedures manipulated by the well-to-do to their own advantage added to the burdens of the peasants: "The end result of our miserable system is always that the poor man becomes a soldier, the rich man remains free." To exempt all sons of wealthy families, he added, was just in the eyes of neither God nor man, and socially dangerous besides, since a poor peasant was usually the breadwinner of his family or the sole support of his parents. If exemptions were to be given at all, they should be reviewed by a commission made up of inhabitants of other districts so that the effect of family influence or local interest could be avoided. When a young peasant asked Clausewitz whether *everyone* had to serve in the *Landwehr* until he was thirty-two, and if this was not the case how exemptions were allocated, Clausewitz pretended to be an overage lieutenant in the regulars who knew nothing about the *Landwehr:* "That is how the chief of staff of the Rhine army had to crawl behind his incognito to hide his deep embarrassment." Gneisenau, to whom Clausewitz sent a long, emotional account, had parts of it copied and forwarded to Hardenberg, who in turn promised to pass it on to the king.[8] But by fall, when the second annual contingent of recruits for the army and *Landwehr* was chosen, little had changed, and Clausewitz could only repeat: "In my opinion it is an incredible burden that someone is made dependent on the caprice [*Willkür*] of a *Landwehr* Major and a county councillor until he has reached his thirty-third year." Even a good cause could be spoiled if inequities made the people turn against it.[9]

   That conscription was retained despite its flaws was due to the support of the king and of most of the senior generals, who could see no feasible alternative for maintaining a significant military establishment on the limited human and financial resources of the state. The same support was not forthcoming for the *Landwehr*.[10] Efficiency and political reliability of the new force were both suspect, and it is sometimes difficult to identify the real motives in the moves that intensified from 1817 on to reconstitute or even abolish the *Landwehr*. Its military effectiveness gave grounds for concern, particularly after the veterans of the Napoleonic wars had left its ranks. That many of its officers fell short of the professional competence of

8. Clausewitz to Gneisenau, 28 April 1817, Pertz-Delbrück, v, pp. 213–217; the quoted passages are on pp. 215–216. Gneisenau to Hardenberg, 12 May 1817, and Gneisenau to Clausewitz, 13 May 1817, *ibid.,* p. 217. Clausewitz referred to the economic crisis in the Eifel in his essay "Umtriebe," which was written during the early 1820's; see p. 6 above and pp. 298–306 below.
9. Clausewitz to Gneisenau, 26 September 1817, Pertz-Delbrück, v, 248. Cf. the similar arguments in the strongly egalitarian report of a Rhenish official, January 1818, quoted in Koselleck, p. 300, n. 39.
10. The debate over the *Landwehr* is ably summarized by D. Showalter in "The Prussian *Landwehr* and Its Critics, 1813–1819," *Central European History*, IV (1971), No. 1. His article is a useful corrective to the standard liberal interpretation that all opposition to the *Landwehr* was politically motivated, but errs by falling into the opposite extreme and unduly minimizing the ideological element. The memoranda by Clausewitz, which I discuss on the following pages, leave no doubt that he at least was convinced that the *Landwehr* issue was largely political; but Showalter fails to take account of them.

their comrades in the line could hardly be doubted, nor could one deny the inconveniences resulting from the *Landwehr's* separate organization. In an emergency the time needed to integrate *Landwehr* and regular formations might prove dangerous. Boyen and other supporters admitted these weaknesses, but accepted them for the sake of the political and social advantages they expected from a military force that existed in close contact with civilian life, that was led by an officer corps with strong middle-class representation, and that furthered the sense of mutual responsibility between state and citizen.

In the political climate of 1819 these benefits no longer carried much weight with the king. The moderates among his advisers found it increasingly difficult to support measures rooted in the reform era; by the end of the year Frederick William felt able to insist that the peacetime organization of the *Landwehr* be brought into closer accord with that of the line. This meant redrawing the *Landwehr* conscription districts, closing or moving the *Landwehr* armories—feared by some conservatives as centers of armed insurrection—abolishing a number of units, and reorganizing the remainder into regiments matching these of the line. Henceforth two *Landwehr* regiments formed a *Landwehr* brigade, which combined with a line brigade to constitute a division under the command of a major-general on the regular establishment. Witzleben, the king's expediting general adjutant, persuaded Frederick William to retain enough of the former *Landwehr* inspectors to provide commanding officers for the new *Landwehr* brigades, but the relative autonomy of the force, as well as its links with local society and its agencies of self-government, came to an end. Boyen was not prepared to carry out the destruction of his cherished system of national education through military service, and resigned. In the weeks following, Grolman also resigned, and Humboldt left office, having been defeated in his struggle with Hardenberg over the constitutional issue, and having lost his most powerful military allies.

It was far from certain at the end of 1819 that the *Landwehr* would continue to exist even in its reorganized form. Prince August, for one, openly advocated its complete abolition, and Clausewitz, who may have hoped that his former superior was more farsighted than the ideological enemies of the people in arms, sent the prince a memorandum which argued that while from a purely professional point of view the standing army was superior to the *Landwehr*, Prussia's position in the center of Europe, and her poverty, demanded military institutions and policies related to, and drawing on, the spirit and life of the population. The memorandum ended: "I cannot conclude without once more warmly reminding Your Royal Highness of Scharnhorst's legacy: a standing army, as perfect and powerful as circumstances permit; joined by a *Landwehr*, so universal, so encompassing, in its forms so closely linked to civilian life, that the institution becomes one with the nation. ... I tremble for Scharnhorst's work; I see that for theoretical reasons and from theoretical convictions people disturb the venerable edifice that was erected jointly by his profoundly creative spirit and the great need of the times. It proved itself in a stormy epoch; and this historical proof, which should suffice for centuries, is not to last for five years!" [11] The note failed in its intention. Prince August remained skeptical; a year and a half later he was still suggesting that the reconstituted *Landwehr* was inappropriate to Prussia's conditions and needs. [12]

On the day that Grolman resigned, Clausewitz sent Gneisenau a longer study, "On the political advantages and disadvantages of the Prussian *Landwehr*," with the suggestion that it be forwarded to the chancellor, who might find it useful ammunition in the continuing debate with the political rather than the military opponents of the *Landwehr*. [13] The memorandum begins abruptly, with a list of arguments most frequently raised against the *Landwehr:*

"The institution of the *Landwehr,* by organizing a significant part of the population, about one-third of all able-bodied males, into regular regiments, by giving them officers out of their own ranks, and by depositing arms in open armories in their midst, *obviously places weapons in the hands of the people.*

"The people, like any people, can hardly be entirely content. We can even say that logically this [contentment] is quite impossible. But we live in an age that is characterized by unquiet aspirations and a spirit of disaffection with government; *thus it is now doubly dangerous to place weapons in the hands of the people.*

"In times of internal disquiet and disaffection of the lower classes, any government must regard the sword as the ultimate support of law and sovereignty after all means of persuasion and wisdom have proved to no avail. But the sword is a weak support if it is not solely in the hands of the government, if the rebellious masses are armed just as well."

Clausewitz continues that he does not wish to question these propositions and conclusions, but that there are other realities that are more important: first, arming the people raises the defensive strength of the state to a level beyond anything obtainable by regular forces alone. Secondly, "the *Landwehr* increases the danger of revolution; abolishing the *Landwehr* increases the danger of invasion. On the historical evidence, which is the greater danger?" Clausewitz answers his own question by arguing that even in the recent past Germany has been free of revolutionary movements: "We

11. Memorandum, [?] December 1819, Clausewitz, *Politische Schriften und Briefe,* p. 242.
12. See Müffling's defense of the *Landwehr* in his report of 5 July 1821 to Prince August, in "General Müffling über die Landwehr," *Historische Zeitschrift,* LXX (1893).
13. "Über die politischen Vortheile und Nachtheile der Preussischen Landwehr," Schwartz, *Leben des Generals Clausewitz,* ii, 288–293. Clausewitz to Gneisenau, 17 December 1819; Gneisenau to Hardenberg, [?] December 1819, Pertz-Delbrück, v, 400–401.

know nothing of any revolution, of any genuine rebellion. Do we know nothing of invasion? If in a certain sense it may be risky to have a people in arms, isn't it far more dangerous to rule an unarmed people?" [14]

After pointing out that weapons have little to do with revolutions, that standing armies constitute no "talisman against revolutionary flames," and that *Landwehr* and line are not the true political opposites they are often claimed to be, he proceeds to what he regards as the central issue: "The source of all this concern. What is this source? The government's sense that it is isolated." The government feels that in difficult times it can rely only on the standing army. "We believe we have shown that this is no true support. [Instead] let the government gather around it representatives of the people, elected from those who share the true interests of government and are known to the people. Let this be the government's principal support, friend and ally, as Parliament has been for a century the support of the king of England." [15]

The memorandum concludes with a survey of Prussia's international position, which, Clausewitz argues, can be maintained only through modern institutions of government and defense, suffused with the vitality and spirit that the reforms introduced to the country: "And so let the men of 1806, who seek salvation in the decrepit forms of that period, search their consciences and honestly face the questions that we have raised here. Let them feel the enormous responsibility they assume when their hands, which perhaps have never done serious work, begin to destroy the edifice on which our magnificent fate rested in 1813, 1814, and 1815, like the goddess of victory rests on her chariot." [16]

Quite apart from its political message, the essay offers a good example of Clausewitz's developed dialectical style. He seeks understanding—or, which may be different, seeks to make his point—not by depriving the opposing arguments of all validity, but by testing their probability against historical and contemporary evidence and by opposing them with other, weightier truths. This manner of proceeding, and the attempt to pry the debate loose from dependence on such givens as "standing army" and *Landwehr* by inquiring into their substance and implications, characterizes the theoretical and historical writings as well as the political essays of his maturity. Unusual in this essay and in the message to Prince August are merely the passages of impassioned rhetoric, reminiscent of the *Bekenntnisdenkschrift;* such notes are rarely sounded in the manuscripts written after the wars. They appear in the memoranda of December 1819 because Clausewitz feared for the achievement of Scharnhorst and of the reform era,

14. Schwartz, *Leben des Generals Clausewitz*, ii, 289–290.
15. *Ibid.*, pp. 290–291.
16. *Ibid.*, p. 293.

which he was convinced had been right and necessary, and whose intense personal meaning to himself he was never to deny.

It was very likely in the same weeks in which he wrote to Prince August and Gneisenau that he produced a third, longer manuscript, entitled "Our Military Institutions." He may have written it to clarify his own ideas, or may have intended it for Gneisenau, Groeben, and other trusted friends; such passages as the observation that the reforms were carried out in the face of the king's distrust suggest that he did not envisage a broader circulation. Nevertheless, after an interval of a year or more, in 1821, he submitted the manuscript to a military periodical, whose editors, not surprisingly, filed it away until more auspicious times. Thirty-seven years later a new generation at last published it.[17]

The essay opens with an explanation of the reforms, points to their success, and defends them against the reaction, "which has gained more weight than might reasonably have been supposed." The ultras owe their success to their tactic of emphasizing details while ignoring the total picture. This objection, which Clausewitz liked to raise against opposing views, and which is still echoed in the opening chapter of *On War,* was only partially justified in the present instance. It applied to men who were troubled by such matters as the sloppy drill of civilians in uniform. Ideologically committed conservatives kept the total picture as firmly in mind as did Clausewitz, only from a different point of view: monarchical absolutism and a legally structured, hierarchical society were more important to them than the power of the state.

In "Our Military Institutions" Clausewitz does not try to change their minds. Instead he musters arguments that demonstrate the weakness of the conservative case by appealing to the objective standards of international power, and to the realistic need for more equitable treatment of the classes in modern society, not for reasons of absolute justice but because "the times demand it." The essay first makes the case for the rationality of the reforms, then lays bare what the author regards as the irrationality or selfishness of the conservative opposition: only the reforms of the years 1807 to 1814 can maintain Prussia in the ranks of major powers. To the objection that the state ought to descend to the second magnitude for which its population and territory qualify it, Clausewitz responds that such a reversal goes against logic and the trend of recent history, and furthermore, that in measuring effort and strength it is necessary to distinguish between offen-

---

17. "Unsere Kriegsverfassung," Clausewitz, *Politische Schriften und Briefe,* pp. 142–153. The article first appeared in the *Zeitschrift für Kunst, Wissenschaft und Geschichte des Krieges* (1858), No. 7. The time of writing is indicated by references to the current debate over Prussia's military policy and by an allusion to the beginning of Frederick II's reign "eighty years ago" (p. 144). The wording is strikingly similar to that of the other two memoranda.

sive and defensive policies. Prussia must exert all her energies simply to remain safe. Under present circumstances, her financial and human investment in her defense are not excessive.

The *Landwehr* plays a special role in the country's defense since it touches all of society. "The *Landwehr* is a regional institution. ... The standing army is an institution of the state." It alone makes possible a large defensive force, suffuses the people with martial spirit, merges the productive elements of society with the armed forces, and brings the weight of the entire people to bear whenever the nation is attacked.[18]

Having made his by now familiar case for the *Landwehr,* Clausewitz proceeds to analyze what he believes to be the three principal motives of the opposition. The first is dislike of conscription: "Our nobleman finds it an unbearable thought to serve in the ranks with his peasants." If the values of the *ancien régime* still prevailed, that would be an impossibility, "but the feudal system has waned, here as elsewhere." The second reason is fear that the new officer corps, which is no longer completely dominated by the nobility, is inefficient: "But basically opposition is caused not so much by patriotic concern over the technical inadequacy of the *Landwehr* officers as by the disagreeable feeling of seeing the former character of the corps changed by so many alien additions, to see the son of a nobleman serve with the son of a grocer, or even under him. This feeling—response to an unfamiliar way of doing things—deserves no special consideration." In any case, *"esprit de corps,* the manners of good society, even a certain military uniformity of behavior," are not really essential for making good soldiers, as was proved by the revolutionary armies in Poland, Spain, and France.[19]

The third reason is the fear of revolution: "It is said that the *Landwehr* system arms the people, and thus lends every revolution far greater strength, total superiority over the standing army. Here people are being misled by vague conceptions, and we have the following to say in opposition: (1) All recent revolutions were made in conjunction with the standing army; but the mother of all, the most important of all, the French Revolution, took place without any national guard. Though the standing army did not play a major role in the Revolution, neither did it provide a bulwark against it. ... (2) The brute force of the people, employed as a revolutionary tool, centers on the capital; but here the *Landwehr* has little or no impact. ... (3) It cannot be denied that in a true civil war the *Landwehr* organization would facilitate the arming of rebellious segments of the population. But such wars, which are caused by recklessness and factionalism [*Übermut und das Faktionswesen*], are extremely rare in history. Whenever they do occur they have profound motives that would have caused the break even without the *Landwehr.* ... To believe in the possibility of such a break

18. Clausewitz, *Politische Schriften und Briefe,* pp. 148–149.
19. *Ibid.,* pp. 149–152.

in our present condition would be to believe in ghosts; and to ignore external danger because of this illusory evil would be embracing death out of fear of dying.

"Prussia has the need to arm her entire people so that she can withstand the two giants who will always threaten her from east and west. Should she fear her own people more than these two giants?" [20]

However much these two memoranda strengthened the resolve of supporters of reform, they had as little impact on opinions in other circles as did the plea to Prince August. Hardenberg sent a brief note to Gneisenau: "The more I am in accord with the thoughts on the *Landwehr* developed in your memorandum, the more it pleases me to be able to tell you that everything that people in town have been saying about the abolition of this organization is empty gossip, without the least foundation, and that the king has never for a moment had this intention ... ." [21] Hardenberg said nothing about the subordination of *Landwehr* to the army, nor did he respond to Clausewitz's suggestion that the best defense against revolution was an assembly of elected representatives of various classes of society—a statement which at this juncture must have struck him not only as impolitic but also as absurd. Apparently Gneisenau transmitted the chancellor's assurance to Clausewitz, who wrote his friend Groeben a few days after Gneisenau had received Hardenberg's note that while the abolition of the *Landwehr* remained a possibility, he, Clausewitz, did not consider it likely. He added that if it should be destroyed, then not in consequence of Metternich's influence—it was an article of faith among the reformers that foreign powers feared the *Landwehr* and Clausewitz himself repeatedly alluded to their concern—but because "this institution remains a horror [*Greuel*] to the more elevated classes of our state." [22]

The principal message of the memoranda, addressing the immediate crisis that caused them to be written, is clearly that foreign policy, which centers on the issues of self-preservation and the maintenance of the state's international position, should not be conducted according to the particular interests of small groups in society. On the contrary, social arrangements and their reflection in the institutions of government must conform to the requirements of foreign policy. It may be asked whether Clausewitz was not unduly pessimistic in his view of the international situation as being fraught with peril for the state. In 1819 he did not believe war to be imminent, but he was concerned about the future. "Sooner or later," he wrote in the last of the three memoranda, "we shall really have to defend our skin." [23] As a prophecy of the course Prussian history would take in the

20. *Ibid.*, pp. 152–157.
21. Hardenberg to Gneisenau, 22 December 1819, Pertz-Delbrück, v, 401.
22. Clausewitz to Groeben, 26 December 1819, Kessel, "Zu Boyens Entlassung," p. 52.
23. Clausewitz, *Politische Schriften und Briefe,* p. 146.

succeeding two or three generations this was hardly accurate; neither was it inappropriate advice.

If Clausewitz's memoranda rejected the subordination of foreign policy to social considerations, he did not deny the reality of social differences. Since they did in fact exist, no government could or should ignore them completely. Differences in education, cultural standards, sensitivity to the challenges of the age, so his ideas may be paraphrased, were significant in society and important to the state. But they were not rigidly linked to the traditional hierarchies. On the contrary, as the true function of the nobility diminished and middle-class achievements increased, old forms of precedence and privilege had to be discarded. Even the majority of the population, which had not risen far, if at all, above its former condition, could no longer be treated as an inert mass. To do so would gradually poison society, and nothing in the social and political contributions of the upper and middle classes justified such inequities.

The memoranda as well as his letters of the period make it apparent how impressed Clausewitz was by the pervasive force of self-interest in society, and by the equally widespread indifference toward the ideal of political community. This seemed to him more pernicious among the influential and well-to-do than among the poor, who could not yet be expected to comprehend the abstraction called nation, and who were at the same time almost defenseless before the authority of the state. But his insistence that they deserved protection should not be mistaken for paternalism. He believed as strongly that all men should be treated with a modicum of fairness—that some attention must be paid to their innate value as human beings, their potential and achievements—as his brother-in-law Marwitz believed that, individual differences notwithstanding, men should be treated according to the estate or social group to which they belonged.

The specific arrangements by which the demands of the state and the just interests of the individual could be assured and reconciled were, as we know, of less interest to Clausewitz. He advocated a council of state and some kind of parliament as means for diminishing the gap between government and people, and for educating society by an increase in political activity, just as he championed the *Landwehr* not only for military reasons but also in order to bring army and people closer together in the service of the emerging nation. His manuscripts refer only vaguely, if at all, to organizational details of the *Landwehr,* to the authority and duties of a representative assembly, to qualifications for the vote. What interested him were the new opportunities for political and social development afforded by these institutions. As in his operational and strategic theories, his faith in the possibilities generated by a new situation far outweighed his concern for form—an attitude that was perhaps less realistic in politics than in war.

Some time after the *Landwehr* crisis his essay "Umtriebe"—a word not as awkward in German as its approximate equivalent, "Agitation," sounds in English—reconsidered several of the issues treated or alluded to in the memoranda of 1819.[24] This fragment of some 14,000 words is the most puzzling of all of Clausewitz's works. It would be interesting to know precisely when it was written, because in it Clausewitz moves away from the support for parliamentary government expressed in the memorandum for the chancellor; but the date can only be guessed at. Specific references, for instance, to Görres's book *Teutschland und die Revolution* indicate it must have been after 1819, and the Clausewitz papers contained notes for the essay on a sheet that also refers to Hardenberg's death, which occurred on 26 November 1822.[25] Possibly the manuscript was written not at once but with interruptions over a period between 1820 and 1823. Its purpose is equally obscure. In the text Clausewitz occasionally refers to himself in the third person as the author, and there are other indications that he meant to participate with a pamphlet or short book in the debate over Germany's political future; however, some acerbic comments on current policies of Prussia's ally Austria make it unlikely that he wrote for immediate publication. Perhaps a revision would have toned down these passages, and would also have removed the discrepancies of treatment and approach between various sections, which in the present state of the work are difficult to reconcile.

The essay lacks an introductory, programmatic statement. The first quarter consists of a carefully worked-out interpretation of the rise and decline of the European nobility, and of the more immediate causes of the French Revolution, to which I shall return further on. On the eleventh page of the printed text, the purpose of this account is explained: "We have deemed this commonsense review of the history of our social conditions necessary so that we can see clearly in what political conditions we really find ourselves." [26]

This assertion of the impossibility of interpreting the present without understanding the past, which is characteristic of Clausewitz's thought, is succeeded by an analysis of the differences between French and German conditions during the *ancien régime,* and of the impact of the French Revolution on Germany, which, he argues, was intensified because in Austria the reign of Joseph II had raised more hopes than were satisfied, and in Prussia men were disgusted at Frederick William II's "wastefulness, his mistresses, his immoral officials, his absurd visions, his religious edicts." The excesses of the Revolution and Napoleonic imperialism compromised the cause of republicanism in Germany. If the country did not return to calm

---

24. "Umtriebe," *ibid.,* pp. 153–195.
25. See Rothfels's editorial note, *ibid.,* p. 244, which erroneously gives 1823 as the year of Hardenberg's death.
26. "Wir haben diesen Blick des gesunden Menschenverstandes auf die Geschichte unserer gesellschaftlichen Verhältnisse für nötig gehalten, um deutlich einzusehen, in welchem politischen Zustande wir uns denn eigentlich befinden," *ibid.,* p. 164.

after Napoleon had been defeated it was because "a part of educated society had set itself two new goals: one was the unity of the German people; the other, constitutions." [27]

A discussion of the early Restoration follows, which is less firmly structured than the first part of the work, and more subjective and argumentative in tone. Clausewitz sympathizes with the feelings of Germany's "academic and nonacademic youth," but calls their goal of unity absurd under present conditions: "Germany can reach political unity in *one* way only, through the sword, when one state subdues all others. The time has not arrived for such subjugation, and if it should ever come it is impossible to predict at present which of the German states will become master of the others." [28] The political efforts of the students and of their academic mentors are ridiculed, as are their motives for supporting the constitutional cause, which leads to a digression in which Clausewitz develops his ideas on the role of parliaments and of popular political participation, before returning to the recent German past. [29]

The Wartburg celebration of 1817 and the murder of Kotzebue two years later are mentioned to introduce a discussion of the immaturity of German students, their faith in abstractions, their intolerance of opposing views, and their glorification of medieval Germany, which they imagine as "a magnificent entity, full of brilliance, glory, strength, and virtue." Clausewitz adds: "In short, the world must change again. Youth must be taught to grasp the idea of the state; a sturdy citizen of medieval Augsburg or Nuremberg is to be the ideal type; for the time being one can make a start with some nuances of dress, or hairstyle, of demeanor, and of speech. Germany must regain her unity; if it can't be done with an emperor then as a republic." [30] Illustrative of these attitudes he considers to be the book *Germany and the Revolution* by Görres, whom he describes as "brilliant but consumed by a passionate democratic lust for power." A thousand words are devoted to an outline of Görres's life and ideas, the latter being severely condemned while the honesty and simplicity of his private affairs are praised. The tone is conversational, personal, anecdotal; in style as well as in scope the section is the antithesis of the scholarly analysis with which the essay opens. [31]

Having concluded his survey of the students' political agitation, and stated his opinion that governments could not afford to leave it unchecked, Clausewitz asks whether Germany, and in particular Prussia, faced a real danger of revolution in 1818. His answer is unequivocally negative. Dis-

27. *Ibid.*, pp. 164–170.
28. *Ibid.*, p. 171.
29. Clausewitz, *Politische Schriften und Briefe*, pp. 172–177.
30. *Ibid.*, p. 183.
31. *Ibid.*, pp. 177–183.

content could be found in Prussia that was far more significant than student unrest—the reactionary movement among the nobility, the response of the well-to-do to the burden of high taxes and to the disruption of trade caused by the redrawing of the frontiers—but these dissatisfactions were not conducive to revolution, rather the opposite.[32]

The falling off of international trade introduces a further lengthy digression, as the essay itself calls it: a discussion of the recent history and present circumstances of the Rhineland, which ends with the emotional account of the near-starvation that Clausewitz observed in the rural districts in 1817.[33] Clausewitz returns to his main argument with the observation that while the failure of the Prussian government to relieve their economic distress gave the Rhinelanders the impression that the government was weak, its good intentions were too apparent to turn even this episode into a cause for revolution. But if no danger of revolution existed in Germany, what measures, if any, should Prussia take to counter the student agitation? Clausewitz argues that on the one hand, the government should have been aware of its complete security; on the other hand, it could not tolerate revolutionary propaganda among its own future officials and teachers. The state "owed it to itself and to its effectiveness in the future to step in, and would have been held to account by the people had it not done so." This equivocal conclusion is elaborated with a paragraph that characterizes the point of view apparent throughout those parts of the essay that deal with contemporary events: "That, to be sure, was not the judgment of the academics, who regarded this youthful striving merely as the expression of noble sentiments; even if the ideas were essentially silly and wrong, they thought it beneficial for the common good that they were expressed, and they considered it truly obscurantist not to allow the young people to play with their ideas. Such nonsense seduced even the most reasonable and fair-minded individuals into wrong ideas and untimely anger against the government. Almost the only supporters of the government's measures were passionate reactionaries; those who on reasonable grounds recognized clearly not only the duties of government but also how much in such cases a government can tolerate were few indeed." [34] The essay breaks off in the middle of an attack on the Austrian government and on Metternich specifically for exaggerating the threat of revolution in Germany, in which connection the Austrian fear of the independent spirit of the Prussian army and *Landwehr* is mentioned once again.[35]

The loose structure, the shifting focus, and the lack of proportion between various sections of the text are evident. In part this is due to prob-

32. *Ibid.,* pp. 184–185.
33. Clausewitz, *Politische Schriften und Briefe,* pp. 185–191.
34. *Ibid.,* p. 193.
35. *Ibid.,* pp. 193–195.

lems that always arise when serious historical interpretations are combined with analyses of contemporary phenomena. One may believe as strongly as Clausewitz did that past and present are linked, and that history provides an essential avenue to the understanding of one's own age; but the psychological conditions of the two fields of study are different, as are their methodological demands and possibilities. A revision might have brought Clausewitz nearer to solving the problem of fusing the separate parts of his discussion into a more unified whole, and especially to bringing the personal, polemical character of the second half of the text into closer accord with the remarkable objectivity of his interpretation of events before the fall of Napoleon. And, to be sure, the text's subjective approach to contemporary events is of a special, circumscribed kind: it does not express the views of a party or faction; it criticizes even the side it supports, the Prussian government. Nevertheless, the gap between the historical and the contemporary sections of the work is wide; more than stylistic corrections—a rethinking of the central issues—would have been required to bridge it.

An example is the treatment of German intellectuals and students after 1815, which is full of insights. Clausewitz observes, for instance, that the uncompromising declarations of the radical students resembled the extremism of Cromwell's Puritans and of the Jacobins, with the difference that the English and French revolutionaries developed this quality gradually and asserted it openly only after they had achieved power, while the German students began with intolerance.[36] But the analysis of the basic situation is clouded. Even while affirming that a German revolution was out of the question, Clausewitz attributed a power to the political statements of academics that he himself elsewhere says they do not deserve. His sense of realism was betrayed by his tendency to take ideas seriously, and perhaps the example of the French Revolution made it difficult for him to discount the impact of rhetoric. He recognized the immaturity of the *Burschenschaften,* but it seems not to have occurred to him that the noisy young men who wore odd clothes and were rude to their betters had more enthusiasm than staying power, and that after a brief summer of glory the rebels would scurry for professional and economic security. Instead, he took them seriously—not only because they stimulated and helped to justify reactionary measures but also because they were subversive to political stability, which he himself had difficulty believing.

This raises the question of the changes Clausewitz's political views had undergone since 1819. In his editorial note to "Umtriebe," Rothfels writes that the essay treats the constitutional issue in a far more conservative vein than had the memorandum "On the political advantages and disadvantages of the Prussian *Landwehr.*"[37] It may have been this same essay that led

36. *Ibid.,* pp. 177–178.
37. Clausewitz, *Politische Schriften und Briefe,* p. 244.

Meinecke to talk of "Gneisenau's (and also Clausewitz's) strange development" toward "a more aristocratically tinged way of thinking," although Meinecke mentions no specifics and we can only guess at what he had in mind.[38] A further question is to what extent the essay really reflects Clausewitz's opinions. If he wrote for immediate publication—which is far from certain—it would help to explain the more conservative tone of some of the sections, which alone would have made publication possible in the early 1820's. His private correspondence, which might serve as a check, provides little help. For some years after the departure of Boyen and Humboldt from office, his letters rarely mention internal politics; the few political references that do occur are vague, but indicate no change from his former political attitudes.[39] During the same period Frederick William and the conservatives at court and in the ministries continued to regard him as too liberal to be entrusted with a diplomatic assignment. In this respect, as in others, "Umtriebe" remains puzzling.

Clausewitz's general political observations are grouped in the digression that interrupts his discussion of the student movement's support for the constitutional cause. He begins: "The wish to limit the pure, or if one likes, the absolute monarchy through participation of the estates is an idea that is particularly natural when great abuses, incompetence, and partiality bring about the desire to return to order and justice through an increase in the political dialogue [*Mehrseitigkeit der Stimmen*].

"Although the German governments cannot be accused of major abuses, nevertheless at a time that demanded so much effort on the part of the subject [i.e., 1813–15] it was natural to wish that a number of responsible men of different classes assist the government, prevent error and injustice, and give everyone a greater sense of security. ...

"But improvement of the administration was not the main reason why men were so eager for a constitution. In their opinion the main fault of which the German governments stood accused was their weak and shameful foreign policy." Clausewitz agrees that shortsighted actions of the German states facilitated French domination of Europe, but doubts that constitutional government would have made a difference. This introduces a paragraph that touches on his basic concern: "The role played by a state toward other powers is only indirectly and by no means significantly linked to its

38. Meinecke, *Boyen*, ii, 385, and n. 2.
39. E.g., a letter to Gneisenau of 14 January 1820 argues that the government must recognize that its actions against members of the reform group are unjust, and hopes that "little by little more of a public [i.e., political] life will develop." The previously cited letter of 23 October 1820 to the same recipient includes a defense of the French Revolution as a necessary political act, refers to the bitter opposition of the nobility to the changes in Prussia since 1806, and repeats a play on words concerning the political calm in Berlin: The Prussian minister in Dresden replied, when asked whether he had news from Berlin: "Yes, I have news, i.e., I have none .... The people there are neither motivated nor agitated [*Die Leute haben weder Triebe noch Umtriebe*]." Pertz-Delbrück, v, 409, 443–444.

constitution, and although one might believe that a certain steadiness, consequentiality, and security in foreign policy should naturally result from a constitution, history—unless we are very much mistaken—does not bear this out." [40]

After a brief historical and geographic survey, which finds assemblies more suitable to countries whose location offers them some security than to German states, surrounded by dangers that can be avoided only by a secretive, determined, and flexible policy, qualities that he believes are not in accord with the procedures of deliberative bodies, Clausewitz offers as his opinion that the institutions best suited to strengthen and improve policy are a responsible ministry and a council of state. He finds selfish interests, demagoguery, turbulence, and domination of the passive majority by the active minority as characteristic of republics, and instead offers a quiescent alternative: "If the subject is properly to pertain to the state, he must understand the main interests of the state; these must be great and permanent; and the citizen's support of this permanent direction must constitute his participation [*und in dieser bleibenden Richtung muss sich die Teilname des Bürgers befinden*]. The government must be so organized that it deserves his confidence; this confidence need not be blind or absolute; he can evaluate the government's actions, and his heart can give them greater or lesser approval. In this judgment and greater or lesser approval of the subject the government can recognize the stars that guide it and enable it to travel more easily and quickly." He concludes that the purpose of government is to induce energy and honesty in the private affairs of the citizen as well as comprehension of the major interests of the country. "It is not our intention to show what institutions lead to these goals ... ." [41]

If genuine, this was a striking reversal indeed of his advocacy, in December 1819, of the British Parliament as the model for Prussian political development. He may have meant every word; or the essay may have been written to demonstrate his political reliability at a time when his hopes for a diplomatic appointment made it important to disarm conservative opposition to his candidacy. But, as we know, the manuscript was not completed, and remained unread in his drawer. Unless new evidence emerges, the questions raised by the work cannot be definitely answered. But it is worth pointing to one facet of the essay in which it does not differ from its author's earlier or subsequent opinions. His retreat from constitutional government to an autonomous executive composed of crown and high bureaucracy is not linked to any change in his view of the rights and duties pertaining to different classes in society. The essay opposes special privilege of any group as firmly as Clausewitz had opposed it in the reform era, or in his letters to Gneisenau from the Eifel Mountains.

40. "Umtriebe," Clausewitz, *Politische Schriften und Briefe*, pp. 172–173.
41. *Ibid.*, pp. 176–177.

This absence of social partiality, which runs through the essay, is one of the impressive features of its opening historical passages; indeed, it helps to make Clausewitz's historical interpretation possible. The rise and decline of the European nobility, the growth of what he describes as the *nouveau peuple* in the 17th century, the spread of governmental authority, are detailed with complete ideological detachment, purely on the basis of functionality. Clausewitz does not depict the dominance of the military nobility and the enserfment of large numbers of peasants in the early Middle Ages as a crime against the social contract—a concept he regards as unhistorical and just as artificial as that of positive law—but as soon as the nobility's position no longer coincides with its real functions, no defense can be advanced for it. When the nobility lost much of its military significance and became subservient to the new centralized state, its privileges were no longer tenable. Attempts to retain its former dominance were, he thought, understandable, but in the long run hopeless—they could only lead to injustice, abuses, and "ignoble profits"—while the growth of the bourgeoisie and the gradual economic strengthening of the rural population demanded changes in their respective positions in society. Thus, Clausewitz writes in a characteristic passage, "in our opinion the French Revolution came about for two main reasons. The first is the strained relationship between the classes, the great favoritism shown the nobility, the great dependence and, it must be said, in part the great oppression of the peasants; the second is the disorganized, partial, and wasteful administration." A few sentences further he concludes: "When the enormous majority challenged the minority, the nobility had to give way. It was no longer strong enough to resist this force; the old conditions collapsed—and collapsed forever; because once something organic has been broken it may be glued together again, but can never be returned to an organic whole." [42] So much for legitimacy and other social concepts of the Restoration!

Clausewitz realized that opinions such as these, which today strike us as the self-evident basis for any interpretation of the late 18th century, were scarcely to be expected from a senior officer in the service of a monarchy, and he added: "Not a few scholars will shrug their shoulders at this glance at history, and come forward with a hundred objections. How many might not be cited from Möser alone!" This was an allusion to Möser's last essays in the *Berliner Monatsschrift* before his death in 1794, which interpreted the

42. *Ibid.*, p. 164. It may be noted that during the reform era Clausewitz predicted that vast social changes would occur in Europe whatever the outcome of the political and military conflicts: "Europe cannot escape a great and universal revolution, whoever emerges victorious [from the war of 1809], but it will certainly be less bloody and of shorter duration if Austria and Germany win. If not, our generation might well perish before the true crisis occurs. Even a general German insurrection would be merely a precursor of this great and universal revolution (which, by the way, need not be another French Revolution). Only those kings who can enter into the true spirit of this great reformation, and lead it, will be able to survive." Clausewitz to Marie v. Brühl, 21 May 1809, *Correspondence*, p. 234.

Revolution as an artificial "philosophic" interference with tradition and property rights, an unjustified assault on those organic, hierarchic forces that Clausewitz, on the contrary, wrote were destroyed because they were no longer functioning and inhibited the maturation of more vital elements. In the beginning 19th century, as the emergence of the nation-state, the expanding population, and economic change destroyed the old enclaves of privilege, political development might take different paths, but society, he believed, could only—and therefore should—become more egalitarian.

IV. BERLIN

In Berlin, Clausewitz's existence soon fell into a routine, whose orderly pattern incorporated a number of diverse social groups, ranging from the families of his old friends, the princes Wilhelm and Radziwill, to essentially middle-class circles of scholars and professors. With his major-general's pay of 3,000 taler and allowances, he found himself for the first time in his life in comfortable economic circumstances, the more so since his duties did not carry with them extensive social obligations. As one of two dozen or more generals stationed in the capital, occupying a post that neither affected policy nor lay in the mainstream of administration, he played only a minor role in the military world. During his first year he resumed giving occasional tutorials on war and military history to the crown prince, who again treated his old teacher with good-natured respect since their joint tour of the Rhineland. The two men remained on superficially amicable terms without Clausewitz ever entering the prince's intimate circle. In 1821 his connection with the general staff, which had been broken when he quit his post as chief of staff in Coblenz, was partially restored by his being appointed an associate member of the central staff organization in Berlin, the Great General Staff. As *aggregirter Officier des General-Stabes,* his duties were limited to such matters as assisting in evaluating the annual maneuvers, but at least the relationship enabled him to keep in touch with current strategic planning.[1]

His duties as director of the *Allgemeine Kriegsschule* took up no more than a part of every morning, their inconvenience being further ameliorated by the fact that Clausewitz lived in the college.[2] The War College had taken over the entire building in which Scharnhorst's old school had once been housed together with other army offices—a vast Frederician structure, designed in the shape of an E, with the three short bars forming two rear

1. Hahlweg, *Clausewitz,* pp. 47–48, refers to two memoranda on strategic and organizational subjects, written in 1819 or soon afterwards: "Über einen künftigen Krieg mit Russland," evaluating the possibilities of defending East Prussia against a Russian offensive; and an essay on the composition and command-structure of the army of the Germanic Confederation, "Deutsche Streitkräfte." Clausewitz was to treat the latter subject again in the winter of 1830. See pp. 402–405 below.
2. The account of the internal arrangements of the *Allgemeine Kriegsschule* and of Clausewitz's life there is based principally on the above-cited works by Poten, Scharfenort, Steinmann v. Friederici, Brandt, and Kessel's *Moltke,* on B. Schwertfeger, *Die grossen Erzieher des deutschen Heeres,* Potsdam, 1936, and W. Erman, *Paul Erman,* Berlin, 1927.

courtyards. The steep stairs leading from the foyer to auditoriums and classrooms were famous throughout Berlin; Alexander von Humboldt, who occasionally lectured at the college, compared their ascent to that of the Chimborazo. The building was located in the center of official Berlin, on the banks of the river Spree, opposite the royal palace and the dome. Clausewitz had been assigned a flat in the short wing facing the river, Burgstrasse 19, which also housed his office, the living quarters and offices of the administrative staff and of some of the teachers, the main auditorium, and a library of 15,000 volumes. His administrative duties, which included such matters as supervision of the school's budget and payroll, were not burdensome.[3] His relations with the directorate of studies proved more difficult, particularly when its area of competence came into conflict with his disciplinary authority over the students. Stützer, who was the most active and influential member of the directorate, was an unremitting opponent; but friction continued even after his death in 1824, and led to complaints about Clausewitz to the inspector-general of military schools and to the ministry of war. Official contact between the director and the officers attending the college was limited. Many came in closer touch with him only when they required an advance on their monthly pay: in the college they were referred to as *Pumpiers,* a typical Berlinese word formation, combining the slang meaning "to borrow" of the word *pumpen,* "to pump," with the French personal suffix *ier.* Clausewitz's adjutant during this period has left some telling reminiscences of these encounters, which also cast light on the program that Clausewitz followed for twelve years.[4]

Every weekday morning at nine, by which time Clausewitz was already working on his manuscripts at a desk in his wife's drawing room, the doorman, a one-armed veteran, announced his adjutant. "The adjutant, his files (which were usually very few) under his arm, entered the anteroom. Soon the door leading to the room of the general's wife opened, and the general appeared; the adjutant bowed silently, as did the general. The latter turned to his so-called office—as already mentioned, his real work table was in his wife's room—opened the door, and motioned the adjutant to enter first. The papers to be presented rarely called for discussion; usually they were signed without one word being exchanged. At the end the general rose, silently made another bow, which the adjutant respectfully returned, and left the room. If the general saw a letter, report, or something similar that was not drafted to his liking, he crossed out the text without saying a word, and at once wrote a new version."

3. However, he was sometimes occupied with the most insignificant of details. The archives of the Staatsbibliothek, Berlin-Dahlem (2f 1820), contain a communication, dated 13 February 1824, from Clausewitz to the head of the royal library concerning the transmission of an unnamed volume for the use of a lieutenant.
4. Steinmann v. Friederici, pp. 36–41.

After the adjutant had finished, the *Pumpiers* wishing an advance on their pay came one by one into Clausewitz's office, where each made his request in the fewest possible words, offered a receipt, which Clausewitz signed silently, and was dismissed. This frequently repeated scene, the adjutant adds, was borne by the director with unfailingly silent stoicism. Once, however, a *Pumpier* was announced "who asked for an advance nearly every month, and thus had become somewhat familiar to the general. It was in July, shortly before the end of the college year. 'Sir,' he began his request, 'after completing the three-year course I am returning to my regiment, and am obliged to outfit myself again. I beg to request an advance of sixty taler.' "

The conversation continued:

GENERAL: How do you intend to repay the sixty taler?
OFFICER: From my pay.
GENERAL: But, my dear man, you will draw your pay only one more time here, on the first, and it doesn't even amount to half that sum.
OFFICER: In that case, Sir, I should like to request thirty taler.
GENERAL: But that doesn't change anything. You can't spend your entire pay. What are you going to live on?
OFFICER: In that case, Sir, I would request only an advance covering the period until the first.
GENERAL: Since we have entered negotiations, in God's name, bring me your receipt for endorsement!
OFFICER: I already have it prepared.

And from several receipts for different sums he drew out the one that was wanted.

In this manner, the adjutant continues, "the general's scholarly work was interrupted in the mornings, but never for long. Then he resumed work until noon ... . From 12 o'clock on, visits were received and returned. Field Marshal Gneisenau usually called several times each week, and would stay until 2:00 in the afternoon. Lunch was served around that time. Frequently the general had guests, but never more than six or eight persons, usually men of intellectual distinction. Then the general's mind, his wit, his slashing sarcasm blazed in bright flames ... . The afternoon was again devoted to writing. Evenings, with rare exceptions, were spent at the home of Count Gneisenau or Count Bernstorff, unless there was an invitation to court or to a large dinner. The general and his wife would almost always return by 11 o'clock."

That Clausewitz wrote in his wife's salon rather than in his office is only a further indication of their very close relationship and of the part assumed in it by his scholarly work. He often dictated to her; she checked references and excerpted texts that he needed, and when he wrote he did not isolate himself from her, as he isolated himself from everyone else, but sought her company—a manner of working that might have been awkward in the director's office. It would in any case have seemed desirable to him to separate his scholarly and personal concerns from his official environment. In some respects, however, the *Kriegsschule* proved to be not a burden but of assistance to his scholarship. It must have been convenient to live across the hall from one of the largest military libraries in the state. Perhaps for that reason his private library was small, though he bought some standard authors and major reference works.[5] The college possessed an even more valuable intellectual resource in some of its civilian and military faculty. Of particular interest to Clausewitz was the physicist Paul Erman, who held professorships both at the University of Berlin and at the college, and was a member of the Royal Academy of Sciences. Erman's scientific contributions were not of lasting value. His best-known early achievement—a theory of the unipolarity of electrical conductors, for which he received a prize of 3,000 francs from the *Institut* in Paris—was disproved by Faraday; but he advanced the design and construction of scientific instruments, and did useful work on such questions as the influence of galvanic currents on adhesion. His most important contribution to the progress of physics in Germany was his refusal to follow the newly fashionable Romantic philosophy of nature, whose mysticism he opposed with an insistence on experimentation and exact observation. As a teacher he was outstanding. Clausewitz attended his course at the *Kriegsschule* for a year without missing a single lecture; presumably some of the scientific allusions and parallels in *On War* can be traced back to this experience.[6] Erman, who had married Karoline Hitzig, a sister-in-law of Captain O'Etzel, Clausewitz's associate in Coblenz, lived with his family in the college; after O'Etzel himself was appointed to the faculty in 1820, the relationship between the two families and Clausewitz must have been cordial. Erman's son Adolph also studied physics, and in 1828 commenced a voyage around the world to determine the effect of magnetic forces at different latitudes. In 1830 Erman published a preliminary report of his son's experiments and general experiences, including an account of a visit to Buddhist priests in Siberia, and sent copies to Clausewitz, which evoked the following charming response:

"My warmest thanks for the agreeable present with which you surprised me the day before yesterday. To be sure, I can digest only the blue

---

5. E.g., the subscription list of K. A. v. Zedlitz's important statistical work, *Die Staatskräfte der Preussischen Monarchie unter Friedrich Wilhelm III*, Berlin, 1828, includes Clausewitz's name on p. vii.

6. See, for example, this description of battle: "The major battle is ... to be regarded as concentrated war, as the center of gravity of the entire conflict or campaign. Just as the focal point of a concave mirror causes the sun's rays to converge into a perfect image and heats them to maximum intensity, so all forces and circumstances of war are united and compressed to maximum effectiveness in the major battle." *On War*, book IV, ch. 11 (p. 366).

pamphlets [containing accounts of Erman's travels; another pamphlet reported on his scientific work], but these are indeed delightful. That the little boy who ten years ago played his pranks in our courtyard (and now plays them with the *Chamba Lama*) has for some years been a European scientist who feels nature's pulse is certainly no common matter, and must greatly please his father. That, too, is what I, with my strong regard for excellence, can prize most highly. May I return your New Year's wishes with this delayed note, together with a more powerful wish: with the wish that you will live anew in your son, to whom—as with the successor of the *Chamba Lama*—the soul of his predecessor and father transmigrates while both are living." [7]

Far more creative than Paul Erman was Karl Ritter, one of the founders of the comparative study of geography. Ritter sought to integrate the different relevant disciplines into a comprehensive approach to physical and cultural geography, and his emphasis on the historical element "finally led him to universal cultural history as a grandiose synthesis of geography and history in their most fundamental implications." [8] Clausewitz's topographical discussions in his histories and in *On War* employ concepts of such 18th-century geographers as Buache, which he had presumably learned as a student, and which Ritter was now demolishing as overly descriptive and insufficiently analytic. [9] But Clausewitz must have regarded Ritter's insistence on the permanent interaction of all aspects of nature with man, and their basic harmony, as welcome scientific support of long-held beliefs. In addition, the two men shared an interest in progressive education; Ritter himself had worked with Pestalozzi and written several essays on the application of Pestalozzi's methods to scientific training. [10] A third scholar of international reputation at the college was Gustav Köpke, an immensely gifted and popular teacher of the history of classical and modern literature, who incidentally had written a book on the art of war in Homeric Greece.

Clausewitz received less stimulation from the officers on the staff of the *Kriegsschule,* though at least five among them were men of more than average ability, whose scholarly interests coincided with some of his own pursuits. O'Etzel and Rühle von Lilienstern have already been mentioned. O'Etzel's expertise in the field of military geography may have been tapped by Clausewitz for his historical studies; after Clausewitz's death he not only read the proofs of the collected works but also prepared the maps. Rühle's

7. Letter of 24 January 1830, Erman, p. 210.
8. Kessel, *Moltke,* p. 39.
9. E.g., the discussion of watersheds in *On War,* book VI, ch. 17 (p. 623).
10. The catalogue prepared for the auction of Ritter's extensive library after his death contains only a very few titles on military topics, but among them are the ten volumes of Clausewitz's works and a reprint of his short biography of Scharnhorst. *Verzeichnis der Bibliothek und Kartensammlung des Professors Dr. Carl Ritter,* Leipzig, 1861, i.

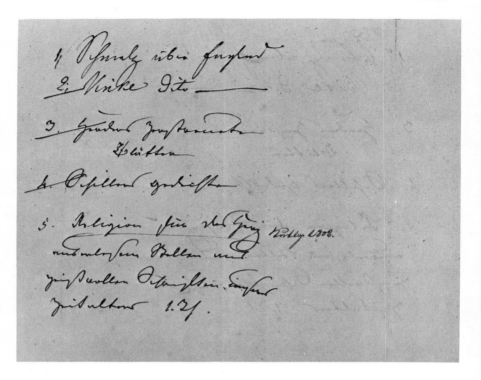

A note to a librarian, written in 1820.

In the note Clausewitz requests two books on England: *1. Schmalz über England; 2. Vinke ditto*—
i.e., T. A. Schmalz [Scharnhorst's brother-in-law], Staatsverfassung Grossbritanniens, Halle, 1806, and
L. v. Vincke, Darstellung der innern Verwaltung Grossbritanniens, ed. R. Niebuhr, Berlin, 1816; *3.
Herders Zerstreute Blätter*, a collection of Herder's essays and his anthology of Greek lyrics and epigrams; *4.
Schillers Gedichte;* and 5. *Religion für das Herz* [oder Bekenntnisse des Glaubens, der Liebe und der
Hoffnung, in] *auserlesene*[n] *Stellen aus geistvollen Schriften unseres Zeitalters*, a collection of thoughts on
religion from the works of various authors. Place and date of the last publication are noted in the librar-
ian's hand: *Stuttg*[art] *1802.* Collection of the author.

military interests were far broader. In his writings he addressed himself to
some of the same problems that Clausewitz was exploring; but after Clausewitz's initial setback at the college the relationship between the two men
remained distant. That did not prevent Rühle from publishing a very favorable review of the first two volumes of *On War,* which included a sympathetic appreciation of the dead author's personality and talents.[11] Clausewitz frankly disliked one of Rühle's gifted associates, Joseph Maria von
Radowitz, who decades later was to play an important role in efforts to

11. *Jahrbücher für Wissenschaftliche Kritik*, II (August 1833), nos. 26–28.

create a German federation under Prussian leadership. After attending French military schools, including the *École Polytechnique* in Paris, Radowitz had served in the Westphalian artillery, and as a sixteen-year-old lieutenant was wounded and awarded the Legion of Honor. When Jerome's kingdom dissolved, Radowitz joined the Hessian contingent of the allied forces and saw service in France. In 1823, still only twenty-six, he entered the Prussian army, and in the following year was appointed both to the general staff and to the directorate of studies of the *Kriegsschule*, where he was also assigned living quarters. His interests ranged from the study of mathematics to the iconography of saints, and he published books in both fields. Clausewitz seems to have been irritated by his demonstrative, rather romantic Catholicism, and by the rapid success at court and in Berlin society of a man who had fought for Napoleon.[12] It must have tested even Clausewitz's stoicism when the applicatory method, which he had vainly recommended in 1819, was adopted by the college seven years later on the urging of Radowitz, who had himself been taught in this method, and that Rühle and his protégé received credit for the reform.[13]

Two other instructors at the *Kriegsschule* were well-known interpreters of the Napoleonic wars, Karl von Decker and Karl von Canitz und Dallwitz, both a few years younger than Clausewitz. Canitz had been a student of Clausewitz in 1810 and 1811. In 1820 he became teacher of the history of war at the *Kriegsschule*, a position he retained even after he was appointed first adjutant to Clausewitz's friend, Prince Wilhelm. During these years he published two volumes on the history of cavalry, which contained passages that went beyond the technical treatment of the subject to speculate on fundamental elements of war and on their connection with history in general. Canitz went on to a distinguished career in the army and the diplomatic service, and between 1845 and 1848 served as Prussia's minister of foreign affairs.[14] Clausewitz appears to have valued his knowledge and judgment, as, to begin with, he respected Decker's. Grandson of an army chaplain and son of a bourgeois artillery officer who retired with the courtesy-rank of major-general, Decker had distinguished himself as an officer in the horse artillery and later on the general staff. He and his father were ennobled in 1819. The younger Decker taught tactics both at the Combined Artillery and Engineering Academy and at the *Kriegsschule*, supervised one of the general staff's topographical projects, together with Rühle edited the army's semiofficial periodical, the *Militair-Wochenblatt*, and still found time to write five books between the end of the war and

12. Clausewitz's antagonism is described in the memoirs of Countess Bernstorff, ii, 39, 102.
13. On Radowitz's part in introducing the applicatory method to the *Kriegsschule*, see his memoirs published by P. Hassel in *Joseph Maria v. Radowitz*, Berlin, 1905, pp. 24–27, and Hassel's comments, *ibid.*, pp. 192–194.
14. G. Dallinger has written a good biography of Canitz which stresses his diplomatic and political activities: *Karl von Canitz und Dallwitz*, Cologne and Berlin, 1969.

1822, when he briefly went to prison for killing another officer in a duel. His most successful work of this period was a practical, clearly written study of the little war, which after its first appearance in 1822 was reprinted three times and translated into French.[15] A comparison with Clausewitz's lectures of 1810–11 on the same subject shows that Clausewitz would have found little, if anything, new in Decker's treatment. Decker's career and literary activities were not seriously interrupted by his prison term. In 1824 he became editor of a new journal, and in the following year he published a book on Napoleon's campaign of 1796, at the very time when Clausewitz was planning a similar project. That Clausewitz no longer had the same regard for Decker's work he had earlier expressed in his memorandum to Boyen is suggested by a note added to his manuscript on 1796: "The most recent history of this campaign by Major von Decker is less useful than anything else that has appeared, and deserves no serious mention." [16]

Clausewitz's relations with the military authors gathered at the *Kriegsschule* were thus ambiguous. He could reasonably point to an insufficiency of systematic analysis in the work of some, to a lack of realism in the writings of others, and he was probably correct in thinking that he had little to learn from a clever popularizer of Decker's type. Yet many of the ideas on war that occupied him were common currency to the entire group. To varying degree Rühle, Canitz, Decker, and Radowitz grasped essential elements of Napoleonic operational practice, and sought to depict them in their writings. An example of their understanding of contemporary conditions is provided by the extensive revision of an earlier work by Scharnhorst, his *Handbuch für den Offizier,* which Rühle published shortly after the war.[17] Many of the themes familiar to us from Clausewitz's writings during the preceding decade are repeated. The work opens with the words "Krieg ist Kampf." Its author accepts as a matter of course that the destruction of the enemy's armed forces is the aim of military operations. The political purpose of war, the importance of initiative and intelligence in exploiting the unforeseen, the limitation of theory, the false security offered by rules

15. C. v. Decker, *Der kleine Krieg,* Berlin and Posen, 1822. On Decker, see Priesdorff, vi, No. 1704, and M. Jähns, "Das Militär-Wochenblatt von 1816–1876," in *Militärgeschichtliche Aufsätze,* ed. U. v. Gersdorff, Osnabrück, 1970.

16. C. v. Clausewitz, *Der Feldzug von 1796 in Italien; Werke,* iv, 4. Until the fourth volume of the collected works appeared in 1833, Decker seems not to have been aware of Clausewitz's opinion. On the first anniversary of Clausewitz's death he gave a memorial lecture which was fulsome in its praise of Clausewitz's genius, kindness, and uncorruptible judgment. An incomplete version of the talk is printed in Schwartz, *Leben des Generals Clausewitz,* ii, 500–504. That Decker's understanding of Clausewitz's theories did not rise above the conventional wisdom of the Prussian army is indicated by his comment on Clausewitz's proposition that the defense is a stronger form of war than the attack: "I would give much if the great philosopher of war had not written that sentence." Quoted in W. M. Schering, *Die Kriegsphilosophie von Clausewitz,* Hamburg, 1935, p. 15.

17. R. v. L. [Rühle von Lilienstern], *Handbuch für den Offizier,* 2 vols., Berlin, 1817–18.

and principles, the analysis of purpose, means, and circumstances to determine specific decisions—all are discussed. But, to be sure, when Rühle writes that "individual actions have *military purposes;* war as a whole, however, always has an *ultimate political purpose,*" the proposition lacks any analytic function. It appears suddenly, in a section on the little war, and is dropped after a few paragraphs.[18] Rühle and other theorists in the college as well as throughout the army rarely went far beyond the recognition of facts. They were content to record the empirical data of the wars from the French Revolution to 1815, and consequently in their writings statements on the political function of war, on the unpredictability of events, the significance of psychological factors, etc., are enveloped in tactical and organizational matter. To far lesser extent that is also true of Clausewitz's analyses, which move back and forth between major and minor elements. But these are always clearly distinguished, and when Clausewitz does discuss tactical details he tries to do so on the basis of the concepts of violence, chance, genius, and politics that underlie his view of war. He interprets the detail as an expression of fundamental forces, and the links that connect the part with the whole are never dropped.

Rühle's concern with operational and tactical methods indicates his overwhelming interest in the present—that is, in the application of very recent experience to the near future. When he refers to the past it is usually to define the present more sharply. For Clausewitz, on the contrary, the differences between Napoleon and Frederick, between citizen-soldier and mercenary, are the elements from which a universal theory must be constructed, rather than one that is time-bound. It was the failure of his contemporaries to see beyond the present, not their specific doctrines, that he castigated most vehemently. His decision to introduce the essays on strategy that he wrote after 1815 with a long, derisive quotation from Georg Christoph Lichtenberg, the wittiest critic of intellectual narrowness in German literature, indicates better than anything else how much contempt Clausewitz felt for the common run of military theorists. This contempt was valid if war was ever to become comprehensible beyond the level of the barrack square; but in a more immediate, personal sense Clausewitz was too harsh. If he had been more forthcoming, if exchanging views with his colleagues had been easier for him, he too might have benefited.

Some of the intellectual stimulation that he found lacking at the *Kriegsschule* he was given in other quarters. Gneisenau continued to be both an inspiration and a sounding board. His friend Groeben often visited Berlin. Among the small number of more junior officers who sought his guidance was Johannes von Tümpling, an associate from the time in Coblenz, and Carl von Roeder, a friend of long standing, over whose personal

18. *Ibid.,* ii, 8.

and professional development he watched with "sympathy and affection." [19] To an inquiry by Roeder in 1827, Clausewitz responded with an
exposition on the interaction of politics and strategy that remains a valuable addendum to *On War*. [20]

Membership on the committee formed to raise money and supervise
the design for a monument to Scharnhorst led to his acquaintance with
Prussia's foremost architect, Karl Friedrich Schinkel, and the two sculptors
Rauch and Tieck. [21] After Meusebach, with whom he had been on good
terms in Coblenz, moved to Berlin in 1820, Clausewitz was introduced to
another segment of the intellectual and artistic life of the capital. In his
memoirs, the poet and editor of early German literature Hoffmann von
Fallersleben writes that in Meusebach's house he occasionally met Gneisenau, Clausewitz, and Tümpling—the latter two sometimes accompanied
by their wives. Other regular callers were Georg Anton von Hardenberg,
brother of the poet Novalis, who himself wrote poetry under the pseudonym Rostorf; the legal philosopher and historian Karl von Savigny; and
Hegel, who generally devoted the second half of the evening to playing
cards with his host. [22]

Already familiar to Clausewitz in Meusebach's circle was Privy Councillor Eichhorn, now a senior official in the ministry of foreign affairs, and
the writer Achim von Arnim, both of whom he had known since the days
of the *Christlich-Deutsche Tischgesellschaft*. Arnim and his wife Bettina would
occasionally pass a day or an evening with the Clausewitzes, sometimes in
the company of Amalie von Helvig, a minor poetess, who had been a friend
of Schiller and was on close terms with Gneisenau. In the summer of 1818,
before Clausewitz had moved to Berlin, Bettina wrote Baroness Helvig that
Meusebach had told her a great deal about his friend, who, he said, did not
deserve his reputation of being a "cold, sarcastic hero" but possessed a
"warm, tender, deep nature." [23] Three years later she had occasion to write
to her absent husband about a picnic on the shores of the Wannsee near
Berlin, in the course of which "Clausewitz slipped from the little ferry into
the water and immediately sank beneath the surface, but suffered no consequences other than shock."

Other old acquaintances were Sophie Schwerin, widow of an officer who

19. Roeder, p. 306.
20. Published under the title *Zwei Briefe des Generals von Clausewitz: Gedanken zur Abwehr* as a special
issue of the *Militärwissenschaftliche Rundschau*, II (1937). See below, p. 379.
21. *Karl Friedrich Schinkel: Lebenswerk; Berlin*, ed. P. O. Rave, Berlin, 1962, iii, 327.
22. H. Hoffmann von Fallersleben, *Mein Leben*, Hanover, 1868, i, 311–312. In a letter of 5 October
1807 to his fiancée, Clausewitz mentions reading a collection of poems edited by Rostorf; *Correspondence*,
p. 147.
23. Undated letter in H. v. Bissing, *Das Leben der Dichterin Amalie von Helvig*, Berlin, 1889, p. 399.
The biography contains a few other references to the Clausewitzes, as does the correspondence of Achim
and Bettina v. Arnim, *Achim und Bettina in ihren Briefen*, ed. W. Vordtriede, Frankfurt, 1961, i. The
quotation which follows is from a letter of 14 May 1821, *ibid.*, p. 273.

was killed at Waterloo, and Varnhagen von Ense, with whom Clausewitz had attended Kiesewetter's lectures on Kant nearly twenty years earlier. For some years Clausewitz was a regular visitor to Countess Schwerin's soirées, where among other Berlin notables he came to know a special friend of the hostess, the popular novelist Henriette Paalzow, and her brother, the artist Wilhelm Wach, a former *Landwehr* officer, who had studied in the ateliers of David and Gros, and subsequently was appointed court painter in Berlin. In 1830 Clausewitz sat for him, the result being a tamely elegant Berlin Biedermeier portrait, which nevertheless catches something of the spirit and inwardness of its subject. Varnhagen was now married to Rahel Levin; his diplomatic career in which he had risen to the rank of Prussian minister-resident at one of the smaller German courts had ended, but he remained in close touch with the senior bureaucracy and the diplomatic corps, and was an assiduous and highly critical observer of politics and society in the capital. In the early 1820's Clausewitz is repeatedly mentioned in his diary: the two men met at Varnhagen's house or elsewhere, and seemed to be fairly open with each other; but as time goes on the references to Clausewitz grow less frequent, as they also diminish in the correspondence and diaries of other members of Berlin society. Clausewitz appears increasingly to have restricted his social life to the relatives of his wife—her mother still lived, and one of her cousins was now intendant of the royal theaters—and to the families of his friend Gneisenau and of a new acquaintance, Count Bernstorff, the minister of foreign affairs.

The bond between Gneisenau and Clausewitz became even closer in these years. The two men admired and completely trusted each other, their feelings being amplified by the firm friendship that had grown up between Gneisenau and Marie von Clausewitz. Gneisenau, married to a country squire's daughter who was happiest in her domestic concerns, valued the charm and intellectual energy of his friend's wife, and freely confided in her. In turn, the affection in which she held him was not inhibited by the façade of formality that Clausewitz retained even toward his best friend. Plans for the three to travel together to England or Italy came to nothing; but for many years the Clausewitzes spent part of every summer at Gneisenau's Silesian estate, which he had received from the state as a reward for his services during the Wars of Liberation. In 1828 the connection between the two families was given a formal note when Marie von Clausewitz's brother, twelve years her junior, married Gneisenau's third daughter.

Clausewitz's relations to the Bernstorffs were of very different character; but what began as an acquaintance between two mutually sympathetic couples soon attained a level of genuine, if limited, intimacy. Christian Günther Bernstorff belonged to a family whose members had for generations occupied important positions in the service of Hanover, Lüneburg, and especially Denmark. Between 1797 and 1810 he had been Danish minister of foreign affairs, then served as ambassador to Vienna, Danish representative to the Congress of Vienna, and ambassador to Berlin, until he was appointed Prussian minister of foreign affairs in 1818. The choice met with a mixed reception. Friedrich August von der Marwitz may have expressed a more common point of view than was his wont when he commented: "The country and all of Europe were offered the scandal that in the entire Prussian monarchy none was deemed competent to guide the state's foreign affairs, but that a Dane had to leave the diplomatic service of his country in order to head Prussia's the following day. Even if we concede every possible virtue to such a changeling [*Überkömmling*], he could never possess the quality on which alone everything depends in this position: *Prussian character, Prussian honor,* and *a Prussian heart."* [24]

In fact, Bernstorff's appointment had much to commend it. Until 1818 Hardenberg had acted as his own foreign minister as well as secretary of the treasury. Now the burden of work had become too great, and at the age of sixty-eight the chancellor was losing his former resilience; clearly foreign affairs and the treasury should be made into separate ministries, with Hardenberg retaining supreme control. The obvious choice for the ministry of foreign affairs was Humboldt; but his relationship with Hardenberg had deteriorated, he was suspect to the adherents of enlightened conservatism and anathema to the men of the far right, let alone to Marwitz and others with neofeudal views. Other liberal or moderate candidates—Boyen and Gneisenau were mentioned as possibilities—would have encountered almost as much opposition. On the other hand, Hardenberg did not want to appoint an ultraconservative. He had not given up his hopes for a constitution; he needed a man versed in diplomatic routine, who had no close ties to any of the political factions in Prussia—someone in whom he could rely both in an administrative and a political sense. The appointment of a foreigner, who resembled the chancellor in his belief in progress through administrative reforms if not in his concern for constitutional development, thus gave little away to any side. [25]

Clausewitz first met Bernstorff at the Congress of Aachen. After the two men were settled in Berlin, the Clausewitzes regularly visited the minister and his wife, and came to be regarded as friends of the family, though in her recollections the countess, who tended toward superlatives in describing her social life, may have exaggerated the depth of the relationship. [26] She was a harmless, lachrymose lady of distinguished lineage,

24. Marwitz, p. 678.
25. The historical picture of Bernstorff has long been dominated by Treitschke's forceful but irresponsible interpretation. The recent dissertation by L. Baack, "Christian Bernstorff and Prussia, 1818–1830," Stanford, 1973, corrects numerous misconceptions on the basis of very extensive archival material.
26. A tenuous connection already existed between Clausewitz and the Bernstorffs. A son of Clausewitz's grandfather by his first marriage, Carl Christian Clauswitz, studied theology and law at the University

sensitive to the feelings of those in her immediate circle, but conventional and intellectually insignificant. Her memoirs, which often mention Clausewitz and his wife, are almost devoid of tangible information about them. Count Bernstorff, too, could adopt the sentimental mode. After Clausewitz's death he eulogized his friend in verses which were as shallow and flawed in the original German as they are in English translation:

The deepest strivings of the clearest mind,
the fullest loving of the warmest heart,
in him were gracefully combined.[27]

But Bernstorff was also a highly knowledgeable and efficient diplomat, whose professionalism Clausewitz respected, and with whom he found himself at one in recognizing the weaknesses and limitations that hedged in Prussia's position in the world.

The connection with Bernstorff acquired special significance for Clausewitz when he himself became candidate for a diplomatic assignment in the spring of 1819. As so often before, the effort to improve his position owed much to Gneisenau's encouragement. On 12 May, Gneisenau suggested to Hardenberg that Clausewitz be appointed ambassador to London. The chancellor, he reported immediately after their meeting, had spoken favorably of Clausewitz's qualities, and had authorized Gneisenau to inquire whether Clausewitz would accept the post if it were offered.[28] This elicited an emotional reply, in which Clausewitz thanked Gneisenau for having "dared" to make such a suggestion, and expressed the writer's sense of inadequacy but also his willingness to accept if the chancellor should on further reflection decide to make the offer official.[29]

For a time it appeared that Clausewitz would be appointed. In November, Gneisenau wrote to Groeben that the matter was settled, adding, "He is very pleased; Frau von Clausewitz less so."[30] Clausewitz enjoyed strong support, not least Humboldt's, who wrote to Hardenberg that Clausewitz's "balanced, intelligent character would make him acceptable" to the English, and also recommended him to Bernstorff.[31] On 29 November,

---

of Halle, and became tutor to Counts Christian and Leopold Stolberg, poets and friends of the young Goethe. In the 1770's, Clauswitz entered Danish service, in which he rose to the rank of councillor of state. After his death in 1795, two of his children, Gottlob and Charlotte, were adopted by Elise Bernstorff's parents and brought up with her. Gottlob became a senior official in the Danish forestry service; Charlotte died unmarried in 1816. Clausewitz made her acquaintance in Holstein at the end of the fall campaign of 1813.

27. Schwartz, *Leben des Generals Clausewitz*, ii, 262.
28. Letter of 12 May 1819, Pertz-Delbrück, v. 370.
29. Letter of 14 May 1819. Gneisenau sent it on to Hardenberg with a strong covering note, *ibid.*, pp. 371–372.
30. Letter of 18 November 1819, *ibid.*, p. 388.
31. Humboldt to Hardenberg, 8 September 1819; Humboldt to Gneisenau, 15 October 1819, in *Wilhem v. Humboldts Politische Briefe*, ii, 329, 337.

Varnhagen noted in his diary that Clausewitz had been given the appointment: news which he repeated on 2 December, and interpreted as a victory of Humboldt or possibly Gneisenau over the new minister of foreign affairs.[32] But only a week later he wrote that the appointment was being violently opposed, and that Clausewitz's future remained uncertain.[33] By the 18th it was rumored that the appointment had not only been withdrawn but that Clausewitz's position at the *Kriegsschule* was being given to another officer.[34] Other rumors more favorable to Clausewitz also circulated, but Varnhagen continued to hear that Clausewitz was being opposed for his radical sympathies. On 3 January 1820, Varnhagen noted: "General Clausewitz visits me; he is still not certain whether he is being sent to London."[35]

Clausewitz's hope of exchanging the *Kriegsschule* for a diplomatic assignment had become enmeshed in the conflict over the constitution and the *Landwehr,* which at year's end reached a resolution of sorts with the departure from office of Humboldt, Boyen, and Grolman. The defeat of the most active of the remaining reformers was accompanied by a campaign to seek out all enemies of monarchical supremacy, which hounded its victims in ways that were alternately vicious and ludicrous. It was difficult to remain serious when someone of the character of Count Groeben, now chief of staff of an army corps, was subjected to a high-level investigation because the police had found a note he had written in 1816, warning Görres in jocular terms of unexpected guests for dinner.[36] Clausewitz, marked as another member of the reformist faction that was being neutralized, knew the identity of many of his opponents. On 18 December he wrote Gneisenau that, according to Boyen, the spokesman of the court party in the ministry of foreign affairs, Privy Councillor Ancillon, was working against him.[37] A week later he wrote to Groeben that he was opposed not only by Ancillon but also by the Duke of Cumberland and the British minister in Berlin, while with a few exceptions the whole Prussian diplomatic corps was grumbling about his nomination.[38] He recognized that his prospects were jeopardized, but thought that at worst he would receive a consolation prize: membership in the council of state or a senior position on the general staff. He counted heavily on the good opinion in which he was held by the head of the king's military cabinet, Job von Witzleben, and seems to have exaggerated the strength of Hardenberg's support.[39] In reality his op-

---

32. K. A. Varnhagen von Ense, *Blätter aus der preussischen Geschichte,* Leipzig, 1868, i, 8, 11.
33. *Ibid.,* p. 14. See also the entries for 10 and 16 December, pp. 15, 22.
34. *Ibid.,* p. 23. See also the entries for 22 and 29 December, pp. 28, 34.
35. *Ibid.,* p. 41.
36. Groeben to Gneisenau, 8 January 1820, Pertz-Delbrück, v, 405–406.
37. *Ibid.,* p. 400.
38. Clausewitz to Groeben, 26 December 1819, Kessel, "Zu Boyens Entlassung," p. 51.
39. The military cabinet, established in June 1814, was an important step in the conservative reversal of the reformers' efforts to detach the army from complete and direct control of the monarch. Its

ponents meant to keep him from any position of influence, and they were too numerous and powerful not to get their way. Not only Ancillon but also Prince Wittgenstein, head of the police and minister of the royal household, and almost certainly the commander of the guards, Duke Karl of Mecklenburg, regarded Clausewitz as a secret radical. In persuading the king to reverse a decision that had not yet been officially announced, they received valuable help from the Duke of Cumberland, who had recently taken up residence in Berlin. Cumberland, the future King of Hanover, outdid even Duke Karl in his hatred of social and political change, and added to the impact of Karl's views on the king, which in these years was considerable. The weight of Cumberland's opposition, fortified by the British minister in Berlin, Rose—who was a political ally of the duke—can be gathered from a dispatch that the Danish diplomat Eugen Reventlow, Bernstorff's son-in-law, sent his government on 3 December: "I was assured yesterday that it was very possible that the designation of General Clausewitz to the London position will be withdrawn. The Duke of Cumberland has repeatedly declared his strong opposition, nor has M. Rose for his part painted the most favorable portrait of him. Not to mention other factors that could fault this choice, M. de Clausewitz is reputed to have belonged at all times to the democratic party, and to have been, for example, one of the foremost partisans of the *Tugendbund*." [40]

That the official representative of a foreign power and a member of its royal family spoke against an ambassadorial candidate should have been enough to end the matter. But in the ministries and at court the conflict over policy and personnel had not abated, and for the time being the London embassy remained in charge of subordinate officials. Clausewitz's position was embarrassing, Varnhagen noted on 1 May 1820; the appointment had obviously run into great difficulties, but his was still the name most frequently mentioned for the post. [41] Shortly afterwards, a compromise attempt by his supporters to secure for him the lesser appointment of minister to Switzerland came to nothing. [42] It was not until the summer of 1821 that the post in London was filled, and in a manner that meant a double

predecessor was the expediting general adjutant, who functions had been abolished in 1808. Witzleben, head of the *Militärkabinett* from 1817 on, was an exceptionally gifted, realistic officer, who repeatedly prevented ultraconservative excesses in the army and the ministries, but his daily access to the king and his great influence, unchecked by institutional accountability, meant a return to the earlier system of personal rule.

40. Eugen v. Reventlow to minister of foreign affairs, 3 December 1819, Dpt. f. u. A. 1771–1848, Preussen II, Depecher 1819; Rigsarkivet, Copenhagen.

41. Varnhagen von Ense, i, 129. See also the entries for 16 January, 23 February, 11 and 27 March, 19 April, the long discussion of Clausewitz's opponents on 7 May, and the entries for 8 and 31 July 1820; *ibid.*, pp. 55, 87, 99, 110, 124, 132, 164, and 175.

42. Stein reacted angrily to the news that Clausewitz, "a man of great merit," had not been given the Swiss assignment; Stein to the President of the Swiss Diet, N. F. v. Mülinen, 3 October 1820, *Briefe und Amtliche Schriften*, vi, ed. A. H. v. Wallthor, Stuttgart, 1965, 314. Two years later Varnhagen reported that Stein sent greetings to Gneisenau, Grolman, and Clausewitz: "Men, he says, who are not in fashion, but on whom he will always count ...." Entry for 13 June 1822, Varnhagen von Ense, ii, 139.

defeat for Clausewitz. He was notified by Bernstorff that the king planned to sign a cabinet order holding out the prospect not of the London embassy but of an unspecified diplomatic appointment at a future date. When the king's order did not arrive, Clausewitz appealed to Bernstorff to raise the matter once more with the chancellor. A few days later he sent Bernstorff a second letter, the friendly and reasonable tone of which could not hide his mortification at the treatment he had received. The increasing doubts concerning his person, he wrote, "make it impossible for me still to want the appointment. ... I am driven to tell Your Excellency how sorry—yes, how pained—I am at having made myself into an object of criticism." He was reluctant to withdraw officially, since he had earlier informed the chancellor and the king that if the appointment were offered he would accept; but now he begged Bernstorff and the chancellor to come to a decision without regard to his feelings: "Just as I never sought the position [presumably an allusion to Gneisenau's initiative in putting his name forward] so I never want to occupy it against Your Excellency's judgment, and in opposition to the power of circumstances." [43] It was in these days that a conservative career diplomat was given the embassy—a decision, Varnhagen reported, "that is considered a victory of Count Bernstorff over the chancellor." [44]

Bernstorff's role in this long-drawn-out affair is obscure. Clausewitz's candidacy was only one of many problems that faced him when he arrived in Berlin, and one that could not be isolated from the ideological conflict in Prussia, to which, indeed, he owed his own appointment. It suited neither his political orientation nor his need to establish good relations with the court party to champion a man who was out of step with the restorative spirit of the day. On the other hand, Bernstorff soon realized that Clausewitz was anything but the democrat of ultra rumors. He came to consider him a friend, and seems to have been prepared to lend his support so long as this did not entail disagreeable confrontations with the Ancillons and the Wittgensteins. Varnhagen was certainly mistaken in regarding Clausewitz as a pawn in a struggle between Hardenberg and Bernstorff; indeed, whatever disagreement existed between the chancellor and his minister amounted to little more than the friction that inevitably accompanies the gradual transfer of day-to-day control over foreign policy to the new man. Whenever Bernstorff considered the time propitious, he did try to satisfy Clausewitz's persistent wish for a diplomatic assignment. In 1822 and again the following year there was talk of an appointment to one or the other minor power, and in November 1823 Bernstorff actually proposed Clausewitz for the Munich embassy, but was compelled to inform Clause-

43. Clausewitz to Bernstorff, 30 September 1821, and undated letter of October, 1821; Schwartz, *Leben des Generals Clausewitz*, ii, 255–258.
44. Entry for 8 October 1821, Varnhagen von Ense, i, 352. Compare the entry for 4 July of the same year, *ibid.*, p. 334.

witz that the king had rejected his suggestion.[45] As usual, Varnhagen was informed quickly but not quite accurately of what had transpired. "General von Clausewitz is to be ambassador to Copenhagen," he wrote in his diary, "since his attitude is believed to disqualify him for Munich; he is far too liberal, it is said. 'Not to Munich,' the king is supposed to have said, 'but Copenhagen seems more suitable—that may be all right.' " [46] But Copenhagen, too, turned out to be a delusion.

What appears most interesting in Clausewitz's efforts to gain a diplomatic appointment is the strength of his longing for it. It was not simply a matter of leaving the disagreeable administrative duties at the *Kriegsschule:* he could have obtained another assignment in the army, though not one that would have fully satisfied him. Disgust with conditions in Berlin, the appeal of a more stimulating, freer life elsewhere, an increasing concern with foreign affairs to the exclusion of earlier hopes for domestic change— all combined in his wish to become an agent of Prussia's foreign policy. The wish was so intense that he was willing to suffer the hurt of appearing to society not as Boyen or Grolman, who silently accepted the consequences of being out of political favor, but as someone who repeatedly put himself forward for prestigious and attractive employment, and repeatedly was turned down. In this sense, too, the episode was unique in his life.

These equivocations and disappointments did not noticeably diminish his scholarly energies. As he came to realize that he would never receive a diplomatic assignment, he withdrew still further from society and for some years devoted himself wholly to bringing together earlier ideas on war, developing and revising them into a comprehensive theory of conflict. Intermittently he was in poor health. On 3 June 1822, his wife's birthday, he suffered a "strokelike" attack which temporarily paralyzed his right arm; it is impossible to say whether or not this was a psychosomatic incident. At least twice—in 1825 and again the following year—he received extensive leaves to take the waters at Ems and Marienbad, the latter trip giving him the opportunity of revisiting the battlefields of Auerstedt and Jena and of spending a few days in Prague. In 1827 he became so severely ill that he feared he would die. The nature of this illness is not known. He appeared to make such a good recovery that no doubt was expressed concerning his ability to remain on the active list; but it is likely that the illnesses of this period brought about the "completely ruined nervous system" to which his death was attributed four years later.[47]

His career had come almost to a standstill. In 1822 he received the

---

45. Bernstorff to Clausewitz, 21 November 1823; Schwartz, *Leben des Generals Clausewitz,* ii, 258.
46. Entries for 1 and 12 October 1823, Varnhagen von Ense, ii, 417, 424–425.
47. On Clausewitz's illnesses see Bernstorff, i, 326; Priesdorff, v, No. 1429; Clausewitz's diary of his journey to Marienbad in Schwartz, *Leben des Generals Clausewitz,* ii, 269–288; and Kessel, "Zur Genesis der modernen Kriegslehre," *Wehrwissenschaftliche Rundschau,* III (1953), No. 9, 412.

Order of the Red Eagle, third class, a decoration appropriate to his rank and seniority. Varnhagen wrote in his diary that the same decoration was received by Clausewitz's brother-in-law Marwitz, but also by the composer Spontini and by a subaltern official of the king's household: "Everyone comments on this association, and it is thought that especially Marwitz must foam at the mouth with anger." [48] Six years later Clausewitz was awarded the second class of the same order with oak-leaf cluster, which indicated that he might still have a future in the service. On the other hand, when the position of chief of staff fell vacant in 1829 he was considered neither for it nor for the subordinate position of chief of the staff's central body, the Great General Staff. [49]

It was in these years of outward quiescence that a French agent visiting Berlin wrote a profile of Clausewitz as part of a comprehensive report on the Prussian army for the French minister of war. With its fund of accurate information, as well as its omissions and errors, the sketch offers a good summary of the knowledge contemporaries had of Clausewitz's past and present life, and their opinion of him:

"Clausewitz (Charles de) was born in Burg near Magdeburg in 1780. His father had been an officer. In 1792 he was placed as cadet in a regiment, in which he served during the campaign[s] of 1793 and 1794. Then he entered the Military Academy in Berlin, where he remained until 1803. He became the favorite and later the friend of General Scharnhorst, director of the academy (who has since become known through the creation of the *Landwehr*).... .

"Clausewitz served in the campaign of 1806 as aide de camp of Prince August of Prussia, was taken prisoner at the engagement of Prenzlau, and sent to France. After his return to Prussia he served there until 1812 on the general staff with the rank of major, and in particular acted as assistant to General Scharnhorst. Among his duties was that of teaching military theory to the *Crown Prince of Prussia* and to *Prince Frederick of the Netherlands*.

"At the beginning of the war against Russia, Clausewitz openly declared himself against the French. Disapproving of the alliance that Prussia had concluded with them, he shed the Prussian uniform and took up arms against his country by entering Russian service. He was appointed quartermaster general in Wittgenstein's corps, and it was he who secretly treated with General Yorck, leading him to defect.

48. Entry for 20 January 1822, Varnhagen von Ense, ii, 15.
49. A few officers, Gneisenau among them, believed Clausewitz to be the best possible choice for chief of the general staff—a position, incidentally, which in the 1820's was primarily concerned with plans for mobilization and war, and still fell far short of the executive power it acquired under Moltke. The man who was actually appointed—Johann Wilhelm Krauseneck—had, however, amply proved his technical and administrative proficiency and his ability to lead troops in the field, and since he was also senior to Clausewitz his choice could not be regarded as an injustice. Once again Clausewitz suffered from the circumstance that had characterized his position in the military hierarchy since 1806: even if the king had found him more sympathetic, he was too junior by a few years to be the obvious candidate for important appointments.

"Clausewitz served in the campaign of 1813 as Russian officer attached to the headquarters of Marshal Blücher. At the invitation of General de Gneisenau, to whom he was linked by friendship, and who at that time shared his hatred of the French, Clausewitz wrote the history of the campaign of 1813 (published in Leipzig in 1814, and for a long time believed to be by General Gneisenau himself).

"When the Prusso-Russian [*sic!*] Legion was formed under General Wallmoden, Clausewitz became its chief of staff, and brought himself to favorable attention at the engagement on the Göhrde.

"In 1815 he returned to Prussian service and became chief of staff of General Thielemann [*sic!*], who fought at Wavre (at the battle of Waterloo) against General Grouchy.

"Then he was assigned to the Rhenish provinces. Subsequently promoted to major-general he was appointed director of the Military Academy at Berlin, a post he still occupies today.

"For some time he pushed his ill will against France so far that, following the example of his friend General Count Gneisenau, he no longer wished to talk French. His wife, whose opinions were even more extreme than his, encouraged him for a long time in that attitude. However, when he saw General de Gneisenau abandoning his rudeness and associating with the French minister [to Berlin] in order to counter the rumor of his extreme liberalism, Clausewitz followed his example. He has remained friend and confidant of General Count Gneisenau, who did all he could in 1820 and 1821 to have him appointed Prussian minister to London. The king does not like General Clausewitz, and the effort was in vain. But since that time these two officers have remained on very intimate terms with the minister of foreign affairs, Count Bernstorff.

"General de Clausewitz has the reputation of being a very good general staff officer." [50]

Early in 1830 Clausewitz at last left the *Kriegsschule.* An officer who had recently joined its faculty subsequently wrote that Clausewitz had been a complete failure there, and that his position had become untenable.[51] Clausewitz himself told the minister of war that after eleven years in an administrative post he wanted to return to service with the troops. On 27 December 1829 he submitted a request for a new assignment to Frederick William, who responded positively on 7 January.[52] A major-general holding Clausewitz's seniority might have expected command of a division, but since he had not served in the line for thirty years, this was scarcely a possibility. Opportunities did, however, exist in the artillery, where technical

50. "De l'état militaire en Prusse," a 327-page manuscript, dated 1826; Carton No. 1529, "Mémoires et Reconnaissances," folder 10, *Archives de la Guerre,* Vincennes. The cited text is contained in the section "Notices biographiques."
51. Brandt, ii, 19–20.
52. Priesdorff, v, No. 1429.

expertise mattered more than it did in the infantry or cavalry. While Clausewitz had never served in this arm, he possessed some knowledge of its mechanics and tactics, and could be trusted to acquire the rest quickly. In 1830 the artillery, commanded since the reform years by Prince August, was organized into three groups of three brigades each, an officer with the title of inspector heading each group. Clausewitz was designated commanding officer of the 3rd Inspection, with headquarters in Breslau, the capital of Silesia. To familiarize himself with the service, he was temporarily attached to the 1st Inspection in Berlin.[53] Before turning his whole attention to his new duties, he separated the unfinished manuscript of *On War* into bundles, which he sealed and put away until such time as he could return to the manuscript and complete it. In early September 1830, Clausewitz left Berlin for Breslau, where his wife joined him some weeks later.

53. On 9 March 1830. Until he received his new permanent appointment, Clausewitz continued as administrative head of the *Kriegsschule*. In April he was also made a member of the army's evaluation commission of scientific and mechanical proposals.

11

THE MAJOR HISTORICAL AND THEORETICAL WORKS

I. INTRODUCTION

The four years of intermittent warfare that destroyed French hegemony in Europe had interrupted Clausewitz's theoretical and historical studies but had not halted them completely. At the outset, shortly before the invasion of Russia, his essay for the crown prince summed up the ideas on strategy and military leadership that he had developed during the era of reform. These ideas he expanded and amended in the wars that now began. During the armistice in the summer of 1813, he wrote his account of the campaign that had just been concluded, and it was most probably during the fall of the following year that he wrote the sections dealing with his personal experiences in Russia that were later included in his history of the war of 1812. On his return to Germany after the final defeat of Napoleon, writing again became a regular part of his existence. In the two years he was stationed in Coblenz he wrote a long study of the campaign of 1814, the biography of Scharnhorst, and a collection of essays on strategy, besides the usual memoranda on organizational and operational matters. The twelve years in Berlin that followed, he gave over largely to research and writing. During this period he wrote the reform proposal for the pedagogic program of the *Kriegsschule* and the political essays that are discussed in the previous chapter; studies of the wars of Frederick the Great; the analysis of Prussia before and during 1806 that has been repeatedly cited in this book, *Observations on Prussia in Her Great Catastrophe;* histories of the campaigns of 1796, 1799, and 1815; and he completed the history of Napoleon's invasion of Russia. In the same years he expanded his essays on strategy into a comprehensive theoretical treatment of war, which in turn he began to revise after 1827 as he developed new concepts that seemed to call for a recasting of *On War*. This long and productive period came to an end with his departure from the *Kriegsschule.* In the last year of his life, when he once more participated in the formulation and execution of the state's military policies, he wrote the strategic memoranda and political essays that are discussed in the following chapter.

The alternation between history and theory that characterized Clausewitz's writings before 1812 became more pronounced after peace returned. During the reform era he had discontinued writing long historical studies on the order of his earlier history of Gustavus Adolphus. In these years his historical work consisted of such briefer pieces as his articles on the campaign of 1806 published in *Minerva,* or outlines of events in Spain or the Vendée; much of it was also subsumed in his political discussions—the essay on national character, for instance, or his letter on Machiavelli to Fichte. With the defeat of Napoleon his political output diminished, without ceasing altogether, and he returned to the detailed narrative and analyses of extended sequences of events. His longest historical work, the history of the campaign of 1799 in Italy, is nearly 950 pages in print.

Not only did Clausewitz shift back and forth between history and theory; his historical writings contain theoretical discussions, and his essays and chapters on theory are filled with historical material. Their interaction was determined by the concepts of the two disciplines that he began to develop in his early twenties, and which by 1812 he had brought to completion in all essential aspects. As we know, he believed that it was not the business of theory to generate doctrine. Our aim, he wrote in a characteristic passage in *On War,* "is not to provide new principles and methods of conducting war; rather we are concerned with examining the essential content of what has long existed, and to trace it back to its basic elements." [1] The task of theory was to clarify reality; or, more accurately, to help men clarify it by stimulating their minds and making them more sensitive to their surroundings—in Clausewitz's case, to their military surroundings. If theory interposed itself between the individual and his world, both theory and man failed. Reality appeared in two different forms: as experience and as history. To search the past for laws to apply to action in the present was useless: "We cannot formulate principles, rules, or methods: history does not provide a basis for them. On the contrary, at almost every turn one finds peculiar features that are often incomprehensible and sometimes astonishingly odd. Nevertheless it is useful to study history in connection with this subject [war] as with others. While there may be no system, no mechanical way of recognizing the truth, truth does exist. To recognize it one generally needs seasoned judgment and an instinct born of long experience. While history may yield no formulae, it does provide an *exercise for judgment,* here as everywhere else." [2] If the historian deals honestly and competently with the evidence, if his first concern is with specifics rather

1. *On War,* book VI, ch. 8 (p. 562).
2. *Ibid.,* book VI, ch. 30 (p. 756).

than with the larger, artificial periodization of the past—its division into campaigns, reigns, or eras—his work, to varying degrees, becomes recorded reality. Together with experience, which it depersonalizes and immeasurably enlarges, history serves as the starting point for theoretical speculation.[3] History also illustrates the arguments and propositions posed by the theorist: "Historical examples clarify everything and also provide the best kind of proof in the empirical sciences. This is particularly true of the art of war."[4] History serves to test theory, confirms genuine advances in cognition, and makes further progress possible. It was primarily his reflection on the historical evidence that induced Clausewitz, after having nearly completed *On War* in 1827, to amend his fundamental theories by developing the hypothesis of the dual nature of war.

A discussion of his mature historical work will reveal more about the role history played in Clausewitz's effort to understand the external world; but before turning to these writings we should note that the dominance of history over his theories is more comprehensive than the influence which theory exerted on his historical analyses. The formal conceptualization of certain factors—genius, for instance, or friction—contributed to the precision and emphasis of Clausewitz's historical interpretations, but these were never shaped by theoretical elements. Clausewitz did not depict the campaigns of 1630 to 1632 or the invasion of Russia from the exclusive point of view of the psychology of Gustavus Adolphus or Napoleon. In his eyes, the commander's genius was a highly significant element, but only one among several factors; he did not compress the evidence into a single explicatory pattern based on personality traits or—in Jomini's manner—on the commander's adherence to, or neglect of, an operational system. He sought to structure his analyses, not from the outside but by exploring the forces at work within single episodes and by tracing the connections between episodes. In his histories he imposed no theoretical limitations on reality as he perceived it; just as he insisted that theory should not form a closed system but remain open, susceptible to change. Here, too, may be found the explanation for the abruptness with which he concluded some of his longer historical works—the study of 1815, for example. What needed to be said, and could be said, is contained in the chain of narrative and analysis: no extensive summary is necessary; the work blends into the continuum of life.[5]

---

3. Occasionally Clausewitz came close to suggesting that a sense of reality could be equated with experience and reflection on the past. See, for example, the characterization of Phull in his history of 1812; *Werke*, vii, 7. Even the empirical soldier who had no interest in theory would, he thought, find history invaluable; nothing, for instance, proved more conclusively the "often incredible effect" of moral and psychological factors; *On War*, book III, ch. 3 (p. 255).

4. *Ibid.*, book II, ch. 6 (p. 233).

5. Other instances of abrupt conclusions can be found in the "Campaigns of Frederick," the *Observations on Prussia*, and the "Campaign of 1814." The final chapters of *1796* and *1799* contain extensive political and strategic analyses; the "Campaign of 1812" ends with an interpretation of Napoleon's strategy.

APPROXIMATE CHRONOLOGY OF CLAUSEWITZ'S WRITINGS, 1813–31

The three stages in the genesis of the manuscript to which Clausewitz eventually gave the name *On War* are identified as "ON WAR 1, 2, & 3."

1813	"The Campaign of 1813 to the Armistice"	
1814	Parts of "The Campaign of 1812 in Russia"	
1816–18	Essays on strategy	ON WAR 1
	"The Campaign of 1814 in France"	
	"On the Life and Character of Scharnhorst"	
1819	Memorandum on the *Kriegsschule*	
1819–23	Political essays	
1819–27	The first six books of *On War;* drafts of books VII & VIII	ON WAR 2
early 1820's	"The Campaigns of Frederick the Great"	
1824–25	*Observations on Prussia in Her Great Catastrophe*	
after 1824	Completion of "The Campaign of 1812 in Russia"	
1827–30	Revisions of *On War*	ON WAR 3
	The Campaign of 1796 in Italy	
	The Campaigns of 1799 in Italy and Switzerland	
	The Campaign of 1815 in France	
1831	Political essays	

With the exception of the long memorandum on the *Kriegsschule,* the many service memoranda and shorter studies in military history and theory that Clausewitz wrote during this period are not included in the table.

II. HISTORY

In his collection of essays "Die Reorganisatoren des Preussischen Staates," Wilhelm Dilthey praised Clausewitz's account of the Russian campaign and of the Convention of Tauroggen, and added: "No German historian can be compared to this supremely gifted pupil of Scharnhorst." [1] Dilthey did not elaborate on this astonishing judgment, and it left scarcely a trace in German historiography, just as a few years later Delbrück's comparison of Clausewitz to Tocqueville failed to stimulate the profession's interest in Clausewitz's histories. At most some writers noted the affinity between Clausewitz's treatment of the past and that of the precursors and pioneers of historicism, without, however, proceeding to substantive analyses. [2] In such surveys of German historiography as Srbik's *Geist und Geschichte* Clausewitz's name does not appear.

Greater attention has been paid to the relationship between Clausewitz's historical and theoretical work, principally by Delbrück, whose interpretation is discussed below, and more recently by Eberhard Kessel. [3] These scholars were primarily concerned with his theories, and consequently treated the histories as sources rather than reading them for their own sake.

On War has overshadowed everything Clausewitz wrote; but there are other reasons for the neglect his histories have suffered. The greater part appeared in his posthumous *Werke*, whose subtitle, *Über Krieg und Kriegführung*, seemed to suggest that the contents were addressed to the military professional rather than the scholar. From the 1850's on, comprehensive histories and biographies of the Napoleonic era appeared, based on the extensive archival research that had now become possible, which completed the relegation of Clausewitz's volumes to the shelf of technical documentation. Other of his writings remained unknown for decades. It was not until 1888, for example, that his study of the collapse of Prussia was published, by which time its interpretations had become common property—some-

---

1. W. Dilthey, *Zur Preussischen Geschichte*, Leipzig and 1936, pp. 119–120. The essays originally appeared in 1872.
2. E.g., Kessel, *Zeiten der Wandlung*, pp. 259, 264–265; P. Paret, "Clausewitz," *International Encyclopedia of the Social Sciences*, 1968, II, 512.
3. See Kessel's introduction to his edition of Clausewitz's *Strategie*, and his article "Zur Genesis der modernen Kriegslehre," in the *Wehrwissenschaftliche Rundschau*.

times directly through the borrowings of historians to whom Clausewitz's manuscripts had been made available.[4]

Clausewitz is one of that small group of historians writing in the early years of the 19th century who had learned to treat political, diplomatic, and military events in analytic narratives, undidactically, with a feeling for the ways of practical life—often gained through personal experience—and a sense of the sources, but still without a comprehensive theoretical armory. He drew on letters, other unpublished material, and sometimes on conversations with participants when he worked on the recent past; but he relied primarily on printed documents and secondary sources. These he evaluated critically, comparing one with another, considering a statement's origin and purpose, and judging it in the light of experience and common sense. He tried to put himself in the position of the people he wrote about, although he knew that an approximation was the best that could be achieved. His constant discussion of alternatives open to governments and individuals is one expression of this effort. At the same time he sought to discover what almost always lay beyond the knowledge of the historical actor: the larger connection of events. This search for patterns and form reflected neither a teleological view of history nor the acceptance of a more or less mechanistic causality but his belief in the ultimate unity of all phenomena. An example of his manner of shaping interpretation and presentation of the material is his study of Scharnhorst, in which a few major issues—the relationship of a creative individual to society, to the state, to the changing and unchanging forces of his age—are carefully worked out. It is instructive to compare this essay with such characteristic biographies of the period as Varnhagen von Ense's *Biographische Denkmale,* whose anecdotal treatment of statesmen, scholars, and soldiers is usually structured around the single theme of the subject's success in life.

Clausewitz's historical writings can be divided into studies of wars in which he took part and those in which he did not, whether they occurred during his life or earlier; works that focus on institutions, politics, and the influence of personality rather than on military operations; and the extensive historical surveys, illustrations, and digressions contained in *On War.* One long manuscript does not fall within these categories: his analysis of the campaign of 1814, which, as its full title indicates, was intended as a "strategic critique" of the war. Clausewitz wrote the study at the time he resumed serious theoretical work after the Wars of Liberation, to test his conceptualizations against a chain of events on which he was thoroughly informed through conversations with Gneisenau and other participants. It is neither history nor theory but forms a transition between the two, and thus is best discussed after the true historical writings.

---

4. Clausewitz, *Nachrichten über Preussen,* introduction of the anonymous editor, p. 418.

Clausewitz's manuscript on Frederick the Great consists of short discussions of major issues in the first two Silesian Wars—campaign plans, fragmentation of forces, Austrian superiority in light troops, etc.—and of a chronologically structured treatment of the Seven Years' War.[5] Even this latter account, however, is essentially analytic rather than narrative. For each year of the war, the strengths and intentions of the opponents are outlined and compared; the ensuing discussion of the significant maneuvers, battles, and sieges of the campaign is interspersed with brief essays bearing such titles as "Numbers were less significant in the former tactical system than in today's tactics," "Consequences of a siege that is not preceded by a victorious battle," or "Envelopments." Clausewitz emphasized the distribution of forces, their assignments and movements, the personalities of their commanders, and the relationship between military action and political concerns. Here, as in most of his historical writing, he had relatively little to say about the fighting itself. As he noted repeatedly, the sparse and contradictory sources available on any war were especially unreliable when it came to battles. Besides, he argued, a battle was generally decided by factors external to it: numbers; the training, discipline, and morale of the troops; the function of the encounter in the opposing strategic plans; the character of the commanders. "Subtleties of elementary tactics," he thought, usually played a lesser role.[6] Consequently he eschewed detailed accounts of the behavior of units and individuals in combat. The anecdotes, suspense, and drama of battle descriptions, which form a staple of the literature, are largely missing in his histories, though *On War* contains graphic accounts of a typical modern—Napoleonic—battle, and close investigations into personality traits and their suitability to various aspects of war. What Clausewitz found impressive and important to understand in the Seven Years' War was above all the consequentiality and "naturalness" of Frederick's strategy—a term of approbation that recurs throughout his histories—and the close agreement between the king's political aims and military actions. Frederick exemplified the effectiveness with which genius could function even in unfavorable conditions; at the same time, Clausewitz freely criticized him for errors of planning and execution, which he ascribed in part to his passionate, stubborn nature. But though far from a blind admirer, Clausewitz did not share the sometimes emotional antagonism of many reformers, for whom Frederick was the symbol of the old Prussia that needed to be reshaped and modernized. He treated the king with the same sense of realism and objectivity with which he wrote about the Seven Years' War as a whole.

The study of the wars by which Prussia gained European stature bears the imprint of the work of a specialist, fully conversant with his subject,

5. "Die Feldzüge Friedrich des Grossen von 1741–1762," *Werke*, x, 29–254.
6. *Ibid.*, p. 91.

who assumes an almost equal familiarity on the part of the reader and feels free to compress his treatment of the essential facts in order to concentrate on analysis. The histories of the campaigns of 1796 and 1799 are far more descriptive. The major operations are explored in detail, and greater attention is paid not only to general political developments but also to the marches and expeditions of marginal significance, which were very frequent in the Italian wars. Clausewitz felt somewhat handicapped by the scarcity and inadequacy of his sources. He complained repeatedly of poor maps, confusing or contradictory accounts by other historians such as Jomini, and of the refusal of the Austrian government to publish documents clarifying the operational decisions and the underlying strategic and political deliberations. Whenever possible, in his analysis of accounts written by participants, he compared their reports and statements at the time with subsequent accounts, giving preference to the former when they disagreed. This seemed to him particularly necessary in the case of Napoleon, whose character was responsible for his military success but at the same time contributed to the obfuscation of the truth in his memoirs. "It is a sad necessity for us," Clausewitz wrote in his history of the campaign of 1796, "not to accept fully the commander's evaluation of his own decisions; and yet someone who seeks the truth must be genuinely convinced, and if he finds this conviction in the circumstances rather than in the commander's statement, he cannot sacrifice his opinion to the mere authority of the commander. Bonaparte wrote his memoirs fifteen or twenty years after the event and with reference to the criticisms of particular aspects of his campaigns with which he had become acquainted, for he seeks to refute them. Under these circumstances he is no longer unbiased, especially since he cannot tolerate any kind of censure and finds it quite impossible to admit mistakes, though other great generals have frequently been able to acknowledge their errors. For these reasons we must be very cautious in our use of his memoirs, and necessarily place greater reliance on contemporary sources and on the results that emerged from the circumstances and the course of events at the time." [7]

Napoleon's apologia provided only the most striking illustration of the weakness of memoirs as historical sources, and also of the relationship between a general's conduct and his subsequent analysis of events. In an examination of the reasons for Archduke Charles's failure to destroy the far weaker French army under Jourdan at the beginning of the campaign of 1799, Clausewitz wrote of the archduke: "First he lacks enterprise and the hunger for victory. Secondly, as we have already said, while his judgment is otherwise sound he has in the main a completely false idea of strategy: he

7. *Der Feldzug von 1796 in Italien; Werke,* iv, 342. Cf. the related statement on p. 334, and similar comments at the beginning of *Der Feldzug von 1815 in Frankreich; Werke,* viii, 8.

takes the means for the purpose, and the purpose for the means. In war everything should be done to bring about the destruction of the enemy's forces; but destruction does not exist as a separate task in his range of concepts; he accepts it only insofar as it is also a means of driving the enemy from this or that position. To him success is solely the occupation of certain positions and areas; but these cannot ever be anything but a means for achieving victory—that is, for destroying the physical and moral strength of the enemy. We can recognize how far the archduke pursues this false course from the fact that in his victorious battles his opponents never suffer a significant loss of prisoners and guns ... , but we can recognize it even more clearly in the failure of the archduke's accounts to mention enemy casualties in any battle at all." [8]

In short, through an element missing in his description and analysis, the archduke unconsciously reveals a central feature of his generalship. The historian, by recognizing and interpreting the negative evidence, transforms his treatment into a more accurate depiction of the reality of the campaign than is offered in the statements of those who fought in it.

Since his sources were sparse, Clausewitz found it easier to reach "genuine conviction" on strategy and generalship than on the events of a particular engagement, to which in any case, as I have suggested, he ascribed less significance. Some comments at the conclusion of his chapter on the battle of Arcola in November 1796 indicate his position: "In this survey of the battle we have included only matters contained in the accounts of Jomini and of [the Austrian] General Neiperg, or in the original reports of Bonaparte and Berthier, and we only arranged the existing data in such a way as to achieve the greatest possible coherence for the whole. Therefore we are far from believing that our depiction is necessarily true; when the data are so few and so confused, even the most careful comparison cannot guard against error, nor can even far greater discernment than we believe ourselves capable of save us from a totally false view of things. Still less do we think that our narrative renders the development of the various incidents completely natural and comprehensible. On the contrary, we ourselves find a number of things quite inexplicable—for example, the employment of entire brigades and divisions on the causeways. Most probably the ground on either side was not as impassable as was the case in the Dutch inundations in the campaigns of 1672 and 1787, but firm in some places. Only a very accurate map, or one's own inspection of the area, can clarify this point. The plan used by General Jomini, on which we have based our description, is barely adequate, better suited to obscure than to explain the

---

8. *Die Feldzüge von 1799 in Italien und der Schweiz,* part I; *Werke,* v, 152–153. Some years earlier, in *On War,* book VI, ch. 16 (p. 615), Clausewitz had praised Charles as being "a good historian, a good critic, and above all a good commander in one."

matter. Nevertheless the battle developed more or less as the various reports state; consequently local circumstances must have made this course of events possible, and that must satisfy us.

"It is quite different with the decisions of the two commanders. Occasionally these, too, might have been modified slightly by minor circumstances of which we know nothing, but their main features can derive only from the overall conditions at the time, and it is thus a natural demand of our intelligence to conceive of these decisions as existing in some kind of conceptual connection with those conditions." [9]

Thus even in the expanded, detailed narratives of the campaigns of 1796 and 1799, Clausewitz's treatment of the course of operations is analytic in the true sense of the term. Consequently no break occurs between the sections on marches and battles, and those dealing with strategic and political decisions. The historian investigates and interprets every aspect of his subject with the same questions in mind: What are the external and the psychological conditions of the act described? What is the real purpose of the act, whether it be a patrol or an entire war? What are the means available to achieve the purpose? What are the characteristics of these means? And how well do the commanders, officers, and soldiers, as well as their governments, master the means and comprehend the purpose?

Two examples of strategic and political analysis will illustrate the supple precision of historical inquiry and interpretation that Clausewitz had attained in his maturity. The first is the evaluation of the last phase of the war of 1796, a French offensive from the Venetian plain into the Tyrol, with which his study of this war concludes. Clausewitz notes that one's view of the strength and weakness of a strategic constellation must vary according to one's own situation and intentions. He develops this idea by arranging the reality and assumptions of the French and Austrian commands into a series of concentric circles, beginning with the narrow compass of Napoleon's Army of Italy: "When Bonaparte crossed the Julian Alps, his situation appeared extremely dangerous if there was reason to believe that in Styria the Austrians were assembling superior forces to defeat him. But if the horizon expands and we know that these forces do not exist, the danger disappears, and now it is the Austrians who are threatened by defeat under the walls of Vienna, if they still wish to risk a battle to save their capital. The Army of Italy approaches like a storm cloud. If, however, we expand our view still further and delay the decisive battle—waging it not to save the capital but to win the war—then it becomes immediately apparent that the French army is too weak. Considering that army in isolation, it is seen to face disaster simply because the decision has been delayed. The probability of ultimate success is now against the French. However, if we

9. *Der Feldzug von 1796; Werke,* iv, 225–226.

do not limit our evaluation to this single army, but expand it to include the two French armies on the Rhine, we discover such a degree of French superiority that it seems inevitable for the fighting to shift from the Rhine to the interior of Austria. Now the inadequacy of the Army of Italy is made up for by the superiority of the other two armies. An invasion of all three forces toward the heart of the monarchy is no longer beyond their strength, and that is the threat now facing Austria.

"The Austrian government may regard this invasion as a danger that should be avoided, if possible, by quickly making peace. But if this is not their attitude, the French will have to regard the invasion merely as a means to achieve a further purpose. If we suppose this further purpose to be the total defeat of the Austrian state—that is, if the invasion is continued to the eastern frontier in order to defeat the last Austrian forces there—the outcome, the probability of ultimate success, will change again. For all our recent experiences tell us that as long as the Austrian population remains loyal to its rulers, the French forces would be too weak for such an enterprise, and the forward movement of the invasion would by itself bring about a reversal. But if we also consider a second possibility, that the French do not push their invasion to the far borders of the empire but come to a halt earlier, then the Austrians can no longer hope for an inevitable reversal, because now the French would have time to bring up the necessary reinforcements. Even under these conditions the probability of final victory rests with the Austrians, but it would require great sacrifice, appropriate effort, and activity.

"Among these different options, the reality of the situation will determine the particular position from which the strategic issue is to be judged. Either one cannot see beyond a certain line, which was Bonaparte's situation when he crossed the Julian Alps, or the ultimate object in view, on which all lines of action should concentrate, has supreme significance—which, for example, the protection of Vienna or preventing an invasion might have had for the Austrians. In 1814 and 1815 the occupation of Paris possessed such supreme significance, and Paris necessarily formed the focus on which all strategic lines converged.

"If the significance is so overwhelming that the peace terms with which the evil can be averted do not constitute too high a price, then simple logic must lead to peace.

"Whether this significance is recognized or not, and how it is interpreted, will affect our evaluation of the final consequences of a strategic plan. That character and emotions, which play such a great role in war, also greatly influence judgment on the highest level of reflection is self-evident. A firm, courageous individual will judge his situation differently than will the timid. That is especially true of men who must act. Among those who merely judge—in particular in the tribe of authors, where everyone is courageous and firm—differences of opinion usually are caused by a misunderstanding of the conditions that prevailed, often from an absence of data, still more often from an absence of the genuine spirit of critical analysis." [10]

The second, briefer illustration of Clausewitz's method of interpretation is a passage from the last chapter of his history of the war of 1799, in which he reflects on the ultimate reasons for the breakdown of the collaboration between Austria and her allies. After tracing them to Austria's secret political aims, which also inhibited her operations in Italy, he launches into a series of generalizations on the difficulties of political leadership in war before returning to the specific conditions of 1799, which he hopes are now better understood: "Ministers and policy advisers never clearly see the effect that their decisions have in the theater of operations. But in war more than elsewhere, purpose and means exist in permanent *reciprocal relationship*. However valid it is for political intentions to give events their initial direction, the means—that is, fighting—can never be regarded as an inanimate instrument. Out of the rich vitality of war grow a thousand new motives, which may become more significant and dominant than the original political considerations. War resembles a ship contending against storm and waves. One must be aboard to steer it competently, to take advantage of the elements, and so complete the journey as well as may be. If, in addition, we recall that most well-conducted wars in the past were waged on the basis of the *subjective convictions* of the commanders, and how few clear conceptions of grand strategy existed before today; when we further consider that a *government official* other than the commander, not stationed in the theater of war, who wants to influence the conduct of operations regularly, must have sound ideas on strategy because from a distance he can only consider the issues objectively [i.e., unaffected by the subjective impressions gained from fighting]—when all this is kept in mind we cannot be surprised to find that in this war the measures of the Austrian government constantly skirted the edge of disaster." [11]

This was very different from the usual campaign narrative of the time, and objections were voiced when the manuscripts were published soon after Clausewitz's death. The most severe condemnation was contained in two long reviews of the histories of 1796 and 1799, signed "Al....," which appeared in the *Oestreichische militärische Zeitschrift*, the principal service journal of the Habsburg monarchy. [12] The anonymous author's dislike of Clau-

10. *Ibid.*, pp. 351–354. Cf. the preliminary study of the last phase of the campaign of 1796–97 in *On War*, book II, ch. 5 (pp. 215–218).

11. *Die Feldzü*ge von 1799, part II; *Werke*, vi, 382.

12. Al....., "Der Feldzug 1796 in Italien. Hinterlassenes Werk des Generals Karl von Clausewitz. Berlin, 1833," *Oestreichische militärische Zeitschrift* (Vienna, 1834), no. 7, pp. 67–96; "Die Feldzüge von 1799 in Italien und der Schweiz. Hinterlassenes Werk des Generalen [*sic!*] Karl von Clausewitz. 2

sewitz's method was intensified by his pain at the criticism to which the Austrian army and especially Archduke Charles were subjected. He claimed that Clausewitz had worked from inadequate sources—though the additional titles he suggested were either irrelevant to Clausewitz's purpose or appeared after the manuscripts had been concluded—and accused him of almost plagiaristic reliance on Jomini. The article on 1799 observed that "from a historian who pieces together a new work out of printed studies, a third book from two others, one naturally cannot expect to gain more factual enlightenment than was already offered by his predecessors." [13] In his earlier review the critic characterized Clausewitz's work as sparing with facts and largely analytic: "The reader is to be relieved of the effort of studying the evidence, and thus tracing the connection between events and finding the causes of decisions for himself." [14] Clausewitz's comments on Austrian policy and generalship were labeled insulting and degrading: "With the certainty of a professor who leads his students across the bridge to mathematical wisdom by demonstrating the Pythagorean theorem for the twentieth time—dictatorial, with rare confidence in the infallibility of his statements—General Clausewitz accompanies every order of the Austrian commander with his unreserved disapproval." [15]

It is not surprising that the reviewer found it difficult to tolerate Clausewitz's matter-of-fact conviction that in Italy, Napoleon and the French were superior to Charles and the Austrians, the more so since he was able to show that Clausewitz had committed some errors of detail; but he was also troubled by the absence of the customary didactic material. Clausewitz's books on the wars of 1796 and 1799 did not contain what he expected from military history; indeed, his expectations were so pronounced that he imputed doctrinal intent where none existed. Citing a statement in which Clausewitz weighed the options open to an advancing army that is itself attacked, he commented scornfully: "It must be feared that this regulation provides little help for action in an individual case." [16] It was a

Theile. Berlin, 1833," *ibid.,* (Vienna, 1835), nos. 5 & 6, pp. 200–216, 304–334. Without identifying the reviews, Marie v. Clausewitz mentions them in her introduction to the seventh volume of Clausewitz's *Werke,* 1835, pp. vii–viii. See also C. v. d. Gröben's comment in his introduction to the ninth and tenth volumes, *Werke,* ix, 1837, pp. xiv–xv. Simultaneously with these reviews, the *Oestreichische militärische Zeitschrift* (1834, no. 2; 1835, nos. 5, 11, & 12) printed a very positive discussion of the first volume of *On War* by Gebler, a junior officer on the Austrian general staff. It is an interesting indication of the rapidity with which Clausewitz's reputation grew that the hostile reviewer, writing in the summer of 1834, already refers to Clausewitz as a "celebrity in the military literature."

13. Al....., "1799," *Oestreichische militärische Zeitschrift,* 1835, no. 6, p. 333.
14. Al....., "1796," *ibid.,* 1834, no. 7, p. 67.
15. Al....., "1799," *ibid.,* 1835, no. 5, p. 210.
16. Al....., "1796," *ibid.,* 1834, no. 7, p. 72. The reviewer's strictures on Clausewitz's inaccuracies notwithstanding, a comparison with the chapters on the wars of 1796 and 1799 in D. Chandler's *The Campaigns of Napoleon,* New York, 1966, shows Clausewitz's account of the operations and his statistics to be in general agreement with those of the modern work.

misreading that foreshadowed a century and a half of misinterpretations of Clausewitz by those who searched his writings for answers to their specific operational and tactical problems.

The wish to understand events, rather than to prescribe doctrine, does not assure accuracy of interpretation; neither does impartiality, which in the case of the Franco-Austrian conflicts may have been easier for Clausewitz to maintain than for his Viennese critic. They are helpful attributes, nevertheless, and it must be noted that the same objectivity of tone and method, even toward events that touched Clausewitz personally, marks his histories of 1812, 1813, and 1815. These works have already been referred to in the chapter "Napoleon's Destruction," and it will be sufficient here to add a few comments on the most mature and unified interpretation of the three, the history of 1815. Clausewitz himself had fought throughout the Waterloo campaign, his nearest friend had played a decisive role in its strategic and operational crises, any number of relatives and associates had taken part in the climactic struggle with the emperor, whose genius and boundless aggressiveness had dominated much of Clausewitz's life and thought.

Nevertheless, his study remains detached, objective, its author never shedding his willingness to give the benefit of the doubt to men acting under great difficulties. More even than in his analysis of Napoleon, this refusal to see events through spectacles of national or personal preconceptions is apparent in his treatment of Wellington's failure to assist Blücher at the battle of Ligny, after having given a qualified promise to do so. The episode caused bad feelings among many contemporaries and remained a major issue for later German historians; but Clausewitz barely mentioned it. He expressed himself puzzled by the broad dispersal of the Anglo-Dutch army, but added that the duke must have had his reasons; perhaps the fact that he had never faced Napoleon in person explains why he did not expect the French to concentrate in force against one point in the allied positions. His vague promise on the 16th of June to support the Prussians within a few hours could have referred only to a small part of his army; the Prussians erred in thinking that Napoleon would not divert some troops against Wellington, and in counting on Wellington's help.[17] Insufficient information makes firm judgment on specific decisions difficult and sometimes impossible; on many essentials, he wrote, there is still as little known about the Waterloo campaign as about wars in the 17th century. But even under the most favorable circumstances, the historian would find judging men's behavior nearly as doubtful an enterprise as offering them instruction: both can easily interfere with true understanding. His critique of the battle of Ligny gave him the opportunity to repeat this belief in terms reminiscent

17. *Der Feldzug von 1815 in Frankreich; Werke,* viii, 29–35, 64, 67–68.

of the fuller statements in such works as the history of 1812 or *On War:* "It hardly needs observing that today, with maps and surveys of every kind in front of us, and with the events behind us, it may be easy to discover the reasons for the [Prussian] failure and to emphasize those reasons that were recognized as mistakes after we have thought through all the complexities of the episode; but at the time this could not be as simple. Action in war resembles movement in an impeding element; uncommon qualities are needed to attain even average results. Therefore, in war more than elsewhere criticism exists only to recognize the truth, not to act as judge." [18]

Objectivity of interpretation extended not only to difficult allies but also to one's enemies. Clausewitz's hatred of the cruelties and aggressiveness that were part of the French Revolution and of French imperialism under Napoleon was accompanied, as we know, by a sense of the historical processes that had led to the upheaval, and by admiration for the energies and genius for which the Revolution had paved the way. Certainly after 1815 his personal dislikes very rarely surface in his treatment of French history. A passage in his essay on Scharnhorst exemplifies his dispassionate concentration on the point that seemed to him to be essential: "The old military system had collapsed in the wars of the French Revolution; its forms and means were no longer appropriate to the changed times and new political ways. That lesson everyone had been taught by the French sword. As usually happens in such situations, feelings outstripped fact, and faith in the old system was undermined even more than reality justified. The revolutionary methods of the French had attacked the traditional instruments of warfare like acid; they had freed the tremendous element of war from its ancient diplomatic and economic bonds. Now war stepped forth in all its raw violence, dragging along an immense accumulation of power, and nothing met the eye but ruins of the traditional art of war on the one hand, and incredible successes on the other. ... War was returned to the people, who to some extent had been separated from it by the professional standing armies; war cast off its shackles and crossed the bounds of what had once seemed possible." [19]

By the time Clausewitz came to write *On War,* this interpretation had led to a theoretical conclusion: "War . . . again became the concern of the people as a whole, took on an entirely different character, *or rather closely approached its true nature, its absolute perfection* [my italics]. There seemed no end to the resources mobilized; all limits disappeared in the vigor and enthusiasm shown by governments and their subjects. ... War, untrammeled

---

18. *Ibid.,* p. 94.
19. "Über das Leben und den Charakter von Scharnhorst," *Historisch-politische Zeitschrift,* I, 196. The third sentence in the passage, concerning the tendency of men to react unthinkingly, expresses a belief of Clausewitz's that played a role in his historical interpretations. It is discussed below, pp. 349–350.

by any conventional restraints, had broken loose in all its elemental fury." [20]

Napoleon he admired for perfecting—as he put it—the military and political innovations of the Revolution; indeed, in contrast to Scharnhorst, Clausewitz showed more interest in the man than in the Revolution. To him the emperor was the contemporary who best personified military and political genius, who most clearly recognized the realities of the age, and therefore was able to a degree to liberate himself from their constraints. He was also the man whose defeat was the supreme illustration of the fallibility of genius—that is, of its general human characteristics. Clausewitz noted Napoleon's occasional inefficiencies, his inability as time went on to read the intentions of his opponents, his dishonesty and vanity; but he never questioned his supremacy. This fact seemed so self-evident that it did not require stressing; he expressed it casually, almost marginally, as something that goes without saying. In a study of 17th-century warfare, for example, he praised the conduct of the French Marshal Turenne, but added that his strategy would have proved disastrous 150 years later: "What would Bonaparte have done—or, not to choose the very best—what would Blücher have done if he had confronted Turenne with the concepts and methods of our own days?" [21]

The histories of the great conflicts of the Frederician and Napoleonic eras constitute major investments of their author's time and intellectual energy. They are complemented by the large number of shorter studies of campaigns and entire wars that Clausewitz wrote, from the days when he was a student at Scharnhorst's Institute almost to the end of his life. Sometimes these were little more than outlines, designed to strengthen the writer's command of the material course of events—the thirteen pages on the Russo-Turkish War in the 1730's, for example, or the two slightly longer surveys of the wars of Louis XIV and of the uprising of the Vendée against the French Republic. [22] More extensive studies of the campaigns of Turenne and Luxembourg examine particular features of the strategy and tactics of the time, which are frequently contrasted with practices of the Frederician and Napoleonic periods. [23] Other essays attempt to bring out clearly one particular aspect of war. The short study on the wars of Sobiesky

---

20. *On War*, book VIII, ch. 3B (p. 870). The image of war, freed from its chains, moving in its natural, raw force or crossing Europe like a wild, unshackled element, occurs in other manuscripts as well—for instance, in the memorandum of 1818 on Motz's project of a territorial exchange, and in the essay of the following year, "Unsere Kriegsverfassung."

21. "Turenne," *Werke*, ix, 228.

22. "Übersicht der Kriege unter Ludwig XIV.," *Werke*, ix, 126–152; "Krieg der Russen gegen die Türken von 1736–1739," and "Übersicht des Krieges in der Vendée," *Werke*, x, 15–28, 321–348. Even these surveys range beyond the geographic and military data to touch on the character and attitudes of the populations and armies, and on the personalities of the commanders.

23. "Turenne," and "Die Feldzüge Luxemburgs in Flandern von 1690–1694," *Werke*, ix, 153–228, 229–272.

against the Turks, for instance, which Clausewitz wrote sometime during the last two years of his life, takes as its theme strategies that seek the destruction of the enemy armies. "We should like to say," Clausewitz wrote, "that the intelligent use of the decisive battle has never been demonstrated more clearly than in this war." [24] By contrast, the detailed study of the militarily uneventful Prussian expedition in Holland shortly before the French Revolution is a thorough exploration of the characteristics of limited war. Clausewitz's account of the operations is preceded by an analysis of the internal conflict in the Netherlands, and of the attitude of the foreign powers to the Patriot movement and the Orange party; the conclusion suggests the reasons why this obscure episode seemed to him of great historical and theoretical interest: "Without the survey of political conditions that we have attempted here, the campaign of 1787, and especially its strategic features, would be incomprehensible. Every war simply continues the threads of political intercourse between peoples and between states, and no war can be fully understood if we do not pay attention to its political context. But this is especially true if, as in the present case, the political conditions are far removed from sharp antagonism, and the war itself is more than commonly interwoven with threads of peace." [25]

The objectivity that characterizes the military histories of Clausewitz's maturity had become so much part of his method that the equally detached reader soon takes this dispassion for granted. It appears to be neither unusual nor difficult to attain. The texts reveal no struggle on the author's part to be evenhanded, no sign of the grudging or defensive recognition that there may be two sides to a question; the effort to achieve insight, to progress from lesser to greater understanding of reality, pervades his organizing and analyzing of the data. Partisanship has faded as an issue of historical interpretation. Nothing like that can be said of the *Observations on Prussia in Her Great Catastrophe* or of the essay on Scharnhorst. Here Clausewitz is not seeking knowledge; he already knows everything that really matters to him, and his purpose is to review his opinions and present them to his readers as forcefully and persuasively as he can.

The *Observations* seek to demonstrate that the Frederician state could not have continued unchanged, that Prussian absolutism had corrupted the good sense and creative energies of society to such an extent that for the

---

24. "Sobiesky," *Werke,* x, 1–14. The quotation is from p. 6.
25. "Der Feldzug des Herzogs von Braunschweig gegen die Holländer 1787," *Werke,* x, 255–320. The quotation is from p. 267. It is not known when Clausewitz wrote this study. Caemmerer, p. 77, suggests that it may have been one of his earliest works, which is conceivable since the single source mentioned in the text was published in 1790. However, tone and style, as well as the author's interest in the problem of limited war, suggest a later date. It would be surprising to find the young Clausewitz state the connection between war and politics as firmly and definitively as he does in the passage cited above. See also the references to the 1787 campaign in *On War,* for instance, book VII, ch. 14 (pp. 799–800).

sake of both individual and state it had to be abolished. The essay on Scharnhorst offers a firm defense of the reform program that was launched after 1807, and of the character of its military leader. The *Observations,* especially, are polemical, with sarcastic descriptions of men and institutions; nothing restrains the author from moral judgments and condemnations expressed in language so strong that the work remained unpublished until the Wilhelmine period. The essay on Scharnhorst, although couched in more reserved terms, presumably because it was written for immediate publication in 1818, is equally subjective in its basic attitude.

Clausewitz wrote a first draft of the *Observations* between 1824 and 1825, and revised it in 1828 after he had once more visited the battlefields of Jena and Auerstedt. He intended the manuscript to form part of a longer work—never completed—which was to extend from 1805 through the campaigns of 1806 and 1807 to the dismemberment of the state, and perhaps even through the reform era and the Restoration to Hardenberg's death.[26] The published version, 120 pages long, is divided into four chapters: (1) "Some Glances at the Spirit of the Army and the Government," (2) "Characteristics of the Most Important Personalities," (3) "Causes of the War, and Preparations for It," and (4) "The Campaign of 1806." Clausewitz drew on numerous German and French sources, though he did not use all that were available, particularly in his account of the fighting, in which he seems to have relied to a considerable extent on his own recollections and on talks with other participants. Nevertheless, his treatment of the complex autumn campaign is shown to be remarkably accurate when tested against the French and Prussian army documents, which were published after his death. Some of his strength figures, march distances, and dates were incorrect, and his strategic commentary was necessarily subjective; but his grasp of the strategic essentials of the campaign and of the psychology of the Prussian commanders and their troops has never been surpassed.[27]

26. *Nachrichten über Preussen in seiner grossen Katastrophe; Kriegsgeschichtliche Einzelschriften,* x, Berlin, 1888. On Clausewitz's plans for a longer history of Prussia, see the unsigned editorial introduction, *ibid.,* p. 418, and the note by Rothfels in his edition of Clausewitz's *Politische Schriften und Briefe,* pp. 244–245.

27. In his introduction to the *Nachrichten* the anonymous member of the Historical Section of the Great General Staff who edited the manuscript for publication refers to minor factual errors committed by Clausewitz and corrects them in footnotes throughout the work. Some of his emendations are justified, but by no means all, as is indicated by a comparison with O. v. Lettow-Vorbeck's definitive study, *Der Krieg von 1806 und 1807,* 4 vols. Berlin, 1891–96, which appeared some years later and made use of the French documents that had been published in the interval. In general, Clausewitz appears to have slightly overestimated Prussian strengths and underestimated the number of French troops, no doubt to emphasize the debility of the Prussian system and leaders, while his editor tends to do the reverse. The following representative examples suggest the essential accuracy of Clausewitz's interpretation: Clausewitz accuses the Prussians of mismanaging the two opening engagements of the campaign. He blames the commander of one force, General Tauenzien, for the first defeat; his editor (*Nachrichten,* p. 496, n. 1) justifies Tauenzien; Lettow-Vorbeck, i, 213, holds Tauenzien responsible. Clausewitz condemns Prince Louis Ferdinand's generalship in the second engagement; his editor (*Nachrichten,* p. 499, n. 2; p. 500, n. 1) argues that Louis Ferdinand acted correctly and that Clausewitz's figure of 10,000 men for

A comparison of the fourth chapter, "The Campaign of 1806," with his articles on the same subject published in *Minerva* only a few months after the battles reveals a striking difference: the articles that the young officer wrote at a time when he was despairing over his state were far less critical, certainly less openly emotional, than was the analysis of two decades later.[28] No doubt the articles were intended to be published at once, and Clausewitz was not the man to join in the invective and accusations of such Prussians as Massenbach, Scharnhorst's fellow general-quartermaster. But no pamphlet or article of the time was as damning as Clausewitz's interpretation in the 1820's, and the text does not hide its author's disgust at the confusion and lack of realism in large matters and small that pushed the Prussian army into disaster.

This attitude is supported by careful analyses of institutions and personalities, and expressed in a biting, frequently epigrammatic style. The initial discussion of the army, "which more than any other institution had succumbed to the lassitude of tradition and detail," piles one antithesis on another: "In the Berlin armory the artillery equipment was stored with such care that every last rope and nail was at hand; but ropes and nails were equally useless. The soldier's weapon was kept scrupulously clean, barrels painstakingly polished with the ramrod, stocks varnished every year; but the muskets were the worst in Europe. The soldier was never in arrears in pay and clothing; but the pay was not sufficient to satisfy his hunger, the clothes did not cover him." The result of assigning overage veterans to important posts was summed up in this way: "The senior engineer officers and the fortress commandants were as decrepit as most of their fortresses." The army's tactical system, with its preoccupation with terrain features, was characterized as one in which "the army was married, so to say, to the ground. The battalion defends the hill; the hill defends the battalion." The stages by which the original plan for the Prussian offensive in 1806 was

the Prussian force is too high; Lettow-Vorbeck, i, 226, 239, writes that the prince was temperamentally unsuited to fight a cautious advance-guard action, and gives his strength as 9,700 men. Clausewitz states that Napoleon had no more than 60,000 men in action in the battle of Jena; according to his editor (*Nachrichten,* p. 505, n. 1), this should be over 78,000 men; Lettow-Vorbeck, i, 371, n. 1, accepts the French figure of 54,050. The Prussians were certainly outnumbered at Jena, but Clausewitz's editor (*Nachrichten,* p. 512, n. 1) appears to place more confidence in the self-justifying estimates of the Prussian commanders than in Clausewitz's somewhat higher totals, while Lettow-Vorbeck, i, 371, n. 1, writes that Prussian estimates were "far too low." Clausewitz claims that at the battle of Auerstedt 50,000 Prussians faced 25,000 Frenchmen, a figure that in the course of the battle rose to 27,000 (*Nachrichten,* pp. 434, 517). His editor adjusts this to 48,000 against 33,000; Lettow-Vorbeck, i, 400, estimates 48,000 and 26,300, etc. See also the favorable comments on Clausewitz's interpretation by Schlieffen in his long study "1806," *Gesammelte Schriften,* Berlin, 1913, ii, 167–168, 180, 190–192.

28. Clausewitz also changed his opinion on the strategic possibilities of the main Prussian position at Jena. In his articles he argued that even at the last moment a Prussian attack across the Saale River against the advancing French might have succeeded. Twenty years later he believed that a defensive followed by a counterattack held out the most promise.

reduced to impotence and passivity were described as the plan's medical history, the body that brought about the change as the headquarters-congress, and so forth.[29]

It accords with this manner of treating institutions and events that the description of individuals, too, becomes intensely personal. The most detailed portrait in the *Observations* has already been mentioned—the analysis of Prince Louis Ferdinand.[30] In spite of his weaknesses, the prince seemed more sympathetic to Clausewitz than did most of Prussia's leading figures because he was energetic and enthusiastic, and rebelled, though vainly, against his environment. Clausewitz showed less tolerance for those who felt at ease in the Prussia before Jena. His characterization of a senior general, Ernst von Rüchel, contains this passage: "Frederick the Great was his every third word. The spirit that the old king raised to dominance after the Seven Years' War and in Potsdam personally infused into the army—a certain sternness and precision, which occasionally picks on an insignificant detail to show that nothing is being overlooked, a certain thunder-and-lightning military rhetoric—all this was exaggerated almost to the point of caricature in Rüchel. He was not without superficial polish and learning, read whatever notable was being published, had himself appointed head of the cadet corps, joined a learned military society founded by Scharnhorst, and his writings were full of imagination and energetic rhetoric. But he lacked the capacity for solid, orderly thought to such an extent that what he wrote was nearly always absurd. Of course he had not seriously followed the changes in the art of war, and was convinced that courageous and determined Prussian troops, employing Frederician tactics, could overrun everything that had emerged from the unsoldierly French Revolution. ... General Rüchel might have been termed a concentrated distillate of pure Prussianism." [31]

The foreign minister, Count Haugwitz, Clausewitz dismissed as "a short man of some fifty years, with pleasant features and agreeable manners that expressed superficiality, irresponsibility, falseness, but these blended so perfectly with the man's calm, gentlemanly behavior that there was nothing comic about him. Such was his demeanor; and that was also his personality." [32] The not unfavorable description of Lombard, one of the king's cabinet-councillors, began: "He was a member of the French [Huguenot] colony [in Berlin], and of low birth. His father had been a wig-maker. He married the daughter of a regimental-surgeon. As is well known, in the old Prussian army men of this calling began their careers as

29. *Nachrichten*, pp. 425, 426, 442, 447, 482.
30. See p. 108 above.
31. *Nachrichten*, p. 435. See also the comment on Rüchel in *On War*, book II, ch. 4 (p. 209).
32. *Nachrichten*, p. 448.

company surgeons and barbers. This caused Lombard one day to make fun of his wife, who was somewhat more sensitive about matters of background than he, by asking her: 'Quel vers préférez-vous, ma chère? "L'hirondelle d'une aile rapide frise la surface des eaux" ou "... rase la surface des eaux?" Le premier me rappelle mon père, et le second le tien.' I relate this anecdote because it helps to characterize the man." [33]

Finally, the king himself, more aware of the state's problems than many of his officials, but incapable of resolute decision and action, was introduced with these words: "Frederick William III, from youth distinguished for his serious and firm principles, had too little trust in his own abilities and the abilities of others, was too full of that cold, Nordic sense of doubt that undermines the spirit of enterprise, opposes enthusiasm, and inhibits every kind of creativity." At this point the tense changes into the present: "His invincible tendency to doubt everything points his accurate intelligence and powers of observation narrowly toward human weaknesses and imperfections, which he soon perceives. As a result his lack of confidence almost turns into contempt of mankind." [34]

In Clausewitz's view, these men were less the leaders than the victims of a system no longer in accord with its social and international environment. Some of the most important sections of his work analyze the nature of Prussian government at the time, the interpretation moving back and forth between institutions and inviduals. Clausewitz concluded that the system could never work unless the man at its head was a true autocrat. But even that was no longer adequate in the 1790's, in the face of French expansion and social change at home: "The state had almost doubled in size, the variety and complexity of social conditions and of social demands had greatly increased, and not everyone could reign like Frederick the Great." [35] Lacking such a ruler, it was preferable to govern with a cabinet of responsible ministers who could not simply be dictated to.[36] Further reforms were needed, although they might not have prevented a defeat: "Major changes in the laws and in the organization of government could hardly be expected in such a brief and critical period [the years between Frederick William III's accession and the war of 1806]. In fact, significant changes would have risked creating dissatisfaction at home, which could not have been resolved in time, and which would have been dangerous when the support of all segments and classes of the population was essential." Nevertheless, the first chapter concludes, a responsible ministry, improvements in the bureaucracy and army, and the willingness to resort to

33. *Ibid.*, p. 450.
34. *Ibid.*, p. 422.
35. *Ibid.*, p. 422.
36. *Nachrichten*, p. 423.

exceptional measures to defend the state would have made it possible "*to exist with honor or to succumb with honor.*"[37]

The portraits of Prussia's political and military elite in chapter 2 are followed in the third chapter by an analysis of the diplomatic background of the war, which stresses Prussia's ambiguous situation—that of a power of the second rank acting as a major power. Such an artificial position could be maintained only by flexible and opportunistic policies, but "the necessary energy for deceit and cunning, for consequential dishonesty, was lacking." [38]

Clausewitz ended his discussion of Prussia's diplomacy by restating the concluding argument of the first chapter in terms of foreign policy: "No matter how difficult the political role of a state that finds itself in the ranks of far stronger nations, and regardless of how difficult the condition of Europe ever since the French Revolution advanced on its destructive course with a hitherto unheard-of degree of state power, Prussia's despairing position in 1806 was due entirely to her own poor policies. Perhaps the most effective policies could not have prevented her collapse, but defeat would have been accompanied with more honor, respect, and sympathy, which together with the greater expenditure of her energies would have prepared a better basis for future resurgence." [39]

The bias that is evident in Clausewitz's treatment of Prussia's leaders and their policies fades when he comes to analyze the character—not the effectiveness—of the state's institutions, and disappears entirely in his historical interpretation of the institutions' antecedents. He regarded the Frederician system in itself as neither good nor bad; in the middle of the century it had demonstrated its effectiveness and then had become outdated. Ideas on social structure or on military organization and doctrine were in his eyes equally lacking in the absolute quality of being right or wrong; what he tried to establish was the degree to which they suited their conditions and how adaptable they proved. Unlike a Burke or a Thomas Paine, he did not resort to an ideological standard in his writings about the past. Conversely his essentially historicist position did not make him a conservative in contemporary affairs; his concern for the diplomatic and military efficiency of any political community saw to that, as did his profound empathy with the many men on all social levels about whom he wrote. That he did not consider the past either as a model or as a warning example to the present emerges with particular clarity from his more extensive historical surveys—for instance, from the longest historical interpolation in *On War,* the outline tracing the development of political societies and their military institu-

37. *Ibid.,* p. 431.
38. *Ibid.,* p. 455.
39. *Ibid.,* pp. 465–466.

tions from nomadic tribes to nation-states that he included in his discussion on the relationship between purpose and effort in war.[40] No value judgments are offered; no ideological praise or criticism is accorded to any system. On the contrary, the eleven-page essay is marked by such passages as this comment on the failure of medieval German emperors to combine their repeated invasions of Italy with efforts to gain true control of the country: "It would be easy to regard these [expeditions] as a chronic error, a delusion born of the spirit of the times; but there would be more sense in attributing them to a host of major causes, which we may possibly assimilate intellectually [*in die wir uns allenfalls hineindenken können*], but whose dynamic we will never comprehend as clearly as did the men who were actually obliged to contend with them." [41] Observations such as these suggest the extent to which Clausewitz himself had assimilated the historicist approach.

His ideological and historical detachment seems to be linked with his view that all societies are made up largely of individuals who cannot rise above fashion and the forces of circumstance. He obviously believed that most men, even those who were principled and industrious, lacked the ability to think critically, and he expected no greater understanding from particular groups, corporative bodies, or classes in society. Neither the landed gentry, nor the officer corps, nor the enlightened bourgeoisie, nor the free peasants as a group are ever depicted in his writings as possessing explicit or implicit insights on which the political community could rely. On the contrary, their susceptibility to fashion, to form rather than substance, was an important part of the destructive inertia that he identified repeatedly in the history of societies. He found it entirely understandable—indeed, to be expected—that in the last decades of the 18th-century Prussian society, its government and its army gradually degenerated, that its institutional machinery shriveled up, as he put it. But the decline, though perhaps inevitable, need not be accepted, either by the young officer in prewar Berlin or by the mature man who set about writing the history of those years.

Crises also provided opportunities for the exceptional individual to reverse the process and lead society toward new goals. That juncture—the encounter between the average man and the reformer—was one of the two main themes of Clausewitz's essay on Scharnhorst, the other being the mystery of a creative, fundamentally uncompromising and yet politically effective personality. The essay, thirty-five pages in print, is divided into two parts: the first outlines Scharnhorst's life and career; the second, almost equally long, is entitled "Characterization of Scharnhorst," and contains

40. *On War*, book VIII, ch. 3B (pp. 860–871).
41. *Ibid.*, p. 863.

sections on his mind and his theories, on his emotions, his character, and finally a discussion of Scharnhorst the soldier, with which the whole work is once again brought to an abrupt end.[42] The text is filled with references to the envy, opposition, and intrigues that Scharnhorst encountered "as was to be expected," to "the great mass that did not appreciate his unshowy genius" or that "constantly misjudged him," to "obstacles that true innovation meets everywhere," to mankind, "which loves to attire its mind like its body with shiny fashions; when for once men find themselves in the situation of having to acquire ideas from someone else they prefer those that they believe will *suit their features,*" and to Scharnhorst's own conviction that "most people can be floated off the sandbank of their prejudices only by imperceptible levers." [43] It was Scharnhorst's ability to educate society without its being aware of it—for instance, letting men gradually accustom themselves to the idea of the *Landwehr*—that made his success possible. Clausewitz naturally saw this achievement as largely political in nature. In the six-year-long crisis after Jena, he wrote, Scharnhorst "may be regarded as the core and fulcrum of political resistance, as the seed and the most vitally creative force for spreading the ideals and attitudes of citizenship. The rebirth of the Prussian army, the bringing together of the various classes of society, the creation of the *Landwehr,* the tenacious resistance to the defeatism of the times and the mistrust of the parties, are so many anchors that this able pilot tossed into the threatening seas, anchors that enable the royal vessel to defy the storms that now broke out." [44]

Clausewitz's estimation of the great majority of mankind as fad-ridden and unreflective contributed to his already unteleological view of the past. He rejected the claim that history expressed ethical or ideological progress—a denial that, no doubt, had emotional as well as intellectual roots; but perhaps his intense concern with the specifics of effectiveness and failure in particular situations was itself enough to rule out a belief in overarching trends of social and political morality. Certainly they played no part in his interpretations. The survey of political societies in *On War,* which I have already mentioned, concludes with the thought that the politicization of society which had taken such a long step forward in the French Revolution was unlikely to be reversed in the future—not because the closeness between people and government might be regarded as morally

---

42. "Über das Leben und den Charakter von Scharnhorst," *Historisch-politische Zeitschrift,* I, 175–222. The text is accompanied by two appendices, containing letters from Scharnhorst to Clausewitz, and a sketch of Clausewitz's life by his widow. Clausewitz had written the essay for publication in England. When Gneisenau doubted that at a time of social and political tension in their country English readers would be interested in Scharnhorst, Clausewitz decided to postpone publication to a more auspicious day. Gneisenau to Clausewitz, 7 April 1817; Clausewitz to Gneisenau, 28 April and undated (May) 1817. Pertz-Delbrück, v, 203–204, 213, 221.
43. The last two quotations, *Historisch-politische Zeitschrift,* I, 200, 204.
44. *Ibid.,* 190–191.

desirable but, characteristically, because this interaction generated a measure of power that men would be reluctant to do without once they had come to know it: "The reader will agree with us when we say that once barriers—which in a sense consist only in man's ignorance of what is possible—are torn down, they are not so easily set up again." [45] Clausewitz, however, not only would not interpret history teleologically; he did not even hold the ideal of progress as a beautiful, if unrealizable dream. Like Wilhelm von Humboldt, he combined his commitment to the perfectibility of the individual as an ethical and intellectual imperative with deep skepticism of the capacity of mankind to raise itself to new moral heights and remain there for long.

A comparison with Tocqueville, another historian who felt strong distaste for conventional wisdom and academic preconceptions, ideologically motivated or not, may bring out Clausewitz's attitude more explicitly. The two men held not dissimilar views on the nature, dynamics, and history of the state, though Clausewitz had developed his ideas from reading a relatively small number of secondary sources, not in the archives. Both men also resembled each other in their pessimism, with Tocqueville perhaps more heavily influenced by the social and cultural changes he observed in the present and could identify in the past. And yet, despite his horror of the apparently inevitable mass society of the near future, with its ignorance and brutality, Tocqueville continued to hope, and continued to regard the currents of contemporary life as not only intellectual and political but also ethical challenges, which men such as he himself were obliged to face and attempt to overcome. His strong religious tendencies, which find no counterpart in Clausewitz, certainly contributed to this sense of commitment. It is not the least of Tocqueville's achievements in *L'Ancien régime et la Révolution* that, its concern for liberty notwithstanding, his interpretations remain essentially uncolored by hopes and convictions strong enough to affect his day-to-day intellectual position. In his study of *L'Ancien régime,* Richard Herr cites an incident that exemplifies this side of Tocqueville, and demarcates his standpoint from that of Clausewitz. After Tocqueville had read Gobineau's "Essai sur l'inégalité des races humaines," he wrote the author to reject what he considered the book's "fatalism and materialistic predestination." Gobineau's arguments, he feared, would only corrupt people. He added: "Perhaps you are right, but you have seized on the thesis that has always seemed to me the most dangerous possible to uphold in our day." [46] Who can deny that the sense of anxiety Tocqueville expressed in these words was justified; and who can be blind to their ambiguous implications? Clausewitz's position was simpler. It is almost unthinkable that he could ever have said that a thesis on the fundamental condition of humanity

45. *On War,* book VIII, ch. 3B (pp. 870–871).
46. R. Herr, *Tocqueville and the Old Regime,* Princeton, 1962, p. 92.

might well be correct, but ought nevertheless be suppressed on moral grounds.

That is not to say that he excluded ethical considerations from his work. His view of the nature and function of the state was based in part on the ethical imperatives of individual and social perfectibility. He took seriously such issues as the conflict between equality and liberty in the modern age, or—on another level—questions of looting or the treatment of prisoners and civilians in war. But although they are alluded to, he does not discuss them in depth. Essentially, both his historical and his theoretical writings are concerned with results, which are judged in terms of energy and force, though these are conceived broadly, as incorporating traditional tendencies of a society, its current attitudes, psychological qualities of its leaders and armies, and so on. Put differently, Clausewitz showed great interest in the way men's beliefs affected their behavior, but rarely measured their behavior against the standards of moral absolutes.

In *On War* he openly disavowed competence to resolve ethical issues raised by organized violence. Discussing the recent development of large-scale partisan warfare and the *levée en masse,* he writes: "Any nation that uses it [arming the population] intelligently will, as a rule, gain some superiority over those who disdain its use. If this is so, the question only remains whether mankind at large will gain by this further expansion of the element of war; a question to which the answer should be the same as to the question of war itself. We shall leave both to the philosophers." [47] In his theoretical work the need to understand the nature of war as precisely as possible compelled him to exclude any extraneous factor: "Moral force has no existence save as expressed in the state and the law," he wrote in the opening chapter of *On War.* [48] As Werner Hahlweg has observed: "Obviously he thought that entering into problems of moral behavior in war ..., or exploring the centuries-old question of the 'just' and the 'unjust' war, were 'digressions' that would interfere with his conception of a comprehensive analysis of war as an instrument of state policy." [49] This statement might be even more accurate if amended to read: " ... digressions that would interfere with his conception of a comprehensive analysis of the essence of organized violence." In this instance, in any case, a fundamental requirement of theory affected his historical work, and undoubtedly resulted in a narrowing of focus.

When Schwartz's biography of Clausewitz appeared in 1878, Hans Delbrück used the occasion to write a long article on Clausewitz's mind and work. In his discussion of the essay "Umtriebe," which Schwartz had

47. *On War,* book VI, ch. 26 (pp. 697–698). Cf. related statements in book I, ch. 3, and book VI, ch. 26 (pp. 129, 698).
48. *Ibid.,* book I, ch. 1 (p. 90).
49. Hahlweg, *Clausewitz,* p. 62.

published for the first time, Delbrück compared Clausewitz's interpretation of the origins of the French Revolution to that of Tocqueville, and continued: "It alone would suffice to assign Clausewitz a place among the great historians, and in a sense it must suffice, even though Clausewitz also wrote histories of several major wars. But that is exactly my point: although his historical attitude is constantly demonstrated in these works, he treated his themes in accordance with his purpose, entirely as a writer on military affairs, not as a historian." [50] The following paragraphs clarify this distinction. Delbrück employed the term *Militärschriftsteller* in the sense of military critic, who if he dealt with the past at all did so for a theoretical or possibly didactic purpose; he wrote about historical events critically—evaluating, praising, and condemning. The true historian, Delbrück declared, must approach the past with reverence; it is not his business to judge. He concluded: "By vocation and intent Clausewitz was a writer on military affairs, and solely a writer on military affairs. The eminently historical bent of his mind shows itself only in occasional brief analyses, and in that extraordinarily rare faculty of absolutely objective perception. He sees things as they really are; therefore he can also understand why they took this or that form in the past." [51]

At the time Delbrück wrote, many of Clausewitz's manuscripts had not yet been published; knowledge of such studies as the *Observations on Prussia* might have caused him to modify his views. It is also apparent from the essay that Delbrück's irritation at the "majority of historians" of his own day, whom he castigated as "political or party-authors," capable only of producing a "bastard type of work," played a role in the absolute distinction he drew between critic and historian—a separation that his own historical writings could not have supported. But these considerations do not touch his main argument that Clausewitz's purpose was ahistorical. Obviously this is true of the theoretical works. It does not apply, it seems to me, to many of his other writings, in which criticism and the evaluation of alternatives serve the purpose of reaching a better understanding of aspects of the past. Undoubtedly Clausewitz's historical method was more openly analytic and speculative than would have been found desirable fifty years later, in the heyday of German archival historicism, but that does not affect the method's cognitive purpose. It is nevertheless likely that from this dated, somewhat abstract approach, Delbrück drew an unduly narrow conception of criticism, which in his essay he equated with passing judgment, while Clausewitz took a more comprehensive view of criticism, and explicitly subsumed large parts of it into the historical enterprise, as he understood it. In the chapter "Criticism" in *On War*, he wrote:

"We distinguish between the *critical approach* and the plain narrative

50. Delbrück, "General von Clausewitz," reprinted in his *Historische und politische Aufsätze*, Berlin, 1887, pp. 214–215. See also p. 20, n. 1 above.
51. *Ibid.*, p. 218.

of a historical event, which merely arranges facts one after another, and at most touches on their immediate causal links.

"Three different intellectual activities may be contained in the critical approach.

"First, the discovery and interpretation of equivocal facts. This is historical research proper, and has nothing in common with theory.

"Second, the tracing of effects back to their causes. This is *critical analysis proper*. It is essential for theory; for whatever in theory is to be defined, supported, or simply described by reference to experience can only be dealt with in this manner.

"Third, the investigation and evaluation of means employed. This last is criticism proper, involving praise and censure. Here theory serves history, or rather the lessons to be drawn from history." [52]

Although this typology was written with reference to theory and appeared in Clausewitz's major theoretical work, the historical functions of criticism, as Clausewitz envisaged them, are clearly delineated. All play a part in his histories—but the discoveries of new facts less so than their interpretation and the search for causes. The fluid, undogmatic interpretation of the campaigns in Italy and France shows that it was no pose for Clausewitz to insist that only the exploration of the past for its own sake made it possible to evaluate the fitness of any action, let alone its exemplary quality. But as we know, he considered judgment in the sense of approval and disapproval to be in any case infinitely less significant than understanding what had occurred. As he wrote in the passage cited earlier from his history of 1815: "In war more than elsewhere criticism exists only to recognize the truth, not to act as judge." [53]

If these and similar comments on intent and methodology in his manuscripts and letters deserve credence, he himself was far from limiting the purpose of his histories to the illustrative or didactic. Delbrück's thesis of the *Militärschriftsteller* whose *Kritik* aimed at the reduction of events into propositions and categories, to whom the study of the past is merely the means to a contemporary end, is inaccurate because it responds only to one aspect of Clausewitz's purpose. The empirical concerns of the serving officer and strategic analyst were encompassed in the larger purpose of understanding reality, which for him extended far beyond the present. Clausewitz might believe that theory was more dependent on history than history on theory, since history captured the past dimension of reality, while theory could never be more than an imperfect abstraction; but fundamentally the study of the past and the searching out of the timeless aspects of war fulfilled the same need of cognition; both were allied in the same emotional and intellectual quest.

52. *On War*, book II, ch. 5 (pp. 210–211).
53. *Der Feldzug vom 1815; Werke*, viii, 94. See above, p. 341.

To be sure, that quest called for critical history rather than simple narrative. It once again demonstrates the unity of Clausewitz's ideas and his writings that the critical approach by which he sought to separate and analyze the components of an event or of an argument—exactly as did the young Ranke, who in 1832 stated: "Kritik ist Unterscheidung"—was also the way by which historical interpretation led to theory.[54]

54. Ranke, "Über einige französische Flugschriften aus den letzten Monaten des Jahres 1831," *Historisch-politische Zeitschrift*, I, 144. Compare Ranke's entire statement with the concluding sentence of the first chapter of *On War*. Ranke: "Criticism is differentiation; its ultimate purpose is to assign the element it has differentiated to the appropriate place in one's overall perception." Clausewitz: The "concept of war we have formulated casts a first ray of light on the basic structure of theory, and enables us to make an initial differentiation and identification of its major components."

III. THEORY

The purpose of Clausewitz's theoretical writings was to develop not a new doctrine but a truer understanding of the phenomenon of war. Theory should show "how one thing is related to another, and keep the important and the unimportant separate. If concepts combine of their own accord to form that nucleus of truth we call a principle, if they spontaneously compose a pattern that becomes a rule, it is the task of the theorist to make this clear." [1] In contrast to principles—the nuclei of truths—scientific laws are difficult to establish in an activity such as wars, and laws for action can never exist; but theory does accommodate rules since there are exceptions to every rule. [2] To the theorist the past was as significant as the present. Tradition, the insights and feelings of generations of statesmen and soldiers, their sense of the ways in which policy and strategy interacted with fighting—all needed to be examined and placed in an analytic structure that would be sufficiently specific not to fade under changed conditions and sufficiently elastic to accommodate future advances of theory. Such an analysis was feasible, Clausewitz thought, only if the investigator approached the total phenomenon of war and its component parts as closely as possible, removing to the best of his ability whatever screens of custom and preconception stood between him and his object. The terminology of purpose, aim, and means that Clausewitz devised to differentiate the elements of grand strategy can also be applied to his analytic procedure: better understanding was the purpose, direct observation the aim; studying war from the points of view of experience, history, and logic were the means. The intellectual immediacy with his object to which Clausewitz attributed so much significance was, however, accompanied by a second, subsidiary relationship between himself and other military theorists. Criticism of Bülow and others stands at the beginning of his theoretical work, and he carries on debates with the past and present literature throughout his life. *On War* is an attempt to penetrate to the essence of its subject; but what I have elsewhere called the combative posture of the work is unmistakable. [3]

1. *On War,* book VIII, ch. 1 (p. 849).
2. *Ibid.,* book II, ch. 4 (pp. 203–205). These ideas are reiterated in different formulations throughout *On War.* See, for instance, the statement that the constant search for laws must lead to constant error, book II, ch. 3 (p. 201), or: "There are hundreds of cogent local and special conditions to which the abstract rule must yield." Book V, ch. 5 (p. 421).
3. "Clausewitz and the Nineteenth Century," in *The Theory and Practice of War,* ed. M. Howard, Lon-

Such authors as Lloyd and Jomini remained lifelong targets, not only because Clausewitz thought them wrong but also because they seemed to him to express a far too common tendency toward the doctrinaire and prescriptive. From youth on he had been skeptical of authority that laid down rules concerning military, political, and social relationships—the interaction of two opposing armies, of strategic planner and soldier in the field, of state and individual. He objected that their rules were ineffectual, and, far worse, falsified the reality of the relationships they tried to control. Not only the need for knowledge but also opposition to recognized authority stimulated and continued to inform his analyses. In *On War,* to give one example of the impact the author's antagonisms had on his writings, the importance of battle is emphasized more often than the theoretical argument demands because, as the context shows, Clausewitz felt that even after the Napoleonic experience, strategy continued to be influenced by the traditional preference for maneuver and position warfare.

Even as a young man, while the armies of the French Revolution and of Napoleon confronted him with enormous tangible challenges, he had begun to work his way toward the two prerequisites for a comprehensive interpretation of war: a firm view of the relationship between theory and reality, and the development and mastery of a logically sound method of analysis. By the end of the Napoleonic era he had reached both preliminary goals. The stages of his progress, and his conceptualization of aspects of reality into such analyzable components as friction and genius, have been discussed in earlier chapters and need not be retraced here. It may, however, be useful to recall the analytic method he had adopted by describing its characteristics from a new point of view.

What Clausewitz attempted to do might be called phenomenological in the modern, Husserlian sense of the term. Briefly and perhaps too simplistically, it may be said that the phenomenologist holds that it is possible to give a description of phenomena, which at the same time reveals their essential structure. He does this by distinguishing phenomenological abstraction from inductive generalization. The latter approach scans a number of separate phenomena, notes what they may have in common, and then generalizes that feature as the property all individuals have in common.

Jomini proceeded somewhat in this manner. A prominent feature in a category of phenomena—for instance, operating on interior lines in Napoleonic strategy—is turned into a universal or a prescriptive ideal, without much concern about either the structural function or true necessity of this feature. Such generalizations are, of course, only probable: it would go against logic to claim certainty for them. Phenomenological abstraction, on

don, 1965, p. 26. See also my introduction, "The Genesis of *On War,*" in C. v. Clausewitz, *On War,* Princeton, 1976.

the other hand—*Wesenschau,* Husserl called it—seeks the essence of things, tries to establish the properties a thing must have to be that kind of a thing. It begins not with many phenomena but with the single phenomenon, and it need not investigate others, though it was the special strength of Clausewitz's approach that he combined intensive analysis of the structure of war itself with broad historical comparisons. Basically, however, he took a single phenomenon, varied it in imagination to see what properties were essential to it and what properties could be removed in thought without affecting its essence.

The opening chapter of *On War* reveals this process with special clarity. The social conditions of states, Clausewitz wrote, and "their relationships to one another ... are the forces that give rise to war; the same forces circumscribe and moderate it. They themselves, however, are not part of war; they already exist before fighting starts. ... War is an act of force, and there is no logical limit to the application of that force." After suggesting three dialectical relationships, or "interactions," between opponents that tend to lead to the extreme in violence, the argument returns to the initial proposition: "Thus in the field of abstract thought the inquiring mind can never rest until it reaches the extreme, for here it is dealing with an extreme: a clash of forces freely operating and obedient to no law but their own." [4]

Clausewitz insisted—sometimes with vehemence—that social and ethical reality could only dimly reflect absolute truth; but he nevertheless believed that to understand this reality it was essential to determine the logical extreme, the philosophic ideal, which alone could provide a reliable basis for measurement and analysis. As he was to argue in *On War,* after pointing to the countless occasions in the history of warfare when fighting had fallen far short of extreme effort and violence: "Theory must concede all this; but it has the duty to give priority to the absolute form of war and to make that form a general point of reference, so that he who wants to learn from theory becomes accustomed to keeping that point constantly in view, to measuring all his hopes and fears by it, and to approximating it *when he can* or *when he must.*" [5]

In 1816, when he first set out to assemble his theoretical findings and develop them further, he wrote a separate study in which he tested once more his ideas on the relationship between theory and reality: "The Strategic Critique of the Campaign of 1814 in France." [6] The very first sentences of the introduction reveal his use of the ideal to understand the real: "The campaign of 1814 in France, more than any other, is suited for use as a specific example to clarify strategic thought. First of all, the campaign

4. *On War,* book I, ch. 1 (pp. 90–93). For Clausewitz's complete argument, see below, pp. 382–395.
5. *Ibid.,* book VIII, ch. 2 (p. 853).
6. "Strategische Kritik des Feldzugs von 1814 in Frankreich," *Werke,* vii, 357–470.

belongs to a period in which the element of war moved rapidly and with all its natural energy. Although the actions of the Allies are not free of diplomatic considerations, which resemble water slowing the blazing fire, the overall view of the essence of war and of its purpose is not dominated by diplomatic concerns as most recent wars were before the French Revolution. Each side is driven by a great motive, and neither resorts to those temporizing measures with which earlier generations sought to give the impression of respectable activity." The introduction continues by restating the theme of the limitation of theory that Clausewitz had stressed since his first disputes with other theorists: "No one needs to remind us that we find ourselves in a realm that is ill-suited to absolute truth. We are far from claiming absolute validity for our principles of war, nor for the conclusions drawn from the way the principles operated in this specific case.[7] Both [propositions and conclusions] differ from ordinary speculation on such matters only in that they emerged from the striving for an absolute truth, that the conclusions are based directly on the propositions, and the propositions directly on the phenomena from which they have been abstracted."

Clausewitz ended the introductory chapter with a statement that offers the key to his attitude toward the study of war: "Not what we have thought seems to us to benefit theory, but the *manner* in which we have thought." He added: "Incidentally, we repeat again that here, as in all the practical arts, the function of theory is to educate the practical man, to train his judgment, rather than to assist him directly in the performance of his duties."[8]

The critique itself follows a methodical, formal approach that is unusual in a work by Clausewitz; yet it reads as smoothly as an extended essay. The first chapter proposes eight considerations that Clausewitz regards as basic to the Allies' plans: reasons for their offensive; how far the offensive can be pushed before the French, by withdrawing and concentrating, gain significant strength; purpose and goal of the strategic offensive within this range; etc. The second chapter lists the basic considerations for the defense: purpose, aim, and means of the defense; importance of gaining time; strategic options. In the third chapter the conclusions of the first and second chapters are compared with the actual plans of both sides in 1814. The second half of the study traces and analyzes the events themselves. The treatment is characterized by remarkable independence of judgment. It is, to say the least, startling to see Clausewitz employing one of the most successful offensives in the history of war to illustrate the potential strength of the defensive. As always, he feels no inhibition whatever in criticizing the actions of his own side, even decisions made by his friend Gneisenau in

7. *Grundsätze der Kriegskunst* can hardly be translated other than "principles," but Clausewitz's point may emerge more clearly if "principles" is replaced by "propositions."
8. *Werke*, vii, 359–361.

Blücher's name, or in acknowledging the "natural, logical, realistic" generalship of Napoleon, which nevertheless could not overcome his political handicaps and psychological weaknesses. Although personalities are not emphasized, they form an element in every interpretation, and sometimes provide the basis for more general observations. The emperor's reluctance to yield territory, for instance, becomes the occasion for a two-page digression in which historical and psychological analyses are blended to contrast the schematic use of psychological terms in the military literature with the complexities of strengths and weaknesses that in real life make up such qualities as firmness in adversity or willingness to yield to circumstances.[9] The whole text gives the impression of a writer who has acquired mastery over his material and his stylistic and analytic techniques, and consequently pursues his ideas with complete freedom.

In the "Critique of 1814," Clausewitz integrated history and theory with the aim of illustrating and testing theoretical propositions. Had all his writings been of this character, Delbrück would indeed have been justified in describing Clausewitz's point of view as that of a military critic rather than historian; but among his longer manuscripts it is unique. In the essays on strategy that he wrote during the same period, and that benefited from the critique, Clausewitz dealt exclusively with theory. The collection, which was never printed, has an introduction that quite inappropriately was included in the first edition of *On War* as the "Author's Preface," and has remained associated with the work. It describes the character and intent of the essays, which by combining "analysis and observation, theory and experience" seek to establish the essence of various strategic phenomena; they are not meant to form a comprehensive, "complete" system of the kind offered by rationalist theorists and their latter-day spiritual descendants. Clausewitz scoffs at the absurdities that result from compulsive but illogical detailing by quoting Lichtenberg's "Extract from a Fire Regulation," which begins: "If a house is on fire, one must above all seek to save the right wall of the house on the left, and on the other hand the left wall of the house on the right ... " and proceeds from this opening platitude in one monstrous sentence through every option, possibility, and danger contained in the situation until the terms "left," "right," "house," and "fire" have lost all meaning. Instead, Clausewitz was content to analyze individual aspects of strategy, his selective approach resulting in "chapters that stand only in loose external relation to one another, but which, it is hoped, do not lack an inner connection."[10] In a subsequent note on the project,

9. *Ibid.*, note on pp. 379–381.
10. "Vorrede des Verfassers," *On War* (pp. 82–84). Our knowledge of the development and revisions of *On War* derives to a considerable extent from four introductory notes by Clausewitz that are customarily included in editons of *On War*. The first, the "Author's Preface," was written between 1816 and 1818. The second, included in his wife's preface, deals with the original collection of essays and discusses the expansion of this scheme. The third, dated 10 July 1827, constitutes the first of two further

Clausewitz stated that he had planned to proceed in somewhat "the manner in which Montesquieu dealt with his subject ... . I thought that such concise, aphoristic chapters, which at the outset I simply wanted to call kernels, would attract the intelligent reader by what they suggested as much as by what they expressed; in other words, I had an intelligent reader in mind, who was already familiar with the subject." [11]

None of the essays of this earliest version of *On War* seems to have survived. But we possess at least one preliminary study out of which Clausewitz hoped to distill the concise, aphoristic chapters he was aiming for. It is an essay of some two thousand words, "On Progression and Pause in Military Activity," which was to provide the basis for chapter 16 of book III of *On War*, and contains ideas that are fully explored in various other chapters—for instance, chapter 3B of book VIII. [12] The essay is enlightening not only because it reveals Clausewitz's struggle to discover the form best suited to the presentation of his theories but also for the intermediary place it assumes between his earlier theoretical work and *On War*.

The essay opens with a psychological observation: a comparison of gambling and war. The reason a gambler hesitates to risk everything on one card, preferring instead to extend his game, is fear—besides pleasure in the game itself. In war, fear may similarly prolong the duration of the conflict. However, Napoleonic war, with its push for the decisive battle, seems to suggest that any interruption in violent activity goes against the nature of war. But can we analyze war—not the way men fight but the essence of war itself—in terms of mechanics, with mass, velocity, and time measured as absolutes? No, because war consists in a relationship of two opposing sides, whose perceptions, emotions, and judgment affect each other's actions and reactions. History makes that clear enough. But even if war is regarded unhistorically, as a phenomenon of mechanics, it contains elements that like "ratchet wheels, pendulums, or counterweights" act as retarding forces. One is the problem of cognition, the difficulty of evaluating one's own strength and that of the opponent, which is affected by emotions and can never be wholly accurate. Whatever its accuracy, however, an appreciation of the operational or strategic situation may induce one side or the other, or even both, to renounce the initiative. Another retarding force is the greater strength of the defensive. Beyond a certain point the offensive

introductions by Clausewitz, the so-called "Notes," and mentions the plan for a complete revision of books I to VI, and of the sketches and drafts of books VII and VIII. The second of the "Notes" was written subsequently, perhaps in 1830, and indicates that Clausewitz had not progressed very far with the revision.

11. Second introductory note, included in Marie v. Clausewitz's "Vorrede," *On War* (p. 73).

12. The essay "Über das Fortschreiten und den Stillstand der kriegerischen Begebenheiten" was first published by H. Delbrück in the *Zeitschrift für Preussische Geschichte und Landeskunde*, XV (1878), pp. 233–240. Another preliminary study, far less significant, may be the essay on army organization that is often included as an appendix to *On War*. Its essential points are incorporated into chapter 5 of book V.

slackens: action slows down and may even cease altogether. The attack requires more force than the defense. In this essay Clausewitz even suggests that the advantage of the defense may be as two to one, though obviously he intends to illustrate the dynamics of the process rather than propose a fixed ratio: "The addition that gives strength to the defensive form of war is not only deducted from the side that moves from the defensive to the offensive, it also accrues to the opponent, so that this addition in strength must be figured twice, just as the difference between $A + B$ and $A - B$ is the same as $2B$." [13] It is true that since the rise of Napoleon, "the most daring of gamblers . . . all campaigns have gained such a cometlike swiftness that a higher degree of military intensity is scarcely imaginable." [14] But this need not always be the case. So, after all, there are two types of war, because in war one must consider not only mass, velocity, and time, which are conducive to continuity of violence, but also purpose, feelings, ability, and chance. A comparison between different wars, and the evaluation of specific wars, demands the methodical analysis of all of these elements.

The brief essay, with its highly compressed argumentation, is at once a summary and review of earlier ideas and themes, and a preliminary statement of their subsequent resolution in *On War*. It alludes to the possibility of two types of conflict, which Clausewitz first broached in 1804, though still without pursuing the theoretical and political implications of this insight. [15] It emphasizes the difficulty of acquiring accurate knowledge and the power of friction to reduce the energy of military activity, thoughts familiar to us from his essay for the crown prince. Once again there is an insistence on the importance of psychological factors and of chance. Nor is the use of terms borrowed from mathematics and mechanics an innovation; but now they are given greater prominence. Together with the essay's evaluation of the reciprocal relationship between opponents and of the decisions to act and not to act that flow from it, these terms and their application suggest the approach taken by modern game theory. In an effort to save as much precision, quantification, and comparability for theory, without making theory unrealistic, Clausewitz sought to combine mathematical concepts with such imponderables as the psychological and intellectual qualities of the men engaged in conflict, and the historical condition and the social and political context in which they acted. But the essay's most significant contribution to the development of his ideas was the further short step it took toward explaining why and how the absolute violence that is the essence of war was modified in reality. The concept of friction was here expressed in the language of mechanics as being a ratchet wheel or counterweight, so that at least in a terminological sense friction became part of

13. *Ibid.*, p. 235. The illustration is repeated in *On War*, book III, ch. 16 (p. 307).
14. *Zeitschrift für Preussische Geschichte und Landeskunde*, XV, 237–238.
15. See above, pp. 90–91.

a comprehensive theoretical system. But it must have been obvious to Clausewitz that this was more illustrative than a genuine integration of the factors of chance, emotions, politics, force, and time.

Clausewitz sent the manuscript to Gneisenau with a covering letter, the first part of which dealt with the essay while the remaining longer portion expressed his anguish and rage at the continuing refusal of the Prussian state to grant a pension to Scharnhorst's children. "I take the liberty," he wrote, "of sending Your Excellency a brief essay, whose subject needs to be clearly understood if we wish to illuminate and bring coherence to [the study of] strategy. When, as in this case, a discussion has become too lengthy, I incorporate only the compressed concise conclusions into my little work, and toss the preliminary draft like scraps and chips of wood into the fire. If I make an exception this time and dare send Your Excellency such a chip, it is because this piece will best indicate the structure of the wood from which the work is carved." [16]

As always, Gneisenau responded with praise and encouragement: "Don't throw the chips away, dear friend; I want to have them to enjoy and to keep. It is always good to know how a noble structure has been created; the French history on the building of the Neuilly bridge is as beautiful as the bridge itself, and more instructive. Your essay on progress and pause in military operations expresses my very feelings. You really do possess the ability to discover the sources and develop them. What I vaguely felt about this particular topic, you have now made clear to me." [17]

Gneisenau's suggestion to Boyen at this time that Clausewitz should be given the assignment of writing a treatise on strategy was presumably linked to Clausewitz's plan for his "little work," for which the essay was a study.[18] Other friends reacted less favorably. Carl von der Groeben wrote to Leopold von Gerlach: "As far as it has been written—i.e., a few sheets— I am familiar with the work Gneisenau mentions. But in all honesty, I cannot fully agree with the judgment of our admirable Gneisenau. It [the work] is more critical than definitive, which is good; but the irritated, sickly mood in which it was written comes through, and that is bad." [19] Clausewitz himself felt frustrated by the compressed, fragmented character of the essays, which could satisfy neither his intellectual nor his aesthetic demands. In the previously cited note that his wife included in her preface to *On War,* he wrote: "My nature, which always drives me to develop and systematize, at last asserted itself here as well. From the studies I wrote on various topics in order to gain a clear and complete understanding of them,

16. Clausewitz to Gneisenau, 4 March 1817, Pertz-Delbrück, v, 192.
17. Gneisenau to Clausewitz, 6 April 1817, *ibid.,* pp. 199–200.
18. See above, p. 270.
19. Groeben to Gerlach, 18 May 1817, Schoeps, p. 575.

I managed for a time to lift only the most important conclusions and thus concentrate their essence in smaller compass. But eventually my tendency completely ran away with me; I elaborated as much as I could, and of course now had in mind a reader who was not yet acquainted with the subject.

"The more I wrote and surrendered to the spirit of analysis, the more I reverted to a systematic approach, and so one chapter after another was added.

"In the end I intended to revise it all again, strengthen the causal connections in the earlier essays, perhaps in the later ones draw together several analyses into a single conclusion, and thus produce a reasonable whole [*ein erträgliches Ganze*], which would form a small volume in octavo. But here too, I wanted at all costs to avoid every commonplace, everything obvious that is stated a hundred times and is generally believed. It was my ambition to write a book that would not be forgotten after two or three years, and that possibly might be picked up more than once by those who are interested in the subject." [20]

By discovering through trial and error that compression would not serve his purpose, Clausewitz came to recognize what appears obvious to us: the distillation of complex ideas not only made his treatment too abstract; he had to overcome too many preconceptions and develop too many ideas almost from scratch to follow Montesquieu's pattern comfortably. Once he had moved to Berlin he greatly expanded his original scheme. By 1827 he had written a manuscript of some one thousand pages, which, barring the revisions he undertook after he had recovered from his illness that year, was essentially *On War* as we know it today.

On War is divided into eight books: (I) "On the Nature of War," which defines the basic tendencies of war and the difference between absolute and real war, and discusses such topics as purpose and means in war, genius, and friction; (II) "On the Theory of War," which contains the major methodological analyses; (III) "On Strategy in General," which includes not only chapters on force, time, and space but also a detailed treatment of psychological elements; (IV) "The Engagement," which together with operational questions treats the interaction between moral and material factors; (V) "Military Forces," (VI) "Defense," and (VII) "The Attack"—the three most conventionally military books of the work; and (VIII) "War Plans," which expatiates on the relationship between absolute and real war, and analyzes the political character of war and the influence of politics on strategy.

The material is thus arranged in a relatively straightforward sequence, beginning with a survey of the whole in the first chapter, proceeding to the

20. Second introductory note, included in Marie v. Clausewitz's "Vorrede," *On War* (pp. 73–74).

nature of war and to the purpose and problems of theory. Books III through VII discuss strategy and the conduct of military operations. The work ends with an analysis of the most important functions of military and political leadership in war, and integrates war into social and political life. *On War* is, in short, an attempt both to penetrate to the essence of true war, to use Clausewitz's term—that is, ideal war—as well as to understand war in reality on the various levels of its existence: as a social and political phenomenon, and in its organizational, strategic, operational, and tactical aspects.[21]

On War contains little on the ethics of violence and barely refers to the possibilities of irrational political leadership, though passages point to the importance of these issues. Presumably it was Clausewitz's special sense of realism that prevented him from dealing with the former. He never questioned the right of political communities as living social organisms to defend themselves, and even to increase their strength if this could be achieved without seriously damaging the international environment. He could conceive of no ethical force that could effectively inhibit this process other than opinions held *within* each particular society—certainly not such supranational bodies as organized religion or great-power vehicles for international morality like the Holy Alliance. The question of rational, responsible political leadership pertained to the theory of politics, not of war, even if the delusions of a dictator or of an entire society led to insane and suicidal destruction.

Nor does the work treat the naval side of war, though it makes some interesting comparisons between land and sea tactics. Clausewitz lacked the expertise to discuss naval operations in detail, and he seemed to feel reluctant to extend his analysis of strategic planning and execution to naval warfare. His propositions on the nature of war, on the role of theory, and on the interaction between war and politics apply to the seas as much as to land, without this needing to be explicitly stated.

Within the eight books and 128 chapters and sections of *On War* dozens of major and minor themes are introduced, developed, compared, and combined. Arguments are repeated and tested in different contexts; two or more theses are brought into interaction; an idea is defined with extreme, one-sided clarity, to be varied chapters later and given a new dimension as it blends with other propositions and observations. Discussions of the nature of war in the abstract alternate with the application to real war of such analytic devices as the theory of purpose and means, of the major concepts of friction and genius, of propositions of lesser magnitude such as those concerning the relationship of attack to defense, and with detailed operational and tactical observations—all embedded in historical evi-

21. W. M. Schering, in *Die Kriegsphilosophie von Clausewitz*, Hamburg, 1935, presents a complicated outline of the "systematic structure" of *On War*. Some of his comments are interesting, but in the main his analysis pretentiously underlines the obvious.

dence.[22] The text is characterized by movement, cross-references, and allusions not only to other parts of the book but also to the experiences of the author and of his generation. Through the entire work, creating an internal unity surpassing that of its external design, run the two dialectical relationships between absolute and real war, and between reason, chance, and violence. It was more than vanity and self-consciousness that caused Clausewitz to doubt that many readers were capable of following his overarching argumentation, which demanded concentration on each detail with a simultaneous sense of its place in the whole.

The fluid, open form that Clausewitz had finally chosen suited his purpose perfectly. How much he gained by isolating particular arguments and pursuing them as far as possible, without concern for space or aphoristic formulation, can be seen by comparing chapter 16 of book III, "The Suspension of Action in War," with the essay of 1817, parts of which provided the basis for the chapter.[23] Chapter 16 is one of the steps in the process by which Clausewitz clarified the relationship between absolute and real war. He started with the thesis that once war broke out a suspension or diminution of violence could in theory not be justified: in a general sense both parties to the conflict are permanently in action, but at each particular moment one side acts while the other waits because circumstances rarely appear equally favorable to both at the same time. Even if circumstances are balanced, or seem to be, the political motives of the opponents continue to differ: one must necessarily be the aggressor. So even if we assume equal opportunity, one side will be under greater pressure to act. Consequently inactivity of both sides at the same time appears contradictory to the nature of war. But that does not mean that war is made up of constant activity: "No matter how savage the nature of war, it is chained by human weaknesses; and no one will be surprised at the contradiction that man seeks and creates the very danger that he fears." [24] History shows that pause is the rule and action the exception in war. On the other hand, recent experiences prove that we are correct in regarding war essentially as activity. What would be the point of all preparation and effort if they did not lead to action?

The general principle stands: in war both sides are in permanent activity and seek to destroy each other. Now we must consider the modification of the principle. There are three factors that inhibit constant action: human fear and indecisiveness, which are intensified in war; imperfect insight into

22. Clausewitz argues that historical *examples* (not history in general) have four functions in theory. An example may be used to interpret an idea; it may be used to discover how an idea can be applied in practice; it may provide proof that a phenomenon or effect is possible; and a tenet or proposition may be derived from the detailed, circumstantial treatment of a historical event. *On War*, book II, ch. 6 (p. 235).
23. "Über den Stillstand im kriegerischen Akt," *On War*, book III, ch. 16 (pp. 304–309).
24. *Ibid.*, p. 305.

reality, which leads to errors in judgment; and the greater strength of the defensive: "Thus in the midst of the conflict itself concern, prudence, and fear of excessive risks find reason to assert themselves and to tame the elemental fury of war." [25]

But there are still other reasons for inactivity: weak political motives, which may be so feeble that they turn war into a fragmentary thing [*dass sie den Krieg zu einem Halbdinge machen*]. Theory finds it difficult to deal with such wars; as the reasons for action and violence diminish, the random and incidental are given greater scope. Such wars, which invite artificial, insignificant actions, also tend to mislead people about the nature of war itself.[26] The chapter concludes: "All of these reasons explain why action in war is not continuous but spasmodic. Violent clashes are interrupted by periods of observation, during which both sides are on the defensive. But usually one side is more strongly motivated, which tends to affect its behavior: the offensive element will dominate, and will usually maintain its continuity of action." [27]

In miniature, this chapter reflects the method and tone of the whole work. The dialectical argument progresses from thesis to antithesis, but without seeking a synthesis; rather, theory and reality are compared, and blend only to the extent that reality seems to permit. War and politics are seen as a continuum. History, psychology, and common sense are called on to guide and control logic; even an attack on the rationalist theorists of war, who misconstrue conflicts fought for insignificant motives as "the true war," is not lacking.

The theoretical explanation for the obvious fact that war does not consist in a single blow or in a group of simultaneous actions, but extends over time with activity and inactivity alternating, was combined by Clausewitz with discussions in other chapters to bring out as clearly as he could the modification that the concept of absolute, true war undergoes in reality. Absolute violence, though logically valid, was a fiction, an abstraction that served to unify all military phenomena and helped make their theoretical treatment possible. The power of friction reduced the abstract absolute to the modified forms it assumed in reality. The analytic power generated by this dialectical relationship between the absolute and the real, between philosophy and history, was enormous. But, as Clausewitz had already sensed when he wrote the essay "On Progression and Pause," the concept of absolute violence as the true war and of its inevitable modification and reduction in practice was too narrow. It needed to be developed further, a

25. *Ibid.*, p. 307.
26. Here Clausewitz makes three points, typically interdependent, which in different form recur throughout the book: A war with weak motivation presents difficulties to a theory based on the essential violence of war; it may confuse the judgment of the men engaged in it; and it may mislead theorists to see war as consisting essentially of maneuver and the occupation of key positions rather than of fighting.
27. *On War*, book III, ch. 16 (p. 309).

task he was not to engage in systematically until he began the last revisions of the manuscript in 1827 or later.

True war was absolute violence because organized mass violence was the only feature that distinguished war from all other human activities: "Essentially war is fighting [*Krieg in seiner eigentlichen Bedeutung ist Kampf*]; for fighting is the only effective principle in the manifold activities generally designated as war." [28] Real war was both more and less than absolute. *Less,* because rarely if ever did it attain absolute violence, though in the extermination of one prehistoric tribe by another, or in the Napoleonic campaigns, reality had come close to the ideal. The various elements grouped under the concept of friction reduced the level of violence, which, on the other hand, tended to be increased by the process of escalation, by the likelihood that one antagonist would respond to the actions of the other by trying to outdo him. [29] Real war was more than pure violence because it was not an isolated phenomenon, but pertained both to the individual and to the social world.

Real war, Clausewitz declared, was a composite of three elements: violence and passion; the scope afforded by all human intercourse to chance and probability, but also to genius, intelligence, courage; and its subordination to politics, which, Clausewitz characteristically argued, made it subject to reason. [30] An adequate theoretical understanding of war—one that did not fly in the face of reality—must incorporate all three of these elements. Theories that dealt only with the military aspects of the second—how planning, leadership, and effort might succeed in the uncertain business of defeating the enemy army—were inadequate, as were theories that interpreted war primarily as a political or psychological phenomenon. By remaining suspended between the three magnets or energy fields of violence, of politics, and of chance and creativity, which to varying degree interacted in every war, theory gained the universality that allowed it to analyze all wars, past and present, as well as the flexibility that would enable its major propositions to accommodate whatever social and technological changes the future might bring. Permanence and change did not confuse theory, but became equally comprehensible. Indeed, each illuminated the other.

The tripartite definition of war alone made it possible for Clausewitz to advance from partial studies to a comprehensive and integrated analysis of war. But although he created what may be regarded as the archetype of any theory that seeks to proceed beyond the specialized and mechanical to a balanced interpretation of the nature, use, and techniques of violence, his personal condition and opinions naturally tilted his analysis. This is not so

28. The opening sentence of book II, "On the Theory of War," *ibid.,* (p. 167).
29. For Clausewitz's development of the concept of escalation, see below, pp. 384–385.
30. For Clausewitz's complete description of the "remarkable trinity" of war, see below, pp. 394–395.

much the case with specifics; Clausewitz's supposed preference for the major, decisive battle, in particular, is an erroneous assumption, based on the very inability to follow his dialectic that he had predicted.[31] What I refer to is rather a general tendency of his work. Of the three elements that he identified as making up war, he associates the "blind natural forces" of violence primarily with society as a whole, with the people, the individual. The "scope that the play of courage and talent will enjoy in the realm of probability and chance" he relates primarily to the armed forces. The political element of war, the area he considers most subject to deliberate reasoning, is the business of government. Clausewitz explicitly does not set up discrete divisions; his argument employs relative terms and rejects exclusive affinities. As an example, he observes that all military activities, not only guerrilla warfare but even actions carried out by regulars, are influenced by hatred and aggressiveness, since the army is part of the people, made up of individuals with feelings of their own. Nevertheless, in *On War* his fundamental analytic distinctions coexist with some strongly subjective assumptions: the raw emotions that provide energy for all effective action rest in society. It is the task of the political leadership to abstract these energies without succumbing to their irrational power. Government transforms psychic energy into rational policy, which the army helps carry out. The view is that of the professional soldier, who regards himself as protector and servant of the political community, as well as that of the aristocrat who has come to terms with the centralized state, or who, as in the case of Clausewitz, is its product. It is true that Clausewitz insisted—more often after 1815 than before—that the state should not give the soldier impossible missions. "In its relation to policy," he wrote in 1827 to Müffling, then chief of staff, "the first duty and right of the art of war is to keep policy from demanding things that go against the nature of war, to prevent the possibility that out of ignorance of the way the instrument works, policy might misuse it." [32] But he judged correctness of use by political standards: the sacrifice of an army is appropriate if it truly answers the political purpose, which in *On War*—though not in his political essays—Clausewitz assumes to be generally realistic and responsible: "Policy, of course, is nothing in itself; it is simply the trustee for all interests [of political society] against the outside world." [33] Certainly, governments constantly made

---

31. See, for instance, the italicized passage in *On War,* book I, ch. 2, "Purpose and Means in War" (p. 119): "We can now see that in war many roads lead to success, and that they do not all involve the opponent's outright defeat. They range from *the destruction of the enemy's forces, the conquest of his territory, to a temporary occupation or invasion, to projects with an immediate political purpose, and finally to awaiting passively the enemy's attacks."* Each may be the appropriate means for the particular purpose and circumstance.

32. Clausewitz to Müffling, [?] 1827, quoted in H. v. Freytag-Loringhoven, *Kriegslehren nach Clausewitz,* Berlin, 1908, p. 16.

33. *On War,* book VIII, ch. 6B (p. 891).

mistakes; but he could only assume that usually they tried to express the true concerns of the state, which they were more likely to recognize than the ill-informed and thoughtless populace, who could too easily be seduced by fashion or emotion.[34] Since the theory of war deals with the use of force against external enemies, Clausewitz was logically correct in not exploring the problems posed by irrational or mistaken political leadership—questions he left to political theory. Still, the structure of *On War* is sufficiently expansive not to have suffered from a discussion of these issues that went beyond his arguments for the need of close political and military interaction and of military subordination to the political leadership presented in book VIII.

And yet, whatever the pitfalls of his rigorous logic and of the view of the political and social world contained in *On War,* they did not prevent Clausewitz from developing an analytic scheme whose decisive characteristics are realism, balance, and comprehensiveness, and that is sufficiently flexible to accommodate opinions very different from those held by its originator—just as, it might be thought, Freud's cultural pessimism did not prevent him from inventing a theory of human feelings and behavior that expresses far more than his personal predilections.[35]

Having postulated the tripartite nature of war, outlined its three primary elements, and indicated the properties that a genuine theory of war should possess, Clausewitz proceeds to explore and integrate these four major themes. As long as the dialectic, the constant merging and separation of his arguments is kept in mind, it is possible to identify groups of topics and levels of interpretation that more accurately reflect the approach taken in *On War* than does its formal organization: (1) The discussion of theory and methodology, based largely on Clausewitz's studies during the reform era, constitutes a distinct concern of the work. The principal agent of his methodology, the thesis of means and purpose, borrowed, as we know, from late-Enlightenment aesthetics, guides the analysis of war in reality. (2) What actually occurs when men fight is defined and rendered subject to analysis through the formulation of such concepts as friction and genius. (3) Other concepts refer more narrowly to the dynamic of

---

34. During the Third Reich, Clausewitz's emphasis on the rationality of political leadership embarrassed some of his interpreters. In his book *Wehrphilosophie,* Leipzig, 1939, the Clausewitz scholar W. M. Schering, who worked the meager vein of National Social Existentialism, argued that to understand Clausewitz the modern reader should substitute "will" for "purpose" (p. 91). He tried to qualify Clausewitz's assertion that theory could never offer a positive doctrine for action (pp. 249–250) and finally acknowledged that he could not agree with Clausewitz that reason determined policy. Rather, Schering claimed, decisions find their roots in the will, which has been forged and tempered in previous conflicts (p. 276).

35. Without suggesting true theoretical or functional similarities, I cannot refrain from pointing to the obvious parallel between the trinity of Id, Ego, and Superego, and Clausewitz's trinity of Violence, Creativity, and Reason—with the army, the expression of creative genius operating in the realm of the imponderable, reconciling the demands of violence and of reason in war.

fighting—that of escalation, for example. (4) These analytic components are supplemented by a secondary category of propositions, which further identify and interpret both the elements of war and their place in its dynamic structure.

The distinction between true and real war had given Clausewitz one basis for developing his theory; another was provided by his differentiation between the physical and nonphysical aspects of war. When theory of any kind deals with the physical and concrete it faces no exceptional difficulties: "Architects and painters know precisely what they are about as long as they deal with material phenomena. Mechanical and optical structures are not in dispute." [36] But theory becomes vague as soon as it tries to explain perceptions and feelings. Clausewitz employs a highly suggestive analogy to make his point: "Medicine is usually concerned only with physical phenomena. It deals with the animal organism, which, however, is subject to constant change and thus is never exactly the same from one moment to the next. This renders the task of medicine very difficult, and makes the physician's judgment count for more than his knowledge. But how greatly is the difficulty increased when a mental factor is added, and how much more highly do we value the psychiatrist!" [37] Since war is a mixture of the physical and of the mental, moral, and emotional, a theory of war becomes very difficult. Certainly it is impossible to lay down valid rules for the conduct of war: "A positive doctrine is unattainable." [38]

Two solutions exist for this dilemma: First, those aspects of war in which the physical predominates are more susceptible to theoretical treatment than those activities in which intelligence and emotions play major roles: organization and tactics pose far fewer difficulties to theory than do strategy and the political function of war. Secondly, theory need not be a guide for action. It can be an intelligent analysis that familiarizes the student with the subject and educates his judgment. Theory "is meant to educate the mind of the future commander, or, more accurately, to guide him in his self-education, not to accompany him to the battlefield, just as a wise teacher guides and stimulates a young man's intellectual development but is careful not to lead him by the hand for the rest of his life." [39] If the theorist adopts Clausewitz's views of the proper role of the teacher, a realistic theory of war, combining logic, observation, and experience, becomes possible.

Knowledge, once gained, is still difficult to apply. Any action in war poses problems, which increase with responsibility. For the soldier, knowl-

---

36. *On War*, book II, ch. 2 (p. 182). This paragraph and the two following are based primarily on book I, ch. 2, and book II, chs. 1 and 2.
37. "... und wieviel höher stellt man den Seelenarzt!" *ibid.*, book II, ch. 2 (p. 182).
38. *Ibid.*, book II, ch. 2 (p. 187).
39. *Ibid.*, book II, ch. 2 (p. 189).

edge must turn into ability.[40] Ability is achieved when knowledge almost ceases to exist independently and is assimilated into the individual's attitudes and habits. As the physician in Clausewitz's analogy, so the soldier: his judgment, derived from study and experiences, replaces knowledge. He no longer goes by the book, but follows his "insight and tact of judgment." The dialectic between theory and practice, in which one affects and informs the other, is resolved—one of the rare syntheses in Clausewitz's arguments.

Theory must study the nature of means and purpose. We are already familiar with Clausewitz's use of these concepts in his histories. In theory as well as in history, the identical phenomenon may be either means or purpose, depending on the context and one's point of view. In tactics—the part of war related to the particular battle—the fighting forces are the means, victory is the purpose. In strategy—the part of war related to the use of battle for the purpose of the war—victory is the means to attain this purpose. War as a whole is the means to fulfill the political purpose. In actual fighting, the military aim—to defeat the enemy or to weaken him significantly—temporarily replaces the political purpose. But the military aim, and military considerations in general, must never conflict with the ultimate political goal. By analyzing each aspect of military planning and execution for its relationship to the military aim, and by extension to the war's political purpose, theory can assign each particular means to its proper place in the over-all structure of war, and evaluate its effectiveness.[41] Much of On War consists of such analyses; but before 1827 Clausewitz treated the political dimension less systematically than other areas of war. It was not until he formulated the thesis of the dual nature of war in his final revisions that he fully succeeded in fitting various levels of violence into the continuum of government policy.[42]

The two major analytic devices, friction and genius, which Clausewitz developed in the years preceding and immediately following the War of 1806, reappear essentially unchanged in On War, though he greatly expands their treatment and places them in permanent interaction: "Friction is the only concept that more or less corresponds to the factors that distinguish real war from war on paper. The military machine—the army and everything pertaining to it—is basically very simple, and therefore seems easy to manage. But we should bear in mind that none of its components is of one piece, each part is composed of individuals, every one of whom retains his potential of friction. ... A battalion is made up of individuals, the least important of whom may chance to delay things or somehow make them go wrong. The dangers inseparable from war and the physical exertions war

40. "Das Wissen muss ein Können werden." *Ibid.*, book II, ch. 2, (p. 197).
41. *Ibid.*, book I, ch. 2, and book VIII.
42. See below, pp. 377–381.

demands can aggravate the problem to such an extent that they must be ranked among its principal causes. ... This tremendous friction, which cannot, as in mechanics, be reduced to a few points, is everywhere in contact with chance, and brings about effects that cannot be measured, just because they are largely due to chance. ... Action in war is like movement in a resistant element. ... Moreover, every war is rich in unique episodes, each is an uncharted sea, full of reefs." [43] Not only the psychological element but friction and the signularity of events forbid general laws.

Under the "general concept" of friction are grouped friction in the narrow sense—the impediments to smooth action produced by the thousands of individuals who make up an army—but also danger, physical exertion, the difficulty of gaining accurate information, and other impersonal as well as psychological factors. A battle-hardened, experienced army may be compared to a lubricant that reduces the friction of the various human and organizational parts of the machine; but for the engine to operate efficiently more is required: intellectual and psychological forces, "moral qualities," genius.

These forces are, of course, themselves primary contributors to friction. Every aspect of war is suffused by psychological qualities in a negative as well as in a positive sense: "All war presupposes human weakness, and seeks to exploit it." [44] But it is the creative employment of intellectual and psychological strengths that alone can overcome friction, exploit chance, and turn the imponderable into an asset: Physical causes and effects are to moral factors "little more than the wooden hilt [is to] the real weapon, the finely honed blade." [45]

These factors, which Clausewitz termed *moralische Grössen*—moral and psychological values—reside in the talents of the commander, the military virtues of the army, and the spirit of society as reflected in its soldiers, popular influences which Clausewitz enumerates as enthusiasm, fanatic energy, faith, political beliefs. [46] Theory must therefore analyze emotional forces of all kinds: the psychology of the individual and the psychology of the group. In the 1820's such an effort would necessarily fall far short of the firm conclusions he desired. Clausewitz himself complained of contempo-

43. *On War*, book I, ch. 7 (pp. 160–161). Cf. the passage from "The Campaign of 1812 in Russia," *Werke*, vii, 177: "In war everything is simple, but the simplest thing is extremely difficult. The military instrument resembles an engine with enormous friction, which cannot, as in mechanics, be reduced to a few points, but is everywhere in contact with a host of imponderables. Besides, war is activity in a resistant element. A movement easily executed in the air becomes very difficult to do in water. Danger and effort are the elements in which the spirit operates in war, and these elements remain alien to the classroom and study. For these reasons one never does as much as one had intended; just to maintain an average level of achievement already calls for more than ordinary strength."
44. *On War*, book IV, ch. 10 (p. 363).
45. *Ibid.*, book III, ch. 3 (p. 255).
46. *Ibid.*, book III, ch. 4 (p. 257). This and the following three paragraphs are based primarily on book I, ch. 3, and book III, chs. 3–6.

rary psychology's inadequate understanding of human emotions, "this obscure field," into which we have no business to go farther "with our slight scientific knowledge [*Philosophie*]." [47] He was reduced to two partial solutions: to enumerate and differentiate psychological qualities and character traits that were significant in war; and to subsume a large part of his interpretation of these factors under the concept of genius.

His taxonomy follows conventional patterns. [48] He discusses moral and physical courage, different kinds of determination, energy, firmness, ambition, etc. These qualities are placed in different contexts to determine their specific meanings. Courage, for example, is influenced by the way men perceive reality, which in turn is affected by their position and responsibilities. Four basic personality types are outlined: men who are phlegmatic or indolent; vital but calm; lively and easily stimulated, but lacking in staying power; and those who have strong but deeply hidden emotions. All of these traits, Clausewitz suspects, are closely linked to physical characteristics. [49] Each type seems better suited to some duties than to others. The easily stimulated officer may prove useful in a subordinate position "simply because the action controlled by junior officers is of short duration. Often a single brave decision, a burst of emotional force will be enough. A daring assault is the work of a few minutes, while a hard-fought battle may last a day and a campaign an entire year." [50] Best suited to supreme command are the men who keep their strong feelings deeply buried—one of the frequent allusions to Scharnhorst throughout the book.

These and other categories differ from the standard typology of Clausewitz's day only in the attempt to test a given feature against a variety of concrete situations, and in the fact that no discernible philosophy of human behavior seems to underlie Clausewitz's descriptions.

Genius, as we know, had become Clausewitz's favorite device to conceptualize the various abilities and feelings that affected the behavior of or-

47. *Ibid.,* book I, ch. 3 (p. 140).

48. See above, pp. 158–159. It is not known how familiar Clausewitz was with the technical psychological literature of his time. The only writers mentioned in his works and correspondence who may be considered psychologists or pedagogues without being philosophers are Pestalozzi, Jean Paul, and Lichtenberg. Schering, *Geist und Tat,* p. xxix, suggests that Clausewitz derived his psychology from such French authors as Chamfort and Vauvenargues, but gives no evidence for this statement, which has in fact nothing to recommend it. The sections on psychology in *On War* reflect opinions that are very general and that were widely accepted at the time: free will exists, feelings are a positive force, enthusiasm and determination are praiseworthy, etc. Whether Clausewitz derived these beliefs directly or at second or third hand from the writings of Shaftesbury, Moses Mendelssohn, Kant, or such contemporary academics as Johann Georg Heinrich Feder, who developed a realistic psychology emphasizing the will, can no longer be determined and does not really matter. On the other hand, it is neither insignificant nor surprising that Clausewitz quoted Lichtenberg. The irony, earthiness, and supreme commonsense of the man whom Max Dessoir has rightly called the most outstanding practical psychologist of the 18th century could hardly have failed to appeal to him.

49. *On War,* book I, ch. 3 (pp. 139–140).

50. *Ibid.,* book I, ch. 3 (pp. 140–141).

dinary men as well as that of the exceptional individual. In agreement with aesthetic theories of the late Enlightenment, he meant by genius the harmonious combination of qualities needed for supreme achievement in a particular area of activity. Individual creativity, the ability to overcome the impediments of spirit and matter, reaches its highest level in genius, and theory must try to follow it to those heights.

In one sense, the discussion of psychological elements constitutes the weakest part of *On War*. Clausewitz's speculations on the suitability of different psychological qualities for different tasks are marked by common sense, but different combinations and affinities are equally conceivable. Its insights and realism notwithstanding, his taxonomy is basically impressionistic. The vagueness of the treatment is compounded by the confusion introduced by the two overlapping analytic concepts of genius and of moral and psychological values. To interpret genius as the intensification and integration of universal qualities is satisfactory as a base for further investigation into this specialized condition; but Clausewitz's general analysis of psychological forces suffers because too often these are discussed only in the context of genius.

But if Clausewitz was precluded by the state of psychology in his time from incorporating a clinically and logically consistent theory of feelings and behavior into *On War,* the importance and originality of his attempt to do so is not diminished. Writers on war had always stressed the significance of emotions in battle, and psychological taxonomies of various kinds were not unusual in the literature. But earlier authors always treated feelings as essentially unfathomable; their importance was noted, and then ignored. Clausewitz, on the contrary, contends that psychological factors form a major element of war—at times he even regards them as the most important force—and that consequently theory must deal with them. He tried to fulfill this obligation by formulating the concepts of moral qualities and of genius, which in conjunction with the concept of friction at least enabled him to fit psychology and creativity into his analysis of the structure and processes of war.

Friction and creativity help determine the character and rate of progress of military operations. This progress itself, or the failure to progress, assumes a variety of specific forms. A group of concepts in *On War* separates the dynamic of violence into its constituent parts: the thesis of the reciprocal relationship of the two opponents; the thesis of the tendency of their efforts to escalate; the thesis of the interdependence of attack and defense; the thesis that for reasons of time, space, and energy the offensive gradually weakens until a "culminating point" is reached, after which the defense may gain superiority; the thesis that the defensive contains both resistance and counterattack, just as in the offensive attack, pause, and resistance interact. With these concepts we have reached the category of secondary propositions. To varying degrees they are suggestive of factors that might obtain in all conflicts, but they reflect the specific conditions of the Napoleonic era far more directly than do Clausewitz's thoughts on the basic nature of war. They and the discussion of detailed topics that grow from them—retreat after a lost battle, defense of a mountain range, crossing a river, and so forth—constitute the immediate reality that provided much of the raw material for Clausewitz's theories. They also demonstrated to his satisfaction that while the higher reaches of war, where reason, emotion, and imponderables resolve the fate of states and peoples, might pose almost insuperable difficulties for theory, large if relatively subordinate areas of war were susceptible to analysis, and thus proved that a theory of war was in fact possible. As he wrote in the "Note" of 1830: "A whole range of propositions can be demonstrated without difficulty: that defense is the stronger form of fighting with the negative purpose, attack the weaker form with the positive purpose; that major successes help bring about minor ones, so that strategic results can be traced back to certain turning-points; that a demonstration is a weaker use of force than a real attack, and that it must therefore be clearly justified [appropriate use of means for the purpose]; that victory consists not only in the occupation of the battlefield but in the destruction of the enemy's physical and psychic forces ... ; that success is always greatest at the point where the victory was gained, and that consequently changing from one line of operations, one direction, to another can at best be regarded as a necessary evil; that a turning movement can only be justified by general superiority or by having better lines of communication or retreat than the enemy's; that flank-positions, therefore, are governed by the same considerations; that every attack loses impetus as it progresses." [51]

These themes and approaches concerning the nature of theory, the interaction of theory and practice, the conceptualization of the more important aspects of war in real life, the definition of its dynamic processes, and the differentiation of the constituent parts of strategy, operations, and even tactics, are shaped by the three basic interpretive positions formulated in the tripartite description of war: War is essentially violence; war is the realm of chance in which only disciplined and creative psychological qualities—ability, talent, genius—can act effectively; war has political purposes and effects. Behind these realistic propositions, the thesis that true war is absolute violence stands as the regulative idea, the ultimate analytic authority.

51. *Ibid.*, "Note" (pp. 80–81). The proposition that the attack gradually weakens, stated in *On War*, book VII, ch. 4, is linked with the concept of the culminating point—the point beyond which the attacker can no longer effectively defend himself against a counterattack, *ibid.*, book VII, ch. 5. In his essay "Umtriebe" Clausewitz used the term *Kulminationspunkt* to mark the beginning of the irrevocable decline of the power of the European nobility.

But was it actually true that the abstract ideal always suffered modification in real life? And, secondly, was it valid to deduce from the concept of the absolute, as Clausewitz did for many years, that all wars, whatever their cause and purpose, must be waged with supreme effort? In 1804 he had already distinguished between wars fought "to destroy one's opponent, to terminate his political existence," and wars waged to weaken the opponent sufficiently so that one could "impose conditions [on him] at the peace conference." [52] Yet while drawing this distinction, he denied that limited aims justified a limitation of effort. In his notes for *Strategy* as well as in the essay for the crown prince some years later, he argued that even if no more were intended than compelling the opponent to agree to terms, his power and will to resist must be broken. For political and social as well as for military reasons, the preferred way of achieving victory was the shortest, most direct way, and that meant using all available force.[53] In this view, which cavalierly passed over the possibility that excessive mobilization could also have counterproductive effects, Clausewitz's personal experiences buttressed the demands of his logic: it was not difficult to believe that from the first campaign of the Revolution to the wars of 1806 and 1809 France emerged victorious because her opponents would not exert themselves to the utmost. And it was in part because contemporary reality seemed to confirm the view that every war was a modification of the absolute and that every war should be waged without restrictions being placed on the rational application of force that these arguments retained what might be called a formal supremacy in Clausewitz's writings even as he was coming to appreciate that they were one-sided.

His essay "On Progression and Pause" indicates that by 1817 he was no longer content to impute the modification of military activity wholly to the force of friction. Because war consisted in a series of interactions between opponents, it was proper not only in reality but also in logic that not every minute should pass at the highest pitch of effort and violence. Numerous hints in books I through VIII of *On War* point in the same direction. His historical research supported the logical hypothesis. By the middle of the 1820's Clausewitz was convinced that often in the past limited conflicts had occurred, not because the protagonists' means precluded greater effort or because their leadership or will had faltered but because their intentions were too restricted to justify anything more. A war fought for limited goals was not necessarily a modification or corruption of the theoretical principle of absolute war. Consequently, Clausewitz declared in his "Note" and in his last version of chapter 1 of book I, a second type of war

52. See above, pp. 90–91.
53. See above, pp. 195–196. This concept is analyzed in various contexts in *On War*. See, for example, book III, ch. 8 (p. 274), or book III, ch. 11 (p. 289), where the strategic benefits of overall strength are outlined.

existed that was as valid as absolute war, not only in the field but also philosophically. Limited wars might be a modification of the absolute, but need not be, if the purpose for which they were waged was also limited. Violence continued to be the essence, the regulative idea, even of limited wars fought for limited ends; but in such cases the essence did not require its fullest possible expression. The concept of absolute war had by no means become invalid and it continued to perform decisive analytic functions; but it was now joined by the concept of limited war.

The dual nature of war, as Clausewitz formulated it in the last years of his life, is expressed in two pairs of possible conflicts, each defined according to the purpose involved: war waged with the aim of completely defeating the enemy, in order (a) to destroy him as a political organism, or (b) to force him to accept any terms whatever; and wars waged to acquire territory, in order (a) to retain the conquest, or (b) to bargain with the occupied land in the peace negotiations. Other, defensive, combinations were also possible. With this redefinition the proposition that war is the continuation of politics by other means, or that war is the continuation of policy with an admixture of other means, becomes theoretically and empirically accurate.

In the "Note" of 1827 Clausewitz stated his intention of revising the entire text of *On War* to develop the different types of conflict systematically. But he went further. The revision would more firmly establish as a second major theme the political character of war, "that war *is nothing but the continuation of government policy with other means.*" [54] The distinction he drew between the two themes is puzzling since only a few sentences earlier the "Note" declares that political motives determine whether a conflict is limited or not. Clausewitz did not explain why he separated the dual nature of war and the political character of war in his programmatic statement, but Eberhard Kessel has suggested a reason based on arguments and observations that recur throughout Clausewitz's writings: war is influenced by objective and by subjective political factors. The objective factors comprise the specific characteristics and strengths of the state in question, and the general characteristics of the age—political, economic, technological, intellectual, and social. The subjective factors consist in the free will of the leadership, which should conform to the objective realities, but sometimes does not, or sometimes rises above them. Put differently, Clausewitz separated the political consequences of general conditions and those arising from individual intelligence, emotions, genius. He may have sought analytic clarity by linking his discussion of the objective political realities mainly to the concept of the dual nature of war, and the issues of leadership mainly to the concept of the political character of war. [55] But however

---

54. "Note," *On War* (p. 77).
55. Kessel, "Zur Genesis der modernen Kriegslehre," pp. 415–417. See also the same author's "Die doppelte Art des Krieges," *ibid.*, IV (1954), No. 7.

Clausewitz's statement is interpreted, the reader of *On War* will find himself in accord with its author if he gives the political motives and character of war more prominence than they receive in much of the text, and, further, if he amends the unrevised sections to the effect that limited wars need not be a modification, but that theoretically as well as in reality two equally valid types of war exist.

The practical point that emerged from the concept of the dual nature of war was not the commonplace that men fight for political reasons but that each specific conflict should be shaped and guided by the kind and intensity of its political motives. Violence should express the political purpose, not replace it. Men who readily acknowledged the political roots of war found it difficult to follow Clausewitz to this conclusion. Six months after he had outlined his plans for the revision of *On War*, his friend Roeder sent him two strategic excercises, which Müffling had set his subordinates on the general staff. What did Clausewitz think of the problems and of Roeder's solutions? The problems assumed that Austria, allied with Saxony, was about to attack Prussia; but while specifying in detail the military means of the opposing sides they offered no further information on the aims of the various governments and the international situation in general.[56]

On 22 December Clausewitz answered Roeder that he could make little sense of the first problem. Two days later he dismissed the second in similar terms. As posed, they were too incomplete to permit a meaningful solution since they failed to state even the military aim of the two sides: "This aim is largely the result of mutual political relations of the two parties and of their relationship to other states that could participate in the [diplomatic and military] action. If these matters are not established, a [strategic] plan of this type becomes nothing more than a combination of a few factors of time and space, directed toward an arbitrary goal." [57] Any other combination might be equally valid. Clausewitz nevertheless outlined the strategic and operational alternatives in some detail; but he preceded his discussion with a declaration of basic principles:

"War is not an independent phenomenon but the continuation of politics by different means. Consequently the main lines of every major strategic plan are *largely political in nature,* and their political character increases the more the plan applies to the entire campaign and to the whole state. A war plan results directly from the political conditions of the two warring states, as well as from their relations to third powers. A plan of campaign results from the war plan, and frequently—if there is only one theater of operations—may even be identical with it. But the political element even

56. The problems, Roeder's solutions, and Clausewitz's comments were published in 1937 under the title *Zwei Briefe des Generals von Clausewitz: Gedanken zur Abwehr,* as a special issue of the *Militärwissenschaftliche Rundschau.*
57. *Ibid.,* pp. 8–9.

enters the separate components of a campaign; rarely will it be without influence on such major episodes of warfare as a battle, etc. According to this point of view, there can be no question of a *purely military* evaluation of a great strategic issue, or of a purely military scheme to solve it." [58]

That was the reality. How could men be taught to understand it? Clausewitz thought that it was enormously difficult to construct a didactic problem with even a semblance of realism because reality consisted of a "mass of individual circumstances," ranging from details to "very important points [*sehr grosse Hauptsachen*], which until today have nevertheless almost always been ignored. For instance, Bonaparte and Frederick the Great are often compared, sometimes without keeping in mind that one had forty million subjects, the other five. But let me call attention to another, less noticeable but very significant distinction: Bonaparte was a usurper ... while Frederick the Great disposed of a true inheritance. Had nature given both men identical psychological qualities, would they have acted in the same manner? Certainly not, and that alone makes it impossible to measure them by the same standard." [59]

The comparison between Frederick and Napoleon, which had occupied Clausewitz since his youth, underlined the importance of the reciprocal relationship between the psychological qualities of the individual and his specific historical situation. What one man found possible and desirable was not so for the other. The special circumstances of his times almost always allowed Napoleon to seek the total destruction of his opponent's armies. That led people "to assume that the plans and actions that *emerged from these circumstances* were *universal norms.* But such a view would summarily condemn the entire history of war, which is absurd. If we wish to derive an art of war from the history of war—undoubtedly the only way an art of war can be established—we must not minimize the testimony of history. ... We must not allow ourselves to be misled into regarding war as a pure act of force and of destruction. ... We must recognize that war is a political act, which is not wholly independent, that it is a true political instrument, which does not act on its own but is controlled by something else: by the hand of politics." [60]

The final correction of the regulative idea on which his theories of war were based—the theoretical acceptance of gradations of violence—is perhaps Clausewitz's most impressive intellectual and psychological achievement. His thought had been formed and continued to be strongly influenced by the philosophy of German idealism; but in his forties he liberated himself from its authority in the very manner advocated by idealist philosophy, not by destroying but by expanding it. Instead of a single absolute, he

58. *Ibid.*, p. 6.
59. *Ibid.*, pp. 6–7.
60. *Zwei Briefe des Generals von Clausewitz*, pp. 7–8.

now posited a pair of absolutes. Reality, the limitation of violence, need no longer be an imperfect version of the ideal; depending on the purpose of the particular war, and on the manner in which it was waged, reality might closely reflect the ideal—even more closely in a limited than in an absolute conflict.

Even after he had rewritten the first chapter of *On War* and revised other sections, Clausewitz recognized that his ideas needed to be developed further, and passages in the book and in the letters of his last years point to important additions to theory that he never worked out in detail.[61] For instance, book VI of *On War* states that the dual nature of war applies to defensive as well as offensive war, but the definition in the opening chapter of the work refers only to the side that initiates the conflict. Again, his opening propositions assume that ultimately political and military goals were in accord, even though elsewhere he stated that the relationship between political purpose and military aims tended to be more complex, and that in the course of the conflict each might affect and change the other. Despite his remarkable invention of the concept of escalation, he never sufficiently explored the various ways in which two opponents influence each other. At least some of these problems would have been further resolved and some inconsistencies removed had he lived long enough to carry out the enormous task of revising the entire manuscript. As it was, he left behind what he thought could "only deserve to be called a shapeless mass of ideas. Being liable to endless misinterpretation it would be the target of much half-baked criticism... . Nonetheless, I believe an unprejudiced reader in search of truth and understanding will recognize the fact that the first six books, for all their imperfection of form, contain the fruit of years of reflection on war and diligent study of it. He may even find they contain the basic ideas that might bring about a revolution in the theory of war." [62] With the last phrase he may have meant no more than to express his confidence that *On War* indicated what questions ought to be asked, and the kind of answers, combining specificity with universality, that should be sought.

---

61. The extent of Clausewitz's revisions after 1827 is uncertain. Besides the first chapter, he may also have revised chs. 2 and 3 of book I, and ch. 2 of book II, as well as parts of book VIII, without, however, considering these to be in final form.
62. "Note," *On War* (p. 79).

IV. "WHAT IS WAR?"

After the work of an innovative mind such as Clausewitz's has been analyzed, after the context and genesis of his writings have been discussed and their author's cultural and emotional roots suggested, the historian can do no better than let the work speak for itself. All history is reconstruction, but the history of ideas not in the same manner or to the same extent as the history of political, economic, or military activity. Much of the material that most concerns the historian of ideas has retained something close to its original condition; the historical substance of a manuscript by Clausewitz is different from that of a political or military act of Napoleon, regardless of how many memoranda, dispatches, and decrees surround the latter. The manuscript is an artifact, the decision at best a fossil. The historian of ideas is in the enviable position of dealing with material that is both past and present. I have quoted Clausewitz more frequently in discussing his histories and theories than in earlier chapters; any remaining screen of interpretation between reader and subject should now be removed altogether.

The opening chapter of *On War,* the text of which follows, is not characteristic of the work as a whole. No other chapter is as comprehensive, and few chapters are as formally structured; its numbered sections and paragraphs have greater affinity with German philosophic writing of the time and even with Montesquieu's *De l'Esprit des lois* than with the rest of *On War.* It is the only chapter that Clausewitz regarded as complete. But he also expressed the confidence that it would "at least serve the whole by indicating the direction I meant to follow everywhere." [1] In his eyes the opening chapter was the best introduction to his book, and thus it is also the best imaginable guide to his entire theoretical work.

WHAT IS WAR?

1. Introduction

I propose to consider first the various *elements* of the subject, next its *various parts* or *sections,* and finally *the whole* in its internal structure. In other words, I shall proceed from the simple to the complex. But in war more than in any other sub-

---

1. "Note," *On War* (p. 79).

ject, we must begin by looking at the nature of the whole; for here more than elsewhere the part and the whole must always be thought of together.

2. Definition

I shall not begin by formulating a crude, journalistic definition of war, but go straight to the heart of the matter, to the duel. War is nothing but a duel on a larger scale. Countless duels go to make up war, but a picture of it as a whole can be formed by imagining a pair of wrestlers. Each tries through physical force to compel the other to do his will; his *immediate* aim is to *throw* his opponent in order to make him incapable of further resistance.

War is thus an act of force to compel our enemy to do our will.

Force, to counter opposing force, equips itself with the inventions of art and science. Attached to force are certain self-imposed, imperceptible limitations, hardly worth mentioning, known as international law and custom, but they scarcely weaken it. Force—that is, physical force, for moral force has no existence save as expressed in the state and the law—is thus the *means* of war; to impose our will on the enemy is its *object*. To secure that object we must render the enemy powerless, and that, in theory, is the true aim of warfare. That aim takes the place of the object, discarding it as something not actually part of war itself.

3. The Maximum Use of Force

Kind-hearted people might of course think there was some ingenious way to disarm or defeat an enemy without too much bloodshed, and might imagine this is the true goal of the art of war. Pleasant as it sounds, it is a fallacy that must be exposed: war is such a dangerous business that the mistakes which come from kindness are the very worst. The maximum use of force is in no way incompatible with the simultaneous use of the intellect. If one side uses force without compunction, undeterred by the bloodshed it involves, while the other side refrains, the first will gain the upper hand. That side will force the other to follow suit; each will drive its opponent toward extremes and the only limiting factors are the counterpoises inherent in war.

This is how the matter must be seen; it would be futile—even wrong—to try and shut one's eyes to what war really is from sheer distress at its brutality.

If wars between civilized nations are far less cruel and destructive than wars between savages, the reason lies in the social conditions of the states themselves and in their relationships to one another. These are the forces that give rise to war; the same forces circumscribe and moderate it. They themselves, however, are not part of war; they already exist before fighting starts. To introduce the principle of moderation into the theory of war itself would always lead to logical absurdity.

Two different motives make men fight one another: *hostile feelings* and *hostile intentions*. Our definition is based on the latter, since it is the universal element. Even the most savage, almost instinctive, passion of hatred cannot be conceived as existing without hostile intent; but hostile intentions are often unaccompanied by any sort of hostile feelings—at least by none that predominate. Savage peoples are ruled by passion, civilized peoples by the mind. The difference, however, lies not in the respective natures of savagery and civilization, but in their attendant circumstances, institutions, and so forth. The difference, therefore, does not operate in every case, but it does in most of them. Even the most civilized of peoples, in short, can be fired with passionate hatred for each other.

Consequently, it would be an obvious fallacy to imagine war between civilized peoples as resulting merely from a rational act on the part of their governments and to conceive of war as gradually ridding itself of passion; so that in the end one would never really need to use the physical impact of the fighting forces—comparative figures of their strength would be enough. That would be a kind of war by algebra.

Theorists were already beginning to think along such lines when the recent wars taught them a lesson. If war is an act of force, the emotions cannot fail to be involved. War may not spring from them, but they will still affect it to some degree, and the extent to which they so do will depend not on the level of civilization but on how important the conflicting interests are and on how long their conflict lasts.

If, then, civilized nations do not put their prisoners to death or devastate cities and countries, it is because intelligence plays a larger part in their methods of warfare and has taught them more effective ways of using force than the crude expression of instinct.

The invention of gunpowder and the constant improvement of firearms are enough in themselves to show that the advance of civilization has done nothing practical to alter or deflect the impulse to destroy the enemy, which is central to the very idea of war.

The thesis, then, must be repeated: war is an act of force, and there is no logical limit to the application of that force. Each side, therefore, compels its opponent to follow suit; a reciprocal action is started which must lead, in theory, to extremes. This is the *first case of interaction and the first "extreme"* we meet with.

4. The Aim Is to Disarm the Enemy

I have already said that the aim of warfare is to disarm the enemy and it is time to show that at least in theory this is bound to be so. If the enemy is to be coerced you must put him in a situation that is even more unpleasant than the sacrifice you call on him to make. The hardships of that situation must not of course be merely transient—at least not in appearance. Otherwise the enemy would not give in but would wait for things to improve. Any change that might be brought about by continuing hostilities must, then, at least in theory, be of a kind to bring the enemy still greater disadvantages. The worst of all conditions in which a belligerent can find himself is to be utterly defenseless. Consequently, if you are to force the enemy, by making war on him, to do your bidding, you must either make him literally defenseless or at least put him in a position that makes this danger probable. It follows, then, that to overcome the enemy or disarm him—call it what you will—must always be the aim of warfare.

War, however, is not the action of a living force upon a lifeless mass (total nonresistance would be no war at all) but always the collision of two living forces. The ultimate aim of waging war, as formulated here, must be taken as applying to both sides. Once again, there is intraction. So long as I have not overthrown my opponent I am bound to fear he may overthrow me. Thus I am not in control: he dictates to me as much as I dictate to him. This is the *second case of interaction and it leads to the second "extreme."*

5. The Maximum Exertion of Strength

If you want to overcome your enemy you must match your effort against his power of resistance, which can be expressed as the product of two inseparable factors, viz. *the total means at his disposal* and *the strength of his will.* The extent of the means at his disposal is a matter—though not exclusively—of figures, and should be measurable. But the strength of his will is much less easy to determine and can only be gauged approximately by the strength of the motive animating it. Assuming you arrive in this way at a reasonably accurate estimate of the enemy's power of resistance, you can adjust your own efforts accordingly; that is, you can either increase them until they surpass the enemy's or, if this is beyond your means, you can make your efforts as great as possible. But the enemy will do the same; competition will again result and, in pure theory, it must again force you both to extremes. This is *the third case of interaction* and *the third "extreme."*

6. Modifications in Practice

Thus in the field of abstract thought the inquiring mind can never rest until it reaches the extreme, for here it is dealing with an extreme: a clash of forces freely operating and obedient to no law but their own. From a pure concept of war you might try to deduce absolute terms for the objective you should aim at and for the means of achieving it; but if you did so the continuous interaction would land you in extremes that represented nothing but a play of the imagination issuing from an almost invisible sequence of logical subtleties. If we were to think purely in absolute terms, we could avoid every difficulty by a stroke of the pen and proclaim with inflexible logic that, since the extreme must always be the goal, the greatest effort must always be exerted. Any such pronouncement would be an abstraction and would leave the real world quite unaffected.

Even assuming this extreme effort to be an absolute quantity that could easily be calculated, one must admit that the human mind is unlikely to consent to being ruled by such a logical fantasy. It would often result in strength being wasted, which is contrary to other principles of statecraft. An effort of will out of all proportion to the object in view would be needed but would not in fact be realized, since subtleties of logic do not motivate the human will.

But move from the abstract to the real world and the whole thing looks quite different. In the abstract world, optimism was all-powerful and forced us to assume that both parties to the conflict not only sought perfection but attained it. Would this ever be the case in practice? Yes, it would if:

(a) war were a wholly isolated act, occurring suddenly and not produced by previous events in the political world;
(b) it consisted of a single decisive act or a set of simultaneous ones;
(c) the decision achieved was complete and perfect in itself, uninfluenced by any previous estimate of the political situation it would bring about.

7. War Is Never an Isolated Act

As to the first of these conditions, it must be remembered that neither opponent is an abstract person to the other, not even to the extent of that factor in the power of resistance, namely the will, which is dependent on externals. The will is not a wholly unknown factor; we can base a forecast of its state tomorrow on what it is today. War never breaks out wholly unexpectedly, nor can it be spread instantaneously. Each side can therefore gauge the other to a large extent by what he is and does, instead of judging him by what he, strictly speaking, ought to be or do. Man and his affairs, however, are always something short of perfect and will never quite achieve the absolute best. Such shortcomings affect both sides alike and therefore constitute a moderating force.

8. War Does Not Consist of a Single Short Blow

The second condition calls for the following remarks:

If war consisted of one decisive act, or of a set of simultaneous decisions, preparations would tend toward totality, for no omission could ever be rectified. The sole criterion for preparations which the world of reality could provide would be the measures taken by the adversary—so far as they are known; the rest would once more be reduced to abstract calculations. But if the decision in war consists of several successive acts, then each of them, seen in context, will provide a gauge for those that follow. Here again, the abstract world is ousted by the real one and the trend to the extreme is thereby moderated.

But, of course, if all the means available were, or could be, simultaneously employed, all wars would automatically be confined to a single decisive act or a set of simultaneous ones—the reason being that any *adverse* decision must reduce the sum of the means available, and if *all* had been committed in the first act there could really be no question of a second. Any subsequent military operation would virtually be part of the first—in other words, merely an extension of it.

Yet, as I showed above, as soon as preparations for a war begin, the world of reality takes over from the world of abstract thought; material calculations take the place of hypothetical extremes and, if for no other reason, the interaction of the two sides tends to fall short of maximum effort. Their full resources will therefore not be mobilized immediately.

Besides, the very nature of those resources and of their employment means they cannot all be deployed at the same moment. The resources in question are *the fighting forces proper, the country,* with its physical features and population, and its *allies.*

The country—its physical features and population—is more than just the source of all armed forces proper; it is in itself an integral element among the factors at work in war—though only that part which is the actual theatre of operations or has a notable influence on it.

It is possible, no doubt, to use all mobile fighting forces simultaneously; but with fortresses, rivers, mountains, inhabitants, and so forth, that cannot be done; not, in short, with the country as a whole, unless it is so small that the opening action of the war completely engulfs it. Furthermore, allies do not cooperate at the mere desire of those who are actively engaged in fighting; international relations being what they are, such cooperation is often furnished only at some later stage or increased only when a balance has been disturbed and needs correction.

In many cases, the proportion of the means of resistance that cannot immediately be brought to bear is much higher than might at first be thought. Even when great strength has been expended on the first decision and the balance has been badly upset, equilibrium can be restored. The point will be more fully treated in due course. At this stage it is enough to show that the very nature of war impedes the *simultaneous concentration of all forces*. To be sure, that fact in itself cannot be grounds for making any but a maximum effort to obtain the first decision, for a defeat is always a disadvantage no one would deliberately risk. And even if the first clash is not the only one, the influence it has on subsequent actions will be on a scale proportionate to its own. But it is contrary to human nature to make an extreme effort, and the tendency therefore is always to plead that a decision may be possible later on. As a result, for the first decision, effort and concentration of forces are not all they might be. Anything omitted out of weakness by one side becomes a real, *objective* reason for the other to reduce its efforts, and the tendency toward extremes is once again reduced by this interaction.

9. In War the Result Is Never Final

Lastly, even the ultimate outcome of a war is not always to be regarded as final. The defeated state often considers the outcome merely as a transitory evil, for which a remedy may still be found in political conditions at some later date. It is obvious how this, too, can slacken tension and reduce the vigor of the effort.

10. The Probabilities of Real Life Replace the Extreme and the Absolute Required by Theory

Warfare thus eludes the strict theoretical requirement that extremes of force be applied. Once the extreme is no longer feared or aimed at, it becomes a matter of judgment what degree of effort should be made; and this can only be based on the phenomena of the real world and the *laws of probability*. Once the antagonists have ceased to be mere figments of a theory and become actual states and governments, when war is no longer a theoretical affair but a series of actions obeying its own peculiar laws, reality supplies the data from which we can deduce the unknown that lies ahead.

From the enemy's character, from his institutions, the state of his affairs and his general situation, each side, using the laws of *probability,* forms an estimate of its opponent's likely course and acts accordingly.

11. The Political Object Now Comes to the Fore Again

A subject which we last considered in Section 2 now forces itself on us again, namely the *political object of the war*. Hitherto it had been rather overshadowed by the law of extremes, the will to overcome the enemy and make him powerless. But as this law begins to lose its force and as this determination wanes, the political aim will reassert itself. If it is all a calculation of probabilities based on given individuals and conditions, the *political object,* which was the *original motive,* must become an essential factor in the equation. The smaller the penalty you demand from your opponent the less you can expect him to try and deny it to you; the smaller the effort he makes, the less you need make yourself. Moreover, the more modest your own political aim, the less importance you attach to it and the less reluctantly you will abandon it if you must. *This is another reason why your effort will be modified.*

The political object—the original motive for the war—will thus determine both the military objective to be reached and the amount of effort it requires. The political object cannot, however, *in itself* provide the standard of measurement. Since we are dealing with realities, not with abstractions, it can do so only in the context of the two states at war. The same political object can elicit *differing* reactions from different peoples, and even from the same people at different times. We can therefore take the political object as a standard only if we think of *the influence it can exert upon the forces it is meant to move.* The nature of those forces therefore calls for study. Depending on whether their characteristics increase or diminish the drive toward a particular action, the outcome will vary. Between two peoples and two states there can be such tensions, such a mass of inflammable material, that the slightest quarrel can produce a wholly disproportionate effect—a real explosion.

This is equally true of the efforts a political object is expected to arouse in either state, and of the military objectives which their policies require. Sometimes the *political and military objective is the same*—for example, the conquest of a province. In other cases the political object will not provide a suitable military objective. In that event, another military objective must be adopted that will serve the political purpose and symbolize it in the peace negotiations. But here, too, attention must be paid to the character of each state involved. There are times when, if the political objective is to be achieved, the substitute must be a good deal more important. The less involved the population is, the less serious the strains within states and between them, the more political requirements in themselves will dominate and tend to be decisive. Situations can thus exist in which the political object will almost be the sole determinant.

Generally speaking, a military objective that matches the political object in scale, will, if the latter is reduced, be reduced in proportion; this will be all the more so as the political object increases its predominance. Thus it follows that without any inconsistency wars can have all degrees of importance and intensity, ranging from a war of extermination down to simple armed observation. This brings us to a different question, which now needs to be analyzed and answered.

12. An Interruption of Military Activity Is Not Explained by Anything Yet Said

However modest the political demands may be on either side, however small the means employed, however limited the military objective, can the process of war ever be interrupted, even for a moment? The question reaches deep into the heart of the matter.

Every action needs a certain time to be completed. That period is called its duration, and its length will depend on the speed with which the person acting works. We need not concern ourselves with the difference here. Everyone performs a task in his own way; the slow man, however, does not do it more slowly because he wants to spend more time over it but because his nature causes him to need more time. If he made more haste he would do the job less well. His speed, then, is determined by subjective causes and is a factor in the actual duration of the task.

Now if every action in war is allowed its appropriate duration, we would agree that, at least at first sight, any additional expenditure of time—any suspension of military action—seems absurd. In this connection it must be remembered that what we are talking about is not the progress made by one side or the other but the progress of military interaction as a whole.

13. Only One Consideration Can Suspend Military Action, and It Seems That It Can Never Be Present on More Than One Side

If two parties have prepared for war, some motive of hostility must have brought them to that point. Moreover, so long as they remain under arms (do not negotiate a settlement) that motive of hostility must still be active. Only one consideration can restrain it: *a desire to wait for a better moment before acting.* At first sight one would think this desire could never operate on more than one side since its opposite must automatically be working on the other. If action would bring an advantage to one side, the other's interest must be to wait.

But an absolute balance of forces cannot bring about a standstill, for if such a balance should exist the initiative would necessarily belong to the side with the positive purpose—the attacker.

One could, however, conceive of a state of balance in which the side with the positive aim (the side with the stronger grounds for action) was the one that had the weaker forces. The balance would then result from the combined effects of aim and strength. Were that the case, one would have to say that unless some shift in the balance were in prospect the two sides should make peace. If, however, some alteration were to be foreseen, only one side could expect to gain by it—a fact which ought to stimulate the other into action. Inaction clearly cannot be explained by the concept of balance. The only explanation is that both are waiting for a better time to act. Let us suppose, therefore, that one of the two states has a positive aim—say, the conquest of a part of the other's territory, to use for bargaining at the peace table. Once the prize is in its hands, the political object has been achieved; there is no need to do more, and it can let matters rest. If the other state is ready to accept the situation, it should sue for peace. If not, it must do something; and if it thinks it will be better organized for action in four weeks' time it clearly has an adequate reason for not taking action at once.

But from that moment on, logic would seem to call for action by the other side—the object being to deny the enemy the time he needs for getting ready. Throughout all this I have assumed, of course, that both sides understand the situation perfectly.

14. Continuity Would Thus Be Brought About in Military Action and Would Again Intensify Everything

If this continuity were really to exist in the campaign its effect would again be to drive everything to extremes. Not only would such ceaseless activity arouse men's feelings and inject them with more passion and elemental strength, but events would follow more closely on each other and be governed by a stricter causal chain. Each individual action would be more important, and consequently more dangerous.

But war, of course, seldom if ever shows such continuity. In numerous conflicts, only a very small part of the time is occupied by action, while the rest is spent in inactivity. This cannot always be an anomaly. Suspension of action in war must be possible; in other words, it is not a contradiction in terms. Let me demonstrate this point, and explain the reasons for it.

15. Here, a Principle of Polarity Is Proposed

By thinking that the interests of the two commanders are opposed in equal measure to each other, we have assumed a genuine *polarity*. A whole chapter will be devoted to the subject further on, but the following must be said about it here.

The principle of polarity is valid only in relation to one and the same object, in which positive and negative interests exactly cancel one another out. In a battle each side aims at victory; that is a case of true polarity, since the victory of one side excludes the victory of the other. When, however, we are dealing with two different things that have a common relation external to themselves, the polarity lies not in the *things* but in their relationship.

16. Attack and Defense Being Things Different in Kind and Unequal in Strength, Polarity Cannot Be Applied to Them

If war assumed only a single form, namely, attacking the enemy, and defense were nonexistent; or, to put it in another way, if the only differences between attack and defense lay in the fact that attack has a positive aim whereas defense has not, and the forms of fighting were identical; then every advantage gained by one side would be a precisely equal disadvantage to the other—true polarity would exist.

But there are two distinct forms of action in war: attack and defense. As will be shown in detail later, the two are very different and unequal in strength. Polarity, then, does not lie in attack or defense, but in the object both seek to achieve: the decision. If one commander wants to postpone the decision, the other must want to hasten it, always assuming that both are engaged in the same kind of fighting. If it is in A's interest not to attack B now but to attack him in four weeks, then it is in B's interest not to be attacked in four weeks' time, but now. This is an immediate and direct conflict of interest; but it does not follow from this that it would also be to B's advantage to make an immediate attack on A. That would obviously be quite another matter.

17. The Superiority of Defense over Attack Often Destroys the Effect of Polarity, and This Explains the Suspension of Military Action

As we shall show, defense is a stronger form of fighting than attack. Consequently we must ask whether the advantage of *postponing a decision* is as great for one side as the advantage of *defense* is for the other. Whenever it is not, it cannot balance the advantage of defense, and in this way influence the progress of the war. It is clear, then, that the impulse created by the polarity of interests may be exhausted in the difference between the strength of attack and defense, and may thus become inoperative.

Consequently, if the side favored by present conditions is not sufficiently strong to do without the added advantages of the defense, it will have to accept the prospect of acting under unfavorable conditions in the future. To fight a defensive battle under these less favorable conditions may still be better than to attack immediately or to make peace. I am convinced that the superiority of the defensive (if rightly understood) is very great, far greater than appears at first sight. It is this which explains without any inconsistency most periods of inaction that occur in war. The weaker the motives for action, the more will they be overlaid and neutralized by this disparity between attack and defense, and the more frequently will action be suspended—as indeed experience shows.

18. A Second Cause Is Imperfect Knowledge of the Situation

There is still another factor that can bring military action to a standstill: imperfect knowledge of the situation. The only situation a commander can know fully is his own; his opponent's he can know only from unreliable intelligence. His evaluation, therefore, may be mistaken and can lead him to suppose that the initiative lies with the enemy when in fact it remains with him. Of course such faulty appreciation is as likely to lead to ill-timed action as to ill-timed inaction, and is no more conducive to slowing down operations than it is to speeding them up. Nevertheless, it must rank among the natural causes which, *without entailing inconsistency, can bring military activity to a halt.* Men are always more inclined to pitch their estimate of the enemy's strength too high than too low, such is human nature. Bearing this in mind, one must admit that partial ignorance of the situation is, generally speaking, a major factor in delaying the progress of military action and in moderating the principle that underlies it.

The possibility of inaction has a further moderating effect on the progress of the war by diluting it, so to speak, in time, by delaying danger, and by increasing the means of restoring a balance between the two sides. The greater the tensions that have led to war, and the greater the consequent war effort, the shorter these periods of inaction. Inversely, the weaker the motive for conflict, the longer the intervals between actions. For the stronger motive increases willpower, and willpower, as we know, is always both an element in and the product of strength.

19. Frequent Periods of Inaction Remove War Still Further from the Realm of the Absolute and Make It Even More a Matter of Assessing Probabilities

The slower the progress and the more frequent the interruptions of military action the easier it is to retrieve a mistake, the bolder will be the general's assessments, and the more likely he will be to avoid theoretical extremes and to base his plans on probability and inference. Any given situation requires that probabilities be calculated in the light of circumstances, and the amount of time available for such calculation will depend on the pace with which operations are taking place.

20. Therefore Only the Element of Chance Is Needed to Make War a Gamble, and That Element Is Never Absent

It is now quite clear how greatly the objective nature of war makes it a matter of assessing probabilities. Only one more thing is needed to make war a gamble—chance: the very last thing that war lacks. No other human activity is so continuously or universally bound up with chance. And through the element of chance, guesswork and luck come to play a great part in war.

21. Not Only Its Objective But Also Its Subjective Nature Makes War a Gamble

If we now consider briefly the *subjective nature* of war—the means by which war has to be fought—it will look more than ever like a gamble. The element in which war exists is danger. The highest of all moral qualities in time of danger is certainly *courage*. Now courage is perfectly compatible with prudent calculation but the two differ nonetheless, and pertain to different psychological forces. Daring, on the other hand, boldness, rashness, trusting in luck are only variants of courage, and all these traits of character seek their proper element—chance.

In short, absolute—so-called mathematical—factors never find a firm basis in military calculations. From the very start there is an interplay of possibilities, probabilities, good luck and bad, that weaves its way throughout the length and breadth of the tapestry. In the whole range of human activities, war most closely resembles a game of cards.

22. How in General This Best Suits Human Nature

The intellect always craves what is clear and certain, but uncertainty often fascinates us. It is our nature, rather than joining the intellect on its narrow, tortuous path of philosophical inquiry and logical deduction, from which it emerges—hardly knowing how—in strange and alien surroundings, where all familiar landmarks seem to have disappeared, to prefer to daydream in the realms of chance and luck. The world of narrow necessity is left behind and it revels in a wealth of possibilities. Courage, inspired, rises up and leaps into daring and danger, as a fearless swimmer dives into the current.

Should theory leave us here, and cheerfully go on elaborating absolute conclusions and prescriptions? Then it would be no use at all in real life. No, it must also take the human factor into account, and find room for courage, boldness, even foolhardiness. The art of war deals with living and with moral forces. Consequently it cannot attain the absolute, or certainty; it must always leave a margin for uncertainty in the greatest things as much as in the smallest. With uncertainty in one scale, courage and self-confidence must be thrown into the other to correct the balance. The greater they are, the greater the margin that can be left for accidents. Thus, courage and self-confidence are essential in war, and theory should propose only rules that give ample scope to these finest and least dispensable of military virtues, in all their degrees and variations. Even in daring there can be method and caution; but here they are measured by a different standard.

23. But War Is Nonetheless a Serious Means to a Serious End: A More Precise Definition of War

Such is war, such is the commander who directs it, and such the theory that governs it. War is no pastime; it is no mere joy in daring and winning, no place for irresponsible enthusiasts. It is a serious means to a serious end, and all its colorful resemblance to a game of chance, all the vicissitudes of passion, courage, imagination, and enthusiasm it includes are merely its special characteristics.

When whole communities go to war—whole peoples, and especially *civilized* peoples—the reason always lies in some political situation and the occasion is always due to some political object. War, therefore, is an act of policy. Were it a complete, untrammelled, absolute manifestation of violence (as the pure concept would require), war would of its own independent will usurp the place of policy the moment policy had brought it into being; it would then drive policy out of office and rule by the laws of its own nature, very much like a mine that can explode only in the manner or direction predetermined by the setting. This, in fact, is the view that has been taken of the matter whenever some discord between policy and the conduct of war has stimulated theoretical distinctions of this kind. But in reality things are different, and this view is thoroughly mistaken. In reality war, as has been shown, is not like that. Its violence is not of the kind that explodes in a single discharge, but is the effect of forces that do not always develop in exactly the same manner or to the same degree. At times they will expand sufficiently to overcome the resistance of inertia or friction; at others they are too weak to have any effect. War is a pulsation of violence, variable in strength and therefore variable in the speed with which it explodes and discharges its energy. War moves on its goal with varying speeds; but it always lasts long enough for influence to be exerted on the goal and for its own course to be changed in one way or another—long enough, in other words, to remain subject to the action of a superior intelligence. If we keep in mind that war springs from some political purpose, it is natural that the prime cause of its existence will remain the supreme consideration in conducting it. That, however, does not imply that the political aim is a tyrant. It must adapt itself to its chosen means, a process which can radically change it; yet the political aim remains the first consideration. Policy, then, will permeate all military operations and, in so far as their violent nature will admit, it will have a continuous influence on them.

24. War Is Merely the Continuation of Policy by Other Means

It is clear, consequently, that war is not a mere act of policy but a true political instrument, a continuation of political activity by other means. What remains peculiar to war is simply the peculiar nature of its means. War in general, and the commander in any specific instance, is entitled to require that the trend and designs of policy shall not be inconsistent with these means. That, of course, is no small demand; but however much it may affect political aims in a given case, it will never do more than modify them. The political object is the goal, war is the means of reaching it, and means can never be considered in isolation from their purpose.

25. The Diverse Nature of War

The more powerful and inspiring the motives for war, the more they affect the belligerent nations and the fiercer the tensions that precede the outbreak, the closer will war approach its abstract concept, the more important will be the destruction of the enemy, the more closely will the military aims and the political objects of war coincide, and the more military and less political will war appear to be. On the other hand, the less intense the motives, the less will the military element's natural tendency to violence coincide with political directives. As a result, war will be driven further from its natural course, the political object will be more and more at variance with the aim of ideal war, and the conflict will seem increasingly *political* in character.

At this point, to prevent the reader from going astray, it must be observed that the phrase, the *natural tendency* of war, is used in its philosophical, strictly *logical* sense alone and does not refer to the tendencies of the forces that are actually engaged in fighting—including, for instance, the morale and emotions of the combatants. At times, it is true, these might be so aroused that the political factor would be hard put to control them. Yet such a conflict will not occur very often, for if the motivations are so powerful there must be a policy of proportionate magnitude. On the other hand, if policy is directed only toward minor objectives, the emotions of the masses will be little stirred and they will have to be stimulated rather than held back.

26. All Wars Can Be Considered Acts of Policy

It is time to return to the main theme and observe that while policy is apparently effaced in the one kind of war and yet is strongly evident in the other, both kinds are equally political. If the state is thought of as a person, and policy as the product of its brain, then among the contingencies for which the state must be prepared is a war in which every element calls for policy to be eclipsed by violence. Only if politics is regarded not as resulting from a just appreciation of affairs, but—as it conventionally is—as cautious, devious, even dishonest, shying away from force, could the second type of war appear to be more "political" than the first.

27. The Effects of This Point of View on the Understanding of Military History and the Foundations of Theory

First, therefore, it is clear that war should never be thought of as *something autonomous* but always as an *instrument of policy;* otherwise the entire history of war would contradict us. Only this approach will enable us to penetrate the problem intelligently. *Second,* this way of looking at it will show us how wars must vary with the nature of their motives and of the situations which give rise to them.

The first, the supreme, the most far-reaching act of judgment that the statesman and commander have to make, is to establish by that test the kind of war on which they are embarking, neither mistaking it for, nor trying to turn it into, something that is alien to its nature. This is the first of all strategic questions and the most comprehensive. It will be given detailed study later, in the chapter on "War Plans."

It is enough, for the moment, to have reached this stage and to have established the cardinal point of view from which war and the theory of war have to be examined.

28. The Consequences for Theory

War is more than a true chameleon that slightly adapts its characteristics to the given case. As a total phenomenon its dominant tendencies always make war a remarkable trinity—composed of primordial violence, hatred, and enmity, which are to be regarded as a blind natural force; of the play of chance and probability within which the creative spirit is free to roam; and of its element of subordination as an instrument of policy, which makes it subject to reason alone.

The first of these three aspects mainly concerns the people; the second the commander and his army; the third the government. The passions that are to be kindled in war must already be inherent in the people; the scope which the play of courage and talent will enjoy in the realm of probability and chance depends on the particular character of the commander and the army; but the political aims are the business of government alone.

These three tendencies are like three different codes of law, deep rooted in their subject and yet variable in their relationship to one another. A theory that ignores any one of them or seeks to fix an arbitrary relationship between them would conflict with reality to such an extent that for this reason alone it would be totally useless.

Our task therefore is to develop a theory that maintains a balance between these three tendencies, like an object suspended between three magnets.

What lines might best be followed to achieve this difficult task will be explored in the book on the Theory of War. At any rate, the preliminary concept of war we have formulated casts a first ray of light on the basic structure of theory, and enables us to make an initial differentiation and identification of its major components.

✠ 12 ✠

THE LAST YEAR

I. THE REVOLUTIONS OF 1830

In the last days of July 1830, some weeks before Clausewitz left Berlin for his new post in Breslau, Charles X was overthrown in France. The replacement of the elder Bourbon line by the Duke of Orleans in defiance of the principle of legitimacy, to which the congress of Vienna had attached such profound significance, was followed toward the end of August by the Belgian uprising against the Dutch. To many observers in Berlin the threatened dissolution of the United Netherlands, keystone in the defense of Germany against France, appeared only as the first stage in a revolutionary process that might again engulf Europe. Among those who were outraged at the general spirit of insurrection, Clausewitz commented, "were many who were not accustomed to think with clarity and precision, and who considered Prussian intervention in the Belgian affair as highly feasible, and consequently as necessary." [1] He was referring to the Legitimist groups around Duke Karl of Mecklenburg and the king's sons; later in the year he dismissed the princes' political bombast as a disagreeable and painful spectacle. [2] Equally hostile to Louis Philippe but showing greater reserve were such ultraconservatives as Ancillon, who during the first weeks of the crisis acted as Bernstorff's deputy at the foreign office, and Prince Wittgenstein. In the regimental messes, naturally enough, the opinion prevailed that a Prussian expeditionary corps could soon settle matters in

---

1. Undated introductory note to his journal covering the period from 7 September 1830 to 9 March 1831. Schwartz, *Leben des Generals Clausewitz,* ii, 299. The journal entries were evidently written some time after the events to which they referred. As early as 20 August, Clausewitz had written to Gneisenau that "in the beginning the party of the ultras wanted nothing better than to march and subjugate France; but little by little their blood has somewhat cooled." Pertz-Delbrück, v, 607.
2. Clausewitz's response of 13 November 1830 to a letter of 5 November by Gneisenau, who mentioned a hunt dinner given by the crown prince at which the political conversation was climaxed with a toast to the good cause, followed by the smashing of glasses. Pertz-Delbrück, v, 616, 620. Treitschke devotes an interesting and characteristic paragraph to this episode in his *Deutsche Geschichte,* iv, 196–197.

Brussels. Clausewitz, on the contrary, thought that a Prussian move would only lead to French intervention and a European war. However, his caution was accompanied by the pessimistic belief that Prussian neutrality was unlikely to prevent a general conflict. In the middle of August, even before the Belgians rebelled, he wrote to Gneisenau, who as usual was spending the summer in Erdmannsdorff, his Silesian estate, that he would rather hang himself than remain in the artillery when war came. He conveyed his feelings to Witzleben, who as the head of the king's military cabinet now exerted more influence than ever, and was assured that he would be given a different assignment if hostilities seemed imminent.[3] On the eve of Clausewitz's departure, Witzleben asked him to travel by way of Erdmannsdorff and convince Gneisenau that an earlier suggestion of the king's—he would be delighted to see Gneisenau in the capital—was more than a polite gesture to the army's senior officer in a time of crisis. The implication was that Gneisenau would receive command of the field army if Prussia mobilized. On the day Clausewitz began his journey, 7 September, Duke Karl of Brunswick, whose "limitless egotism"—to use Bernstorff's characterization—had made his reign a public scandal, was driven from his state by a popular uprising. It was obvious to Clausewitz that, contrary to the fears of the Prussian Legitimists, Germany was not seething with revolutionary fever; but the tumult in Brunswick, together with disturbances in Hesse and Saxony, reinforced the impression he gained from events beyond the Rhine that suddenly the political stability of Europe had come into question.

The possibility of war was real enough, although the unwillingness of any power to act unilaterally eventually proved an effective brake. The tsar urged observance of the Vienna treaties on Russia's allies of 1814 and 1815, offered the services of his army, and sent Field Marshal Diebitsch —the man who had signed the convention of Tauroggen with Yorck— to Berlin to press for intervention. Austrian policy was more ambiguous. Metternich made it plain that he would employ force to maintain the status quo in Italy; on the Rhine he wanted Prussia to take the military lead, so long as this would not unduly increase her influence in Germany. The British government considered neither the change of regime in Paris nor the Belgian revolution as a cause of war, but was cognizant of the fact that the conflict between Dutch and Belgians could spread, especially if the French volunteers who had joined the insurgents were succeeded by French regulars. As late as the following summer, when a French corps responded to a call for help from the new Belgian king, Palmerston declared that unless

---

3. Clausewitz to Gneisenau, 20 August 1830, Pertz-Delbrück, v, 607. During the same days the king pessimistically wrote that war seemed inevitable sooner or later. Frederick William III to his daughter Charlotte, Empress of Russia, 4/14 August 1830, "Aus dem letzten Jahrzehnt Friedrich-Wilhelms III.," ed. P. Bailleu, *Hohenzollern-Jahrbuch*, XX (1916), 152.

the French withdrew a general war would be inevitable. In the London conference on the future of Belgium, which opened early in November 1830, French proposals for partitioning the country did nothing to reduce tension. The French themselves feared the dynamic of their internal politics, which placed conflicting pressures on their foreign policy. In Prussia, Frederick William and Bernstorff were prepared to intervene only if they could count on British support, which they soon recognized would not be forthcoming. But, as they saw it, the real danger was French aggression. It seemed almost inconceivable to them that France would not take advantage of the opportunities created by the Belgian uprising. They feared even more that Louis Philippe would fall as the revolution was radicalized.

On this point their anxieties coincided with those of Gneisenau and Clausewitz, whose views on foreign affairs during these months can be reconstructed in detail from their correspondence and from Clausewitz's diary. Gneisenau may have had a more favorable opinion of Charles X—after the revolution he acknowledged that Marie von Clausewitz had read Charles's character more accurately than he; but on the whole the two friends were in agreement. Both opposed a preventive war. Not only could Prussia ill afford to act alone; she would require two months to mobilize the forces necessary for a major conflict, and any mobilization measure "would immediately fan the flames of war." [4] Even such a purely precautionary move as putting the Rhenish fortresses in readiness to withstand a siege must be avoided, they held, since France could use it as a pretext for war. Indeed, their great fear was that Prussia would be attacked, and that she would have to bear the brunt of the fighting, as she had in 1806. For the moment the country's security rested less with her soldiers than with the diplomats. If the Prussian government reached firm agreements with its allies, the French might be dissuaded from war altogether. At the very least, time was gained during which the liberal monarchy could establish itself as a secure and reliable member of the international community; alternately, civil war might break out in France, which would render foreign adventures out of the question. But wasn't it in the nature of any state to

---

4. Gneisenau to Clausewitz, 18 August 1830, Pertz-Delbrück, v, 604. I have slightly revised the earlier view expressed in my article "An Anonymous Letter by Clausewitz on the Polish Insurrection of 1830–1831," *Journal of Modern History*, XLII, No. 2 (June 1970), pp. 184–185 and note 3, that Clausewitz initially favored intervention but changed his mind. I based my opinion on a letter of 21 October 1830 to Gneisenau, in which Clausewitz criticized attempts to influence the Prussian government to intervene, and continued: "If in the first days of August we had possessed a force of 150,000 men on the French frontier, I would certainly have been of the opinion that we should at once march on Paris. . . ." Now, he concluded, there was nothing to be done but wait. Pertz-Delbrück, v, 609. Since a force of such magnitude could be available only in time of war, it makes better sense to interpret this passage as demonstrating the practical impossibility of intervention, the more so since Clausewitz's first letter to Gneisenau after receiving news of the revolution unequivocally opposed intervention. *Ibid.*, p. 607. Treitschke's assertion in his *Deutsche Geschichte*, iv, 45, 202, that Clausewitz favored a preventive war, which has become generally accepted in the literature, now seems to me even less valid than I thought a few years ago.

fill a power vacuum on its borders? In November, Clausewitz wrote that "if one wishes to be objective one can hardly blame the popular movement now dominating Paris for imposing as a prime condition on any government claiming authority that it must not renounce such enormous advantages." [5] The natural tendency of France, as that of any powerful state, to expand, appeared to Gneisenau and Clausewitz all the more likely to become reality because they expected the July Revolution to repeat the course that events had taken after 1789. Despite Clausewitz's conviction that each episode in history was unique, it was difficult for him not to believe that "in France new revolutions will develop from the loins of the first revolution, and that this country [France] will then break the peace." [6] The impressions of 1792 and 1793, when he had first put on uniform and when the new energies of France began to burst through the confines of the *ancien régime,* continued to captivate the judgment of the mature man—as the concepts of *raison d'état* and power too exclusively dominated his evaluation of foreign affairs. He found the dynamics of those days thirty-five years ago so readily understandable and historically justified that their recurrence seemed to him highly probable, almost inevitable.

In the latter half of September, Gneisenau traveled to Berlin, keeping in frequent touch by letter with Clausewitz, who had taken up his post in Silesia. Marie von Clausewitz remained in the capital for the time being, but her brother, husband of Gneisenau's second youngest daughter, was stationed in Breslau, and the companionship the young couple offered Clausewitz made his new existence more agreeable; during the first weeks he called on them every day.[7] Throughout October he inspected the three artillery brigades of his command, a tour that took him to East Prussia, to the "Grand Duchy of Posen"—the belt of formerly Polish territory given to Prussia in 1815—and to various towns in Silesia. Toward the end of the month he returned to Breslau, where he and his wife settled in an apartment provided by the state. He was repeatedly indisposed, but felt able to remain on duty. On 5 December he received the news that an insurrection had broken out in Warsaw. Shortly afterwards a letter from Gneisenau informed him that the king had asked Gneisenau to command the army about to be mobilized, and had approved Gneisenau's request that Clausewitz be appointed his chief of staff. On 12 December, Clausewitz and his wife returned to Berlin.

The uprising of cadets and students in Warsaw on 29 November, almost unopposed by the small Russian garrison, quickly led to the collapse of Russian authority throughout the country. For some weeks the rela-

5. Clausewitz to Gneisenau, 13 November 1830, Pertz-Delbrück, v, 618.
6. Clausewitz to Gneisenau, 21 October 1830, *ibid.,* p. 609.
7. Brühl to Gneisenau, 25 September 1830, published by H. v. Sybel in "Gneisenau und sein Schwiegersohn, Graf Friedrich Wilhelm v. Brühl," *Historische Zeitschrift,* LXIX (1892), 264.

tionship between Poland and the Empire remained in doubt, but by January the break was complete and war had become inevitable. By preventing Russia for the time being from intervening on the Rhine these events contributed to the continued peaceful resolution of the Belgian issue. On the other hand, the enthusiasm with which Italian and German liberals greeted the insurrection increased tensions in central Europe. Prussia was faced with the immediate problem that the rebellion might extend into Posen. More than three-fifths of the inhabitants of the province, which linked Silesia and East Prussia, were Poles, and at least among the nobility support for the new regime in Warsaw seemed nearly universal. Prussia's security as well as concern for her Russian ally demanded the closing of the long Prussian-Polish frontier. More active measures of support for the Russians were considered, but these were rejected in favor of a policy of benevolent neutrality. To be prepared for any eventuality, units in the eastern provinces of the monarchy were mobilized or placed on alert; four regiments that drew their rank and file from largely Polish districts were transferred to the west to preclude mutinies in support of the insurgents; and mobilization plans were prepared for the corps stationed along the Rhine. Although Gneisenau and the army's senior officers had a low opinion of Russian efficiency, they expected that Diebitsch, who had returned to Russia to take command of the force assembled to reconquer the country, would encounter few difficulties. Until the Poles were defeated, however, they feared the possibility of Prussia having to fight simultaneously in the east and west, perhaps against opponents who coordinated their actions.

Once arrived in Berlin, Clausewitz became less concerned about potential foreign enemies than about conditions at home. The state with the most disciplined civil and military institutions in Europe still lacked a central body that could develop and implement policy. Power and accountability were no longer as disjointed as they had been before 1806, but particularly in those areas of government in which the king took a special interest, royal prerogative and personal influence continued to inhibit the energetic, consistent conduct of business. Though frequently ill, Bernstorff retained his sure hand as foreign minister, but increasingly he relied on two very dissimilar subordinates. The first of these was the archconservative Ancillon, who dealt with non-German matters, while relations with the German courts and the German Confederation were the responsibility of Eichhorn, whom Metternich insisted on regarding as a revolutionary in disguise, and who had indeed retained his moderate reformist principles from the days he had assisted Stein. The foreign ministry did not, however, have sole management of foreign affairs. Duke Karl, the president of the Council of State, claimed a voice, as did Prince Wittgenstein. Opposed to these ideological adherents of the Russian alliance was the Prussian ambassador at St. Petersburg, General von Schoeler, who never ceased to warn of the Tsar's unreliability and lack of realism in his direct reports to the king. Any number of other officials, experts, and interested personalities participated in molding foreign policy, which nevertheless was conducted with greater efficiency than could be found on the military side. Since the king did not consider himself competent in the areas of strategic planning and higher military organization, he left these matters to others while keeping a close watch on the army as a whole. Hake, Clausewitz's former superior in Coblenz, was still minister of war, his talents fully taken up with problems of equipment and supply, while the relatively junior Witzleben in effect made the major decisions regarding organization and appointments. On strategic issues Witzleben was advised by the chief of the general staff, Krauseneck, whose counsel reflected his fear that strong measures might antagonize the smaller German states and compromise the turn toward more liberal policies that he favored for Prussia. Since the general staff disposed over few sources of news from abroad, Krauseneck labored under the additional handicap of depending for foreign intelligence on Bernstorff and on Witzleben himself, neither of whom kept him regularly and fully informed. Knesebeck, the king's senior general adjutant, assumed a roving commission in the fields of foreign affairs and strategy. His Austrian sympathies made him in the king's eyes a useful counterweight to such men as Krauseneck and Rühle, and to a lesser extent Witzleben and Gneisenau, who believed that recent events afforded Prussia new opportunities in Germany if she would only reject Austrian dominance over the military arrangements of the Confederation and adopt more liberal policies in regard to the press laws and on constitutional issues. Gneisenau, who had not yet received his appointment as commander in chief, found himself with Clausewitz at the edge rather than at the center of affairs. Krauseneck wanted Gneisenau to be given overall authority for the duration of the emergency; but to bring this about Gneisenau would have had to approach the king in his own behalf, and Clausewitz felt compelled to advise the chief of staff that Gneisenau was not the man to push himself forward. With his vast moral authority and great charm Gneisenau quickly became the uncrowned head of the military world in the capital even as its official leadership continued to be denied him. Otherwise little changed throughout December and January.[8]

Clausewitz's own situation was painfully ambiguous. His friendship with Gneisenau and Bernstorff, and the good relations he enjoyed with Witzleben, Krauseneck, Eichhorn, and others, were balanced by the indifference or antagonism he encountered from such men as Knesebeck, An-

---

8. Complaints about the confusion at the apex of the military hierarchy came from all factions but were particularly strong among former members of the reform party. For characteristically blunt comments see Grolman's statements in E. v. Conrady, *Leben und Wirken des Generals Carl von Grolman*, Berlin, 1894–96, iii, 116–119.

cillon, who had strongly opposed his entry into the diplomatic service, and the king himself. A minor episode at the beginning of his stay in Berlin indicated clearly enough that Frederick William had approved his new appointment without enthusiasm. Senior officers transferred to the capital were obliged to report to the king at the first levee held after their arrival. If, as happened in Clausewitz's case, the levee was canceled, the officer in question could expect a command to appear at the palace. But two weeks passed without such an invitation, and Clausewitz had resigned himself to the snub, when he encountered the king at a concert in the crown prince's residence. "When he saw me," Clausewitz wrote in his diary, "he crossed the room, greeted me pleasantly, and more or less apologized for not yet having been able to receive me; but then said nothing further. However, he talked for a good ten minutes with my wife, who stood next to me—about politics, to be specific. The world could well assume that we both were much in the king's favor, and that I was an important figure in the state." In reality, Clausewitz continued, "I passed six weeks in Berlin without any real duties. Only a report that Prince August had me draft for the evaluation commission of scientific and mechanical proposals, concerning the changed construction of our supply wagons, occupied me to some extent." [9]

He spent his leisure time familiarizing himself with the situation in Poland by studying the history of Prussian operations during the Second Partition and working out contingency plans for a Prussian offensive on Warsaw in collaboration with the Russians, as well as plans for defensive measures to prevent Polish troops from crossing Prussia to reach Belgium or France—a possibility that caused some concern in Berlin. [10] But much of his time was given to the far more difficult problems posed by a war with France. As early as August he had written a long evaluation of the political and strategic alternatives of such a conflict, and sent it to Gneisenau, who passed it on to Witzleben soon after his arrival in Berlin, with the comment that the views Clausewitz expressed were his own. [11] Toward the end of the year Clausewitz drew up a second memorandum, which took account of the political changes that had occurred in the interval—particularly the loss of Belgium as a base of Prussian or allied operations. [12]

The two essays have a feature in common: their author's doubt that an

9. Schwartz, *Leben des Generals Clausewitz,* ii, 302.
10. *Ibid.*
11. "Promemoria über einen möglichen Krieg mit Frankreich." The text is printed in "Zwei Denkschriften von Clausewitz 1830/31," *Militär-Wochenblatt,* 1891, Nos. 29–30.
12. "Betrachtungen über den künftigen Kriegsplan gegen Frankreich," printed as appendix in *Moltkes Militärische Werke,* first series, iv, Berlin, 1902. The Historical Section of the German General Staff published the essay in this context to illustrate the differences between Clausewitz's plan and Moltke's plan for a war with France of 1859. It may be noted that Clausewitz's memorandum repeats arguments developed in the final chapter of book VIII of *On War:* "The Plan of a War Designed to Lead to the Total Defeat of the Enemy."

attack on France was more than a remote possibility in view of the political constellation and the forces available.[13] In August Clausewitz posited two logical alternatives for war: an alliance of major powers attacking France; and a French attack on Prussia, the most exposed member of the alliance. He argued that the Allies should take the offensive only if they were strong enough to reach Paris. Otherwise the French should be permitted to attack; after their advance had reached its culminating point and spent itself, a counteroffensive would have excellent chances. Even without the Russians, who needed many months to become operational, it should be possible for the Allies to raise over 500,000 men, of whom 350,000 would be available for a major offensive from the low countries by Prussian, British, and Dutch forces, and secondary thrusts by the Austrians and minor German states across the Rhine. If political and financial factors precluded such co-ordinated moves in sufficient strength, the Allies should opt for the stronger alternative, the defensive. To secure communications with England, cover the Netherlands and the Rhineland, and threaten Paris, the main allied army should assemble in southern Belgium. The French would have to seek it out there; any attacks they might launch against central and southern Germany would only weaken their main effort, and therefore should not be strenuously resisted—though undoubtedly there would be heavy political and psychological pressures to do so.

By the time Clausewitz wrote the second essay, the already favorable position of France had become even stronger. The loss of Belgium meant that an allied offensive on Paris would have to proceed from southern Germany or the middle Rhine—approaches that presented exceptional difficulties.[14] A limited offensive was more realistic, but there was no natural defensive line between the Rhine and Paris where the advance could halt and take up strong positions. Belgium remained the strategic key as well as the true object of any war with France, consequently the Allies should aim for Belgium rather than Paris. An offensive against Belgium would be facilitated by the highly developed transportation network of the area; it would protect northern Germany and generate Dutch and British support. If the Austrians covered northern Italy and southern Germany, Prussia could devote most of her forces to the offensive—a division of labor that accorded with the political and strategic interests of the two powers. Clausewitz knew, however, that Krauseneck and Witzleben advocated the formation of three armies: an Austrian army in Württemberg; a central force consisting of south-German and Prussian contingents; and a northern army of Prussians and Hanoverians. They feared that the formation of two main forces would destroy the unity of command—a handicap Clausewitz was willing

---

13. This basic theme of Clausewitz's strategic writings in 1830 and 1831 is further proof of his opposition to a preventive war. Evidently Treitschke did not read the memoranda in question.
14. Clausewitz, "Betrachtungen," *Moltkes Militärische Werke*, pp. 181, 182.

to accept since in his plan the southern army acted as a holding force, leaving the war of movement to the Prussians. Krauseneck and Witzleben, on the contrary, argued that if Prussian troops made up the major part of two armies out of three, unity of command would extend over two-thirds of the total force. At the same time, the smaller German powers would be bound more closely to Prussia. Clausewitz analyzed their proposal, which became Prussian policy, and concluded that no strategic purpose would be served by it; on the contrary, "it would be a great mistake, and prove detrimental to the whole war." Nevertheless, he continued, "we will admit that particular political conditions may exist that could lead us to accept this disadvantage, for he who asserts—as so often happens—that politics should not interfere with the conduct of war has not grasped the ABC of grand strategy." [15] To encourage the south-German states, Prussia might have to reduce her Belgian force, and contribute two or three corps to a third army on the middle Rhine. This third force, created for political purposes, could not be expected to gain a strategic victory, but for that very reason should be aggressive and take risks: "Daring is always in order when one wants to achieve something beyond one's means and when failure would not constitute a major disaster." [16] A detailed analysis of the offensive in Belgium concludes the study.

A shorter memorandum sent to Witzleben in February 1831, "Some aspects of a future war against France," repeats the previous argument that unless the Allies have the forces for an offensive that can reasonably be expected to carry to Paris, they should attack Belgium. But the emphasis is now clearly on a defensive war, to which Clausewitz devotes three times the space he gives to offensive operations. He concludes that as long as Prussia can rely on her allies, the French will find it as difficult to reach Berlin and Vienna as the Allies to reach Paris. [17]

The interest of the memoranda lies both in their theoretical aspects and in the manner in which they reflect a specific historical situation. They are filled with echoes from Clausewitz's earlier writings: the declaration that political considerations control strategy, coupled with the recognition that it may be difficult to reconcile political interests with operational needs; the argument that in a major war all forces should be mobilized at once regardless of cost and effort, which repeats the "first principle" of the essay for the crown prince of 1812; the careful differentiation of limited and

---

15. *Ibid.*, p. 188. On the general issue of the organization of allied forces for a war with France, see H. v. Treitschke, "Preussen und das Bundeskriegswesen 1831," printed as an appendix in vol. iv of his *Deutsche Geschichte*.
16. Clausewitz, "Betrachtungen," *Moltkes Militärische Werke*, p. 190.
17. "Einige Gesichtspunkte für einen gegen Frankreich bevorstehenden Krieg," printed in "Zwei Denkschriften von Clausewitz 1830/31," *Militär-Wochenblatt*, 1891, No. 31. According to Clausewitz's diary, the memorandum was completed before 17 February; Schwartz, *Leben des Generals Clausewitz*, ii, 311.

unlimited war, exemplified by the choice of Belgium and Paris, respectively, as the strategic target; the pervasive emphasis on the strength of the defensive. In these and other instances the essays represent the practical application of earlier theoretical findings. But they also document Clausewitz's interpretation of Prussian capabilities and weaknesses after the July Revolution. Neither in the summer and fall of 1830 nor early the following year did he believe it feasible for Prussia to go to war other than as a member of a grand alliance. At most, the essay of February 1831 hints at the possibility of Prussia having to face a French attack unsupported. It was his awareness of the state's relative weakness that led him to insist on the primary importance of the Austrian alliance. Only the presence of strong Austrian forces in southern Germany gave the Prussian army operational freedom in the north. Regardless of the objectionable character of Austrian policies in Germany, the alliance had to be preserved so that Prussia could retain a range of military options in regard to France, Belgium, and Poland. On this point, as we have seen, he disagreed with Krauseneck, who believed that Prussian opposition to Austria would bring about "moral conquests" in the German Confederation. For Clausewitz the French threat took precedence over the rivalries and disagreements between conservatives and moderates in Germany.[18]

In February, Clausewitz started to take a more active part in the work of the army's leadership. His participation began on the 4th, when Hake gave Gneisenau the option of including Clausewitz in a meeting with Krauseneck and Witzleben. The group, which met to consider measures against a French surprise attack, was persuaded by Clausewitz that such an attack could not be imminent. At the same time he called attention to the need of improving the gathering of strategic intelligence. Three days later he attended a second conference, which was joined by Bernstorff and Eichhorn, to discuss the implication of an announcement by the French government that the calling up of 80,000 conscripts was under consideration. On 10 February he submitted a plan for reorganizing the intelligence service. At a third meeting, with Gneisenau, Hake, Witzleben, and Krauseneck, on the 16th, Clausewitz reported on the likelihood of a Polish army crossing into Prussia, which he discounted. The following day he proposed the establishment of a standing committee with the authority to make major political and military decisions, and repeated his call for improvements in the information services. On the 21st, Witzleben announced that Clausewitz would be placed in charge of collating intelligence, but factionalism was too entrenched in Berlin to permit this decision to be implemented.

18. A clear summary of the differences on this issue between Krauseneck and himself is contained in a letter Clausewitz wrote to his wife on 23 June 1831, in which he continued to stress the need for a united front against France; *Correspondence*, pp. 456–457. See also the earlier letter to Marie v. Clausewitz of 9 June 1831; *ibid.*, pp. 446–447.

Clausewitz nevertheless submitted a second plan for the establishment of a central intelligence agency in the general staff. Further discussion on mobilization measures followed with the foreign minister and Eichhorn, as well as with Witzleben and Krauseneck. By the beginning of March, although the system of *ad hoc* meetings was retained, Gneisenau and Clausewitz had gone some way to filling the void in the high command.[19]

As Clausewitz became involved in the technicalities of army organization and mobilization timetables, the political issues that stimulated these measures exerted their accustomed strong pull on him. His frequent meetings with Bernstorff and Eichhorn provided him with fairly detailed knowledge of the diplomatic exchanges between Berlin and the other capitals, and reinforced the general ideas on Prussia's position in the international community that he had held for many years with specific and current information. In January and February, after he had familiarized himself with the issues, he wrote two papers on the international situation. The first, "The Condition of Europe Since the Polish Partitions," was apparently intended for private circulation; the other, "Reduction of the Many Political Questions Occupying Germany to the Basic Question of Our Existence," Clausewitz hoped to publish.[20] He submitted his manuscript anonymously to the most prestigious newspaper in Germany, the *Augsburger Allgemeine Zeitung*, which, however, rejected it. A second attempt by Eichhorn to persuade Cotta, the liberal publisher of the *Augsburger Allgemeine*, to accept the piece also failed. The specific grounds for the rejection are not known, but, as Hans Rothfels suggests, at a time when most educated Germans tended to interpret international affairs as a conflict between the principles of autocracy and liberalism, an analysis based wholly on the concept of *raison d'état* would hardly be welcomed.[21]

That Clausewitz wanted to influence liberal opinion, rather than merely state his position, is indicated by his sending the manuscript to the Augsburg newspaper, which enjoyed a large readership among the educated middle classes in all German states, and also by a comment in his diary: "I sought to make it clear to the good people [*Leutchen*] that something besides cosmopolitanism should determine our position on the Belgian, Polish, and other questions, that German independence was in the gravest danger, and that it was time to think about ourselves." [22] The condition of

19. Diary entries from 4 February to 2 March; Schwartz, *Leben des Generals Clausewitz*, ii, 304–317.
20. "Die Verhältnisse Europas seit der Teilung Polens" and "Zurückführung der vielen politischen Fragen, welche Deutschland beschäftigen, auf die unserer Gesamtexistenz" were first published *ibid.*, pp. 401–417. They were reprinted with a valuable commentary by H. Rothfels in his edition of Clausewitz's *Politische Schriften und Briefe*, and are also included in the volume of selections edited by W. Schering. The following is based on my previously cited article. "An Anonymous Letter by Clausewitz," *Journal of Modern History*, 1970.
21. Clausewitz, *Politische Schriften und Briefe*, ed. Rothfels, pp. xxxii–xxxiii.
22. Diary entry for 21 February 1831, Schwartz, *Leben des Generals Clausewitz*, ii, 313. See also Clausewitz's letter to his wife, 18 March 1831, *Correspondence*, p. 418. Months later he was still toying

Europe, he wrote in the first of the two essays, had undergone a change since the disappearance of Poland as an independent state. This change, however, was due not to the partitions but to the concurrent growth of French power. The widespread support that the Polish insurrection enjoyed among Germans was a fad, based less on moral than on aesthetic principles—neither of which was a consideration that should be substituted for one's political interests. Poland could be restored only at the future expense of Austria and Prussia: any war with France would necessarily involve these powers in a conflict with the new Poland. Polish independence thus imposed the strategic handicap of a two-front war on Prussia. The root of the problem was French aggression, which since 1789 had rarely abated. Today France continued to be the dominant power on the Continent, facing states that were divided by separate interests and that also were threatened by their particular neighbors—Turkey, Poland, and Sweden.

Clausewitz returned to the relation between French power and Prussian *raison d'état* in the manuscript submitted to the *Augsburger Allgemeine Zeitung*. Ever since the Burgundian buffer had disappeared, Germany was under attack by France. Belgium, as long as Austria controlled her, had served as a bastion for Germany and Europe, and as a foothold for England, whenever the British wanted to defend the threatened Continent. German policy toward the new independent Belgium must be guided by concern for German security, which should also determine policy in the questions of Italian and Polish independence. A free Italy would undoubtedly ally herself with France, as would a free Poland. The Poles claimed that they could serve as a buffer against Russia, but this called for two conditions that did not exist: Poland was not a modern state, and would not be for many years; and the Poles would have to establish friendly relations with Germany, which was unlikely for psychological as well as for political reasons.[23] In any case, "so long as *everything* must be feared from France, nothing is to be feared from Russia." Poles and Frenchmen always regarded themselves as natural allies, and the object of their alliance obviously was the man in the middle, Germany. France, on the other hand, had nothing to fear: England, Austria, and Prussia would never launch a preventive war against her because, among other reasons, France was so strong that a struggle with her could not be waged as a cabinet war but must be imbued with the same just enthusiasm that motivated the German people in 1813. Clausewitz ended with a denial of two liberal articles of faith. If Germany should again have to fight France, the French would be defeated because, for one, their

with the idea of publishing the manuscript as a separate pamphlet; Clausewitz to his wife, 13 August 1831, *ibid.*, pp. 477–478.
23. Clausewitz had expressed similar views on Polish history several years earlier, interestingly enough as part of a discussion on the means of defending large areas in *On War*, book VI, ch. 6 (pp. 539–541). See also pp. 418–420.

military institutions were no longer superior to Germany's, which had improved since the days of Napoleon, and, further, because the French were no longer a united people: "Nothing is more common today than to conceive of a capital's radical party [*Volkspartei*] as representing the entire people, and yet this is always more or less illusory, and this more or less serious misconception will always have consequences in real life." [24]

The realistic appreciation of historical and current phenomena that marked many of these observations—the truth of the last point, for example, was underscored even more strongly in the French Revolution of 1848 than in 1830—should not be permitted to obscure the peculiarly single-minded nature of Clausewitz's outlook. He evaluated internal affairs of France, Belgium, Poland, and, of course, Germany almost entirely according to the effect they might be expected to have on Prussia's position in Europe. How can this attitude be reconciled with his critical view of Prussian conditions, his opposition to reaction, his belief in the intentions and achievements of the reform party, which are evident in his biography of Scharnhorst, the political essays of the early 1820's, the *Observations on Prussia,* and form a major theme of his correspondence? Throughout these years, in a variety of ways, he expressed lack of confidence in the personal rule of Frederick William, and distaste for the government's timid illiberalism. His letters also indicate, however, that like Gneisenau, Boyen, Grolman, and other friends he had come to accept the impossibility, for the time being, of detaching Prussia from the spirit of the Karlsbad Decrees. All that could be attempted was to defend the basic institutional changes that the reform era had brought to the army, the bureaucracy, the courts, and the schools, and little by little to extend their reach. Even his essay on Scharnhorst, which he had written not to put in a drawer but for publication, was less an appeal for the completion of Scharnhorst's program than a reminder to an ungrateful state and an unaware society of one man's achievements that underlay the revival of Prussia's independence and power.

His unwilling acceptance of a political reality too firmly ensconced to alter for the present, made foreign affairs seem more important to him than ever. If little could be done at home, it might still be possible to influence foreign policy. Here, too, there are parallels between Clausewitz's attitude and that of other men who had been associated with Scharnhorst. It is not difficult to see how the reformers' impotence at home might be compensated for by greater concern with foreign relations. No doubt Clausewitz's ambition to enter the diplomatic service was in part nourished by such considerations. He could still scoff bitterly at the Legitimist fantasies of a Radowitz or the naïve liberalism of journalists who knew nothing of the ways of government and the great world, but his diary and corre-

24. Clausewitz, *Politische Schriften und Briefe,* ed. Rothfels, p. 238.

spondence—and even his essays—show clearly that his political imagination was now mainly engaged by Prussia's foreign relations. Indeed, one of his main complaints of the ideologues at both extremes was that their tenets disregarded the vital interests of the Prussian state. He, on the contrary, would have considered France as the major source of danger to Prussia even if she had been a second Tsarist autocracy. The vitality of French revolutionary traditions simply added a dynamic and unpredictable element to the *raison d'état* of the greatest power on the Continent. National self-determination and the extension of political participation in societies abroad must be opposed if they promised to strengthen France unduly, and political reform in Germany must be postponed—regardless of how desirable and even necessary it might be—if such changes threatened to confuse the purpose and sap the energy of Prussia's dealings with her neighbors.

If Clausewitz's article had been accepted by the *Augsburger Allgemeine Zeitung,* his appeal for the primacy of state power over ideology and cosmopolitan sympathies would no doubt have been quickly submerged in the flood of enthusiasm for Polish independence that swept central and southern Germany, and even penetrated Prussia, where, particularly in the eastern provinces, it was strongly tinged with dislike and fear of Russia. And yet, at the very peak of liberal fervor, other views were beginning to influence middle-class attitudes. Had Clausewitz survived his illness in the fall of 1831 even for a short time, he would have witnessed the increasing currency that opinions related to his belief in the individuality of national development and the need for national strength were gaining among the German public. The classic formulation of the uniqueness of each nation's history and of the primacy of foreign affairs was achieved in 1833 when Ranke's *Historisch-politische Zeitschrift,* which had been founded under the sponsorship of Bernstorff and Eichhorn, printed its editor's essay on "The Great Powers." [25] In the previous year Ranke had published the biographical study of Scharnhorst by Scharnhorst's recently deceased associate. The events treated in Clausewitz's essay now lay two decades and more in the past, and their political divisiveness was lessening, although Ranke still felt compelled to excise two passages in which Clausewitz stated his condemnation of the old system with particular bluntness. [26] But gradually the reform era, with its energy and its elements of idealism and self-sacrifice, was becoming part of Prussia's historical substance, which strengthened the state, whatever the direction in which the state might move.

---

25. C. Varrentrap suggests that failure to place Clausewitz's article in the *Augsburger Allgemeine Zeitung* contributed to Eichhorn's wish to establish a political journal in Berlin: "Ranke's Historisch-politische Zeitschrift und das Berliner Politische Wochenblatt," *Historische Zeitschrift,* LXXXXIX (1907), 47, n. 1.
26. Max Lehmann compared the manuscript of the essay, in Marie von Clausewitz's handwriting, with Ranke's version, and published the suppressed passages in the second volume of his *Scharnhorst,* pp. 639–640. Ranke also deleted some lines from a letter of Scharnhorst to Clausewitz, which he printed in one of the appendices to the article.

II. OBSERVER ON THE FRONTIER

In the first days of February, Diebitsch entered Poland with 127,000 men, and marched toward Warsaw. Early thaws and forward units of the Polish army slowed the Russian progress, but within three weeks Diebitsch's main columns had reached the Grochów plain, across the Vistula from Warsaw. On 25 February they attacked the Polish army drawn up before the river. Poor leadership on both sides turned the fighting into a primitive test of strength. In the early evening the Poles fled across the Vistula, but retained control of the single bridge, while the Russians were too exhausted and disorganized to pursue them, and thus lost the opportunity of ending the war at once. A few days later, Diebitsch withdrew some miles to the east to rest and resupply his troops.

In East Prussia the first reports of the battle were interpreted as a decisive Russian victory. The local commanders thought it likely that Polish troops would soon attempt to cross the frontier, either to surrender or to make their way to France, and redistributed their units to meet these contingencies. Contrary orders from Berlin caused some confusion, and Frederick William decided the time had come for Gneisenau to take up his command. On the evening of 7 March, accompanied by a small staff that included Major O'Etzel, Clausewitz's friend since their tour of duty in Coblenz, Gneisenau and Clausewitz left Berlin, and two days later reached Posen, where Clausewitz found quarters for them in the town's best hotel, the Hotel de Vienne. Rooms and location were ideal, Clausewitz told his wife in his first letter, but the streets so muddy that walking was a trial.[1] He was exhilarated with his new assignment, potentially the most important of his career, and his pride and sense of pleasure were not to leave him for some months, even though the absence of a military decision in Poland condemned him to essentially administrative duties, and "to drink tea and wait."[2] He and Gneisenau regarded Posen as an interlude before they assumed their duties in the west, and they observed events in Poland with France always uppermost in their minds. When early in April, Skrzynecki, the Polish commander in chief, defeated two Russian columns, and news arrived at the same time suggesting that war with France was imminent,

---

1. Clausewitz to his wife, 10 March 1831, *Correspondence*, pp. 411–412.
2. The words are those of Grolman, who commanded a division under Gneisenau; Grolman to his wife, 21 March 1831, Conrady, iii, 124.

Gneisenau and Clausewitz reacted by proposing an attack on Warsaw with 51,000 men, so that the fighting in the east could be ended at once and the Prussian army appear in full strength on the Rhine.[3] The crisis passed, and their plan was relegated to the mountain of files that was one of the more notable monuments to the July Revolution.

Gneisenau had four corps under his command—about 145,000 men, not quite half the field strength of the entire army—stationed in a broad arc that curved from Tilsit and Königsberg in the northeast over Danzig and Thorn west to Posen, and then to Silesia in the southeast. Parallel to the Prussian frontier, and enfolded by it, ran the smaller curve formed by the Narew and Vistula rivers, which defined the main area of fighting, with Warsaw near the point farthest west. After the initial Russian advance had come to a halt, Diebitsch's plan of operations was reduced to a holding action before the capital, while other forces attempted to cross the Narew and the northern stretch of the Vistula, their right flank protected by the Prussian frontier. The Russians pushed reliance on their ally of 1813 and '14 to the point of asking permission to enter East Prussia and cross the Vistula in Prussian territory at Thorn, which would provide them with a safe base for an attack on Warsaw from the rear. This request, which brutally disregarded Prussia's difficult position toward the western powers, was rejected by Frederick William in unusually forceful terms.[4] Left to his own resources in hostile country with the weather continuing to inhibit movement, Diebitsch had difficulty supplying his dispersed forces and coordinating their actions, while in Posen, Gneisenau and Clausewitz could only marvel at the slowness and indecision of Russian operations. To Clausewitz the campaign soon became an illustration of how wars should not be fought—the stronger side fragmenting its forces, and failing to seek a decision regardless of local setbacks. By the end of May he described Diebitsch's performance as "a disgrace from which the Russians will not soon recover."[5]

The absence of adequate information that had troubled Clausewitz in Berlin persisted in Posen. Among his earliest concerns after arriving there was to insure the flow of detailed reports from the various garrisons and from observers stationed at the frontier. It also seemed desirable to gain information directly from the opposing sides. On 12 March he wrote to

---

3. Pertz-Delbrück, v, 648–653; Caemmerer, pp. 122–123, n. 12.

4. T. Schiemann, *Geschichte Russlands unter Kaiser Nikolaus I.*, Berlin, 1913, iii, 111.

5. Clausewitz to his wife, 23 May 1831, *Correspondence*, p. 438. Five days later he wrote that the war constituted a bottomless source of irritation to him; *ibid.*, p. 439. According to a member of Gneisenau's staff, Heinrich v. Brandt, except for overestimating Polish determination and strategic sophistication, Clausewitz predicted the movements of their forces with considerable accuracy throughout the campaign. Brandt, ii, 107. The second volume of Brandt's above-cited memoirs provides independent confirmation of the account Clausewitz gives in his correspondence of his activities and opinions in Posen. Brandt's characterization of Clausewitz at the *Kriegsschule* is mentioned on p. 325 above. See also p. 211, notes 7 and 9.

End of a letter by Clausewitz to Canitz.
The German reads:

*Das ist alles was ich Euer Hochwohlgeboren mitzuteilen weiss; er-
lauben Sie mir noch den Wunsch Ihrem fernern freundschaftlichen
Wohlwollen empfohlen zu sein. Der FeldM. trägt mir die
besten Grüsse für Sie auf.
Mit der wärmsten Hochachtung*

Euer Hochwohlgeboren

Posen den 12ᵗMärz 1831   *ergebenster Freund u Diener*

Clausewitz

(GStA, Rep. 92 v. Canitz Nr. 4) Berlin,
Staatsbibliothek Preussischer Kulturbesitz,
früher Preussische Staatsbibliothek.

Canitz, his former colleague at the *Kriegsschule* who now commanded a regiment in East Prussia, that efforts were under way to establish liaison with
Diebitsch's headquarters: "For this task the field marshal has chosen Major
v. Brandt of the General Staff, because he is not only fluent in Polish but
also a very knowledgeable and sensible officer. He hopes that Field Marshal
Count Diebitsch will take him into his confidence to the extent the mission

requires, and I do not want to fail to ask you to do the same. Naturally the field marshal does not expect Count Diebitsch to give Major Brandt information that is highly secret; but even news of the general circumstances of the war and assumptions concerning its probable course are of definite value to us." [6] This circumspect approach had little effect. Brandt was succeeded by other representatives, among them Canitz, but the Russians saw no reason for keeping Gneisenau up to date, and on occasion even such elementary information as the location of Diebitsch's headquarters was not known in Posen. [7] Communications with Warsaw were even more tenuous, so that Clausewitz complained that the war was being carried on "behind a curtain." [8] The Prussians were compelled to rely on spies, whom Clausewitz did not trust, on reports of travelers, letters from Warsaw and other Polish towns—the mail continued to function with few interruptions—and on the eleven Warsaw daily newspapers, copies of which reached Posen regularly on the three weekly post days.

Only a few days after he had taken up his command, the Polish press brought Gneisenau into a dispute with Berlin, which touched on the army's policy toward Prussia's Polish inhabitants. Frederick William had ordered that for the duration of hostilities the eastern provinces adopt the special security policies that the Austrian government had introduced in Galicia, "to the extent suitable to Prussian conditions." [9] The Austrian measures, which sought to seal off Galicia completely from the insurrection, included the prohibition of all Polish newspapers. The requisite order by the Prussian minister of the interior, Brenn, however, was opposed by the Civil Governor of Posen, Eduard von Flottwell, who argued that the newspapers had not had an adverse effect on public opinion, and that prohibiting them could not stop smuggled copies from reaching the province but only interfered with the legitimate desire for information on the part of the general public. Brenn responded with a compromise: the newspapers were to be screened before distribution and any issue containing politically dangerous material should be confiscated. Flottwell again objected that censorship was ineffective as well as detrimental to public opinion, but tried to carry out the order, which resulted in the usual inconsistencies and absurdities. On 13 March, Gneisenau asked Flottwell to suspend censorship

6. Clausewitz to K. W. v. Canitz, 12 March 1831. Dallinger prints parts of the letter in his biography of Canitz, pp. 113–115, but the sentences quoted here are not included. The original is deposited in the Geheime Staatsarchiv, Berlin-Dahlem, GStA, Rep. 92 (v. Canitz Nr. 4).
7. It did not help communications that Diebitsch had taken a dislike to Clausewitz, his companion in the last stages of the campaign of 1812. Clausewitz could discover no personal grounds for this but supposed that Diebitsch, himself once a Prussian cadet, resented Germans who had served in the Russian army and then, like Clausewitz, returned to Prussia. Clausewitz to his wife, 1 April 1831, *Correspondence*, p. 426.
8. Clausewitz to his wife, 17 March 1831, *ibid.*, p. 418.
9. M. Laubert, "Die polnischen Zeitungen in der Provinz Posen 1831," *Forschungen zur Brandenburgischen und Preussischen Geschichte*, XL (1927), 150.

until he could settle the question with Brenn. Not only was it impossible to prevent newspapers from reaching Posen, he wrote, but censorship often deleted innocuous matter, only whetted people's appetite for speculation, caused rumors, and gave the government an image of frightened pettiness that was beneath its dignity.[10] His letter, reminiscent in tone and wording of his defense fifteen years earlier of Görres's right to publish what he wished, caused Flottwell to rescind censorship once more; but the dispute with Brenn persisted and some rather loose controls were applied until the papers ceased publication with the Russian recapture of Warsaw. The episode—characteristic of the continuing conflict between the relatively liberal high bureaucracy and the adherents of a rigid absolutism—was a prelude to the effort by Bernstorff and Eichhorn to moderate and even abolish Prussian censorship, in the belief that the middle classes should be given greater political scope; in the following year this was to be the immediate cause of Bernstorff's departure from office.

Gneisenau's advocacy of the freedom of the press was caused by his lifelong distaste for narrow governmental controls, rather than by confidence in the loyalty of the Polish nobility and bourgeoisie in Posen. "The general state of mind in this province is not gratifying," he wrote to Groeben in April. "The old Polish hatred of Germans is asserting itself more openly and is intensified by the events near Warsaw [recent defeats of units of the Russian covering force]. Prussian officials are intimidated and regard their assignment in this land as an exile. Without the presence of troops insurrection would already have broken out, and then woe to our officials and to the Jews, who find themselves in the same state of perdition with the Prussians here." [11] On these grounds he also opposed a new partition of Poland, which a Russian emissary had tentatively proposed to Bernstorff. It would be too difficult, Gneisenau thought, to integrate more Poles into the Prussian state.[12] Clausewitz went further. After he had seen the Posen magistrate attempt to sabotage sanitary procedures ordered by Flottwell, he complained to his wife of the "Polonizing spirit of the local population. The Germans are even worse than the Poles because they imagine that in the new thousand-year Polish realm everything will be arranged equitably and democratically. This German disloyalty toward one's own people, which unfortunately is a true national weakness, as we can see from the case of Alsace and other examples, outrages me more than any other error; here, where in the long run one nationality must completely replace the other, it reaches the acme of stupidity and danger." [13] With Gneisenau

10. *Ibid.*, p. 152.
11. Gneisenau to C. v. d. Groeben, 18 April 1831, Pertz-Delbrück, v, 665.
12. Schiemann, iii, 123.
13. Clausewitz to his wife, 24 July 1831, *Correspondence*, p. 468. The letter echoes the criticism of German selfishness in his essay on German and French character twenty-three years earlier.

he regarded it as one of their main tasks to convey to the inhabitants of the eastern provinces a sense of the permanency of Prussian authority, which in their view called for a discreet show of force and evenhanded, businesslike administration. Significant anti-Russian activity had to be punished, but mere expressions of opinion, the Polish patriotism of the salons, could be ignored. For themselves, they made a point of avoiding society, German as well as Polish, except on official occasions, so as not to be drawn into political arguments and have their names associated with this or that faction.[14]

Their consequent isolation, which the small headquarters staff did little to alleviate, threw the two men into daily intimacy for a longer period than ever before—a test their friendship easily passed. Clausewitz continued to stress the gap in rank between Gneisenau and himself with an insistence that Gneisenau may have thought excessively pedantic, but their friendship shone through all protocol. It was strengthened rather than limited by the differences in their characters, which the passage of time had only accentuated. Clausewitz admired, to the point of idealization, the older man's natural authority, his gaiety—now somewhat subdued by age—the intuitive, almost miraculously accurate judgment he retained on strategic and operational issues, his harmonious humanity. When Clausewitz found something to criticize in Gneisenau—a seeming unfairness to a relative, for instance—it was in the way Eckermann did when commenting on a failing of the old Goethe: the enormous superiority of the man was not affected by such flaws. Gneisenau in turn was awed by Clausewitz's creativity, his seriousness, and his passionate logic, which never failed to lead to insights even if these did not always coincide with haphazard reality. "Clausewitz must have much patience with me," he wrote his son-in-law Brühl in April, expressing as he had so often before his humility before Clausewitz's power of sustained and systematic thinking.[15] The discrepancies in their fortunes struck him as inappropriate. Accustomed as he was to success, he felt affronted by the difficulties Clausewitz had experienced, and continued to experience, in his career. He resented the king's refusal to promote Clausewitz to lieutenant-general, an advancement that could reasonably have been expected in view of his friend's seniority and record. His last ambition, he wrote to Brühl, was to help Clausewitz assume his rightful position as chief of the army's general staff.[16] Each man accurately read

---

14. To Clausewitz's regret, one result of the restrictions he placed on his social life, as well as of his opposition to Polish nationalism, was a slight estrangement between himself and his old friend Prince Radziwill, who occupied the largely ceremonial post of governor-general (*Statthalter*) in Posen, and advocated more sympathetic treatment of his Polish compatriots; Clausewitz to his wife, 16 April 1831, *Correspondence*, pp. 430–432.

15. Gneisenau to F. W. v. Brühl, 19 April 1831, Sybel, p 275.

16. *Ibid.*, p. 275; Gneisenau to his son-in-law W. v. Scharnhorst, 5 April 1831, published by A. Pick, "Briefe des Feldmarschalls Grafen Neithardt v. Gneisenau an seinen Schwiegersohn Wilh. v. Scharnhorst," *Historische Zeitschrift*, LXXVII (1896), 252. Clausewitz himself commented with some

the other. Whatever the circumstances, Gneisenau dominated his environment; Clausewitz had created a world of the mind that he ruled with equal authority. He was flattered and embarrassed when he came across a passage in the Parisian *Journal des Débats* that Gneisenau had marked "Clausewitz": "It is certain that the most serious and enlightened minds are those which question the most, and that those which question the most have the firmest convictions." [17]

Their days in Posen were uncrowded. Official business occupied the morning, after which they and their staff lunched together, and work continued through the afternoon. Once the weather turned fair they rode regularly in the surrounding countryside. The evenings were usually spent apart. Clausewitz wrote letters and read—Barthold's new work in medieval history and a political essay by Schleiermacher are mentioned in his correspondence, as are the memoirs of Mme. Du Barry, which rather shocked him—and a great number of German, English, and French newspapers with which he supplemented the reports and letters on the international situation he received from Bernstorff and others in Berlin. [18] French politics and their impact on foreign policy continued to hold his greatest attention. Despite his suspicion of successive French cabinets, he hoped that Louis Philippe's rule would be sustained. After the scare early in April he thought that until the new chamber was elected France would probably not go to war with Germany, and in July he was troubled by hints in the press that the voting seemed to be going badly for the government. Against this backdrop—always linking events elsewhere in Europe to the energy-field centered on Paris—he followed the course of the Italian uprisings, the continuing struggle over Belgium, and the sudden flaring up in June of the crisis over Luxembourg.

In March he wrote Canitz, after summarizing the latest information in the Polish papers: "The storm is again rising in the west. The *Journal des Débats* contained the report of Maison [the French ambassador to Austria] on his interview with Metternich, in which the latter declared that under no condition could Austria be prevented from repressing the Italian rebellions. Maison added: 'You know how strongly I have advocated peace, but now I think it high time to march an army into Piedmont.' " Clausewitz continued: "If I combine this news with the decree issued on the 10th of this month concerning the calling up of 80,000 conscripts of the class of 1830 (which brings the French army to 500,000 men) and further with the statement already printed in the *Gazette* that a regiment stationed in St.

bitterness on his lack of advancement, which in a letter to his wife of 6 April 1831 he ascribed to influences emanating from Monbijou, the palace of Duke Karl of Mecklenburg. *Correspondence*, p. 428.

17. Clausewitz to his wife, 23 June 1831, *ibid.*, p. 455.

18. F. W. Barthold's *Der Römerzug König Heinrichs von Lützelburg* appeared in Königsberg in 1830 and '31. It is a facile, excessively long narrative, based on secondary sources. Clausewitz called it "somewhat overburdened with major and minor themes, but an intelligent book." Letter to his wife, 24 March 1831, *ibid.* p. 423.

Denis has suddenly left for the Piedmontese frontier, I can no longer doubt the early outbreak of war in Italy. I can't understand why the Austrians prefer to issue statements rather than fight. If they had intervened immediately in Bologna, they would have met with far less opposition in Paris than their threatening statements encounter now." [19] The election of Leopold of Coburg to the Belgian throne seemed to him the best solution of an unfortunate tangle, but he feared for the security of the fortress of Luxembourg, which since 1815 was garrisoned by troops of the German Confederation, though the duchy itself was part of the Netherlands. Whether Belgium could now claim Luxembourg depended, he believed, to some extent on the history of the duchy's sovereignty—one of the rare occasions on which he invested ancient treaties and dynastic contracts with contemporary political authority. In June he asked his wife to trace for him the changes in Luxembourg's political status since the 15th century so that he could puzzle out the matter for himself.[20]

In the meantime the fighting in Poland went badly for both sides. The Russians failed to make significant progress, while the Poles were unable to improve their almost hopeless strategic position. Increasingly they placed reliance on help from France and England, but only a major victory could conceivably have stimulated effective diplomatic support. The cholera that broke out with great violence in the second half of April inhibited both armies, the Poles perhaps less than the Russians, who in April and May reported 9,000 cases, of which over 3,000 were fatal.[21] A major battle was nevertheless fought on 26 May at Ostrolenka on the Narew. It ended in a Polish defeat. The Russians had also suffered heavily, however, and again failed to pursue their enemies, who retreated in fair order toward Warsaw. An insurrection in Lithuania threatened the Russian lines of communication, but was itself in danger of collapse unless strongly supported by Polish regulars. While awaiting reinforcements that would make possible a new offensive on Warsaw, Diebitsch died of cholera on 10 June.

The new commander in chief, Paskevich, arrived at army headquarters in Pultusk in the last week of June. Supplies for twenty-five days had been accumulated, much of them purchased in East Prussia, and the Prussian government had agreed to ship further foodstuffs from Thorn once the Russians penetrated to the lower Vistula. On 4 July the army began to march slowly to the west, reaching Osiek on the Vistula on the 16th. At the same time Russian reserves extinguished the uprising in Lithuania. On the 15th the last Polish regulars in the area escaped to East Prussia and surrendered. The crossing of Paskevich's army to the southern bank of the Vistula took

---

19. Undated letter to Canitz, presumably written between 19–21 March, Geheimes Staatsarchiv, Berlin-Dahlem, GStA, Rep. 92 (v. Canitz Nr. 4). See also Clausewitz to his wife, 18 and 21 March 1831, *Correspondence,* pp. 418–421.
20. Clausewitz to his wife, 23 and 27 June, and 9 July 1831, *ibid.,* pp. 454–455, 459, 463–464.
21. Schiemann, iii, 111.

four days. "One might think it were the army of Xerxes," Clausewitz wrote to Krauseneck, "and yet, according to Colonel Canitz's statement to Major von Brandt, they are only 65,000 men ..., but—6,000 wagons. Of course, these 65,000 men and 300 guns ought to make a Polish defeat in battle a certainty." [22] With Russian forces to the east and west of Warsaw, the situation had become desperate for the Poles; but Paskevich refused to hurry, and it was not until 18 August that he arrived before the capital.

Prussia's qualified support of Russia in the conflict that was now entering its ultimate phase was the occasion of Clausewitz's last appearance in print during his life. It was largely reliance on East Prussia as a secure and convenient source of supplies that made possible the Russian army's strategy of ponderous accumulation and application of force. During the buildup of matériel before Paskevich assumed command, the full significance of this assistance had become apparent, and on 19 June, Skrzynecki, the Polish generalissimo, addressed a letter of complaint to the Prussian king. After this note had been rejected on the ground that the king could not accept communications from an authority whose status he did not recognize, it was published in Warsaw in July, and reprinted in several German newspapers. [23]

Skrzynecki complained that Berlin's policy of neutrality to the contrary, Prussian officials on the Polish border supplied Russian forces with food, ammunition, and uniforms; a Prussian engineer was helping the Russians to construct a bridge across the Vistula; and Prussian gunners had been detached to serve with Russian units. Some of these charges were without foundation; perhaps they were included to defend Skrzynecki against his many Polish critics, but that did not invalidate the main point: the Russian army was obtaining valuable help from Prussia.

The appearance of the Polish note in the German press caused Clausewitz to write a brief anonymous reply, which first appeared on 21 July in the local German newspaper, the *Zeitung des Grossherzogtums Posen,* from which it was immediately copied by other German papers. When Frederick William came to read the reply, he inquired after the author's identity and, on learning it was Clausewitz, sent a cabinet order to Gneisenau, praising the content and form of his chief of staff's defense of government policy. [24]

Skrzynecki's letter, Clausewitz wrote, "is apparently a device to renew certain ridiculous and wholly imaginary assertions, and serve them up to a credulous public. Nothing is true in these statements except that the Rus-

22. Clausewitz to Krauseneck, approximately 23 July 1831, *ibid.,* 126–127.

23. The official text is published in D'Angeberg (i.e., J. L. Chodz'ko), *Recueil des traités, conventions et actes diplomatiques concernant la Pologne,* Paris, 1862, pp. 825–826. For a contemporary German version see the *Staats und Gelehrte Zeitung des Hamburgischen unpartheiischen Correspondenten,* No. 174, 26 July 1831, pp. 2–3. The following is based on my previously cited article "An Anonymous Letter by Clausewitz," *Journal of Modern History,* 1970.

24. The text of the order was cited by Clausewitz in a letter to his wife, 20 August 1831; *Correspondence,* p. 483.

sians bought foodstuffs and supplies for cash from private dealers in the Prussian provinces—mainly grain, hay, and straw—that they shipped their purchases on rented barges and wagons to the points where they needed them, that in addition they wanted to use the barges to transport troops across the Vistula, and now have in fact done so. Everything else is a deliberate lie. One must be very ignorant in the history of international law to find a breach of neutrality in such actions, if, indeed, it is possible to apply the concept of neutrality to an insurgent power that is not recognized by a single government in the world. When the French army crossed the Rhine during the Seven Years' War, it employed vessels of the neutral Dutch Republic, and subsisted on Dutch wheat. When, in turn, Duke Ferdinand of Brunswick crossed the Rhine in 1758, he did exactly the same. It is probably asking too much that a Warsaw journalist should be aware of such matters. But the Poles must know little of their own history, or be deeply ashamed of certain pages in it, if they cannot recall the depots which Russia established on the territory of their magnificent neutral republic during the Seven Years' War. At that time, after all, Poland was still a populous nation; the partitions had not yet occurred. Indeed, the partitions were made necessary by the disorderly, almost Tartar-like administration of the vast areas the Poles possessed. The commercial dealings with Prussian subjects to which reference is made in no way involve the Prussian government. If such traffic were to be in the nature of an intervention, how would one have to categorize the active help by means of money, arms, and volunteers that other countries have tolerated in order to give a boost to the Belgian and Polish rebellions?" [25]

In the battle over German public opinion, Clausewitz's letter struck a blow for Prussian *raison d'état* and German self-interest against a hopeless and troublesome cause that was trying to maintain itself by what the writer took to be spurious legalisms. While laying bare the inconsistencies and weaknesses of Skrzynecki's arguments, Clausewitz passed over the fact that Prussian help was of far more than marginal value to the Russians. Since no government had recognized the Polish state, the issue of Prussian help was in any case not a legal but solely a political problem. Judged by international custom, Prussia's actions were unexceptional; certainly they did not equal the range of French support of the Belgians. That other powers, even Russia, did their best to ignore the extent of French support only bore out his implied point: if states were sufficiently powerful, or otherwise favored by circumstance, the laws of neutrality could be bent with impunity, in the 19th century as well as in earlier times. Clausewitz's letter, in short, applied to a specific instance the general ideas that he had developed some months earlier in his two essays on Germany and Poland.

That his rebuttal is filled with a sense of impatient superiority, and

25. I have used the text published in the *Staats und Gelehrte Zeitung des Hamburgischen unpartheiischen Correspondenten*, No. 174, 26 July 1831, p. 3.

couched in violent, insulting language, may reflect his old dislike of Poles—or at least of Polish political society—for his letters in the spring of 1831 repeatedly acknowledge Polish bravery and energy, and in his essay "On the basic question of Germany's existence" he referred to the Poles as "a very able people." But, he added immediately, "a people that had remained half-Tartar in the midst of civilized European states." [26] In one sense it was the political weakness of Poland, which, he wrote in the same essay, he did not believe could be made good in less than a century, that he regarded as the real issue. A power vacuum on Prussia's eastern frontier would always be exploited by her enemies: Russia had done so in the Seven Years' War, and France might do so today. The possibility that a weak buffer could be preferable to a strong neighbor he evidently rejected on the basis that the disappearance of the Polish state would reduce the scope for mischief of French diplomacy, and that swallowing Poland would cause Russia problems. Finally, Russia was not as strong as she appeared: the poor showing of her army and administration in the present campaign testified to that.[27].

These political considerations notwithstanding, it is striking how little tolerance the hopeless fight for Polish independence evoked in a man who twenty years earlier had rejected the likelihood of success as a proper measure for political action. In 1831 Clausewitz judged the Polish insurgents in much the same way that Napoleon had condemned Scharnhorst and Stein, and would have condemned Clausewitz had he known of his existence: as irresponsible and quite possibly dangerous visionaries. For once Clausewitz's empathy and imagination fell far short in his interpretation of another people's history and concerns. That he scorned Polish idealism simply because it was Polish and not his own—that his rejection expressed a narrowly German point of view—would be the obvious explanation; but it would be mistaken. During these same months he reacted quite differently to a newly activist France. The French state represented a far greater threat to Germany than did Poland; but although he criticized the French for being vainglorious political gamblers, he never thought of denying that from their point of view their policies—dangerous to Germany though they were—might appear reasonable and often were justified, not only by their standards but by the standards of the international community as well.

It was not in a spirit of brutal nationalism, granting no validity to the ambitions of others, that he judged this community. Rather, his views were filtered through his particular conception of political realism. He con-

---

26. "Zurückführung der vielen politischen Fragen ...," *Politische Schriften und Briefe*, p. 233. See also Clausewitz to his wife, 24 March, 6 April, 28 May, 4 June 1831, etc.; *Correspondence*, pp. 422, 426, 441, 444.
27. Clausewitz to his wife, 23 May 1831, *ibid.*, pp. 438–439.

tinued to feel a deep sympathy for the primacy of power in international affairs, which suggested that a state's enlightened self-interest could turn
into a significantly *active* agent in international relations only if the state
possessed a measure of power sufficient to support action. Otherwise *raison
d'état* called for inactivity, for preserving one's existence by depending on
the tolerance or support of others. But as a young man his sense of realism
had been coupled with intense political idealism. He was willing for himself and for the state to take the greatest risks—in part to rectify the historical and human injustices of Napoleon's domination of Germany, but also
because at that time he attributed moral and psychological qualities to the
state, which, all evidence to the contrary, he insisted must personify
heroism and justice. We have found elements in his background and family
life, and in his emotional and intellectual development during the early
years of his military career, that help explain why for Clausewitz the personification of the state took on such strong and demanding forms. We
have also seen that the original emotional attachment to the state waned
after he left Prussia in 1812, after Scharnhorst died and Napoleon was defeated, and after the Restoration brought the triumph of *Ordnung* over idealism.

Clausewitz continued to be a Prussian and German patriot. But he
had learned to accept state and people for what they are—suffused with
flaws and shortcomings of all kinds. His psychological demands on the outside world were scaled down. Only the intellectual recognition of power retained its old purity. His interpretation of the political world reached new
heights of realism, with power the decisive feature in his analysis. It need
hardly be said that neither in his youth nor in maturity was his concept of
power primarily materialistic: political as well as military force was generated and shaped by psychological and historical elements, cultural values,
enthusiasm, intelligence, principles, idealism. But these elements needed a
materialistic base to become effective. By 1831 his more objective view of
the state, but also the history of his disappointment with the ideal state of
his youth, and its renunciation, made it more difficult, even impossible, for
him to accept the hopeless political idealism of others, which he may even
have felt as a reproach to his own resignation.

During the weeks before Clausewitz wrote his rebuttal to Skrzynecki,
a new problem had arisen in his area of responsibility, complicating his
duties and adding a further disagreeable dimension to the waiting for the
Polish adventure in freedom to end: the cholera was approaching the Prussian frontier. At the beginning of May, Clausewitz had drawn up plans to
control the disease, should it reach Prussian territory.[28] In the corre-

28. Clausewitz to Grolman, 9 May 1831, Conrady, iii, 129–130.

spondence with his wife the disease was first mentioned on 9 May, not to be referred to again until June, when two letters in quick succession discussed the epidemic in Warsaw and Diebitsch's death. His wife replied that since the cholera was moving west she wanted to come to Posen so that she could care for him if he became ill, but Clausewitz forbade it: "Do you believe that I would take you to a battle? And yet that would be no more than an intensification of this sudden danger ... . In this brief illness, during which physicians and surgeons constantly attend one, nursing by ladies is almost out of the question in any case. And don't you believe that I am ten times more likely to fall victim to the disease when I am afraid of infecting you than when I have no need to worry? No, if anything protects me, it is my complete composure. Next door is a room for transient visitors. Yesterday evening, when I was already in bed, I heard someone vomit violently; what could be more natural than to think of cholera, and yet I fell asleep at once." [29] In the same letter of 16 June, he wrote of organizing the sanitary cordon on the frontier and around Danzig, the main port in the area. He expected criticisms of his measures, the more so since, as he wrote, he knew that he was unpopular in Berlin. Objections were not long in coming but the king backed up the decisions. The cordons interfered with travel and commerce, at times stopping trade altogether; on a few occasions peasants trying to break through the controls were shot. The purely military aspects were also troublesome. The cordons required thousands of soldiers, and weakened Gneisenau's mobile forces; the gathering and transmission of information became even more difficult. As physicians held different theories on the cause of cholera, there was no agreement on the suitability of the quarantine measures. "We find ourselves here in the greatest possible controversy over the usefulness of cordons," Clausewitz began a letter to his wife. "It is true that they have great disadvantages; but I believe they reduce the disease, or rather its spread, so that if the disease is constantly confronted with new cordons to the west its prongs will spread out more thinly, and at last vanish altogether." Here Clausewitz was at least partly wrong, since, as a modern student of the epidemic of 1831 has written: "Quarantine regulations without an understanding of the mechanism of cholera's extension, and particularly of the need to control and purify water sources, were bound to fail." [30]

On 13 July, Clausewitz wrote that the cholera had crossed the frontier cordon in three places, but that only a few fatalities had been reported. On the following day the first soldier of the Posen garrison died of the disease. When it became known that the corpse had been buried without being dis-

29. Clausewitz to his wife, 16 June 1831; *Correspondence*, p. 452. See also his letter of 27 June; *ibid.*, pp. 458–459.
30. Clausewitz to his wife, 12 August 1831; *ibid.*, p. 475. R. McGrew, *Russia and the Cholera, 1823–1832*, Madison and Milwaukee, 1965, p. 8.

sected, as cholera regulations required, Gneisenau ordered the body exhumed and dissected in the presence of Clausewitz and two other witnesses. Clausewitz's letter of the 24th dealt with complaints by Posen citizens about isolating the infected soldiers of the garrison, an incident that gave rise to his previously mentioned reference to the "Polonizing spirit" of the local German population. Two days later he wrote that the total number of cases in Posen had risen to sixty-nine, though he thought the epidemic remained rather mild. On the 29th he traced the progress of the epidemic toward Berlin, which he estimated it would reach in the fall, and suggested that his wife and her mother be ready to leave the capital as soon as the first case appeared.[31]

This letter, which deals with many things besides cholera, shifting abruptly from general topics to the writer's feelings, is unusually somber in tone. Clausewitz sees only confusion and new political difficulties in Belgium and Italy. Reports of the cholera riots in St. Petersburg recall to him Manzoni's *I Promessi Sposi:* "In the two centuries that have passed since the period he described, the populace seems not to have changed at all. The same doubts, the same suspicion, the same rumors of poisonings, the same mixture of fear and foolishness that existed in Milan occur here every day; in Petersburg things appear to have been even worse." He writes that he has no news to give her of the war; but apparently the letter was interrupted, to be continued the following day: "Today it is said that the Russian army has begun to move on Warsaw. Then the ultimate great decision will soon take place, which I look forward to with alarm. If I should die, dearest Marie, that is part of my profession. Don't grieve too deeply over a life that could no longer lead to much. Stupidity is spreading; no one can defend himself against it, just as no one can defend himself against the cholera. At least it takes less time and suffering to die from the latter than from the former. I leave the world with so great a contempt for mankind's sense and judgment that I cannot express it. This illness must rage on to its conclusion, a conclusion I would never have witnessed in any case, so not much is lost." [32]

Its unrestrained pessimism, which overshadows any earlier expression of discouragement, makes this paragraph exceptional in Clausewitz's correspondence, as does the extent to which it breaks down the barriers between the writer's inner life and the external world. The grammatical structure reflects his emotional turmoil. Clausewitz's letters to his wife very rarely contain passages with a similar profusion of interlocking sentences and am-

31. *Ibid.,* pp. 466–468, 471. See also Clausewitz's letter to Countess Bernstorff of 22 July 1831; Bernstorff, ii, 209–210, and Brandt, ii, 126. Toward the end of July, Clausewitz's orderly died of cholera, Countess Gneisenau to her grandson August, 13 August 1831, Pertz-Delbrück, v, 681. Either Clausewitz did not give his wife the news or the letter has been lost.
32. Clausewitz to his wife, 29 July 1831, *Correspondence,* pp. 471–472.

biguous key terms. The "ultimate great decision" obviously means the struggle for Warsaw; but Clausewitz could hardly be in doubt as to its outcome, and it may be guessed that he was writing of another kind of end as well—especially since the following sentence refers to his own death. The impending battle for Warsaw, however, presented no threat to the observer in Posen; it seems that the reference was to serve merely as a way of introducing the paragraph's major theme: the writer's profound discouragement and his presentiment of death. His life could no longer amount to much since the men in authority over him did not recognize his true worth, but their blindness is only part of a broader, impersonal stupidity— which he nevertheless felt was killing him. With the final assertion that his premature death would be no great loss because he could never have survived long enough to witness the coming of a saner world, the paragraph reaches the extreme position that life in a world dominated by false values was not worth living.

Taken as a whole, the letter is an extraordinary reflection of the anxieties that Clausewitz had accumulated during months of relatively passive waiting on the Polish border. As time passed, his evaluation of international affairs must have gone far to convince him that there would not be a major European war, and that his appointment as Gneisenau's chief of staff, which at first appeared so promising, would not, after all, lead to important achievements. Hints of this recognition and of occasional dejection can be found in several of his letters before the end of July. On receiving the news of Stein's death early in the month, he replied that he thought his old friend "was glad to leave this world, for he was as despondent as I about many things, and felt that he could no longer avail against the evil in the world." [33] Other passages recall his bitter view of mankind as a herd moved by fashion rather than understanding. And yet, not too much should be made of these statements. Nothing suggests that they expressed a dominant mood. Generally they are embedded in texts of very different character: the writer is self-confident, takes pleasure in his duties and knows he is appreciated, even while he is angry that he has not yet been advanced in rank—which, as he also knew, would have meant a degree of preferential treatment. [34] His anonymous letter in the Posen newspaper

33. Clausewitz to his wife, 9 July 1831, *ibid.*, pp. 461–462.
34. An analysis of the careers of Prussian senior officers based on the army lists and on Priesdorff's biographical dictionary indicates that Clausewitz, one of approximately sixty major-generals on active service in 1831, was still relatively young for his rank, and that his decorations were somewhat above par for his rank and seniority. He possessed only one Prussian award for service against the enemy, but five Russian and Swedish decorations; the Prussian Order of the Red Eagle second class, with oak-leaf cluster, awarded for peacetime service, placed him in the top tier of officers of his rank. He had reached the rank of general at a very early age. Many able officers of his age and length of service were not promoted to major-general until they were past fifty. Advancement slowed considerably after the Wars of Liberation, and it was nothing unusual to wait twelve years or more for promotion from major-general to lieutenant-general. Of the officers who had been promoted to major-general in the same year as Clausewitz,

suggests that he had not given up trying to enlighten the public, as does his continuing wish to publish as a pamphlet the essay that had been turned down by the *Augsburger Allgemeine Zeitung*. Even more important, the sadness and depression of the letter of 29 July are succeeded by very different sentiments in later correspondence. The letters Clausewitz wrote to his wife on the 2nd, 6th, 16th, and 20th of August are generally optimistic, contain plans for the future, and report praise he had received from the king and others.[35] On the 13th he repeated the earlier theme that he was disgusted at the stupidity of mankind and looked forward to nothing but an honorable death. The letter continued, however, with an objective evaluation of his prospects. He and Gneisenau daily expected orders to leave Posen. He was not certain that Gneisenau would accept command of the army in the west; perhaps the field marshal lacked his old spirit, but if he took up his new duties with confidence, Clausewitz would be happy to serve as his chief of staff—though ideally he preferred command of a division, which would give him greater independence. If Clausewitz's letters in the spring and summer indicate that life had its difficulties and that he was sometimes disappointed, they do not suggest that he had lost hope and renounced ambition.

This changed on 23 August. During the previous night Gneisenau had fallen ill. His physicians diagnosed a relatively mild case of cholera, but his constitution was too weak to bear the strain, and he died the following evening.

Clausewitz spent the 24th arranging the funeral, helping to draft an obituary notice for the Posen newspaper, and writing extensive reports on Gneisenau's final illness for the king, the crown prince, and numerous other military and civil notables.[36] His report to Frederick William ended with a few lines, verging dangerously on the personal, that stressed the loss that the monarch and state had just suffered. The routine business of the high command also demanded his attention. He hoped that no one would

1818, seven eventually reached higher grade. Of these, one was promoted in 1832; another, who was senior to Clausewitz, was given the title of lieutenant-general in 1831, but had to wait eight more years for his substantive rank and the raise in pay that went with it. The remaining five were promoted in 1831. Three of them had several years' seniority over Clausewitz; the fourth was rewarded for important diplomatic services; the fifth was Witzleben, one of the most influential men in the army, and a favorite of the king. It can be concluded that while Clausewitz had a right to expect special consideration for his performance as Gneisenau's chief of staff, the fact that he was not promoted in 1831 was normal under prevailing conditions. He could confidently look forward to advancement within the next year or two, which would have made him one of the youngest lieutenant-generals in the army; but he did not measure himself by ordinary standards, and, disclaimers to the contrary, did not want ordinary standards applied to him.

35. *Correspondence*, pp. 472–484.
36. On the first days after Gneisenau's death, see Clausewitz's diary, *ibid.*, pp. 487–488, and his letter to his wife of 5 September 1831, *ibid.*, pp. 488–491. Additional documents are printed in W. Kuhn, "Der Tod des Feldmarschalls Gneisenau," *Forschungen zur Brandenburgischen und Preussischen Geschichte*, L (1938), 136–141; and Priesdorff, iv. No. 1236.

be sent to succeed Gneisenau. The war in Poland was about to end; the army would soon be disbanded; until then he felt capable of managing affairs in Posen.[37] He made no attempt to deny to himself or to others that he had suffered a devastating shock, but the increased activity helped him over his initial grief. After a few days, however, his emotions found an outlet in anger. He took it as an insult that the king did not personally reply to his report, that the semiofficial *Berliner Staatszeitung* did not carry a memorial article but was content with reprinting the brief notice that his own office had prepared for the "miserable provincial sheet" in Posen; he feared that the king would not adequately convey his condolence to Gneisenau's family or provide his widow with a decent pension; and the disappointing response elicited by his letters to the royal family and to the senior generals confirmed him in his suspicion that one more gigantic injustice was being perpetrated on those who had once saved the state and continued to represent its highest standards. A comrade suggested that the expressions of regret in his reports created resentment—an observation that he thought showed great understanding of the human psyche.[38] At least his old friend Prince Wilhelm, the king's younger brother, sent him a beautiful note, "indeed not in his own hand, but surely of his own authorship"— though after copying the text for his wife he thought it probable that the note had, after all, been drafted by an adjutant. Still, that was preferable to Duke Karl's stilted response, and the crown prince had not answered at all.[39]

Much of this was exaggeration. Duke Karl's note was unexceptional, considering that it was addressed to someone the writer disliked, concerning a man he had once believed to be a threat to the king's authority. The crown prince did write, after two weeks, a sympathetic letter, which also reassured Clausewitz about the financial security of Gneisenau's widow and children.[40] But Clausewitz was too bitter not to feel that anything that was done was inadequate. Fifteen years ago he had deeply resented the failure to honor Scharnhorst's memory; now the same vindictiveness and disregard seemed to follow on the death of his other close friend. To add to his anger and frustration, when he did hear from the king it was to receive an order to go into quarantine, which greatly increased the difficulties of his work. For ten days he and his staff moved to an estate on the outskirts of Posen. "Here I sit," Clausewitz wrote to his wife, "a prisoner in a Polish country house, whose original slovenliness has been reinforced by the decaying ele-

37. "I presume, and in my interest I add *it is to be hoped,* that his [Gneisenau's] position here will not be filled again, since the Polish affair has reached the point where new crises and further changes are hardly conceivable." Clausewitz to Müffling, 30 August 1831, Hahlweg, *Clausewitz,* p. 52.
38. Clausewitz to his wife, 5 September 1831, *Correspondence,* p. 489.
39. Clausewitz to his wife, 9 September 1831, *ibid.,* pp. 491–492.
40. Duke Karl of Mecklenburg to Clausewitz, 25 August 1831, in Priesdorff, iv, No. 1236; Crown Prince Frederick William to Clausewitz, 9 September 1831, Pertz-Delbrück, v, 700–701.

ments of time and of confusion. Nor am I certain who has a better claim on my quarters, the army of mice that grew up here or I." [41] Now that he had gained some distance from Gneisenau's death he could express concern over his own future: "If our dear friend had left his post here in good health he would have been the first to tell the king that everything that was so highly praised [in Berlin] was my work, for whenever he received a cabinet order complimenting him he gave it to me with the words: 'That is only for you.' I confess that my soul is so full of mistrust that I lack all joy and courage to carry on my duties." On the 8th, Warsaw surrendered to the Russians. When Clausewitz heard the news, he responded with a mixture of gratification and continued depression. He was pleased that he remained in charge, and was winding down the affairs of the army on his own, but he feared that without Gneisenau's support he would not be given due credit. "He would certainly have praised me to the king, and if only out of consideration for him I would not have been left without a mark of recognition. Now the debt that is owed me has gone up in smoke . ... In all important things in my life I have had great luck, but not in such matters. Well, one must accept it, and that is easily done if one says with the Preacher: 'All is vanity.' " [42]

He returned to Posen on the 11th. Four days later he was stunned to learn that Knesebeck, a man whose politics and personality he found equally distasteful, had been appointed commander of the army in the east in Gneisenau's place. Clausewitz had expected that his successful assumption of responsibility would obviate the appointment of a new commanding general; and yet this decision, like the delay in his promotion, should not have come as a surprise. For any number of reasons it was awkward to leave affairs in Posen in the hands of an officer who was junior in rank to the army's four corps commanders and some of the divisional commanders as well. Even though the assignment could last only a few weeks and would no longer call for difficult decisions, orderly procedure made it preferable to send a senior general to Posen. Knesebeck was an obvious choice for this post. He was one of the highest-ranking officers in the service, but his duties were largely honorific and he would not be missed from his regular assignments; on the contrary, Witzleben was probably anxious to put an end to his diplomatic missions, in which he was once again demonstrating his customary ineptitude.

To Clausewitz, however, "the appointment of General Knesebeck was a thunderbolt from the clear sky." [43] After the first shock, his resilience

41. Clausewitz to his wife, 5 September 1831, *Correspondence*, p. 488. The following quotation is from the same letter, p. 490.
42. Clausewitz to his wife, 11 September 1831, *ibid.*, p. 495.
43. Clausewitz to his wife, 16 September 1831, *ibid.*, p. 497. The following quotation is from the same letter, pp. 497–498. In a letter of 21 September he repeated that Knesebeck was cordial and seemed to have full confidence in him; *ibid.* p. 498.

nevertheless reasserted itself once more. Knesebeck, who had never held a major command and had no knowledge of local conditions, was forced to rely heavily on his chief of staff, and was clever enough to know it: "He obviously sensed that the mistrust that had existed between us had to be put aside for the time being . ... Consequently he behaved as though we were the oldest of friends, and since his arrival he has done nothing but praise my performance and the excellent organization of our work here. In short, we are on very good terms. Nevertheless, I find it horrible to carry on the same tasks with another man, and especially to sit with him at the same table where we often were so gay with the field marshal. This feeling turns food and drink to gall. Well, *il faut passer par là,* and I imagine it won't last for more than a few weeks."

What Clausewitz did not allude to in his letters, though he and his wife could not help but be painfully aware of it, was the political irony that lay in Knesebeck's appointment. The man whom Scharnhorst had castigated as a hypocritical and dangerous opponent of innovation, and whom Clausewitz had called "Scharnhorst's and my own sworn enemy," who in 1813 had advocated strategies that avoided battle at all cost, and whose influence with Frederick William had in 1814 nearly ruined Blücher's and Gneisenau's plan to destroy Napoleon by marching on Paris, a strikingly successful representative of everything conservative, was given charge of an enterprise that for a brief period had returned the survivors of the reform movement to activity and influence.[44] Nothing could better symbolize the course that the Prussian state had taken since 1815 than the replacement of Gneisenau and Clausewitz by Knesebeck, once the danger of serious fighting had passed. For Clausewitz personally, the sudden, needless elevation to a position of authority over him of a man whose greatest talent lay in playing on the anxieties and prejudices of the king could only be a further instance of the general stupidity and ill will by which he felt engulfed.

On 5 October the remnant of the Polish field army crossed into Prussia and surrendered. The capitulation of the last Polish fortresses followed, and on the 20th the Prussian army was demobilized. Some days later the king expressed to Clausewitz "complete satisfaction with the efforts with which he sought to justify the confidence placed in him."[45] The headquarters at Posen was disbanded, and on 7 November Clausewitz returned to Breslau, where his wife joined him two days later. Although the epidemic had reached Berlin at the end of the summer, she had remained in the capital to care for her mother, who was now in her seventies. Cholera cases had also been reported in Breslau; but, she writes, the prospect of

44. Clausewitz's characterization of Knesebeck occurs in a letter of 26 March 1813, to his wife, *Correspondence,* p. 321.
45. Priesdorff, v, No. 1429.

being reunited with her husband pushed anxiety over sickness, the future, even grief at Gneisenau's death, into the background.[46] On the voyage to Silesia the lines from Goethe's *Iphigenia:*

> Golden sun, lend me your rays,
> thankfully lay them at Jupiter's throne

kept running through her mind.[47] To celebrate her return, Clausewitz's servants had decorated the entrance and hall of their apartment with wreaths and festive arches of fir branches. At first Clausewitz appeared to his wife to be in high spirits; he had gained weight and seemed younger. He was cheered by the prospect of returning to *On War,* and perhaps completing it in the course of the winter, and also believed he had reason to expect a new and more important assignment.[48] But soon she realized that he had not overcome the shocks of the past months. In particular, he could not forgive the coldness with which he thought the king treated Gneisenau's memory. After his death she wrote: "Because his nerves were already so irritated he took these things perhaps too tragically, and attached more importance to them than they deserved."[49] Nevertheless, husband and wife passed "eight on the whole very happy days" together. On the morning of the 16th Clausewitz received reports from subordinates for two hours in his study, then he said he thought he had caught a cold and would stay home. His wife and her brother Count Brühl, who called on the couple shortly before noon, felt that there was no cause for serious concern, but sent for his physician. Early in the afternoon he began to vomit, suffered cramps in his calves, and showed other symptoms of cholera. After three hours he seemed to be more comfortable, but only a short time later he complained of severe pains in the spine, which were followed by cramps in the chest, and finally by what was described as a "nervous stroke"—which in the medical parlance of the 1830's signified a sudden paralysis of the nervous system without clearly attributable cause. He died just before nine o'clock in the evening. Medical opinion held that his general condition,

---

46. The first case of cholera in Breslau was reported on 20 September 1831; the epidemic continued for three months. Of the town's approximately 90,000 inhabitants, 1,347 were infected, of whom 795 died. R. Kayser, *Zur Geschichte der Cholera, speciell der Choleraepidemien in Breslau,* Breslau, 1884, pp. 7–8.

47. "Goldne Sonne, leih mir Deine Strahlen/Lege sie zum Dank an Jovis Thron." *Iphigenie auf Tauris,* III, 1. The quotation, cited from memory, is not quite accurate. Marie v. Clausewitz to Countess Bernstorff, 17 or 18 November 1831; Bernstorff, ii, 225–226.

48. M. v. Clausewitz, Preface, *On War* (p. 75); Second Appendix to Clausewitz, "'Über das Leben und den Charakter von Scharnhorst," *Historisch-politische Zeitschrift,* I, 221.

49. Marie v. Clausewitz to Countess Bernstorff, undated, written soon after 20 November 1831; Bernstorff, ii, p. 228. The two letters by Marie v. Clausewitz to Countess Bernstorff are our only reliable sources on Clausewitz's last days. The account of his illness and burial in Schwartz, *Leben des Generals Clausewitz,* ii, 440–441, is incomplete and inaccurate.

more than the cholera, had led to his death; from Marie von Clausewitz's description of the last hours, it seems probable that he died of a heart attack.

When the threat of cholera had first become apparent in the late spring of 1831, the Prussian government issued a set of public-health measures, which included regulations for the burial of victims of the disease. The corpse was to be transported only at night, in a special hearse, with attendants wearing protective smocks; interment was restricted to isolated cholera cemeteries; no one was permitted to attend the funeral. The absurdity of these prohibitions had led to their being quietly disregarded in Berlin.[50] When Hegel died of cholera on 14 November he was buried in daylight, in the old cemetery on the Chausseestrasse, next to Fichte's tomb, in the presence of hundreds of friends and students. In Breslau, however, the rules continued in force, except for a recent decision that military personnel could again be buried in the regular army cemetery. Clausewitz's relatives did not want to disobey the law openly by accompanying the hearse, but Count Brühl bribed the gravediggers to allow him to be present at the burial; after nightfall he evaded the guards stationed around the cemetery, and before the coffin was closed placed a laurel wreath on the dead man's chest. Two days later the Breslau garrison paraded for a brief memorial service. In the following months Marie von Clausewitz, assisted by Brühl and Clausewitz's friends Groeben and O'Etzel, arranged for the publication of at least some of her husband's manuscripts. The first volume of his *Posthumous Works,* books I–IV of *On War,* appeared in 1832. Seven more volumes were issued before Marie von Clausewitz's own death in 1836; the last two appeared in the following year. Their publication did not signify the start of a triumphal march of ideas universally accepted; but the systematic, historical study of organized violence in human affairs had begun.

50. A. Streckfuss, *Berlin im neunzehnten Jahrhundert,* Berlin, 1868, ii, 372, 379–383.

BEYOND THE NATION-STATE

THE LETTER THAT MARIE VON CLAUSEWITZ WROTE TO her friend Countess Bernstorff immediately after Clausewitz's death joined an evaluation of his life to the description of his dying: "It is a great comfort to me that at least his final moments were calm and painless, and yet the expression and tone with which he expelled his last sigh were heart-rending; it was as though he pushed life away like a heavy burden. Soon afterwards his features became calm and peaceful; an hour later, when I saw him for the last time, they again expressed the deepest pain. And indeed, life for him had consisted of an almost unbroken chain of effort, sorrow, and vexation. Certainly, on the whole he had achieved much more than he could have hoped for at the outset; he felt this deeply and acknowledged it with a grateful heart. But he never did scale the highest peak, and every pleasure that he experienced contained a flaw that clouded his enjoyment. He lived through great, glorious years, but never had the good fortune of fighting in a victorious battle. The night from the 18th to the 19th June 1815, which the field marshal, who spent it pursuing Napoleon, used to call the most beautiful of his life, was among the most terrible for him, after the battle of Wavre. To a rare degree he enjoyed the friendship of the most noble men of his time, but he never received the recognition that alone would have enabled him to be genuinely useful to his country. And how did he not suffer with and for his friends!" [1]

These lines have had great impact, directly and indirectly, on subsequent interpretations of Clausewitz's life. For some historians the letter has served as a magnet, gathering the sporadic instances of disappointment, anger, and depression Clausewitz expressed over nearly thirty years in his correspondence with friends, and with his fiancée and wife. Marie von Clausewitz seemed to confirm and emphasize their impression of a life that

1. Letter of 17 or 18 November 1831, Bernstorff, ii, 227.

in important respects they regarded as a failure. The most influential of these scholars was Hans Rothfels, at least so far as his early works are concerned; later he appeared to modify his original conceptions, without, however, explicitly rejecting them.[2]

In the preface to his important edition of Clausewitz's political essays, which I have repeatedly cited, Rothfels wrote that in Clausewitz's psychological makeup, "the energy of the will and of activity was not resolved in the energy of contemplation," and that Clausewitz died "with the feeling of having missed his true vocation"—without, however, citing evidence for this statement or identifying the vocation.[3] Similarly, Werner Hahlweg, whose bibliographical research has so greatly added to our knowledge of Clausewitz's writings, holds that the last half of Clausewitz's life was marked by "disappointment, bitterness, and final resignation," and even asserts that "what came after 1812 meant a fading away [*Abklingen*] without genuine fulfillment, a forced, even tortured renunciation."[4]

In their claim of unrelieved bleakness these interpretations go far beyond anything Marie von Clausewitz expressed even in hours of deepest grief; nor would Clausewitz have agreed that his life after 1812 was barren of genuine fulfillment. On the contrary, he had a healthy regard for his achievements, intellectual and otherwise, though being sane he could be dissatisfied with himself. What he suffered from was that his true value, as he saw it, was not sufficiently recognized. The failure to draw this distinction with the necessary clarity is the first factor to be noted in the judgments of Rothfels and Hahlweg, together with a disturbing vagueness in their argumentation. They point to genuine issues, to the severe disappointments that were part of Clausewitz's life; but for reasons that will become apparent when we consider the assumptions underlying their analyses, they misinterpret Clausewitz's defeats, while paying insufficient attention to his external successes and internal triumphs.

At the base of Rothfels's interpretation lies a romantic nationalism that reflects the young historian's attitude at the time he published his major studies on Clausewitz, during and immediately after the First World War. It characterizes this attitude that he found nothing extreme in Clausewitz's concept of the state in the years after Jena, or in his simultaneous denigration of the French national character; he would scarcely have agreed with the present study that these opinions represented a temporary exaggeration of Clausewitz's earlier ideas, brought about by the shock of defeat, and soon replaced by an ever-increasing objectivity. For him Clausewitz is primarily the German patriot before his time. Rothfels has the great merit

2. Note his valuable chapter on Clausewitz in *Makers of Modern Strategy*, ed. E. M. Earle, Princeton, 1961.
3. Clausewitz, *Politische Schriften und Briefe*, pp. ix, xi.
4. Hahlweg, *Clausewitz*, pp. 7, 22.

of being the first scholar to attempt a detailed psychological portrait of Clausewitz, but regrettably he relied on a mystical causality. His analysis stressed one aspect above others—that Clausewitz was an outsider, not in the sense that every genuinely creative individual stands in some respects apart from his contemporaries, but with the special meaning of his not being an indigenous, land-owning Prussian noble. Rothfels speculates that Clausewitz must have suffered severely from his ambiguous background. All available evidence, however, indicates that the lasting significance of Clausewitz's antecedents lies elsewhere. The Clausewitzes were not just outsiders, they also belonged to the new men who in large numbers served and strengthened the state, and indeed made the modern state possible. Socially induced feelings of inferiority may well have been part of their makeup at first, but there is little sign of this in Clausewitz's actions and letters, while his entire life documents the concept of the state that emerged among the new elite. Rothfels, nevertheless, regards the social inferiority of Clausewitz's family as a source—or even as the source—of what he terms Clausewitz's pessimism, of always expecting the worst. This attitude in turn is said to have condemned Clausewitz to exist at the edge of events, and explains the "military fiasco" that he suffered: "It is the lack of organic, indigenous roots [*der Mangel organischer Bodenständigkeit*], the inevitable need to absorb externals with unusual receptivity and excitation without the power to confront them with the instinctive imperturbability of a sovereign ego: it is this special relationship to objects, this inner ambiguity of his existence, that determines Clausewitz's fate in the realm of action." [5] This almost *Völkische* interpretation fails to explain why "rootlessness" must lead to pessimism—it did nothing of the sort in the case of Scharnhorst and Gneisenau—nor does Rothfels indicate how the family's spurious nobility or Clausewitz's supposed insecurity caused his assignment to that part of the Prussian army in 1815 that was not present at the climax of Waterloo.[6]

When faced with interpretations of this kind, it may not be amiss to point out that if the main French attack at the battle of Ligny had been directed against the Prussian left wing rather than against the center, another corps, not Clausewitz's, would almost certainly have covered the Prussian retreat, with the consequence that two days later Clausewitz could easily have found himself at the head of the column hurrying to support Wellington, rather than fighting a holding action against Grouchy. Surely it was not the fateful extension of his social background and of his uncertain ego that prevented Clausewitz from sharing in the triumph of Waterloo and receiving the usual honors awarded a senior staff officer after a

5. Rothfels, *Carl von Clausewitz: Politik und Krieg,* p. 170.
6. See also Kessel's cautiously stated objections—perhaps influenced by German conditions at the time of writing—in his previously cited article, "Carl von Clausewitz: Herkunft und Persönlichkeit," *Wissen und Wehr,* XVIII (1937).

decisive victory—thus demolishing Rothfels's interpretation—but simply chance, which historians, like soldiers, do well to treat with respect.

Less fate-ridden, more cautiously realistic is the evaluation of Werner Hahlweg, who finds the key to what he regards as the "inner imbalance in Clausewitz's personality, the inability of realizing the unity of ideas and action," not in social conditions but in the individual himself: "The diverging complexity of his character traits prevented Clausewitz in the final analysis from developing into a harmonious personality. The tension between the reality of the age, as he experienced it, and his sense of the goals that could be achieved or should be fought for was perhaps too pronounced. Apparently he suffered throughout his life from the duality of his nature: from the discrepancy between ambition and reality, from wanting to achieve something for which he perhaps lacked the necessary preconditions, or which at least was denied to him." [7] This ambition, according to Hahlweg, was to lead armies in battle—an aim that he links with the question, also raised by Rothfels, of whether Clausewitz would have been a great commander. That this is scarcely a fruitful topic for historians had already been observed by Delbrück in his devastating critique of Schwartz's pioneering biography. Delbrück nevertheless took pains to explore the different aspects of the question, and arrived not at an answer but at an evaluation of probabilities. He took note of comments by Clausewitz's contemporaries, Thielmann and Brandt, that Clausewitz tended toward caution in the field, since he tried to weigh all possibilities; he agreed that for the great commander rigorous logic might be less valuable than instinct—which was also Clausewitz's opinion—but thought that there could be no doubt that "Clausewitz as an active, courageous, unusually prescient man and experienced soldier would have made a better than average general." He concluded: "For still higher excellence, absolute standards probably do not exist. Conditions must be taken into account as much as individuals. In particular, wars vary greatly and call for different leaders . ... Whether Clausewitz could have lived with and overcome the grinding personal frictions of the leaders and nations in the campaign of 1813 may be doubted. For the precise computations of the war of 1870 he might well have been the right man." [8]

If the question of Clausewitz's potential for senior command has any validity at all, it is only to the extent that it illuminates the issue of the reasonableness of his ambitions. Both Rothfels and Hahlweg posit a basic conflict between action and scholarship that tore Clausewitz apart; but that is yet another assumption derived less from the evidence than from their

7. Hahlweg, *Clausewitz*, pp. 30–31.
8. Delbrück, *Historische und Politische Aufsätze*, p. 226. Cf. the discussion of Clausewitz's potential for leadership in the valuable article by K. Linnebach, "Clausewitz' Persönlichkeit," *Wissen und Wehr*, X (1930).

own preconceptions. Rothfels, in particular, seemed to believe in the years after 1918 that the conflict between the two realms could never be reconciled—a belief that reflects ideas current in his own generation more accurately than it does those of the early 19th century. When he further asserts that Clausewitz's desire for activity was not resolved by his scholarship, he is suggesting that writing served as an inadequate substitute for fighting, which is, to say the least, difficult to reconcile with the fact of intense, satisfying, and almost uninterrupted scholarly activity that is documented from Clausewitz's twenty-third year on. However fascinating these and similar generalizations may seem, they are defective history. Historians may consider it useful to attempt interpretations of the psychological elements and dynamics of their subjects. But unless they and their readers are content with purely subjective speculations, their interpretations will not only have to deal critically with all the evidence, and be prepared to admit ignorance when necessary evidence is lacking; their analytic structures must also consist of firm causal links that the reader can comprehend and test. Argument by apposition and assumption, as exemplified by Rothfels's paragraph cited above, obscures rather than clarifies the past.

As a young man Clausewitz was very ambitious. In a letter written during the period of his internment he even voiced the fantasy of achieving supreme command, regretting that this could not occur when he was young, but only when his arm trembled with the feebleness of age.[9] His hopes differed little from those held by countless junior officers in all armies; and like most of them he, too, came gradually to accept that he would never rise to the highest position. In letters to his wife and to Gneisenau he continued to express his ambitions frankly, but now on a more realistic scale. His career was interrupted by internment, but when he returned to active service advancement was rapid.[10] What he himself regarded as satisfactory progress was stalled, this time seriously, when in 1812 he chose to quit Prussia. Under the circumstances, promotion to general six years later was a remarkable recovery.

The objective aspects of a man's career need not, of course, determine his sense of achievement; but historians should not ignore them, particularly when Clausewitz himself acknowledged his successes, while wishing they had been greater. That his longing for victory in battle was not an obsession, which alone might justify Rothfels's judgment of his career as a failure, is borne out by a further change in attitude. In his early letters he associated military success with leadership in battle; but even before he

9. Clausewitz to Marie v. Brühl, 2 April 1807, *Correspondence*, pp. 105–106. See above, p. 127.
10. Some comparisons: The ages at which Clausewitz was promoted to captain, major, and colonel were 29, 30, and 35 respectively. The corresponding ages for Boyen were 36, 37, 41; for Grolman, 30, 30, 36; for Krauseneck 32, 35, 39; and for Gneisenau, who belonged to an earlier generation, 35, 46, 49.

turned thirty he had come to regard himself, without apparent misgivings, as primary a staff officer. When he applied for an Austrian commission in 1809, he explicitly preferred the staff to the line, a preference that he was to repeat in later years, though at other times he wished for the command of a regiment or brigade.[11] In the last months of his life he could complain about the lack of recognition and independence that was the lot of a chief of staff, but was prepared to continue in that position under suitable conditions; otherwise he hoped for command of a division. His expanding scholarly interests—from 1808 on closely associated with his staff duties—contributed to this development. His statement that if he were economically independent he would like to be a civilian scholar, and his attempts to enter the diplomatic service, scarely bear out interpretations of Clausewitz as a man who could find satisfaction only in the army and in war.[12] Finally, his life, far from being torn by irreconcilable conflicts between scholarship and war, demonstrates a far-reaching unity of purpose and achievement. Trying to excel in more than one area of activity is likely to lead to difficulties, but Clausewitz combined two very different callings—service to the state and scholarship—with remarkable success.

If interpretations of Clausewitz's inner life ought to take account of his external successes and failures, they must also show regard for the circumstances that accompanied the increased incidence of pessimism that his letters reveal after 1815. Some of these statements expressed dissatisfaction with an unsympathetic superior, slow advancement, or his failure to gain a diplomatic post. But most refer to a broader development, which, to be sure, also handicapped his further career: the conservative resurgence in Prussia and Germany. It would have argued a peculiar estrangement from reality for a man committed to reform not to be offended and depressed by the Restoration, with its parochialism, injustices, and absurdities. Clausewitz was compelled to renounce strong hopes for the Prussian state and society, and he resented the men he considered responsible for the loss, from the king down. In certain crises—when political intrigue deprived him of an ambassadorship, or when he watched Polish insurgents reenact his own struggle for a free fatherland—his disappointment errupted in anger and depression. But even the most telling evidence of his feelings that we possess—his correspondence with the two individuals who were closest to

11. Clausewitz to Marie v. Brühl, 19 June 1809, *Correspondence*, p. 248.
12. Cf. his letters to Gneisenau of 27 February 1815 and 16 September 1820, quoted on pp. 245 and 281 above. Similar sentiments can be found in his correspondence with his wife, before and after marriage—for example, his statement in a letter of 15 September 1807, *Correspondence*, p. 138: "You err if you think that the idea of quitting the service is abhorrent to me. As long as there is no war, I regard it as completely unimportant whether one is a soldier or not, and if I had enough means to do without any work at all I would gladly retire to the country, devote myself to the study of history and of war, and calmly await the moment when it is time to return to the service. But that is out of the question since I have no other property than the sword on my side."

him, his wife and Gneisenau—show these moods only occasionally. Depression is not an unusual condition; what matters is its comprehensiveness, depth, and frequency. Neither his letters nor his actions indicate that Clausewitz's personality was essentially depressive, just as they do not indicate that he was torn by irreconcilable conflicts. On the contrary, the occasional episodes of open or repressed anger appear as wholly reasonable, positive reactions of a sensitive, intelligent man to normal internal stress and sometimes severe external difficulties, both of which, in general, he managed effectively. His ability to work steadily, productively, and with pleasure, and his equally pronounced gifts for friendship and love, scarcely convey anything but the impression of a strong, essentially healthy psychological constitution.

It is of the greatest significance that one of Clausewitz's major disappointments—his disappointment in the Prussian state—was also the occasion of an important advance in emotional independence and maturity. In discussing the ideas that Clausewitz expressed in his writings and personal letters before the War of 1806 and during his internment, I have suggested that he developed an idealized, unusually demanding concept of the state, whose pronounced personal overtones and pervasiveness in his thought point to far earlier roots, though not enough is known about his childhood to allow for more than hypotheses. That a strong personal identification with the state was more than rhetoric was in any case confirmed by Clausewitz's behavior during the years of reform, culminating in his radical attempt in 1812 to save the Prussian monarchy in spite of herself, at great and lasting personal cost. Writing the *Bekenntnisdenkschrift* and quitting the Prussian service constituted the emotional high point of Clausewitz's relationship with the state and the extreme of his idealization. These actions also marked the nadir of his disappointment in the real state, and during the following years a process of psychological separation took place which eventually enabled him to think of Prussia with nearly the same objectivity that he applied in his judgment of any major power.

Renouncing his identification with the idealized state was undoubtedly a long step forward in his personal maturation. But very little evidence exists for the dynamics of this process. To what extent was Clausewitz's renunciation a relatively independent act, in which the maturing individual gradually detached himself from childhood fantasies and adopted values that allowed him to live in greater freedom and self-sufficiency? To what extent was it a response to external conditions, a realistic recognition of the flawed nature of the state, and of its increasingly undesirable policies, which repressed earlier demands but left them more or less unresolved? Obviously both forces were at work, but their relative strengths and the precise nature of their interaction cannot be determined on the evidence. That the external detachment occurred is certain; the emotional equation that made it possible remains largely obscure: another reason why a detailed psychological interpretation of the last twenty years of Clausewitz's life presents great difficulties.

A more openly intellectual concern also benefited from his detachment from the state—his ideal of human perfectibility, the belief that education and work would bring the individual nearer to autonomy and to a harmonious integration of talents and feelings. Experience persuaded Clausewitz that this was not likely to occur for the great majority of mankind; but he retained his belief in the applicability of the principle to exceptional individuals at all levels of society. We noted before that his denial of the teleological view of history did not disturb his faith in the possibility of personal perfectibility. His own progression from the instinctual existence of childhood through dependence on the state toward independence reads like a paraphrase of Fichte's late fragments on political theory, his *Staatslehre*—a confirmation, it may be thought, of the psychological insights contained in the philosophy of German idealism. That in Clausewitz's case emotional liberation was not accompanied by withdrawal from state service was due perhaps not only to his limited financial means but also to his continued fascination with the reality of the state, though had he possessed a small income he might have followed Wilhelm von Humboldt's example on a modest scale and lived the life of a private scholar. As it was, he continued to serve the state even as he recognized the inadequate, "pauvre" manner in which the state responded to the ethical and cultural obligations that the reform movement had ascribed to it. Under the pressure of circumstance he put off earlier hopes for pedagogic, social, and political development, and now interested himself primarily in the diplomatic and military power of the state. His sense of realism, which had been a pronounced feature of his thought from the time he began to write, rose to new dominance. His demand for the ethical sanctity of the state might abate, but not his recognition of its place in the world, nor of its mechanics of power. These factors had to be accepted, whether or not they could be reconciled with one's idealism. For Clausewitz the Prussian state ceased to be what it continued to be for Hegel: the realization of an ethical idea. Instead, he regarded it as a historical reality whose first duty is to maintain itself.

His feelings as a Prussian subject and the approach he chose in interpreting the Prussian state and the state in general have much in common. Both as citizen and as political analyst he appeared relatively free of ideological preconceptions, apart from his belief that a political organism claiming independence and true sovereignty must above all be strong. His essays in the early 1820's and again in 1831, and his historical analysis of the collapse of the Frederician state, were highly argumentative, but their theme was institutional efficiency and political realism, not such concepts as absolutism, legitimacy, the social contract, or nationalism. In essence they represent a return to Machiavelli, in whose writings national and cultural considerations were also far from absent but who emphasized the primacy of the structure and mechanics of power. Even during the years of conflict with Napoleon, a detached appraisal of possibilities and risks accompanied Clausewitz's call for heroism. The realistic element in his thought was too fundamental ever to be wholly pushed aside; and, to be sure, the adventurous policies he advocated aimed at restoring and increasing the strength of the state. After the *Bekenntnisdenkschrift* it became the principal theme of his political writings that men should recognize the realities and responsibilities of power and act accordingly.

This also characterizes his writings on war. A parallel presents itself between the genesis of his studies of the state and the genesis of his studies on war: a rabid patriot comes to see the state as a pure organism of power, bare of all ideological decoration, whether they are those of traditional values or of the burgeoning nationalism of his age, while his speculations on the emergence of the modern state transcend the German experience in their search for generalities. A passionate soldier comes to regard war as an activity from which assumptions, convention, doctrine must be stripped, so that war can be studied and understood as an expression of social and political life, as a compound of violence, creative genius, and reason. The idealization of the nation-state gives way to acceptance of political reality. The theoretical demand for absolute violence is relinquished in favor of joining the ideal and the real in the proposition of the dual nature of war.

Both lines of intellectual effort reach realistic appraisals, realistic in the sense that the analyst tries to the best of his ability to eliminate all extraneous values and concepts from the subject under investigation. Clausewitz restricted his view to that which exists, even if he could not see it fully, clearly, or accurately. But if his writings on the state and on war shared a common outlook, they differed vastly in form and content. Although war was only one among several expressions of state power, it was the one he chose to investigate in detail, and for which he developed a comprehensive theory; on the state he wrote as historian and commentator, not as theorist. His theories of war did not require the context of a political theory as long as he was clear in his mind on the essential element of the state's existence. The bond between his political and military writings, which assume such different forms, lies rather in their common motive— the search for understanding. The specific psychological foundations of this need are obscure; we cannot know what longings and anxieties of the child were sublimated in the scholarly research and the struggle for scientific method of the grown man. But it is evident that his need to explore certain components of his existence in a logical, objective manner was as strong as his drive to demolish the military dogma of the society and state in which he grew up. Together they helped him shed the emotional trappings of the idealization of the state, which earlier had exerted such compelling power over him. And they enabled him to formulate the first theory of war that looked beyond the operational to include its political and psychological aspects, and that rejected all time-bound and geographic standards. The development of his theory of war was influenced by his ideas on the absolute monarchy as well as on the nation-state of the coming industrial age, but the result transcends both. He never completed his theoretical work, even in the limited sense in which he considered completion possible and desirable; nor did he achieve his highest ambitions for external recognition. Nevertheless, his life demonstrates a unity of motives and effort, a harmonizing of inner needs and achievements, a mastery of reality through understanding.

A NOTE ON SOURCES

CLAUSEWITZ WAS A PROLIFIC WRITER WHO PUB-
lished little during his lifetime; the ten-volume edition of historical and
theoretical works that appeared soon after his death began a process of posthumous publication that continues to this day. Within the last two decades
Werner Hahlweg has printed the manuscript of a course of lectures Clausewitz gave during the reform era, and Hahlweg, Eberhard Kessel, and I
have published shorter pieces and letters that were not known before.
Research for this book uncovered further items—for example, Clausewitz's
letter to Boyen of 29 November 1816, which indicates with exceptional
clarity his bitterness at the treatment of Scharnhorst's memory in the Restoration, or the French intelligence appraisal of Clausewitz, cited in chapter
10, section iv. Presumably, additional material by and on Clausewitz will
turn up in the future.

Piecemeal publication of an extensive *Nachlass* and correspondence
that are now widely dispersed has made available to scholarship a vast but
disorganized body of sources. Even the more important editions of Clausewitz's writings partly duplicate and partly supplement one another:
Schwartz in 1878, Linnebach in 1917, Rothfels in 1920 and 1922, and
Schering in 1941 published some of the same essays and letters; each also
printed items not found elsewhere—to the point that several editions contain different extracts from the same manuscript while none has the complete text. Werner Hahlweg's recent edition of Clausewitz's papers—
Schriften—Aufsätze—Studien—Briefe, Göttingen, 1966,—of which one 760-
page volume has already appeared, will not bring order to this confusion.
The edition, a masterpiece of transcription and presentation, contains previously unpublished material as well as corrected readings of material already known, but for reasons of economy excludes other pieces that in subject matter and time of writing are closely related to its contents. Thus
Hahlweg prints Clausewitz's answer to an examination question of 1803,

and a strategic study of 1805, but not Clausewitz's notebook on politics and war of the same period, the entries of which are scattered among several works now out of print. Nor does he include Clausewitz's manuscript on strategy of 1804, or his first published article, written in 1805. Any analysis of Clausewitz's thought and of his political and military activities must continue to draw together and reconcile the fragments of his publications and correspondence, as well as the imprints that his ideas and personality left in the diaries and memoirs of his contemporaries.

A comprehensive edition of Clausewitz's letters does not exist. His correspondence with his wife, before and after marriage, has appeared separately; his correspondence with Scharnhorst and Gneisenau is contained in their biographies and published papers. Letters to other individuals are dispersed through the literature dealing with the period; a few—notably the discussion of Machiavelli addressed to Fichte—constitute sources of primary importance to the genesis of his ideas. Few letters that he exchanged with civilian correspondents have survived, and in general his name does not figure prominently in the correspondence and memoirs of the time. Among the exceptions is the diary of Countess Bernstorff; but far more interesting acquaintances rarely mention him. His sojourn at Coppet in 1807 in the company of Mme. de Staël, Mme. Récamier, and August Wilhelm Schlegel left only a thin residue in their profuse literary output, and even that is lacking in the papers of such men as Heinrich von Kleist and Fichte, whom he must have seen occasionally during the following years. The absence of comments is a reflection of Clausewitz's reserved personality, which usually failed to make an impression on people who did not know him well. Nevertheless, the writings of the time do contain references to him that scholarship has ignored until now, which add to the relatively sparse data on certain periods of his life. Wilhelm von Humboldt's correspondence, for instance, reveals that Clausewitz was engaged on a fairly important political mission in Frankfurt in 1816. Again, Humboldt's London diary indicates that Clausewitz visited England the following year—a visit that must have deepened his appreciation of the diversity of European social and political development and that evidently spurred his desire to be appointed Prussian ambassador to the Court of St. James. The papers of such figures in Berlin society and literary circles as Bettina von Arnim and Varnhagen von Ense tell us something about his life in the Prussian capital in the 1820's.

Much of the voluminous literature on Clausewitz deals with the impact that his theories had on war in the later 19th and 20th centuries, or with their validity today, topics that fall outside the scope of this book. Those interpretations of his ideas, activities, and personality that seem significant to me are discussed in the text and footnotes, and only a brief survey of secondary works basic to any study of Clausewitz need be given here.

Any such list must begin with the early biography by Karl Schwartz, *Leben des Generals Carl von Clausewitz und der Frau Marie von Clausewitz geb. Gräfin von Brühl*, 2 vols., Berlin, 1878. Schwartz's historical analysis is negligible and his narrative contains many errors, but he prints material still not available elsewhere. Two valuable short studies of the man and his influence are Rudolf Karl von Caemmerer's *Clausewitz*, Berlin, 1905, and Werner Hahlweg's *Carl von Clausewitz*, Göttingen, 1957. Hans Rothfels, who spent a lifetime publishing and interpreting Clausewitz's work, wrote a sophisticated analysis of Clausewitz's first thirty-five years, to which—despite disagreements on fundamental issues—I am greatly indebted: *Carl von Clausewitz: Politik und Krieg*, Berlin, 1920. Rothfels's integration of the history of ideas with cultural and military history was further developed by Eberhard Kessel in his introduction to Clausewitz's *Strategie aus dem Jahr 1804, mit Zusätzen von 1808 und 1809*, Hamburg, 1937, and in a number of remarkable biographical and theoretical articles, among them "Carl von Clausewitz: Herkunft und Persönlichkeit," *Wissen und Wehr*, XVIII (1937), and "Zur Genesis der modernen Kriegslehre," *Wehrwissenschaftliche Rundschau*, III (1953). Some of the themes developed by Rothfels and Kessel are reinterpreted from a more exclusively military and political point of view by Gerhard Ritter in the chapter "Revolution und Kriegsführung: Napoleon und Clausewitz," in the first volume of his *Staatskunst und Kriegshandwerk*, Munich, 1954.

A special place in the Clausewitz literature is occupied by the three works of Walther Malmsten Schering: *Die Kriegsphilosophie von Clausewitz*, Hamburg, 1935; *Wehrphilosophie*, Leipzig, 1939; and his selection of Clausewitz's writings, *Geist und Tat*, Stuttgart, 1941. Schering, who taught philosophy at the University of Berlin during the Third Reich, had the inestimable benefit of disposing over the entire body of Clausewitz papers before they were dispersed and disappeared at the end of the Second World War. A planned edition of Clausewitz's unpublished manuscripts never materialized, although he included some hitherto unknown essays in his volume *Geist und Tat*. Schering's analyses of Clausewitz's methodology clarified some of its elements; but he was error-prone, not only with dates and names but also in his readings of the texts, and it is difficult to know how to characterize his effort, by means of word substitutions and modernizations of terms and concepts, to bring Clausewitz's theories into agreement with the National Socialist cult of the leader.

Among works on Clausewitz that I have cited only rarely, or not at all, five should be mentioned here. Shortly before the First World War, Paul Roques published an elegant but superficial study *Le Général de Clausewitz*, Paris, 1912. Much inferior is Roger Parkinson's *Carl von Clausewitz*, London, 1971, a poor specimen of popular biography, full of factual errors, howlers, and references to nonexistent works. In the early 1930's two dissertations on Clausewitz were published in Germany, neither of which contributed anything to the understanding of his life or his writings: Richard Blaschke's *Carl von Clausewitz: Ein Leben im Kampf,* Berlin, 1934, and Arnold Brügmann's *Staat und Nation im Denken Carls von Clausewitz,* Heidelberg, 1934. Blaschke's work, originally an Erlangen dissertation, substitutes romantic patriotism for research. Brügmann has a better sense of the historical issues, but his treatment is confused, replete with errors and misquotations, and never develops an identifiable thesis. Finally, Maria Hartl has written a brief, stimulating monograph on Clausewitz's literary style, *Carl von Clausewitz: Persönlichkeit und Stil,* Emden, 1956.

More detailed introductions to the publication history of Clausewitz's writings and to the literature concerning him may be found in Werner Hahlweg's essay and notes in the 16th edition of *Vom Kriege,* Bonn, 1952, and in my article "Clausewitz: A Bibliographical Survey," *World Politics,* XVII (1965).

MANUSCRIPTS, BOOKS, AND ARTICLES CITED

MANUSCRIPTS

Berlin. Geheimes Staatsarchiv Preussischer Kulturbesitz, Rep. 92 (von Canitz Nr. 4).

Staatsbibliothek Preussischer Kulturbesitz, Clausewitz (2f. 1820).

Copenhagen. Rigsarkivet, Dpt. f. u. A. 1771–1848, Preussen II, Depecher 1819.

Merseburg. Deutsches Zentralarchiv, Historische Abt. II, Rep. 92 (Boyen d. Ä.).

Vincennes. Archives de la Guerre, Carton No. 1529, "Mémoires et Reconnaissances."

CLAUSEWITZ: WORKS AND CORRESPONDENCE

Note: Editions cited are those used in this book.

"Bemerkungen über die reine und angewandte Strategie des Herrn von Bülow," *Neue Bellona,* IX (1805), no. 3.

"Historische Briefe über die grossen Kriegsereignisse im Oktober 1806," *Minerva,* I and II (1807), issues for January, February, and April.

"Kriegsartikel für die Unter-Officiere und gemeinen Soldaten (der königl. preussischen Armee). ... Verordnung wegen der Militär-Strafen. ... Verordnung wegen Bestrafung der Officiere. ... Reglement über die Besetzung der Stellen der Port-epée Fähnriche und über die Wahl zum Officier. ..." *Jenaische Allgemeine Literatur-Zeitung,* no. 238, 11 October 1808.

[With Gneisenau] "Nachruf." "Nekrolog" [of Scharnhorst], *Preussischer Correspondent,* 12 and 14 July 1813.

Der Feldzug von 1813 bis zum Waffenstillstand [Glatz, 1813]. A free translation of this work is incorporated in J. E. Marston, *The Life and Campaigns of Field-Marshal Prince Blücher*. London, 1815.

"Über das Leben und den Charakter von Scharnhorst," *Historisch-politische Zeitschrift*, I (1832).

Hinterlassene Werke des Generals Carl von Clausewitz über Krieg und Kriegführung. 10 vols. Berlin, 1832–37.

    Vols. 1–3: *Vom Kriege;* "Übersicht des Sr. Königl. Hoheit dem Kronprinzen ... ertheilten militärischen Unterrichts."

    Vol. 4: *Der Feldzug von 1796 in Italien.*

    Vols. 5–6: *Die Feldzüge von 1799 in Italien und in der Schweiz.*

    Vol. 7: "Der Feldzug von 1812 in Russland"; "Der Feldzug von 1813 bis zum Waffenstillstand"; "Der Feldzug von 1814 in Frankreich."

    Vol. 8: *Der Feldzug von 1815 in Frankreich.*

    Vol. 9: "Gustav Adolphs Feldzüge von 1630–1632"; "Historische Materialien zur Strategie"; "Turenne"; "Die Feldzüge Luxemburgs in Flandern von 1690–1694"; "Einige Bemerkungen zum spanischen Erbfolgekriege ...."

    Vol. 10: "Sobiesky"; "Krieg der Russen gegen die Türken von 1736–1739"; "Die Feldzüge Friedrich des Grossen von 1741–1762"; "Der Feldzug des Herzogs von Braunschweig gegen die Holländer 1787"; "Übersicht des Krieges in der Vendée 1793."

"Über das Fortschreiten und den Stillstand der kriegerischen Begebenheiten," publ. by H. Delbrück, *Zeitschrift für preussische Geschichte und Landeskunde*, XV (1878).

Nachrichten über Preussen in seiner grossen Katastrophe; Kriegsgeschichtliche Einzelschriften, x, Berlin, 1888.

"Zwei Denkschriften von Clausewitz 1830/31," *Militär-Wochenblatt* (1891), nos. 29–31.

"Betrachtungen über den künftigen Kriegsplan gegen Frankreich," *Moltkes Militärische Werke*, first series, iv, Berlin, 1902.

Karl und Marie von Clausewitz: Ein Lebensbild in Briefen und Tagebuchblättern. Ed. K. Linnebach. Berlin, 1917.

"Ein kunsttheoretisches Fragment des Generals Carl von Clausewitz," publ. by H. Rothfels, *Deutsche Rundschau*, CLXXIII (1917), no. 3.

"Ein Brief von Clausewitz an den Kronprinzen Friedrich Wilhelm aus dem Jahre 1812," publ. by H. Rothfels, *Historische Zeitschrift*, CXXI (1920), no. 2.

Politische Schriften und Briefe. Ed. H. Rothfels. Munich, 1922.

Strategie aus dem Jahr 1804, mit Zusätzen von 1808 und 1809. Ed. E. Kessel. Hamburg, 1937.

Zwei Briefe des Generals von Clausewitz: Gedanken zur Abwehr, special issue of the *Militärwissenschaftliche Rundschau,* II (1937).

"Clausewitz über den Gedanken eines Ländertauschs zur Verbindung der Ost- und West-Masse der Preussischen Monarchie nach den Befreiungskriegen," publ. by E. Kessel, *Forschungen zur Brandenburgischen und Preussischen Geschichte,* LI (1939).

Geist und Tat. Ed. W. M. Schering. Stuttgart, 1941.

Principles of War. Trans. and ed. H. Gatzke. Harrisburg, 1942.

Vom Kriege. Ed. W. Hahlweg. Bonn, 1952.

"Clausewitz bei Liddell Hart" (letter to the *Allgemeine Jenaische Literatur-Zeitung,* 23 May 1806), publ. by W. Hahlweg, *Archiv für Kulturgeschichte,* XLI (1959), no. 1.

Schriften—Aufsätze—Studien—Briefe. Ed. W. Hahlweg, i, Göttingen, 1966.

"An Anonymous Letter by Clausewitz on the Polish Insurrection of 1830–1831" (letter printed in the *Zeitung des Grossherzogtums Posen,* 21, July 1831), publ. by P. Paret, *Journal of Modern History,* XLII (1970), no. 2.

On War. Trans. and ed. M. Howard and P. Paret. Princeton, 1976.

Note: Additional letters, memoranda, and diaries are contained in such books and articles, listed below, as K. Schwartz, *Leben des Generals Carl von Clausewitz,* Berlin, 1878, and E. Kessel, "Zu Boyens Entlassung," *Historische Zeitschrift,* CLXXV (1953), no. 1.

OTHER PRIMARY SOURCES

Al..... . "Der Feldzug 1796 in Italien. Hinterlassenes Werk des Generals Karl von Clausewitz. Berlin 1833," *Oestreichische militärische Zeitschrift* (1834), no. 7.

———. "Die Feldzüge von 1799 in Italien und der Schweiz. Hinterlassenes Werk des Generalen [*sic!*] Karl von Clausewitz. 2 Theile. Berlin 1833," *Oestreichische militärische Zeitschrift* (1835), nos. 5 and 6.

Arndt, E. M. *Ein Lebensbild in Briefen.* Eds. H. Meissner and R. Geerds. Berlin, 1898.

———. *Zwei Worte über die Entstehung und Bestimmung der teutschen Legion.* N. p., 1813.

Arnim, A. and B. v. *Achim und Bettina in ihren Briefen.* 2 vols. Ed. W. Vordtriede. Frankfurt, 1961.

August, Prince of Prussia. *Aus dem kriegsgeschichtlichen Nachlasse Seiner Königlichen Hoheit des Prinzen August von Preussen; Kriegsgeschichtliche Einzelschriften,* ii. Berlin, 1883.

"Aus dem letzten Jahrzehnt Friedrich-Wilhelms III." Ed. P. Bailleu. *Hohenzollern-Jahrbuch,* XX (1916).

Aus den Jahren Preussischer Not und Erneuerung. Ed. H. J. Schoeps. Berlin, 1963.

Aus den Papieren der Familie von Schleinitz. Berlin, 1905.

Aus der Zeit der Not. Ed. A. Pick. Berlin, 1900.

Beguelin, H. and A. v. *Denkwürdigkeiten von Heinrich und Amalie von Beguelin.* Ed. A. Ernst. Berlin, 1892.

Berenhorst, G. H. v. *Aus dem Nachlasse von Georg Heinrich von Berenhorst.* Ed. E. v. Bülow. 2 vols. Dessau, 1845–47.

Bernstorff, E. v. *Gräfin Elise von Bernstorff.* Ed. E. v. d. Bussche-Kessell. 2 vols. in 1. Berlin, 1896.

Bignon, L. P. de. *Histoire de France sous Napoléon.* 14 vols. Paris, 1829–50.

Blumen, C. F. v. *Von Jena bis Neisse.* Ed. C. M. v. Unruh. Leipzig, 1904.

Boyen, H. v. *Beiträge zur Kenntnis des Generals von Scharnhorst und seiner amtlichen Thätigkeit in den Jahren 1808–1813.* Berlin, 1833.

———. *Erinnerungen aus dem Leben des General-Feldmarschalls Hermann von Boyen.* Ed. F. Nippold. 3 vols. Leipzig, 1889–90.

Brandt, Heinrich v. *Aus dem Leben des Generals der Infanterie z. D. Dr. Heinrich von Brandt.* Ed. H. v. Brandt. 3 vols. Berlin, 1868–82.

Bray, S. v. "Aus der Berliner Hofgesellschaft der Jahre 1805 und 1806," *Deutsche Rundschau,* XXIX (1903), no. 5.

"Briefe des Feldmarschalls Grafen Neithardt v. Gneisenau an seinen Schwiegersohn Wilh. v. Scharnhorst," publ. by A. Pick, *Historische Zeitschrift,* LXXVII (1896).

Brünneck, M. v. *Von Preussens Befreiungs- und Verfassungskampf.* Ed. P. Herre. Berlin, 1914.

[Bülow, H. D. v.] *Lehrsätze des neuern Krieges.* Berlin, 1805.

Bülow, H. D. v. *Militärische und vermischte Schriften von Heinrich Dietrich von Bülow.* Eds. E. Bülow and W. Rüstow. Leipzig, 1853.

[Bülow, H. D. v.] *Neue Taktik der Neuern.* 2 vols. Leipzig, 1805.

C———r. "Über die wissenschaftliche Bildung des Officiers," *Jahrbücher der preussischen Monarchie* (1800), no. 1.

"Circular-Verordnung Sr. Königl. Majestät von Preussen an Allerhöchstdero sämtliche Regimenter und Bataillons den Unterricht in den Garnisonschulen betreffend," *Jahrbücher der preussischen Monarchie* (1799), no. 3.

Chodz'ko, J. L. [D'Angeberg]. *Recueil des traités, conventions et actes diplomatiques concernant la Pologne.* Paris, 1862.

Decker, C. v. *Der kleine Krieg.* Berlin and Posen, 1822.

Dorow, W. *Erlebtes.* 4 vols. Leipzig, 1843–45.

Eisenhart, F. v. *Denkwürdigkeiten des Generals Friedrich von Eisenhart.* Ed. E. Salzer. Berlin, 1910.

Estorff, E. O. v. *Fragmente militairischer Betrachtungen über die Einrichtung des Kriegswesens in mittlern Staaten*. Frankfurt and Leipzig, 1780.

Fichte, J. G. *Briefwechsel*. Ed. H. Schulz. 2 vols. Leipzig, 1925.

———. *Philosophie der Maurerei*. Leipzig, 1923.

———. *Reden an die deutsche Nation*. Munich, 1922.

———. *Volk und Staat*. Ed. O. Braun. Munich, 1921.

Fouqué, F. de la Motte. *Lebensgeschichte des Baron Friedrich de la Motte Fouqué*. Halle, 1840.

Frederick II. *Hinterlassene Werke Friedrichs II*. 15 vols. in 5. Frankfurt and Leipzig, 1788.

———. *Oeuvres de Frédéric le grand*. Ed. J. D. E. Preuss. 31 vols. in 27. Berlin, 1846–56.

Gebler. " 'Vom Kriege.' Hinterlassenes Werk des Generals Karl von Clausewitz," *Oestreichische militärische Zeitschrift* (1834), no. 2 (1835), nos. 5, 11, 12.

Goethe, J. W. v. *Werke*. 14 vols. Hamburg, 1956–60.

Görres, J. v. *Gesammelte Briefe*. 3 vols. Munich, 1858–74.

———. *Teutschland und die Revolution*. Teutschland [i.e., Coblenz], 1819.

Gomm, W. M. *Letters and Journals of Field Marshal Sir William Maynard Gomm, G.C.B.* Ed. F. C. Carr-Gomm. London, 1881.

H. "Nachricht von der bei dem Infanterie-Regiment Prinz Ferdinand zu Neuruppin errichteten militärisch-wissenschaftlichen Bildungsanstalt für künftige Offiziere, und der damit verbundenen Regiments-Schulkommission," *Jahrbücher der preussischen Monarchie* (1799), no. 3.

———. "Nachricht über den Fortgang der militärisch-wissenschaftlichen Bildungs-Anstalt, bey dem Regiment Prinz Ferdinand zu Neu-Ruppin," *Jahrbücher der preussischen Monarchie* (1800), no. 2.

H[ahn], J.Z.H. "Bescheidene Prüfung der Circularverordnung Sr. Königl. Majestät von Preussen ... den Unterricht in den Garnisonschulen betreffend, sowie der darin enthaltenen Grundsätze über Volksschulen und Volksunterricht überhaupt," *Monatschrift für Deutsche* (1800), nos. 5–7.

Hardenberg, K.A.v. *Briefwechsel des Fürsten Karl August von Hardenberg mit dem Fürsten Wilhelm Ludwig von Sayn-Wittgenstein, 1806–1822*. Ed. H. Branig. Berlin, 1972.

Herrmann, E. *Diplomatische Correspondenzen aus der Revolutionszeit 1791–1797*. Gotha, 1867.

Hoffmann von Fallersleben, H. *Mein Leben*. 6 vols. in 5. Hanover, 1868.

Hohenzollernbriefe aus den Freiheitskriegen 1813–1815. Ed. H. Granier. Leipzig, 1913.

Humboldt, W. v. *Gesammelte Schriften*. Ed. A. Leitzmann. 15 vols. Berlin, 1903–20.

————. "Politische Jugendbriefe Wilhelm von Humboldts an Gentz," publ. by A. Leitzmann, *Historische Zeitschrift,* CLII (1935).

————. *Wilhelm von Humboldts Politische Briefe.* Ed. W. Richter. 2 vols. Berlin, 1936.

Hüser, J. G. v. *Denkwürdigkeiten aus dem Leben des Generals der Infanterie von Hüser.* Ed. M. G. Berlin, 1877.

Jomini, A. H. *Histoire critique et militaire des guerres de la Révolution.* 15 vols. Paris, 1820–24.

————. *Précis politique et militaire de la campagne de 1815.* Paris, 1839.

————. *Résumé des principes généraux de l'art de la guerre.* Glogau, 1807.

————. *Traité de grande tactique.* 4 vols. Paris, 1805–7.

————. *Traité des grandes opérations militaires.* 6 vols. Paris, 1811.

Journal des opérations des IIIe et Ve Corps en 1813. Ed. G. Fabry. Paris, 1902.

Kant, I. *Werke.* Ed. E. Cassirer. 11 vols. Berlin, 1912–22.

Kiesewetter, J. G. C. *Immanuel Kants Critik der Urtheilskraft für Uneingeweihte.* Berlin, 1804.

Kleist, H. v. [C. J. Levanus]. "Allerneuester Erziehungsplan," *Berliner Abendblätter* (1810), nos. 25–27, 35–36.

————. "Epigramme," *Phöbus,* I (1808), no. 6.

Klöden, K. F. v. *Karl Friedrich von Klödens Jugenderinnerungen.* Ed. K. Koetschau. Leipzig, 1911.

Kosmann, J. W. and Heinsius, T. *Denkwürdigkeiten der Mark Brandenburg,* III (1797).

Krisenjahre der Frühromantik. Ed. J. Körner. 3 vols. Bern, 1969.

Lebensbilder aus dem Befreiungskriege. Ed. J. F. v. Hormayr. 3 vols. Jena, 1841–44.

Le Mesurier, H. *Reflections on Modern War by the French General Latrille.* London, 1809.

Machiavelli. *Discourses.* Trans. and ed. L. J. Walker. New Haven, 1950.

Marston, J.E. *The Life and Campaigns of Field-Marshal Prince Blücher.* London, 1815.

Marwitz, F.L.A. v. d. *Lebensbeschreibung.* Ed. F. Meusel. Berlin, 1908.

Marx, K. and Engels, F. *Briefwechsel.* 2 vols. Moscow and Leningrad, 1936.

Menu von Minutoli, J. H. *Beiträge zu einer künftigen Biographie Friedrich Wilhelm III.* Berlin, 1843.

Montesquieu, C. L. de Secondat. *De l'Esprit des lois.* Leyden, 1749.

Müffling, P.F.C. v. [C. v. W.]. *Betrachtungen über die grossen Operationen und Schlachten der Feldzüge von 1813 und 1814.* Berlin and Posen, 1825.

————. "General Müffling über die Landwehr," *Historische Zeitschrift,* LXX (1893).

————. *Die preussisch-russische Campagne im Jahr 1813.* N.p., 1813.

Pestalozzi, H. *Heinrich Pestalozzis Lebendiges Werk.* Ed. A. Haller. 4 vols. Basel, 1946.

Puttkammer, L. v. *Erinnerungsblätter aus dem Leben Seiner Königlichen Hoheit des Prinzen August von Preussen.* Gotha, 1869.

Radziwill, L. *Quarante-cinq années de ma vie.* Ed. M. Castellane-Radziwill. Paris, 1911.

Ranke, L. v. *Hardenberg und die Geschichte des preussischen Staates von 1793–1813.* 3 vols. Leipzig, 1879–81.

————. "Über einige französische Flugschriften aus den letzten Monaten des Jahres 1831." *Historisch-politische Zeitschrift,* I (1832).

Raumer, K. v. *Karl von Raumers Leben von ihm selbst erzählt.* Stuttgart, 1866.

"Reglement für die Junkerschule des Infanterie-Regiments Prinz Ferdinand zu Neu-Ruppin," *Jahrbücher der preussischen Monarchie* (1799), no. 3.

Die Reorganisation des Preussischen Staates unter Stein und Hardenberg. Part I, *Allgemeine Verwaltungs- und Behördenreform.* Ed. G. Winter. Publikationen aus den Preussischen Staatsarchiven, xciii. Leipzig, 1931.

Die Reorganisation des Preussischen Staates unter Stein und Hardenberg. Part II. *Das Preussische Heer vom Tilsiter Frieden bis zur Befreiung: 1807–1814.* Ed. R. Vaupel. Publikationen aus den Preussischen Staatsarchiven, xciv. Leipzig, 1938.

Roeder, C. v. *Für Euch, meine Kinder! Erinnerungen aus dem Leben des Königlichen General-Lieutenants Carl von Roeder.* Berlin, 1861.

Rochow, C. v. and Fouqué, M. de la Motte. *Vom Leben am preussischen Hofe.* Ed. L. v. d. Marwitz. Berlin, 1908.

Rühle von Lilienstern, J. A. [R. v. L.] *Handbuch für den Offizier.* 2 vols. Berlin, 1817–18.

————. "Vom Kriege. Hinterlassenes Werk des Generals Carl v. Clausewitz," *Jahrbücher für wissenschaftliche Kritik,* II (August 1833), nos. 26–28.

Rüstow, W. *Die Lehre vom kleinen Kriege.* Zurich, 1864.

Scharnhorst, G. v. *Scharnhorsts Briefe.* Ed. K. Linnebach. Munich and Leipzig, 1914.

————. *Militärische Schriften.* Ed. C. v. d. Goltz. Dresden, 1891.

————. *Militairisches Taschenbuch, zum Gebrauch im Felde.* Hanover, 1792.

————. "Die Vertheidigung der Stadt Menin und die Selbstbefreiung der Garnison unter dem Generalmajor von Hammerstein," *Neues Militärisches Journal,* XI (1803).

[Scharnhorst, G. v.] *Verfassung und Lehreinrichtung der Akademie für junge Offiziere, und des Instituts für die Berlinische Inspection.* Berlin, 1805.

Schinkel, K. F. *Karl Friedrich Schinkel: Lebenswerk.* Eds. P. O. Rave et al. 12 vols. Berlin, 1950–62.

Schleiermacher, F. *Erziehungslehre.* Ed. C. Platz. Berlin, 1849.

Semler, J. S. *Lebensbeschreibung von ihm selbst verfasst.* N. p., 1781.

Seydlitz, A. v. *Tagebuch des Königlich Preussischen Armeekorps unter Befehl des General-Lieutenants von York.* 2 vols. Berlin and Posen, 1823.

Staat und Erziehung in der preussischen Reform 1807–1819. Ed. K. E. Jeismann. Göttingen, 1969.

Stein, K. v. *Freiherr vom Stein: Briefe und amtliche Schriften.* Eds. W. Hubatsch et al. 10 vols. in 11. Stuttgart, 1957–74.

[Steinmann von Friederici] *Was sich die Offiziere im Bureau erzählten.* Berlin, 1853.

Stuve, J. "Nachrichten von einer musterhaften Garnisonschule," *Berlinische Monatschrift,* II (1783).

Valentini, G. v. *Der kleine Krieg.* Berlin, 1833.

Varnhagen von Ense, K. A. *Biographische Denkmale.* 5 vols. Berlin, 1845–46.

————. *Blätter aus der preussischen Geschichte.* 3 vols. Leipzig, 1868.

————. *Denkwürdigkeiten des eigenen Lebens.* 3 vols. Leipzig, 1843.

Verzeichnis der Bibliothek und Kartensammlung des Professors Dr. Carl Ritter. 2 vols. Leipzig, 1861.

Voss, J. v. *Heinrich von Bülow.* Kölln [i.e., Berlin], 1806.

Wachholtz, F. L. v. *Aus dem Tagebuch des Generals Fr. L. von Wachholtz.* Ed. C. F. v. Vechelde. Braunschweig, 1843.

Wedel, K. v. *Lebenserinnerungen.* Ed. C. Troeger. 2 vols. Berlin, 1911–13.

Weishaupt, A. *Geschichte der Vervollkommnung des menschlichen Geschlechtes.* Frankfurt and Leipzig, 1788.

————. *Über die Selbstkenntnis, ihre Hindernisse und Vortheile.* Regensburg, 1794.

Wolzogen, L. v. *Memoiren.* Leipzig, 1851.

Zedlitz, K. A. v. *Die Staatskräfte der Preussischen Monarchie unter Friedrich Wilhelm III.* Berlin, 1828.

ARMY LISTS,
BIOGRAPHICAL DICTIONARIES,
AND OTHER REFERENCE WORKS

Adress-Kalender der Königlich Preussischen Haupt- und Residenz-Städte Berlin und Potsdam, Berlin, 1805.

Allgemeine Deutsche Biographie, iv, Leipzig, 1876.

Allgemeines Gelehrten Lexicon. Ed. C. G. Jöcher, i, Leipzig, 1750.

Banniza v. Bazan, H. and Müller, R. *Deutsche Geschichte in Ahnentafeln,* ii, Berlin, 1942.

Boiteau, P. *État de la France en 1789*. Paris, 1861.

État militaire de France. Paris, 1789.

Gieraths, G. *Die Kampfhandlungen der Brandenburgisch-Preussischen Armee*. Berlin, 1964.

Kurzgefasste Stamm- und Rangliste der Königlich Preussischen Armee für das Jahr 1789. Berlin, 1789.

Neues allgemeines Deutsches Adels-Lexicon. Ed. H. Kneschke. iv, Leipzig, 1929.

Priesdorff, K. v. *Soldatisches Führertum*. 10 vols. Hamburg, 1936–42.

Rangliste der Königl. Preussischen Armee für das Jahr 1805. Berlin, 1805.

Rang- und Quartierliste der Preussischen Armee von 1812. Reprinted, Osnabrück, 1968.

Rang- und Quartierliste der Königlich Preussischen Armee für das Jahr 1818. Berlin, 1818.

Rang- und Quartierliste der Königlich Preussischen Armee für das Jahr 1831. Berlin, 1831.

Stammliste aller Regimenter und Corps der Königlich Preussischen Armee. Berlin, 1798.

SECONDARY SOURCES

Alger, J. I. *Antoine-Henri Jomini: A Bibliographical Survey*. West Point, 1975.

Anderson, E. "Die Wirkung der Reden Fichtes," *Forschungen zur Brandenburgischen und Preussischen Geschichte*. XLVIII (1936).

Baack, L. "Christian Bernstorff and Prussia, 1818–1830." Ph.D. dissertation, Stanford University, 1973.

Bailleu, P. *Königin Luise*. Berlin and Leipzig, 1908.

Barthold, F. W. *Der Römerzug König Heinrichs von Lützelburg*. 2 vols. Königsberg, 1830–31.

Bergmann, E. *J. G. Fichte der Erzieher*. Leipzig, 1928.

Bernfeld, S. *Sisyphus or the Limits of Education*. Ed. P. Paret, trans. F. Lilge. Berkeley and Los Angeles, 1973.

Bissing, H. v. *Das Leben der Dichterin Amalie von Helvig*. Berlin, 1889.

Blaschke, R. *Carl von Clausewitz: Ein Leben in Kampf*. Berlin, 1934.

Bratring, F. W. A. *Statistisch-Topographische Beschreibung der gesamten Mark Brandenburg*. 3 vols. Berlin, 1804–9. Reprinted, Berlin, 1968.

Brügmann, A. *Staat und Nation im Denken Carls von Clausewitz*. Heidelberg, 1934.

Büsch, O. *Militärsystem und Sozialleben im alten Preussen*. Berlin, 1962.

Burg, P. *Feder und Schwert: Der Philosoph des Krieges, Carl von Clausewitz*. Berlin, 1939.

Caemmerer, R. v. *Clausewitz*. Berlin, 1905.

Chandler, D. *The Campaigns of Napoleon.* New York, 1966.

Colin, J. *Campagne de 1793 en Alsace et dans le Palatinat.* Paris, 1902.

———. *La Tactique et la discipline dans les armées de la Révolution.* Paris, 1902.

Conrady, E. v. *Leben und Wirken des Generals Carl von Grolman.* 3 vols. Berlin, 1894–96.

Czygan, P. *Zur Geschichte der Tagesliteratur während der Freiheitskriege.* 3 vols. in 2. Leipzig, 1909–11.

Dallinger, G. *Karl von Canitz und Dallwitz.* Cologne and Berlin, 1969.

Delbrück, H. "General von Clausewitz," *Historische und politische Aufsätze.* Berlin, 1887.

Dilthey, W. *Studien zur Geschichte des Deutschen Geistes.* Leipzig and Berlin, 1927.

———. *Zur Preussischen Geschichte.* Leipzig and Berlin, 1936.

Drewitz, I. *Berliner Salons.* Berlin, 1965.

Elkan, A. "Die Entdeckung Machiavellis in Deutschland zu Beginn des 19. Jahrhunderts," *Historische Zeitschrift,* CXIX (1919), no. 3.

Elze, W. *Der Streit um Tauroggen.* Breslau, 1926.

Engel, L. *Geschichte des Illuminaten-Ordens.* Berlin, 1906.

Erman, W. *Paul Erman,* Berlin, 1927.

Fontane, T. *Sämtliche Werke.* 27 vols. Munich, 1959–70.

Freytag-Loringhoven, H. v. *Kriegslehren nach Clausewitz aus den Feldzügen 1813 und 1814.* Berlin, 1908.

Friederich, R. *Die Befreiungskriege 1813–1815.* 4 vols. Berlin, 1911–13.

———. *Geschichte des Herbstfeldzuges 1813.* 3 vols. Berlin, 1903–6.

Friedländer, G. *Die Königliche Allgemeine Kriegs-Schule und das höhere Militair-Bildungswesen 1765–1813.* Berlin, 1854.

Gall, L. "Liberalismus und 'bürgerliche Gesellschaft'. Zu Charakter und Entwicklung der liberalen Bewegung in Deutschland," *Historische Zeitschrift,* CCXX (1975), no. 2.

Goltz, C. v.d. *Von Rossbach bis Jena und Auerstedt.* Berlin, 1906.

Hagemann, E. *Die deutsche Lehre vom Kriege; I: Von Berenhorst zu Clausewitz.* Berlin, 1940.

Hahlweg, W. *Carl von Clausewitz.* Göttingen, 1957.

Harraschik-Ehl, C. *Scharnhorsts Lehrer: Graf Wilhelm von Schaumburg-Lippe in Portugal.* Osnabrück, 1974.

Hartl, M. *Carl von Clausewitz: Persönlichkeit und Stil.* Emden, 1956.

Hassel, P. *Joseph Maria v. Radowitz.* Berlin, 1905.

Herr, R. *Tocqueville and the Old Regime.* Princeton, 1962.

Heydemann, F. *Die neuere Geschichte der Stadt Neu-Ruppin.* Neuruppin, 1863.

Hinrichs, C. *Preussen als historisches Problem.* Ed. G. Oestreich. Berlin, 1964.

————. *Preussentum und Pietismus.* Göttingen, 1971.

Höhn, R. *Revolution—Heer—Kriegsbild.* Darmstadt, 1944.

Ibbeken, R. *Preussen 1807–1813.* Cologne and Berlin, 1970.

Jähns, M. *Geschichte der Kriegswissenschaften vornehmlich in Deutschland.* 3 vols. Munich and Leipzig, 1889–91.

————. *Militärgeschichtliche Aufsätze.* Ed. U. v. Gersdorff. Osnabrück, 1970.

Janson, A. v. "Ein vergessener Zivilstratege," *Militär-Wochenblatt* (1907), Beiheft 12.

————. *König Friedrich Wilhelm III. in der Schlacht.* Berlin, 1907.

Jany, C. *Geschichte der Preussischen Armee.* 2nd ed. 4 vols. Osnabrück, 1967.

Jeismann, K. E. " 'Nationalerziehung'," *Geschichte in Wissenschaft und Unterricht,* XIV (1968), no. 4.

Kayser, R. *Zur Geschichte der Cholera, speciell der Cholera-Epidemien in Breslau.* Breslau, 1884.

Kelly, W. Hyde. *The Battle of Wavre and Grouchy's Retreat.* London, 1905.

Kessel, E. "Carl von Clausewitz: Herkunft und Persönlichkeit," *Wissen und Wehr,* XVIII (1937).

————. "Die doppelte Art des Krieges," *Wehrwissenschaftliche Rundschau,* IV (1954), no. 7.

————. "Georg Heinrich von Berenhorst," *Sachsen und Anhalt,* IX (1933).

————. *Moltke.* Stuttgart, 1957.

Zeiten der Wandlung. Darmstadt, 1953.

————. "Zu Boyens Entlassung," *Historische Zeitschrift,* CLXXV (1953), no. 1.

————. "Zur Genesis der modernen Kriegslehre," *Wehrwissenschaftliche Rundschau,* III (1953), no. 9.

Klein, E. *Von der Reform zur Restauration.* Berlin, 1965.

Klippel, G. H. *Das Leben des Generals von Scharnhorst.* 3 vols. Leipzig, 1869–71.

Koselleck, R. *Preussen zwischen Reform und Revolution.* Stuttgart, 1967.

Krieger, L. *The German Idea of Freedom.* Boston, 1957.

Krosigk, H. v. *Karl Graf von Brühl und seine Eltern.* Berlin, 1910.

Kuhn, W. "Der Tod des Feldmarschalls Gneisenau," *Forschungen zur Brandenburgischen und Preussischen Geschichte,* L (1938).

Laubert, M. "Die polnischen Zeitungen in der Provinz Posen 1831," *Forschungen zur Brandenburgischen und Preussischen Geschichte,* XL (1927).

le Forestier, R. *Les Illuminés de Bavière et la franc-maçonnerie allemande.* Paris, 1914.

Lehmann, M. *Knesebeck und Schön.* Leipzig, 1875.

————. *Scharnhorst.* 2 vols. Leipzig, 1886–87.

Lehmann, R. *Geschichte der Niederlausitz.* Berlin, 1963.

Lenz, M. *Geschichte der Königlichen Friederich-Wilhelms-Universität.* 4 vols. in 5. Halle, 1910–18.

Léonard, E. *L'Armée et ses problèmes au xviiie siècle.* Paris, 1958.

Lettow-Vorbeck, O. v. *Der Krieg von 1806 und 1807.* 4 vols. Berlin, 1891–96.

————. *Napoleons Untergang 1815.* 2 vols. Berlin, 1904–6.

Linnebach, K. "Clausewitz' Persönlichkeit," *Wissen und Wehr,* XI (1930).

McGrew, R. *Russia and the Cholera, 1823–1832.* Madison and Milwaukee, 1965.

Marx, A. *Die Gold- und Rosenkreuzer.* Zeulenroda and Leipzig, 1929.

Meinecke, F. *Cosmopolitanism and the National State.* Ed. F. Gilbert, trans. R. B. Kimber, Princeton, 1970.

————. *Das Leben des Generalfeldmarschalls Hermann von Boyen.* 2 vols. Stuttgart, 1896–99.

Meyer-Benfey, H. "Kleists politische Anschauungen," *Schriften der Kleist-Gesellschaft,* xiii-xiv, Berlin, 1932.

Montheilet, J. *Les Institutions militaires de la France.* Paris, 1932.

Nohn, E. A. *Der unzeitgemässe Clausewitz; Wehrwissenschaftliche Rundschau* (1956), Beiheft 5.

Palmer, R. R. "Frederick the Great, Guibert, Bülow: From Dynastic to National War," *Makers of Modern Strategy.* Ed. E. M. Earle. Princeton, 1961.

Paret, P. "Clausewitz: A Bibliographical Survey," *World Politics,* XVII (1965), no. 2.

————. "Clausewitz and the Nineteenth Century," *The Theory and Practice of War.* Ed. M. Howard. London and New York, 1966.

————. "Clausewitz," *International Encyclopedia of the Social Sciences,* ii, 1968.

————. "Education, Politics, and War in the Life of Clausewitz," *Journal of the History of Ideas,* XXIX (1968), no. 3.

————. "Nationalism and the Sense of Military Obligation," *Military Affairs,* XXXIV (1970), no. 1.

————. *Yorck and the Era of Prussian Reform.* Princeton, 1966.

Parkinson, R. *Carl von Clausewitz.* London, 1971.

Pertz, G. H. and Delbrück, H. *Das Leben des Feldmarschalls Grafen Neithardt von Gneisenau.* 5 vols. Berlin, 1864–80.

Petersdorff, H. v. *General Johann Adolph Freiherr von Thielmann.* Leipzig, 1894.

Pirmasens und Kaiserslautern; Kriegsgeschichtliche Einzelschriften, xvi, Berlin, 1893.

Poseck, E. *Louis Ferdinand, Prinz von Preussen.* Berlin, 1943.

Poten, B. v. *Geschichte des Militär-Erziehungs- und Bildungswesens in den Lan-*

den deutscher Zunge, iv, *Preussen; Monumenta Germaniae Pedagogica,* xvii, Berlin, 1896.

Das Preussische Heer im Jahre 1812. Ed. Kriegsgeschichtliche Abteilung II of the Great General Staff. Berlin, 1912.

Das Preussische Heer im Jahre 1813. Ed. Kriegsgeschichtliche Abteilung II of the Great General Staff. Berlin, 1914.

"Das Projekt der deutschen Union der XXII," *Latomia: Freimaurerische Vierteljahrsschrift,* XXI (1862), no. 1.

Quistorp, B. v. *Die Kaiserlich Russisch-Deutsche Legion.* Berlin, 1860.

Raif, A. *Die Urteile der Deutschen über die französische Nationalität im Zeitalter der Revolution und der deutschen Erhebung.* Berlin and Leipzig, 1911.

Ritschl, A. *Geschichte des Pietismus.* 3 vols. Bonn, 1880–86.

Ritter, G. *Frederick the Great.* Ed. and trans. P. Paret. Berkeley and Los Angeles, 1968.

———. *Staatskunst und Kriegshandwerk.* 4 vols. Munich, 1954–68.

———. *Stein.* Stuttgart, 1958.

Röder, R. "Zur Geschichte der Konvention von Tauroggen," *Das Jahr 1813.* Ed. F. Straube. Berlin (East), 1963.

Roques, P. *Le Général de Clausewitz.* Paris, 1912.

Rothfels, H. *Carl von Clausewitz: Politik und Krieg.* Berlin, 1920.

———. "Clausewitz," *Makers of Modern Strategy.* Ed. E. M. Earle. Princeton, 1961.

Scharfenort, L. v. *Die Königlich Preussische Kriegsakademie, 1810–1910.* Berlin, 1910.

Schaumburg-Lippe, F. C. zu. *Zur Ehre des revolutionären Menschen: Wilhelm Regierender Graf zu Schaumburg-Lippe.* Stadthagen, 1960.

Schering, W. M. *Die Kriegsphilosophie von Clausewitz.* Hamburg, 1935.

———. *Wehrphilosophie.* Leipzig, 1939.

Schib, K. *Johannes von Müller, 1752–1809.* Schaffhausen, 1967.

Schieder, T. "Niccolò Machiavelli. Epilog zu einem Jubiläumsjahr," *Historische Zeitschrift,* CCX (1970), no. 2.

Schiemann, T. *Geschichte Russlands unter Kaiser Nikolaus I.* 4 vols. Berlin, 1904–19.

Schlieffen, A. v. *Gesammelte Schriften.* 2 vols. Berlin, 1913.

Schnabel, F. *Deutsche Geschichte im neunzehnten Jahrhundert,* 4 vols. Freiburg, 1929–37.

Schneider, H. *Lessing: zwölf biograpische Studien.* Bern, 1951.

Schowalter, D. "The Prussian *Landwehr* and its Critics, 1813–1819," *Central European History,* IV (1971), no. 1.

Schrader, W. *Geschichte der Friedrichs-Universität zu Halle.* 2 vols. Berlin, 1894.

Schultze, J. "Bischoffwerder," *Mitteldeutsche Lebensbilder,* III (1928).

———. *Geschichte der Stadt Neuruppin.* Neuruppin, 1932.

Schwartz, K. *Leben des Generals Carl von Clausewitz und der Frau Marie von Clausewitz geb. Gräfin von Brühl.* 2 vols. Berlin, 1878.

Schwartz, P. *Der erste Kulturkampf in Preussen um Kirche und Schule: 1788–1798; Monumenta Germaniae Pedagogica,* lviii, Berlin, 1925.

Schwertfeger, B. *Das Treffen an der Göhrde; Militär-Wochenblatt* (1897), Beiheft 5/6.

————. *Die grossen Erzieher des deutschen Heeres.* Potsdam, 1936.

Seidel, P. "Karl Adolph Graf von Brühl," *Hohenzollern-Jahrbuch,* I (1897).

Sembdner, H. *Die Berliner Abendblätter Heinrich von Kleists; Schriften der Kleist-Gesellschaft,* xix, Berlin, 1939.

Sens, W. "Die Schulen der Stadt Burg, Bez. Magdeburg, zu Beginn des 19. Jahrhunderts," *Geschichtsblätter für Stadt und Land Magdeburg,* LXVI-LXVII (1931–32), no. 1.

Srbik, H. v. *Geist und Geschichte vom Deutschen Humanismus bis zur Gegenwart.* 2 vols. Munich and Salzburg, 1950–51.

Stadelmann, R. *Scharnhorst: Schicksal und Geistige Welt.* Wiesbaden, 1952.

Steig, R. *Heinrich von Kleists Berliner Kämpfe.* Berlin and Stuttgart, 1901.

Streckfuss, A. *Berlin im neunzehnten Jahrhundert.* 2 vols. Berlin, 1866–68.

Sybel, H. v. "Gneisenau und sein Schwiegersohn, Graf Friedrich Wilhelm v. Brühl," *Historische Zeitschrift,* LXIX (1892), no. 2.

Thile, G. *Geschichte der Preussischen Lehrerseminare; Monumenta Germaniae Pedagogica,* lxii, Berlin, 1938.

Treitschke, H. v. *Deutsche Geschichte im 19ten Jahrhundert.* 5 vols. Leipzig, 1923.

Tschirch, O. *Geschichte der öffentlichen Meinung in Preussen vom Baseler Frieden bis zum Zusammenbruch des Staates (1795–1806).* 2 vols. Weimar, 1933–34.

Varrentrap, C. "Rankes Historisch-politische Zeitschrift und das Berliner Politische Wochenblatt," *Historische Zeitschrift,* LXXXXIX (1907), no. 1.

Venzky, G. *Die Russisch-Deutsche Legion in den Jahren 1811–1815.* Wiesbaden, 1966.

Wahl, H. *Prinz Louis Ferdinand von Preussen.* Weimar, 1917.

Waller, J. *Wellington at Waterloo.* London, 1967.

Weniger, E. *Goethe und die Generale der Freiheitskriege.* Stuttgart, 1959.

————. "Philosophie und Bildung im Denken von Clausewitz," *Schicksalswege deutscher Vergangenheit.* Ed. W. Hubatsch. Düsseldorf, 1950.

Wienecke, F. *Das preussische Garnisonschulwesen.* Berlin, 1907.

Windelband, W. "Die neuere Philosophie," *Allgemeine Geschichte der Philosophie.* Ed. P. Hinneberg. Leipzig and Berlin, 1913.

Wohlfeil, R. *Spanien und die Deutsche Erhebung, 1808–1814.* Wiesbaden, 1965.

————. *Vom Stehenden Heer des Absolutismus zur Allgemeinen Wehrpflicht.* Frankfurt, 1964.

Wuppermann, L. *Prinzessin Marianne von Preussen, geborene Prinzessin von Hessen-Homburg in den Jahren 1804–1808.* Bonn, 1942.

NAME INDEX

INDEX OF CLAUSEWITZ'S WRITINGS